SAND CREEK AND THE TRAGIC
END OF A LIFEWAY

SAND CREEK AND THE TRAGIC END OF A LIFEWAY

LOUIS KRAFT

University of Oklahoma Press : Norman

Publication of this book is made possible through the generosity of Edith Kinney Gaylord.

Library of Congress Cataloging in Publication Control Number: 2019049558
ISBN 978-0-8061-6483-0 (hardcover)

The paper in this book meets the guidelines for permanence and durability of the Committee on Production Guidelines for Book Longevity of the Council on Library Resources, Inc. ∞

1 2 3 4 5 6 7 8 9 10

For
Glen Williams, my brother throughout time. Our friendship
began in 1990 in a software company, and he soon became my best male
friend ever. Our relationship has experienced a world of change
that neither he nor I ever dreamed possible, but we
have survived it. He is with me in life as he
will be in death—forever linked.
And for
Pailin Subanna-Kraft, my lady, best friend,
wife, and love, who has accepted my
life and world without question.
Without her I would
have no life.

Contents

List of Illustrations   ix

Acknowledgments   xi

1. Emerging from the Mists of Time   3

2. Riding into the Future   17

3. Dominating a New World   31

4. A Failure to Grasp the Future   53

5. Bent's Fear Becomes Reality   72

6. Welcome to the White Man's World   91

7. White Man War and Dissonance   109

8. Unjustified Actions   126

9. A Frantic Summer   142

10. A Disobedient Play for Peace   159

11. A Peace in Name Only   175

12. The White Man's Word   199

13. Vengeance and Outrage   220

14. The Cost of Glory   241

15. The Beginning of the End   261

   Epilogue: The Tragic End of a Lifeway   280

Notes   337

Bibliography   399

Index   413

Illustrations

⟨⟩

FIGURES

High Back Wolf, painting by George Catlin 13
Yellow Wolf, watercolor sketch by Lieutenant James W. Abert 21
Bent's Old Fort National Historic Site (La Junta, Colorado) 29
William Bent 32
Owl Woman, watercolor sketch by Lieutenant James W. Abert 39
John Evans with daughter Josephine 57
Woodcut of Little Raven, Albert Deane Richardson,
 and Horace Greeley 82
Elizabeth M. Byers 88
William N. Byers 99
Governor John Evans 115
Neva and Spotted Wolf 121
John Smith with Cheyennes Lean Bear, Standing-in-the-Water,
 and War Bonnet in group photograph 123
Nancy Morton 151
Major Ned Wynkoop, painting by Louis Kraft 164
Laura Roper, Daniel Marble, Isabelle Eubanks,
 and Ambrose Asher 172
Southern Cheyenne Ivan Hankler 176
Cheyenne and Arapaho chiefs arriving in Denver,
 September 28, 1864 179
Participants in the Camp Weld Council, September 28, 1864 191
Colonel John Chivington 207
Colonel George L. Shoup 218

Illustrations

Sand Creek, painting by Gordon Yellowman   222

Second Lieutenant Harry Richmond   230

Lieutenant Colonel Samuel F. Tappan   242

Captain Silas Soule   251

Hersa Coberly Soule   255

Black Kettle, painting by Jeroen Vogschmidt   271

Cheyenne–Dog Man–Lakota Pawnee Fork village site in Kansas, and woodcuts of Ned Wynkoop, Dick Curtis, and Little Raven   286

Magpie Woman and George Bent   290

Little Raven holding Grass Woman, William Bent, and the chief's sons Little Bear and Shield   297

Charley Bent, woodcut by Theodore R. Davis   303

George Armstrong Custer charges into the Washita Village, detail of mural by Steven Lang   315

Black Kettle and Medicine Woman Later in the Washita village, detail of mural by Steven Lang   316

Wichita Agency, I.T., detail of watercolor by Vincent Colyer   327

Little Raven, painting by Robert Lindneux and Juan Menchaca   328

Maps

Nebraska Territory, Kansas Territory/State, and Indian Territory   xvi

Colorado Territory and vicinity   xvii

Sand Creek village, three sand pits, and the escape routes on November 29, 1864   214

Acknowledgments

CHARLES (CHUCK) RANKIN, former University of Oklahoma Press editor in chief, has perhaps played *the* major role in my nonfiction life. We met, I think, at the beginning of the twenty-first century. He helped me with *Lt. Charles Gatewood & His Apache Wars Memoir.* It was not a book for OU Press, but it opened the door to conversations about a Ned Wynkoop book, which he supported every step of the way.

As *Ned Wynkoop and the Lonely Road from Sand Creek* moved toward publication, Chuck pitched me to write a book about the Sand Creek Massacre. I told him, "No, I don't write books about war; I write about people." He did not accept this, and over the next year-plus, we continued this discussion in person, on the phone, and via email. We eventually agreed that it would not be a book about the massacre; rather it would be about the lead-up to the November 29, 1864, attack, the assault, and the aftermath. We talked about our views, about my fears, about how perhaps this manuscript could be written. If not for Chuck, *Sand Creek and the Tragic End of a Lifeway* would have never happened.

IN 1987 I DELIVERED A TALK at the "First Annual West Coast Order of the Indian Wars Conference" (regrettably it was also the last OIW conference) in Southern California. There I met Mike Koury, who has not only become a friend but has gone out of his way to help me. I also met former Custer Battlefield National Monument (now Little Bighorn Battlefield National Monument) ranger Chris Summit. He said something that I never forgot:

"If you're going to write about the Cheyennes, you must see the George Bird Grinnell Collection at the Southwest Museum."

Liza Posas, head librarian at the Braun Research Library (Southwest Museum), Autry National Center of the American West, Los Angeles, California, played a large role in my continued research of the Grinnell Collection. Grinnell's research is invaluable for anyone writing about the Cheyennes, and I hope I am not out of line when I say that his papers are more important than his classic Cheyenne books. Braun research assistant Manola Madrid printed and later digitized my requests. The Southwest and Autry merged in 2003, and the Autry National Center is now the Autry Museum of the American West. The Autry's archive library and the Braun closed at the end of 2014. Both archives will be housed in a magnificent state of the art 100,000-square-foot building now called the Resources Center of the Autry in Burbank, California. It is scheduled to open in late 2020 or early 2021.

The Colorado Historical Society in Denver, which I have mined for decades, began its transfer to its new home not far from its original site after I concluded my Wynkoop research. Although the images used in the Wynkoop book were cited as History Colorado (per their request) the notes were cited as Colorado Historical Society (CHS). This means that citations listed in the Wynkoop book as CHS are now History Colorado.

Over the years the Western History Collection at the Denver Public Library and the Fray Angélico Chávez History Library, History Museum of New Mexico, Santa Fe, have been favorite sources for much of my research. Recently Marty Vestecka Miller of History Nebraska provided documents, a roll of microfilm, and two images of great value. I must mention Kevin Mohr, chief of interpretation and operations at the Washita Battlefield NHS in Cheyenne, Oklahoma. In spring 2018 I contacted him about the possibility of using two details from Steven Lang's magnificent mural that is at the battlefield. Kevin was totally in agreement with this from this first time we spoke, but it took until May 2019 before I had the permissions I needed from the National Park Service, and this would not have happened without Kevin's ongoing efforts. I also want to mention Cheyenne peace chief Gordon Yellowman, whom I met when we both spoke at Fort Larned, Kansas, in 1999. During the event, he and Cheyenne chief Lawrence Hart blessed the Cheyenne–Dog Man–Lakota village site that was destroyed in 1867. Gordon was selling prints of his art, "Sand Creek," and I bought one. It has been displayed at Tujunga House ever since. His painting was the only choice I had for this dust jacket. When I contacted Gordon about using his art, he was honored. When he said, "yes," I was more honored.

My association with the National Park Service began in 1990, when now chief historian George Elmore (Fort Larned NHS) played a key role in bringing my novel about Cheyenne-white relations in 1867 Kansas to life. A friend ever since, he has been a key player in all my Cheyenne-white research (books, articles, and talks). He kindly forwarded a question on John Chivington's first-trip mileage to Denver to Scott Gillette (chief of interpretation, Sand Creek Massacre NHS), and he forwarded it to Dr. Gary Roberts, the foremost Sand Creek expert. Gary graciously provided information. Others have also offered support: Jeff C. Campbell (Sand Creek Massacre NHS ranger–interpretation) has provided invaluable information at the massacre site, in phone conversations, and by sharing his documentation and commenting on mine; Craig Moore (former Sand Creek Massacre NHS ranger and Cheyenne genealogical expert); former Oklahoma Historical Society research expert Bill Welge; John M. Carson (park ranger–interpretation at Bent's Old Fort NHS) played a major role in my understanding the fort's dating, which is all over the place in published works; historian Gregory F. Michno shared his research on the Jicarilla Apaches, which was of massive help in understanding one of Black Kettle's raids; and Indian wars historian Paul Hedren supplied an in-depth review of the Sand Creek manuscript.

Leo Oliva is a historian, writer, speaker, and one of the major players in protecting key Cheyenne sites in Kansas, such as the Pawnee Fork village site in Kansas. He has been aided by many, including the Fort Larned Old Guard. I have known him since the 1990s, and he has not only been instrumental in bringing me to Kansas time and again, but has been one of my go-to people on the 1860s Cheyenne wars. This brings me back to George Elmore and Fort Larned NHS, for they are responsible for constructing the building that Ned Wynkoop rented from the post trader for his Indian agency from original plans.

John Monnett, first-class historian, Northern Cheyenne expert, and friend, and his wife Linda opened their home to Pailin and myself in fall 2014. During our visit he escorted us to numerous libraries, museums, and historic sites. On October 3 he and Linda took us to the Sand Creek Massacre NHS in southeast Colorado (my previous visit dated to the 1990s-era privately owned land that was not where the actual battle took place). We walked the bluffs to the west of the massacre site, which is immense, as we took photos of where the village circles once stood and discussed what we saw. What I observed, heard, and learned on that day has been invaluable.

Historian Dee Cordry and I connected a number of years back due to our mutual interest in mixed-blood Cheyennes that we researched and wrote about. This ranged from primary source to obscure photos and art as we studied their lives. We shared leads, long conversations, and detailed emails as we separated facts from fiction and misconceptions that have snowballed throughout time. This has led to a friendship with Dee, and a connection with Cheyenne chief Harvey Pratt (Dee's friend, and a direct descendant of Julia Bent and Edmund Guerrier), who has kindly assisted our research.

Two people played large roles in my development as a writer and historian. Over what seems like a lifetime, *Wild West* magazine editor Greg Lalire has not only put up with me but has kindly printed my articles. Tomas Jaehn, previously of the Fray Angélico Chávez History Library, History Museum of New Mexico, Santa Fe, and now the director of special collections at the Center for Southwest Research, University of New Mexico Libraries, a lifetime ago created the Louis Kraft Collection at the Chávez. Before and since that time he has done everything possible to support my research, writing, and speaking projects. He is a good friend, and we visit whenever I am in Santa Fe or he is in Los Angeles.

Other writers and artistic people have constantly supported my ongoing writing projects of the 1860s Cheyenne Indian wars. They include Dr. Henrietta Mann and Minona Littlehawk; director and writer Tom Eubanks; writers Thomas McNulty and Johnny D. Boggs; historians Gary Leonard, Layton Hooper, Deb Goodrich, Michelle Marie Martin, and Eric Niderost; artist Jeroen Vogtschmidt, who painted a portrait of Black Kettle for me; publishers Dick and Frankie Upton; Errol Flynn expert David DeWitt; and great friends Kim Walters and Veronica Von Bernath Morra.

My daughter, Marissa Kraft, is always present in my life and our trips to the American West. I cannot begin to tell you how many good times and travels we have shared together. She has been with me when we explored the Anasazi, Navajos, Apaches (Geronimo), and Cheyennes (Black Kettle and Stone Forehead), and when we tracked Kit Carson, Charles Gatewood, George Custer, and Ned Wynkoop. She knows all of them, as she has walked with them. Our trips have been some of the best times in my life, and hopefully also in hers.

Glen Williams and Pailin Subanna-Kraft have played special roles in the creation of this book but in different ways. Glen has helped with research and document creation, and has offered major support of my writing—critical and complementary. More important for this book, Glen, who is one-quarter Cheyenne, alerted his large family of my difficulty finding a number of images. They dug into their photo collections and found a few prints that might be useful and donated them to the Louis Kraft Collection. Thanks, Bro. Pailin is Thai. I met her at a dinner party I hosted for five. One of the guests insisted that she bring a coworker named Pailin. Both she and I said no, but each of us eventually gave in. That June 15, 2013, day and evening changed my life forever, for not only did Pailin and I meet, but I met a special person who would become my wife. She has done research with me in the field, as well as in libraries and historic archives, and she has always been totally supportive of my writing.

Current OU Press editor in chief Adam Kane has not missed a beat during the transfer of leadership at the press. Like Chuck, he has been in my corner at all times. He listened to me, advised me, and did all he could to improve the manuscript as he moved it toward production. Thank you, Adam. Managing editor Steven B. Baker repeated what he had done for the Wynkoop book, with his insightful edits, comments, and thoughts as he smoothly pushed the manuscript through the editorial process. He has again been key in the creation of this book—which I consider the most important one that I will ever write. Design and production manager Tony Roberts's design of the book cover is magnificent and surpasses his terrific work on the Wynkoop cover. I have nothing but praise for him and his production team. Cartographer Bill Nelson has again created terrific maps. Copyeditor Kerin Tate's running list of comments raised terrific questions, observations, and clarifications. This was a massive task, and I am grateful for her effort, which helped improve the readability of the book.

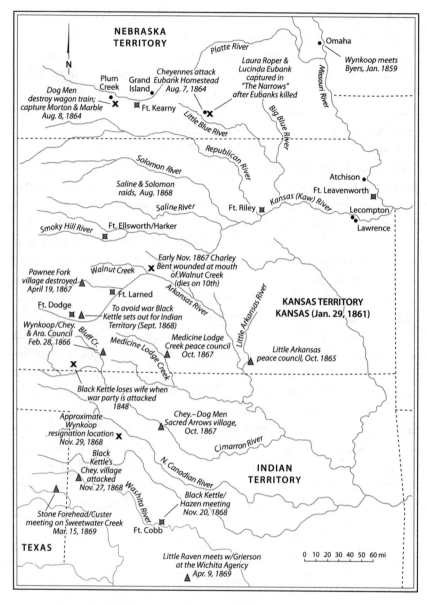

The map contains the following labels:

NEBRASKA TERRITORY

Platte River

Omaha

Wynkoop meets Byers, Jan. 1859

N

Laura Roper & Lucinda Eubank captured in "The Narrows" after Eubanks killed

Cheyennes attack Eubank Homestead Aug. 7, 1864

Plum Creek

Grand Island

Dog Men destroy wagon train; capture Morton & Marble Aug. 8, 1864

Ft. Kearny

Little Blue River

Missouri River

Big Blue River

Republican River

Solomon River

Saline & Solomon raids, Aug. 1868

Atchison

Ft. Leavenworth

Saline River

Ft. Riley

Kansas (Kaw) River

Lecompton

Lawrence

Smoky Hill River

Ft. Ellsworth/Harker

Early Nov. 1867 Charley Bent wounded at mouth of Walnut Creek (dies on 10th)

Pawnee Fork village destroyed April 19, 1867

Walnut Creek

Ft. Larned

Arkansas River

Little Arkansas River

KANSAS TERRITORY KANSAS (Jan. 29, 1861)

Ft. Dodge

To avoid war Black Kettle sets out for Indian Territory (Sept. 1868)

Wynkoop/Chey. & Ara. Council Feb. 28, 1866

Bluff Cr.

Medicine Lodge Creek

Medicine Lodge Creek peace council Oct. 1867

Little Arkansas peace council, Oct. 1865

Black Kettle loses wife when war party is attacked 1848

Approximate Wynkoop resignation location Nov. 29, 1868

Chey.–Dog Men Sacred Arrows village, Oct. 1867

Cimarron River

INDIAN TERRITORY

Black Kettle's Chey. village attacked Nov. 27, 1868

N. Canadian River

Washita River

Black Kettle/ Hazen meeting Nov. 20, 1868

Stone Forehead/Custer meeting on Sweetwater Creek Mar. 15, 1869

Ft. Cobb

TEXAS

Little Raven meets w/Grierson at the Wichita Agency Apr. 9, 1869

0 10 20 30 40 50 60 mi

Nebraska Territory, Kansas Territory/State, and Indian Territory. *Map by Bill Nelson*

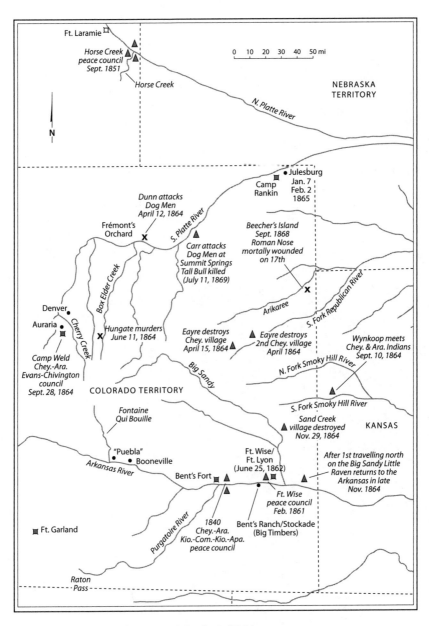

Colorado Territory and vicinity. *Map by Bill Nelson*

SAND CREEK AND THE TRAGIC
END OF A LIFEWAY

ONE

Emerging from the Mists of Time

A GROUP OF WHAT WOULD BECOME Algonquian-speaking people began an exodus at least twenty thousand years ago. Originally from Siberia, they traveled south and then west to what would become southwestern Europe (today's France, Portugal, and Spain). This did not end their wanderings, for somewhere near the southernmost part of this land, which butted up to a never-ending mass of water, these Europid-Asiatic groups continued moving with no set destination in mind.[1]

Totally dependent on the terrain they meandered through, they moved first one way and then another as they lived off what the ground and streams provided. They ate vegetables and fruit when they found it. Their weapons were minimal, mainly sticks and stones that they used to kill small game or fish. They had little clothing, and their shelters offered little protection from the elements, especially during the cold moons. Life was precarious, as many would not survive the changing seasons. In small groups they walked north, then west or south, and again north. During the millennium that it took them to arrive at the northern reaches of the earth (northern Europe), they faced a frozen tundra to the west. As the harsh terrain provided shrubs, lichens, moss, and grasses when warmer moons thawed the top layers of ice, they dared to cross it. But, as in the past, they would reverse their travel, and then recross again, before they reached the northeastern portion of a land that someday would be called North America. By this time they had further developed their weaponry and had improved their method of killing game, except for large animals and fish. Ice and cold remained constant and hindered their struggle to provide the life essentials for their families. More time passed and small groups of these people reached solid land. They moved southward and again northward, before again turning south and continuing until they reached an area of large lakes. During this time they began to unify into Algonquian family circles and then into specific clans that would eventually become tribes. Still their lives remained shrouded in mystery, with little more than hints of a past long gone and forgotten by the passing of eons.[2]

Still they survived.

By this time—and centuries had passed—the Algonquian people had divided into separate tribes, and loyalties based on linguistics had emerged. The largest and most powerful of the tribes were the Crees. They kept peace with other Algonquian tribes or warred with any that angered them. Other Algonquians that ventured farther to the west included the Blackfeet and the Gros Ventres, but only a small portion of this tribe continued westward.

Two other Algonquian groups—actually three—would form two tribes and would complete the migration.

One was the Arapahos. This tribe's name may have derived from a Crow term for "tattooed people" or a Pawnee word that meant "trader." The Arapahos call themselves *Hinono'ei* (singular) and *Hinono'eino'* (plural), a term that has been translated to mean "Our People," "Cloud People," or "Wrongrooters."[3]

The Arapahos' migration over the now-extinct land mass that separated Europe from the Americas happened about the same time as other Algonquian passages over the frozen tundra. However, once they crossed the Great Lakes, evidence of their existence disappears—for almost another century. It would not be until the late 1600s that the Arapahos would emerge again from the mists of time. The reason they did not appear in early records and were only hinted at in oral traditions was that their migration westward took place earlier. They perhaps also chose different migration paths onto the Great Plains and the land of the buffalo. With only dogs to serve as beasts of burden, they abandoned growing crops in permanent villages west of the Great Lakes and moved across the Missouri River sometime around the beginning of the seventeenth century. They crossed the upper Missouri between the Big Dry Ford and the mouth of the Musselshell River, or in the Milk River country. They then either walked onto the plains or traveled along a northern route to perhaps as far as present northwestern Montana.[4]

Another Algonquian-speaking people migrated from Europe at roughly the same time as the Cloud People. They also reached the lakes after a centuries-long migration, but unlike the Hinono'eino', they had begun to step from obscurity. Although small in numbers, they met and realized that they were distantly related to the Crees as their language was similar, enough so that they could communicate with the larger tribe. This smaller grouping of people would eventually be known as the Cheyennes. As they were able to communicate with the Crees, they were accepted as kin. The Crees called them "Ka-nea-hea-was-tsik," which meant "Those with a language somewhat like us," and "Cree Talkers."[5]

The Cheyennes called themselves the *Tsistsistas*, which among other things means "the People."[6] Over the years the Tsistsistas' name "has been translated to mean . . . 'people alike,' 'our people,' [or possibly] 'related to one another,' or 'similarly bred.' [Sometimes] their name has also been translated as 'gashed' or 'cut people.' The white man came up with the word 'Cheyenne,' from the [Siouan] word, 'Shai ena,' which translates to 'people who speak with a strange tongue.'"[7] "Tsistsistas" also means "beautiful people."[8] There is one more translation of their name, and it has an extraordinary meaning.

BETWEEN 1673 AND 1680 the Tsistsistas lived on the Wisconsin River to the west of Lake Michigan in farming villages that consisted of earthen lodges, with perhaps fifteen people living in each lodge. So did the Chongasketons and Oudebatons, who whites on the early frontier thought had been of Sioux descent. They were wrong, for the Sioux had migrated from Asia to the North American continent over the Bering land bridge in ancient times. The Tsistsistas had no connection with them. Instead, there were other people who crossed the land bridge between Europe and the Americas, and these "proto-Cheyenne groups . . . were later incorporated into the Cheyenne [tribe]."[9] The Chongasketons spoke a similar dialect of the language that the Tsistsistas spoke, confirming that both tribes were descendants of Algonquian lineage. Actually the Chongasketons—as they were listed on early French maps—were Sutaios (Sutai is singular). There were four "bunches" to the Sutai band at this time, and each was named after a leader. The Oudebatons were also erroneously thought to be related to the Siouan people, that is, the Wahpeton Sioux, but like the Chongas-ketons, their native dialect made them relatives to the Tsistsistas and not descendants of those who had crossed the Bering land bridge. They would become known as "Omisis, 'Eaters,' or Naomisis, 'Northern Eaters,'" and would eventually become the Wuh´tapiu (Wotapio) band.[10]

Although the Tsistsistas, Omisis, and Sutaios camped near each other and knew one another, they did not migrate between the upper Missis-sippi River region and in the direction of the Missouri River between 1680 and 1730 as one group. These migrations were separate journeys made by smaller "bunches" of people that belonged to the same bands. The people did not camp or travel together within their own grouping. Although these people spoke the same or similar dialects, the various bands moved west-ward independently and at their own pace. At the same time intermarriage between the Tsistsistas, Omisis, and Sutaios had begun to create links be-tween these people, but they were not yet one tribe or one nation.[11] Ac-cording to Cheyenne memory, farther back in time before they began their westward migration, the Tsistsistas and Sutaios were enemies. Although they spoke a language that both could understand, the Sutaio's dialect was "rougher, harsher, and more guttural."[12]

At various times during the eighteenth century the Tsistsistas, Sutaios, and Omisis arrived at the Missouri River. Here they found the Hidatsas, Mandans, and Arikaras (Rees), three sedentary tribes who cultivated crops and had become allied with one another. At this time the Tsistsistas still grew corn, but their days as farmers were nearing an end, at least for most of them, as their migration continued west and south. Also at this time they were often in contact with bands of Sioux near the Missouri.[13]

Their travels and settlement along the upper Missouri opened the Peo-ple's eyes to what they had previously seen and desired, but for the most part did not realize or have—trade with the white man and the valuable objects they had to offer: guns, guns, and more guns, and do not forget the horse—that magnificent animal that some of them realized could change their lives.

Again in small groups, the Tsistsistas, Omisis, and Sutaios began to in-dependently cross the Missouri River. After the crossing, the Tsistsistas and Sutaios parted company for a third time. While the Tsistsistas continued farther west, the Sutaios moved north.[14] Until this time the Tsistsistas had not been aggressors—had not sent out war parties. This changed, for now small war parties set out on foot. This marked the beginning of a life change that had been slowly coming. From this time forward the transformation from a pastoral people to a warrior-based society evolved quickly.[15]

The exodus continued moving west until the Tsistsistas reached the Sheyenne River around 1750. They did not remain there long, and their travels next sent them south and slightly east to the Minnesota River, which they reached by 1766.[16]

MAHEO WAS AND IS "the All Father, the Sacred Persons, and the Powers" of the Tsistsistas.[17] "Maheo is [also] the ancient Cheyenne name for the All Father, the Supreme Being."

Sometime in the Tsistsistas' prehistory, Maheo told them that animals would come from the south and would influence their lives. These animals would have "round feet" and "long hair on their necks," that their "tails would drag on the ground," that they would eat grass, and that "they will be on the watch continually, raising their heads all the time as they feed."[18] These animals, Maheo said, would change the Tsistsistas' lives, for now they would be able to travel far and wide quickly. He called the animal "Mö-î't-nök" or perhaps "Mo-it-nok." The Mo-it-nok, Maheo said, had no relatives and married his own kind.

Although everything their God told them had an upside and hinted at a future they could not imagine, Maheo also told them that there would be dark times ahead, and that the People would be like Mo-it-nok; that is they would marry their own when young and would not live long. Moreover, they would forget the old ways as they moved into their future. Then, shockingly, Maheo pointed at a figure who sat on the ground and had hair over his face. The Tsistsistas had never seen this person before and did not know where he came from. Maheo told them: "He will always make trouble for you."

It was at this time that the Tsistsistas' name took on yet another meaning: the "Called Out People."[19]

TSISTSISTAS CLAIMED THAT THIS MOVEMENT to the Missouri and then south to the Black Hills and yet farther south and onto the plains was motivated by their desire to have the horse.[20] But this did not prove to be completely true. Survival and war had influenced much of their travels, but now they had another motivation—the buffalo and trade.

To this point in time the Tsistsistas and the Hinono'eino' were little more than ghosts. They were people that white men had encountered but barely noted or simply ignored. The end of the eighteenth century marked the beginning of the decline of the egotistical Anglo-European refusal to accept, or at least recognize, a people who not only lived but who would create an extraordinary future.

One of the most important Tsistsistas of all time was born into the Aorta band about 1795. He was called Ho'honaeve'ohtanehe. His name translated to Rock Forehead and to a lesser degree Stone Forehead.[21] He would be the firstborn of a new generation of Tsistsistas that would not only realize the Called Out People's future but in the coming decades would play a major role in it.

By the dawning of the nineteenth century Tsistsista leaders had remained nameless faces not recorded by time. When chance circumstances created an encounter with the white man, the foreigners in their land jotted short notes of the event, sometimes even attempting a physical description of the Called Out People, but they never seemed to have an interest in recording the names of the Tsistsistas that they met. Exploratory outfits, Canadian or American, reached their campsites, which they usually shared with other Indians, and spent time with them. But they could not communicate, as no one could translate the Tsistsista language. The whites knew only that they had met a different Indian people who stood out and camped with or near Indians they knew; at times called them "Shawyens," "Schians," or "Shiennes." Charles Mackenzie, along with Alexander Henry, came in contact with the Tsistsistas twice in the early 1800s. During the second meeting at a camp on the Knife River the Tsistsistas camped with Sioux and Arapahos. They had painted their horses and had covered the animals' heads with masks that included horns and red cloth that decorated them to represent red deer, antelope, and buffalo.[22]

The times had begun to change. Tsistsista boys aspiring to become warriors, and their brethren not yet born, found a brave new world awaiting them, at least for those who dared to reach into the unknown. Their lifeway would expand, grow, and sparkle across the night skies. Nothing would seem impossible, and within a short time they would become the masters of their world.

Years passed—between two and three generations—before the Sutaios decided to reverse their direction and travel south toward the Black Hills country. By now it was near the end of the eighteenth century. When they reached the Cheyenne River, which was east and south of the Black Hills, they again crossed paths with the Tsistsistas, who "at once recognized [them] by their speech."[23] Even so, the Tsistsistas called them "the Strange Talkers" as "many words were quite different."[24] Soon the two tribes would merge, and the Sutaios became a Tsistsista band.

Early in the new century, between 1812 and 1815, Black Hawk (or Hawk-Stretched-Out), who was not a chief, and his wife Little Brown Backed Hawk Woman (or Sparrow Hawk Woman), both of whom were Sutaios, saw the birth of their first child. Although this youngster's parents were Sutaios, this newborn was a Tsistsista due to their smaller tribe merging into the larger tribe. This boy, who would be the oldest of four children, was born into the Hairy People clan (Hí-vāi-tä-nü). He would eventually have many names documented as his in the future. Many moons would pass before he would meet white men. When he did, they had trouble pronouncing and phonetically spelling his Tsistsista name. It would take even more years before he met a white man who made an effort to say his name correctly—"Make-tava-tah." According to his sister, Wind Woman: "Black Kettle was ten years older than Gentle Horse and . . . Gentle Horse was four or five years older than she."[25] The fourth child, Black Hawk (or Stone Teeth) died soon after his birth. Wind Woman was born east "of the Black Hills on the Cheyenne River" about three years before the stars fell in 1833 in what would become Dakota Territory (perhaps as early as 1830), which made Black Kettle's birth about 1815.[26]

Wind Woman remembered that when she was four or five, her Sutai band began to venture south onto the plains to trade. She claimed that it was still later when some of the bands moved to the south to live, but it could not have been much later.[27]

Black Kettle had many Tsistsista names, but the one closest to an English phonetic pronunciation was "Make-tava-tah." Other attempts at recording his name included Mokatavatah and Mo-ta-va-to.[28]

THE KEY ARAPAHO LEADER was born somewhere between 1809 and 1810. Although there has been some confusion over where, there should not be, as the Hinono'eino' had reached the North Platte River about 1800. His name was Little Raven (Oh-has-tee, Hosa), and his life's path would be similar to Make-tava-tah's, with whom his name would often become attached in the distant future.[29]

The other major Arapaho leader, Left Hand (Niwot, Nor-wan-che) was born on the central plains around 1823, which shows without a doubt that when the Hinono'ei and Tsistsista warriors ventured south to trade, hunt buffalo, and obtain horses, that at times their wives accompanied them. His brother, Neva (Nevah), was also born on the plains two years later. Over time as the brothers grew from childhood to adulthood they remained close, a closeness that remained throughout Left Hand's life. They also had another thing in common: beginning about 1833 they both began to learn and speak English. Left Hand became fluent in English, and he also mastered speaking the Tsistsista and Lakota dialects. The boys gained their knowledge of English when the Arapahos visited fur trading posts on the Upper Arkansas and overlooking the South Platte (but this was in the future).[30]

ALTHOUGH SOME TRADING TOOK PLACE with the white man, for the most part the Tsistsistas had almost no contact with the bearded foreigner from 1804 until the mid-1820s. At this time their weapons consisted of bows and arrows, war clubs, lances, and knives. Warriors used "the heaviest part of a buffalo bull's hide" to create their shields.[31] After creating the framework and adding the buffalo hide, the warriors covered their work with buckskin that was of the best quality. To finish their art, which would serve as their physical and spiritual protector, they painted it and decorated it with eagle feathers.

This soon changed, for now a Tsistsista chief walked into the white man's world, and although his life would not last long after the initial meeting, he did not fade with the mists of time. He stood proud and tall, and impressed the invaders. By 1824 a fair amount of Tsistsistas still lived and farmed on both sides of the Missouri River, but tradition placed the more adventurous of the bands roaming to the west and south of the river as the horse culture began to accelerate.[32] About this time High Back Wolf had become the head chief of the council of forty-four and the Sweet Medicine chief.

Back in Tsistsista history they selected forty-four chiefs who may have been war chiefs but now only worked for the welfare of all their people. "All the peace chiefs are proven warriors, but when a chief of a [warrior society] is raised to the rank of peace chief . . . [h]e retains his membership, but he is no longer a war chief."[33] Once chosen as a council chief they could no longer organize war parties or ride the war trail. Their goal was now peace and protecting the Called Out People. They were chosen for ten years and they could again serve for an additional ten years. These leaders represented all the bands, but there were five that had much more power than the rest, and they were without doubt the elite leaders of the People. "The personal requirements for a tribal chief, reiterated again and again by the Cheyennes, are an even-tempered good nature, energy, wisdom, kindliness, concern for the well-being of others, courage, generosity, and altruism. These traits express the epitome of the Cheyenne ideal personality. In specific behavior this means that a tribal chief gives constantly to the poor." These were the council chiefs of the Tsistsistas.

IN 1825 BREVET GENERAL HENRY ATKINSON, who functioned as a special commissioner, led an expedition of nine keelboats up the Missouri River. His goal was to make treaties of friendship that included trading items of worth as well as protection. Although not stated to the tribal leaders he met, there was also an underlying goal: to protect the fur trade that existed since Lewis and Clark's epic journey at the beginning of the century. Whenever Atkinson saw a band of Indians, he pulled to the shore and attempted to meet with them. When Atkinson's small fleet reached the mouth of the Teton River, he met Oglala Sioux and other Siouan people. He also learned of a nearby Tsistsista village that was friendly with the Sioux.[34]

At that time a portion of the Tsistsistas still lived near the western bank of the Missouri year-round while others spent time on the Great Plains following the Ésevone—the buffalo herds—but still returned to the river to trade. This Tsistsista band was one of the latter.

At the beginning of the Moon when the buffalo bulls are rutting (July), High Back Wolf heard from Lakotas that American white men wanted to sign a treaty with the Tsistsistas. He asked other chiefs to go with him and speak with them. When they refused, High Back Wolf set out with those who followed him. Two chiefs, Buffalo Head and The One Who Walks Against the Others, changed their minds and rode after him. Before reaching the Lakota village on the Missouri, he was joined by White Antelope, who then led either the Dog Men or Elkhorn Scrapers warrior society, and Chief Little Moon. After they reached the Sioux village, which also included Tsistsista warriors, the People moved upriver until they reached the confluence of the Teton River.[35]

On July 4 High Back Wolf became the first Tsistsista chief to step from the shadows, for on that day he and other leaders of the People met Atkinson. High Back Wolf and Lousy Man invited the general, Major Benjamin O'Fallon (U.S. Indian agent, Indian Affairs), Major Stephen W. Kearny (First Infantry), Lieutenant William S. Harney (First Infantry), G. H. Kennerly (U.S. special Indian agent), and the other commissioners to sit on buffalo robes while they feasted on thirteen boiled dogs. Afterward the Tsistsistas lit a pipe, and as it was passed around the circle the chiefs and officers smoked. When the ceremony ended, the Indians presented the pipe to Atkinson and then gave their guests the buffalo robes that they sat upon.[36]

At the council High Back Wolf wore impressive-looking scalp leggings and a scalp shirt. Atkinson presented him with a bay horse with a saddle and bridle, two revolvers, a saber, and a suit, which was most likely a uniform.[37] The journalist traveling with Atkinson's expedition described the chief as "one of the most dignified and elegant looking men I ever saw." In a letter home, an unnamed officer with Atkinson described the Cheyennes as "genuine children of nature, they have[,] unlike other Indians, all the virtues that nature can give, without the vices of civilization."[38]

The following day High Back Wolf, the Tsistsistas, and Sioux watched in wonder as Atkinson paraded his soldiers before them, and even more so when the visitors speedily transported two howitzers across the prairie. That night Atkinson's men presented a light display in the dark sky when they shot twenty rockets into the air and fired six howitzer shells across the water. Impressed by what he had seen, High Back Wolf presented Atkinson with a mule and a Spanish saddle.[39]

While High Back Wolf's appearance and demeanor demanded attention, his presence meant that the Tsistsistas no longer hovered on the edge of reality. Now whites could translate their words. When he stepped forward and spoke, his words and stature dominated. Over time the whites also called him High Wolf (Hoh´ ni kya´ he yo) or Tall Wolf (Hon i´ o hkha´ ho i yis´), High-Backed Wolf, and Wolf on the Hill (Né-hee-ó-ee-wó-tis).[40] He led the way, and from 1825 onward Tsistsista leaders no longer existed in a vast

Artist George Catlin painted this portrait of High Back Wolf (he called him Wolf on the Hill, Né-hee-ó-ee-wóo-tis) at Fort Pierre (present-day South Dakota) in 1832, a year before he was murdered just days before the "night when the stars fell" in 1833. The chief had painted his face red for this portrait. When I have seen his portrait printed in black and white in other books, his face has often been lightened; most likely because the publisher did not want to state that Wolf on the Hill had painted his face.

Smithsonian American Art Museum, Washington, D.C. / Art Resource, N.Y.

wilderness of nameless souls lost to history. Instead, they appeared as tall (about six feet) physical specimens, dignified, and in control of their lives.

On July 6 Atkinson presented High Back Wolf and his band with a friendship treaty. It offered the Tsistsistas protection and the opportunity to trade with the United States for items that they might deem important such as blankets, guns, and ammunition. Whether the chief understood the details or not, trading would only happen when convenient to the Americans—most likely whenever white men stumbled upon Tsistsistas and had items to trade. Before the agreement became official, High Back Wolf and the other leaders had to agree that they would protect American traders, give up tribal members guilty of crimes, and most important, not trade or sell guns and ammunition to tribes hostile to the United States.[41]

High Back Wolf made his mark and was listed on the treaty paper as "The Wolf with the High Back" (and Sho-e-mow-e-to-chaw-ca-we-wah-ca-to-we), as did three other chiefs (including The One Who Walks Against the Others) and eight warriors (Lousy Man and White Dear were listed as warriors) on July 6.[42]

There were two people at this historic meeting that began a relationship that would last throughout time: Lieutenant Harney, just shy of his twenty-fifth year, and a thirteen-year-old Sutai boy called Make-tava-tah. Circumstances brought them together at the council and for some reason they bonded—a young officer at the beginning of his career and a teenaged boy destined to become a major player in his people's future. Harney adopted the boy as his son—if only for a few days. When walking between races, the major problem is language; not only having the words translated correctly but understanding the cultural meaning behind them. Harney thought that Make-tava-tah was High Back Wolf's son.[43]

Make-tava-tah was not High Back Wolf's son, and yet he was. Language and culture and how it was translated is directly responsible for Harney believing that the boy was the chief's son. Make-tava-tah's father died while he was still young and the chief looked after him, but it was more than that. The Sutaios' and the Tsistsistas' kinship has a language of sisters and brothers and uncles and aunts and fathers and mothers that can be confusing, and even more so when there is a language barrier.[44]

As the Cheyennes and Arapahos rode into their future, so did a handful of white men, or as the Tsistsistas would come to call them, *vihio* or *ve'heo* (now spelled *vi'ho' i*), which originally meant "spider," as the first white men they saw were hairy and covered themselves with clothing, which concealed them as a spider hides in the center of its web. The Arapahos called white men *a'tha*, and it also meant "spider" for the same reason.[45] As the years would pass, the transformation of the meaning of the word made sense. One of these men, John Simpson Smith, no later than his twentieth birthday in 1830, had left Kentucky and had become a trapper in the upper Rocky Mountains.[46]

During this time Smith came into contact with numerous tribes including the Blackfeet, Sioux, Crows, Cheyennes, and Arapahos. Smith was a survivor and fully capable of taking care of himself in the wilderness. At an unknown date but around this time Smith cached his furs and avoided the yearly mountain man rendezvous of drink, gambling, and perhaps sex, which could result in the loss of all his hard work. Instead, the following spring he built a bullboat that he had learned from Indians, a tub-like boat of willows with a buffalo hide stretched over the framework. As he moved down the Missouri River and closed on Fort McKenzie, the boat overturned and pitched him into the freezing water. He saved his hides and guns, but feared lighting a fire, as he was in Blackfeet country. After a miserable night he awoke with a toothache and a neurological attack. Needing help he continued down the Missouri to the fort, where he obtained a bottle of laudanum and jug of alcohol.

The laudanum worked its magic, and Smith continued his journey. Drowsy, he did not realize that Blackfeet warriors tracked him. At a bend in the river, Smith's boat came too close to the bank and the Blackfeet captured him at gunpoint. They took all he had, gutted the bullboat and led him onto the prairie. He knew that they intended to kill him, but first they cooked his meat. They also found his alcohol but it was too strong for them to swallow. Smith showed them how to dilute it with water. He watched as they drank and drank. Finally the laudanum had worn off and his pain returned. Smith drank from his bottle of laudanum, drawing the Blackfeet to him. By this time he had some knowledge of their words and warned them that it was bad medicine. They tried to grab the bottle and he fought to keep it. Finally he made them understand that he would give them a little to try. Smith knew exactly what he was doing and doled out portions that put them to sleep. When all lost consciousness, he broke their bows and arrows and tossed them into the fire; their guns and knives he tossed into the river. He then packed their lead and powder, meat, and his hides and some that they had onto horses, keeping the best for him to ride.

But Smith had not moved quickly enough, for Blackfeet on horses appeared in the distance. He waited until they drew close enough to see that their comrades looked dead. Before one could shoot Smith he shot the warrior. The other turned and ran. Smith shot his horse, which dropped. Before the warrior could recover from the fall Smith was on him and killed him with his knife. It is unknown if these were the first people he killed, but then he dispatched all. Smith gathered their scalps while taking care to retain the shells, trinkets, and brass wire attached to their hair.[47]

Smith would prove to be a man beyond his times. Although not the first mountain man to do so, he certainly accepted the various tribes as human beings, and people that he honestly enjoyed knowing. Although he knew that at times his life might be at risk when dealing with them, he learned their ways and their languages. He spoke the Cheyenne, Arapaho, Sioux, and Blackfoot (Siksika) dialects, as well as French and Spanish, which was his mother's native language.[48]

AT THIS TIME MANY TSISTSISTAS were coming of age and making their mark as warriors. Some would become leaders, one a mystic and Keeper of the Sacred Arrows—Lean Bear, White Antelope, and Stone Forehead—but it would be another who would come to play the most important role in the People's future. Make-tava-tah—Black Kettle to the invading whites—was now a budding warrior but still a youngster when he joined the Bowstring warrior society. It did not take him long to prove himself a warrior, but apparently he was not pleased with his choice, and soon after becoming a man he left that society and became a member of the Bone Scrappers (also known as the Crooked Lances). While still young he married Little Sage Woman. Due to a matrilineal clan structure, he left the Hairy People clan and became a member of his wife's clan, the Wuh´tapiu.[49]

TWO

Riding into the Future

THE DARING PORTION of the Tsistsistas had gambled on their future by breaking away from those of their tribe who had decided to remain in the north and along the rivers to the east. They sought a new life and felt that it was before them on the central and southern plains. Not that many moons had passed since the Tsistsistas began to obtain horses. Once they mastered the exceptional skills and mobility that the horse gave them, they were well on their way to creating a new lifeway beyond their wildest imagination. The horse allowed them to trail the buffalo herds that ranged deep into this new land. This majestic beast had become key to their life and provided much of their needs from food to clothing to blankets to lodge and shield covers to a commodity that had great trade value.

The horse, combined with the buffalo, allowed them to turn their backs on living in stationary villages and dependent upon growing food. No longer would their immobile settlements be targets for larger Indian groups that wanted to kill and steal their women and children.[1] The horse also meant that they were no longer subservient to the Sioux and other powerful or more plentiful tribes that could on a whim decimate their numbers.

The future had arrived. Although still unknown and indefinite, the plains offered them a new life in a new land. It was theirs for the taking, and those who seized the day entered a golden age with the horse. Still, they had no idea what would happen other than that they could hunt buffalo and provide for their families. The horse also gave them the ability to trade for what they did not have. They already knew that the white man in the northeast had guns and powder and fancy cloths, while the Southwest of the Spanish-speaking people offered different items that were also of value such as the horse. The Tsistsistas created their own northeast-southwest diagonal corridor to the east of the Rocky Mountains. Controlling trade in their new land between the Platte and Arkansas Rivers would change their lifeway as never before.

At the same time they were aware that other Indian peoples inhabited the land they began to dominate. This undoubtedly meant warfare, or perhaps not. They had now become an aggressor and could attack tribal enemies to obtain not only horses and supplies, but also women and children, as birth rates and the size of bands within the tribe remained small.

ALTHOUGH THE TSISTSISTAS AND THE SUTAIOS realized that the white man would be a part of their future, they never dreamed that a trio of them would soon enter their lives.

Brothers Charles and William Bent (b. November 11, 1799, in Charleston, West Virginia, and May 23, 1809, in St. Louis, Louisiana Territory) were in Sioux country by 1823 or 1824 when William was fourteen or fifteen. They focused on the beaver trade with its ready-made market for pelts in the East. In 1826 they partnered with Ceran St. Vrain (b. May 5, 1802, near St. Louis, when the area still belonged to France). Although their early partnership still included trapping beavers, it now expanded to hauling goods from St. Louis to trade for skins and then hauling the hides back to civilization to sell.[2] Because of its location to three major rivers, the Missouri, Mississippi, and Ohio, St. Louis had become the perfect hub for traders.

YELLOW WOLF, WHO EMERGED as a daring warrior in the early 1820s, became the leading chief of the Hairy Rope People by 1826. He was described as a man of high intelligence, a small, wiry war leader, but also someone with a vision of the future. Lured by wild horses and buffalo aplenty, he had already led hunting parties south of the Moon Shell River (Platte). That year he and those of the Hairy Rope People who followed his lead moved from the Black Hills to south of the Platte permanently. Not satisfied with following the Ésevone (buffalo), and the horses that ran wild, that same year he crossed the Flint Arrowpoint River (Arkansas) and traveled farther south to raid the Kiowas and Comanches. His objective: horses.[3]

This would put him on collision course with the *vi'ho' i* and a meeting that would affect the Southern People's future beyond their wildest imagination.

During their first years of partnership the Bents and St. Vrain had seen failure and success as they trapped and traded for beaver skins along the Upper Missouri River. At some point they decided to explore Santa Fe, the city that dominated the southern trade. Since Mexico had won its independence from Spain in 1821, the city was no longer off-limits to Americans, and by this time Charles and Ceran had been to Santa Fe. Actually they hauled the goods to and from civilization, while William remained in the wilderness and took care of business during their absences. As William Bent aged toward manhood and managed the company's employees, he began to consider what he and his partners had and what perhaps they should have, and the gap was huge. William came up with the idea to cut out the trappers that pulled profits from their trading enterprise and deal directly with the tribes that dominated the plains between the Platte and Arkansas Rivers.

Charles and St. Vrain had discussed opening a trading post in Santa Fe. While St. Vrain handled this portion of their partnership, the two Bents reached the mouth of the Purgatoire River by 1829. Not satisfied with what they saw, they continued until they reached the source of the Arkansas River in the Sangre de Cristo Mountains, the southernmost of the ranges in the Rocky Mountains. Thinking that the nomadic Plains Indians would come to them and trade buffalo hides for their goods, they built their first wooden stockade.[4] The Bents and St. Vrain had formed a partnership, but the legality hinged totally upon the then United States–Mexico border. This area, at the southern portion of the Rocky Mountains, was known as the East Range, and at the mouth of the Arkansas it dropped about 4,600 feet as the water moved rapidly east and onto the upper plains and flowed to the Mississippi River.

It was still 1829 when Charles and William Bent and their trappers moved back down the Arkansas and stopped at the Fontaine Qui Bouille (Fountain Creek), a tributary of the Arkansas.[5] At this time William Bent, now nineteen or twenty, spoke with brother Charles and St. Vrain about his idea to create permanent trading posts to trade with the Plains Indians. They liked the idea and built a second stockade at the confluence, but there were no Indians with whom to trade.[6] Any trading that they may have done would have been illegal, as they did not have a license.[7] Charles set out for St. Louis, and St. Vrain traveled to Santa Fe, while William took charge at the log fortress.

The timing was fortuitous, for that year Tsistsista chief Yellow Wolf and a war party, which also included Wolf Chief and Little Wolf, traveled south of the Arkansas to capture wild mustangs. Unsuccessful, they moved into Texas. After raiding a Comanche horse herd on the Red River, they hustled north. Yellow Wolf had been aware of the *vi'ho' i* invaders and was curious. Certain that Comanches did not follow him, he approached the white man's stockade at the Fontaine Qui Bouille. William greeted the Tsistsistas gracefully. As they communicated mostly with sign language, the two men saw a potential partnership and were open to the possibilities that it might present.[8] Yellow Wolf's warriors were thrilled with what Bent had to trade. They also liked his open and friendly manner. Over the next three days Yellow Wolf questioned the *vi'ho' i*'s intentions and was pleased with the answers.

When the chief and his warriors resumed their journey to their village on the Fat River (South Platte), two young warriors, infatuated with the white man's trinkets and way of life, refused to depart with Yellow Wolf and the war party, as was their right. Instead they remained behind at Bent's stockade.

Yellow Wolf had misjudged the Comanches' anger over the raid, and never realized that Comanche chief Bull Hump and a war party tracked the Tsistsistas' trail northward. Luckily for him and those with him, they headed north when they did. Not so for the two young warriors, as they were trapped within the white man's wooden fortification. William Bent found himself in the same pitiful position, as Tsistsistas' moccasin prints were all over the ground, and worse, he had two warrior guests—a combination for disaster. With the gates to the fort shut, William walked toward Bull Hump and his war party to see what he wanted. Using sign language, Bull Hump made it clear that his horses had been stolen, and he wanted them back. He demanded to know which way the Tsistsistas traveled. Bent said that the Tsistsistas had ridden to the northeast. It was not quite true, but Bull Hump would figure that out for himself. Although livid, Bull Hump accepted what he understood of the white man's signs before he and his war party rode off.

Yellow Wolf's initial meeting with William Bent, during the tail end of a raid on a Comanche horse herd in 1829, led to a follow-up meeting with Bent and his brother Charles. He told them that if they moved down the Arkansas River and closer to the land where the Cheyennes hunted buffalo, that his and other bands would trade with them. According to George Bent, High Back Wolf was present at the second meeting. Lieutenant James W. Abert painted at least two watercolor portraits of Yellow Wolf at Bent's Fort in 1845. Abert tipped this watercolor of Yellow Wolf into his personal copy of *Message from the President . . . Communicating a Report of an Expedition Led by Lieutenant Abert, on the Upper Arkansas and through the Country of the Camanche Indians, in the Fall of the Year 1845*. Washington, 1846. The other painting he did of Yellow Wolf was of him sitting facing forward.

Abert, J. W. (James William). Watercolor plates, Yale Collection of Western Americana, Beinecke Rare Book & Manuscript Library. Call number: Zc20 846un, Image number: 1244715.

The two Tsistsista warriors were grateful for what Bent had done to save their lives, and when they rejoined Yellow Wolf's band they shared the story. Bent had done what he did to remain alive. At the same time he had unwittingly paved the way for his and the Tsistsistas' future.

Yellow Wolf had not finished with the short *vi'ho' i* he had met on Fontaine Qui Bouille. As the white man plotted his future, so did Yellow Wolf. That summer the chief returned to the trader's stick fort. This time he brought other chiefs (High Back Wolf and Standing on Hill as well as Little Wolf and Wolf Chief), as it was important that they viewed and experienced what he did. During this meeting they smoked a pipe, shared gifts, and as William Bent now knew a smattering of Tsistsista words, which he mingled with sign language, they talked—good talk that benefited both sides. When Bent stated that he and his partners intended to build a permanent trading post at Fontaine Qui Bouille, Yellow Wolf told them that this was too far from the buffalo hunting grounds. His people did not like to venture away from the plains during the snow moons, as they did not like moving far from where the buffalo roamed. He told the whites to build their trading post on the Flint Arrowpoint at the Purgatoire. If they did this, Yellow Wolf said he would bring the Hairy and Scabby bands to winter in the Big Timbers. Of more importance, Yellow Wolf said that his people would have plenty of buffalo robes to trade. Charles Bent, who was present, liked the idea and accepted it immediately.[9]

That year Charles and William Bent traveled to the confluence of the suggested rivers and began building a mud and stone adobe fortress on the banks of the Arkansas River. But before it was complete, William Bent obtained what would be the first of many names. Yellow Wolf named him "Little White Man" because of his height. Soon the Arapahos, Kiowas, Comanches, and Kiowa-Apaches began calling him "Roman Nose." Many years later—long after William Bent's death—the ethnologist James Mooney wrote about the Kiowas. Mooney insisted that a white man called "Roman Nose" was the first white man to trade with the Kiowas on the Arkansas, but did not know his name. George Bent, William's then-aging son, asked Mooney if this "Roman Nose" was also called "Mo-ta-ho-kiah," and Mooney answered, "yes that was it."[10]

This solitary outpost that would eventually be called "Bent's Fort" would soon change the future of the Cheyennes, Arapahos, and Bent, St. Vrain & Company.

In the early 1830s the Tsistsistas became associated with the Hinono'eino', or the *Nŭm o sĭn' ha nhĭ' a*, a name the Tsistsistas called the Arapahos (which means "build their fires to the south"). As George Bird Grinnell wrote, "The account of the Arapahoes' joining the Cheyennes is vague though much has been written on the subject. A milder and more easy going people than the Cheyennes, the Arapahoes yet fought side by side with them in many a stubborn battle. There is a large infusion of Arapaho blood in the Cheyenne tribe, for many Cheyenne men married Arapaho women. On the other hand, it is my impression that comparatively few Cheyenne women have married Arapaho men."[11] Intertribal marriage played a major role in the close association between the two tribes. Zdeněk Salzmann provided a reason for this vagueness: "[T]he presence of the Arapaho west of the Missouri River is not conclusively documented until the end of the eighteenth century, by which time they began to be referred to as having hunted in an area extending from present-day northwestern Montana to western South Dakota and Nebraska and as far south as the Arkansas River in Colorado."[12]

The Cheyennes that would become the Southern Cheyennes had pulled the Arapahos in with them as trading partners with the Bents, and around 1830 they and the Arapahos began sharing the land between the Platte and Arkansas Rivers.

This three-way association (Southern Cheyennes–Arapahos–Bents/St. Vrain) gave the Indians what they needed to complete their dominance in and across their land, for it allowed them to become the middleman and trade with Hispanics, whites, and Indians to the south and with whites, Sioux, Arapahos, and Cheyennes, along with other Indians in the north and northeast. It was also at this time that William Bent became aware that gold was in the region, for occasionally he received it as payment. Again, if the payment was for goods that he sold, he was functioning as a trader illegally. Bent rightfully feared that a gold rush would mark the end of the Cheyennes and Arapahos as their "home and hunting grounds will be appropriated by the white man and they themselves . . . finally exterminated."[13]

Early in 1830 a Tsistsista war party traveled to the lower Platte River to raid the Pawnees but instead were surrounded by the Wolf People and killed. Afterward the Skidi Pawnees scalped and cut the dead into pieces, and left the hacked-up meat in a stream or pool of water for wolves to devour. The Tsistsistas learned of their end when either a Hinono'ei or Tsistsista war party found what was left of the remains. The Tsistsistas wanted revenge. The council chiefs for Omisis, also known as Ohméséhesos (Northern Cheyennes), and the Southern People met and discussed this. Once in agreement, they approached the keepers of the Sacred Buffalo Hat and the Sacred Arrows to see if they would lead the attack. The holy men agreed. At this time White Thunder (b. ca. 1763), a Sutai who had married a Tsistsista woman (Tail Woman), was the Keeper of the Sacred Arrows, and had been since about 1820.[14]

The entire tribe did not join together often for the purpose of going to war.[15] When it did happen, the Tsistsistas' two sacred objects, Maahótse (Sacred Arrows) and Is´siwun (Sacred Buffalo Hat) led the way.[16] The Tsistsistas had a defined religion and sacred ceremonies that guaranteed their safety, longevity, and success in battle. If the Keeper of the Sacred Arrows or a war leader broke a taboo it could lead to tragedy for the People.

Moons passed. Finally in summer of that year the Northern and Southern People joined as one and, along with Arapahos and Sioux, moved east toward where the Skidi Pawnees hunted buffalo. White Thunder led the exodus eastward as it skirted the Platte River. These sacred objects almost never went to war, but when they did, all the Tsistsistas merged to confront an enemy. White Thunder was confident that scouts would find the hated Wolf People. For centuries the Tsistsistas had survived enemy assault after enemy assault. Constant relocations to the south and then west, and their adaptation to their new environment, gave them strength, life, and their two sacred objects. The mobility of the horse gave them power over the buffalo, the animal that provided much of the essentials of life, and when combined with the knowledge that trade provided most of what else they needed, it gave them a confidence in themselves.[17]

High Back Wolf and his wife, She Who Bathes Her Knees, and their band accompanied the procession, which advanced in small groups. But, contrary to the Tsistsistas' confidence, all would not go as planned. Scouting parties returned to the tribe and announced that they found no sign of the Pawnees. A large war party replaced them. They, too, failed to locate the target.

Unknown to the Tsistsistas, Chief Big Eagle's Skidi Pawnees camped at the head of the South Loop in what would eventually become Nebraska Territory. They had traveled to this land to sacrifice an enemy captive to the Morning Star.

A hunting party from the Skidi village discovered four Tsistsistas, including Roasting (High Back Wolf's brother) and Light while they camped on a stream called Bird Timber Creek (since known as Birdwood Creek), which ran into the North Platte River above the forks of the river. These Tsistsistas had been part of the scouts searching for the Pawnees. The hunters attacked. After an attempt to defend themselves behind the stream bank failed, the Tsistsistas retreated onto the prairie with the enemy in pursuit.

At this time the main village of the Tsistsistas and their allies moved to meet the scouting parties at a predetermined location. One of the advance groups stumbled upon Roasting's camp, and quickly realized what had happened. The fight had ended on the prairie, but the bodies had been dragged about after death. The advance party found the warrior's decomposing bodies by a "little stream" near where the fight had begun. The Tsistsistas called the place "where the scouts were killed and rotted."[18]

The tragic news spread quickly among the tribe, and the advance came to a halt. While the Called Out People set up camp and mourned, the chiefs, who sensed the urgency to learn the location of their tribal enemy, met in council. After smoking a pipe they decided to increase the search for the Pawnees. Additional scouting parties were sent out, and they followed the Skidis' trail.

By this time the Pawnee hunting party had returned to the main Skidi village and announced that they had killed Tsistsistas. Although unsure if the enemy was near, runners rode to outlying camps and directed their brethren to join the main village.

The Tsistsista scouting party that followed the Pawnee trail moved stealthily and discovered the main Pawnee village without detection. Days had passed before they returned to the Tsistsista village. They pointed to a high blue ridge in the far-off distance and said that the village camped at the head of a creek below the ridge. They also reported that they saw Pawnees converging on the village from all directions and that the enemy built breastworks.

The People wanted vengeance. The rest of that day and throughout most of the night, the entire village moved toward the Pawnee camp. Before dawn, Tsistsista warriors had formed a line outside the Skidi village and waited for first light. However, before the attack began, a large party of Pawnees set out to hunt buffalo. They rode near where the warriors hid, but instead of letting the Pawnees pass, young warriors attacked them.

This was too early for the attack. The Sacred Arrows were present, and they had to lead the assault. Worse, White Thunder had not completed attaching the arrows to the lance that Bull would carry. When he saw the excited Tsistsista warriors charging toward the enemy, he screamed for them to halt, to come back, for what they did was taboo. They did not hear him, and certainly they did not obey him.

At this time an old Skidi warrior who was ill, depressed, and had a terrible skin disease that he realized would never heal, knew that his end of life was near. Wanting it now, he asked warriors in his family to move him from the village and onto the ground where the fight would soon take place, as he could no longer walk. They did, carrying him on a blanket and placing him in front of the growing Pawnee line. He had a bow and arrows, but he would not use them. When his brothers retreated, he expected to be killed.

When White Thunder finally finished attaching the sacred bundle, Bull mounted and urged his horse to catch his brethren who had totally ignored the law of the Called Out People. As the entire tribe had moved to kill the Pawnees, he and the arrows should have been at the front of the attack. But he never overtook them, so the battle began without him. White Thunder must have cringed, for he knew that something evil would happen.

Seeing the old Skidi warrior on the ground, a number of other Tsistsistas charged him and touched him with their lances or bows as they counted coup.

They did not kill him.

Bull had failed. In disgust he yanked his mount away from the fight. When he saw the Pawnee on the ground, Bull galloped toward him. Other Tsistsistas saw his attack and yelled that there were no more coups to count on this man. Angry and wanting to kill, he ignored what he heard. When he reached the Skidi, he attempted to ride over him, but his horse shied away from the Pawnee. Bull leaned backward and thrust the lance with the arrows tied to it at the man. The Wolf warrior dodged the death stroke, grabbed the weapon, and yanked. Bull lost hold of the lance but did not fall off his mount.[19]

A hated Pawnee had the arrows! This could not be, for the arrows represented the Tsistsistas' power over the buffalo and their enemies. Instead of leaping off his horse and killing the man on the ground, Bull panicked. He had foolishly placed the arrows at risk to count a coup that could no longer be counted. Unsure what to do, perhaps even fearful for his life, he made no attempt to regain possession of the arrows. He turned his horse around and raced back toward the Tsistsistas' line, screaming that the arrows had been captured.

The Skidi on the ground realized from the Tsistsista's reaction that the lance and the arrows attached to it represented something special. He examined what he now held. "A coyote hide was wrapped upon the spear. About the middle of the spear was a bundle, and in this bundle were the four sacred medicine-arrows of the Cheyenne."[20] The sick Skidi knew he held something sacred. He shouted for Pawnee warriors to ride to him and take it. Hearing the old warrior's demand Skidi warriors rushed toward him.

Moments later, the Tsistsistas realized what had happened. They also rode toward the man on the ground, but they were too late. Before they got near him, he passed the lance to a Skidi warrior who then galloped away, as did the other Pawnees. In anger and frustration, the Tsistsistas killed the man on the ground.

The Skidi warrior handed the lance with the arrows to Big Eagle. The chief immediately charged the Tsistsistas. But instead of meeting him and attempting to retrieve the arrows, they fled in fright. All except for one. He yanked his mount to a halt, turned, and rushed toward the Skidi chieftain. Big Eagle turned and retreated with the lone Tsistsista in pursuit. Big Eagle allowed the warrior to almost catch up to him. He then turned his mount abruptly and again became the aggressor. The Tsistsista changed direction and rode for his life. Big Eagle charged after him. When close, the Pawnee chief struck him in the buttock with the lance, counting coup.[21]

Bull's attempt to count coup had turned potential victory into tragedy, for the arrows were gone. He had lost the People's power.

Soon after, the Tsistsistas pulled away from the Pawnee village, ending the fight. They did not know how many of their own or of the enemy had been killed. But that did not matter. All that mattered was that Pawnees had the four Sacred Arrows. The entire tribe retreated back to where they had camped before marching toward the Skidi camp.

As shock set in, the immensity of what had happened covered the People with a darkness. Many cried openly, fearful of the future.

Two winters passed, maybe three. The Called Out People were still without the Sacred Arrows. These were not good times, and something had to be done. At this time the entire tribe gathered within view of the Sacred Mountain to await the decision of the council of forty-four. Each of the chiefs wore an eagle feather, carried a pipe in a fringed bag, and sat in positions representing their status within a double-sized lodge. Facing the tipi's entry and in the place of honor sat High Back Wolf. He "was the Sweet Medicine Chief himself. His seat represented Ma[heo]'s home at the heart of the universe, and he, the greatest of the Chiefs, was to be as wise, as generous, as good a father to the People on earth, as the Creator Himself was to the People from above. The office of Sweet Medicine Chief was one of great holiness, for he bore under his left arm the sacred bundle containing the holy sweet root into which Sweet Medicine transformed himself before he left earth. Thus, through the Sweet Medicine Chief, the Prophet continued to guide the People with both wisdom and justice."[22] On each side of him sat the keepers of the Sacred Arrows and the Sacred Buffalo Hat.

The chiefs had gathered to decide if "four new Arrows [should] be made," as the Called Out People "could not exist without the Sacred Arrows." They decided that they should.

By 1832, and certainly by 1833, William Bent saw the completion of Bent's Fort, which was at first called Fort William. Although he and his partners had been stocking it during its construction, and improving their relationship with the Southern Cheyennes and Arapahos, they undoubtedly engaged in illegal trade. During this time William polished his ability to talk not only with Cheyennes and Arapahos in their language, but also with Comanches and Kiowas. By 1833 the three partners had fine-tuned their duties within Bent, St. Vrain & Company. Charles handled the business operations out of St. Louis including the caravans, and St. Vrain was in charge of the company's Santa Fe trade, while William managed all business at the fort.[23] Still, they operated outside the law; most likely feeling safe, as Bent's Fort was basically a nonentity far from civilization in a land populated by Indians. Charles would not be granted a license to trade with Indians until December 18, 1833.[24]

High Back Wolf, although respected and acclaimed, did something that, according to George Bent, displeased the People. Two or three days before the stars fell in 1833 some of the chief's relatives quarreled "in a dispute over a stolen wife" near his lodge.[25] Or was it that his relative, the mother of Hail, was mistreated by her husband? High Back Wolf heard the argument, rushed from his tipi, pulled the woman away and took her to her family and safety. One story has it that a Tsistsista named Flint stabbed and killed him. There is a second scenario a day or two later; in this one Flint knifed High Back Wolf after the husband's relatives got him drunk. Regardless,

Bent's Old Fort National Historic Site (La Junta, Colorado) is a replica of the trading fortress that the Bent brothers and St. Vrain built on the Arkansas River in the 1830s. They built at this location because they agreed with Yellow Wolf's request to build a trading post closer to the buffalo hunting grounds. This led to a partnership between the Cheyennes, Arapahos, and Bent, St. Vrain & Company that benefited all of them, albeit during the early years illegally. Charles St. Vrain did not receive a license to trade until December 18, 1833.

Photo © 1987 by Louis Kraft. Louis Kraft Collection, ACP010. Chávez History Library, Santa Fe, N.Mex.

Bent made it clear that "the Indian idea of a chief is not a fighter but a peace maker. . . . The Cheyennes said he deserved this [his death]; he was a chief and had no business to fight even in aid of his closest kinsmen."[26]

Stark, sudden, final. The death of a man who sought not to kill or harm but only to end an argument. That the People could accept the sudden demise of a chief simply because he had no business interfering is a harsh statement of a culture that cherished life.

Justified murder or not, the Tsistsistas lost a leader who used his brain and had been capable of working with the *vi'ho' i*. Although totally unknown at the time, the future would divide the Tsistsistas farther apart than the split caused when part of the tribe decided to live in the south. This separation would create two divergent views on how to deal with the *vi'ho' i* invasion and would ultimately create a chasm between warrior society leaders and council chiefs so strong that in the future, even the welfare of their very existence could never again bring them together.

A few days after High Back Wolf was murdered, an extraordinary event happened, and it was so huge that it was seen over the entire North American continent. On the evening of November 12–13, 1833, the Tsistsistas saw what they forever after called "the night when the stars fell." They also claimed that it happened in sadness to the murder of High Back Wolf. According to a newspaper account at the time, "it looked as if the heavens were pouring down showers of fire—others, that it resembled the falling of brilliant and burning snow—not an occasional spit here and there, but as it would look in a storm—save only, that the flakes flew in an opposite direction to the wind."[27]

THREE

Dominating a New World

BEFORE BENT'S FORT had been licensed to sell or trade goods to the Cheyennes and Arapahos, the relationship between William Bent and the Indians grew. As Yellow Wolf had promised, several Tsistsista bands moved south to the Arkansas and began wintering thirty-five miles below the fort in the Big Timbers. This gave both the Tsistsistas and Bent the opportunity to visit each other. Bent met White Thunder's oldest daughter, Mis-stan-sta or, as she was known to the white man, Owl Woman. She is "a remarkably handsome woman," Lieutenant James Abert later wrote, "[who] has not been obliged to work; therefore her hands are in all their native beauty, small, delicately formed, and with tapering fingers. Her wavy hair, unlike the Indians' generally, was fine and of silken softness. She put on her handsomest dress in order to sit for me. Her cape and undergarment were bordered with bands of beads, and her beautiful leggins, which extended only to the knee, were so nicely joined with the moccasin that the connection could not be perceived, and looked as neat as the stockings of our eastern belles; and the modest attitude in which she sits is characteristic."[1]

Stepping between the races and marrying at this time was taboo in the Anglo-American world, but it had much less censure on the frontier. Trappers had been doing it for years. There were numerous reasons: it added a bond and protection between the whites and the tribes into which they married. In Bent's case, it sealed his relationship with the Cheyennes. Owl

Trader William Bent (ca. early 1830s) near the time he married Owl Woman, a marriage into the Cheyenne tribe that would link them and history for all time.

The Denver Public Library, Western History Collection, Call No. 1F-21677.

Woman and Bent married in 1835. Although he did not partake in the male's portion of the Cheyenne marriage ritual, he did present many presents to his bride's family including horses, guns, powder, and other trade items. Owl Woman performed her part of the ceremony as if she was marrying a man of her race.

IN 1837 A WAR PARTY from the Bowstring warrior society wanted to raid Kiowa horse herds. According to George Bent, "next to the Prophet," seventy-four-year-old Keeper of the Sacred Arrows, White Thunder, "was the most venerated man in the tribe."[2] His word was law, and he told them that this was not a good time to perform an arrows renewal ceremony, which was necessary to bless the raid. The Bowstring warriors disrespected him, damned him, and worse, they beat him with their quirts, lashing him time and again until he surrendered to their dominance.

Before White Thunder performed the ceremony he warned the warriors that the raid would fail if they went to war as a previous tribal murder in 1836 had not yet been cleansed because the time was not yet right. "Wherever you go, you will be powerless!" he said.[3] They ignored his warning, his curse. Soon after, forty-two Bowstring warriors set out on horseback.[4] They had little luck and moons passed. Finally after a long search they came upon a grouping of Comanche, Kiowa, and Kiowa-Apache camps between Red and Canadian Rivers on the Washita River. As it was still day, two Bowstring scouts crept forward and hid on a hill above the Kiowa camp. Suddenly a mounted Kiowa hunter approached them from behind. Instead of remaining hidden they stood and fired at him. They missed and he charged into the camp shouting warning. The scouts ran back to where the rest of the dismounted warriors waited on the prairie. It was still light when mounted Kiowas found, killed, and scalped them.

Near the end of 1837 a Kiowa-Apache who had an Arapaho wife visited a Hinono'ei village and told the story of what happened to the long-missing Bowstrings.[5] When these Cloud People shared the news with the Tsistsistas, the camp went into mourning. Relatives begged the council chiefs and leaders of the warrior societies to take vengeance. Eventually word reached Porcupine Bear, chief of the Dog Man military society. "Dog Soldiers" is a white-man term.[6] Actually not all the Dog Men were Tsistsistas. Many were mixed-blood Tsistsista-Lakotas, as Dog Men and their children intermarried with the Sioux who ranged along the Republican River. Many of their leaders in the coming the years would be of mixed blood. As the intermingling of the warrior society increased over time, many men and women spoke both languages.[7]

Winter had arrived. Porcupine Bear refused to wait for spring and carried the war pipe to Tsistsista camps, even though he braved snow that covered Mother Earth. At each village the headmen smoked with him, agreeing that they would join him when he carried the Sacred Arrows against the Kiowas.

Finally he reached an Omisis/Ohméséheso village that was on the South Platte. For the events that happened next, either Porcupine Bear provided the impetus, or his timing was simply poor. If the former, Porcupine Bear presented the war pipe to chiefs and soldier society headmen, smoked with them, and obtained their pledge to join the war against the Kiowas. At this point Porcupine Bear began distributing whiskey.[8]

If the latter—it was Porcupine Bear's timing, and it could not have been worse. Brokers from the American Fur Company were present when he arrived at the village. These white men had traded liquor to the People and many of them were already drunk.[9] Worse, Porcupine Bear visited friends and relatives, including cousins Around and Little Creek. They had whiskey when he joined them, and soon thereafter everyone was drunk.

At that point, Little Creek and Around began pushing each other. At first it was in fun, but it quickly grew to anger. Little Creek pulled out a knife and leaped at him. They fell to the earth with Around below his attacker. Porcupine Bear, who sat by himself, drank and sang Dog Man songs. He was oblivious to what played out before him until Around screamed for someone to help him. Not thinking clearly, Porcupine Bear drew his butcher knife and rushed to protect the young man. Within seconds he plunged his blade into Little Creek several times. Suddenly sober, Porcupine Bear knew he had broken a major Tsistsista taboo: he had killed one of his own. He pushed either his or Little Creek's knife into Around's hand and ordered him to thrust it into the dying man. It had to be self-defense.

The Tsistsista way did not see it as the chief had hoped. He and Around had committed a heinous offense. The Ohméséheso council chiefs gathered and decided on banishment.[10] Porcupine Bear had been stripped from his membership and ranking within the Dog Men. He and those with him were now outlaws and outcasts, they were not welcome in any Tsistsista village or any Tsistsista council, and they were not to travel with the Called Out People.[11]

Worse, the Tsistsistas still needed to avenge the deaths of forty-two warriors. Yellow Wolf knew that the effort to secure revenge could not end because of Porcupine Bear's crime. He handed the leadership to the chief of the Bowstrings. Little Wolf, in turn, asked the other soldier societies to help him avenge his brothers' deaths. After the Ohméséhesos arrived at the Southern People's huge camp on the Arkansas below Bent's Fort—and they were the last Tsistsistas to appear—the arrows were renewed. The council of forty-four met and voted for war. As snow still covered the ground, the bands did not move south of the Arkansas until summer approached. The Hinono'eino' had already arrived at the Sand Hills, and the Tsistsistas pitched their village circles a short distance away. The chiefs of both tribes met and feasted. To this time the Cloud People had mostly avoided war with the Kiowas and Comanches, but now they accepted the war pipe from Little Wolf. Soon after, the tribes found their target when scouts followed a party of Kiowa and Comanche warriors returning from a buffalo hunt. They led the Tsistsistas to a large camp on Wolf Creek close to where its mouth met Beaver Creek to the northeast. Kiowa-Apaches and Comanches were in the village, and a large Comanche village was close.[12]

Porcupine Bear and those with him dogged the combined tribes as they moved south while camping some distance away. Early on the day that the Tsistsistas and Hinono'eino' planned to attack, Porcupine Bear was to the west of the attacking force when he moved out. The disgraced Dog Man chief's line of march put him on a collision course with the enemy.

Tsistsista taboos no longer meant anything to him. When he saw a Kiowa buffalo hunting party in the distance, he yelled to his warriors, "keep out of sight. I will deceive them."[13] Porcupine Bear knew that before blood could be drawn, that Maahótse and Is'siwun had to be uncovered for the blinding ceremonies. He knew this, and yet he ignored it. Mounted and with his back turned to the enemy, Porcupine Bull waved his arms as if signaling that he saw buffalo in the distance. The ruse worked, and the Kiowas rode toward him. Not expecting to be attacked, they did not exchange their travel ponies for their buffalo horses, nor did they prepare for battle. When his prey was close, Porcupine Bear grabbed his lance from the ground, yanked his mount around, and charged. The surprise was complete, and Porcupine Bear and six warriors killed the entire party of thirty men and women, all of whom they scalped.[14]

Although unknown at this time, Porcupine Bear had destroyed a piece of tribal custom and instigated actions that would eventually lead to a third division within the tribe.[15]

Unaware of Porcupine Bear's actions, the Tsistsistas prepared for battle. They left their lodges and belongings at their village circles. When they neared the Kiowa village, they left their women, children, and old ones in nearby hills; the Hinono'eino' did the same. The warriors, chiefs, and holy men rode onward, eager to begin the attack. What happened during the course of the day was confusing, but warriors on both sides died. According to the Tsistsistas, the Kiowas, Comanches, and Kiowa-Apaches lost warriors and women.[16]

The battle was a scramble of isolated incidents, and most have conflicting tellings of what happened. Walking Coyote, who rode a horse that Yellow Wolf gave him, and the warriors with him, saw a Kiowa man and woman. When he charged toward them, they turned and rode for their lives. The Kiowa warrior was on a fast horse and quickly outdistanced her. She yelled for him to come back and get her. He ignored her and rode on. Walking Coyote reached her. He counted coup and then killed her. Other Tsistsista warriors caught up with the Kiowa warrior and killed him.[17]

This battle continued through the morning and into the afternoon. One side advanced, charged, and killed, and then the other side did. There was bravery spread over the land, coups were counted, and people died.[18] But the key for the Tsistsistas was that the power of Maahótse had been broken once again.

White Thunder had remained true to what the Sacred Arrows embodied to the People. He had become one of the most important people of the Tsistsistas throughout time. He was a man of peace, a man with a vision, but on this day he stopped walking Mother Earth. White Thunder died when a Comanche and Kiowa charge breached Tsistsista lines and rode over older leaders. He was crushed to death under the pounding hooves of the enemy's horses.[19]

By 1840 THE TSISTSISTAS had become the dominant tribe on the central plains. As they amassed horses through trade and war, they were able to trade from the northeast to the southwest. With the addition of Bent's Fort on the Arkansas at the Purgatoire, they and the Arapahos increased their trading with other tribes while also obtaining their requirements, such as guns, rounds, powder, blankets, cloth, and beads. Their horse culture quickly evolved into an importance equal to that of the buffalo, as it represented wealth and manhood, for often they obtained this cherished animal by raiding enemies. The best horse-hunting grounds were below the Arkansas in the land of the Comanches, Kiowas, and Kiowa-Apaches. This meant that Tsistsista raids often targeted their enemies. Horse raiding became a showplace for young warriors who needed to prove that they were worthy, to show their courage by counting coup, and most important, to capture horses for themselves.

All was not as it appeared in the Tsistsista and Hinono'ei world. Worse, although both tribes thought they were in control of their future, they were not, as they did not adapt to a constantly changing environment. There were years with plenty of rain, and there were years of drought. Regardless of which, the horses they cherished always struggled to survive the freezing moons. Annually they lost weight and many died. Most never regained their previous weight or strength once the grasses began to grow again. During years of drought, and there could be many in a row, there was not enough grass or water to nourish their animals, and this often led to disease and death. Large horse herds required care and grooming, which was not sufficiently performed and led to other health issues including insect infestations.

But it was more than just adapting to the ever-changing weather conditions. The Tsistsistas and Hinono'eino' did not attempt to conserve their resources. Without considering the consequences, they degraded "their winter camps," especially the two Big Timbers (on the Arkansas and a tributary of the Smoky Hill). At first this was not a problem as there was "no infectious threat." But the ongoing "thinning of trees" for fuel, and the increasing lack of saplings as additional fodder for their herds created a growing worm problem that added to the reduction in size of these and other areas. Although aware that Bent's Fort harvested "riparian grasses for hay" and "winter forage," the Tsistsistas failed to see the importance of this.[20]

That summer of 1840 Kiowa-Apaches visited Arapaho chief Bull.[21] This came about because one of Hinono'ei warrior Little Raven's relatives had married an Apache woman, which in turn opened the door to friendly relations between the two tribes, even though the Tsistsistas remained mortal enemies. Bull's guests announced that the Comanches and Kiowas, who were then camped on the North Canadian River's north fork (Beaver River), wanted to make peace with the Hinono'eino' and Tsistsistas.

A Tsistsista war party had stopped at the village on their way south to raid the Comanches and Kiowas. Bull invited Seven Bulls and eight young warriors to meet the Kiowa-Apaches in his lodge. When they arrived, Bull filled a pipe. As Seven Bulls was not a chief and could not make peace, he refused to smoke, but said that he would listen to the offer. The Apaches explained that the Kiowas and Comanches offered to return the Bowstring scalps wrapped in cloth and that they would give each Tsistsista and Hinono'ei man, woman, and child a horse.

Seven Bulls called off the raid and returned to his village on Shawnee Creek, a northern tributary of the Republican River, and told High Backed Wolf of the offer.[22] On the second morning of Seven Bulls's return, an oversized lodge was created so that the council chiefs who were present could hear the proposal. After discussing it they decided to defer to the Dog Men. After High Backed Wolf told White Antelope and Little Old Man of the proposal, he said, "[C]all together your Dog Soldiers and talk this matter over, and let us know what you think of it; what is best to be done."[23]

This was a bold move by High Backed Wolf to allow the Dog Men to decide upon war or peace. "The Cheyenne had become dependent upon the horse, and any warrior's path to glory and wealth lay most easily and quickly in raids upon the rich horse herders to the south, these same Kiowas and Comanches. Acceptance of the proposal meant that the young men would be blocked in one of their main and favorite avenues of activity."[24]

White Antelope and Little Old Man called the Dog Men to council and explained that they had been chosen to decide upon peace or war. A Dog Man leader deferred to White Antelope and Little Old Man's decision, and the other chiefs and warriors agreed. White Antelope and Little Old Man chose peace, and returned to High Backed Wolf, the council chiefs, and Kiowa-Apaches and shared their decision. Runners spread across the land to alert the bands of the ruling.

Not long after the Tsistsistas set up camp on Two Butte Creek, Comanches Shavehead and Bull Hump, Kiowa-Apache Leading Bear, and Kiowas Satank, Little Mountain, Eagle Feather, and Yellow Hair, and a boy (Yellow Boy, Yellow Hair's son), appeared on a hill. They slowly advanced and entered the Tsistsista camp circle. After dismounting they sat in a line. "After they were seated all the chiefs of the Cheyennes, carrying their pipes, went to where the strangers were sitting and sat down beside them, making a long row. Eagle Feather carried a filled pipe. As soon as the Tsistsistas had seated themselves, he lit it, stood, and offered the pipe to each one, and all took a puff. Thus the peace was declared."[25]

The emissaries carried forty-two Bowstring scalps held in a Diné (Navajo) blanket, but High Backed Wolf refused to accept them. He did not intend to insult anyone; instead he wanted to move forward with peace and knew that the scalps would anger the Tsistsistas. High Backed Wolf stood. "Now we have smoked and made peace with these tribes," he said, "if any of you have any presents that you wish to give these men, bring them here."

Both sides decided upon a meeting ground for all five tribes—a few miles below Bent's Fort on high ground on both sides of the Arkansas. The Tsistsistas and Hinono'eino' on the north while the Comanches, Kiowas, and Kiowa-Apaches camped on the south side. "It is good," Little Mountain agreed. "There we will make a strong friendship which shall last forever. We will give you horses, and you shall give us presents." And it happened as stated; peace for all time.

YEARS PASSED. ON JULY 7, 1843, William Bent and Owl Woman's third child was born at Bent's Fort.[26] The timing could not have been more prophetic,

Owl Woman was Keeper of the Sacred Arrows White Thunder's oldest daughter. This watercolor sketch of her was created by Lieutenant James W. Abert in 1845, ten years after she married William Bent. Abert tipped his colored portrait of her into his personal copy of *Message from the President . . . Communicating a Report of an Expedition Led by Lieutenant Abert, on the Upper Arkansas and through the Country of the Camanche Indians, in the Fall of the Year 1845* (Washington, 1846). It is one of at least two portraits that he created of Mis-stan-star, as he spelled Owl Woman's Cheyenne name. Halaas and Masich, *Halfbreed* (2004), claim the correct spelling of her name was Mis-stan-sta.

Abert, J. W. (James William). Watercolor plates, Yale Collection of Western Americana, Beinecke Rare Book and Manuscript Library. Call number: Zc20 846un, Image number: 1182327.

for George Bent would come of age at a time when mixed-bloods needed to choose which race was best for them. Although not known at this time, his life would be unique.

AN ENTREPRENEUR WHO LIVED IN INDIANA but was destined to make his mark in Chicago, Illinois, experienced a major loss but then saw a total renewal to a life that would be rife with tragedy. His name was John Evans (b. March 9, 1814), and he had luckily been born into a well-to-do family, which allowed him to pursue his desires. Originally his studies had been medicine. Over the coming years he would make his mark not only in the medical world but also in education, and in avenues not yet imagined. By 1844 Evans and Hannah (m. 1838) enjoyed a life of success that was beyond their wildest dreams. But that year their two sons perished, Joseph Canby (b. 1839) and David (b. 1841). The loss must have been devastating. Evans had luckily found his perfect match in life with Hannah and their continued intimacy led to the birth of their third child that year—Josephine (b. September 30, 1844), who would become a cherished link between his past and future.[27] Over the next two decades her life would symbolize her father's life.

The following year—1845—Owl Woman gave birth to her last child and William Bent's second daughter, Julia, who was born at Bent's Fort. There were complications during the birth that Owl Woman would never overcome. "My mother[']s name is Owl Woman," Julia would later say in a sworn statement. "My mother died when I was a very small child. Slow Smoking [Yellow Woman] married my father, William Bent, after my mother died."[28] George Bent confirmed his sister's statement when asked about his relationship to Yellow Woman. "She was a sister of my mother, Owl Woman. After Owl Woman died in 1846, my father married Slow Smoking."[29] William Bent also married Yellow Woman's other sister, Island, at this time.[30]

IN JULY 1846 SEVENTEEN-YEAR-OLD Lewis Hector Garrard left his home in Louisiana and traveled by steamer up the Mississippi River to St. Louis, Missouri. There he joined Ceran St. Vrain's train for the famed Bent's Fort. John C. Frémont's expedition of 1842–43 prompted his journey of discovery. He had "letters of credit, cash, a pocket Bible, and a rifle, with a few calico shirts" that his parents gave him.[31] Garrard had a keen eye for what he would experience, and although almost totally unknown to history, he left a treasure trove of written description.

While Garrard inched westward with St. Vrain, major events were in progress—the war with Mexico, which had begun that year (the United States annexed Texas in 1845). On September 22, while in Santa Fe, General Stephen Watts Kearny laid out the law for the land that America had obtained—mainly New Mexico Territory. He also appointed Charles Bent, who lived in the Taos Valley, governor of the newly acquired land. Many Pueblo Indians and Mexican citizens living in the new U.S. territory were not pleased with the change of government.[32]

After reaching Bent's Fort on November 2, Garrard met William Bent. He described the trading post as "a quadrangular structure, formed of adobes, or sun-dried brick. It is thirty feet in height, and one hundred feet squared; at the northeast corner, and its corresponding diagonal, are bastions of a hexagonal form, which are a few cannon. The fort walls serve as the back walls to the rooms, which front inward on a courtyard. . . . The roofs of the houses are made of poles and a layer of mud a foot or more thick, with a slight inclination, to run off the water."[33]

Before nightfall on the eighth Garrard joined a man that he never dreamed of meeting for a trip into an exotic new world. "I started for the Indian village with John Smith," he wrote. "Yes! John Smith! [T]he veritable John Smith! After . . . the civilized world, and traversing the almost boundless plains, here, at the base of the Rocky Mountains, among buffalo, wild Indians, traders, and Spanish mules, have I found a John Smith. And, probably, for fear the name might become extinct, he has named his little half-breed boy John, whom we called Jack."[34]

The former mountain man and current Bent's Fort trader was known along the eastern edge of the Rockies, but Garrard spoke of him as a celebrity whose name and exploits were known east of the Mississippi River. Everyone has good days and bad days, and this is what makes them interesting and worth knowing. John Simpson Smith fit this simplistic definition of humankind to a tee. He lived a life he created out of nothing, doing things that were not accepted in his time. But then again by 1846 Smith was completely entrenched walking between two worlds that did not accept each other. As mixed-blood Tsistsistas would soon do as they reached maturity, so did Smith—he chose which lifeway best suited him.

For Lewis Garrard this trading trip would open his eyes to an unknown world and culture. He may have been young, but his literacy and inherent sense of what he saw were astounding, and he excelled at presenting a first-hand account of what he observed.

"Smith's squaw [Wapoola], a woman of thirty years or about," Garrard wrote, "with prominent cheek bones and other Indian peculiarities, rode astride of a high-pommeled Indian saddle. The horse was decked out with a saddle cover of blue cloth, worked according to fancy, with many-colored beads, and tin pellets pendant from the fringed edges, covering him from w[i]thers to rump. Little Jack, three or four years of age, clung behind his mother, plainly showing in his complexion and features the mingling of American and Indian blood."[35] Wapoola's son, a full-blood Tsistsista about ten, rode a horse and traveled with them.

That night all of them, including a Canadian named Pierre, who drove the wagon that hauled trade goods, their bedding, and provisions, and two others (Drinker and Lee), camped near the mouth of the Purgatoire (or Animas) River. Before calling it a day they ate pounded buffalo meat, drank coffee, smoked a pipe, and talked until the blaze of their fire faded.

The next morning everyone awoke wet and uncomfortable. After setting out, Smith and Garrard spent time together—one craved news of the States while Indians dominated the other's queries. Smith spoke about Tsistsista food, customs, and what he called their *easy life.*[36] Night had not yet arrived when Smith's train reached its destination—the Tsistsista village of Vip-po-nah, or "Lean Chief," as Garrard called him. To ensure they would sleep in the place of honor in Vip-po-nah's lodge, Smith and his party placed their "possibles bags" inside it. Wapoola and Jack might have been included, as the chief only had one wife and an unknown number of daughters. While Vip-po-nah's wife and daughters rearranged the chief's tipi, Smith and Garrard were surrounded by women and children as they unsaddled their mounts. The seventeen-year-old Garrard was surprised that the boys were naked, a custom that he learned continued from birth until six or seven (save for a necklace), while the girls were fully clothed from early in life onward. When Smith and the others entered the lodge a second time, Vip-po-nah said, "Hook-ah-hay! Num-whit!" which meant "Welcome, how do you do," as he knew Smith came to trade and would share his coffee.[37] Everyone drank water, ate meat, and passed a pipe. While Smith and Vip-po-nah updated each other on news, a crier announced that "Blackfoot [Smith] had come for mules; and all who wished, to come and trade; that [h]e had tobacco, . . . blankets, knives, and beads."

The following morning the village broke camp and traveled toward the Big Timbers on the north bank of the Arkansas. Young warriors rode back and forth as they kept the entire village moving. "The young squaws take much care of their dress and horse equipments," Garrard wrote. "[T]hey dashed furiously past on wild steeds, astride of the high-pommeled saddles. A fancifully colored cover, worked with beads or porcupine quills, making a flashy, striking appearance, extended from w[i]thers to rump of the horse, while the riders evinced an admirable daring, worthy of Amazons."[38] He continued:

> Their dresses were made of buckskin, high at the neck, short sleeves, or rather none at all, fitting loosely, and reaching obliquely to the knee, giving a relieved, Diana look to the costume; the edges scalloped, worked with beads, and fringed. From the knee downward, the limb was encased in a tightly fitting leggin, terminating in a neat moccasin—both handsomely worked with beads. On the arms were bracelets of brass, which glittered and reflected in the radiant morning sun, adding much to their attractions. In their pierced ears, shells from the Pacific shore were pendant; and, to complete the picture of *savage* taste and profusion, their fine complexions were eclipsed by a coat of flaming vermilion.

Garrard found himself mesmerized by his introduction to Cheyenne women.

> Altogether it was a pleasing and desirable change from the sight of the pinched waists and constrained motions of the women in the States, to see these daughters of the prairie dressed loosely—free to act, unconfined by the ligatures of fashion; but I do not wish to be understood that I prefer our women dressed *à la Cheyenne*, as it is a costume forbidden by modesty, the ornaments gaudy and common and altogether unfit for a civilized woman to wear; but here, where novelty constitutes the charm, 'twas indeed a relief to the eye.

The village traveled two hours before halting for the women to set up the new camp. A couple of days passed while Smith traded with the Cheyennes. After he acquired four mules he departed for Bent's Fort, reaching it on the evening of the thirteenth or fourteenth. The timing had been perfect, as William Bent was about to set out on a trading mission, again to

Vip-po-nah's village. Smith and Garrard joined the train, which delighted the young man, as he craved more time with the Tsistsistas. Upon their arrival at the chief's campsite, Bent slept in his own tipi, while Smith and Garrard were again the chief's guests. It bothered Garrard that women performed all of the work while the men sat around talking, smoking, and eating; that from childhood onward males were cherished while females were not. "The girls do not receive much attention from the father; they are reared to implicit obedience, and with a feeling of inferiority to the males."

As November sped toward conclusion, Garrard had seen the Tsistsistas' trading negotiations with Bent and Smith. Remaining near Smith, he came to know a man who was exceedingly intelligent, and according to Garrard spoke six languages: English, Cheyenne, Arapaho, Sioux, French, and some Spanish. The Tsistsistas liked and respected him. At the same time he saw a man with a ferocious temper and not one to cross. He had watched Smith pour cup after cup of freezing water onto Jack's face to stop him from crying. Summing up the trader, Garrard wrote: "Smith was strange in some respects; his peculiar adaptation to surrounding circumstances and perceptive faculties enabled him to pick up a little knowledge of everything, and to show it off much to his own credit—an unaccountable composition of goodness and evil, cleverness and meanness, caution and recklessness!"[39]

As Garrard enjoyed his time in the land of exotic people, events hastened toward conclusion. On December 26, 1846, New Mexico territorial governor Charles Bent wrote that on the seventeenth a former Mexican citizen informed him "that a conspiracy was on foot among the native Mexicans, having for its object the expulsion of the United States troops and the civil authorities from the territory."[40]

In early January 1847 Bent returned to his home in San Fernando de Taos in the Taos Valley to spend time with his family. Although he knew that some rabble-rousers attempted to stir up emotions in the Pueblo of the Taos Indians, many of whom had already been converted to Catholicism, some three miles north of the valley, he apparently thought all was under control, as several of the leaders had been arrested.[41]

Unaware of the growing tensions on the frontier, early in January 1847 Smith and Garrard continued to partner; the master and his student. The weather was freezing and snow blanketed the ground. First light on the third week found them back on the move. By afternoon their progress had slowed as they worked at cutting a trail through snow drifts. Due to the frozen state, Smith left his rifle in the wagon. Garrard would later comment, "a most foolish thing, not to be expected of a mountaineer."[42] Garrard, who rode, carried his long gun. They were so far in front of the wagon they could not see it. Smith's keen eye saw riders approaching. "Wagh! Indians, 'by beaver!'" he said. "[K]eep your eye skinned." The only weapon Smith carried was a knife.

The approaching riders were Arapahos. Smith and Garrard offered to shake hands, but the leading warrior ignored them. "Ten-o-wast?" Smith asked, meaning, "What is it you wish?" Hearing no answer, Smith repeated the question.

"Ni-hi-ni, veheo, matsebo, esvone Arapaho," came the reply, meaning, "[W]hite man was bad, that he ran the buffalo out of the country, and starved the Arapaho."

Smith explained that he loved and traded with the Tsistsistas, that his wife was Tsistsista, that he only killed meat he ate, and that he was not like the white man. "It [has] always [been my] intention to live and die with the Cheyennes," Smith said, "for [I have] thrown away [my] brothers in the States. The Cheyenne lodge [is my] home."

The Arapaho warrior (Garrard call him a chief) disagreed. "The white man has a forked tongue."

"I-sto-met, wah-hein," Smith said, which meant "P'shaw, no."

Smith's words changed the warrior's opinion. "Ni-hi-ni, ni-hi-ni, Hook-ah-hay," the Arapaho replied, meaning "Yes, yes," and "Goodbye." He and thirty warriors rode off.

John Simpson Smith did not yet know his future, but he was comfortable in his present, and this had given him confidence with the passing years. As Garrard surmised, Smith had a strength and a will to do as he desired.

Unknown to Smith and Garrard, Mexican citizens unhappy with American rule supplied alcohol to the Taos Indians and urged them to destroy the newly placed American government officials then living in the Taos Valley. In the early hours of January 19 a mass of angry and drunk Taos Indians along with Mexican citizens that opposed American dictum began a day of terror. This included an assault on Governor Bent's adobe home. Curses, screams of hate, and the firing of guns awoke everyone inside. The young women and children in the Bent adobe clutched each other in fear for their lives. Charles Bent dressed, while Maria Ignacia Jaramillo, his wife, loaded two guns. Instinctively he knew that if he fired on the mob, they would explode with rage and kill every living being in his home: his wife and their three children; Ignacia's younger sister Josefa Jaramillo Carson, who was then eighteen and married to famed mountain man and scout Kit Carson

(February 6, 1843); Thomas Boggs's young wife; and a Mexican woman in the governor's employ. He could not allow them to be massacred and refused the guns. His lone hope was to negotiate, and he waited until the mob bashed in the door and confronted him. Bent tried to soothe matters but failed, for the rabble shot him with rounds and arrows. Still, the invaders did not kill any of the women or children, perhaps because Bent did not attempt to kill anyone. After the invaders left, Bent's family struggled to ease his pain and save his life. They failed, and fearful for their lives, they began to dig a hole through the twelve-inch adobe wall and into the home of a French Canadian and his Mexican wife. Their woman neighbor chipped away at the joining wall from her side. Once the hole was large enough for Mrs. Carson and Mrs. Boggs to escape, the neighbor hid them until an elderly Mexican took them into his house. After dressing them as Indians, he had them grind corn in his kitchen. Ignacia and her children remained in the house with their dead husband and father.[43] Sheriff Lee and others died on that day.

On the morning of January 19 John Smith and Lewis Garrard traded beads with an elderly Indian woman for a piece of meat in one of William Bent's log houses in the Big Timbers. While she negotiated for more beads, she pointed to a man approaching on horseback. "Po-ome!" she said, [N]um-whit veheo." ("Blackfoot! [L]ook yonder, there's a white man.")[44] Smith greeted the visitor, whom he called, "Louy." The newcomer quickly shared what he knew of Governor Bent's murder and the uprising at "Touse" (Taos). The news shocked everyone and spread quickly. William Bent, who was at his cabins downriver of the fort, met with Louy. "We pitied William," Garrard stated. When the Indians that were present heard, they wanted to send a war party to the Taos Pueblo and avenge Charles's death. Bent said no, but that if needed, he would organize a force at the fort. "The news had quite a depressing effect upon us," Garrard recalled. "We were even apprehensive of our own safety in case the Santa Féan forces were overpowered; for it was probable the country, from El Paso to El Valle de Taos, had revolted; and, as Bent's Fort contained much of value and was an important post, a Mexican expedition might well be expected."

IT WAS SOMETIME AFTER the January 1847 Taos revolt when Thomas Fitzpatrick, the famed plainsman who had many Indian friends during his time as trapper and mountain man, began to question life in the Southwest. According to him, "many volunteers should die of disease."[45] With Bent's Fort his final destination, for safety Fitzpatrick joined a caravan that traveled to Santa Fe. John Smith, his wife Wapoola (who was Chief Yellow Horse's sister), and their son Jack (who looked white and Cheyenne in adulthood) were in the city.[46] "Before leaving Santa Fe, I met with the man who I had all along intended to engage as interpreter for the Cheyennes and Arap[a] hos," Fitzpatrick reported.[47] "I engaged him for three months . . . at twenty-five dollars per month."

After joining a wagon train accompanied by discharged soldiers, Fitzpatrick, Smith, and his family reached Bent's Fort in late August 1847. As they approached the trading post they saw that not much had changed since it had been completed about 1832 other than an enormous American flag that fluttered in the breeze.[48] The agreement between the Bents, Tsistsistas, and Hinono'eino' continued to thrive: buffalo robes and furs for the white men, and beads, cloth, coffee, and the all-important weapons and ammunition for the tribes.

Fitzpatrick's mission was to meet with two of the five tribes for whom he had recently become agent. And he was a good choice, for they knew and respected him. As Fitzpatrick reported, soon after his and Smith's arrival at Bent's Fort, "a large portion of the Ch[e]yennes, and a few of the Ar[a]p[a] hos, who, on hearing of my arrival, hastened to see me, no doubt expecting to receive presents, but in this they were sadly disappointed."[49] Not missing a beat, Fitzpatrick, with Smith interpreting, told them to arrange a council, as he wanted to meet with them.

Soon after, Fitzpatrick, Smith, and their entourage, which included Bent's Fort staff, traveled to the meeting ground. The trading post provided bread, coffee, and other necessities for a celebration before sitting in council. When the meeting began, Fitzpatrick spoke about the United States' "kind intentions" toward the tribal bands of the Tsistsistas, the Hinono'eino', and the Sioux (who were not his wards) that remained at peace with the white man. He made it clear that he intended to learn "what Indians were engaged in plundering and robbing travellers on the Santa Fe road, and throughout the country."[50]

The council was long, but Fitzpatrick only featured one Indian speaker from the three tribes that attended the powwow. Already the number of buffalo and other game that the Plains Indians depended on for their survival had begun to noticeably decrease. The three tribes knew what was happening. If not, Fitzpatrick "reminded them," which showed why the tribes liked and respected him. He had the gift of not only accepting those of another race but could see and understand their dilemma. He spoke of "the great diminution and continual decrease of all game."

Returning to "the murdering and plundering [of] his people," Fitzpatrick threatened punishment of warriors that committed these acts. At this time his agenda was in line with the U.S. government's goal, telling his wards they should "turn their attention to agriculture, it being the only means to save them from destruction." The People and Cloud People did not want this—not then and not anytime in their future.

Fitzpatrick had not finished. He had yet another problem to address. He spoke of "the many evils arising from the use of spirituous liquors," and advised abandoning them "altogether" as they were a "degrading and abominable . . . practice."

Southern Tsistsista chief Yellow Wolf stood and said he would share Broken Hand's words with the Called Out People, and that they would be cherished. He also said (and this is only if Smith's translation was accurate), "[W]e are very poor and ignorant, even like the wolves [o]n the prairie; we are not endowed with the wisdom of the white people. Father, this day we rejoice; we are no more poor and wretched; our great father [in Washington] has at length condescended to notice us, poor and wretched as we are; we now know we shall live and prosper, therefore we rejoice." There was no reason to grovel and beg, for they dominated their land. The white man had become the intruder, but at this time he was little more than a nuisance. The much-needed herds of buffalo, antelope, and deer had shrunk, but the three tribes remained in total control of their lifeways and future. Still, they craved presents that the *vi'ho' i* more often than not gave to warring bands when hostilities ended. The People were angered and hurt that they, who were friends with the *vi'ho' i*, did not receive these gifts. Before discussing the murder of Old Tobacco by whites the previous year, Yellow Wolf stated "that the Ch[e]yennes are ready and willing to obey him [the great father] in every thing; but, settling down and raising corn, that is a thing we know nothing about, and if he will send some of his people to learn us, we will at once commence, and make every effort to live like the whites."

Yellow Wolf's words were ignored, if even considered.

Was 1847 the first time the Tsistsistas and Hinono'eino' heard the request—or demand—to turn their back on their lifeways? Yellow Wolf not only addressed it but replied that the People would do as told. His words were his, but if he meant what he said, only those who followed his lead would consent to them. The Dog Men and the other warrior societies had not agreed to walk away from their life of the horse and buffalo, and neither had any of the council chiefs who were not present.

"I believe the Ch[e]yennes are serious in the professions of friendship; they plainly see what must befal[l] them on the extinction of game, and therefore wish to court the favor of the United States government, hoping to obtain assistance." Either the Tsistsistas present at the council presented a false image of their desire to do as told, or Fitzpatrick totally misread what he saw and heard. Continuing, he stated: "Many of them appear very desirous to commence raising corn, but I fear the effort will be found too laborious for them, unless they are encouraged and assisted." It mattered not, for the demand and the return offer to comply floated off in the wind, even though it was in Fitzpatrick's report. The Cheyennes' and Arapahos' futures loomed before them, but much time would pass before this "big talk" demand would again be made.

The agent also reported the various tribes' sizes and approximate warrior counts (and his numbers included only those people then living below the Platte River). According to Fitzpatrick the Cheyennes had 280 lodges or less and not more than 500 warriors; the Arapahos had approximately 350 lodges and 800 warriors; the Sioux then living near the north fork of the Platte River but who roamed to the south had 800 lodges and between 2,000 and 4,000 warriors.

Fitzpatrick's opinion of the Arapahos was not close to his view of the Cheyennes. "The Ar[a]p[a]hos are most to be dreaded, not on account of their superior bravery and courage, as they do not excel the others in that respect; but [from their] . . . defeat of the whites on the Santa Fe road."

IN 1848 TSISTSISTA BANDS from the north and the south met on what they called the Sand Hill Timbers on the south side of the Arkansas River. Violence had happened within the tribe when Walking Coyote had killed White Horse at St. Vrain's Fort on the South Platte after White Horse ran off with his wife, White Horse Stealing. But the Sacred Arrows were not renewed, as no one had requested that it be done. As always, a large number of people could not live in the same location for an extended amount of time, as there was not enough game to sustain them or enough grass for their livestock. The bands needed to separate to procure food, so the Scabby band moved down the Arkansas and toward the Cimarron River, and two warriors set out to hopefully locate a herd of buffalo, which were scarce. Moons passed and they did not return. Worried relatives asked the chiefs to send a war party to find them. These warriors found the remains in recently dug graves in a Mexican buffalo hunters' camp in New Mexico Territory. Many Tsistsistas spoke against making war, as the Sacred Arrows had not been renewed. Council chiefs met and agreed that a war party should not avenge the killing, as the Mexicans had strong medicine that could make those who attacked them sick. This had happened when Kiowas and Kiowa-Apaches had raided into Mexico, and later their tribes had been struck with smallpox, with fully half of their people dying.[51]

Not happy with the decision, relatives approached leading warriors to avenge the murders, as council chiefs only ruled those that followed their lead. Any warrior could have a dream that told him to lead a war party. If other warriors believed that the raid would be successful they would join the war party, and the chiefs had no power to stop them. Black Kettle, who had married Little Sage Woman years before and had since proved himself one of the leading warriors of the Wuh´tapiu band, did not hesitate. He agreed with the relatives' request, telling them that he would avenge the two warriors' demise. Almost immediately Wolf Chief, Feathered Shin, and Frog agreed to join the raid into New Mexico Territory.[52] Fifteen warriors joined them, and surprisingly Black Kettle and Frog brought their wives on the raid. The goals: kill Mexicans, acquire horses, and obtain spoils of war.

The war party cautiously skirted the Purgatoire River that flowed into the Arkansas near Bent's Fort from the south, and which was a natural path southward, as Jicarilla Apaches hunted mountain sheep and elk in the Raton Mountains. The Jicarillas were Athapascans, people that had migrated to the Americas from Asia and then moved southward, like other Apaches, Navajos, and Pueblo Indians. As they had plenty of contact with Taos and Picuris, which were Tiwa-speaking, they adopted some of their ways. Divided into two parts, mountain people (called Olleros) and plains people (called Llaneros), Jicarillas were hunter-gatherers who grew vegetables. Those that cultivated vegetables in the mountain foothills mostly lived in permanent villages; their homes were hogans similar to those of the Navajos—who called themselves the Diné. But for most, surviving between the mountains and the plains and finding subsistence for large numbers of people was almost impossible, and they often split into small bands. When hunters stalked buffalo onto the plains of New Mexico Territory and Texas, elders and children remained in permanent villages, while warriors and their wives lived in tipis and hunted their major meat source in the fall.[53] They were natural enemies of the Tsistsistas, and Black Kettle wanted nothing to do with the Jicarillas.

After avoiding contact with the Jicarillas, Black Kettle's raid traveled south as far as they could until they were still north of Mexico but close to where he wanted to begin the raid. Moving east into the land north of the United States–Mexico border, they struck at the people they thought had murdered their warriors, killing and capturing horses and other plunder.

Satisfied that the two warriors had been avenged, Black Kettle moved northward, traveling on the west side of the South Canadian River. As he approached the mountains leading toward Raton Pass, the Tsistsista war party crossed to the east side of the river. Black Kettle headed toward the Cimarron River with the intention of returning to the Arkansas on the central plains.[54] He was attempting to bypass where the Jicarillas hunted elk, deer, and mountain sheep north of the Raton Pass and along the Purgatoire River south of Bent's Fort while at the same time avoiding an Apache or Ute village on the prairie. The route Black Kettle chose happened to be on the western side of a roughly two-hundred-mile-wide expanse where the southern of the two great buffalo herds migrated south in the fall to the Texas Panhandle and east and north in the spring to the prime hunting grounds of the Tsistsistas and Arapahos. The western side of this corridor was where the Jicarillas hunted buffalo, sometimes with the Utes. It was a "natural passageway through the arm of the mountains which swings eastward from [the Raton Pass]."[55]

As Black Kettle moved the captured pony herd toward where the People camped on the Arkansas, he kept scouts watching for enemies in all directions. Those in the lead saw a warrior on foot pulling his horse. They thought that he looked for something on the ground. When informed of this, Black Kettle directed two young warriors, Red Moon and Timber, to approach the warrior. They mounted and rode off. When they neared the warrior, he mounted and galloped off. They gave chase, but the rider rode over a bluff and disappeared. Red Moon and Timber reached the top of the bluff, and to their shock, the rider had ridden into a Ute-Jicarilla camp. Timber and Red Moon turned their mounts and raced back to Black Kettle and shouted the alarm.

With no time to waste, Black Kettle and his party turned the herd and pushed it in the opposite direction. As they did, Utes and Jicarillas appeared at the crest of the bluff and charged in their direction. Before long, Black Kettle realized that they could not retain their plunder and the herd while outrunning the enemy. But by then it was too late, for the Utes and Apaches were upon them. Black Kettle and Little Sage Woman, Frog and Red Eye Woman, and Wolf Chief engaged their foe up close as they attempted to flee.

A running fight ensued. At that time it could have gone either way, as the Tsistsistas struggled to break free and put separation between themselves and their enemies. It was not to be, for as they rode, the cinch on Little Sage Woman's saddle broke, and she fell to the ground. The Tsistsistas wheeled around to save her while Black Kettle rode after her horse, which he caught. By the time he rejoined the *mêlée* the Utes and Apaches had surrounded Little Sage Woman and those who defended her. When he brought the animal to his wife, he and Red Moon were not able to protect her as she attempted to mount the now bareback animal. The skittish horse bucked and Little Sage Woman again fell to the ground. By this time the Ute and Jicarilla assault was relentless. Feathered Shin fell from his mount, dead. Black Kettle and Red Moon received wounds. With the enemy closing in for the kill and with no way to save his wife, Black Kettle fled, and Red Moon followed him. Satisfied with their prize, Little Sage Woman, the Utes and Apaches did not give chase. But Little Sage Woman would not die on that day.

Although Black Kettle and his war party had lost their plunder, the horse herd, and Little Sage Woman, the running fight had not ended. Other Utes and Jicarillas continued their running assault on the rest of their war party. Frog's wife became the next target. Frog refused to run as the foe closed in on Red Eye Woman, their intention clear. He fought to save her until he met his end. Wolf Chief also died while trying to save Red Eye Woman. This ended the fight, for the Utes and Apaches had what they wanted: the Tsistsistas' loot, a horse herd, and two women.[56]

The war party limped back to the Arkansas and to their people. They had administered vengeance, taken blankets and other valuables, and gained the richest prize of all—horses. Still, the raid was a failure. Two women had been lost and three warriors had been killed. The next time Black Kettle saw William Bent, he shared the loss of his wife. Bent said that he would do what he could to find out what had happened to her. Kit Carson said that he, too, would help, but over time they would learn nothing.[57] Did she rebel against those who now owned her, against the rape and unwanted marriage that would become fact, and was she then killed? Or was she traded or sold to other Apaches, or perhaps to the Mexicans, there to be raped and sold until her end? Little Sage Woman's fate remained a mystery, and one to which Black Kettle would never learn the answer.

FOUR

A Failure to Grasp the Future

By 1848 John Evans, who still lived in Indiana, resigned as "superintendent of the Indiana Hospital for the Insane."[1] But then he again experienced personal tragedy when his third son, John, died. At this time he was still almost a decade and a half away from a career choice that would alter his life for all time.

Already William Bent had accepted Owl Woman's younger sisters into his household. After Yellow Woman (Slow Smoking) and Island became Bent's wives, they performed traditional wifely duties, and also raised and cared for his offspring. Yellow Woman (Slow Smoking), who was the youngest of the sisters, seldom stayed at Bent's Fort. Still, she provided William with his last child, a son, whom he named after his oldest brother. Charles (Charley) was born in 1848.[2]

As the 1840s neared an end, much had changed to the east of the Rocky Mountains. The glory days of the beaver trappers were gone, replaced by traders, with Bent's Fort being the foremost trading post near the Santa Fe Trail. But it was not as before. William Bent had lost his three brothers who had partnered with him in the mountains—Robert was killed by Comanches in October 1841 while hunting buffalo, Charles was murdered during the Taos revolt, and George died of consumption at Bent's Fort in

October 1847.[3] Moreover, Bent had tired of his disagreements on how to run the business with Ceran St. Vrain, and was outraged when his partner offered to sell Bent's Fort to the U.S. Army in 1847. A disgusted Bent bought St. Vrain's portion of the ownership of their bastion of trade on the Arkansas. But the profits had vanished. Realizing that the magnificent partnership that he and his partners had enjoyed with the Southern Cheyennes and Arapahos was at risk, he offered to sell his magnificent adobe structure to the army. The exact price he asked may have been an outrageous $50,000 or a modest $16,000. The military presented him with a $12,000 take-it-or-leave-it offer, which he rejected.[4]

In summer 1849 Bent set out with a wagon train of hides to Westport and St. Louis with his oldest son, Robert, who was eight or nine. Soon after he left, Yellow Woman took eleven-year-old Mary, six-year-old George, one-year-old Charley, and their grandmother, Tail Woman (White Thunder's widow), to a Tsistsista Sun Dance with the Kiowas near the Cimarron River on Bluff Creek (Mule Creek to the Kiowas). But it was a bad time to travel, as cholera, the "big cramps," spread like a prairie fire as it moved south from the Platte Road and killed at random. Tsistsistas on the Platte fell from their horses and died horribly where they landed as they attempted to escape from the unseen killer. William never reached his destination. News of the deadly disease stopped him cold, and he immediately changed direction and headed back to Bent's Fort. It was worse for Yellow Woman, for in the joint village, people began to collapse and die. A Tsistsista chief realized what was happening. "The Big Cramps!" White Face Bull shouted. "Everyone run!"[5] Panic seized the village as Indians left their possessions and lodges and ran for their lives. This included Yellow Woman, Tail Woman, and the three children, who had just arrived at the Tsistsista camp. As Julia was four, there was no way Bent would take her and Island on such a long trip. At the same time, Yellow Woman had to deal with taking care of her one-year-old son, Charles. Island and Julia remained behind at Bent's Fort, where Julia's early years were spent with Island, never with Yellow Woman. Julia would later state "that soon after my mother[']s [Owl Woman's] death some people took me and raised me until I was a grown woman and I never lived near Slow Smoking [Yellow Woman]."[6]

Yellow Woman, along with many of Yellow Wolf's Rope Hair band, and the Aorta band, fled in terror. George rode on a travois pulled by a mule that was surrounded by the Called Out People as they urged the horses from the village of death. He held his infant half brother Charles while

Mary rode on a horse. By late morning the following day they reached the Cimarron River (Many Pipe Dance River) and camped. While Tail Woman relaxed against a tree, she suddenly curled up in pain. She died of the cramping cholera at noon, and was quickly wrapped in a blanket and placed in the tree. Everyone hastily fled the campsite.[7]

The Kiowas called that summer of 1849 the "Cramp sun dance."[8] They remembered this time "as the most terrible experience with their history, far exceeding in fatality the smallpox of nine years before. It was a disease entirely unknown to them, and was particularly dreaded on account of its . . . suddenness, men who had been in perfect health in the morning being dead a few hours later." It was just as deadly for the Tsistsistas, for almost half of their entire population died.

Soon after reuniting with his family at Bent's Fort, William recalled his meeting with Yellow Wolf, when the chief had asked him to build a trading post closer to the buffalo range. He had done so, but what had been was no more. Hoping he could revive his glorious trading past, Bent decided to move closer to the migration path of the buffalo herds. He sent his children with Island (and most likely Yellow Woman) down the Arkansas to the Big Timbers, where he intended to build a log fortress and continue dealing with the Tsistsistas and Hinono'eino'. He had no intention of abandoning his adobe fortress to whomever claimed it, and stayed behind with trusted employees. Together they removed everything of value that remained, and then torched his prized fort. Much was destroyed, but not all, and from this time forward the ruins would be known as "Bent's Old Fort."[9]

By late winter 1849 the cramping sickness had ended. At this time the Southern Tsistsistas camped near Bent's trading fortress in the Big Timbers. Within the Sacred Arrows lodge at the center of the village, Lame Medicine Man, whose face had begun to swell, executed the "throwing it at him" ceremony. Unfortunately he made a mistake while performing the rite, and instead of spitting out the piece of sweet root in his mouth, he swallowed it. Soon after, the Keeper of the Arrows became deathly ill. The People believed that this happened because Lame Medicine Man swallowed the root. As he had no immediate relative to replace him as keeper, the chiefs hastily called for the council of forty-four to meet and choose his successor. This meant that the council chiefs in the north needed to travel to the south. Urgency dictated that they act, for it was mandatory that the current arrows keeper perform the operation that created his successor, which had not happened in his case, for White Thunder had died when the arrows were lost. When they met, they smoked the pipe to Maheo, to Mother Earth, and to Sweet Medicine. Afterward they chose Stone Forehead, the warrior who had become a mystic and council chief.[10]

The time had arrived, and Stone Forehead welcomed it. It had been ordained that he would become the Keeper of the Arrows. He had been a warrior, but those days had passed. Since then he had become a medicine man and leader that Tsistsistas followed. Now he would be become the spiritual head of the People and eventually the most powerful Tsistsista on the central and southern plains. Stone Forehead fasted, and on that special day Lame Medicine Man fasted. Just before the operation began, Stone Forehead lay on white sage that covered the ground with his head to the east. A buffalo head faced him and the medicine pipes were next to the skull.

At sunrise the dying Lame Medicine Man began to carve up Stone Forehead's body with a knife. The procedure, actually a mutilation which might be considered tattooing, was intricate and took time to complete, and throughout it the current keeper paused and both he and his successor smoked. Lame Medicine Man marked one-and-a-quarter-inch strips on Stone Forehead's arms and legs with charcoal. He drew a moon on his chest and below it the sun. Other markings included a strip that began at the wrist of each arm and ran up to the shoulder and then down to the moon and sun; two-inch lines two inches apart on the back of the arms; and finally lines on the outside of the legs that ran from the ankles to the waist and slanting lines between his knees and the waist. When ready, Lame Medicine Man used an awl to lift Stone Forehead's skin within the charcoal markings, which he then cut with a knife. After each slice, he used the awl to raise the severed skin and pointed to the east, south, west, north, above, and finally down, where he set the skin on the ground.[11]

By 1850 JOHN EVANS lived in Chicago with his family. That year he suffered yet another personal tragedy when he lost his cherished wife Hannah. She had not been thrilled with the move, which, related or not, led to her tuberculosis. Evans's business ventures thrived in Chicago, but Hannah's demise pitched him into the depths of hell. His young daughter Josephine had become his muse, his lone attachment to his family now gone. After Hannah's death Evans considered placing Josephine in a home while he toured Europe to come to terms with the destruction of his family. But Josephine brought him so much joy that he could not desert her. There would be no

John Evans with daughter
Josephine in the early 1850s.
Regardless of how history
praises or damns the second
territorial governor of Colorado
Territory one thing was
certain: he loved his family,
and especially Josephine,
who became a cherished link
between his past and future.
She was eight or nine in this
image.

*John Evans and daughter Josephine,
1853. History Colorado. Accession
89.451.1369.*

trip. Evans rented out his house while he and Josephine continued to live
in part of it. Around this time Evans, who was still clean-shaven, had a portrait of himself and his daughter taken. This precious time with Josephine
signaled a telling point in Evans's life; that regardless of how successful he
had become, it was the people in his life that counted most to him.[12]

By 1848 Thomas Fitzpatrick was aware of the U.S. government's effort
to build forts along the Platte River and to equip a regiment of mounted
riflemen to patrol the route, which was a part of the Oregon Trail. President Polk had presented this idea on December 2, 1845, and by the end
of the year the U.S. Senate and Congress had introduced bills. The process
began, with Fort Kearny established in 1848. But to Fitzpatrick's dismay,
the forts were undermanned. In his view the soldiers assigned to the various posts could not defend the forts, much less protect whites heading
westward.[13] This was not a new thought for Fitzpatrick, as he had previously stated (January 11, 1847): "[A] post at or in the vicinity of Laramie is
much wanted. It would be nearly in the vicinity of the buffalo range, where
all the most formidable Indian tribes are fast approaching, and near where
there will eventually (as the game decreases) be a great struggle for the ascendancy."[14] What Fitzpatrick stated was not new, but it had been ignored,

mainly because the U.S. government could not envision the Indians of the plains as any more than a nuisance. There were also obstacles, such as the Mexican war.

A year passed, and by then the U.S. had bought Fitzpatrick's former trading site, sometimes known as Fort Laramie, from the American Fur Company. Fearful of the growing aggression along the Platte River Road by the Cheyennes, Sioux, and other tribes, Fitzpatrick pushed for a "great" council with peaceful and aggressive Plains Indian tribes. Colonel David D. Mitchell, superintendent of the Central Superintendency of Indian Affairs, then stationed at St. Louis, had supported Fitzpatrick's idea but had no power to make it happen. He told Fitzpatrick to travel to Washington and pitch the council. The year 1850 arrived, and the U.S. Senate approved $200,000 for a council, but the House of Representatives killed the proposal. In 1851 Fitzpatrick returned to Washington and secured the backing of the Missouri delegation in Congress, and with their support the proposal met with approval on February 27, but the expenses had been reduced to $100,000. The date of September 1, 1851, was set for the council, with Mitchell and Fitzpatrick serving as commissioners.[15]

After his return to the frontier, Fitzpatrick traveled to the Arkansas River, which he reached on June 1, and in the vicinity of the Cimarron Crossing and at a place he called Fort Sumner (more often known as Fort Atkinson), he spoke to small groups of Arapahos, Cheyennes, Comanches, Kiowa-Apaches, and Kiowas. His goal was to invite these tribes to the council, and he sent runners to announce the news. The word spread quickly, and by the end of the second week all five tribes had set up camp circles. After their arrival Fitzpatrick met with each tribe separately. He served coffee, pork, and bread at feasts before passing out gifts to each tribe. After the various distributions, he spoke about the upcoming grand council that would be held at Fort Laramie on the North Platte and invited them to attend. The Southern Cheyennes and Arapahos said that they would attend, but the other tribes declined—the Crows and Sioux were infamous horse thieves, and the trip would be too long and hazardous for their ponies and mules.[16]

As the distance was six hundred miles, Fitzpatrick advised the Tsistsistas and Hinono'eino' to travel in small groups, "and procure as much food on the way as possible. . . . buffalo, elk, deer, antelope, and grizzly bear, besides a great variety of the different kinds of water-fowl indigenous to the United States." However, before the two tribes departed the area, Colonel Edwin Vose Sumner and his command, who were en route to New Mexico

Territory, camped one and a half miles above the fort. Sumner was about to assume his new position as military governor of New Mexico Territory.

Although Sumner's stop was short, it would not be without incident. His escort included wives of officers. What followed disturbed Fitzpatrick. Sumner's command allowed "the Indians . . . free intercourse in and about the military camp, a privilege, in my opinion, which should never have been allowed." He was both astonished and upset as "'familiarity breeds contempt' [no] better exemplified than in that country and its natives. Such free and unrestrained intercourse, carried on between officers, privates, squaws and Indians . . . was certainly a new thing to me." He rarely saw traders allow such contact between the races.

Fitzpatrick's fear was justified. Lean Bear (also known as Starving Bear and A' wōn ī nāh ' kū among others), was still a warrior at age thirty-eight.[17] Glittering stones attracted the Tsistsistas, and often they traded hides for them. A ring belonging to an officer's wife grabbed Lean Bear's attention. He stepped to her and took hold of her wrist to get a close look at it. George Bent claimed more than once that he removed the ring from her finger. She screamed in fright, and her husband stepped from one of the sod buildings with a carriage whip and viciously struck Lean Bear repeatedly. Although Fitzpatrick stated Lean Bear received "a good, sound flogging," he dismissed the beating as little more than "unseemly conduct towards the wife of said officer, and of a character which I have never known the Indians of that country to be guilty of before at least such as have the least pretension to friendship." He also had a strong opinion on how whites should act when dealing with Indians. "I have frequently witnessed a want of self respect exhibited by men in high positions on such occasions, thereby inviting the disrespectful and rude treatment of the untutored Indian; and I regret that the idea prevails, to a more or less extent, among many persons, that, to receive the respect and attention of Indians, one must cast off the restraints of civilized society, and assume conduct and manners entirely the reverse; such, however, is a great error, and I do, without hesitation, assert, that there is no course more proper for a white man to pursue among Indians than an upright, virtuous, and moral one, both in conversation and conduct; and moreover, that the very rules of decorum which govern a gentleman in civilized society, are both suitable and applicable in his intercourse with the Indian race."

Fitzpatrick presented one side of the incident, which was Lean Bear stepping beyond Anglo-American culture and touching a white woman. There was another side to what happened; the Tsistsistas considered it an insult to strike a warrior with a whip. The Called Out People never struck a male child—for any reason—for fear that it would break his spirit and destroy his chances of becoming a brave warrior.[18] Lean Bear had been struck by a whip and the Tsitsista warriors did not like it.

But the incident had not ended. According to Bent, "A great Warrior by name of 'Bear' was on his fine [white horse] urging young Warriors to get ready for fight. [H]e wore Bear Robe and 2 Bears Ears on his head with a big Tomahawk[.] [H]is face was all painted with black Clay and White Clay."[19] Bent went on to describe "Bear" riding through the village and yelling for Tsistsistas to kill the hated *vi'ho' i*. Bull Bear, born about 1835, was Lean Bear's younger brother. Bent's description shows sibling love and a readiness to fight against what he considered wrong, as he did thirteen years later, but he never called him "Bull" Bear.

The Bear had ignited the warriors to attack Sumner's camped caravan, for the insult upon his brother (physical or kinship) had to be avenged. That night, Tsistsistas asked the Kiowas and Comanches to join them, but they refused. The next morning Fitzpatrick, with William Bent interpreting, spoke with aroused warriors and soothed tempers while Sumner's command continued their journey to Santa Fe. As soon as the meeting ended, Fitzpatrick set out for Fort Laramie.

As the proposed treaty council at Fort Laramie loomed, many of the major tribes on the plains realized its importance to their well-being. Not wanting to miss the council, Stone Forehead and the Tsistsistas traveled north and set up their camp circles near the fort by late July. Although a major portion of the council was to secure peace between the tribes, the Tsistsistas did not hesitate to attack, kill, and scalp two Shoshone (Snakes) scouts during their journey to the council ground. Other tribes also arrived early, including the Hinono'eino' and the Brûlé and Oglala Sioux.[20]

Colonel Mitchell arrived at Fort Laramie on September 1. Colonel Samuel Cooper (adjutant general of the army), A. B. Chambers, editor of the *St. Louis Missouri Republican*, and Robert Campbell, one of the original owners of Fort Laramie, accompanied him. Although not all the Indians had arrived, and ten thousand were expected, Mitchell saw two problems. Due to the continuous flow of wagon trains heading for the California gold fields and Oregon Territory, the land surrounding the fort was almost devoid of vegetation. The recent arrival of the Indians and their huge horse herds meant that the Indians' livestock could not live off the land. Worse, that day, the caravan of gifts had not yet arrived. Mitchell wisely moved the council thirty miles down the North Platte to the mouth of Horse Creek. The massive procession began on September 4, and reached Horse Creek two days later. To ensure the peaceful relations between the tribes, Mitchell assigned camp areas that kept tribal enemies apart from each other. He camped at the junction of the creek with the North Platte, the Cheyennes camped upriver of the confluence and above Mitchell's camp, and the Shoshones camped to the east of Mitchell. Fitzpatrick and John Smith camped upriver on the creek.[21]

Editor Chambers described the Cheyennes as "a stout, bold, athletic set of people" who were "better supplied with horses and implements of war, than the other tribes." He claimed that the peace commissioners and military officers treated them respectfully, only to be looked upon by the Cheyennes with "great contempt," which they did "not hesitate to express . . . freely."[22]

The council began officially on September 8, and the white delegation made a mistake that would be repeated time and again during the coming years. They insisted that each tribe choose one chief to represent them in the treaty negotiations. The Tsistsistas designated Stone Forehead.[23] Unfortunately few whites that dealt with the Plains Indians, specifically the Cheyennes, ever understood that council chiefs were once great warriors and often leaders of the warrior societies, but were now past the age of going to war (usually between their late thirties and late forties). Council chiefs were men of peace. They might camp with the warrior societies but did not ride the war trail with them, for "the chief's authority was primarily a moral authority, subject to the respect accorded him by the people."[24] Cheyenne leaders only spoke for the people that followed them, which meant that no Tsistsista chief could speak for all the People. Fitzpatrick had spent too many years walking among the Cheyennes. He knew that Stone Forehead could not speak for all the People. He should have spoken up, but did not.

Article 5 of the treaty stated, in part: "The aforesaid Indian nations do hereby recognize and acknowledge the following tracts of country, included within the metes and boundaries hereinafter designated, as their respective territories."[25] Specifics for the Southern Cheyennes and Arapahos included:

> The territory of the Cheyennes and [Arapahos], commencing at the Red But[t]e, or the place where the road leaves the north fork of the Platte River; thence up the north fork of the Platte River to its source; thence

along the main range of the Rocky Mountains to the head-waters of the Arkansas River; thence down the Arkansas River to the crossing of the Santa Fé road; thence in a northwesterly direction to the forks of the Platte River, and thence up the Platte River to the place of beginning.

It is, however, understood that, in making this recognition and acknowledgement, the aforesaid Indian nations do not hereby abandon or prejudice any rights or claims they may have to other lands; and further, that they do not surrender the privilege of hunting, fishing, or passing over any of the tracts of country heretofore described.[26]

John Smith's translation to Cheyenne and John Poisel's to Arapaho must have been decent, for in the future, Cheyenne and Arapaho leaders would speak of this treaty and what they understood to be their land.

AT AN UNKNOWN TIME after the loss of Little Sage Woman, Black Kettle married Medicine Woman Later (Ar-no-ho-woh), who also belonged to the Wuh´tapiu band.[27]

SOMETIME DURING THE YEARS 1851 OR 1852 the Pawnees killed Alights-on-the-Cloud, a Tsistsista chief, while he wore an old Spanish breastplate. In 1853 the People sought revenge for his death. Dog Man chief Little Robe (Ski´o mäh´), whose son also died, carried the pipe to a large encampment of Tsistsista bands on Beaver Creek where it merged into the South Platte. He eventually met with soldier societies and Ohméséhesos, and then the Hinono'eino', Brûlé Sioux, Kiowa-Apaches, and Kiowas, as well as the Crows (as the last two tribes still respected the 1851 treaty). It was the sixth and final movement of the Sacred Arrows against an enemy. As they approached the Pawnee village, a Pottawatomi camp that included a few Sacs, perhaps anticipating a retaliation by the Tsistsistas, had moved near the Pawnees on the Republican River.[28]

Medicine men played an important role in the Tsistsistas' lifeway. If a man wanted to become a medicine man, custom demanded that he "pass" his wife or a female relative to the medicine man who would share his knowledge. The involved process included not sleeping with his wife or having sexual contact with her, and she had to consent to be passed. The medicine man's payment was large for sharing his power or medicine, and it was "a complete [sexual] connection with the woman" on the prairie.[29] The Tsistsista's wife (or female relative) would inform mystics to smoke and wait until the intimate act became fact. If nothing happened, the medicine man would announce this by touching her with sagebrush.

The Dog Men also have a ceremony wherein a chief or a warrior may pass his wife to obtain one of four "dog ropes." Little Robe passed two of his wives so he could wear one rope on each side when he danced.

On the morning of the attack, but before the ceremonial preparation had been completed, Big Head and seven warriors left the huge camp and rode undetected toward the Pawnees. All eight of them knew that no Tsistsista could advance beyond the Sacred Buffalo Hat or the Sacred Arrows until every portion of the blinding ceremony had been completed. Still, they broke this taboo, as they wanted to claim the first coup and first scalp.

In preparation for the upcoming onslaught on the Pawnees, Stone Forehead handed one of the arrows to a warrior named Wooden Leg. The women were not allowed to view this and turned away. Wooden Leg stood "in front of the [battle] line, [and] pointed [the arrow] toward the enemy, singing the arrow song and dancing in time to the singing, and, as he sang and danced, thrusting the arrow point of the arrow toward the enemy."[30] The warriors waved their shields and weapons toward the Pawnees as they stamped their feet in beat with the song. When finished, Wooden Leg returned the arrow to Stone Forehead.

Stone Forehead then walked to his cousin Black Kettle, who sat on his horse at the front of the battle line, and offered the Sacred Arrows to him to carry into battle.[31]

With the arrows ceremony complete and as the attack neared, Tsistsista Long Chin rode to the front of the battle line. He began to secure the buffalo cap on his head, but the string under his chin broke. Realizing his situation, he called for the entire battle movement to halt. In front of everyone "he pledged [that he would] give away his wife to have her passed after getting back to the village." Satisfied that all would be well when his wife was passed for his power, he reattached the broken string to the buffalo hat and tied it under his chin.

Black Kettle held the Sacred Arrows. Usually they were attached to a lance or a medicine stick. As he began to secure them to what he would hold, and knowing that he, too, needed power to defeat the Pawnees and more important, to protect the arrows, he also proclaimed that he would pass his wife after the battle.

The Tsistsistas and their allies moved forward. When they saw Pawnees near their village, they charged, not knowing that Big Head had broken with tradition and had broken the power of the Sacred Arrows. The Pawnees, with the support of their allies, the Pottawatomis, who joined the battle after it began, along with the Sacs, won the day with their rifles. They killed eleven Tsistsistas, including Wolf Tongue, who was married to Black Kettle's sister, Wind Woman, and one Arapaho.

Also in 1853 a war party of Tsistsistas attacked the Pawnees. Bull's son, Pheasant Tail, saw a warrior and charged him on his horse. The Pawnee held his ground and waited. When Pheasant Tail reached the enemy and counted coup with his lance, the Pawnee shot him. Black Kettle saw the encounter, and as Pheasant Tail fell from his horse, he rushed forward and killed the warrior.[32]

Soon after, the mixed-blood boy George Bent attended the ceremony that honored those who had died while counting coup on an enemy. The war party, which included Black Kettle, painted their faces black and lined up holding drums. Scalp carriers, warriors that held the scalps taken in the fight, stood on both sides of the war party. Everyone waited, for the dance could not begin until all those who had lost a family member while counting coup arrived. Bull, who had painted his entire body black, arrived with his wife. Bent remembered that he looked as if nothing bad had happened, for Pheasant Tail had died an honorable death. Bull signaled for the dance and singing to begin.

Not long after the Tsistsistas' fights with the Pawnees in summer 1853, the Comanches and Kiowas invited Big Head, Curly Head, and War Bonnet to visit them with the lure that they could show them where many "spotted horses" were available for the taking in Mexico, along with the possibility of captives, "silver mounted bridles," silver dollars to adorn their ponies' tails, and Mexican blankets.[33] This was an offer not to be refused. The Tsistsista leaders crossed the Arkansas and traveled south to the Cimarron River (Bull River to the Indians) with perhaps fifteen young warriors, where they met with a Kiowa named Black Eagle. Two Comanche and Kiowa war leaders (Heap of Bears and Sleeping Wolf) led the way south. The war party entered Mexico, avoiding Mexican villages and troops, and all looked good as they saw returning Comanche and Kiowa war parties with plunder and horses (the Kiowas were supposedly at peace with Mexico at this time). They continued south until they reached the mountains north of Chihuahua. Here Sleeping Wolf and Heap of Bears showed War Bonnet where he would find the spotted horses. Instead of remaining hidden, War Bonnet chose to take the direct route to the plunder. Curly Hair and Big Head demurred and argued for caution. War Bonnet called them cowards, which stung. The next morning before they departed, Heap of Bears and Sleeping Wolf warned them that they were about to ride to a dangerous place and that they should choose a meeting place in case they had to scatter.

Two days later War Bonnet saw herds of cattle and horses in the distance as the Comanches and Kiowas said he would. He directed Mad Wolf and Young Bear to kill a fat steer while he and the rest of the war party gathered horses and took captives. All had gone well, and War Bonnet and the Tsistsistas moved northward. In the meantime Young Bear and Mad Wolf found the cattle to be as wild as buffalo. They ran with the animals until Mad Wolf's arrows dropped a large steer. The point fell off one of his arrows when he pulled it from the kill. While Mad Wolf looked for it on the ground, his pony bolted.

At the same time, Mexican soldiers began to chase War Bonnet's war party along with the stolen horses and mounted prisoners. The soldiers were so intent upon killing that they did not see Mad Wolf climb up behind Young Bear on his horse and ride in another direction. The pursuit forced War Bonnet's raiders toward a stockade long in ruins. They reached it and were quickly surrounded, but held the soldiers off until deep into the night. Knowing they could not remain in the ruins, War Bonnet and the rest made a break for freedom. Big Head was shot as he stepped from the ruins, but War Bonnet and the others were able to get out of the stockade. They split up, only to be run down and killed. Wolf Foot and Head Fox were the last two to emerge from the stockade, and they galloped toward timber in the distance. Soldiers chased them. Soon a Mexican caught up to Wolf Foot and lanced him. Head Fox held a slight lead when he reached the deep shadows that trees provided. Visibility was nonexistent. When he rode into a low-hanging branch, the impact knocked him to the ground. On foot, he scrambled to avoid soldiers searching for him.

In the meantime, Mad Wolf and Young Bear had come upon a Comanche war party, who took them to a Comanche camp. Days later, Head Fox arrived with another Comanche war party. Time passed before the three of them joined a Kiowa war party that moved north with a herd of horses. The leaves turned yellow before Kiowas on the Cimarron River provided them with blankets, saddles, and horses for their return to the People, who were then camped near Bent's trading stockade in the Big Timbers. The tragedy affected many families. Women, men, and children cried. Dogs joined the chorus and howled. Women used flint to slash their arms and legs. Those who had lost loved ones lined up to hug the chiefs and head men of warrior societies, which meant that they wanted retribution. The council chiefs and warrior-society leaders discussed the matter and decided that a war party would enter Mexico at the beginning of the following summer.

The year 1853 also proved to be big for George Bent, as he turned ten on July 7. That fall his father, who owned a farm in Westport, Missouri, sent him and his siblings to live there. Robert was thirteen, Mary was fifteen, and Julia was eight. They would live in what George would later call a nice house while they attended school.[34]

BY THE TIME THAT LATE SPRING 1854 arrived, Black Kettle was in his early forties. His status as a warrior and his prestige among the Tsistsistas had grown over the years, but he had not become a council chief. Still the warrior, Black Kettle stepped forward and announced that he would lead the raid into Mexico during the summer moons to avenge War Bonnet and the others. His valor and courage guaranteed that others would join him, including Big Jake, an up-and-coming Tsistsista warrior named Little Robe, and approximately one hundred other warriors. Head Fox volunteered to lead the war party into Mexico, but Young Bear and Mad Wolf refused to put their lives at risk a second time. Supposedly council chief White Antelope wanted to join the war party, but his advanced age of sixty-five would have prohibited this.[35]

The war party moved south to a Kiowa–Comanche village, and then the mixed war party entered Mexico without incident. This time, avoiding detection was of paramount importance. As they continued southward they struck Mexican pueblos and caravans, and when approached by Mexican soldiers, they usually won the firefights, but not always. They continued southward as they collected plunder, horses, and prisoners, which included girls and boys. Mexican soldiers guarded a wagon train they came upon, but they fled when they saw the Tsistsistas. This capture gave Black Kettle's war party many Mexican blankets, something the People desired.

The trek south continued, but Black Kettle and his war party never reached the stockade ruins, for a successful raid suddenly turned deadly.

Mexican soldiers attacked the war party. The Tsistsistas must have been surprised, for the attack overwhelmed them and they split into small groups and fled. The Mexicans secured all that they had won in battle—everything—horses, plunder, and prisoners. Black Kettle had escaped uninjured, but as he headed northward, all he had to show for the entire raid of revenge was one mule. The raid had failed. Luckily most of the warriors who had ventured south with him made it back to the Arkansas and their people.

By her own hand, Elizabeth Minerva Sumner proclaimed herself perfect to brave new frontiers. Although born in Chillicothe, Ohio (August 31, 1834), she would spend sixteen years in Iowa. Although she considered her father, Horatio Nelson Sumner, a farmer, he bought and sold cattle to the Chicago market. "There were nine children in our family," she wrote, "five boys and four girls. I was the third oldest, spent my early life out of doors, and lived very close to nature. I was what you would call an athletic girl. There was nothing my five brothers and I could not do."[36] She would later describe Iowa at the time of her youth as wild and uncultivated.

Although unknown to Elizabeth Sumner when she was about sixteen, a young man named William Newton Byers (b. February 22, 1831) emigrated from Madison County, Ohio, to Iowa, with his family in 1850. His professional life began two years later when the U.S. government employed him as a surveyor. This led him to Oregon, Washington, and California. He returned to Iowa in 1854, most likely to Muscatine, and this placed him in contact with Elizabeth. After a short courtship they married on November 16, 1854. By this time Byers was both a surveyor and civil engineer. They had discussed their future and knew that it would be on the frontier. Shortly after their marriage they set out for Nebraska Territory. At Council Bluffs, Iowa, Elizabeth and Byers found the Missouri River rough, almost violent, forcing them to leave their stock and wagon on the eastern shore. Heavy winds made the crossing perilous, and by the time they reached the opposite bank, night had arrived. They had no wagon, no team, and no way to continue their journey to Omaha. Because they could not carry their trunks, this left them one choice: Byers would walk to Omaha, about two miles away, and employ a wagon to retrieve Elizabeth and their belongings, while she sat on the west bank of the Missouri. "To say I was frightened as I sat there in the dark . . ." Elizabeth wrote, "would be putting it mildly."[37]

Omaha had but one house when the Byerses arrived, but the settlement became their home. William continued working in his field as he began to survey a good portion of what would become the city of Omaha as well as eastern Nebraska Territory. At this time Elizabeth claimed that "my" home, meaning her home with William, was a "little house . . . surrounded by Indians."

WHEN THE CHIEF OF THE WUH´TAPIU BAND, Bear Feather (also known as Old Bark), died during the winter of 1854–55, a council met to select the next chief. Black Kettle's courage had been extraordinary, and like cousin Stone Forehead, he stood out. Black Kettle became chief of the Wuh´tapiu in 1855.[38]

Black Kettle knew the responsibility that now rested on his shoulders, and he would never waver from it. Never. Like a white man that he would not meet for another nine years, he would face criticism, threats, and hatred when he refused to back away from what he felt was the right course for the Tsistsistas to follow. Most of the Called Out People failed to see that their lives had begun to change, but there would be no turning back. The reality was that each year they saw more and more of the white invaders. This was a problem, but they could not decide how to deal with it.

EIGHTEEN FIFTY-SIX MARKED THE BEGINNING of a nervousness among the Called Out People. The Tsistsistas that lived on the North Platte joined with the Arkansas River bands who were then camped on the Republican River. This time would affect their future, although they did not realize it. As the moons moved toward hot days and beyond, the Tsistsistas became aware of a discernible division within the tribe. The threat of the invading *vi´ho´ i* was real, and many of the young warriors wanted to fight (and it did not matter if they lived in the north or south). On the other side, council chiefs such as Lean Bear (who became one in 1854), worked for a peaceful solution to the People's dilemma.

By the fall of that year Anglo-American parties traveling along the Platte River road en route to the California and Oregon Territories risked attack by Cheyenne and Kiowa warriors. People were murdered, scalped, and mutilated. Learning of what had *supposedly* happened, the U.S. government placed the blame on the Southern Cheyennes and decided to show the tribe the might of the American military. By April 10, 1857, Secretary of War John B. Floyd set in motion expeditions "to keep the peace of the plains and to punish past offences against the United States, especially those committed by the Cheyenne and Kioway Indians."[39] Colonel Edwin Vose Sumner, who then commanded Fort Leavenworth in Kansas Territory, would lead one of the expeditions. His orders were simply to attack, destroy, and if possible, to kill. He also had orders to cut off annuity distributions to the Southern Cheyennes responsible for the murders.

Sumner would lead a two-pronged expedition against the culprits. Major John Sedgwick, with four companies of the First U.S. Cavalry Regiment, set out from Fort Leavenworth on May 18. He led his command up the Arkansas River. Two days later Sumner departed the same post with two companies of cavalry. He marched up the Platte River. At Fort Kearny two companies of the Second Dragoons joined his command. Even though his "hair and beard [were] white as snow," as a contemporary stated, "he was still quite vigorous, every inch a soldier, straight as an arrow, and could ride like a Cheyenne."[40]

While Sumner continued his march toward Fort Laramie, word placed the Cheyennes camping between the Arkansas and Platte Rivers. At Fort Laramie, rumors spread of Indian depredations. Per orders, the colonel left the dragoon companies at the post and replaced them with three companies of the Sixth Infantry. On June 27 Sumner set out to meet Sedgwick's command; this happened at the confluence of the South Platte and Crow Creek on July 5. Reports placed Cheyenne villages congregating near the Republican River. Knowing that time was important, Sumner sent his wagons and tents back to Fort Laramie with instructions to meet his command on the South Platte near the lower crossing in twenty days. With pack mules hauling supplies and troops driving a herd of cattle, the colonel began his hunt in earnest.

At first light on July 29 Tsistsistas and Lakotas, painted and dressed for battle, led war horses from the village on the Saline and followed medicine men Ice and Dark a few miles northeast of the Saline valley to a lake that had a panoramic view of the surrounding plains. The awakening sun created a sparkling and fluctuating shine on the water's surface, and gave everyone confidence that they would defeat the oncoming *vi' ho' i* army. They dismounted, and as Dark and Ice sang "to the Sacred Powers," the warriors washed their hands in the clear water.[41] The medicine was powerful, for "when they raised their hands toward the weapons of the white men, their bullets would drop and roll harmlessly at the feet of the Cheyennes." The ceremony complete, Ice and Dark remained behind while chiefs and war leaders led warriors to where the battle would take place—"the east end of the valley on the south fork of the Solomon." Here they unsaddled their mounts and set them free to graze and drink water while they rested under the shade of cottonwood trees.

At ten o'clock that morning, Sumner's Delaware Indian scouts sent back word that they had discovered fresh signs. At this time Sumner neared the headwaters of the Solomon River in Kansas Territory. He marched his command in three columns, so he could quickly repulse an attack from either flank, front, or rear. The colonel now feared that if these were the Cheyennes that he hunted, that they might scatter. He immediately ordered his six companies of cavalry to advance. Before long it became obvious that the warriors—who were indeed Cheyennes—had used a decoy party to lure the soldiers to chase them, spreading them out over a large area before the warriors attacked "with their whole force."[42]

Sumner placed the warrior count at three hundred. He moved toward the foe, and, according to him: "[W]e suddenly came upon a large body of them drawn up in battle array, with their left resting upon the stream [Solomon's Fork of the Kansas] and their right covered by a bluff."[43] The colonel did not waste time and yelled for his command to form a battle line. With his flanks protected he moved forward.

"When the Cheyennes were almost in rifle-shot they were outflanking us both right and left," Robert M. Peck wrote. He was a seventeen-year-old private in Company E of the First Cavalry, and he kept a journal of the expedition.

> Our right was moving along the bank of the river. A larger party of the Indians had crossed the river, and, after passing our right, was about to recross and come on our pack-train in the rear. They were also turning our left, all the while keeping up that infernal yelling. Noticing that the Cheyennes were turning our left, [Sumner] ordered Captain Beall (the left company) to deploy his company to the left and head them off. He seemed to have determined to offset the disparity of numbers by a bold dash that would create a panic in the enemy's ranks, and roared out, "Sling—carbine!" then immediately, "Draw saber!" and we knew the old man was going to try a saber charge on them.[44]

Surprisingly the warriors did not break and run. Just the contrary. They desired a confrontation. But this ended almost immediately as Ice and

Dark's prayers and spell that morning failed. There were no soldier bullets to fall harmlessly, as it was a *vi'ho' i* long sword charge.[45] The reason, although unknown to Sumner, was simple. The Tsistsistas had power against the white man's guns but not his swords. They fled, but were not demoralized as the colonel claimed.

The fight on the Solomon ignited infighting within the military, which was protecting the roads to California and Oregon. Colonel William F. Harney (commanding the army for Utah) was one of the instigators. "Colonel Sumner's action took place some sixty or seventy miles south of Fort Kearny on the 29th of July—and the fact, that in four days after, 150 of these Indians attacked [a] cattle party within twenty-eight miles of Fort Kearny, shows they not only had no fear for their families from Colonel Sumner's Command." He pointed out that Sumner made "no mention of the number of [Indians] killed & wounded . . . which I judge to be small from the . . . facts & from private reports of the affair. . . . Colonel Sumner should have sent at least two companies of his mounted force, to Fort Kearny, immediately after his action to protect the millions of both public and private property on [the Platte] road, which is without a single mounted soldier from this to Fort Laramie; as I have stated before, Infantry is useless to pursue mounted Indians."[46]

BY THE LATE 1850s and certainly by the early 1860s the Dog Men were no longer outlaws, no longer unwelcome members of the Tsistsista nation. They had evolved into a third, or central, division within the tribe. They ranged between the Republican and Smoky Hill Rivers and acted as a base for any warrior willing to fight white aggression.[47]

FIVE

Bent's Fear Becomes Reality

BANKS IN ENGLAND suffered a large decline in gold reserves during the 1857 summer, pushing up discount rates in London, which in turn caused investors to sell American securities and purchase short-term English bonds. This had an immediate effect on the American stock market, and especially railroad shares. United States stocks fell at an alarming rate, and on August 24 the stock market crashed. A panic gripped the country, and created an enormous excess of merchandise, outrageous prices, and a bacchanalia of railroad construction totally out of control. Banks failed, and the panic plunged into depression. The South was the least affected, as their cotton crop had an ongoing market across the country. Even so, many people suffered and lost everything. Forty thousand people lost jobs in New York City. Still the Northeast and Mid-Atlantic states did not suffer as much as the frontier borderlands.[1] "With the massive influx of immigrants to western territories, the land market should have continued to boom, but low prices combined with the abundance of prime land marked the end of a promising future."[2]

POTENTIAL MINERS AND LAND DEVELOPERS from Lawrence, Kansas Territory, arrived at the confluence of Cherry Creek and the South Platte River in 1858. They wanted to try their luck at William Green Russell's Dry Creek diggings, which were then deserted, but quickly realized that it had been picked clean. Not deterred, they laid out their first town-site north of Dry Creek, which they called "Montana," but soon realized that it was not a good location and abandoned it.[3] During this time they heard of two traders who had married Indian women and resided on the south bank of the South Platte. Although they did not know them, they had heard of their reputations—especially John Simpson Smith's, whom they met first. Although not large, he was known as a deadly man to cross. Adnah French and his land development partners discussed their town proposal and asked Smith to join the company, which he did. On September 24, 1858, Smith took the group to William McGaa's "residence." McGaa (who at times called himself Jack Jones) lived with his Sioux wife and mixed-blood children. Smith and McGaa were neighbors, friends, and at times partners. He also joined the company, and on that day the members created the bylaws for the St. Charles Town Company.[4]

The next day Smith and McGaa traveled to their new partners' camp to "Survey Two ¼ quarter Sections, or 320 acres of the Public Domain for Town purposes."[5] On the twenty-sixth the company decided that McGaa, Smith, and Charles Nichols would build a cabin on each quarter section of the staked-out land. Two days later the town company held an election: French became president, McGaa vice president, and Smith treasurer. On October 2 French and the other five members of the town company departed for Lecompton, the capital of Kansas Territory, to file the legal paperwork and purchase supplies.

But then the unexpected happened.

On November 2, 1858, the combined William Larimer–H. P. S. Smith–Ned Wynkoop land group reached where Cherry Creek flowed into the South Platte—the land of gold, riches, and their future fortunes. The terrain was just as they envisioned, but with one problem. They were too late, as the St. Charles Town Company had claimed the land.[6]

The new arrivals set their sights on what was not legally theirs; the mostly vacant and yet staked land to the east of the South Platte. The members of the Lecompton Town Development Company had specific duties, all except for one: Edward Wanshaer Wynkoop (b. June 19, 1836). He had been designated "sheriff of Arapahoe County," but there was no county and no law. Wynkoop—Ned as he preferred to be called—figured the appointment was worthless. He came from a well-to-do Pennsylvania family that had fallen into hard times after his father died when he was two years old.

The last of eight siblings, he was babied but well educated and literate.[7] More important he had a rebellious attitude when he ventured westward to make his fortune—he acted by his own hook and offered no excuses. Although he did not know it, he would become one of the key players in a conflict that reverberates to this day.

That November Larimer, H. P. A. Smith, and Wynkoop approached Smith, McGaa, and Nichols and informed them that McGaa would host a meeting in his log shanty on the west side of the South Platte. At the November 17 meeting Larimer told the gathering, which included the merged Lecompton-Larimer group, the Lawrence and Leavenworth groups, and any other interested parties present, that he had authority to form a new town company called the Denver City Town Company. McGaa stated that the three St. Charles members did not compose a majority of their town company and could not vote to pass the marked land to another group. Larimer asked Nichols, McGaa, and Smith to join the Denver City Land Company. When they refused, he gave them two choices: leave the area or hang. If they left and later returned they would be killed. All three joined.

As a leading player in the claim-jumping, Wynkoop had crossed John Smith, who would not forget the threat on his life.

Five days later, on the twenty-second, a follow-up meeting was held at McGaa's. At this meeting "Golden City" was proposed as the name for the city.[8]

The next month would not pass smoothly, as the Denver City Town Company made known their plans to develop the area and had documentation backing their authority from James W. Denver, the former governor of Kansas Territory. The citizens of the South Platte told Larimer, Wynkoop, and their company to resign their commissions. On December 1 Wynkoop resigned as sheriff while knowing that once he returned from civilization, he would use his worthless commission for all it was worth. McGaa was elected to replace him. On the third, Albert Steinberger and Wynkoop braved the dead of winter as they set out to file the paperwork in Lecompton.[9]

At this time Left Hand's band of Hinono'eino' often camped near the confluence of Cherry Creek and the South Platte. Little Raven's band also camped in the area. The arrival of ever-growing numbers of white men on their land was a growing concern. But they did not threaten the newcomers, nor did they attack and kill them as they built wooden structures or in small groups began to look at rocks that they pulled from the flow of the rivers and streams.

Aware that news of gold had spread east to civilization, on December 1, 1858, William Bent wrote superintendent of Indian affairs A. M. Robinson in St. Louis, and shared his apprehension for the Indians of the plains. He feared the influx of white men to the Indians' land in search of gold might lead to violence, and urged Robinson to push the Indian Bureau to send a delegation of commissioners to meet with the Plains tribes and work out a plan that would be agreeable to them. If this did not happen quickly, Bent knew that gold fever would lead to war. He had discussed a possible alternative to the problem with some of the chiefs, and that was turning their backs on their hunting culture and learning to become farmers like the *vi'ho' i*. Surprisingly, some agreed with him, for he wrote: "They are anxious to get at it. If you will only give them a start they will go ahead."[10] But this was wishful thinking at best.

Robinson agreed with Bent's urgency. He also knew that an agent for the Plains Indians was needed immediately, and that the man had to know his wards as well as be respected by them. Since Thomas Fitzpatrick's death in 1854 none had fit the bill. The superintendent acted quickly and, without consulting Bent, recommended that his superiors in Washington, D.C., appoint the trader agent for the Upper Arkansas Agency.

By 1858 John Smith saw the birth of a second son with Wapoola, but this boy would soon disappear into the mists of time.[11]

As the year 1859 neared, John Smith continued to enjoy the celebrity of walking between the races. This included brains, guts, and survival expertise. Still he constantly watched for potential danger. Surviving in the wilderness took many skills, and over the years Smith had honed them. This included toughness and understanding his surroundings, which in turn gave him a hardness that did not allow deviation from what he expected.

On the first Sabbath in 1859, January 2, an unnamed miner with a Methodist background spoke about the Lord near the Cherry Creek–South Platte confluence. After the prayers, preaching, horse racing, and gambling ended, fiddles appeared along with other musical instruments, and a dance began. It was a time of feasting, of joyous and boastful words, and the constant flow of music as the men danced with each other and a lone woman or two. John Smith and his wife Wapoola attended the celebration. It was an Anglo celebration, but also one that the Tsistsista and Hinono'ei women who had married into the white race observed, welcomed, and embraced. Wapoola liked the melodic flow of the music. More, she wanted to join the dancers as the miners and frontiersmen lifted their legs and moved to the

melody. She asked her husband to dance. He refused. The *vi'ho' i* continued to dance before her and she saw no wrong in joining them. Wapoola
asked a miner to dance, he accepted, and they moved to the beat of the
melody. An outraged John Smith grabbed a three-legged stool that was
called a "creepy," crossed to where his wife danced, and without warning
swung with all his might at her back. The sudden assault disgusted William
McGaa, and he wrote a friend, "[O]ur beloved and most respected friend,
the original John S. Smith[,] breaks his squaw's back . . . for daring without
his permission to trip the light fantastic toe."[12] Lewis Garrard, whom Smith
had befriended in 1846, described the "light fantastic toe" as swinging a
partner "rudely and gently in the mazes of the contra dance—but such a
medley of steps is seldom seen out of the mountains—the halting, irregular
march of the war dance, the slipping gallopade, the boisterous pitching of
the Missouri backwoodsman, and the more nice gyrations of the French-
man—for all, irrespective of rank, age, and *color*, went pellmell [*sic*] into
the excitement, in a manner that would have rendered a leveler of aristocra-
cies and select companies frantic with delight."[13]

As Wapoola crumpled to the ground moaning in agony, Smith glared
at the onlookers, almost as if daring them to speak up or come at him.
None did.

Racism ruled the day, but on that January 2, the miners saw a heinous
act, and Smith's fame could not obliterate what he had just done. Although
no one had challenged him on that night, they would pronounce judgment on his foul behavior. "The original John S. Smith has just been served
notice to leave this town in four days [or face death]; his conduct has been
such of late that the mining community will stand it no longer. His squaw
is suffering severely from the effects of the said creepy. [He] goes into exile
alone, among the Arapahoes, there to recruit his almost shattered fortunes."[14] Smith did not take the threat lightly and left the area without his
sons, Jack and the infant, and without Wapoola, who attempted to recover
from a shattered back.

By LATE 1858 WILLIAM BYERS and John K. Kellom had partnered to write
a book about the gold fields to the east of the Rocky Mountains. When
published in early 1859, it would be titled *A Hand Book to the Gold Fields
of Nebraska and Kansas: Being a Complete Guide to the Gold Regions of the
North and South Platte and Cherry Creek*. Byers, who had been considering

turning his back on his civil engineering profession, announced next to his name on the cover, "Late Government Surveyor."[15] He felt that the area would prove to be an El Dorado and would enable him to secure his family's future. He and Kellom had been gathering information for their publication that would detail the routes to the region, but for the most part had nothing from the gold fields that was little better than hearsay. Actually, a lot of what they would publish about the trails leading to untold wealth was based on guesswork. This had not stopped them from proceeding with their project. Already, books and pamphlets had begun to see print, and they sold. The lure of gold and riches had grabbed a nation struggling after the banking collapse of 1857.

The one thing Byers and Kellom needed was the touch of authenticity. Then they heard that two men from the South Platte River–Cherry Creek region had arrived in Omaha on January 5, 1859, while traveling to Lecompton. Byers made a point of seeking out the two men who had created a sensation when they walked the streets filled with people craving news of the gold finds on January 8. Both men looked like they had long turned their back on civilization, and although the first of the two, Albert Steinberger, presented what still remained of a piece of eight dollars of gold that he had washed up, the other man grabbed his attention.

Byers had just met Ned Wynkoop, who, like himself, was good with words and did not shy away from stating what he believed. At the time of their meeting, the nattily garbed Byers was a far cry from the other man. Wynkoop described himself: "Dressed in buckskin from head to foot, an otter skin cap and Indian moccasins; long matted hair falling below the shoulders; unshaven and dirty face; belt around the waist with Pistols and Bowie Knife attached I seemed to be a cross between a Malay pirate and a Digger Indian."[16] Physical appearance aside, the men immediately liked each other.

Wynkoop had spent less than two months in the gold region, and Steinberger slightly longer. The timing had not been good for mining due to the cold temperatures and the advent of winter; still he provided Byers with positive prose that sounded good but had no basis in fact. "This creek [Cherry] heads in a *mesa*," Wynkoop and Steinberger explained, "or elevated table land jutting out from the mountain range far into the plain, and forming the divide between the waters flowing into the Arkansas on the south and the Platte on the north."[17] As they knew the land, this, along with additional text about the region, immediately gave them credibility.

Byers printed their words, and people hoping for a better future would not only read the Byers-Kellom book but would act upon what they thought truthful. Continuing, they stated: "Gold has been found all along Cherry creek, wherever any prospecting has been done, or nearly to its head." This statement implied that riches were readily available for the taking, dazzling anyone who was considering risking everything and setting out for the gold fields. Wynkoop and Steinberger then named individual men (one German had $60 of gold dust and still another had $350 of the dust that he had not sold) and groups, such as the Georgia Company, which took $392 from a twenty-foot hole, but had since moved to another valley. They provided a large number of specific dollar figures for gold mined, making it sound as if they spent their short time at the base of the Rockies traveling to all the mining sites and interviewing miners. Byers never questioned them, for they provided exactly what he wanted to hear and print. Byers's interview, which he prepared as if Wynkoop and Steinberger had provided him with a written document, filled a little over six pages.[18] Surprisingly, Wynkoop and Steinberger mentioned two men that the Denver City Town Company threatened to hang if they did not support the land jump and join their town company: John Smith (who they said went by the name of "Tashona-hata," or "White Blanket"), a "celebrated Cheyenne interpreter," and William McGaa.[19] Wynkoop and Steinberger had no clue that Smith, whom they had just praised, had become persona non grata in the gold region.

Although it had been reported that William Byers reached Denver City on April 17, 1859, he would, thirty years later, claim that he did not reach the boomtown until after nightfall two days later, when he rode into Denver on horseback. Perhaps the nineteenth presented a better date for his arrival as it, according to Byers, allowed him to place his entrance into his future on the evening "before the celebrated stampede began which carried back, or turned back on the plains, four-fifths of all the people who that year set out for the promised land."[20] Interpreted another way, he would not be threatened by mob law that demanded his lynching, as Ned Wynkoop would be when he returned to Denver City in fall 1859. Unwittingly Byers and Kellom had made him a prominent figure in their gold fields manifesto, which placed a target on his back for the false deception of unimagined riches. Continuing, Byers claimed that the press he purchased in Omaha arrived in Denver on the twenty-first. "[T]wo days later," as Byers stated in 1889, he used this press to print the first edition of the *Weekly Rocky Mountain News* "in the midst of a driving snowstorm." This is either legend, magnificent fiction, or he had written some of his early columns of Denver and the gold fields long before setting out from Omaha. Continuing in that first edition of the *News*, Byers also printed: "Our course is marked out, we will adhere to it with steadfast and fixed determination, to speak, to write and to publish the truth and nothing but the truth."

Byers and Kellom's book influenced many men to chase the dream of untold riches on the eastern slope of the Rocky Mountains. But unlike most of those who read and believed what amounted to little more than propaganda and left their families behind, Byers would eventually send for Elizabeth and their children to join him in the gold region.

Before he sent for his wife, Byers returned to Omaha with several companions, but it was not to gather his family. While in the city, on July 10, 1859, Byers wrote a report that he addressed to the western press. He again touted gold discoveries. "That rich gold deposits exist along the eastern slope of the Rocky Mountain chain is now known to be a fixed and indisputable fact. Fine 'float' gold is found along all the streams emerging from the mountains from the Arkansas river on the south to the Cach-a-la-poudre on the north."[21] He spoke of "gold bearing quartz." He also wrote about John H. Gregory's discovery on May 6, 1859, "on a little tributary of Rallston's or north fork of Vasquez's Fork of the South Platte river." His letter continued documenting discoveries on "the South fork or main fork of Vasquez's river, upon several of the tributaries of St. Vrain's fork of the [South] Platte, and upon the slope of the snowy range" in mid-June. His flowing description of gold discoveries continued as he publicized the riches to be made. But then Byers changed direction and presented much-needed truth and a warning. "The first grand rush to the mines in March last was principally made up of the most reckless adventurers without any of the experience or qualifications requisite to make them successful ones. Hundreds of men set out without any preparation to pull a handcart or carry a pack on their backs, an outfit expected to subsist them on a journey of nearly a thousand miles over a country of which they had not the slightest conception. . . . all these multitudes reached Cherry Creek out of means, at a season when no kind of mining could be advantageously prosecuted, and in the mountains not at all."

Byers then spoke of the masses that had already begun their rush back to civilization. "Many find they have mistaken their calling—mining requiring work, to which they are constitutionally opposed." He also pointed out that many that fled the area missed their farms and families. Finally he advised those thinking of traveling to the gold fields not to travel in the fall, as that was "the commencement of winter when but little work can be done, and all must live and have shelter. Let no one go without the most fixed determination to persevere, use industry, endure hardships, and brave adversity."

On April 27, 1859, President James Buchanan signed a temporary commission naming William Bent as Indian agent of the Upper Arkansas Agency. Bent was not pleased when Superintendent Robinson informed him of the appointment, as it was a thankless job that would deny him much-needed time to manage the log fortress, his traders, and his caravans to St. Louis and back to the frontier. Still, his wards would be the Southern Cheyennes and Arapahos, and they needed him. While in St. Louis in May with his oldest son Robert, he met with Robinson and consented to the assignment. Bent then arranged for runners to invite the Southern Cheyennes and Arapahos to meet him in mid-July at the junction of the South Platte River and Beaver Creek. When Bent and his son reached the designated meeting, he was disappointed to find only forty-five Tsistsista tipis awaiting his arrival. He again sent out runners to his wards, who were then on the prairie hunting buffalo, and he settled down to await their arrival.[22]

A twenty-six-year-old journalist named Albert Deane Richardson, who had recently been a correspondent for the *Boston Journal,* reached Denver City in 1859. His main intention was to document his wanderings in the American wilderness, the gold rush, and as he often called Indians, "the noble savage." He used these words sarcastically, for he mostly found them disgusting, particularly eating animal entrails and vermin, and even selling young daughters. But there was one Arapaho he came to like and respect.

"The savage like Falstaff is a coward on instinct—also treacherous, filthy and cruel," Richardson wrote.[23]

But one chief, the "Little Raven," was the nearest approximation I ever met to the Ideal Indian. He had a fine manly form and a human, trustworthy face. To spend an hour in our cabin was his custom always of an afternoon and, though his entire ignorance of English was only equaled by my utter innocence of Arapahoe, we held pleasant communion together. Our conversations were carried on by signs and the very few words we had in common. The tongue was weak, but the gesticulation eloquent.

Usually by some means we could make each other comprehend; but twice or thrice became, as actors say, hopelessly "stuck." Then my visitor sent for one "Left Hand," a linguist; for as Day & Martin the great blacking manufacturers, "kept a poet," so the chief of the Arapahoes maintained an interpreter. Left Hand spoke English fluently, having acquired it from traders in boyhood, and soon extricated us from our conversational quagmire.

Upon entering Richardson's cabin Little Raven grunted cordially as they shook hands. He would then sit in the only chair while Richardson sat on the table as he filled his guest's pipe with tobacco. Their visits always began with a quiet smoke, but not passing the pipe, as Richardson would light a cigar. Slowly they would begin to converse about various subjects: Utes, mines, weather, until "gradually we become communicative and at last familiar." Little Raven's curiosity about the Great Father and Washington often dominated their time together.

On one occasion Little Raven asked personal questions of the white man while proudly comparing the answers to his own life. Richardson had a wife and one child back East, while Little Raven had seven wives and ten children. When the chief asked how many horses, Richardson weakly replied that he had none. "The Raven answers by pointing triumphantly at his thirty sleek ponies grazing on the adjacent prairie," wrote Richardson, while admitting "that the Raven is becoming directly personal and inferentially abusive." Going on the offensive, he asked how many revolvers Little Raven owned as he passed his "Colt's new patent" to him. The chief studied it "with great curiosity and admiration." When he passed it back to Richardson, he "discharg[ed] the five barrels in rapid succession," which garnered "a childish satisfaction not unmingled with terror."

But their friendship was not one-way, nor was it based upon one-upmanship. On a sweltering 1859 summer day Richardson visited the chief's village. When he reached a ceremonial lodge, two warriors guarding it informed him that he would have to wait. Richardson did. Buffalo horns and a wolf skin were displayed next to the tipi. Eventually Little Raven and seven warriors, all who were naked, stepped outside covered in sweat.

Woodcut of Little Raven and Albert Deane Richardson. In 1859 Little Raven examines journalist Albert Deane Richardson's revolver in his cabin in Denver. Although Richardson looked down at American Indians and recorded some less than savory thoughts about them, he thought highly of Little Raven. After they met, the chief visited him almost daily. They communicated with grunts, a handful of English and Arapaho words, and hand signals, and at times this caused difficulties. When this happened, their conversation came to a halt. Little Raven sent for his friend Left Hand, who translated their words. In the background is Richardson's friend, Horace Greeley, the publisher of the *New York Tribune*, who promoted the slogan, "Go West, young man."

Louis Kraft Collection, ACP010. Chávez History Library, Santa Fe, N.Mex.

Totally exhausted they dropped to the earth. "They had been taking a vapor bath," Richardson wrote, "to propitiate their 'medicines.'"

"That night the entire band including the women paraded through the town, pausing before many dwellings and drumming upon a circular piece of buffalo hide stretched over a wooden frame, while they chanted a weird refrain. Early the next morning the braves started on the war path against the Utes; and this ceremony was an invocation to the whites to protect the squaws and children during their absence."

While in Denver, Richardson made another telling observation, this time dealing with something quite familiar to him. But in this instance he must have shuddered at what he saw. "Denver had its weekly *Rocky Mountain News*," Richardson wrote. "Editor [Byers] and printers cooked[,] ate[,] and slept in the one room of the log building where articles were written, type set and paper worked off."[24] Although the crude log structure would continue to function as the *News's* office for some time, in the not-too-distant future, Byers would not sleep with his staff.

As ELIZABETH BYERS HAD NO DESIRE to purchase and travel on her own prairie schooner pulled by oxen, in July 1859 she and her two children set out with a man whom she paid to transport them to Denver as they traveled with a caravan. On that first night of their trek into the unknown, her children sat near her as she plucked a guitar.

Unannounced and without warning, Indians entered the camp and moved about. "Of course I was frightened," Elizabeth admitted.[25] But having been around Indians before, she remained calm. Her reasoning was simple: "[B]ecause we had learned from our life in Omaha never to let an Indian know you were afraid of him." That night she and the hired man fed their visitors. Eventually they left and the journey continued.

Elizabeth's convoy reached Fort Kearny on the Platte River, which she claimed had three channels at the military post. Although only two or three feet deep, quicksand made crossings treacherous. The men waded in the water, doing what they could to keep the wagons upright and the livestock and wheels from getting caught in the sand. Still, wagons careened hideously as they threatened to capsize, and horses became caught and began to be dragged down. The ordeal frightened her children, and they clung to her as she tried to maneuver the wagon. Elizabeth found the second stream as bad as the first, but the third presented less of a problem. "[W]hen we reached the shore I was exhausted and so were the men that had been in the water," she admitted as she thanked God that they had reached Fort Kearny.[26] By this time Elizabeth was fed up with the man she had hired to transport her, and she sent a message to William in Denver. The trip continued.

William Byers was a multitalented man. He could make major changes in his professional path as he tracked and followed his dream into the American frontier. One of the keys to Byers's success was his ability to meet people from all sorts of life and befriend them, interview them, and use them to his benefit. He received Elizabeth's message, realized the precarious situation, and immediately contacted an agent that he had met from the Overland Stage Company. The agent told him that although the stages were not running, the stations were up and had livestock. More important, he told Byers that when he and his family reached him, if they wanted to brave the trip in a two-seat buckboard that would travel around the clock except for stops to change horses, that he would enjoy them joining him when he traveled to Denver.

Byers jumped at the offer and set out for the stage station. When Elizabeth reached the station, which was just inside what would become Colorado Territory, she fired her hired man. Byers arrived, and the final segment of Elizabeth's journey to Denver began. "You can imagine how cramped we were in a vehicle of that kind, traveling day and night, stopping of course every ten miles. We had our meals at the stations, and came through without accident, or very great discomfort."

Elizabeth, Byers, and their two young children reached Denver City on August 7. She thought that she was "the eighth white woman in Denver," and "I felt that I was the advance guard of civilization at the foot of the Rocky Mountains."

At that time Denver had one hotel, and they moved into it. They slept in the front room of the wood-framed building, which had no plaster. Their room in the establishment of Captain Sopres and Mr. Slaughter was in line with the rest of the building and its accessories, and they slept on mattresses on the floor. During their stay, Slaughter's son proposed hanging a quarter of beef at the entry and naming the hotel "The Slaughter House." Elizabeth enjoyed hearing the suggestion, which she considered "rather smart."

On August 16 William Bent held the first of his two official 1859 meetings with the Southern Cheyennes and Arapahos at the confluence of Beaver Creek and the South Platte. His wards still occupied the land documented as their territory in the 1851 treaty. The area mostly included the land bordering the east slope of the Rocky Mountains from the North Platte, South Platte, and Arkansas Rivers, and continuing eastward into Kansas Territory.

But the area had extended, as the two tribes had also claimed the land south of the Arkansas River to the Raton Mountains in New Mexico Territory.

After the passing of the pipe, Bent informed his wards that the Indian Bureau wanted them to choose "a fixed residence, and occupy themselves in agriculture."[27] Surprisingly, the Indian leaders in attendance supported this idea. "[They] declared with great unanimity to be acceptable to them," Bent continued. "They expected and ask, that [the] department shall supply them with what is necessary to establish themselves permanently." Unfortunately Bent did not list any of the Indian leaders.

As their land was being overwhelmed by whites, William Bent wanted the chosen territory to be in an area where there were no white men. This meant selecting the land that the Southern Cheyennes and Arapahos had recently taken for themselves—between the Arkansas and the Raton Mountains, including the Purgatoire River and Fontaine Qui Bouille Creek. Although he did not push for this land to become their destination, this was the ground that the chiefs unanimously chose, which pleased Bent. As he estimated that 60,000 whites had flooded their territory by midsummer, he was delighted that the two southern divisions of their tribes "scrupulously maintain peaceful relations with the whites and with other Indian tribes, notwithstanding the many causes of irritation growing out of the occupation of the gold region, and the emigration to it through their hunting grounds, which are no longer reliable as a certain source of food to them."

A month later, on September 15, Bent again met with his wards to continue discussing their future away from the land recorded as theirs in the 1851 treaty. "Being Buffalo Indians," as Bent defined them, "they require dwelling-houses to be constructed for them." The chiefs also said that they wanted a treaty and soon, along with "pay for the large district known to contain gold, and which is already occupied by the whites." Satisfied with the meetings, Bent traveled to St. Louis.

ON SEPTEMBER 27, 1859, THREE SISTERS with their mother and stepfather arrived in Denver. The oldest of the sisters, Louise Wakely (b. September 17, 1836), was sometimes, but not always, identified as M'lle Haydee when she appeared on the Denver stage, but even more often her younger sister, Rose (b. November 18, 1842), would also be listed as M'lle Haydee. Louise was an actress while Rose was a dancer.[28] The youngest was Flora (b. about 1845), and she was a singer. They had been a traveling theatrical act, but once they reached Denver they no longer toured, as they found a home in the boomtown.

Soon after Louise, Rose, and Flora trod the theatrical boards in Denver, Ned Wynkoop returned to the city. He had been lucky to survive the journey—not because of an Indian attack, but because his name was recognized by numerous members of the multitudes of men who had failed to strike it rich and who now limped back to their homeland and families. They blamed him for their failures, and once, he had even been threatened with hanging.[29]

Safely back in Denver, Wynkoop soon reconnected with Byers, who was never threatened for writing his book on the gold region. Although he was not a member of the elite class of Denver society, not a man of riches, and not a man with a thriving business, their friendship continued, and even better, his actions provided Byers with good copy for the *News*.

Wynkoop's return also included the beginning of a second relationship. He attended one of the early performances of Louise Wakely on the Denver stage. She excited him, as she did many other men in attendance that night. Wynkoop wanted her. He also realized he had a lot of competition. But he also had guts. He had done some acting when in school, and now with winter closing in, and without any chance of working a mining claim, he tried out for one of the leading parts in *Skatara, or the Mountain Chieftain*. He was tall, good looking, charming, had a mellow, unaccented voice, and was good with the spoken word. His goal was simple—have the upper hand over the other young bloods in Denver City who desired Louise Wakely. He landed the role of Hardicamp, a frontiersman, which was little more than typecasting for Wynkoop. Rehearsals began for *Skatara*, but as an amateur actor he never received a dime for any of his performances; only professionals were paid. Wynkoop did not care, as he found himself in a position to woo the lady. The play premiered in Denver on December 7, 1859.[30] At this time Wynkoop struggled to support himself as a sheriff, a position that only paid upon apprehension and conviction.[31]

AFTER WILLIAM BENT REACHED St. Louis, he drafted his annual report on October 5, 1859. He focused on two main points: (1) "I consider it essential to have two permanent stations for troops, one at the mouth of Pawnee Fork, and one at the Big Timbers, both upon the Arkansas river. A smothered passion for revenge agitates these Indians, perpetually fomented by the failure of food, the encircling encroachments of the white population, and the exasperating sense of decay and impending extinction with which they are surrounded"; and (2) "These numerous and warlike Indians, pressed upon all around by the Texans, by the settlers of the gold region, by the advancing people of Kansas, and from the Platte, are already compressed into a small circle of territory, destitute of food, and itself bisected athwart by a constantly marching line of emigrants. A desperate war of starvation and extinction is therefore imminent and inevitable, unless prompt measures shall prevent it."[32] Bent wanted the Southern Cheyennes, Arapahos, Comanches, and Kiowas totally separated from the migration of the white man and trained to farm.

IN OCTOBER 1859 A WAGON TRAIN delivered the Byerses' belongings, including a cookstove and their silver table utensils. Byers secured a one-room cabin outside of Denver and moved his family into it. Most of the houses at this time had mud roofs, but theirs had a board roof, as they did not want the mud dripping on their belongings after a rain. A month later, in November, they moved into a larger log cabin that they had rebuilt from a cabin that had been torn down. It stood on the west side of Cherry Creek, and the front room functioned as the office for the *Rocky Mountain News*, while Elizabeth kept the two other rooms as their home.[33]

Elizabeth proudly remembered that she entertained and fed men that were famous. Her and William's first dinner party included William Bent's trading partner Ceran St. Vrain, pathfinder Kit Carson, and mountain man James Beckwourth. Elizabeth enjoyed entertaining, and even more so when her guests were "celebrities," as she called them, a fitting term for Carson especially. But as she admitted, her "Virginia blood rather boiled," for Beckwourth was a mixed-blood African American. She confessed, "I hadn't been used to sitting at a table with a colored man, and I hardly knew what to do, but almost instantly decided that there was but one thing to do and that was to ignore it altogether and treat them all alike, which I did."[34]

But Elizabeth was not as unbiased as she claimed. "Observer," who wrote for the *Missouri Democrat*, featured her as one of only eight ladies who were *the* "belles" of Denver. She was slender, exquisite, and definitely belonged on the list. He then named two other young women that he also considered belles. If Elizabeth Byers was ever privy to Observer's list, she must have been outraged. They were Arapahos Alfarita and Heeaweea, "the young and beautiful daughters of his Excellency, Little Raven, President of our Arrapahoe [*sic*] Nation."[35]

Elizabeth Byers was a literate person who documented a small portion of her life. She was descriptive, and some of her memories are gems. At one time, during the early years of Denver, she was named as one of the city's belles. It was an honor, and one she appreciated. However, her actions belied her printed words when it came to race.

Elizabeth M. Byers. Photo by Bradley & Rulofson. History Colorado. Accession # 91.429.128.

Elizabeth supported husband William's opinions of the gold region, Denver, and the ongoing tensions between the states. His view on Indian removal, if not yet in place, would soon be. At this time Elizabeth and her husband were still in love, and she would follow his lead. But her prejudice would not just include Indians, whom she viewed as "savages."

By this time William Byers's goals for Denver City had taken shape. Many agreed with his vision of the future, but some did not. This meant that at times Byers's life was at risk. He used the *Rocky Mountain News* not only to shape Denver's future, but also to attack those he felt needed to be publicly chastised. One such person was L. J. Winchester, who had failed to pay the fee for his continued subscription to the *News*. It just so happened that Winchester, who had just set out for the East, was not aware that Byers had attacked him in print. While Winchester continued his trip, his partner, Mr. Warren, refused to let the insult fade unanswered. Warren published cards that called Byers "*a villain, liar and coward.*"[36] Warren had but one goal, and that was to meet Byers on the field of honor and kill him in a duel. Byers was not a coward. He also was not a fool. Accepting the challenge represented his death, for there was no way he would be able to shoot Warren before his antagonist ended his life. William Byers was in his prime, and he had goals—make Denver a major city, and more, make this portion of Kansas Territory a state in the Union. The standoff of accusations came to a head on November 18, when Byers was forced to face the man who wanted to kill him. Surprisingly, they worked out their differences—there would be no duel and no death. Warren endorsed him as "Mr. Byers, the editor, who attends to his business and mixes not among the rabble, either in the streets or the barrooms, but walks onward, and speaks right onward according to his view of right, justice and independent expression."

Although Elizabeth was a member of the elite Denver society who stood firmly behind the emancipation of the Negro, she harbored a prejudice that went beyond people of race, and it was in total disagreement with William. She had an inherent hatred for women she considered less than her, and this included actresses such as Louise Wakely.

As "Observer" reported, "There was a grand and complementary ball, a few nights since [November 21], at the Jefferson House, in Auraria. . . . The supper was as grand an institution as could be got up in the cities of the States anywhere. There were thirty ladies and fifty to seventy-five gentlemen comprising members of the Senate and House, business men, and goodlooking, well dressed fellows," and this included William Byers.[37] "The ladies in appearance, style and dress, were just as richly got up as you could see them at a fashionable party in St. Louis or Baltimore," and this included Elizabeth Byers.

Louise and her sisters attended the ball. Regardless if she or her sisters realized it, women who considered themselves the privileged of Denver were not happy that they dared to step beyond their station in life. Unwittingly or not, they became targets. This meant that Louise—regardless if she had consummated her sexual bonding with Wynkoop, who was not present and not yet courting her—was considered little more than a whore, as she was an actress. Acting, and that included all forms of presentation on stage at this time, had a stigma that tainted any female's reputation as far as the hoity-toity of society were concerned. Elizabeth Byers was a member of the latter, and when she saw Louise, Rose, and Flora mixing with the men present, she let William know that she would not remain in such company and promptly exited the event along with several other "ladies," but without her husband. Elizabeth and the other women's reason was simple: there were ladies "of the 'art dramatic'" present, and they considered them prostitutes.

ON TUESDAY, JANUARY 17, 1860, the Episcopal minister John H. Kehler arrived in Denver City with his family by stagecoach. Already white-haired, he had become a deacon in Maryland on August 21, 1841. He had served in Shepherdstown, Virginia, and more recently had been the rector of Sharpsburg, Maryland, at St. Paul's Church. As tensions between the northern and southern states escalated, his pro-Union views became unpopular and were ostracized. Realizing that the time had arrived to seek out a new land, Kehler packed up his family in 1859 and set out for the gold fields. Although the arduous trip took its toll, everyone arrived in good health, and Kehler realized that his decision to compel his family to suffer a long trip had been worth every discomfort that he forced upon them. Four days later, on the evening of January 21, he led a gathering of men and women in prayer. Afterward he explained why he had passed out cards announcing the meeting, as he wanted to discuss the possibility of establishing an Episcopal Church in Denver. Before the meeting concluded, thirteen men and women volunteered to locate a building for the first service.[38] Thrilled over the outcome of the meeting, Kehler later said: "A large portion of the community is composed of enterprising gentlemen who give unmistakable evidence of their respect for our ministry and appreciation of the Church."[39] Elizabeth Byers had attended this meeting, and was impressed with Reverend Kehler. That day she and Kehler's daughters decided to meet at her home to create "The Ladies Union Aid Society," in which she presided as president. At that first meeting the group resolved to "aid and assist" the creation "of a Church in [its] midst" as well as "any benevolent purpose which the Association may decide upon."[40] Elizabeth claimed that she and Kehler's daughters created the society to also benefit the poor.

Reverend Kehler delivered his first service in the former *Rocky Mountain News* log cabin office on Sunday, January 29. Elizabeth, William, and their children attended. Many miners also attended, and they afterward greeted him warmly. However, his daughters' presence did not hurt, as all were unmarried and of marriageable age.[41]

SIX

Welcome to the White Man's World

IN EARLY MARCH 1860, the thirty-nine-year-old Methodist Episcopal minister Reverend John Milton Chivington (b. January 27, 1821), who then served as the presiding elder of the Nebraska City District, Nebraska Territory, had, since his appointment in April 1859, traveled to Leavenworth City, Kansas Territory. Beginning in 1856, when the Methodist Episcopal Church held its first Kansas-Nebraska conference, in Lawrence, Kansas Territory, he had found that his imposing presence led to a string of appointments that kept his family in motion between the territories.[1] Chivington had met Martha Rollason in Cincinnati, Ohio, during one of his many trips marketing his family's timber. Although she was two years older than him, he found her literate, attractive, and an expert seamstress. They married in 1840. Thomas was born in 1841, Elizabeth Jane in 1842, and Sarah in 1844.[2]

By this time Chivington had made a name for himself that included much more than his religious beliefs. At the 1859 conference he had been the chairman of a committee that stood firmly against slavery and printed: "God has made of one blood all nations of men," and that the Methodists believed that "every human being [was] the offspring of the common Father."[3] Chivington's allies were antislavery, while his opponents were proslavery. Although a number of the Methodist ministers had fled Kansas Territory to escape tar and feathering or hanging, Chivington had refused to stand down. At this Nebraska-Kansas conference, he had a chance meeting with an entrepreneur named John Evans, who had visions of creating a town called "Oreapolis," which he had modeled after a city he had already created in Illinois, "Evanston," that would be *the* doorway to the West.[4] Neither man knew that this chance encounter would lead to a relationship three years later, one that would link them for all time.

No bishop attended the 1860 conference, but when it met in session on March 15—the last time the preachers of the two territories would meet—the conference created the Rocky Mountain District, which would be headquartered in Denver, and Chivington was appointed the presiding elder of the district. The conference approved a generous amount of funding: Rocky Mountain District ($1,000), Denver and Auraria ($700), Golden City and Boulder ($600), Mountain City ($500), Clear Creek ($500), Blue River ($500), and Colorado City ($200). After the conference ended, Chivington and his family went to Nebraska City to prepare for the move.[5]

Chivington would not be the first Methodist minister in Denver. George W. Fisher had performed the first services in and around Central City and Denver beginning in November 1858. In 1859 William H. Good (whom Chivington replaced in Nebraska City) and Jacob Adriance (whom Chivington knew) were selected by Bishop Levi Scott at the 1859 Kansas-Nebraska Conference to become missionaries to the gold region. After arriving on June 28, 1859, they traveled throughout the area on both sides of the South Platte River and held meetings in Denver, Auraria, Golden, Boulder, and Central City.[6]

Chivington, by now a huge bearded bastion of a man, with his family, departed Nebraska City in two wagons that hauled their belongings on April 23, 1860. They headed almost due west using the newly created Pony Express route until they reached the Platte River Road where it joined with the Overland Trail. Here the traffic increased in both directions, as it reduced the distance. When they reached the confluence of the North and South Platte Rivers into the Platte River, Chivington took the road south, and it skirted the South Platte until his small caravan reached Cherry Creek and his destination on May 19. The trip took twenty-six days.[7]

FIVE MONTHS AFTER CHIVINGTON'S ARRIVAL in Denver something happened that meant nothing to him, even if he was aware of it, but it would lead to his crowning glory. On September 8, 1860, commissioner of Indian affairs Alfred Burton Greenwood received instructions dated August 11, 1860, "to carry out the act of Congress, passed at its last session, appropriating thirty-five thousand dollars to enable the Secretary of the Interior to hold a council with the Cheyenne and [Arapaho] Indians, on the Upper Arkansas."[8] He set out for the frontier four days later. During the trek Greenwood learned of "[c]itizens of the United States . . . [that] were brutally murdered and scalped upon the road [he traveled]." Not finished he stated, "that the murders were committed almost within range of the guns at Fort Larned. The Indian mode of warfare, however, is such that it is almost impossible to detect them in their designs."

On September 8 he reached Bent's New Fort, which was then part of Fort Wise on the Arkansas River. Located on a butte to the east of the post, it served as commissary, jail, and the Indian agency. As he had previously asked Agent William Bent to advise the Cheyennes and Arapahos that he wanted to meet with the major chiefs of the two tribes, Greenwood was angry when he arrived at the isolated post. Half of the Indians he wanted to meet were not present. "I only found the principal portion of the [Arapahos] and a few lodges of Cheyennes." Greenwood met with the Arapahos, but never discussed the results of the meeting. Nor did he name the chiefs who had been waiting since July to speak with him.

Days passed and September became October with no sign of Black Kettle. Greenwood's mission had failure written all over it. Then, within "a few days of my departure," Greenwood reported, "White Antelope, Black Kettle, and four or five sub-chiefs, came in without their bands." Black Kettle claimed that after he received news of the commissioner's coming, that it took him twenty days to travel to Fort Wise. Greenwood met with the Arapaho leaders, along with Black Kettle, White Antelope and the other Cheyenne chiefs. He "informed them as to the object of my visit," which he never recorded in his report. He told the chiefs that the Great Father was happy with their peaceful view toward the white man despite the fact that many of their brothers were warlike. Black Kettle and White Antelope readily responded that they were pleased that "he had heard of their good conduct." They asked Greenwood to tell the Great Father, "that they intended, in every respect, to conform to the wishes of the government."

But did Black Kettle and the others actually say this? Greenwood had an agenda, and his report only documented what he claimed they said. The commissioner then presented them with a map that showed their territory at the time of the 1851 treaty along with a map of proposed reservation lands. If Black Kettle and the others understood what they looked at, they would have immediately realized that all their primary buffalo hunting grounds would no longer be theirs. "[T]hey seemed to understand perfectly," Greenwood claimed, "and were enabled, without difficulty, to give each initial point." The question of translation and understanding must be raised here, as it is totally disjointed from their future treaty dialogues. "I stated to them that it was the intention of their great father to reduce the area of their present reservation, and that they should settle down, and betake themselves to agriculture, and eventually abandon the chase as a means of support." To repeat, Greenwood wanted to *reduce the area of their present reservation*," meaning the area outlined in the 1851 treaty, *which clearly defined their territory*. This appears to mean that the United States had accepted that the land designated as Cheyenne-Arapaho land in 1851 was indeed theirs. But that land had become prime, and the United States now wanted it. Regardless of what Black Kettle and White Antelope felt or thought, they knew that none of their people wanted this.

Still, Greenwood claimed: "They informed me that such was their wish, and that they had been aware for some time that they would be compelled to do so; that game was growing scarce every year." Greenwood then moved into the big lie of his report. "I pointed out to them a country that I regarded as fertile, upon which I desired them to settle." If Black Kettle and White Antelope understood what Greenwood showed them, they would have realized that they would be giving away roughly nine-tenths of their land for a piece on the Upper Arkansas, a large portion of which was not "fertile." Much of it was wide-open prairie without trees and little water.

Regardless of who was present, Greenwood was talking about a lifeway, a culture—their lifeway and culture, and he ignored it. He also ignored the Indians' point of view while he stuffed down the chiefs' throats what the U.S. government ordained—to live where we demand, and to live like white men. The reason was clear why none of Black Kettle's words were documented as translated; they were not in line with Greenwood's task of grabbing almost all of their land. However, the commissioner did record one telling comment in his report. "[T]he chiefs of the Cheyennes present requested that, in order that there should be no trouble amongst themselves in future, that they should have the opportunity of consulting their co-chiefs and branches before executing any agreement." Greenwood claimed that if their people rejected the new treaty, "that they [Black Kettle and

White Antelope], as the principal chiefs, would enter into such agreement, and settle down."

Greenwood hoped to complete the treaty that September. He failed, as Black Kettle and the others refused to touch the paper. Whatever really happened during that one day in September has been lost to time, and was perhaps bogus at best. Black Kettle and White Antelope knew the rules of their people, they knew their powers, and they knew what they could and could not agree to with the white man. What the commissioner would present to his superiors was not, and never was, what they understood or accepted. Greenwood departed for the East on September 20.

WITH THE APPROACH OF THE CIVIL WAR, which by the beginning of 1861 was inevitable, Kansas became a state on January 29, and Colorado Territory was created a month later (February 28). That February a handful of Southern Cheyenne and Arapaho leaders met in council with the United States at Fort Wise. When the new territory was created, Fort Wise was located in the southeastern portion of it. Tsistsista council chiefs Black Kettle, White Antelope, and Lean Bear were present, as were Little Wolf, Tall Bear, and Left Hand (or Namos), who should not be confused with the Southern Arapaho Left Hand, who refused to attend the council. Hinono'ei chiefs Little Raven, Storm, Big Mouth, and Shave Head also took part in the negotiations.

John Smith and Robert Bent (William Bent's mixed-blood Cheyenne son) were employed to translate for the Cheyennes and Arapahos.[9] The fully bearded Albert Gallatin Boone, who was a grandson of the famed trailblazer Daniel Boone, had become agent for the Upper Arkansas Agency on October 17, 1860. When Greenwood was not available for the February council, he served as a "special" commissioner.[10]

Left Hand's absence spoke volumes, especially since it was almost certain that he, along with Little Raven, had met with Commissioner Greenwood the previous September.[11] If he had been present and had spoken in English, he would have shocked the clean-shaven and hawkish Greenwood. More important, he was aware of what was happening and wanted no part of it.

Much has been made that the treaty council was only for the Southern Cheyennes, but this was not accurate. Often Dog Man leader Bull Bear and the Keeper of the Sacred Arrows, Stone Forehead, rode and traveled with their brothers below the Platte and along the Republican and Smoky Hill Rivers. And why not, for this was their prime area for not only hunting buffalo but also deer and antelope. Not to forget, and this was major, both Bull Bear and Stone Forehead considered themselves Southern Tsistsistas. This 1861 travesty of a treaty included them, while also including their brethren the Ohméséhesos (Omisis), for it was their joint land as described in the 1851 treaty.

There were ten chiefs representing the Southern Cheyennes and Arapahos present. But as in the previous September, the white man recorded none of their translated words during the negotiations. Actually, there was no negotiation, and that was why there was no reason to document Indian words.

The main points of the published treaty included the following:

- "The said chiefs and delegates of said Arapahoe and Cheyenne tribes of Indians do hereby cede and relinquish to the United States all lands now owned, possessed, or claimed by them, wherever situated, except" the new reservation boundary, which removed them from a portion of the buffalo migration path.[12] Worse, most of their reservation was situated on barren prairie with little water and almost no trees or wildlife.

- The U.S. government would build houses for the Cheyennes and Arapahos, and would furnish "them with agricultural implements, stock animals, and other necessary aid and facilities for commencing agricultural pursuits under favorable circumstances."

- The two tribes would receive $15,000 each annually for fifteen years beginning when they moved onto the said reservation.

- "Their annuities may, at the discretion of the President of the United States, be discontinued entirely should said Indians fail to make reasonable and satisfactory efforts to advance and improve their condition."

- "[T]he President, with the assent of Congress, shall have full power to modify or change any of the provisions of former treaties with the Arapahoes and Cheyennes of the Upper Arkansas, in such manner and to whatever extent he may judge to be necessary and expedient for their best interests."

- "It is also agreed that all roads and highways, laid out by authority of law, shall have right of way through the lands within the reservation."

Why on earth would Little Raven, or Black Kettle, remain silent? If either chief understood that the treaty was a land grab that removed the Hinono'eino' and Tsistsistas from their land and placed them mostly on barren prairie, or that it was intended to destroy their entire lifeway, they would not have made their marks. It was all for the *vi'ho' i*, nothing for their people, and worse, they would have no say in their future lives. Why did they not attempt to change some of the treaty items if they understood them? There was not one request or input to this treaty by any of the Cheyenne or Arapaho leaders. Not one.

Still Black Kettle, White Antelope, Lean Bear, Little Raven, and the others touched the paper on February 18, 1861. Boone would later state that Black Kettle totally understood the details of the proposed treaty.[13]

That year, and probably after the Fort Wise peace negotiation, the Tsistsistas selected six chiefs who were already members of the council of forty-four to be the head chiefs of the council. They were Lean Bear, White Antelope, Little Wolf, One-Eye, Two Buttes, and Black Kettle. Black Kettle was chosen as the head of the six chiefs, which in turn made him "the spokesman for the tribe."[14] There was something strange here, for from this time forward Black Kettle would be denigrated time and again for his negotiations with the white man. He had just made his mark on a piece of worthless paper that supposedly gave the Tsistsistas' prized land to the increasingly hated *vi'ho' i*. Why would he be selected as one of the six leading chiefs of the Tsistsistas' traditional council of forty-four? Regardless of how his people viewed him, and perhaps because his name was more prominent than those of the other chiefs, the whites considered him the leader of the Called Out People. This was never the case.

WHEN THE AMERICAN CIVIL WAR began on April 12, 1861, the pro-Union side easily outnumbered Southern sympathizers in Denver. By the end of the month the city had become a hotbed of seething hatred with no middle ground. Although nothing other than angry rhetoric had occurred, there was a void in leadership. William Gilpin, the recently appointed governor, had still not arrived, leaving the city to fend for itself. This was fine with William Byers, for by now he and his partners had turned the *Rocky Mountain News* into a political machine for the "stars and stripes," and woe to those who disagreed. Actually Byers and other newspapers received updates on the war of rebellion on a daily basis (albeit late), and reprinted what they received.

Although the pro-Unionists feared a Southern invasion of the Southwest, which would certainly include the territory's gold region, rumors began to circulate of an Indian uprising. They were strong enough that on

April 24 Agent Boone, who located his agency near Denver, sent a dispatch to Fort Wise. He requested two companies of cavalry. He wanted them "held in readiness" at Denver "to obey his call in case Indian difficulties should become threatening."[15]

On that same morning of April 24, Boone appeared at the *Rocky Mountain News* office. He told Byers that he regretted "the deposition manifested in a certain quarter, to inflame the feeling against the Indians."[16] He spoke about "headstrong and impulsive" people that pushed for "an immediate attack upon the Indians in this vicinity." Boone said that such an action could prove "disastrous, and would endanger the peace and safety of every ranchman and settler throughout this region, but the entire Platte route, between this city and the Missouri river would become a theatre of violence and bloodshed."

Although Byers viewed himself as an empire builder, he reported what he learned of the Indians' side in an unbiased manner while making it clear that war was possible. "Let the report once go back to the Missouri river that there is serious trouble here with the Indians, and emigration will cease at once. Shall the folly and rashness of a few inconsiderate persons, who wish to gain a little personal notoriety, be allowed to embroil us in a war with the Indians?"

On April 25 Left Hand, two Arapaho warriors, and John Poisal stepped across the plank bridge that led to the second floor of the building that was built in the dry creek bed and entered the *Rocky Mountain News* office. A French Canadian plainsman and trader in his fifty-first year, Poisal had married into the Southern Arapaho tribe as early as 1833, when he married Left Hand's sister, Mahom (Snake Woman). They sired five children, and lived with her band for years before choosing to reside on Cherry Creek in 1857. During these years he became friends with the chief and played a large role in Left Hand's command of English.[17] Left Hand brought Poisal with him to ensure that Byers understood the meaning of his words.

According to Byers, Left Hand said "his tribe still retain their usual and long standing good feeling and friendship for the whites, and that under no circumstances will they injure or molest the whites."[18] However, fearing war, he also stated "that the Cheyennes are disposed to be troublesome." A strange statement considering the close relationship between the two tribes. Left Hand wanted it known that if there was war, and if it included the Cheyennes, that his people were not involved. Continuing, he said that he would punish all Arapaho warriors that "commit any offence."

William Byers had his vision of Denver in place long before he traveled to the fledgling city and began printing the Weekly and Daily *Rocky Mountain News*. He knew the power of words and used them to help create a great city and territory, and this included attacking his competition and anyone who disagreed with his views.

William N. Byers. History Colorado. Accession # 89.451.342.

More important, he had "fears that in the event of trouble his people will be mistaken for Cheyennes, as many of the whites cannot distinguish between them."

Already whiskey selling to the Plains tribes had become a big issue, and had been since at least the 1830s. Left Hand addressed this, saying that he would "keep his [people] from accepting or buying whisky from the whites." Stories had circulated, and Left Hand had heard them, that Cheyennes had recently "killed one hundred white men below Fort Wise on the Arkansas." This he discredited as untrue. Before leaving he said that Little Raven was en route to Denver to meet with Agent Boone.

Two days after Byers had printed Boone's concern about the Indian situation he returned to it. "Hardly an hour passes that we do not hear the most startling stories about Indian outrages. They are in almost every instance utterly without foundations, or shallow of truth. We caution the public against these flying reports."[19]

Boone met with Arapaho chiefs Little Raven, Left Hand, Shave Head, Storm, and between twelve and fifteen warriors in his office on Monday afternoon, April 29. Byers attended with a few members of the *News* staff.

John Smith translated. "Through him," Byers printed, "we were enabled to understand the object and aims of the meeting."[20] Here, Byers was not just talking to the wind, for Left Hand would have spoken up if Smith's knowledge of the Arapaho language was faulty. He used interpreters whenever it suited him. His reason was simple: he wanted to hear what was said in English while appearing as if his mastery of the language was spotty at best. Left Hand, Little Raven, and the others sat. The calumet was lit and displayed to the four directions, and everyone shared the pipe. Afterward the chiefs and warriors shook hands with the *nih' oo3oo* (or *niatha* and *nihancan*, the last of which is the Arapaho word for their "spider trickster," and is similar to *vi'ho' i*, the Tsistsista word for spider and white man), as they called the white man.[21] Little Raven, whom Byers called the "chief" of all the Arapahos, stood and spoke.

The chief had a lot to say, and a member of Byers's staff recorded Smith's translated words. Little Raven said that he hoped the white man would have the "same kind feelings towards his tribe that the Great Father [President Lincoln] had so often expressed towards them. All his tribe, as well as the Cheyennes, Kiowas and Sioux, have been instructed to treat the whites kindly—to render them assistance when necessary; and they expect the same kind offices in return." He made it clear that the Hinono'eino' had suffered since the *nih' oo3oo* had arrived in their land, that "their game had become scarce and they were compelled at times to ask for food from the whites." Continuing, he said "[h]e knew that the whites were taking large sums of gold from the mountains—that the cities and villages springing up around him were built upon the Indians' land, and with the Indians' timber." Still, he felt "that the Great Father would make adequate returns for all this." He added that "the Government ought to pay the Indians in coin instead of goods."

Changing direction, Little Raven announced that "Next summer [meaning during the upcoming moons] all the friendly tribes of this region would assemble in or near Denver, for the purpose of having a Grand talk, which they hoped would result in a permanent treaty of peace and a good understanding with the whites—to know just what territory they had ceded to the Government." Little Raven had just exposed a key piece of the February 1861 council with Colonel Boone: they did not understand the treaty terms that were forced upon them. When this happened, the chief hoped to lead a delegation to visit the Great Father in Washington.

Little Raven then surprisingly praised Boone, saying that "he regarded him as the Great Chief of this region—one to whom the friendly tribes look for advice, council, and protection." Finished, he sat, and the "pipe of Peace," as Byers called it, was again shared.

Boone then spoke, saying that the "Great Father at Washington never forgot his 'children,'" but the great distance slowed the process. He assured the Arapahos that they would receive what was owed to them. The agent then warned them to destroy whiskey when offered to them and to avoid the white man's cattle that roamed the plains, for taking these animals would lead to trouble. The Arapahos passed the pipe a third time, and afterward they shook hands with Boone, Smith, Byers, and those with him.

Little Raven had spoken of what his people wanted to happen, and Byers published the details of what he said in the *Rocky Mountain News*, but this did not end the Arapahos' efforts to inform the white man that they were willing to work with him peacefully.

On the evening of April 30, Left Hand watched a performance of *The Lady of Lyons* at the Apollo Theatre. According to Byers, "some of his brethren were [also] present."[22] This evening again pointed out that Left Hand carefully chose when he spoke in English to whites. After the performance, the *Rocky Mountain News* reported: "In his vernacular, the Arapahoe Chief [made] a handsome speech." The word "vernacular" clearly refers to his native language, meaning that for his words to be understood, an interpreter had to be present (none were named in the article). Byers would have certainly announced if he had delivered his talk in English, and would not have implied that he spoke in his mother tongue. Continuing, the paper printed that Left Hand "wished his white brethren would stop talking about fighting with his people, because his people had no enmity against them whatever—but looked on them as brethren—that, as they came here hunting for gold, they would hunt after the gold, and let the Indians alone—that, although his white friends intruded on his antelope and buffalo grounds, it was now all right—his people could find plenty more." Like Little Raven's words, so now did Left Hand's see print in the press. The chiefs had realized the power of the white man's talking leaves (paper), and that if they could get their thoughts and words passed around on it, that it might help their cause to retain peace between the races.

Boone lived up to the praise that Little Raven had given him. On May 1 he delivered a note to Byers at the *Rocky Mountain News*, which contradicted "the foolish rumor about the destruction of express stations."[23] He also shared the Indian Bureau's view that it "regards the traffic in liquor with the Indians as most criminal, and endorses any acts of summary vengeance visited by the Indians upon those who furnish them with spirits." In that day's edition, Byers confronted the citizens of Denver: "Parties in our city, who have heretofore sold whiskey to the Indians, will do well to take warning."

Events and perceptions now began to happen in quick succession, and the young Bent brothers joined the cavalcade. Although Colorado Territory was mostly pro-Union, George and younger half brother Charles Bent sided with the South, a view they did not share with their father. They had spent a good portion of their early years with the people of their mothers—Owl Woman and Yellow Woman—among whom they had learned how to ride like warriors. But they also spent part of their school years in Missouri. On May 10, 1861, George and Charles saw an event in the streets of St. Louis that sickened them. When Brigadier General Nathaniel Lyon's four Union volunteer regiments, supported by a regiment of regular troops, rounded up Southern sympathizers at Camp Jackson and marched them through the thriving city, bystanders became outraged. They shouted curses and racist insults at the volunteers, who were mostly Germans. Rocks were thrown at Lyon's men, and then an unknown shot sounded. The untrained volunteers began firing at the spectators. When the massacre ended, twenty-seven men and women and one infant were slain, with more wounded.[24] George, a young man, and Charles, on the cusp of manhood, would never forget what they saw.

At this time Little Raven and Left Hand's bands of Arapahos frequently camped near each other, and often set up their camp circles near the growing Denver City. It was their land—the area had been a natural camping ground for them long before the white invasion. And for the most part they got along well with the miners and city builders. On May 21 both chiefs and many of their band members gathered at Denver's race track on the outskirts of the city. It was a good day as warriors bet and everyone cheered their favorite riders. But, as was happening with increasing frequency, the Cloud People were able to secure spirits in the city. Men and women got drunk despite the warnings to avoid liquor. Later that day two warriors got into a fight with three Mexican traders who sold whiskey, and one of the warriors was hurt. The next day Byers published a short notice for a meeting at the paper's office to discuss how "to adopt some plan for stopping the sale of whisky to Indians."[25] As this was seen as an ongoing problem, Byers printed: "It is the duty of every good citizen to be promptly upon the ground."

DENVER HAD BECOME AN ARMED BASTION of contrasting views. Armed men wandered the streets clutching their guns while avoiding deadly confrontation. The outbreak of war had created enemies of former friends who now wanted nothing more than to draw blood. As May 1861 neared an end, staunch Unionist Ned Wynkoop strolled the streets of Denver as he pondered his future. He still had his lady, actress Louise Wakely, but his nonpaying stage-acting fame—secured by his leading performance as *The Drunkard*—was quickly fading from memory. Although he was still a sheriff, he had stopped working as a bartender for Charlie Harrison at the Criterion, a saloon and hotel. Harrison's temper and inclination for sudden violence was just too dangerous, and the Criterion functioned as an "unofficial headquarters" for those who supported the Confederate States of America.[26] Undoubtedly Wynkoop remembered his early years in Lecompton when Jayhawkers and Border Ruffians seemed intent to kill anyone who disagreed with their viewpoint during the late 1850s.[27]

An explosion seemed imminent.

On May 29, 1861, the territory's first governor, William Gilpin; Secretary of State Lewis Ledyard Weld; Surveyor Francis M. Case; and the chief clerk of the surveyor general's office, Eli M. Ashley, arrived in Denver City.[28]

Rumors of a rebel invasion of the Southwest increased, making Colorado Territory vulnerable to attack. It did not help that as summer approached, Southern sympathizers openly posted advertisements offering to purchase ammunition and percussion caps that would be used to defeat the federal government. That was not all, for the Reverend Chivington had heard that the outnumbered secessionist contingent still in the city bragged that they intended to steal as much gold as possible before ditching the Union hellhole and joining the Confederacy. Chivington did not hide his contempt for slavery and those who supported it. When Gilpin took it upon himself to prepare to repel a Confederate invasion without proper authority, Chivington praised him.[29] Wynkoop felt that if Gilpin had done nothing and had waited for instructions from Washington, that the "delay might have proved fatal" for Colorado Territory.[30]

On June 9 Left Hand's war party that looked for Utes to attack reached A. B. Adams's Ohio House, which was twenty-five miles west of Denver on the South Park road. Apparently warriors approached the building looking for food or water. Something happened that led to an invasion of the building, a threat to white lives, and the theft of property that ranged from a new rifle to food supplies and clothing. This was something that Byers wanted to print, as it would advance the Cheyenne and Arapaho war, which he was convinced would lead to the removal of the Indians from the territory. Byers claimed that "one hundred and sixty" warriors engaged in the takeover of the building.[31] In an event such as this, how was it possible to get an accurate count of the enemy's numbers? They wanted whiskey! It was refused. They wanted clothing. This, too, was mostly denied them. They did receive some items, but it was not enough, and resulted in one warrior pushing his way into the building and charging up a staircase to steal. Adams confronted the warrior, who then attacked him with a knife. "Mr. A. then got a blow at the Indian with a stick and knocked him down." The warrior was pushed out the door and it was secured.

But this was not the end, for soon Left Hand appeared, "assuring the occupants that" they would not be harmed. The chief's words won the day, but as soon as the door was opened, "savages" rushed in, "and the pillage commenced." The theft was massive, but no one was harmed. According to the *News*, other buildings were also invaded and robbed that day. This was a story right to Byers's liking, and he printed it without confirming a word.

This should have been the end to the incident, but it was not. John Poisal read the story and alerted Left Hand to what Byers printed in his June 12 weekly. The accusations and falsifications did not please the chief. On June 19 they walked into Byers's office and confronted him on the story. Left Hand again had Poisal interpret.

As the translation of Left Hand's words tell the story, he and his war party against the Utes stopped near Adams's building for a noon rest. "A white man in the upper story of the house beckoned an Indian boy to come to him. . . . When the boy came to the foot of the stairs leading up [the] outside [of] the house to where the man who called him, Adams knocked him down with a club and beat him until he was senseless."[32] When Left Hand reached the house and recovered the boy, "according to Indian custom, [he] demanded payment for the outrage." The request was valid. Adams's wife realized this and "gave them half a sack of flour, an old gun and" other articles. According to Left Hand, he and his warriors were satisfied with the payment for the assault and departed. Byers printed the story that afternoon, while making it clear that Poisal translated the chief's words.

Left Hand's side of the story was never challenged.

On that same June 19, George and Charles Bent's school term ended in St. Louis. They returned to their home in Westport. By this time Missouri had become a hotbed, as pro- and anti-Union sympathies dominated daily life. Even though Albert Boone had spent much of his fortune over the years supporting slavery, he remained a close friend of the Bent family and was always available to William's children when he and they were in Missouri. Boone's store in Westport served as a meeting house for those who supported secession. George and Charley often visited. Time and again they shared what they knew and felt about the May 10 slaughter. And they did not shy away from using the words "damn Yankees." By this time seventeen-year-old George and thirteen-year-old Charley had experienced multiple lifestyles as mixed-blood Tsistsistas who now lived in the white man's world. Not pleased with what they saw, both sided with the Confederacy.

George, along with other young men who felt as he did, enlisted in a Confederate organization called the State Guard. Soon after, George, with Charles in tow, made his way to Springfield, Missouri. George was a prime candidate for enlistment, having his own horse, weapons, and obvious skills, thanks to his early Tsistsista training. He quickly found himself signing the enlistment paper, a simple process that made him a member of the cavalry that Colonel Martin E. Green commanded in Missouri. Charley was a different matter. He was frail, small, and without even one scraggly hair on his face, but then he was only thirteen. The recruiting officer refused to enlist him. Disappointed, but with the same fire that sizzled through George, he returned to Westport. His school years now part of his past, he returned to the Arkansas with the goal of living in Yellow Woman's village permanently.[33]

That same June 1861, territorial governor Gilpin created the First Regiment of Colorado Volunteers. They included Company A, which recruited in Denver, and Company B, which recruited in Central City.[34] Although Wynkoop was still treading the fine line between law and lawlessness, he no longer meandered aimlessly. He enlisted, and on July 31 received a commission as second lieutenant.[35] "I went into the service to help my country in her time of trouble," he said, "not to play soldier."[36] He was not alone, for others who would play large roles in the upcoming years also enlisted, including John Chivington, Unionist Silas Soule, and former miner and current shop owner Scott Anthony, among others.

With the Civil War raging in the East and ongoing in the borderlands, the threat of a Confederate invasion of the Southwest and Colorado Territory seemed imminent. Samuel Colley of New Hampshire, most recently of Beloit, Wisconsin, had drifted into politics, serving in office as a Republican. However, the lure of gold pulled him to California. After a year with little to show, in 1860 he followed his son Dexter, who had moved to Denver, to again roll the dice, but he would not find luck in mining. However, early in 1861 his cousin, William P. Dole, was appointed commissioner of Indian affairs by President Abraham Lincoln. Colley wrote Dole, and on August 26 landed a position in which he had no experience—U.S. agent of the Upper Arkansas Indian Agency. As Albert Boone still occupied the position, Colley did not arrive at the agency until September, and then waited another two months before posting bond.[37] Colley had no clue what the duties of an Indian agent were, but it did not matter. He had a brain, and it would not take him long to figure out how to strike it rich without spending any time in the freezing water flows of the streams and rivers that the Rocky Mountain snow melts fed.

In November a young bride named Susan Riley Ashley joined her husband, Eli, who had arrived in Denver City the previous spring with Governor Gilpin. She had a terrific sense of description when she wrote about the city that became her home. "East Denver was laid out along the Platte River," and already included such streets as McGaa, Larimer, Lawrence, and Wynkoop.[38] It "was a high plateau with no prospect of growing anything more beautiful than cactus, at that time so plentiful there that its sharp spines penetrated my lady's shoes." Continuing, she wrote: "[The] lower streets were occupied by corrals, hay, grain and sales stables, wholesale supply stores, commission houses, and, what seemed for the size of the town, a plethora of boarding houses, saloons and gambling places. . . . The sidewalks seemed always covered with men, and the roadways were filled with oxen and immense freight wagons. Few women were ever seen on these lower streets." She described the rest of East Denver as it moved out onto the prairie, four churches, and Surveyor General Case and his staff, which included her husband (Eli) and a draughtsman, F. J. Ebert, as they worked out of available rooms and moved across Cherry Creek, a dry sand bed that separated East from West Denver.

When she crossed into West Denver she came alive, as it was where most of the houses were, along with a scattering of businesses, a jail, and the only hotel, the Tremont House. There was one other building, "on piles near [the center of Cherry Creek], and the intersection of Market street, stood the pride of the city, the *Rocky Mountain News* office. From this office was issued, in 1861, a daily newspaper owned by Wm. N. Byers. It was Republican in politics, was clean, wide-awake, patriotic sheet, and though its news of the outside world was obtained only from exchanges a week or more old, current events were so fearlessly told and commented upon that more than once in those troublous times Mr. Byers and his property were roughly handled and threatened with extermination."[39]

Susan lived with Eli at the Tremont House for three months, as she insisted that she wanted a fence and gate surrounding their first home. These early days in Denver opened her eyes as she observed the streets from the safety of their hotel room. "The Cheyenne and Arapahoe Indians could be seen in numbers on the streets almost every day then." She admitted to not being an admirer of "Poor Lo," but at first it must have been odd seeing them up close, and perhaps she had heard unfavorable stories.

As it turned out, advice that a fence and gate would keep her secure in her new house proved false. "Many a time in going about my household duties or sitting quietly sewing or reading," she remembered, "an uncanny feeling took possession of me, and looking up I would discover that one or more panes of my window framed the stolid face of an Indian. On one occasion, having forgotten to lock my outer doors, I entered my front room to find three Indians in it and others entering." Surprise, shock, and perhaps anger took hold. "With assumed bravery I cried out 'Puck-a-chee!' (which I had been told was the Indian way of saying begone!) and I put my hands against the nearest Indian as if to push him out." With surprise, shock, and anger gone, she observed Indians she never suspected. "They left without resistance and took their places at the windows."

Susan Ashley had another story that she enjoyed sharing, and it happened on a Sunday morning during her first year in Denver. "[A] most weird and unfamiliar sound" startled her and she hurried to the door to see the cause. "I saw a band of Indians coming up our street, and a minute later thirty or more Cheyennes and Arapahoes passed by, holding aloft on poles five freshly-taken Ute scalps. The doleful sound disturbing the Sabbath quiet was their chant of victory." The celebration continued into the evening with the Cheyennes and Arapahos in the area of the future Union depot. Susan and many whites watched a ceremony that they did not understand, but did not interrupt. "[O]nly fear of the white man's firearms prevented the Indians from seeking fair locks instead of those tawny scalps," Ashley claimed that she and others believed on that night. She saw, she observed, but she made no attempt to make contact, to befriend, or even more important, to understand. In the early 1860s Arapahos and Cheyennes constantly visited Denver, but her lone takeaway was that while "the Indians of the plains professed friendship for the whites . . . it was deemed advisable in these earlier years for all women living on this frontier to know how to load and use both revolver and rifle."

SEVEN

White Man War and Dissonance

ALTHOUGH JOHN CHIVINGTON had rejected the offer to be the chaplain for the First Colorado and had requested a fighting position, his words were not bluster, for his belief in the Union and the freedom of slaves was real. On March 25, 1862, and with a deadly encounter imminent, the major realized where he was and just what might happen. But as the command led by Colonel John Slough rushed toward a confrontation, Chivington became ill and was forced to fall behind the advance and purchase medicine from a mercantile shop that the Union army passed. Three hours later he mounted his horse and hustled to rejoin his command, reaching its camp at Burnell's Springs, New Mexico Territory, close to nightfall. Here Chivington learned that Slough ordered a battalion that included Company F (First Colorado), which was mounted; 150 cavalry commanded by Captain George Howland (Third U.S. Cavalry); along with 180 infantry from three First Colorado Volunteer companies (A, D, and E). Senior Captain Wynkoop of the First Colorado was set to lead the advance, but Chivington assumed command. A foot-weary Wynkoop with the other 179 officers and men luckily were provided wagons for transport. A night march brought them to Kozlowski's Ranch at the eastern entry to Glorieta Pass at ten that night.[1]

Here Chivington and the other officers learned that six hundred rebels were in the area. Expecting to enter battle for the first time in his life, he spoke openly with officers that were U.S. regulars. Chivington had always been vocal, and over the years had always stood firm against any attack on his view or person. Not so on this evening. "[G]entlemen, I am not a professional soldier," he said, "have never been under fire, never made the science of arms a study, and I am ready to receive and act upon any advice that you may give."[2] None was forthcoming.

On the morning of March 26, Chivington set out from Kozlowski's Ranch and headed for the eastern entrance to Glorieta Pass with 418 men. His command consisted of the First Colorado (Wynkoop, Company A, sixty men; Company C, twenty-eight men; Captain Jacob Downing, Company D, sixty men; and Captain Scott Anthony, Company E, sixty men); First Regiment Cavalry Colorado Volunteers (Captain Samuel Cook, Company F, eighty-eight men); plus twelve additional Colorado Volunteers; as well as the First U.S. Cavalry (Captain Richard Lord, Companies D and G, fifty men); and the Third U.S. Cavalry (Captain George Howland, Company K, ten men; Captain Charles Walker, Company E, fifty men). By early afternoon Chivington reached Pigeon's Ranch, a stage station in Apache Canyon, and entered the pass, which was 7,641 feet above sea level. To the south, Glorieta Mesa towered 500 feet above the canyon floor. Ponderosa pines, juniper, and piñon were everywhere, clogging the hills and ravines and obstructing visibility. The intended objective, Johnson's Ranch, was six miles away at the western entrance to Apache Canyon. Suddenly Chivington halted his advance. Major Charles L. Pyron (Second Texas Mounted Rifles), with 250 to 300 Confederate soldiers, held the ground before him with two cannons. It was a little after two in the afternoon. Pyron opened fire.[3]

Per Chivington's directive, Anthony's Company E, followed by Wynkoop's Company A, acted as skirmishers as they moved through the trees at the base of Glorieta Mesa. On the northern side of the canyon, Downing's company advanced near the base of the mountain. Chivington dismounted Howland, Lord, and Walker's cavalry. Walker joined Wynkoop in forcing the enemy to retreat on the left, and while Lord followed them, Howland joined Downing on the right and they began to flank Pyron's position. Chivington remained behind with Cook and the still-mounted Colorado First. According to Walker the skirmishing was all "at long range," but it was effective, as "the enemy fell back so rapidly that we scarcely got sight of them."[4]

It did not take long before Pyron realized that he might be overrun. As he retreated, Chivington followed, striking the enemy three times.[5] During the second or third clash, Chivington charged Pyron's position with

Company F. "[W]ith a pistol in each hand and one or two under his arms," Private Ovando Hollister wrote, the major "chawed his lips with only less energy than he gave his orders. He seemed burdened with new responsibility, the extent of which he had never before realized, and to have no thought of danger. Of commanding presence, dressed in full regimentals, he was a conspicuous mark for the Texan sharp shooters," but their rounds never touched him.[6] It was "[a]s if possessed of a charmed life, he galloped unhurt through the storm of bullets." But the aggressive action ended, and instead of advancing, Chivington retreated back to Kozlowski's Ranch.

EARLY IN 1862 JOHN EVANS traveled to Washington, D.C., to obtain backing for Chicago, Illinois, to house a federal armory. While in the capital city, he heard that Secretary of War Seward was displeased that Colorado territorial governor Gilpin had created two volunteer infantry regiments without approval or funding. This included obtaining supplies from local vendors with promissory notes that he created without federal backing. It did not matter that Gilpin, whose main goal had been to keep the territory loyal to the Union, believed that this also included preventing invasion. Although Evans had rejected President Abraham Lincoln's offer to become governor of Washington Territory in October 1861, Colorado Territory interested him, as he was constantly involved with railroad development. He sought out the Republican senator from Iowa, James Harlan, among others, to urge the president to select him.[7]

Everything fell into place, and Lincoln appointed Evans the second governor of Colorado Territory on March 26.[8]

THE UNION AND CONFEDERATE ARMIES remained in camp on the twenty-seventh, looked after their wounded, and attempted to rest, while knowing that they would again confront each other. On this day, Union spies discovered 1,200 to 1,400 enemy soldiers camped at Johnson's Ranch.[9] Slough's command reached Kozlowski's Ranch about 2:00 A.M. on the twenty-eighth. He and Chivington discussed a plan of attack, and that morning they led their commands toward Glorieta Pass. About 10:30 A.M. they reached Pigeon's Ranch. Here Chivington's two infantry battalions veered to the left and followed Galisteo Road until they began their ascent of Glorieta Mesa. Captain William Lewis commanded a battalion that included the Fifth Infantry (Companies A and G, sixty men); First Colorado (Company B, seventy-eight men); and the Second Colorado (Captain James Ford, company and strength unknown). Wynkoop commanded the second battalion, which consisted mostly of the First Colorado (Lieutenant James Shaffer, Company A, sixty-eight men; Anthony, Company E, seventy-one men; Captain George Sanborn, Company H, about eighty men; and Lieutenant Colonel Manuel Chávez commanded an unknown number of New Mexico militia).[10]

Two days previous, Chivington, Wynkoop, and Anthony had participated in battle for the first time in their lives. Other men died, but they survived. Chivington and Wynkoop had a religious connection, but now all three of their lives would intersect and would be closely linked for an undetermined future. None of them could have predicted this as they climbed Glorieta Mesa. They had not reached the top of the mesa when they heard explosions and gunfire below. Without being able to see the mortal conflict below, they knew that Slough's command had engaged the rebels somewhere near Pigeon's Ranch.[11]

But all was not right with Slough's advance, as a volley of musket rounds came dangerously close to striking the colonel. This created a problem, as the assault upon his life was "friendly fire." Fearful of assassination, Slough hid from the flank where the rounds had been fired. He later claimed that "this is what gave rise to the report that I acted cowardly."[12] It also provided a darker thought, which frightened him. "I am now satisfied that men now high in rank and command were at the bottom of this thing," he wrote. "I am satisfied that . . . if a chance offered I would be murdered."

Soon after, Chivington's force reached the top of Glorieta Mesa.

The major, Wynkoop, Anthony, and the rest of the command weaved their way through heavy vegetation that hindered their progress. Sounds of the fight far below them continued to drift upward. They walked and staggered a mile, then two. The fight below faded to nothing. The lunch hour passed and still the command zigzagged through the desert-like shrubbery. Feet dragged as they plodded onward. Finally at one-thirty in the afternoon they reached their destination. Chivington, his officers, and a guide crawled to the edge of the mesa and gazed down at Johnson's Ranch. The Confederate supply train consisted of two hundred soldiers, between sixty and eighty supply wagons, and a field piece.

But something was wrong. Chivington anticipated supporting Slough, who was supposed to attack the encampment from the canyon floor.

During this time Captains Wynkoop and Lewis kept their men quiet and out of sight. Chivington waited an hour, perhaps more for Slough. Tired of delaying and afraid of being detected, he ordered the attack. The major remained on the mesa from a position wherein he could see the entire camp. When Lewis led the charge down the north side of the mesa, Wynkoop deployed thirty men on the side of it. With good views of the Texans' camp he waited until the rebels saw the onrushing Union soldiers. Surprisingly Lewis's command stumbled and slid more than halfway down the steep mountainside before they were spotted. As the Confederates opened fire, Wynkoop yelled for his sharpshooters to pick off any rebels shooting their weapons or standing near the six-pounder.

When the Union soldiers reached the bottom of the mesa, they screamed and cursed as they swarmed through the camp and surrounded the wagons and buildings. Lewis and his infantry braved five cannon shots aimed at them before they captured the gun and spiked it. During the mêlée the Colorado Volunteers and U.S. regulars killed three Confederates and wounded others. The firefight ended as quickly as it had begun, as the Texans ran for the western entrance to the canyon or climbed the northern cliffs. "The wagons were all heavily loaded with ammunition, clothing, subsistence, and forage," a pleased Chivington reported, and he burned everything.[13] While his men made quick work of the supply train, a wagon containing ammunition exploded, and resulted in the only Union casualty at Johnson's Ranch. Seventeen rebels were captured, including two officers. Even better, they rescued five of their compatriots who had been captured by the enemy at Pigeon's Ranch that morning. Chivington praised his men, especially Captain Lewis.

Unknown to Chivington, but perhaps an unsaid fear, Scurry's force had driven Slough from the field of battle, and the federals retreated back to Kozlowski's Ranch. As soon as the destruction of the rebels' supplies was complete, Lewis's men reclimbed the mesa.

Chivington's command limped into Slough's camp at ten that night. The colonel, Wynkoop, Lewis, and everyone else were bleary-eyed, footsore, and beat. By this time the Confederates knew that their supply train had been destroyed, and they retreated toward Santa Fe. Chivington claimed that his force had killed 27 and wounded 63. Slough and Scurry would report different casualties for the day's battle. According to Scurry the Confederates killed 75 and wounded many more, while his casualties consisted of 33 dead and 35 wounded. Conversely, Slough claimed one officer killed, two officers wounded, 28 men killed, 40 wounded, and 15 men captured, while his command killed at least 100 rebels and wounded 150 or more, while capturing one officer and several prisoners. The reports made it sound as if Slough had won the day even though he had retreated from the field of battle. Perhaps he thought he had, for at five in the evening that day, he received a flag of truce from Scurry, who requested time to attend to his wounded and gather his dead.[14]

Slough had missed the first fight in the canyon, and his performance on the twenty-eighth had not been sparkling. Volunteers and regulars on both battlefields knew what had happened during both battles that day. They also knew that Chivington's surprise attack on the supply train had turned defeat into victory. The First Coloradans cheered Chivington.

Lieutenant Colonel Samuel Tappan, the second in command of the First Colorado, and who had fought with Slough's command on the twenty-eighth, had the most to gain from the colonel's demise. If Slough resigned or was replaced for cowardice, he was first in line to become the regiment's colonel. Slough never considered Tappan but felt the full power of Chivington's sudden popularity. Knowing that Union bullets had been aimed at him, Slough tendered his resignation, and it was presented to General Canby on April 9 with the result unknown until the twelfth.[15]

Two days after Slough resigned his commission, on April 11, John Evans finally took the oath of office as Colorado territorial governor, which ended Gilpin's tenure. As often happened, territorial governors also served as ex-officio superintendents of Indian affairs in an effort to save money. Even though Evans had no experience with Indians, the governorship also included this unwelcome assignment. His additional duties included overseeing the Indians in his jurisdiction, supervising and regulating traders, and keeping vigilant that Indian agents did not operate in an unethical or illegal manner—an almost impossible task. Soon after, he set out for his home in Evanston, Illinois.[16]

Although unaware that the man who had given him an opportunity to fight for his country had been replaced, Chivington saw his future appear before him and circulated a petition requesting that he be promoted to the regiment's colonel.[17]

While Chivington pushed to become the First Colorado's commanding officer, Sibley, who realized how bad the situation was in New Mexico Territory, called off the invasion and fled southward from Albuquerque and back to Texas. On April 13 the time was perfect to strike the death blow

John Evans during the time
he was the second governor of
Colorado Territory (1862–65).

*Louis Kraft Collection, ACP010.
Chávez History Library, Santa Fe,
N.Mex.*

to the fleeing rebels as they were near Tijeras Pueblo at Carnuel Canyon. Victory was at hand, but Chivington did not strike. Instead, he, Wynkoop, Anthony, and the rest of the Colorado Volunteers continued to celebrate their victory at Glorieta Pass. At Tijeras, Tappan, who craved the colonelcy, realized that he had to bow down to the enthusiasm for Chivington. He agreed that Chivington should command the First Colorado, which in turn allowed Canby to appoint Chivington the regiment's colonel.[18]

In late May 1862, while Chivington's egotism grew, the mixed-blood Cheyenne George Bent fought in what would be his last battle for the Confederacy. Although Bent had refused to be a foot soldier, he had quickly discovered that life as a mounted soldier in an artillery unit had few advantages. On the twenty-ninth of the month, Confederate General Pierre G. T. Beauregard signaled the retreat of his brigade of 66,000, as he could not defeat Major General Henry Halleck's Union force of 100,000 and protect Corinth, Mississippi, from invasion.[19]

While George Bent and the Confederate army were in retreat, Chivington made known his ambition, which craved more than just being the First Colorado's colonel. On June 25, 1862, he wrote his friend the Reverend

Hugh D. Fisher in Leavenworth City, Kansas, addressing him as "Dear Bro." He wanted Fisher to use his influence and "write to Senators Lane and Pumsay at Washington and get them to assist Mr. Bennett Delegote from Colorado in obtaining for me a *Brigadier Generalship*."[20] Chivington thought that he, Slough, or Colonel Jesse Leavenworth, who commanded the Second Colorado Volunteers, were the remaining candidates for the promotion. He did not bother to bad-mouth Slough, but he labeled Leavenworth as a "Democrat" and "the meanest old whore monger and drunkard in all the mountains."

With letters endorsing him, including one written by Governor Evans, Chivington set out for Washington on August 7, 1862. After his arrival, he met with Secretary of War Edwin Stanton, whom he found "crusty, brusque, to outside appearances a very disagreeable man to do business with."[21] Chivington, on their first meeting, presented his application to become a brigadier and to change the First Colorado from infantry to cavalry. Stanton ignored the promotion but told Chivington, "The cavalry arm of the service is a nuisance; they have been nothing but a detriment to us since the war broke out." Chivington persisted, but Stanton stopped him, saying that he had made his decision and that it was final. Chivington had a trump card, and he played it. "[T]he transfer will be made," he said.

"How do you expect to accomplish it without my signature?" Stanton challenged.

Chivington replied that he had spent time with Abraham Lincoln the previous day, and during their meeting the president had asked what was the purpose of his visit. Chivington pitched the first: becoming a cavalry regiment. Chivington then shared the president's words: "That is reasonable, it ought to be done. . . . [See] Mr. Stanton, lay the case before him, and if he refuses to do it, you come to me, and I will see that it is done." Chivington claimed that Stanton "looked as if he would like to bite my head off."

Nevertheless, Stanton set up a second meeting at 8:30 the following morning. "I have taken a notion to you," the secretary said after small talk. "I guess I will make you a brigadier and keep you here to aid in organizing these fresh troops that are coming in."

Chivington refused the offer, saying that he preferred to command the First Colorado over "the best brigade . . . in the army of the Potomac." This was an interesting rejection considering the colonel's ambition. Still, his view of the First Colorado had changed during the last six months. When the regiment marched to confront the Confederate invasion, Chivington claimed that the men "were universally anathematized; now their praise was on every tongue. They were thieves and robbers and murderers and anything else that was mean and bad; but now their campaign" to stop the Texans "had made them everything that was noble, brave and saintly." He was a part of this—a major part of it—and he envisioned even greater glory on the Colorado frontier.

That August John Evans traveled to Chicago on business, and this included attending a Union Pacific Railroad board of directors meeting with the goal of getting the train routed through Colorado Territory. While there, he heard of the Santee Sioux uprising in the Minnesota Valley, and of the massive number of people being killed. This alarmed him, and he traveled to Washington before returning to Denver. His goal: obtain additional troops to be in readiness if the Plains Indians joined together to force the whites from the territory.[22]

While the Sioux uprising in Minnesota continued, on August 26, Union cavalry cut off the Confederate retreat and captured George Bent and about two hundred Missourians. But perhaps Bent and those with him had deserted. Most American Indians—including those in the Southwest and on the plains—totally bought into the idea that if you could not win the fight, you run to survive and fight again when the odds were in your favor. Regardless if he deserted or not, he was now a prisoner of war. By early September he was back in St. Louis and incarcerated. According to Bent, on his first day there, news of his arrival was shared with his brother Robert by school friends who saw him marched through the city's streets. Robert was in the city to sell buffalo robes and other merchandise while purchasing supplies before returning to Bent's Ranch. Robert hustled to the prison, and as expected, the Bent name worked wonders. George was released to his father's custody that day. Regardless if it happened on his first day in St. Louis or not, on September 5 George Bent was "released to report at this office for final discharge on oath and bond."[23]

Shortly after his return to his father in the Big Timbers, George Bent decided to live with Black Kettle's band.

WITHIN A YEAR AFTER OFFICIALLY becoming the Indian agent for the Upper Arkansas Indian Agency, Samuel Colley launched a scheme to get rich. He invited his son Dexter to join him at Fort Lyon—the name of the post had changed when General Nathaniel Lyon became the first Union general to die during the Civil War (August 10, 1861). Dexter did, and brought with him between thirty and forty head of cattle, then worth about $1,500. Dexter quickly became the Fort Lyon trader, and just as quickly invited John Smith, who had already been the official Cheyenne interpreter at two major peace councils, to partner with him. Like the Colleys, Smith saw a golden opportunity and jumped on it, as he knew that his long-going relationship with the Tsistsistas would open the door to a profitable future.[24] The Colleys and Smith merger set in motion a trading monopoly that appeared failure-proof.

WHILE IN ST. LOUIS, MISSOURI, on October 23, 1862, John Chivington continued to relish his hop-jump over Samuel Tappan and his ascendancy to colonel of the First Colorado. Feeling the need to gloat while pounding Tappan with his authority, he admitted that his desires as to the future of the Colorado Volunteers "are still in doubt . . . as to what will be done, but am inclined to the opinion that the 1st will be mounted and remain on the 'Frontier' and that I will be in command of 'Colorado' and will get a Brig Genship."[25] Undoubtedly, Tappan cringed when he read Chivington's words.

On October 31, 1862, Evans wrote a personal letter regarding Chivington to Abraham Lincoln. "I have known the Colonel well for years, first as a leading Methodist preacher, and since as a thoroughly loyal, bold, brave and judicious commander."[26] Then in November 1862 the First Regiment of Colorado Volunteers officially became known as the First Regiment of Colorado Cavalry (First Colorado Volunteer Cavalry).[27] Almost two months passed before Evans again wrote Lincoln on December 24. This letter did the trick, and the president added the hero of Glorieta to his list of promotion recommendations. In January he presented it to the Senate.[28]

By January 23, 1863, Tappan had become aware that Chivington had "in the presence of several [officers] threatened" to have him "put in irons."[29] That morning he called on Chivington to see if what he had heard was true, and Chivington confirmed it. The lieutenant colonel considered this an "injustice." That day he wrote a protest letter to Chivington: "I am desirous of acting together in harmony, as soldiers and as men to work for the unity of our regiment in friendship . . . [but] that I am exceedingly annoyed, and excited to anger when I hear that you in my absence threatened me with this and that, speak of me with contempt. . . . From the earliest organization of our regiment you have done your utmost by outspoken remarks and seemly intimations to destroy my influence as an officer in the regiment." Moving forward, Tappan wanted the colonel to state his complaints in his presence.

On January 26 the *Daily National Intelligencer* in Washington, D.C., published a list of recently minted brigadier generals. To date the Senate had only confirmed one officer from Colorado Territory, John P. Slough, who currently served as military governor for Alexandria, Virginia. He had received his promotion on August 25, 1862.[30]

Chivington, regardless of his and others' efforts in his behalf, was the odd man out.

AS THE WAR BETWEEN THE STATES continued mostly east of the Mississippi River, the U.S. government more and more feared that some of the Plains Indians might join forces with the rebels. This was not idle talk, for the Confederacy had approached a number of tribes. The Sioux massacre of whites and mixed-bloods in Minnesota the previous summer and fall presented another concern, and John Evans was well aware of the results. New Ulm was almost totally destroyed, and the survivors had fled from the ruins and stench of unburied corpses. Over 800 whites died during the uprising while another 267 captives—most of them women and children—were saved soon after an ill-advised attack on soldiers of the Third Minnesota Regiment who were picking potatoes near Wood Lake on September 23. The Santee Sioux warriors were driven into a ravine, and cannon fire killed Chief Mankato. This broke the Sioux's efforts to forcibly remove the whites from their homeland. Evans knew that 303 warriors were tried and convicted for murder and rape and sentenced to hang. But because some trials lasted less than five minutes in length, President Lincoln concluded that due process was not served, and that the warriors had faced a kangaroo court bent on revenge. He reviewed each case and commuted all the death sentences except for thirty-nine men who had been convicted of murder, rape, or both, preventing "a travesty of justice."[31] However, before the condemned were hung at Mankato, Minnesota, on December 26, 1862, one warrior received a reprieve when additional evidence was presented.

Evans did not care about the Santee Sioux who were executed, for he was fearful of an Indian uprising similar to what had happened in Minnesota. He initiated sending Kiowa and Comanche leaders to Washington, D.C., to meet commissioner of Indian affairs William P. Dole and President Lincoln. The reason for a Dole-chieftain meeting was to create a treaty. This

came about when Evans pressed Albert Boone in a January 6, 1863, letter for information of the current Cheyenne and Arapaho land situation.
Boone, who had remained knowledgeable on Indian affairs along the Arkansas River, replied that per the 1851 treaty, Cheyenne and Arapaho land
along and near the Arkansas River "was held in common and all of each and
every band hunted where they [chose]."[32]

Evans focused on what Boone had written about communal property,
and extended it to include other Indians living in the territory. He wanted
changes, including a treaty with the Comanches and Kiowas, and he wanted
Dole to do this. In early 1863 Evans instructed Samuel Colley to gather
leaders from these tribes and send them to Washington. Colley, in turn,
directed John Smith, who then translated for him, to move among the
Kiowas, Comanches, Kiowa-Apaches, and Caddos that were then camped
near Fort Larned and sell them on the idea of meeting Dole and the Great
White Father. Evans later added the Arapahos and Cheyennes to the list.[33]

As the delegation grew, it included Arapahos Neva and Spotted Wolf;
Cheyennes Lean Bear, Standing-in-the-Water, and War Bonnet; Comanches Ten Bears and Prickled Forehead; Kiowas Lone Wolf, White Bull, Yellow Buffalo, Little Heart, Yellow Wolf, and two of their wives—Coy and
Etla; Kiowa-Apache Poor Bear; and the Caddo, Jacob.[34]

While Smith mingled with the tribes in Kansas, Colley approached
Little Raven, who was then camped near Fort Lyon. The chief liked the
idea and agreed to join the delegation. He also wanted Left Hand to meet
the Great White Father. As his friend was then camped near Denver, Little Raven sent a runner to urge him to travel to Fort Lyon as quickly as
possible. However, as the departure time grew near and the chief had not
yet appeared, it became obvious that Colley had no intention of waiting.
Little Raven urged Colley to wait for Left Hand, as his words meant a lot
when speaking for their people. The Indian agent ignored the request. This
angered Little Raven so much that he refused to go. Colley, Smith, and
the Indian delegation set out for the East. Soon after their departure, Left
Hand arrived at Fort Lyon and found a totally disgusted Little Raven.[35] Left
Hand was livid when he heard that Colley had refused to include him or
wait for him.

The selection of chiefs had been hasty, but Colley's reason for not waiting for Left Hand was flat-out stupidity, for he lost the two leading chiefs
of the Arapahos. Surprisingly Neva, a subchief and Left Hand's brother, did
not join Little Raven in protest and chose to travel east and meet the Great

Arapaho chiefs Neva and Spotted Wolf (seated) traveled to Washington, D.C., with John Smith and Samuel Colley in 1863 to meet President Abraham Lincoln. While en route they posed for a photograph at the studio of C. Noell and Alfred Addis in Leavenworth, Kansas. Neva was Left Hand's younger brother. They were close, both spoke English, and as Left Hand refused to have his image captured by the white man, one can only wonder how similar the two brothers looked.

Louis Kraft Collection, ACP010. Chávez History Library, Santa Fe, N. Mex.

White Father. Most likely he did this to learn what he could of the white man's world.

On March 12 the delegation reached Leavenworth, Kansas, where arrangements had been made for them to stay at the Planters Hotel. Although Lean Bear, chief of the Ridge Men band; along with Standing-in-the-Water, chief of the Southern Elkhorn Scrapers; and War Bonnet, chief of the Scabby band, did not have as large of a name value as Black Kettle or Stone Forehead, they were respected leaders. During the stop in Leavenworth, Colley and Smith took the chiefs, who were scalp-shirt wearers (meaning they were brave men), to C. Noell and Alfred Addis's studio, and at least two images of them were created, one with Colley and the other with Smith. The Tsistsistas sometimes called Smith "Gray Blanket."[36]

Smith and Colley, with Lean Bear, War Bonnet, Standing-in-the-Water, and the other Indian leaders, reached the capital city no later than March 22. The next day they met with Commissioner Dole, whose goal was to convince the leaders "to render more safe the routes to the gold mines and the Pacific."[37] The press also hinted at treaty negotiations; if so, this did not include the Cheyennes and Arapahos. The frontier and federal governments feared that additional Indian tribes might join the Confederacy. This made the trip a show and tell to impress the Indian leaders with the massive size of the United States, which would make them aware that they could never defeat such an enemy in battle.

On the morning of March 26 Lean Bear and the others dressed in their finest clothing and regalia before Agent Colley and John Smith escorted them to the White House. Upon their arrival they were led into the East Room, where the Indian leaders sat on the floor in a semicircle. Fifteen minutes later Abraham Lincoln appeared and sat in an arm chair. An audience of white dignitaries and women watched as Smith introduced Lean Bear and the others one by one, and as he did they stood and shook hands with the president before again sitting. With Smith translating, Lincoln invited each Indian to speak, however, there had to be another translator present, as Smith did not speak Comanche, Kiowa, Kiowa-Apache, or Caddo.

When it was his turn, Lean Bear spoke about how he wanted to keep the peace, but that white men on the plains did not want this. Lean Bear said, "[I]t is not always possible for any father to have his children do precisely as he wishes them to do." Lincoln explained that sometimes white "children" ignored his wishes and "sometimes behave badly, and violate these treaties" made between Indians and the U.S. government.[38]

With the Civil War raging, the American Indians were not Lincoln's primary concern. Although he had to deal with the Sioux outbreak in Minnesota in 1862, among other problems, he often left the Indian problem on the frontier to the commissioner of Indian affairs and the secretary of the interior. The Washington *Daily Morning Chronicle* quoted Lincoln saying to Lean Bear and the others: "The pale-faced people are numerous and prosperous because they cultivate the earth, produce bread, and depend upon the products of the earth rather than wild game for subsistence."[39] The president suggested that the Indians learn to live as the white man did, echoing a widespread view.

Sometime in April the Colley-Smith-led delegation of Indian leaders returned from Washington and an extended trip to New York City to the frontier and their bands. Undoubtedly they spread the word of what they saw.

That same April, John J. Saville, a surgeon serving a tour of duty on the frontier, found himself in Colorado Territory. He saw a parched land

John Smith is seen standing second from left while Cheyennes chiefs Lean Bear, War Bonnet, and Standing-in-the-Water are sitting from the left in the front row (all three would be killed in 1864). The image was taken at the President's "Summer House" (a botanical retreat to the west of the White House) by Matthew Brady and Company on the morning of March 26, 1863, after the Indian delegation met with President Abraham Lincoln. Sitting at right in the front row is unidentified. Seated from left in the second row are Coy, a Kiowa woman; White Bull, her husband; unidentified; and Kiowa chief Lone Wolf. The rest of the people in the image are unidentified.

Louis Kraft Collection, ACP010. Chávez History Library, Santa Fe, N.Mex.

decimated with little rain and with creeks and rivers that had little water. He claimed that the Arkansas was almost dry. There was little game for the Cheyennes and Arapahos, and those he saw suffered from hunger and disease. Dr. Saville felt that the American-Indian situation was volatile on the roads that connected the territory with the states. Near the end of the month he met with Left Hand. His first surprise in this meeting was that Left Hand spoke and understood English.

But there was more—much more, for he found Left Hand's outrage over the current white-Arapaho situation disturbing. While they talked, Left Hand made him aware that he had not been present at the Fort Wise treaty talks, that he did not know what the white man's treaty said, and that without his mark on the white man's piece of paper, it meant nothing.

Left Hand's anger over Agent Colley not waiting for him to join the delegation of Indian leaders to meet the Great White Father was evident in his words. He claimed that Colley had stated that he would wait for him. If so, this had to have been what Little Raven's runner shared with him. It is unknown if Colley promised that he would wait, and if Little Raven stated this, perhaps it was just one more pitiful translation from English to Arapaho and back. Or it might have been an out-and-out lie. Finally, Left Hand told Dr. Saville that he knew the reason why he had been excluded from the trip. It was because he spoke English. Worse, the whites feared that he might state that his people's agents and interpreters, and that included Colley, had cheated them. Not finished, he said that the whites had broken their word, but here he was vague.[40] Regardless of what Left Hand said and what Dr. Saville shared, the information went nowhere.

GOVERNOR EVANS'S PRAISE FOR CHIVINGTON'S worth as a commanding officer refused to end. This continued into late 1863. Chivington not only appreciated this, he craved it, as he felt becoming a brigadier general guaranteed his future—which he hoped would be in politics. Unfortunately, Brigadier General John Slough had not finished with him, and Slough would have the last laugh over their bitter infighting. Better, he had a trump card that easily topped anything that Evans or any of Chivington's cronies in the Methodist Church could present, and his timing could not have been better. On September 13, 1863, Slough wrote Secretary of War Stanton, with whom he had a good relationship. "Some months ago I recommended Col. John M. Chivington . . . for promotion. . . . I desire to place myself right by withdrawing my recommendation. . . . Judge Hall late Chief Justice of Colorado has just informed me that when I was Colonel of the Regiment and Chivington Major, he and others conspired for my assassination and the attempt was made when en route to New Mexico in February and March 1862. The object was to secure the Colonelcy to Chivington who was recognized as a better military man than the Lt. Col. and the promotion of the other conspirators. . . . The base attempt upon my life was frustrated by Providence."[41] Surprisingly Slough did not mention the attempt upon his life during the Pigeon's Ranch battle on March 28, 1862. It did not matter, for even though Chivington wrote Methodist Bishop Matthew Simpson on December 30, 1863, stating how his promotion to brigadier general would "help our plans out here [Colorado Territory] of which I have no doubt Gov[.] Evans has informed you," nothing would happen.[42]

By the end of September 1863, Lieutenant Silas Soule had been assigned to recruiting duty for the First Colorado Volunteer Cavalry in Denver. He enlisted three to four men on a daily basis. According to a Denver newspaper, "He is universally liked, which accounts for his success."[43]

EIGHT

Unjustified Actions

THE TSISTSISTAS LIVING in the south became nervous when the Sioux sent them a war pipe during the Light snow moon (March 1864).[1] Fearing the consequences of aligning with the Lakotas, they met with Agent Samuel Colley at Fort Larned, Kansas, and told him that they did not want to ride the war trail. Colley relayed this information to Governor John Evans.[2]

Early in the Spring moon (April) when Southern Tsistsistas came upon some oxen (or cattle) in Bijou Basin that were unattended, they drove the animals to their village. The animals had strayed from a herd that belonged to two government freighters named Jackman and Irwin. When the white men realized their stock was missing, they went to Camp Weld and reported the animals stolen. Lieutenant George S. Eayre (Independent Battery, Colorado Volunteer Artillery) with fifty-four men, two 12-pounder mountain howitzers, and Lieutenant Charles Phillips (First Colorado Volunteer Cavalry), with twenty-six men from Company D, set out on April 8 to recover the missing animals.[3]

While the soldiers set out, the Ohméséhesos (Northern Cheyennes) sent a runner to the south to invite the Southern People to join them in a revenge raid on the Crows, who had killed Brave Wolf, a Northern chief, the previous summer. As the grass had begun to grow and the ponies began to fatten, fourteen Dog Men including Bull-Telling-Tales, Little Chief, Bear Man, Wolf-Coming-Out, and Mad Wolf left the Dog Man camp on

Beaver Creek. George Bent was in the village and joined the raid. As this was a war party, the warriors drove a herd of their horses; some were war mounts while the others were for riding during the trip. On April 11 as they rode northward, Bull-Telling-Tales and another warrior came upon four mules that were not tethered or herded and rounded them up. That evening after the Dog Men made camp below the South Platte River, a *vi'ho' i* named W. D. Ripley, who had a ranch on Bijou Creek, appeared. After seeing the mules, he told the warriors that they belonged to him, and that he wanted them back. Bull-Telling-Tales said he would like to be paid or to receive a gift for taking care of the animals. Ripley, who would claim that the animals were horses, refused to pay anything for what he considered his and left the camp without the livestock.[4]

Ripley rode west to Camp Sanborn, on the south side of the South Platte River. Arriving that evening, he told Captain George L. Sanborn (First Colorado Volunteer Cavalry), who commanded the outpost, that Indians raided along Bijou Creek, "committing depredations," and that he had lost all his livestock.[5] "Depredation" had become the key word when reporting an incident involving Indians, for it implied murder, ravage, damage, or loss by a predatory attack and could lead to a generous financial reimbursement to the aggrieved party. Sanborn ordered Second Lieutenant Clark Dunn (First Colorado) with two companies (H and C, forty men), to set out in pursuit at daylight on the twelfth. Dunn force-marched in a southeasterly direction toward the Indians' camp of the previous night, but Ripley was a poor guide and they never found it, which would have clearly shown which direction the warriors traveled.[6]

When Ripley did not return to pay for the animals on the morning of April 12, the Dog Men continued their journey northward. They crossed the South Platte River below Frémont's Orchard, Colorado Territory. But instead of continuing toward the Ohméséheso camps, they followed the river in a westerly direction toward Elbridge Gerry's Ranch, located on the south side of the river just beyond Camp Sanborn. Gerry, an Indian trader, had twice married into the Sioux tribe. Their reason to detour was to obtain something in return for the animals, which they now knew belonged to a white man. They crossed the river to avoid contact with Camp Sanborn.[7]

After Dunn realized that it would be difficult to find the Indians' trail, he split his command, sending the bulk of it south toward the ranches on Bijou Creek. Keeping fifteen men, the lieutenant moved eastward, skirting the South Platte, searching what he called an "arid waste" of little water, deep ravines, and sandy hills. Failing to find a trace of the Indians, he moved southward and reunited with the rest of his command on Bijou Creek at two o'clock in the afternoon. They also had not seen any sign of the Indians. Continuing the hunt, Dunn again moved northward. An hour later he discovered the Indians' trail and followed it. When he was somewhere between three and four miles from the South Platte River, Dunn saw smoke to his right. He again split his command, sending twenty-five men in the direction of the fire.[8]

Gerry had not been at his ranch when the Dog Men arrived, and they reversed their direction, again keeping to the north side of the river. By late afternoon they again approached where they had crossed the river that morning. After safely passing to the southeast of Frémont's Orchard, they changed direction and began to move northward toward sand hills. Although most of the Indians rode, some led their mounts.[9]

At four in the afternoon Dunn reached the river and saw thirty warriors in the main party with others driving a herd of horses toward sand hills, which Ripley said belonged to him. The Indians were about one mile from Dunn's position; approximately three miles east of Frémont's Orchard. By this time, Dunn had force-marched seventy-five miles over broken country on animals that had little to drink. The lieutenant allowed the horses to quench their thirst in the river before crossing to the north side. After reassembling his command on the opposite bank, he ordered a gallop on jaded and water-bloated mounts.[10]

A warrior saw soldiers with guns in their hands galloping toward the Dog Men and yelled a warning. Little Chief had a rifle over his saddle. His first reaction was to turn and flee. Others followed his lead, but Mad Wolf yelled for them to hold their ground. Little Chief yanked his mount to a halt and turned back toward the soldiers. While some warriors moved the pony herd and mules away from the charging soldiers, the mounted Dog Men formed a battle line to confront the charging soldiers. Mad Wolf held a revolver and Wolf-Coming-Out held a bow and several arrows. Farther behind them Bull-Telling-Tales was also dismounted. All three held their mounts' bridles while they waited on foot. Even though they felt they had done nothing wrong, the warriors strung their bows and had revolvers and carbines ready.[11]

Here the telling of what happened varies dramatically.

Dunn claimed he halted his charge about five hundred yards from a Dog Soldier battle line. After sending Ripley and four soldiers to recover the stock from twenty warriors, Dunn left his command and rode 150 yards forward. After halting, he dismounted and walked toward the Indians. When close to them, he used sign language to indicate that he wanted the Indians to return the animals and surrender their weapons. According to Dunn, without provocation twenty-five warriors began shooting at the soldiers. The twenty warriors herding stock rushed to join the firefight. Even though Dunn only had fifteen men to confront an inflated number of forty-five warriors, the Dog Men halted their charge and fled to the bluffs. With the rest of his command arriving to support him, Dunn chased the warriors on worn-out mounts for fifteen or sixteen miles. Night arrived, it began to rain, and the lieutenant called off the engagement and headed back to Camp Sanborn. He claimed he wounded between ten and fifteen warriors and killed between eight and ten while suffering four casualties, of which two later died from their wounds.[12]

In stark contrast to Dunn, the Dog Men claimed that the soldiers never halted their advance and attacked without making any attempt to talk. When a soldier on horseback charged him with a revolver, Bull-Telling-Tales jumped toward him and shot the *vi'ho' i* with an arrow. As the firefight surrounded him he removed a coat and watch from the dead man, who he thought was an officer. According to the warriors this was the turning point of the fight, for the soldiers turned and fled. Wolf-Coming-Out shot a soldier, as did two others. The warriors did not give chase, and after moving off a safe distance, many of them decided to return to the villages on the Smoky Hill. Mad Wolf, Wolf-Coming-Out, and Bear Man were wounded, but the Indians suffered no deaths. They were not happy, for they felt that the soldiers attacked them without cause.[13]

Dunn and his men limped back to Camp Sanborn, arriving about midnight. By this time Elbridge Gerry, whom Sanborn summoned, had arrived at the post. A report written on April 13 stated that the Indians Dunn fought had captured a herd of cattle, and Dunn began a new pursuit at midnight on April 14 with Gerry acting as scout. But this time he did not engage Indians, for a snowstorm made it impossible to find a trail to follow.[14]

Surprisingly, Chivington wrote a report on the April 12 skirmish on April 15, three days before Dunn wrote his report. He increased the number of Indians Dunn faced to seventy while decreasing the number of miles Dunn traveled to sixty.[15]

While the military reports built up the aggressive attitude of the Cheyennes, Elbridge Gerry downplayed the hostilities after returning to his ranch on the fourteenth. He spoke with Cheyennes who had traveled southward from the north, as well as Cheyennes from the main Beaver Creek village, and he believed that no war parties set out to raid whites.[16] The Tsistsistas did not consider raiding tribal enemies the same as attacking whites, and so when Gerry queried them, they did not consider the Dog Men riding north to raid Crows apropos to the question.

This was just the beginning of unjustified attacks on Tsistsistas.

On the fifteenth, Eayre and Phillips's command neared the headwaters of the Republican River, and as they did, they discovered seventy lodges of Southern Cheyenne Crow Chief's band. The Indians had been hunting buffalo and were not aware that they had become the hunted. According to the Tsistsistas, it was early and people were just beginning to get up. Pony herds were allowed to graze a distance from camp at night, but luckily on this morning, boys had already driven the herd closer to the village. Antelope Skin had ridden out early to hunt alone. When he saw the *vi´ ho´ i* soldiers, he raced back to the camp shouting "Jump on ponies! Soldiers are coming!"[17] He leaped off his horse and hid. As the soldiers charged past where he was concealing himself, he shot one of them with an arrow. The Tsistsistas claimed that the soldiers made no attempt to talk. Antelope Skin's warning had saved the People, as it had given them enough time to run to the pony herd, mount, and flee. The Indian fighters made camp in the abandoned camp for three days, and took what they wanted. Before leaving, Eayre burned the village.

Eayre continued his punitive expedition and found a second village on the Republican, but again the Tsistsistas had an advance warning prior to the attack. They had time to grab some of their belongings, but not enough to disassemble their tipis. No one died in the attack, but Eayre destroyed their lodges.[18]

As racial conflict between the Cheyennes and military heated up, Major Ned Wynkoop returned to Denver via coach from a leave of absence to the states on April 26.[19] His journey had proved peaceful, and he was not aware of the escalating violence. Since he had met William Byers in 1859 and had later become his friend in Denver, the frontiersman had always provided good copy for the *Rocky Mountain News*. Wynkoop, unlike many of his peers, was literate, liked publicity, and used his friendship with the publisher-editor to keep his name in print. At times in the past Wynkoop had straddled the definition of law, but Byers mostly ignored his transgressions. Since the struggle to preserve the Union, his marriage, and the start of his young family, the major had become a hero and model citizen.

Shortly after his return, Wynkoop appeared at Byers's office on Cherry Creek. He was glad to be back in the territory, and Byers printed that "Colorado, State or no State, is good enough for [him]."[20] Although unknown to Wynkoop or Byers, when the major departed the editor's office on that day, his future actions would affect their friendship for all time.

A few days later Major Jacob Downing (First Colorado), a lawyer from Albany, New York, was anxious to engage the Cheyennes. He appeared in Denver and asked the colonel "to give me a force to go against the Indians."[21] Chivington did. With forty troopers, Downing "moved north to Camp Sanborn to assume command." Near the junction of the Platte, Downing claimed: "I captured an Indian and required him to go to the village, or I would kill him." The warrior was named Spotted Horse, perhaps a mixed-blood Tsistsista and Lakota, who considered himself friendly to the whites, as he often camped near Gerry's on Crow Creek. Spotted Horse agreed to scout for Downing, as did a white rancher named Samuel Ashcraft.[22]

Back at Camp Weld, on May 2, Wynkoop received orders to assume command of Fort Lyon, replacing Major Scott Anthony.[23] His initial and only contact with Indians, or lack thereof, was when he led an 1863 punitive expedition against the Utes. It ended without him ever seeing the enemy, and had faded into long-gone memories.[24] He would not arrive at the isolated post until the eighth. The timing could not have been better for the novice Indian fighter, as hostilities between the races were intensifying.

On that same May 2, Major Downing with forty troops set out to find warring Cheyennes. The command "traveled all day and all that night."[25] That was not quite true, for they halted in the afternoon before continuing about ten that night. By six the next morning Downing reached his target. "The canyon at Cedar Bluffs originates high on a rock-encrusted plateau where the spring once flowed from below a rock shelf into a depression which stretches parallel to the valley below. This depression is nearly hidden from view by the zigzag course of the erosion which descends through the canyon."[26] The major saw five lodges; it would later expand to fifteen large tipis "and some smaller ones."[27] This was Downing's target "at Cedar Cañon, twenty miles southeast of the American range on the [north side of the] South Platte."[28]

Downing attacked. "I ordered the men to commence killing them," he proclaimed.[29] The major did not separate noncombatants from warriors; he meant everyone—men, women, and children. "I took no prisoners," Downing continued. "There were women and children among the Indians, but to my knowledge, none were killed." If true, this was a major comment, and cannot be ignored.

After his victory Downing hustled to the American Ranch, which forwarded his report to Junction, which wired his details of the victory to Denver.

Byers published Downing's triumph over "the savages" the following day under "DAILY NEWS" in which he called the *News* "The Official Paper of the Territory." According to Downing his troops killed 25 and wounded between 35 and 40 while losing one soldier killed. He also captured 100 horses. "The Indians were totally routed." That same day the Black Hawk *Daily Mining Journal* printed a similar article, while adding: "The Major thinks [an] Indian war has commenced in earnest. Lively times are looked for in the next two weeks."[30] Actually Downing's exact communication with Chivington stated: "Had a fight with Cheyennes today.—Killed about twenty-five . . . Indians . . . Lost one man killed and one wounded. Captured one hundred head of horses. &c.," and according to Downing, "The war has commenced in earnest."[31]

Less than two weeks later on May 15, 1864, Black Kettle and Southern Tsistsista council chief Lean Bear camped near Fort Larned. The recent attacks on their brethren made them nervous and they moved north, camping thirty miles south of the Smoky Hill on Ash Creek.[32]

The next morning hunters announced that soldiers approached the village of 250 lodges. Lean Bear rode toward the soldiers with Star to tell them that his village was not at war. As soon as Eayre saw the Indians he ordered his men to form a line. Wolf Chief, who was present, shared: "We rode up on a hill and saw the soldiers coming . . . When we saw the soldiers all formed a line, we did not want to fight. Lean Bear . . . told us to stay behind him while he went forward to show his papers from Washington which would tell the soldiers that we were friendly. Lean Bear had a medal on his breast given to him at the time the Cheyenne chiefs visited Washington."[33] When he drew near to the soldiers with Star, they opened fire. Lean Bear fell to the ground, as did Star. The *vi'ho' i* soldiers moved forward and fired additional bullets into the two fallen Tsistsistas, ripping their bodies to pieces. Outraged, the warriors attacked, their numbers growing as more rode out of the village. Not wanting war, Black Kettle rode among the warriors as he attempted to stop the fighting, yelling "Do not make war!"[34] Supposedly there were five to six hundred warriors in the village. If Black Kettle had not acted quickly, Eayre and his men would have died. Facing overwhelming numbers, Eayre retreated. Angry warriors, those Black Kettle could not stop, chased the whites as they retreated toward Fort Larned.

Eayre reached Fort Larned safely and reported that he had driven off the Indians after fighting for over seven hours. At first he claimed the soldiers killed three chiefs and twenty-five warriors, while losing four dead and three wounded.[35] He later admitted he fought a seven-or eight-mile running fight, lost three or four men and killed only one unnamed chief.[36]

On May 17, the day after Eayre's command killed Lean Bear, Tsistsista warriors from the Ash Creek village raided along the stage road that linked Forts Riley and Larned seeking vengeance for the chief's murder. This included surrounding a ranch house where a *vi'ho' i* lived with his Tsistsista wife on Walnut Creek. They forcibly took her from him; then told him to leave and not return as they intended to kill all white men in their land.[37]

Unsure what brought on the attacks, Dog Man chiefs Bull Bear and Tall Bull sent out *wolves* (scouts) to watch the soldiers. Wary, the Dog Men avoided contact with the marauding white men. As tensions grew south of the Platte, the Tsistsistas living along the Arkansas spoke for peace. But events beyond both factions' control moved quickly, and hostilities erupted in the Platte River country.[38]

As WYNKOOP SETTLED IN at Fort Lyon, Silas Soule, who had been promoted to captain in April, found life in Denver quiet. He had been on detached duty from Company D of the First Colorado since August 1863. During that time he performed recruiting duty while also acting as an adjutant. Soule mostly pushed papers, and his contact with his regiment had mainly been through communications. As such he had not taken part in any action between the military and the Cheyennes.[39]

If it had been action that Soule craved, May would provide him and the residents on the west side of Denver more than they could handle. Beginning around the twelfth of the month heavy rains pummeled the city. Cherry Creek, a tributary of the South Platte River, often was little more than a trickle. The ground near the creek became saturated. As the days passed, the water level in the creek rose. By the eighteenth it had become a raging river. And the rains continued.

At approximately 11:30 on the evening of May 19 the creek flooded, as racing water flowed over the banks and swept through Denver near the South Platte. The week of unending rain had soaked the surrounding land.

Soon after the midnight hour all hell burst forth when the roar of raging water jerked people from their slumber. A large two-story brick building provided Soule with his office and lodging. He joined the surprised populace as he struggled to get out of it. The raging waters swept away the earth that Soule's office stood upon, and the building crumbled into the torrent. Soule lost everything; the military's paperwork, his cherished letters from Maine, and all his clothes. "I did not save any thing out of it," he lamented to his sister Annie.[40]

The east bank of Cherry Creek to the west side of the South Platte had become a mass of water, while Cherry, Front, and Ferry streets became rivers. "Houses, trees, fences, cattle, hogs, chickens, wagons, barrels, boxes, tents, baggage, household furniture, wagon beds, and indeed property of almost every description was sailing at the rate of twenty miles or more an hour towards the Missouri River," the *Weekly Commonwealth* reported.[41] The loss of property was massive. People flailed about in the rushing water. Lucky ones clung to trees, huddled on roof tops, or took refuge wherever they could. The First Colorado stationed at Camp Weld, as well as civilians, did what they could to rescue people.

In the early morning of May 20 the staff at *The Commonwealth*, one of the daily and weekly newspapers in Denver, anxiously watched the *Rocky Mountain News* office, which straddled Cherry Creek. They hoped "that it might withstand the fury of the waters. Lights gleamed from its windows, showing that all were astir within [as they worked on the next day's edition]. Hardly had those in this office exchanged opinions as to whether that building would be able to hold out, when the light disappeared, and shortly afterward, and at a quarter o[f] one, a loud crash came booming over the water, and the *News* office was totally demolished, the occupants barely saving their lives."[42]

Although William Byers's *Rocky Mountain News* office had been built on the bank of Cherry Creek, he, his wife Elizabeth, and their children lived at what Elizabeth called their country place on the west side of the South Platte River near Val Verde. Early on the morning of May 20 the family awoke to the roar of Cherry Creek's raging water. They knew that the creek had flooded, and Byers decided not to go to the office that morning. Looking outside they saw that the South Platte waters had also risen. Worse, the surging river was alarmingly close to bursting over its banks, which put their home in danger of being washed away.

According to Elizabeth, "the River suddenly cut through a low strip of land, leaving us marooned on an island. This new stream was very deep and rapid."[43]

Luckily Elizabeth and William Byers had friends who realized their danger, and they requested help. Almost as if a miracle, Colonel John Chivington and an escort of soldiers from Camp Weld appeared on the east bank of the South Platte. Chivington called that he wanted to cross the river on horseback. Byers thought this could lead to disaster and yelled at the colonel not to attempt to cross the violent water, as it was too dangerous. Continuing, he said that the water must rise another two feet before the situation became desperate. Chivington shouted he understood, then rode away with his escort.

Time raced forward, and the water continued to rise until it breached the banks. The charging river swept toward the Byerses' house and began to seep through the door sills. Elizabeth and William frantically attempted to move their belongings above the water. Then, keeping dry, they "sat on the table telling funny stories."[44] But that was merely an attempt to remain calm, for Byers now feared the worst. He wrote a note saying "his wife and babies were clinging to the tree tops, [and were] in danger of flood and starvation." He placed the paper in a bottle and flung it into the South Platte.

Two hours had passed since Chivington had ridden away. By this time the Byerses' situation had become desperate, as the water continued to rise within their house. Worse, the structure had begun to creak as it shifted. Elizabeth, Byers, and their children huddled together as they waited.

Chivington had not forgotten them. He returned with his escort and a newly constructed boat tied to a military wagon that he had ordered built in town. Quickly the boat was lowered from the wagon, and soldiers rowed to the Byerses' island. Elizabeth and Byers carried their children as they rushed toward their rescuers. Elizabeth found the short crossing frightening as they were rowed to land on the east bank of the South Platte. Here horses awaited their arrival, and mounted soldiers of the First Colorado escorted them "through the soft mud for a distance of probably a block, which was worse than the boat ride."[45] Eventually they arrived at their destination— Governor John Evans's house. Evans was not home, but his second wife of over ten years greeted them graciously and invited them inside. Margaret Gray Evans had restored John's "optimism and enthusiasm" that had vanished with the death of his first wife, Hannah.[46] She gave him a second youth, and his love for her was endless, as demonstrated in his letters to her. He placed a daguerreotype of his *Maggie* under his pillow at night and in his pocket during daylight hours.

The connection between Byers and Evans was already in place, as well as their bond with Chivington, but now it cemented a communion of their view of the territory's future, and woe to anyone who attempted to block their vision. The Byerses had survived, but as William would soon learn, his livelihood—the tool that he used to drive Denver and Colorado Territory in the direction he felt best—did not.

Silas Soule had also survived. His financial loss did not come close to that of William Byers, but he was certainly just as emotionally devastated. Still, the captain had no problem making fun of his situation in public. He sent numerous notes to *The Commonwealth* over the "Cherry Creek Telegraph" on May 27. The captain was simply playing with words. For example, he wrote, "in regard to my ruin," even though he was an officer in the First Colorado, "I am a pauper, and begging on the streets." Pushing for laughs, he then wrote, "[I] have been presented with a stray hog, and am recruiting for swill."[47] There was no such-named telegraph. He hand-delivered his "notes" to the paper, and it printed three of them on June 1. He put up a brave show while dealing with his current situation and his desire to stop pushing paperwork around on his desk. Soule proclaimed, presumably to people that did not receive *The Commonwealth*, "You will please send fifty cents for every dispatch from your Island, for *Drinks*, to keep up the reputation of Denver." Captain Soule had fallen into the dregs, and although he presented a cocky persona, he struggled to pull himself from a hole that he wondered if he could ever escape.

Simeon Whiteley, whom Soule knew, had relocated from Washington, D.C., to Colorado Territory in 1862 to become an Indian agent for the Utes. With zero Indian experience, he had actually made the exodus to aid the push for the territory to enter the Union as a free state. Whiteley quickly became fed up serving as Ute agent, claiming that he could not perform his duties in the Middle Park of the Rockies when the land was covered in snow for nine months. He relocated to Denver and landed a position at *The Commonwealth*, as he had been an experienced printer in Wisconsin and Illinois, which was nice for him, as he continued to collect his salary as Indian agent.[48]

Using a more serious tone, Soule continued his comments for public consumption with his tongue firmly planted in cheek: "Will Colonel

Chivington start for the mountains to-day? My company papers were in the office where the coat hangs, and are not in a condition to warrant me in leaving with my Company to-day. I have sent the papers, my watch, and a few hundred dollars worth of other property, to the States, via Platte River."[49]

Soule's life was about to change, for no longer would he be a company commander without one to command.

William Byers did not wallow in a "woe is me" attitude while he and Elizabeth remained guests in the Evans household. Although he and partner John Dailey had often performed in a cavalier way toward their competition, they had not burned all their bridges. *The Commonwealth* did not publicize Byers and Dailey's sad state of affairs. At the same time, the newspaper allowed them space to write columns to inform their former readers of their current status. Surprisingly, the disaster did not decree the death knell to the *Rocky Mountain News*.

On May 30 the Byerses returned to their "ranch" on the west side of the South Platte.[50] At this time Byers and Dailey drafted their view of the *News*'s future. Since the disaster, friends and patrons had offered various amounts of money as gifts or loans at low interest rates. Byers and Dailey used these offers to their advantage while declining some of them. The two men worked their readership well, setting them up for their proposal, mainly to recreate the *News* from scratch with the promise of the most modern printing presses and a better weekly and daily paper if they could secure $2,000 paid-in-advance subscriptions to the *Weekly Rocky Mountain News*. Although confronted with the massive task of cleaning and repairing the water and mud damage to his home, Byers must have felt content with the paper's future, for he knew that the *Weekly Commonwealth* would publish his and Dailey's sales pitches.[51]

But their return would not be permanent, for a week later the South Platte's water level again rose dramatically. Byers and Elizabeth packed up and took refuge in the seminary building on the west side of the river, which had just been completed but was not yet occupied. This became their home until they bought a house on Arapahoe Street that was near 15th Street in Denver.

As May moved toward conclusion, Wynkoop still reported to Colonel John Chivington, who commanded the District of Colorado. The Cheyenne war surrounded him at his new post. "The Cheyennes will have to be soundly whipped before they will be quiet," Chivington wrote Wynkoop on the last day of the month. "If any of them are caught in your vicinity kill them, as that is the only way."[52] These were severe words, but words that Wynkoop understood. At this time Captain Soule received orders that reassigned him and Company D to Fort Lyon, where he would become second in command under Wynkoop.

While still en route to Fort Lyon on June 2, 1864, Soule apologized to his mother for his tardy reply to her. As in the past, he justified his actions; this time he had been busy with paperwork. Soule often spoke of sending her money but did not, as he feared that his cash would not reach her in Maine due to ongoing Indian attacks on stagecoaches. Soule also bragged about the worth of his mining interests near Denver; most likely an overexaggeration, as he placed his fifty mining claims worth somewhere between $10,000 and $50,000.[53] He reached Fort Lyon on June 5. Since 1863 he and Wynkoop had little contact except through military reports. They were acquaintances at best. This changed soon after Soule's arrival at the post.[54]

BY THIS TIME THE TSISTSISTAS AND HINONO'EINO' realized that the white invasion of their homeland threatened not only their lifeway but also their existence. To survive, many of them understood that they needed to remove the *vi'ho' i* and *nihancan*—the spider—from their land. A great proportion of the two tribes subscribed to this view, but Black Kettle, White Antelope, Left Hand, and Little Raven remained notable exceptions. Even though they disagreed with the majority of their people, they continued to wield considerable influence within their bands.

But as always they could not control or stop warriors who rode the warpath, for this was the way of the Called Out People and the Cloud People. Even though Black Kettle and other chiefs time and again stated this, the white man refused to accept it. It was a major cultural difference that the Anglo-American leaders used time and again to point the finger of blame at Cheyenne and Arapaho leaders.

It seemed that the Tsistsistas to the east-southeast of Denver were the only tribe in conflict with the whites, but this was not so. There were a number of war parties in the area that began a series of raids on June 9 that lasted three days. Perhaps as many as 113 mules and seven horses were reported stolen. Just two months before, in early April, Nathan Ward Hungate moved his wife, Ellen Eliza Decker, and two daughters, Laura and

Florence, from Nebraska Territory to Colorado Territory. They secured lodging in a cabin on the Isaac Van Wormer property, and Hungate either worked for him or leased his land.

Suddenly there was an escalation of Indian attacks. Feeling that war had been forced upon them, Tsistsistas, Dog Men, and Hinono'eino' joined forces with the Brûlé Lakotas. They raided along the Platte, running off stock at every opportunity, while Tsistsistas assaulted Coal Creek, which was just ten miles from Denver.[55]

On June 10 or very early on the eleventh, Hungate apparently wounded a warrior attempting to steal his stock. As the string of raids targeted horses and mules, it was obvious that the raiders did not intend to kill whites. However, Hungate's shot required retaliation, and on the morning of the eleventh Arapaho raiders returned to where he lived with his family. This time they came with deadly intent and surrounded the cabin. Unable to draw the whites out of the log structure, they set it afire. This forced Hungate (twenty-nine), Ellen (twenty-five), who held her infant Florence (not yet five months), and Laura (who had not reached her fourth birthday) to flee the flames. An armed Hungate led their race to safety, but they did not get far. About four hundred yards from the burning building, the raiders dropped Ellen to the ground with an arrow or bullet and moved in for the kill. Hungate realized his family was lost and ran to save himself. When the warriors reached Ellen and their daughters, they quickly dispatched the girls by slicing their throats. They then stripped the defenseless mother, sexually assaulted her, cut her throat, and mutilated her body. All three were scalped. The warriors caught up to Hungate about a mile from the cabin. After killing him, they took his scalp and cut his body so that he would have no afterlife.[56]

As the raids escalated, fear intensified among the white population. On June 14 Governor Evans announced that the Platte River route had not been shut down, that the American Ranch had not been destroyed, and that few Indians had been seen near the city for some time. He also distributed an executive order to the daily and weekly newspapers in the area.

> I call upon the patriotic citizens of Colorado to fill up the present volunteer militia companies and organize new ones. Nothing can be done until after organization. Any one who has seen a useless crowd at a fire will understand this. Organize! Organize! Mounted rifle companies are the best. All militia company commanders will put their commands in

readiness to respond promptly to a call at any moment, and if possible fill up to the maximum of eighty men.[57]

(Less than two months later the governor would issue a proclamation that would be little more than an open invitation to murder people.)

The next morning a handful of Denverites approached Evans, and this included a member of the *Commonwealth* staff, which gave the paper an inside scoop. The group got right to the point, mainly that there had been a lot of talk on the streets, and the consensus was that the United States should employ Utes "to fight the Cheyennes."[58] On the surface their logic had merit, mainly that the Utes would help themselves by helping the whites.

If Evans did not smile outwardly, he must have struggled to keep a straight face. He was not an Indian man, and the add-on position to being governor, "ex-[o]fficio Superintendent of Indian Affairs," was not of his choosing. Still, he was not an ostrich with his head buried in the ground. He simply told them that their plan was not wise, as the Ute bands were spread throughout the mountains, and that by the time all were assembled, the Cheyennes would be long gone. "[W]e are as yet only at war with the Cheyennes," Evans said, "while the Utes have for ages . . . been at war with *all* the tribes on the plains." One can only wonder if he smirked when he ended the meeting. "[T]o employ the Utes would put us at war with all of them at once."

Before going to press that day the *Weekly Commonwealth* also became privy to details of the recent raids, and what they had learned did not agree with the rumors that were then rampant throughout Denver. "During the thieving and murdering of the past week, ONLY NINE Indians have been seen. Two Indians stampeded the forty-nine mules of Daniels & Brown—and seven were engaged in the murder of the Hunsgate [*sic*] family. No other Indians have been seen in the vicinity of any of the settlements, near or remote to this city, nor is there any evidence indicating the presence of a large number."[59] These words could not have pleased those who used the avalanche of rumors that foretold of an ongoing and ever-increasing war perpetrated against the white population, as it put the lie to the falsification of reality. More, could this less-than-popular view have led to a drop in sales and threats upon the paper's editorial staff—and eventually the upcoming sale of the paper to none other than Byers and his partners?

News of the Hungate murders had reached Denver, and word had it that the family's remains would reach the city later that day. It had been decided that when the nude and mutilated bodies arrived, that they would be put on display for all to see. As planned, seminary bells announced that the corpses were now available for all to examine.[60]

However the population of Denver had previously viewed the Indian war, most opinions changed as men and women looked at the hideous remains of what had once been four human beings that had been reduced to chopped meat. The far-off possibility of what could happen to them became reality; a living nightmare of horror. Panic, fear, and outrage seized the population with a bloodlust and they shouted for the extermination of the Cheyennes. Residents of Denver prepared for the inevitable and nailed wood planks over their windows. Farmers deserted their land and bolted to the city, and this included many of the homesteaders near Fort Lyon and living along the Arkansas. Without a backward glance they abandoned homes, crops, and lives.

William Byers, John Evans, and John Chivington now found themselves in a position wherein they could advance the war, which, if successful, would result in the elimination of the unwanted Indian population from the territory.

NINE

A Frantic Summer

As SPRING 1864 TURNED TO SUMMER, Governor John Evans was not the only leader on the borderlands fearful of being overrun. Major General Samuel Curtis now faced a similar dilemma as the Department of Kansas shuddered under a twofold threat: bushwhackers and raiding Indians. The general had turned his back on Evans's pleas for reinforcements, and he now refused to listen to John T. Cox, a special Indian agent in Indian Territory, who could not stop illicit trafficking of cattle. Curtis did not mince words and said: "I have not a soldier to spare."[1]

While Wynkoop worked at fortifying Fort Lyon against an Indian attack or a rebel invasion, Evans tried a different approach to the problem. On June 27 he wrote a letter "To the friendly Indians of the plains."[2] Hoping to separate friendly from warring Indians, he directed the Indians not at war to report to specified areas—instructing the Cheyennes and Arapahos on the Arkansas to report to Fort Lyon, the Comanches and Kiowas to Fort Larned, the Arapahos and Cheyennes on the Upper Platte to Camp Collins on Cache-la-Poudre, and the Sioux to Fort Laramie, Nebraska Territory. Two days later he wrote Agent Colley directing him to distribute his letter to the Indians "by every means you can."[3] He was hopeful that "many that are now hostile may come to the friendly camp, and when they all do, the war will be ended." He warned the agent to be stingy in providing for the Indians, as appropriations were limited.

IN LATE JUNE KIOWAS held a scalp dance near Fort Larned after Chief Satanta returned from a raid in West Texas that resulted in the capture of Mrs. Dorothy Field and the killing of several whites.[4] During the festivities Chief Satank and his cousin rode toward the fort. A sentry outside the perimeter of the wall-less post warned them off. Ignored, the guard pointed his carbine at Satank, only to have the chief nock two arrows and shoot him before he could fire his weapon. Satank's cousin shot the guard with his revolver. Soldiers inside Fort Larned scrambled to repulse an attack while the two hustled back to their village. Just as agitated as the soldiers, the Kiowas grabbed some belongings, mounted and rode off. While fleeing, warriors saw that the military's horse herd grazed unattended a distance from the fort and drove it away. They would later state that this incident "was their first hostile encounter with United States troops."[5]

Left Hand, whose band camped near the post, sent word to Captain James W. Parmetar (Twelfth Kansas Infantry) that he and his warriors would help recover the stock.[6] "The offer was not altogether altruistic. No doubt Left Hand saw the Kiowa raid as an occasion to demonstrate his people's friendliness while also keeping his warriors busy recovering government horses instead of joining the raiding Tsistsistas."[7] He was unaware that Parmetar was a drunk, or that recent orders forbade Indians from entering forts unless blindfolded.[8] When he did not receive a reply, Left Hand and some of his warriors approached Fort Larned while displaying a white flag, as he wanted to present his proposal in person. They were fired upon and fled. Most of the village quickly moved up the Arkansas with Left Hand, as he wanted no part of war. But he could not control all of his young warriors, and some rode north to join the Dog Men.[9]

A few days later Satanta sent a message to Fort Larned, "saying that he hoped the quartermaster would provide better horses in the future, as the last lot he had received were inferior in quality."[10]

AFTER RECEIVING EVANS'S DIRECTIONS in early July, Colley summoned William Bent from his ranch in the Big Timbers to Fort Lyon and showed him Evans's letter and the proclamation to the Indians. He wanted Bent to talk the peaceful Southern Cheyennes and Arapahos into relocating to the vicinity of Fort Lyon where he could "feed and protect them."[11] Bent agreed and traveled to Kansas. He found the Arapahos on Coon Creek and asked their leaders to camp within four miles of Fort Larned. He also found the

Kiowas, Comanches, Kiowa-Apaches, and the Southern Cheyennes in the vicinity of the post. After speaking with Black Kettle and Little Rock, he led them to within four miles of the fort.

While his father traveled with the Tsistsistas, George Bent, who said, "My father had more influence over these people than any other white man," reached Medicine Lodge Creek, in Kansas, ninety-two miles southeast of Fort Larned.[12] At the Kiowa–Comanche–Kiowa-Apache encampment he learned that his father had met Tsistsistas at the creek and had taken them to the post, and he immediately set out to see him. He had to be careful, for as he put it: "I did not dare to go to a fort or to any white settlement; for reports had been spread that I was taking part in the Indian raids and I would have been arrested or shot on sight." He slipped into the Arapaho camp and surprised his father, who did not expect to see him.

George was present when his father and others translated Evans's proclamation to the Indian leaders camped near the fort, as was his sister Julia. Mixed-blood Tsistsista Edmund Guerrier (b. January 16, 1840) was also in the village. His father was William Guerrier (d. 1857 or 1858 when a powder keg blew up while he traded with Indians), a French Canadian who had been a trapper and who had worked for Bent. His mother was Tatatoini (or Tatatoiui), a Southern Tsistsista who had died during the 1849 cholera epidemic. That year Guerrier was sent east to study, first at St. Mary's Mission in Kansas Territory and then at the St. Louis University in winter 1857. Although Guerrier had mostly worked with whites since returning to the frontier after completing his education, he had recently found himself among his mother's people and living in Little Rock's village. His timing could not have been more fortuitous, for at this meeting he met George Bent and Julia for the first time. More important, it reintroduced him to a world that he had mostly forgotten.[13]

According to William Bent, the Cheyennes "expressed a great desire to make peace and keep it, and appeared to be perfectly well satisfied with the governor's proclamation."[14] But it may not have gone as well as he claimed. Captain William H. Backus (First Colorado) had replaced Captain Parmetar, who had been cashiered out of the military on the seventh of the month.[15] Most likely Backus was not aware of Evans's letter to the peaceful Indians. However, the standing order of no Indians entering forts still existed. George Bent claimed the commanding officer of Fort Larned "met the advances of the chiefs [for peace] so coldly that the council broke up without anything being decided." Perhaps, but William Bent felt that he had accomplished his mission by mid-July and set out for his ranch.

As WILLIAM BENT RETURNED to Colorado Territory, a different take on the Cheyenne war and the push for statehood began to spark a negativity that came from a totally unexpected area—the First Colorado Volunteer Cavalry. Since Chivington had thrown his hat into the ring and campaigned for Congress, he became a target with growing fervor. On July 14 Ovando Hollister followed William Byers's lead and used the *Daily Mining Journal* as a weapon against what he considered untruths. He took direct aim at Chivington and others who supported statehood. He disputed the colonel's claim that the First Colorado stood firmly behind statehood. The accusation, true or not, certainly had backing. "The soldiers from whose vote so much has been hoped are 'the most incorrigible villains in the World' for daring to think in opposition to these self-constituted regulators of public opinion," Hollister quoted from a letter dated July 11.[16] Continuing, Hollister printed, "The soldiers will vote according to the dictates of their own judgment in spite of the misrepresentations of the delegated authorities. Just watch the vote on the Ides of September, and see what you will see." Near the end of the letter, a one-sentence paragraph sarcastically stated: "Indians are scarce, though rumors of war reach us occasionally."

Hollister caught Byers's attention, but before he could lash out against the threat to the upcoming August vote, Wynkoop became aware of letters sent by the anti-statehood contingent, either because Chivington or Major Scott Anthony had alerted him or because he had received an inflammatory missive. The letters urged the soldiers to vote against the Colorado Constitution in the upcoming election.[17] Wynkoop, who thrived under Chivington, liked and respected his superior, and moved quickly to ensure that the campaign for statehood was not defeated.

Wynkoop intended to control the vote of the members of the First Colorado then stationed at the remote post. On the evening of July 18 he assembled all the members of the regiment then stationed at Fort Lyon in front of his quarters, which was outside the perimeter of the parade ground on the southwestern portion of the post near the Arkansas. This included portions of Companies B, D, E, G, and K, and surprisingly Anthony, who was present. "I have called you together this evening to lay before you important matters," Wynkoop said, "which, as citizens of Colorado . . . you should take action upon. The object of this meeting is to send delegates to represent the troops at this Post, in the nominating convention which meets in Denver on the 2d of August."[18]

After Wynkoop acquainted the assembly "with their rights and privileges" as related to their representation in the upcoming constitution vote, Anthony took the lead and called for Wynkoop to be elected chairman, and a vote quickly backed his proposition. Next, Wynkoop "proposed that three delegates be elected, consisting of two enlisted men and one officer."[19] According to George Caryl, a private who had been voted secretary for the meeting, Wynkoop's proposal "was received without a dissenting voice," and quickly Dr. John F. Hamilton was chosen to be one of the nominees.

According to the *Daily Mining Journal* there was no attempt to nominate two "enlisted men" to represent Fort Lyon. Dr. Hamilton was "empowered to cast the entire vote of the garrison and that of the troops at Larned if their delegates should fail to arrive [in Denver]."[20] For the meeting to have reached this point, Anthony had to have been totally in agreement. The *Journal* pointed out the obvious: "Soldiers, you know, are not at liberty to go when and where they will."

The *Rocky Mountain News* claimed that Captain Samuel Robbins proposed that each company should have its own representative. This was quickly voted on and accepted, meaning the proxies chosen that day would vote for the officers and troops that were not in Denver for the August 2 election. The *Journal* ignored this, claiming that the assembled soldiers realized that Wynkoop and Anthony intended to push through their agenda to select a few to represent the First Colorado troops at Fort Lyon and called out with boisterous opposition. Anger erupted when it was clear that *only* Hamilton would have a vote in Denver. Regardless of which letter accurately described what happened that evening, a call for "Ayes" and "Noes" did not solve the problem. Fully half remained in favor of choosing proxies (perhaps 129) while the other half rejected the proposition (125, or slightly higher). Without a chance of gaining a majority vote and realizing that his and Anthony's push to support Chivington and Evans had failed, Wynkoop adjourned the meeting.

Byers was already fed up with Hollister's *Journal* anti-statehood movement and launched an attack. "Some of the sapient opponents of State organization have been writing letters to the soldiers and officers of the brave and gallant Colorado regiments, urging them to vote against the Constitution, and then without even waiting for a reply, reporting that a majority of the boys would so vote."[21] His overlong pitch droned on until he closed his tirade by accusing a few demagogues of insulting the officers and men of the First Colorado. "This talk . . . that the soldiers are going to vote against the Constitution is all bosh. They will do no such thing." Not finished, the next day Byers published: "We hear a good deal of indignation expressed by all classes of our people . . . at the infamous attempts of the Black Hawk *Journal* to disparage Colorado in the eyes of the world."[22]

Despite Byers's assault aimed at the *Journal*, Hollister refused to allow Wynkoop's failure to obtain proxies that supported Chivington's political activities at Fort Lyon to vanish quietly into the night. He presented what he considered additional proof that Chivington, Evans, and their cronies had created a fake Indian war. Soldiers at the post had written letters to Hollister as he stood up to Byers and the push for statehood, and he quoted some of them. Surprisingly the men's ire was not directed at the Evans-Chivington push for statehood and their political ambitions, but focused on the idea that the Cheyenne war was a political ruse to obtain empowerment over the territory. An unnamed soldier claimed that "This Indian war is nothing but a political hobby, so plain a blind man can see it, and the instigators of it should suffer."[23] Another soldier pointed out that "the bedbug and mosquito tribes" were the only foes that the troops stationed at Fort Lyon had to combat.[24]

While the infighting within the First Colorado and the city of Denver continued, on July 25, 1864, the District of the Upper Arkansas was created. General James G. Blunt assumed command with Colonel James H. Ford as second in command. Wynkoop no longer reported to Chivington, as Fort Lyon moved from the District of Colorado to the new district.[25]

THAT JULY, CHARLEY BENT VISITED Charles Rath at his ranch on Walnut Creek, which fed into the Arkansas River in Kansas. Actually Rath, who had done well for himself as a freighter and trader, also had a trading post on the creek as well as a toll bridge that crossed it. Rath, a German, had immigrated to the United States with his family in 1848 when he was eleven. Like others, he ran away from home five years later and set out for the frontier. He found employment in St. Louis as a freighter with William Bent, who was returning to the frontier with a train of goods. In 1860 he had taken over George Peacock's trading post and ranch after the trader and five others were killed by Kiowas. This was near the Great Bend of the

Arkansas River. Rath had already been trading with Cheyennes, Comanches, and other tribes since the mid-1850s, and by 1863 he and his partners obtained title to the land. Rath got along with the Cheyennes, was good with language, and spoke the Tsistsista's tongue fluently. In 1860 he married Making-Out-Roads (Roadmaker), who had previously divorced Kit Carson, Flat Head, and Wolf Man. When Rath married her, she had four full-blooded Tsistsista children, three sons and a daughter, and together they would have one daughter (Cheyenne Belle) before divorcing.

Charley Bent felt comfortable with Rath, but it had not been a relaxed time. On May 17, Cheyennes had struck Rath's ranch, and he claimed that six mules and two horses were stolen. During Charley's visit, a Comanche and Kiowa war party passed close to the ranch and attacked a wagon train on Walnut Creek.[26] Although Charley did not participate in the raid, he knew what happened.

In early August, George Bent, who had returned to his father's ranch on the Purgatoire to get some of his horses, found a large Tsistsista encampment on the Solomon River in Kansas. While he was there, several war parties left to attack the *vi' ho' i* while he remained in the village. Most of these warriors rode north to the Platte River, where they were joined by Lakotas. They intended to strike wagon trains and other targets. But Dog Man chief Little Robe did not travel to the Platte. Instead he led his war party south toward Fort Dodge. A train that Milton Moore accompanied followed one that had Mexican teamsters. When they were south of the post, a war party attacked. During the engagement a warrior on a yellow horse and four others rode between the two trains. "Our party awarded to him full credit for gallantry," Moore wrote.[27] This warrior, who was not a chief, was about twenty-five in 1864. "I knew this young man well," Bent wrote to Moore, calling him Bear Man. Bent also said that he was a "grand warrior in battles."

At the time of Little Robe's August raid, Charley Bent traveled to the Tsistsista village on the Solomon River and spent time with brother George, who was still in the camp. While there, Charley told him about the Comanche-Kiowa raid near Rath's ranch.

On August 7, 1864, sixteen-year-old Laura Roper (b. June 16, 1848) wanted to see her friend Lucinda Eubanks, who was just a few years older than her. She hitched a ride to the William Eubanks Jr. homestead with her father's partner, Marshall Kelly, who was traveling to Nebraska City,

Nebraska Territory, to buy supplies they sold to emigrants traveling along the Oregon Trail.[28]

This day was much like others that summer of Indian troubles. It had dawned peacefully and Laura had no reason to think otherwise, even though three weeks earlier Indians had stolen horses from her father and had committed other thefts along the Little Blue River. Her father, William, told her to ask Eubanks to accompany her home, as raiding Indians might be close.

At four o'clock, after an enjoyable afternoon at the Eubanks homestead, Laura, with Lucinda, her husband, William Jr., daughter Isabelle (three), and infant son Willie (William J. Eubanks, nine months) started back toward her home.[29] They walked half a mile and entered an area surrounded by bluffs that were called "the Narrows." William, who had been barefoot, stepped on something sharp that penetrated his foot. He told Lucinda and Laura to keep walking, that he would catch up after he pulled the sliver out.

Laura carried Isabelle, whom she called Belle, and Lucinda carried Willie. After walking about fifty yards through the bluffs, they halted to wait for William to catch up. Suddenly they heard horrific yells. Laura yelled that she thought it was Indians. Lucinda and she ran back toward the homestead, only to stop. They saw William Eubanks's sister and Lucinda's sister-in-law, Dora (sixteen), run from the house with warriors in pursuit. William Eubanks saw his sister's distress, but instead of rushing toward her, he turned and ran for the river. Eubanks frantically attempted to get to the other side of the water but did not succeed, for when he reached a sandbar, arrows struck him and he dropped. Two of William's brothers had also been at the house. They ran up a draw, but the raiders chased and killed them. They were not aware that Lucinda's father-in-law "and his little nephew" had run in the opposite direction. Warriors caught up to the elder Eubanks and killed him. The "small nephew," whom Laura called Ambrose Asher, had been taken prisoner. Dora ran in the direction of the Narrows and toward where Laura and Lucinda had concealed themselves as they watched people die. A warrior caught up to her and it looked as if he wanted to take her prisoner. Instead Dora resisted and fought to escape. The Indian pulled out a knife and jammed it into her head. She dropped to the ground.

Horrified, the two young women ran for the timber and hid.

As soon as the raiders finished the attack they made certain that they had not missed any other *vi'ho' i*. With Ambrose Asher in tow they mounted and rode west in the direction of the Roper homestead. Laura and Lucinda watched as the Indians began to pass where they hid. It looked as if they were safe. Suddenly Isabelle screamed and Laura could not stifle her. The Indians yanked their horses to a halt and looked toward the timber. Laura pulled off her slippers and she and Lucinda attempted to escape with Isabelle and Willie in their arms. Their actions proved futile, for the mounted warriors quickly caught up to them. Neither Laura nor Lucinda resisted. A warrior dismounted and whacked Laura's hat from her head and grabbed her slippers.

The warriors placed the young women on horses and with the children in their arms they rode back toward the Eubanks homestead with the warriors. About one hundred yards from the structure they passed where Dora had fallen. Laura saw that she was still alive. Just minutes after they reached the house, a warrior rode up with a scalp dripping blood. According to Laura, he yelled "like a madman." She thought that the scalp belonged to Dora, but she was mistaken.[30]

The warriors dismounted and entered the Eubanks house, where they took additional items and destroyed everything else. During this time they totally ignored Laura and Lucinda, whom they had pulled from the horses and allowed to wander about.

Around six the war party departed with the two women holding Willie and Isabelle while mounted behind warriors. It consisted of only seven warriors, as the attackers had split into smaller groups. They crossed the Little Blue and traveled south. It had been dark for hours and still they rode when a warrior rode up to Laura and spoke to her in English, which surprised her. He asked her if "I was afraid the Indians would kill me."[31] "No I wasn't because . . . if they intended to kill me they would have done so," she replied. Before riding off he said words that must have eased her fears. "No, I don't think they will kill you. I don't think they will keep you long before they will give you up." She never saw him again but later learned that he was a mixed-blood Cheyenne named Joe Barroldo.

The next morning, August 8, 1864, nineteen-year-old Nancy Jane (Fletcher) Morton (b. February 8, 1845) and her husband of four years, Thomas F. Morton, awoke in their train's camp near Plum Creek Station on the Platte River Road in Nebraska Territory. This was Morton's fourth freighting trip to Colorado Territory. Nancy had made the journey with him on his first two in 1860 and 1862, but had missed his third in early 1864, as she suffered from measles. She recovered, but they lost their first two children to the illness that April. Even though pregnant with their third child, Nancy had no intention of missing Thomas's fourth trip to the territory.[32]

Nancy Morton was sixteen in 1861 when this portrait of her was taken. Some three years later she was pregnant, and was traveling to Denver with her husband, brother, and cousin. On August 8, 1864, the wagon train they traveled with was attacked, and she was captured by Dog Men. Her story is an amazing one of survival.

History Nebraska. Nancy Fletcher Morton—cased portrait. 20190034, RG3310, 44534.

Their journey had begun in Sidney, Iowa, on July 31. Her brother, William Fletcher, and cousin, John Fletcher, drove two of their three wagons. At the Junction on August 6, the Mortons joined a train with nine wagons, and added at least nine more men to the convoy. One of these teamsters was William D. Marble, whose nine-year-old son, Daniel, accompanied him. Safety in numbers made the nine wagons a welcome addition to the caravan. "The next day we traveled twenty-eight miles in sight of the Plum Creek station and camped over night," Nancy wrote.[33] That night Thomas Morton took the second night shift of guard duty.

In the morning everyone hustled to get the wagons rolling, and on August 8 they broke camp at 6:30. The days for Nancy, Morton, her brother, and cousin had been exhausting as they had pushed to make as many miles as possible each day. On this morning, Morton was worn out and asked if she could handle the team, as he needed more rest. She took the reins as Thomas attempted to sleep.

Hardly any time passed when she saw what she thought were ranchers running buffalo and woke Thomas. He told her that they were herding horses, and tried to return to sleep but she kept talking. Suddenly she realized that they were Indians and called to him. He confirmed that she was correct. "They are for battle," Nancy said. "I think so." "I know they are," she snapped. "They won't kill you," he said, trying to comfort her.

One hundred warriors from Bull Bear's band of Dog Men attacked from all sides when the caravan was one mile from the Plum Creek Station.[34] The Morton's four-mule team began to stampede. By now Morton was out of the wagon and next to his wife. "You can't manage the mules," he yelled as he grabbed the reins and tried to control the animals. Terrified, Nancy leaped from the wagon, and as she did Thomas screamed: "Oh, my dear, where are you going?" These were the last words she ever heard him say. An instant later the wild-eyed team behind theirs plunged past her, and partially rode over her. Injured, she struggled to stand and run as best she could toward the Platte River. William and John Fletcher saw her flee, abandoned their wagons, and raced after her. "We are all going to be killed," John said when they reached her. As he did an arrow plunged into his side. As he fell his blood covered Nancy. "It flowed from his side in a stream as thick as my arm," Nancy remembered. "I could hear the blood running like water from his side."

"Nan, go to the wagon," William yelled as he shot an attacker. Three arrows struck him almost in unison, and the force threw him into Nancy before he dropped to the ground. "Tell Susan I am killed. Goodbye my dear sister."

Warriors on horseback approached her. One demanded that she mount a pony. She refused and he struck her with a whip. Two Cheyennes dismounted and caught her. She fought them but they forced her onto the animal.

The horror was real. What followed would become a nightmare.

Nancy Morton traveled south with the war party. After a mile she pulled off her collar and dropped it and a handkerchief onto the ground. As the miles passed she released a shoe, a glove, and a stocking. She would jettison other articles. After about ten miles the war party halted to rest on the east side of a lake. Nancy dismounted and sat on the ground. Surprisingly a *white man* approached her. "Do you see the arrows?" he asked.[35] Her shock must have been overwhelming as she did not know she had been wounded. When she pulled out an arrow, he indicated another in her thigh. She used a pen knife to "cut it out." The man walked off.

While she sat by herself, a boy whom she knew joined her—Daniel Marble. "What will we do?" he asked—an impossible question. "They have killed my father." They sat for perhaps fifteen minutes, and during this time they cried.

Soon their captors were again moving, but now they rode next to each other. Dan pointed at a warrior wearing Thomas's coat. "[I]s that your husband's[?]" he asked. It was what he wore when killed. Nancy approached the warrior, "and told him to pull it off and he did."[36]

As Nancy continued south so did the war party that held Laura and Lucinda captive. Around noon five warriors joined the group and Laura received a horse to ride. However, that night of the eighth while attempting to climb out of a ravine her saddle broke, her mount fell, dumping her, and when it struggled to regain its feet one of its hooves broke her nose. Warriors cleaned the blood from her face while another whipped the animal. She spent the rest of that night and most of the next day riding behind the warrior who initially captured her.[37]

Nancy and Daniel's captors rode throughout that night, but their experience was not the same as Laura's. All of the warriors except for two got drunk. While moving through the darkness, "they shot [arrows] at Dan seven times, and at me three," Nancy claimed.[38] "The two Indians [not drunk] that we were with made them quit." This was not the first time that Danny had been a target, for during that day a warrior who was already drunk had thrown his lance at him but missed. "Don't kill him," Nancy said, somehow making her words known. "He is my papoose."[39] The war party finally halted perhaps two hours before dawn to sleep. Nancy "held little Dan's head and we cried until morning."

These two or so days of raids along the Platte River Road and the surrounding vicinity was not a coincidence, and many whites at the time thought that it was a joint effort by the Cheyennes and their allies to both cut off travel on a major road to Denver and also make it clear that this was their land and that the *vi'ho' i* were no longer welcome. Their attacks and the lives lost or stolen did not go unnoticed, at least not in Colorado Territory. The terror that had escalated when the nude and mutilated bodies of the Hungate family were displayed in Denver reached a new fever. The war, once for the control of prime land, suddenly had become one of survival.

John Evans knew what the future could be, as did William Byers and John Chivington, and so did the fighting faction of the Tsistsistas, Bull Bear and Tall Bull. Tsistsistas Black Kettle, White Antelope, and One-Eye, and Hinono'eino' Left Hand, Little Raven, and Neva had an idea of what the future held, but they were in the minority within their tribes. Either war or treaties would claim the land in question.

THE RAIDS ALONG THE PLATTE RIVER ROAD exploded with a multitude of shouts for action. Suddenly the loss of life and threat of cutting off the gold fields gave Evans's pleas new life. He no longer found himself crying solo for help to stop the growing Indian war in Colorado Territory. The early August attacks on whites near Plum Creek and elsewhere on the road set off a maelstrom of military dispatches.

Leading the way, Brigadier General Robert B. Mitchell, from Julesburg on August 8, informed Major General Samuel Curtis, who was then in the field: "The Indians are infesting my lines for 500 miles. Have just learned that a train was burned at Plum Creek this morning between Cottonwood and Kearny. I must have at least 800 horses or abandon this line of communication, . . . Please reply immediately."[40] Mitchell quickly sent a second report to Curtis: "[T]his morning there have been two additional attacks on this route. One at Dogtown, east of Kearny ten miles. One mounted company gone in pursuit of Indians from Plum Creek, and the other dismounted. Half the troops in this district on foot."[41] Evans knew that the attacks had caught the military's concern, and he quickly moved to keep their focus on target. "Of course you have news of outrages near Plum Creek," he wrote Curtis on the eighth.[42] "We are in a desperate condition on account of our communications being cut off by Indians. The route will have to be patrolled or we are cut off." Brigadier General James Carleton, who commanded the Department of New Mexico, wrote Curtis and Chivington, that "Owing to Indian troubles upon the plains I have ordered a force of fifty cavalry, fifty infantry, and two howitzers by the Cimarron route to the crossing of the Arkansas, to give assistance to trains en route to New Mexico."[43]

Three days later General Curtis telegraphed Governor Evans, "Arms can be issued to a Federal officer in command of militia in actual service. I wish you would give me facts, so I may know your disasters. . . . All that can be done will be."[44]

Evans immediately replied to Curtis at Fort Leavenworth: "The overland line is about withdrawing stock from the plains for want of protection. Unless troops can be stationed along the line to patrol it our supplies will be cut off. I fear the telegraph will be cut, too. We have but a few arms here, of an inferior quality, with damaged ammunition. The alliance of all the tribes, as I have reported to you, is now undoubted. If they sweep west, as they probably will, we shall be in great danger of being destroyed."[45] He pleaded for five thousand troops to defend "the Overland Stage route," and ended with "What can we expect?"

Curtis quickly replied: "Am fully posted. Do all you can with militia. I will do my utmost to keep lines open."[46]

On that same August 11 Evans issued a proclamation that reneged on his June offer to friendly Indians. "I, John Evans, governor of Colorado Territory, do issue this my proclamation, authorizing all citizens of Colorado, either individually or in such parties as they may organize, to go in pursuit of all hostile Indians on the plains, scrupulously avoiding those who have responded to my said call to rendezvous at the points indicated."[47] This last would be key to the governor's future, as few Indians had responded to his request, and he used this date as a cutoff to delineate peaceful from nonpeaceful. Unfortunately Evans had not taken into consideration the amount of time it might take for the various bands to assemble in one location and make a decision. "[T]o kill and destroy, as enemies of the country, wherever they may be found, all such hostile Indians. And further, as the only reward I am authorized to offer for such services, I hereby empower such citizens, or parties of citizens, to take captive, and hold to their own private use and benefit, all the property of said hostile Indians, that they may capture, and to receive for all stolen property recovered from said Indians such reward as may be deemed proper and just." Evans had created an open invitation for whites to attack any Indians in the territory not then assembled at the aforementioned posts. He went on to state that he would provide arms and ammunition to any who carried out his request.

WHILE EVANS CONTINUED TO PUSH for volunteer troops, on August 13, a frustrated Wynkoop at Fort Lyon reported that he intended "to kill all Indians I may come across until I receive orders to the contrary."[48] Bold words. A war surrounded him, but he had still not fired a shot at the enemy.

In time of crisis, speed was more important than accuracy. Evans's ongoing pleas for military support no longer stunk of false fears and now had validity to support his ongoing request for a volunteer regiment to confront the Indian menace. On August 15 his requests became reality. The next day Byers printed Chivington's announcement of the recruitment of "a Volunteer Regiment of Cavalry to serve one hundred days from date of its organi[z]ation."[49]

Two days after the volunteers began to enlist in the Third Colorado in Denver, Henry Blake, who was from Madison County, Indiana (b. July 2, 1834), mined and prospected near gold mining towns Gold Hill, Central City, and Sugar Loaf. He had left his wife and children in Newton, Iowa, to join the gold rush in Colorado Territory in May 1862, but on August 17 he took the day off from mining to travel to Boulder City for his mail. That day excitement swept across the streets and caught Blake's attention. He mingled with the swarming crowd and with eager ears listened to news that would change his life as he learned about the enlistment of the Third Colorado. Blake's timing to leave Iowa almost hinted at a desire to escape fighting in the Civil War. If so, he did not hesitate a second time. Stepping forward, Blake joined the company being raised in Boulder. In his diary entry on that day he proudly announced that, "I Mad [sic] one of the company."[50]

Blake probably did not realize it, but his mining life had ended forever. The next day he traveled to the Ward District in an August snowfall to recruit volunteers, spending the night in Gold Run. On the nineteenth he returned to Boulder, where he was sworn into the Third Colorado. The next day was free, and he enjoyed Boulder City, including getting "acquainted with a Miss Mollie Jay, a butiful [sic] curly haired lady." Blake's time as a man about town did not last, for he heard of "quite a fright in the eavning [sic]" of the twenty-first, and all the new recruits rushed to the newly constructed Fort Chambers to be issued weapons and did not return to the city proper until thirty minutes after midnight. After a short night of sleep Blake, now a member of the commissary department, distributed uniforms to recruits.

As the number of enlistments in Denver fell far below what was needed to fill the ranks for such a short term of service, on August 18 Chivington created a draft, a conscription of all able-bodied men in Denver. As the colonel needed bodies to fill the ranks of the Third Colorado, on that same day Joseph Davidson, district provost marshal, provided a document that Chivington required: "In compliance with Special Orders, No. 65, Head Quarters, District of Colorado, dated August 18th, 1864, [until] the enrollment of all male citizens of Denver City, Colorado Territory, between the ages of sixteen and upwards is completed; and all such persons, except those already belonging to regularly organized companies, or companies about being organized and recruited, are ordered to meet on Larimer street, Denver, to-morrow, August 19th, 1864, at 9:30 A.M."[51]

Chivington, who was not in Denver, returned four days later, on the twenty-second. To his surprise the special order had been ignored. He approached Byers to reprint Special Orders No. 65, which again stated that an enrollment of all able-bodied male citizens of Arapaho County sixteen years and above were ordered to enlist, and that anyone who evaded this order would be guilty of a military offense and would face punishment.[52] According to Chivington those who did not enlist would upon conscription be assigned to companies wherein they would on a daily basis construct barricades that would protect Denver from invasion. He was not interested in hearing about health issues. The *Rocky Mountain News* reported: "Denver is at last thoroughly military in every respect. Every able bodied citizen over the age of sixteen years is enrolled. Those who have not gone into the Hundred Day service, or enrolled themselves in the volunteer militia companies, are gobbled up by the provost guard."

SOON AFTER BEING CAPTURED, Lucinda Eubanks endured the attentions of "an old chief whose name she" did not remember, as she was forced to move into his lodge.[53] According to Lucinda the Cheyenne wanted her sexually. When she refused, his requests turned to threats of violence. She surrendered her body to his demands. It would get worse, for soon she would suffer every parent's fear. "They took my daughter from me just after we were captured, and I never saw her after." Warriors moved off with her three-year-old daughter, Laura Roper, and her nephew Ambrose Asher, who she claimed was six. After the separation she continued to breastfeed Willie, for fear that if she weaned him the Indians would take him from her.

DURING THE TIME WHEN THE CHERRIES ARE RIPE (August), Tsistsistas Black Kettle, Bull Bear, One-Eye (a council chief), and Hinono'eino' Little Raven, Left Hand, and Neva and other chiefs smoked and discussed the letter that William Bent had delivered to them near Fort Larned.[54] George Bent and Edmund Guerrier were also present. The discussions were lively, as Bull Bear still burned over his brother's murder. Surprisingly the Dog Man chief agreed to discuss ending the war with the *vi'ho' i*.

On August 29 Black Kettle turned to Bent and Guerrier and asked them to translate his words into English on the white man's talking leaves. Bent drafted the letter to Colley. But then, according to Guerrier, George "helped me in writing the letter to Wynkoop to make terms of peace." It was not about English that Bent offered him advice, but as Guerrier put it, his "long absence [from his mother's people caused him to] have forgotten a good deal of Cheyenne." Bent helped him to translate the Tsistsista words to English.[55]

TEN

A Disobedient Play for Peace

ON SEPTEMBER 4, 1864, Major Ned Wynkoop met with post trader Dexter Colley and several officers in his office at Fort Lyon. A commotion outside interrupted the meeting. A sergeant and two troopers who were traveling to Denver to muster out of service had instead returned to the post with three Cheyenne prisoners. This angered Wynkoop, for in mid-May he had issued orders to kill all Indians on sight.[1] Before stepping outside, Wynkoop told the group he intended to rough up the prisoners. Dexter Colley agreed but hustled to be the first out the door.

When Colley saw the Cheyennes, he froze. Wynkoop stepped around him and strode to the mounted group. He ignored the troopers and demanded that the prisoners, two men and a woman, get off their horses. Before the major could "rough up" the Indians Colley told him that he knew these Cheyennes, and that One-Eye supplied "a great deal for information" to his father, Samuel Colley.[2]

Next Wynkoop yelled at the soldiers for not killing the Indians per his orders.[3] The sergeant said that they had shot at the Cheyennes, but they waved pieces of paper and he decided not to kill them. Wynkoop looked at One-Eye, a woman (his wife), and Eagle Head (Minimic, Min-im-mie). The sergeant handed Wynkoop the letters that Guerrier and Bent had written for Black Kettle (but not the free pass Chivington had supposedly written for One-Eye)."[4]

Wynkoop realized the importance of what he held. Before returning to his office he ordered the prisoners brought to him. His officers followed, and then the guarded prisoners. Everyone watched as Wynkoop read the letters. "We received a letter from Bent wishing us to make peace," the Colley letter began.[5] What Black Kettle next offered surprised Wynkoop. "We held a consel [sic] in regard to it & all came to the conclusion to make peace with you providing you make peace with the Kiowas, Commenches [sic], Arrapahoes [sic], Apaches and Siouxs [sic]. . . . We heard that you [have] some prisoners in Denver. We have seven prisoners of you which we are willing to give up providing you give up yours." Although receiving white hostages interested Wynkoop, the next sentence gave him pause. "There are three war parties out yet and two of Arrapahoes. [T]hey have been out some time and expect now soon." To date, Wynkoop had been unable to personally engage the enemy in battle.

Since venturing to the frontier, Wynkoop had survived by a combination of guts and wits, and nothing had changed. The letters in his possession presented an opportunity that he had no intention of ignoring. Although he had no clue of what he should do, he knew he needed to interview the Indians. Unfortunately the only interpreter at the fort was someone Wynkoop wanted nothing to do with—John Smith. He and Smith had kept clear of each other since that eventful November of 1858, when he and the Denver City Town Company threatened to hang him if he did not join their land group. Wynkoop was not privy to Smith and the Colleys' Indian dealings or ethics.[6] He sent for the man he could no longer avoid, and when Smith arrived, Wynkoop appointed him post interpreter.[7]

Wynkoop needed answers and began to ask questions. He wanted to know why the Indians risked their lives to deliver the letters. "I thought I would be killed," One-Eye replied, "but I knew that paper would be found upon my dead body, that you would see it, and it might give peace to my people once more."[8] Wynkoop was not convinced and feared that the Cheyennes might not give up the prisoners. Seeing this, One-Eye offered to forfeit his life if the Called Out People did not do as Black Kettle stated.[9] Twelve years later Wynkoop romanticized his interrogation of One-Eye, saying, "I was bewildered with an exhibition of such patriotism on the part of two savages, and felt myself in the presence of superior beings; and these were the representatives of a race that I had heretofore looked upon without exception as being cruel[,] treacherous, and blood-thirsty."[10] By 1876, when Wynkoop attempted to write a memoir of his Indian experience, he realized that most whites totally rejected his views on race relations, and he was attempting to justify his actions that September of 1864.

Wynkoop's interrogation continued. The tribal bands congregated on a tributary of the Smoky Hill in western Kansas perhaps 140 miles northeast of Fort Lyon. He wanted to meet the warring leaders but knew that it was foolish to even consider it. War raged, and he did not have enough troops to survive treachery. At the same time Wynkoop felt the Cheyennes might free their captives if they could obtain peace. An idea began to form, but he hesitated. Fearing that the white man would not meet Black Kettle, One-Eye told him that there were two thousand people in the combined villages, that the horse herds were large, and that it was impossible to subsist off the land for an extended length of time. He needed to act before the bands split apart and moved in different directions.[11]

Wynkoop had a chance to receive white prisoners and end a war. A heady thought. But as the risk was high, he had no intention of being forced into action. Needing time to think, he incarcerated the Cheyennes. It did not take him long to decide. When he told his officers that he would meet with the warring Indians, they called the mission suicide. Wynkoop refused to listen to their protests. One-Eye's warning was clear: time was essential. As Fort Lyon was isolated and did not have a telegraph, it took a week, and at times much longer, to communicate with his superiors, and a like time for a reply. Following protocol would destroy any chance of meeting the Indians. Not informing his superiors of his intentions also gave him complete control with an outside chance of success.

Even though Wynkoop understood the consequences of acting without orders, he had the foresight to announce his plans. Before setting out for the Smoky Hill, he wrote a letter to Black Kettle informing him of his intention to meet with the chiefs.[12]

Wynkoop set out from Fort Lyon on September 6 with 127 men and two howitzers. He brought the Cheyenne prisoners, whom he threatened with death if he met with treachery, and "The Fool," a Cheyenne Contrary who hung around the fort. Contraries were warriors that "acted by opposites." For example, if asked to walk, they would ride, or if asked to come closer, they would move away. Oftentimes they performed important tasks, including leadership roles in battles. Wynkoop needed an interpreter and continued to employ John Smith. A detachment of infantry that had recently arrived from the Department of New Mexico remained behind to defend Fort Lyon.[13]

By September 9 Wynkoop's letter reached the Tsistsistas' camp on the Smoky Hill. Guerrier read it to Black Kettle, alerting him and other chiefs that the *vi'ho' i* soldier chief at Fort Lyon traveled to speak with them, and that "he did not come out to fight, but to talk."[14]

As if Governor Evans did not have enough to worry about with the statehood election and an ongoing Indian war, early on the morning of September 9 his twenty-year-old daughter, Josephine, set out on horseback to Clear Creek with three girlfriends. About two miles from Denver her mount stepped into a hole, stumbled, and in an effort not to fall leaped forward. The sudden motion threw Miss Evans backward and off the horse. Her companions watched in horror as she landed on the back of her head and shoulders. Immediately Miss Lowell yanked her horse around and raced for home to obtain help. Misses Fisher and Case dismounted and ran to their fallen companion, who had been knocked insensible.

Miss Lowell's gallop to her parents' Denver residence sounded an alarm that something was wrong. Before a carriage could be dispatched to bring Josephine back to the city, rumors quickly spread that the governor's daughter had fallen and that the impact had killed her. This continued until the carriage returned with an alive but obviously injured young lady. "She is suffering greatly but is at times conscious," William Byers published that afternoon, "and there is strong hope of her full recovery at an early day."[15]

Although the near tragedy was of major importance to Evans and his family, Byers refused to ignore the war. That same day he printed that William Bent had abandoned his ranch in the Big Timbers as "the threatenings of the Indians may come true, to wit: That by this moon the red men will make an assault upon all the pale faces of the Arkansas."

The Tsistsistas and Hinono'eino' were aware of the approach of the *vi'ho' i* soldiers. As they neared the massive village, which had just moved closer to Fort Lyon, Neva told Laura Roper that two Tsistsistas had gone to Fort Lyon, and that if they "got into the fort alive," as Laura later stated, "they would tell the commanding officer that the Indians had three prisoners and would give them up if the soldiers would come after [them]."[16] Soon after, Neva told Laura that the soldiers were about a day's ride from the village. More important, he said: "[I]f the Indians and the soldiers could come to an agreement they would give me up." At this time she had been a captive for two days over one month. Her outgoing personality, along with good fortune as to who her captors were, had allowed her to survive without becoming a sexual object.

When Wynkoop began to see signs of Indians on September 9, he sent Eagle Head ahead to announce the purpose of his visit. Later that day, after Eagle Head rejoined the command, Wynkoop moved to the left and set up camp. The next morning, September 10, Wynkoop continued his march toward the village. He had only traveled four miles when an Indian battle line composed of Dog Men, Cheyennes, Arapahos, and Sioux blocked his advance, and this included William Bent's son George. According to Bent the Dog Men wanted to attack and kill the soldiers. Perhaps seven hundred warriors waved their weapons and shouted obscenities.[17] With his officers' unheeded warning of a suicide mission now reality, Wynkoop yelled for his men to form their own battle line. He then slowly advanced toward the warrior line, which agitated them.

Before getting too close to the boisterous warriors, Wynkoop halted a second time. Hoping to avoid a clash, he sent One-Eye to explain that he came because he saw the letters that stated they wanted to discuss ending the war and would give up white hostages. Anxious minutes passed while Wynkoop and his men waited and watched. When One-Eye did not return, Wynkoop felt certain he would be attacked.

Before hostilities commenced, a Tsistsista yelled that he wanted to know what the soldiers wanted. After hearing the translation, Wynkoop replied that he came to talk.[18] The speaker did not believe this. If the *vi'ho' i* wanted to talk, why did he come prepared for war? Wynkoop, through Smith, replied that he intended to defend himself if attacked.

The uproar and anger in the battle line continued to grow, with the Dog Men leading the cry to attack. "Black Kettle and other Chiefs" defused the antagonistic display, Bent claimed, which would have most certainly led to death for some if not all of the soldiers.[19]

The Tsistsista who had spoken up—perhaps Black Kettle—accepted Wynkoop's explanation, and the major agreed for the Indians to lead his command to the village. The warriors closed on the *vi'ho' i*, surrounded them, and with his men little more than prisoners, they moved toward the village. After riding two miles, the warriors halted. Here, Wynkoop received instructions for his command to make camp. Then he, Captain Silas Soule, Lieutenants Joseph Cramer and Charles Phillips, and Smith continued on to an area shaded by trees, which was known as the Big Timbers and

Major Ned Wynkoop confronts a Dog Man–Southern Cheyenne–Arapaho battle line near the Big Timbers in Kansas on September 10, 1864. This happened six days after he received two letters from Cheyenne chief Black Kettle, which stated the Indians wanted to discuss ending the war and had prisoners they were willing to free. As Fort Lyon was an isolated post, and with a minimum of two weeks to request authority to meet with the Indians and receive a reply, Wynkoop— without orders—announced he planned to meet with the Indians. His officers had called it a suicide mission, and now it looked as if they were correct.

Painting of Ned Wynkoop © 2019 by Louis Kraft. Louis Kraft Collection, ACP010. Chávez History Library, Santa Fe, N.Mex.

sometimes the Bend of Timbers. There was no village in sight. Wynkoop, his officers, and Smith sat on one side of a large circle. Chiefs arrived and completed the circle while warriors sat behind them. Wynkoop, who did not know any of the chiefs, found himself totally surrounded. Alert and in-quisitive, he must have asked Smith to point out the chiefs present. Before the passing of the pipe began, Wynkoop found himself face-to-face with Dog Man chief Bull Bear; Cheyenne chiefs White Antelope and Big Wolf; and Arapaho chiefs Left Hand, Big Mouth, Little Raven, and Neva. George Bent sat across from him and next to Chief Black Kettle.

After the pipe ceremony concluded, the council began. With seemingly all Indian eyes watching him, Wynkoop said that he came because he saw Black Kettle's letters, and that he came in "peace and not for war."[20] Smith translated, and Bent confirmed Smith's usage of the Tsistsista language. As Left Hand and Neva were present, they undoubtedly confirmed Smith's usage of their language. Wynkoop hoped that they could work out an understanding between white man and Indian. Continuing, he moved to a major reason for his gamble to end the war. If the chiefs gave him the white captives, it would show that they wanted peace. Wynkoop made it clear that he could not make peace, as he did not have the authority to end the war. He suggested that he escort them to Denver to meet Colorado Territory governor John Evans, who he thought wanted to end the war. If they went with him, he guaranteed their safe return to their villages. Wynkoop then read Evans's proclamation, which William Bent had already shared with them, confirming that Cheyennes and Arapahos who wanted peace should move their villages close to Fort Lyon and end all contact with Indians that continued the war. Not finished (and according to Cramer), Wynkoop told the chiefs that "they could rely upon" what he told them, "that his life was a pledge for his words." He then asked Soule, Cramer, and Phillips individually if they endorsed what he said. Each did.

When Wynkoop finished speaking, the chiefs stood one by one and spoke. They claimed that the *vi'ho' i* held some of their people prisoner, and they wanted them freed. Wynkoop had not heard of any Indian captives. He told them that if some of their people were hostages, that he did not have the power to release them. Wynkoop admitted to the chiefs that he did not have permission to meet with them. He also told them that he knew he had to move quickly if he wanted to see them before they broke up their camp and moved away. He told them that he acted on his own and would not make promises that he could not keep.

If you came to discuss peace, a chieftain asked, "why [did you bring] men and guns?" Wynkoop had already addressed this when he faced the battle line, but did so again. He said that if he faced bad Indians he wanted enough men in case of trouble.

ONE OF THE BARGAINING PIECES that Black Kettle's letter mentioned, and which immediately grabbed Wynkoop's attention, were the seven prisoners that were offered in exchange for peace. Up to this point, they were unnamed, faceless objects. Lucinda Eubanks was not present, for after being traded to Two Face, she and infant Willie appeared to be in constant movement with her Sioux captors, and Laura Roper stated that from that time forward she never saw her friend again. Moreover, Lucinda never stated that she was in this massive camp.[21] The Lakotas had forty lodges at the mostly Tsistsista-Hinono'ei encampment. But, and as always, the village circles were consistent with tribal affiliations—that is, all were tribe- and band-specific. The Sioux did not take part in the negotiations between the Hinono'eino', Tsistsistas, and Wynkoop. Perhaps Black Kettle and the other chiefs who agreed to send the two letters hoped to obtain Lucinda and her child, but they failed.

Nancy Morton had met Lucinda Eubanks shortly after they had been captured in that first main village at the beginning of their incarceration, and perhaps they spent time together over the coming days, but not for long. Nancy was in the village, but the Tsistsista who owned her chose not to sell or give her away. He had every right to do so, and no one—not Black Kettle or Bull Bear—could challenge his decision.

Wynkoop and his troops never saw the massive village, as the Tsistsistas and Hinono'eino' refused to allow the *vi'ho' i* soldiers near their women and children. Still, during the unseen council between Black Kettle, Left Hand, Bull Bear, other chiefs, and Wynkoop, Nancy Morton claimed that she and Lucinda Eubanks were forced upon the ground and covered by a buffalo robe. According to Nancy, she shuddered in fear while Tsistsista warriors stood above her with strung bows and nocked arrows pointed at her in case she dared to scream for help. Even if she had screamed, the soldiers would not have heard her as the distance was too great. Nancy was a young woman who had lived through the horror of seeing her family butchered. What she had just described could not have happened, at least not as she envisioned it, as Lucinda and Willie were not present on September 10.[22]

Although Nancy's captivity was still less than two months, it had been a living hell. Her days were without end, with three thoughts dominating her life: would she be beaten, physically assaulted, or killed? A hard future without end, and worse, for on this day she knew that her mental torture had no chance of ending.

WHILE THE COUNCIL BETWEEN Wynkoop and the Indian leaders dragged on, warriors with strung bows and nocked arrows invaded the soldier's makeshift camp. "[A]bout five Indians to every white man," Sergeant

B. N. Forbes (Company B) claimed.[23] His estimate sounds high, for if correct, over five hundred warriors reduced Wynkoop's escort to little more than prisoners. "They were pretty saucy for friendly Indians," Forbes stated. Warriors who knew a handful of English words, and especially curse words, verbally harangued the *vi'ho' i* soldiers. With an unstated threat of massacre a possibility, the warriors physically forced the white men away from the two howitzers. They then ransacked the provision wagons and took whatever they wanted.

Sensing that the taut situation could explode, Lieutenant George Hardin rode to the council and told Wynkoop that warriors held the men prisoner. The major stood, interrupted the proceedings, and angrily stated that he wanted the Indians out of his camp. Smith and Bent translated his words.[24]

Black Kettle, who had remained silent, left the council and rode to the soldier camp. He found it as Wynkoop claimed and ordered the warriors to leave. Without waiting to see his command obeyed, Black Kettle rode back to the council.

The warriors did as instructed. But as they departed, a number of them moved upwind of the soldiers and fired the prairie. Blazing flames and billowing smoke swept toward the white men. Frantically the soldiers packed their equipage and deserted the area. They traveled roughly twelve miles before they halted and set up camp at Hackberry Creek.

BACK AT THE COUNCIL Dog Man chief Bull Bear still raged over brother Lean Bear's murder the previous May during the time when the horses get fat.[25] Without warning, Bull Bear stood and charged Wynkoop. He ordered the tall soldier to stand. The major did, but refused to cower before his stare. Bull Bear turned to the council. "This white man thinks we are children," he said as he pointed at Wynkoop, "but I tell him we are neither Papooses or Squaws, that we are men, warriors, Chiefs; we have said to him, we want to trade; we have given many horses and many Buffaloe [*sic*] robes to other tribes for these white prisoners; we now say we will trade them for peace. And this white soldier Chief, says, 'give me the White Prisoners, and I will give you nothing in return'; does he think we are fools that he comes to laugh at us."[26]

Bull Bear's words detonated an outburst of anger. With the outcry surrounding him, Wynkoop turned away from Bull Bear and resumed his place next to Smith. He told the trader to tell him what the chief had said.

Smith did, but his attitude had changed. He told the major, "I have now got to talk for my life."[27] The pronouncement caught Wynkoop by surprise. He now felt he could not trust Smith's translation of his words to the Indians or their words to him. He called to George Bent and asked him to confirm Smith's translations and correct them if necessary. Wynkoop's entreaty would not have sat well with Smith, and doubly so, as Bent agreed to it.

The outcry surrounding Wynkoop did not subside. It increased. Warriors and chiefs yelled their support of Bull Bear. Wynkoop did not need a translation to understand the fury directed at him. Perhaps, like Smith, he realized that his life depended upon the immediate future. As the anger grew, Wynkoop likened the Indians to "snarling wolves."[28]

That was all except for Black Kettle, whose quiet demeanor stood out. Instead of joining the outburst, the chief remained calm, dignified, and, according to Wynkoop, smiled at the explosion of pent-up hatred. By this time Black Kettle had become the foremost council chief. His lone goal was to protect the Tsistsistas, especially those who followed his lead. He knew he had to find a way for them to safely walk into the future.[29]

Teetering on the periphery, Wynkoop found himself scrambling for how to proceed, while knowing that his life depended on what he said next. He realized that Black Kettle watched him and felt that the chief not only understood his dilemma but actually encouraged his efforts at the council.[30] This relieved his anxiety and gave him hope to see another day. He felt that he had "come through the fire." Wynkoop realized that his actions and words would determine what would soon happen. One misstep could prove fatal.

With Cheyennes and Arapahos vocalizing their anger for the *vi'ho' i*'s ongoing attempts to kill their people, destroy their villages, and steal their land, Wynkoop controlled his growing unrest. He focused on freeing white captives, convincing the chiefs to travel to Denver to discuss ending the war, and, most important, staying alive.

After Bull Bear ended his tirade, Chief Left Hand stood. At first he vented his anger that soldiers at Fort Larned had fired at him when he approached the post with a white flag in an attempt to help them regain their stolen livestock. The threat of war had led to his band moving up the Arkansas, and had caused the loss of young men he could no longer control when they formed small war parties to seek vengeance. "He, with his main band," Left Hand said, "kept away from them, refusing to fight the whites."[31] Calming, Left Hand said that he still believed "that the difficulty could be settled upon hearing the proclamation of the big chief at Denver." Left Hand "had made every effort to comply with" Evans and "was acting in good faith."

Chief Little Raven spoke next, and he agreed with Bull Bear. "[N]o peace could be brought about." Bull Bear jumped on Little Raven's words, as they gave him another chance to agitate the assembly. "[T]he only thing left [is] to fight," he roared.

Wynkoop's inner nervousness grew as he listened to the continuing fury directed at him. He did not need Bent or Smith to translate these words. Already on edge, the tone of the Natives' voices served as warning that his and his command's well-being depended upon the coming minutes. Despite his inner turmoil he remained calm.

"[T]he whites [a]re not to be trusted," Bull Bear screamed as he tried yet again to ignite violence.

One-Eye pushed forward and demanded attention at the council circle. This surprised Wynkoop, for he had not seen the council chief since he had instructed him to ride between the battle lines that morning. One-Eye told the gathering that he "supposed the chiefs were acting in good faith," and that Tsistsistas "did not lie," referring to his promise that the *vi'ho' i* would not be harmed at this meeting.[32] He now felt "ashamed to hear such talk in the council as that uttered by Bull Bear." He then appealed to the chiefs to "act like men and fulfil[l] or live up to their word." If the Tsistsistas did not do this, "he [w]ould go with the whites and fight with them, and that he had a great many friends who would follow him." Not liking trivial fussing, One-Eye next offered some of his best horses if the chiefs said "no more in council." Bull Bear accepted this and did not speak again. (Later he selected two of One-Eye's horses.)

Black Kettle had remained silent while he listened to the Indian complaints directed at the white soldier chief. No longer. He seized control of the council and spoke quietly to One-Eye, telling him to sit. Turning his attention to the council, he demanded silence. When he had it, he stood and adjusted his blanket around himself. The chief walked to Wynkoop, pulled him upright, and hugged him twice. Black Kettle then led him to the center of the council circle. "This white man is not here to laugh at us, nor does he regard us as children . . . he comes with confidence in the pledges given [him]. [One-Eye] told [him] that he should come and go unharmed."[33] Continuing, the chief said, "[H]is words are straight[.] Had he told us that he would give us peace, [if we gave] him the white prisoners, he would have told us a lie. For I know that he cannot give us peace [as] there is a greater chief in the far off camp of the white soldiers."

That was it. In a sudden turnabout, Black Kettle quieted the nerve-racking situation and ended the council. The chief turned to Wynkoop. "Return upon the trail in which you came with your soldiers," he said, "until the sun has kissed the Prairie, then camp and remain until the sun has gone[.] [B]efore that time passes you will have news from Make-tava-tah." He finished by saying that "our Chiefs will spend the night in council."[34] Wynkoop looked around, and felt that the harsh stares that he had previously seen had mellowed. When Black Kettle finished talking, he again sat. When he did, a number of the chiefs stood and stepped to the soldier chief. They shook his hand, and as Wynkoop remembered, they said "with their usual guttural expression of satisfaction, 'Haio.'" This eased his trepidation.

When the chiefs left, Wynkoop, his officers, and Black Kettle stood. Then the chief shook hands with Wynkoop, Soule, and Cramer, explaining that "he was still, as he always had been, a friend to the whites," and would do what he could to end the war, as he knew "it to be for the good of his people."[35] Continuing, Make-tava-tah said "that there were other chiefs who still thought they were badly treated by their white brethren, [and although they] were willing to make peace, [they] felt unwilling to deliver up the prisoners simply on the promise of [the *vi' ho' i* soldier chief] that he would endeavor to procure them peace." These chiefs, Black Kettle said, wanted the delivery "of the white prisoners [to] be an assurance of peace." He then ensured Wynkoop that the Tsistsistas would not attack his troops when they traveled back to Fort Lyon.

The time to leave arrived. But before going, Wynkoop again told Black Kettle that "it was not in his power to ensure them peace." Black Kettle said he would inform him of the council's outcome the next day. Wynkoop said he would wait.

Wynkoop then mounted, and with his officers, Smith, and One-Eye, he rode to where he thought his camp was and discovered that his men had left. Following the trail, he rode quickly to the bivouac his men set up on Hackberry Creek.[36]

The troops sent for Wynkoop soon after he arrived. The Indians that had been with the command (Eagle Head, One-Eye's wife, and the Fool) had left in the afternoon, and this had caused alarm, as the camp was surrounded on three sides with water and was not defensible. They had discussed "breaking camp and returning to Fort Lyon without orders from the officers."[37] When

Wynkoop met with the troops, he heard their fear of treachery. According to Forbes, who was sergeant of the guard that day, the troops told Wynkoop "that they did not have the confidence in the Indians that he had." The major realized their fright. "[They] demanded to be immediately led back to Fort Lyon," Wynkoop recalled, "[as] they believed that this was but a stratagem on the part of the savages to more effectually hem us in, and by a night attack annihilate us."[38] According to Forbes, Wynkoop took the time to speak with the men, explaining "what the Indians had promised."[39] This eased their fears. They decided "to wait for orders."

Wynkoop thought that the possibility of peace was close, and he had no intention of walking away from the chance. He also realized that he had a potential mutiny on his hands, and "required extreme measure to quell."[40] Knowing that he was "surrounded by thousands of fierce barbarians; whether hostile or not an open question," Wynkoop claimed, "my feelings that long and sleepless night were not to be envied." He, Soule, Cramer, and the rest of his officers took turns at guard duty. When first light arrived, Wynkoop was pleased to learn that none of his troops had deserted.

But on the eleventh, the tension built as the hours slowly passed. Wynkoop waited, and waited. Nothing happened. He heard no subversive words from his men, while at the same time they were not attacked. Finally as the noon hour neared, several Arapahos appeared. Niwot (Left Hand) led the party, and released sixteen-year-old Laura Roper. Left Hand told Wynkoop that the Arapahos had not captured her, but that he had traded for her soon after the Tsistsistas captured her on the Little Blue.[41] Before leaving, Left Hand told Wynkoop that Make-tava-tah would appear on the following day.

Wynkoop sensed that his men wanted to flee. Still, he refused to abandon what he had begun. After dark he and his officers spent another tense night patrolling the perimeter of their camp. The twelfth dawned without incident.

The second day mimicked the first, and hours passed. Finally Wynkoop heard word that Black Kettle approached the camp. He mounted and rode out to meet the chief. John Smith and One-Eye accompanied him. Black Kettle brought warriors and women with him, as well as good news, for the council had decided to end the war. He and other chiefs would travel with him to meet the big chief in Denver.

Wynkoop looked around and saw two boys on horses riding toward him. "Here was the realization of my most sanguine hopes," Wynkoop later

Laura Roper and children. The four prisoners that Chiefs Left Hand and Black Kettle gave to Major Ned Wynkoop on September 11 and 12, 1864. From left: Daniel Marble, Laura Roper, who is holding Isabelle Eubanks, and Ambrose Asher. After Wynkoop brought the children safely to Denver, he asked his father-in-law George Wakely to take this photograph of them at his studio. See the text and notes for the identifications of Daniel and Ambrose.

History Nebraska, 20190034. Laura Roper holding Isabelle Eubanks, Danny Marble, Ambrose Asher. RG1507, 101808.

wrote, "the balance of the poor captives of my race within reach and soon to be under our protection. Such happiness I never experienced before, never since, and do not expect to in this world."[42] Undoubtedly he thought of his young children (Edward Estill and Emily Reveille).

When he reached the larger of the two boys, who rode a pony, Wynkoop asked who he was. "My name's Dan," he said, and then asked if he was the soldier who came for them. The major said that he was. He had just met Daniel Marble, who had been captured near Plum Creek in Nebraska Territory on August 8. After Daniel rode toward the soldier camp, Wynkoop met two children who had been captured with Laura Roper near the Little Blue on August 7. The first was Ambrose Asher, who he figured was two years younger than Marble due to his considerably smaller size. While Wynkoop found Marble talkative, he found Asher silent and uncommunicative.

Then Wynkoop saw a Cheyenne woman holding a child with blonde hair peeking from the folds of a blanket. When he rode to the woman, a little girl reached out to him. This was three-year-old Isabelle Eubanks. He took her from the woman and set her on the front of his saddle. She wrapped her arms around him, and with tears running down her face, sobbed, "I want to see my Mamma." Fearing he might not be able to control his emotions and not wanting do so in front of everyone, Wynkoop rode quickly back to his camp with Isabelle, followed by One-Eye and Smith.

As soon as Wynkoop reached his camp he and his companions were "surrounded by men wild with excitement; shouting[,] cheering, while down the bronzed cheek of many a battle scarred rough soldier coursed a tear," Wynkoop later wrote. "And their pitying looks were cast upon the poor desolate child. Finally, bursting from the throng[,] rushed an old soldier who reached up and took the child, while with a choking voice he asked forgiveness for his former conduct." He had instigated the mutiny that never happened.

Although aware that he put himself at risk for acting without orders, Wynkoop thought that success loomed in his future. He had not obtained all seven prisoners in Black Kettle's letter, but he had four, and seven chiefs traveled with him to Fort Lyon. They included four Arapaho chiefs related to Left Hand: Neva, Bosse, Heap of Buffalo, and No-ta-nee. As expected, Cheyenne council chief Black Kettle made the trip, as did White Antelope, and surprisingly Bull Bear also agreed to go.[43] Even though Left Hand knew that John Smith would interpret for the Hinono'eino', he had refused to meet the white chief Evans, most likely because he still fumed over being fired upon at Fort Larned. Wynkoop set out for Fort Lyon the following morning.

JOHN CHIVINGTON HAD CAMPAIGNED for Congress, and John Evans had campaigned to become a senator in anticipation of Colorado becoming a state. On a daily basis William Byers's *Rocky Mountain News* listed their selections for public office, which also included Abraham Lincoln and Andrew Johnson for president and vice president of the United States.

But time had run out for the Evans/Chivington-led campaign for Colorado statehood. The day of the election—September 13—did not begin as Evans and Chivington had hoped. Instead of becoming the leading candidates for U.S. senator and congressman from the glorious state of Colorado, they watched in anger as the territory's bid for statehood failed.

The "Anti-State conglomeration" handed them a monstrous defeat at the polls that day, much to the chagrin of Byers, who reported anti-statehood threats. Still, nothing would become final until the fate of the proposed Colorado Constitution was decided.[44]

At the same time, both of them knew that the Third Colorado Volunteer Cavalry's enlistment was almost a third over. Already the regiment had been labeled the "Bloodless Third." Evans needed the Third Colorado to score a major victory over the Cheyennes and Arapahos to justify not only its existence, but to vindicate his ongoing cries that the whites in the territory would be wiped out if the regiment had not been created. Chivington's view differed from the governor's, as he saw his chance of becoming an Indian fighter slipping away. Time was of the essence for both of them. They had lost at the polls, but they could not afford to lose the chance for the Third to engage and defeat the enemy.[45]

ELEVEN

A Peace in Name Only

MAJOR NED WYNKOOP, the children, and the seven chiefs reached Fort Lyon on September 17, 1864.[1] Some thirty warriors had followed the soldiers and their leaders, and an even larger number of Tsistsistas and Hinono'eino' had followed them at a distance between 150 and 200 yards.[2] After their arrival the two tribes set up separate camps east of the post.[3]

Unaware of what had happened with the territorial statehood election or that his efforts to end the war could not have been more poorly timed, Wynkoop knew he needed to explain why he acted without orders. On the eighteenth he wrote a report to Major General James Blunt, commander of the District of the Upper Arkansas. Although justifying himself, he shared everything, including facing an Indian battle line, the mixed results of the council, which "was divided, undecided," and that it took two days before Black Kettle announced that seven chiefs would travel to Denver to discuss ending the war, as well as receiving the four prisoners.[4] He also wrote Governor Evans and announced that he would bring the chiefs to Denver to meet with him.[5]

With all hope of becoming a congressional representative gone, on that same September 18, Chivington returned his focus to the Indian war. He informed General Curtis that "Indian warriors congregated eighty miles from Fort Lyon 3,000 strong."[6] His report to Curtis included a copy of a telegram that he had just sent to the secretary of war requesting that he be

Southern Cheyenne Ivan Hankler and his tipi. I met Ivan on April 30, 2004, at the Fort Larned Old Guard annual meeting, and we hit it off. We spent many hours together, which also included time with Kiowa James R. Coverdale, as we hung out in Ivan's fully functional Cheyenne tipi and on the parade ground. That day I gave them some of my books and asked Ivan if I could photograph him in traditional dress inside his lodge. He agreed. On May 1 Ivan gave me a parfleche he made and James gave me a necklace he made. When I gave them the books, I did not realize that I had touched on their culture. Their creations have been displayed in Tujunga House ever since. On the first, Ivan dressed and gave me full permission to use the photos I captured that day (I gave prints of the photo shoot to Ivan and James). While spending time in Ivan's tipi, as well as other fully functional Cheyenne lodges, I have never seen a cross-lodge pole.

Photos © 2004 by Louis Kraft. Louis Kraft Collection, ACP010. Chávez History Library, Santa Fe, N.Mex.

allowed to take supplies currently en route to New Mexico for the Third Colorado Volunteer Cavalry.

While at Fort Lyon and awaiting transport to Denver, Laura Roper spent a little time with Julia Lambert, who was married to a stage line agent at the post. "I knew there were other white women in camp," Lambert claimed Roper told her. "One escaped only to be recaptured and brought back after a chase of several miles. During the night she took off her calico dress, tore the skirt into strips and twisted them into a rope with which she hung herself from the lodge poles. How she accomplished this no one knew as the poles are high in the center."[7]

His preparations complete, Wynkoop set out for Denver on September 20. He took the white children, seven chiefs, Louise (his wife), Captain Silas Soule, Dexter Colley, and John Smith. Lieutenant Joseph Cramer commanded a forty-man escort.[8]

As Wynkoop slowly marched toward Denver, on September 21, Chivington, who had been impressed with First Lieutenant George L. Shoup (Company C, First Colorado), recommended that the lieutenant be promoted to colonel of the Third Colorado Volunteer Cavalry. The clean-shaven Shoup did not waste any time, and on that day he assumed command. By that time the Third's enlistment had swelled to 1,040 enlistees and between 350 and 400 horses. The quartermaster would supply another 400 mounts. At the time he assumed command, the Third Colorado was spread all over the place, with one or more companies at Fort Lupton, Valley Station, and Junction along the South Platte River, and on the Arkansas River five miles below Pueblo. The largest assembly was six companies at Camp Evans, and there were only detachments at Pueblo and Colorado City. Although then sedentary, all would be on the move beginning in mid to late October.[9]

As Wynkoop's caravan traveled through the Arkansas Valley, he saw "a great many farms deserted . . . [and] people congregated together at different points for mutual protection."[10] Although the war still raged in the north, he felt confident that he could safely travel to Denver with a small escort. At Booneville, he, Soule, eight troopers, Louise, the four children, and Dexter Colley, set out for Denver, while Cramer followed at a slower pace with the remainder of the command and the chiefs.

At this time Ovando Hollister wandered the streets of Denver and shipped his articles to Black Hawk. Ever since he and partner Hall had taken control of the paper, he had been a thorn in Byers's side. On the twenty-third Hollister's *Daily Mining Journal* printed: "Election matters are very quiet. It is generally given up that the Constitution is beaten, though some earnestly charge fraud, or the intention of fraud on the part of the Administration. I haven't seen what I deem reliable authority; therefore, I will give no opinion."[11] Byers could not allow this to pass quietly into the night. "The insinuation of the Black Hawk *Journal* that the 'Administration' would countenance election frauds is of a piece with its former outrageous slanders," Byers published. "There is not a man in Colorado, except the political marplot who conducts that paper, that would have the audacity to suggest that the governor is capable of countenancing an election fraud or a fraud of any kind. His uniform course through an unblemished life, and his correct and able administration of the affairs of the Territory ought to shield him from such insinuations."[12]

As soon as Chivington learned of Wynkoop's approach to Denver, he telegraphed General Curtis's headquarters in Kansas. "I have been informed by E. W. Wynkoop . . . that he is on his way here with Cheyenne and Arapaho chiefs and four white prisoners they gave up. Winter approaches. Third Regiment is full, and they know they will be chastised for their outrages and now want peace. I hope that the major-general will direct that they make full restitution and then go on their reserve and stay there."[13]

Wynkoop, Soule, the children, and their escort reached Denver on the night of the twenty-sixth. After Laura and the children had a chance to catch up on sleep, Wynkoop brought them to George D. Wakely's studio. Wakely was his father-in-law, and was also a daguerreotypist. Wynkoop asked him to photograph them, and Wakely did.[14]

On the twenty-seventh, Wynkoop presented himself at the governor's home. Evans, who knew that Wynkoop was in Denver, had arranged to leave the following day for a meeting with the Utes. However, when Wynkoop appeared at his door, he was told that Evans was terribly ill, in bed, and could not see him. Surprisingly, on the morning of the twenty-eighth when Wynkoop descended the stairs of his lodging, he saw Evans and Dexter Colley talking in the lobby. He crossed to them, as he wanted to secure the governor's support to bring about an end to the war. Deathly sick the night before, but now robust, Evans told Wynkoop that he could not meet with the Indians, as he was leaving to see the Utes. Wynkoop pressured him until finally an exasperated Evans exclaimed that the Third Regiment "had been raised to kill Indians, and they must kill Indians."[15] Although

The Cheyenne and Arapaho chiefs arrived in Denver on September 28, 1864, while the mounted Major Ned Wynkoop (the taller of the two officers) and Captain Silas Soule watched the procession on their horses at the lower right of the image. As Wynkoop already knew that Governor John Evans had refused to meet with the chiefs, he approached his father-in-law, daguerreotypist George Wakely, and asked him to document the chiefs' arrival. These photos forced Evans to meet with the Cheyennes and Arapahos that day.

Denver council 1864 (Camp Weld Council). Photo by George D. Wakely. History Colorado. Accession # 89.451.5438.

disappointed, Wynkoop refused to walk away from what he hoped would end the war. He again visited Wakely, and asked him to capture images of the Cheyenne and Arapahos' arrival near the governor's mansion that day. This was pure brilliance by Wynkoop, and as expected, Evans suddenly found himself in a potentially damning situation.

War existed, and it could not end until the Third Colorado scored a major victory. If this did not happen, there would be no way Evans could justify the cost for the Hundred Daysers or could defend his pleas for military reinforcements to prevent the annihilation of whites living in the territory. The governor knew that he could not avoid meeting with the chiefs. He also knew that he could not agree to peace. Evans decided to dominate the council and obtain information that would back his stance that the Indians posed a real threat.

The meeting took place at Camp Weld later that day. Evans, Chivington, Shoup, Wynkoop, Black Kettle, White Antelope, Bull Bear, Bosse, Heap of Buffalo, Na-ta-nee, and Neva, along with Soule and Cramer, were present at the meeting, as was Byers. Simeon Whiteley documented the event.[16] John Smith translated, and other citizens and military personnel attended. Smith's mixed-blood Cheyenne son Jack Smith was also present.[17]

After everyone had assembled at Camp Weld, Evans took control of what he considered his meeting. He opened the council by inviting the Indians to share their thoughts.

Make-tava-tah (Black Kettle) stepped forward to speak, for he had but one goal—secure the peace that the soldier had proposed on the Smoky Hill. Whiteley called Black Kettle the "leading Cheyenne chief." He was the leading chief of the council of forty-four, but that was all. This misconception of one supreme leader of the Cheyenne nation had been addressed many times, but the whites refused to accept it. The Anglo-Americans had a president; so should the various tribes. The white man felt that all indigenous people should have one person that could speak for all their people. From the Plains Indians' point of view, this was incomprehensible. They were from two different cultures with two different views, and neither side could understand or accept the other's interpretation.

"On sight of your circular of June 27, 1864," Make-tava-tah said, "I took hold of the matter, and have now come to talk to you about it." The word usage throughout the meeting was based on Smith's translation of the Cheyenne and Arapaho words, plus Whiteley's jotted notes and his subsequent transcription of them. "I told . . . [William] Bent, who brought it, that I accepted it, but it would take some time to get all my people together—many of my young men being absent—and I have done everything in my power, since then, to keep peace with the whites." Regardless of how much power he wielded, or did not wield, Make-tava-tah had every intention of proving that many Tsistsistas did not ride the war trail.

"As soon as I could get my people together," and here the chief spoke about the large village in the Big Timbers on the tributary of the Smoky Hill, "we held a council." The result was the two letters that Black Kettle directed George Bent and Edmund Guerrier to write. Make-tava-tah could not have dictated the letters of peace if he did not have the support of this village, and Bull Bear was an absolute key for him to move forward. This was approximately one and a half months after Bent delivered Evans's call for peaceful Indians to assemble at forts. This was not a lie by Black Kettle, for he needed to obtain the support of chiefs not associated with his band as well as Left Hand and Little Raven.

Too many of the People had died, including friends. He told the big white chief of Denver of his recent meeting with Wynkoop, a man he did not know but decided to trust. He spoke of the four white children given to the soldier. He also spoke about Mrs. Anna Snyder, who he said had killed herself.

Byers knew that he had a piece of information that had to be printed, and it would happen the next day: "Mrs. Snyder, who was taken near Boonvill[e], on the Arkansas, at the time her husband was killed, has since committed suicide."[18] No one, and certainly not Byers, questioned how Anna Snyder could have climbed high enough on a lodge pole, securely tied a cloth rope to it, and successfully hung herself.

Black Kettle discussed the white captives that he gave to Wynkoop, but the printed meeting details do not ring true, and certainly not from a council chief who was trying to end war. Next Black Kettle stated that Wynkoop suggested this meeting. "We have come with our eyes shut, following his handful of men, like coming through the fire. All we ask is that we may have peace with the whites. We want to hold you by the hand. You are our father. We have been traveling through a cloud. The sky has been dark ever since the war began. These braves who are with me are all willing to do what I say. We want to take good tidings home to our people, that they may sleep in peace."

The chief had reached the absolute point of his talk. "I want you to give all these chiefs of the soldiers here to understand that we are for peace, and that we have made peace [and here he talked about the Smoky Hill meeting], that we may not be mistaken by them for enemies." Black Kettle spoke from his fears of an unknown future. His goal was simple: the People that had accepted the tall soldier chief's offer of peace and camped near him were not at war. All the people with him would do as the *vi'ho' i* chief said they should. He did not want the Hinono'eino' and Tsistsistas that were for peace killed by soldiers.

"I have not come here with a little wolf bark, but have come to talk plain with you." He knew that the white man was trying to push them off their land, the land the buffalo roamed. "We must live near the buffalo or starve." Here Make-tava-tah understated the animal's importance, for it gave the People much more than food—it provided almost everything they needed to survive.

"When we came here we came free, without any apprehension [and again based upon the Wynkoop meeting], to see you, and when I go home and tell my people that I have taken your hand, and the hands of all the chiefs here in Denver, they will feel well, and so will all the different tribes on the plains, after we have eaten and drank with them." This was an overly optimistic statement by Make-tava-tah, who had reached out with words that he hoped would save the Tsistsistas who avoided war.[19]

He waited while Smith translated his words. But it was almost as if Evans had not heard what he said. The governor's words must have confused Make-tava-tah, for they had nothing to do with what he had just said.

"I am sorry you did not respond to my appeal at once," Evans said. "You have gone into an alliance with the Sioux," he then accused, "who are at war with us. You have done a great deal of damage—have stolen stock, and now have possession of it." The governor had no clue of what he spoke of, and yet he placed the war on Black Kettle.

Make-tava-tah had explained that he had responded to Small White Man's (William Bent's) delivery of the *vi'ho' i* letter as quickly as possible.

Moving forward, and without pausing to give Black Kettle a chance to comment, Evans said: "However much a few individuals may have tried to keep the peace, as a nation you have gone to war." His words were vapid, unclear, and spoken only for effect. Wynkoop, an avowed Indian hater, had brought these Indians to Denver and had tried to explain to Evans that they wanted to end the war. He had handed Evans an unwanted gift. The entire statehood election had blown up in the governor's face, and now he had a volunteer regiment—many of whom had been forced into service—that had yet to save the territory from annihilation. Evans stated that the government had done everything possible to save the Cheyennes, feed them, make them comfortable, and protect them.

It is doubtful that Black Kettle understood Evans translated words, for when Evans said, "Bull Bear wanted to come in to see me at the head of the Republican, but his people held a council and would not let him come," Black Kettle replied, "That is true." The council chief had no control over what Bull Bear did or did not do; he had no power to stop Bull Bear from meeting Evans if he had desired to do so, and neither did any other Tsistsista leader.

Evans immediately returned to his view that the Cheyennes wanted war. After making it clear how much time and money he had spent to see the Cheyennes on the Republican, he said: "[I]nstead of this [council], your people went away and smoked the war-pipe with our enemies." Without evidence, the governor had just accused Black Kettle and his band of joining the northern bands of Sioux, Cheyennes, and Arapahos and riding the war trail.

"I don't know who could have told you this," Black Kettle replied.

"No matter who said this," Evans snapped as he dismissed that he had to prove anything, "but your conduct has proved to my satisfaction that was the case."

The accusation must have bewildered Make-tava-tah, for how could he disprove an event that never happened? This almost marked the end of his participation in the meeting.

Realizing that the council chief could not—or would not—address what he knew to be a lie, unnamed chiefs spoke for the first time. Most likely their voices clashed with each other as they denied the charge. Whiteley did not name them, he simply recorded what was said into one sentence: "This is a mistake; we have made no alliance with the Sioux or any one else."

Evans once more stated that the Cheyennes smoked the war pipe, but then said that "smoking the war-pipe was a figurative term." Continuing, he felt "their conduct had been such as to show they had an understanding with other tribes."

Whiteley again combined numerous unnamed speakers to create one response (he never quoted Bosse, Na-ta-nee, or Heap of Buffalo). "We acknowledge that our actions have given you reason to believe this." This statement was the next by Indian leaders and directly after their previous quote. These two quotes—both paraphrases of multiple speakers—are in direct contradiction with each other, and yet this is what Whiteley transcribed for the document.

Evans was exactly where he wanted to be. "So far as making a treaty now is concerned, we are in no condition to do it. Your young men are on the war-path. My soldiers are preparing for the fight. You, so far, have had the advantage; but the time is near at hand when the plains will swarm with United States soldiers."

Did Black Kettle, Bull Bear, Neva, and the others fully understand the translation of the governor's words? Probably not. What about Wynkoop or Soule or Cramer? Certainly a strangely silent Chivington did. Although he said little on that day, he had a good idea what might come, and he had every intention of keeping one of his key subordinates—Wynkoop—under his control whether he reported to the Department of the Upper Arkansas (which Wynkoop now did) or to him. Although he never stated it, Chivington had always been aware of Wynkoop's audacity; the major had courage, guts, and a brain. Chivington must have had a private chuckle when he learned how Wynkoop had forced the meeting on Evans.

"I understand that these men who have come to see me now have been opposed to the war all the time," Evans continued, but it was almost as if he spoke of Indian leaders not present at the conference. Certainly he did not direct his comments at Black Kettle or Neva. "[B]ut that their people have controlled them and that they could not help themselves."

According to Whiteley's transcription, all seven of the Indian leaders said: "It has been so." Why would they agree with his statement? This transcription documented the total misrepresentation of the translation of words. What was said and translated was not understood by the Cheyennes and Arapahos. And this is exactly what Evans grabbed and used to confirm the total Indian war against whites on the frontier.

Evans now had the answer he wanted, and for the rest of the conference it did not matter what he said or how the Indians answered. War existed, and he had proof. Still he desired additional confirmation. "The fact that [you] have not been able to prevent [your] people from going to war in the past spring, when there was plenty of grass and game, makes me believe that [you] will not be able to make a peace which will last longer than until winter is past."

Either Whiteley's capture of Evans's words was poor or the governor totally talked down to the Indian leaders standing before him. If Black Kettle, Neva, White Antelope, and Bull Bear understood what the governor really said, they disguised their feelings, for at no time did Whiteley mention them cringing or reacting poorly to Evans's words.

The meeting, as transcribed by Whiteley, proved to be strange, because the Cheyennes' and Arapahos' singular goal was obtaining peace, while Evans's only stated goal was continuing the war. Yet the Indian leaders only twice objected to any of the *vi' ho' i*'s words. Conversely, the Indian leaders confirmed all of Evans's accusations.

The seventy-five-year-old White Antelope said: "I will answer that after a time."[20]

Evans had no interest in an answer from the ancient council chief, then or later. He continued with his assault: "The time when you can make war best is in the summer-time; when I can make war best is in the winter." If Evans counted upon the newly enlisted 100-daysers to launch a massive winter war, he had trouble counting—for the Third's enlistment would end beginning around November 23, which was almost a month before winter officially began. "You, so far," he continued, "have had the advantage; my time is just coming." He warned the chiefs that the white man's war in the East would soon end. "The Great Father will not know what to do with all his soldiers, except to send them after the Indians on the plains."

The governor then used words that offered hope: "My proposition to the friendly Indians has gone out; [I] shall be glad to have them all come in under it." He would not make any new propositions, but then washed his hands of the situation. "[The] reason that I am not in a condition to make a treaty is that war is begun," Evans said, "and the power to make a treaty of peace has passed from me to the great war chief. My advice to you is to turn on the side of the government, and show by your acts that friendly disposition you profess to me. It is utterly out of the question for you to be at peace with us while living with our enemies, and being on friendly terms with them."

An unnamed Arapaho was confused with the phrase, "on the side of the government." Evans explained that he wanted the friendly Indians to help the soldiers, and the seven chiefs supposedly agreed.

"We will return with Major Wynkoop to Fort Lyon," Black Kettle said, "we will then proceed to our village and take back word to my young men every word you say." He then said optimistic words: "I cannot answer for all of them, but think there will be but little difficulty in getting them to assent to help the soldiers."

Wynkoop had remained silent during the meeting, but now spoke up. "Did not the Dog Soldiers agree," he asked, "when I had my council with you, to do whatever you said, after you had been here?"

"Yes," Black Kettle answered.

Evans retook the lead and repeated that the friendly Indians had to align with the U.S. soldiers or "they would be treated as enemies. You understand," he said, "if you are at peace with us it is necessary to keep away from our enemies." Evans might have been peeved, as Chivington had remained silent. "I hand you over to the military, one of the chiefs of which is here to-day, and can speak for himself . . . if he chooses."

The colonel remained silent.

Not so for the aged White Antelope. "I understand every word you have said, and will hold on to it. . . . The Cheyennes, all of them, have their eyes open this way, and they will hear what you say." He spoke of his trip to visit the Great White Father in Washington and of all the whites he had seen. "I have called all white men as my brothers," he said as he displayed the medal he had received, "[but] now the soldiers do not shake hands, but seek to kill me." Evans's words had confused him. "What do you mean by us fighting your enemies? Who are they?"

"All the Indians fighting us," Evans replied.

"How can we be protected from the soldiers on the plains?" White Antelope asked.

"You must make that arrangement with the Military Chief," Evans stated.

"I fear that these new soldiers who have gone out," White Antelope said, "may kill some of my people while I am here."

"There is great danger of it," Evans said, feeding the chief's trepidation.

"When we sent our letter to Major Wynkoop, it was like going though a strong fire or blast, for Major Wynkoop's men to come to our camp; it was the same for us to come to see you. We have our doubts whether the Indians south of the Arkansas, or those north of the Platte, will do as you say. A large number of Sioux have crossed the Platte in the vicinity of the Junction, into their country." White Antelope wanted to make it clear why he and the other chiefs had traveled to Denver. "When Major Wynkoop came we proposed to make peace. He said he had no power to make a peace except to bring [us] here and return [us] safe."

Evans had stopped listening. He had the information he wanted. "Again, whatever peace [you] make, must be with the soldiers and not me."

After Smith translated the governor's comment, a stillness took over. Chivington continued to remain silent while White Antelope was not sure how to proceed.

"Are the Apaches at war with the whites?" Evans asked, changing the subject.

"Yes," White Antelope said, "and the C[o]manches and Kiowas as well: also a tribe of Indians from Texas, whose names we do not know. There are thirteen different bands of Sioux who have crossed the Platte and are in alliance with the others named." He pointedly did not state that there were Tsistsistas or Hinono'eino' riding with the Sioux.

Evans had new information to follow up on and asked how many warriors were involved. White Antelope did not know, but there were many, and the Sioux had more warriors than all those in the south. It mattered not, for the governor had an opening to query about another raid. "[W]ho committed the depredations on the trains near the Junction, about the 1st of August?"

This took White Antelope by surprise. "Do not know—did not know any were committed." He did not like the direction in which the council had moved. "[We h]ave taken you by the hand, and will tell the truth, keeping back nothing."

The governor did not press for an answer. "Who committed the murder of the Hungate family, on Running Creek?"

Neva stepped forward. "The Arapahoes: a party of the northern band who were passing north—It was Medicine Man, or Roman Nose, and three others. I am satisfied from the time [they] left a certain camp for the north, that it was this party of four persons."

"That cannot be true," Whiteley said. The whites had blamed the Cheyennes, which made Neva's statement unacceptable.

Evans continued to ask about attacks on whites and the theft of livestock, including the murder of a man and boy on Cherry Creek and the theft of military horses at Jimmy's Camp at the beginning of the month. When Neva answered that fourteen Tsistsistas and Hinono'eino' stole the horses, and that the leaders of the raid were Whirlwind and Powder Face, Colonel Shoup quickly corrected him. "I counted twenty Indians." But the most damaging part of this exchange was when Neva said that both Whirlwind and Powder Face currently lived in the Smoky Hill village.

The pace moved quickly as Evans named one Indian attack after another. Once Neva confirmed that Little Raven's son stole Charley Autobee's horses, the governor moved on to Frémont's Orchard. He wanted to know who stole the stock there and then had a running fight with soldiers to the north of the area.

This line of questioning bothered White Antelope. "Before answering this question I would like for you to know that this was the beginning of war and I should like to know what it was for, a soldier fired first."

"The Indians had stolen about forty horses," Evans snapped, "the soldiers went to recover them, and the Indians fired a volley into their ranks."

"This is all a mistake," White Antelope disagreed. "They were coming down the Bijou, and found one horse and one mule." His words made it clear that he did not like what Evans said. "They returned one horse and one mule before they got to Geary's, to a man, then went to Geary's, expecting to turn the other one over to some one. They then heard that the soldiers and Indians were fighting, somewhere down the Platte: then they took fright and all fled."[21]

"Who were the Indians that had the fight?" Evans demanded.

"They were headed by the Fool Badger's son, a young man, one of the greatest of the Cheyenne warriors, who was wounded, and though still alive, he will never recover."

Neva jumped in, as he was concerned where the questioning led. "I want to say something. It makes me feel bad to be talking about these things and opening old sores."

Apparently White Antelope attempted to cut Neva off, for Evans said, "Let him speak."

"[John] Smith has known me ever since I was a child. Has he ever known me commit depredations on the whites?" Neva had a good sense of which way the council was headed and made an attempt to make his case. "I went to Washington last year—receiving good council. I hold on to it. I determined to always keep peace with the whites. Now, when I shake hands with them they seem to pull away. I came here to speak peace and nothing else."

Evans replied, but he did not address what Neva said. "We feel that they have, by their stealing and murdering, done us great damage." It was almost as if he wanted to connect the Indians that came to talk about peace with the warriors that had reacted to the unprovoked attacks. His words turned sarcastic. "[You] come here and say [you] will tell me all, and that is what I am trying to get."

"The C[o]manches, Kiowas, and Sioux have done much more injury than we have. We will tell what we know but cannot speak for others."

"I suppose you acknowledge the depredations on the Little Blue, as you have the prisoners then taken in your possession."

"We . . . took two prisoners," White Antelope admitted, "west of Fort [Kearny], and destroyed the trains," but he spoke of the Plum Creek massacre and not the Little Blue.

"Who committed depredations at Cottonwood?"

"The Sioux," White Antelope said. "What band, we do not know." But he was wrong.

"What are the Sioux going to do next?" Evans wanted to know.

Certainly Black Kettle, White Antelope, Neva, and the other chiefs that had been with Wynkoop for two weeks could not answer the question. Still Bull Bear spoke up for the first time, and if any of the seven would know he would have been the one. "Their plan is to clean out all this country," he said. "They are angry and will do all the damage to the whites they can."

What he said had the ring of truth. But what he said next did not, especially since his verbal assault on Wynkoop and his push to incite the warriors to kill the soldiers on the Smoky Hill. "I am with you and the troops, to fight all those who have no ears to listen to what you say. Who are they?" Bull Bear demanded. "Show them to me. I am not yet old—I am young." Most likely Bull Bear was not aware of white man games of chance, but the Tsistsistas also gambled, and he did at this moment. "I have never hurt a white man," Bull Bear proclaimed (most likely a lie). He had led assaults on *vi′ho′ i* trains, he had taken part in the capture of *vi′ho′ i* women and children, and logically he could have personally killed whites during these times of violence.

"I am pushing for something good," Bull Bear continued. "I am always going to be friends with the whites; they can do me some good."

Evans ignored Bull Bear's words. Instead, he remained aggressive. "Where are the Sioux?"

"Down on the Republican, where it opens out," Bull Bear answered.

"Do you know that they intend to attack the trains this week?"

"Yes; about one-half of all the Missouri River Sioux and Yanktons, who were driven from Minnesota, are those who have crossed the Platte." How did Bull Bear know this? Was he feeding the governor words as he deflected his people's violence? Or did runners meet with him during the journey to Denver?

It was doubtful that Bull Bear knew, but he replied in the affirmative. "I am young, and can fight. I have given my word to fight with the whites." Again, and amazingly, Bull Bear swallowed his pride, his fighting spirit, and basically pledged allegiance with the hated *vi′ho′ i*. "My brother (Lean Bear) died in trying to keep the peace with the whites. I am willing to die in the same way, and I expect to do so."

Neva spoke next, and again for the good of the Hinono'eino' that followed Left Hand's lead. "I know the value of the presents which we receive from Washington," he said. "We cannot live without them. That is why I try so hard to keep peace with the whites."

As he had done during the entire council, Evans continued to ignore what Black Kettle, White Antelope, Bull Bear, and Neva said regarding peace. "I cannot say anything about those things now," he said.

"I can speak for all the Arapahoes under Left Hand," Neva said. "[Little] Raven has sent no one here to speak for him. [Little] Raven has fought the whites."

Evans did not bother to reply, and the chiefs remained silent. As the silence grew, everyone looked around. Colonel John Chivington finally stepped forward and took center stage. "I am not a big war chief," he began, "but all the soldiers in the country are at my command. My rule of fighting white men or Indians is to fight them until they lay down their arms and submit to military authority." He suddenly changed the subject. "[You] are nearer Major Wynkoop than any one else, and [you] can go to him when [you] get ready to do that."[22]

The colonel's words ended the council.

"Black Kettle affectionately embraced the governor," Wynkoop later stated, "then he and the balance of the chiefs shook hands with all those assembled."[23]

Certainly Wynkoop understood everything that Evans said, and that included not one hint of peace from the governor. Then Chivington's last sentence changed his perspective, as he now thought he would be in charge of the Indians at Fort Lyon. "[To] act toward them according to the best of my judgment, until such time as I could receive instructions from the proper authorities."[24] Before leaving Denver, Wynkoop told Evans and later Chivington that "I would bring them back to Fort Lyon and get them to bring their families into the vicinity of the post, until such time as some action was taken by proper authorities in relation to their proposition for peace."[25]

The Tsistsistas and Hinono'eino' thought that the war was over for them—that they would move their camp circles near Fort Lyon. Pleased, they allowed George Wakely to capture their images at the conclusion of the council.

Not so for Governor Evans and Colonel Chivington.

As George Wakely had taken the image of the released children (September 27) and of the Indians' arrival in Denver, it stands to reason that he captured this group image of Major Ned Wynkoop (left front) and Captain Silas Soule at the conclusion of the Camp Weld Council (September 28, 1864) with the chiefs. Sitting are Southern Cheyenne White Antelope (left), Dog Man Bull Bear, Southern Cheyenne Black Kettle, and Arapahos Neva and No-ta-nee. Standing (from left) are unidentified; mixed-blood Cheyenne Jack Smith (per historian Stan Hoig), as he was present and probably standing next to his father (and previously misidentified as Dexter Colley); John Smith; Arapahos Heap of Buffalo and Bosse; trader Dexter Colley; and unidentified.

Camp Weld Council on September 28, 1864. Photo by George D. Wakely. History Colorado. Accession # H.858.4, 89.451.2952.

On that same day Chivington received Major General Curtis's wire. "I shall require the bad Indians delivered up; restoration of equal numbers of stock; also hostages to secure. I want no peace till the Indians suffer more. Left Hand is said to be a good chief of the Arapahoes, but Big Mouth is a rascal. I fear agent of the Interior Department will be ready to make presents too soon. It is better to chastise before giving anything but a little tobacco to talk over. No peace must be made without my directions."[26]

In the next day's edition of the *News*, Byers wrote: "Every one present seemed to be satisfied with the course taken in this most important and critical interview."[27] He, like Wynkoop and John Smith, thought that the war had ended and that Black Kettle, Bull Bear, and Neva "will use their utmost influence to induce their tribes to lay down their arms," which he felt was "a consummation devoutly to be wished for." Byers's take on Chivington's final remark was simple, mainly "an unconditional surrender and laying down of their arms. . . . He referred the whole matter to Major Wynkoop, . . . who was much nearer to their reservation and hunting grounds, and more familiar with their disposition, wants and necessities."

If Wynkoop, the Indians, and even Byers had been duped, both Evans and Chivington felt that their goal and objective was clear, and that they did not hide it. On the twenty-ninth Evans wrote to Agent Colley about the Cheyenne and Arapaho leaders, stating that they "have been heard. I have declined to make any treaty with them."[28]

Wynkoop no longer reported to Chivington, so there was no reason for the colonel to show him General Curtis's September 28 telegram, but he did. This made no sense, as the military backlash to get rid of Wynkoop for acting without orders had already begun. Wynkoop may have been a favorite of Chivington and Byers, but those days were now over. Moreover, there was a possibility that Wynkoop might share the information with the Indians, which was exactly what he did.[29]

Wynkoop departed Denver on October 3 with everyone that had arrived with him except the four children. When his command reached Coberly's road station north of the old "Puebla" ruins above the Arkansas, Wynkoop, Louise, Soule, two other officers, and a small escort left Cramer, most of the troopers, and the chiefs behind and hustled toward Fort Lyon. The major arrived on the eighth; Cramer and the chiefs reached the post on the twelfth.[30] Upon his arrival Wynkoop updated Curtis on everything. "They [the Indian leaders] were perfectly willing to place themselves under my control, for me to dispose of them as I thought proper."[31] He also admitted that he had been "shown a telegram from the major general commanding [the] department, to the effect that no peace should be made with the Indians," while striving to justify his actions and asking for instructions.

During the summer Mollie Dorsey Sanford had lived in the barracks at Camp Weld with her husband, Byron, who was then forage master for the government at the post. Actually, they had lived there off and on over the past three years. Their son, Albert, was born at Camp Weld. However, this time when they moved back to Denver, Byron had resigned his position at the post. He had recently purchased a ranch of 160 acres ten miles west of Denver, and they returned to the city to prepare for the move the following March. At the time of Governor Evans's meeting with the chiefs, he had been on a trip to their property.

Soon after the meeting ended, Mollie learned of the prisoners Wynkoop had brought to Denver. Because Laura, Isabelle, and Ambrose had been captured near her former residence in Nebraska Territory, she opened her home to them. All three lived with her "for a while."[32] "Miss Roper was subjected to all the indignities usually given white captives," she wrote without inquiring, for years later Laura would contradict Mollie without knowing her journal existed. Isabelle and Ambrose "were brutally treated by the squaws."

Isabelle was a gorgeous and striking child although it was obvious that she was a wounded dove. Mollie's heart reached out to her, and when Ambrose and Laura moved on to new families, she kept the child. Belle, according to Mollie, "was scarred all over with the prints of arrow points that the squaws tortured her with." As she did not have a daughter, she thought about keeping Belle, but it would never be as she hoped.

"The mother of little Bell[e] was taken away by some distant band, and the poor little things [sic] left," Mollie wrote. "She saw her father butchered, and only three years old, can and does recount the whole tragedy. I took her, thinking I might adopt her, but I could not stand it. She would wake from a sound sleep, and sit up in bed with staring eyes, and go in detail over the whole thing." Mollie gave Belle to Dr. Brondsall, hoping that the little girl would have a good home and medical care. According to Mollie, Dr. Brondsall adopted her.

EVEN THOUGH WYNKOOP no longer reported to Chivington, on October 16 the colonel wrote him. "I have the best of evidence that there are a large number of Indians on the Republican, and design to go after them. Revolvers have not come. The rascal who started with them left them at Atchison and took on some mining machinery. This leaves us with nothing but our muskets for the Third. Send as quick as possible those Starr carbines. I have moved the Third out sixty miles, and will be after the Indians as soon as we can get those carbines."[33]

On a cold and windy October 30 evening, Captain Silas Soule found himself in a sour mood as he considered the present situation and his future while he attempted to compose a letter in near darkness. He pondered remaining in the service another three years, but then questioned it. As the months passed, Soule longed to visit his family in Maine but knew that the trip would wipe out the saved money for his mother.

Of immediate concern was the perhaps three thousand Cheyennes and Arapahos camped a short distance from Fort Lyon. Considering everything that he had taken part in the past two months, he felt that Black Kettle's and Left Hand's people wanted peace, "but—I think [the] Government will not mak[e] peace with them."[34] If so, he concluded more fighting would follow during the winter months.

Major Wynkoop did not share Soule's concern of more violence. After returning from the Camp Weld meeting, he often traveled to the Arapaho village that was below Fort Lyon and was the closest village to the post. Wynkoop was convinced that Left Hand and Little Raven truly wanted peace, and on occasion when he visited them, he brought Louise and their children with him.[35] Obviously Wynkoop wanted to make a statement that he believed their words. This was unusual behavior, and it certainly influenced George Bent's future.

Major Scott Anthony, who had been removed from command at Fort Larned, Kansas, on October 7, 1864, appeared at Fort Lyon on November 2.[36] Anthony made no attempt to hide the reason for his arrival from Wynkoop. He had orders to investigate any officer who had left his post without authority.[37] No fool, Wynkoop knew that he was the target, and it worsened, for Anthony also had orders to investigate "certain officers" who had disregarded the department commander's order to not issue "goods, stores or supplies to hostile Indians."[38] Anthony also knew that he would replace Wynkoop as commander of the fort, but the orders were dated November 4. On November 5 Anthony presented Wynkoop Special Orders No. 13, which removed him from command of Fort Lyon. Not only did Anthony assume command, but Wynkoop was ordered to "immediately" report to the District of the Upper Arkansas headquarters at Fort Riley, Kansas. Although the directive stated that Wynkoop would report "for orders," the tone implied the opposite.[39] Wynkoop, as he had recently demonstrated, chose to act as he felt best. Although the orders stated that he should directly set out for Kansas, he ignored them. Knowing that his actions might further complicate his future, he intended to remain at Fort Lyon to make the transition of command as smooth as possible.

When Anthony assumed command, he stopped Lieutenant C. M. Cossitt from distributing supplies to the Arapahos under Little Raven, Left Hand, Knock-knee (No-ta-nee), Storm, and Neva on a daily basis from the commissary—the former Bent's New Fort—which was on a hill east of the post. He also began to arrest any Indian found inside the fort's perimeter. On the sixth, Anthony met the chiefs halfway between Lyon and their village, which was about two miles below the commissary. The major began matters with an intimidating manner, demanding to know "by what authority and for what purpose they were encamped" so close to Fort Lyon.[40]

"[We have] been on peaceable terms with the whites," Left Hand replied, "ha[v]e never desired any other than peace, and could not be induced to fight." He claimed that they camped along the Arkansas to avoid the tribes then at war and "to show that they desired peace." At this time the village included 113 lodges and 652 men, women, and children—mostly women and children.

Intending to reverse Wynkoop's course of action, Anthony pressed forward. "I could not permit any body of armed men to camp in the vicinity of the post, nor [allow] Indians to visit the post except as prisoners of war." The chiefs acquiesced to this, "replying that they had . . . very few arms and . . . few horses," and that they would "accept any terms." Ending the meeting, Anthony demanded "their arms and all stock they had in their possession which had ever belonged to white men." According to Anthony, "They at once accepted these terms."

Soon after, the major rode to the Arapaho village, but before reaching it he left troopers hidden in case of need. Then he, Wynkoop, an interpreter, and several soldiers entered the camp, where he demanded their arms. He then "sent out men to look through their herd for United States or citizens' stock." Four horses and ten mules were confiscated. "Their arms are in very poor condition and but few," Anthony reported, "with little ammunition. Their horses [were] far below the average grade of Indians' horses. In fact, these that are here could make but a feeble fight if they desired war."

Anthony agreed with Wynkoop's policy of allowing sanctuary until General Curtis sent word that they were out of the war or still part of it. Then, surprisingly, when Anthony realized how destitute the Arapahos were, he eased up on his hard-line stance and followed Wynkoop's humanitarian lead. "I fed them for some ten days," he later admitted, a change of attitude that pleased Wynkoop.[41]

ON NOVEMBER 15 ANTHONY alerted the officers then stationed at Fort Lyon that he and Wynkoop would meet with Cheyenne and Arapaho chiefs at the commissary. Black Kettle was present, as was Left Hand. At the specified time Anthony, Wynkoop, Soule, Cramer, Lieutenant Phillips, and Second Lieutenant William Minton (First New Mexico Volunteers) walked up the hill. John Smith and John Prowers, who had married One-Eye's daughter (Magon), interpreted. Robert Bent and Agent Colley also joined the meeting. Black Kettle and Left Hand listened as Smith and Prowers stated that the "red-eyed chief"—Anthony had previously had scurvy and his eyes bothered the two chiefs—wanted them to move away from Fort Lyon and camp on the Big Sandy. They had not been pleased with Wynkoop's removal as commander of Fort Lyon, but they understood the demand while realizing their protection had ended. Black Kettle, Left Hand, or both, told the interpreters that they would move their villages as directed. They knew the area, and this was good. After they had agreed to the move, Anthony "guaranteed to them that they could stay there without being molested, until he got some further news from the commander of the department as to what course he should take in regards to them."[42]

Wynkoop's presence helped the meeting go as smoothly as possible, for his previous actions added validity to the safety portion of Anthony's words. More, he attempted to soothe Black Kettle's and Left Hand's fears. "[I]n case he got word from Curtis not to make peace with them," Soule heard Wynkoop say, "he would let them know, so that they could remove out of the way and get to their tribe."[43] Anthony "indorsed Wynkoop's course."

The decision made, Black Kettle and Left Hand returned to their villages and prepared to move to Sand Creek ("Dry Creek" to Tsistsistas).[44] The Hinono'eino' under Left Hand traveled approximately forty miles until they decided where to camp on Sand Creek. According to James M.

Combs, who was not a soldier but was then living at Fort Lyon, Left Hand was sick when he set out for Sand Creek.[45] Little Raven chose not to go to Sand Creek, possibly because he did not trust Wynkoop's replacement. Instead, he and most of the Cloud People selected a camp about twenty miles south of Left Hand.[46]

Black Kettle and the Tsistsistas with him set out for Sand Creek shortly after the Arapahos had moved off, and they reached their destination by November 17.[47] Supposedly they camped about three-quarters of a mile from Left Hand's camp.[48]

With most of the Indians gone from the vicinity of Fort Lyon, and Wynkoop's exit for Kansas imminent, Lieutenant Joseph Cramer began thinking about a letter that Wynkoop had shared with him prior to November 25. It was signed by twenty-seven residents of the Arkansas Valley near Fort Lyon. "In consideration of the danger and risks you have incurred in achieving the rescue of prisoners from [the Cheyennes and Arapahos], the hazard to your own life and the lives [of] your command, we desire to further express our appreciation of your . . . sense of right, and earnestly express the hope that the merit which is justly your due may not go unrewarded in official preferment as well as the gratitude of private citizens."[49]

The letter pleased Cramer, but he felt it needed additional support. That day he drafted a letter that mimicked the affidavit but with greater detail. "[T]he course adopted and carried out by you was the only proper one to pursue, and has sav[ed] the lives of hundreds of men, women, and children, as well as thousands of dollars' worth of property."[50] He praised Wynkoop's efforts to save the captives while mentioning the risk to himself and his command. "For this act alone (even if you had not done more) you should receive the warmest thanks of all men, whether in military or civil life." Cramer felt that the trip with the chiefs to see the governor "was productive of more good to the Indians, and did more to allay the fears of the inhabitants in the Arkansas valley, than all that has been done by all other persons in this portion of the department." Speaking of the area along the Arkansas near Fort Lyon, he wrote, "the people have returned to their houses and farms, and are now living as quietly and peaceably as if the bloody scenes of the past summer had never been enacted." Agent Colley, Soule, Minton, Cannon, and three other officers signed the letter.

Cramer presented it to Anthony the next day. Before forwarding the letter to headquarters, the major wrote: "[I]t is the general opinion here by officers, soldiers, and citizens, that had it not been for the course pursued by Major Wynkoop towards the Cheyenne and Arapahoe Indians, the travel upon the public road must have entirely stopped and the settlers upon the ranches all through the country must have abandoned them or been murdered, as no force of troops sufficient to protect the road and settlements could be got together in this locality."[51]

TWELVE

The White Man's Word

KNOWING THAT HE WOULD SOON DEPART for the East to solicit support for the territory's struggle to combat the ongoing Indian threat, on November 10, 1864, Governor John Evans issued a proclamation of thanks:

> Notwithstanding floods and Indian wars[,] which have temporarily clouded their prosperity, the people of Colorado have abundant cause for gratitude to God for the multiplied blessings and mercies that have crowned the year.
>
> . . . Therefore, I, John Evans, Governor of the Territory of Colorado, do set apart Thursday, the 24th day of November . . . as a day of thanksgiving to God . . . that he will continue to smile upon us[,] and our country.[1]

On the morning of November 16, Evans boarded a coach and set out for Washington, D.C. As the governor did not intend to return to Denver until the legislative assembly convened in January 1865, William Byers praised the man and his mission while taking a shot at his enemies. "No man ever labored more faithfully, more earnestly, or more ably for the good of a people than has Governor Evans for those of Colorado during his administration."[2] Evans was worried about the defense "and the prosecution of the war . . . against the hostile Indians."

Samuel H. Elbert, whom Evans had recommended to become secretary of the territory when he became governor, functioned as acting governor in his absence.[3]

CAPTAIN SILAS SOULE had been upset since Major Scott Anthony had arrived at Fort Lyon and assumed command. On November 25, 1864, Soule presented a formal request to Anthony to be forwarded to General Curtis. He wanted a "leave of absence for thirty days, with permission to apply for an extension. I have been an Officer in the services of the United States for the last three years and have not been off duty or had leave of absence during that time."[4] His request was valid, and Anthony had been pleased that "the veterans who have been on furlough have all returned and that the Company will not in my opinion suffer by his temporary absence."[5] Anthony forwarded the request that day.

On the morning of November 26, Wynkoop, Louise, and their children, Edward Estill and Emily Reveille (three and a half and almost two), with an escort of twenty-eight men, set out for Fort Riley.[6] Although Wynkoop felt that Black Kettle and Left Hand's people would be safe until a military decision had been made in regard to the war, he was nervous for his future. He was also uneasy for the officers who had accompanied him to the Smoky Hill and supported his actions. And well he should have been. As Wynkoop began his journey, Major Benjamin S. Henning, who had temporarily replaced Major General James G. Blunt in command of Fort Riley when he left the district, issued an extensive order addressed to Anthony. Wynkoop "has laid himself liable to arrest and dismissal for absence without leave."[7] Although Henning did not mention Soule or Cramer, he knew that they had gone to the Smoky Hill and were thus "absent without proper authority." But Wynkoop remained the major's main target, and his disdain was evident. Although he tore into Wynkoop's "looseness" while commanding Fort Lyon, he "attribut[ed] it more to ignorance than intentional insult." But that changed in September and October when Wynkoop attempted "to make treaties between a hostile force, and parties that had no authority in the matter." Taking the Indian leaders to Denver (again without orders), and then having the audacity to feed them at Fort Lyon, had sealed the fate of Wynkoop, who had become the perfect scapegoat for the military's failure to end a war with an enemy that refused to give up land they considered theirs.

That same morning Anthony saw an opportunity. He summoned John Smith to his office and asked him to travel to Sand Creek to observe the Indians' attitude and actions and report what he learned—in other words to spy on them. This appealed to Smith, as it would be easy to fulfill the major's request. His twenty-two-year-old son, Jack Smith, currently camped with Black Kettle, as did his second Tsistsista wife, Zerepta, and their three-and-a-half-year-old son, William Gilpin, whom Smith had named after the first territorial governor of Colorado Territory, and his daughter Armama.[8] Smith agreed to the request as long as he had permission to trade. This would allow him to make a profit for himself and Dexter Colley, while providing time to catch up with his family. Smith knew that many of his own race thought of him as little more than a "squaw man." Throughout his adult life he had never walked away from his mixed-race relationships, meaning that although he survived off what he could sell or contribute to the white world, he never denied or turned his back on the Called Out People.

Too many moons had passed to deny that John Smith thrived while walking between two worlds. Based upon his past, he was not afraid to act with violence when threatened. He understood and felt the racial hatred that many in the white world directed toward him for bedding a woman not of his race, much less loving her and calling her wife. Still, his mastery of both languages (and others) gave him money and power, for he knew that he played a key role in the negotiations between the Tsistsistas and the *vi'ho' i*.

Anthony agreed to Smith's request.[9]

For the "trading trip" Smith selected teamster R. Watson Clarke, whom at times Dexter Colley employed, and obtained permission from Anthony to take David Henry Louderback, a member of the First Colorado for three and a half years.[10] Smith wasted little time, and with Clarke and Louderback, he stocked his wagon with goods. Louderback knew of the spying mission, but still Smith's acceptance to report truthfully on the village was questionable, as it would have made his family vulnerable at an uncertain time.

It was still morning when Smith and his companions hitched a mule team and set out for the Sand Creek camp. They did not push the mules and did not arrive at the village until the twenty-seventh. They unpacked the trade goods and stored them in Chief War Bonnet's lodge, set the mules free to graze, and ate dinner.[11]

The Cheyennes that were present at Sand Creek were not just from Black Kettle's band. Beginning upriver were the camp circles of Tsistsistas One-Eye, War Bonnet, White Antelope, Black Kettle, and finally Sand Hill's band on the north (or east side of Dry Creek). Left Hand's Hinono'eino' village was separate from the combined Tsistsista village. There were at least eleven other Tsistsista chiefs present: Little Robe, Little Rock, Yellow Wolf, Standing-in-the-Water, Spotted Crow, Two Thighs, Bear Man, Bear Robe, Yellow Shield, Eagle Head, Whirlwind, and Bear Tongue, and one Hinono'ei chief, Left Hand II.[12] Little Bear (Bear Tongue's son), a close companion of George Bent's, was also in the village.[13] This layout shows the extent and scope of the village. It also shows the separation between the camp circles as they extended along the creek bed. There were about 750 Indians in the village with between 40 and 80 being Hinono'eino'. Using five people per lodge, the combined village circles contained approximately 150 tipis.[14]

That same November 27 evening an unnamed source that had been up-river of Fort Lyon returned to the post and told Anthony that he had seen campfires burning. He also stated that he thought that they were not Cheyennes or Arapahos, as they would have approached the post to talk. Because there had been Kiowa movements in the area, they became the suspects. Indian warriors—especially hostile warriors—presented a threat, so Anthony directed Soule (Company D) to investigate. Lieutenant William Minton (Company K, First New Mexico Volunteers) supported him. It was already dark, and Soule and Minton moved out quickly. Although cautious, Soule pushed the men. Roughly fifteen miles west-northwest of Fort Lyon, his scouts saw riders. Soule thought that the horsemen were Indians but could not confirm this. Not wanting to engage an unknown enemy, he hurried back to the post.[15]

Soule did not have much rest after returning to Fort Lyon, because Anthony had him back in the saddle almost immediately. It was still dark when he led a command of twenty up the Arkansas River. On this predawn morning he did not travel as far as he had the previous evening. At sunrise Soule came upon a mule train. He asked if there were Indians near. The answer was negative. What he heard next surprised him—Chivington approached with the one-hundred daysers. Soule hustled forward, and soon reached Chivington and his command near the watering place at the head of Big Bottom, about twelve miles from Fort Lyon. As soon as Chivington saw Soule, he halted. Soule joined him and they spoke for a few minutes as the command continued toward Fort Lyon. At this time either Chivington or one of his staff, possibly Shoup, asked if the Indians were still at the post. Soule replied "that there were some Indians camped near the fort, below the fort, but they were not dangerous; that they were waiting to hear from General Curtis."[16] Continuing, he said: "They were considered as prisoners." According to Soule, one of the officers stated "that they wouldn't be prisoners after they got there." Soule did not respond to this statement, perhaps because Chivington wanted to know if anyone at Fort Lyon knew of his approach, exactly how far in advance the mule train was, and if he would join him and lead the advance to Fort Lyon. After the conversation ended, Soule dropped back to his command, which marched near the advance of the Third Colorado. Chivington had not shared with Soule why he marched toward Fort Lyon.

Chivington's command of Third and First Colorado Volunteers, along with Soule's patrol, arrived at Fort Lyon that morning. Regardless of how Chivington had approached the post—by straddling the river or using the Santa Fe Stage Route, a road that passed to the north—the only way he could get below the post would be to pass it on the northern side. When Chivington reached the fort, he did not halt. Instead he led the regiment east past the hospital, which was outside the perimeter of the post's parade ground, at the northwestern portion of the fort. The officers' quarters, also outside the parade ground, were due south of the hospital and near the Arkansas.

It was about 10:30 that morning when Anthony, who had heard the approaching column but then realized that it was not halting, hustled across the parade ground and caught up to the regiment as it passed the stage station and corrals, which were at the farthest end of the fort. Chivington's command continued outside the parade ground and near the hill that ran to the river and on which the commissary was located. No mail had reached the post in three weeks. Anthony never reached the head of the column; however, near the stage station he met Second Lieutenant Harry Richmond (Company B, Third Colorado). The meeting was short and took Anthony by surprise. Richmond, after shaking hands and apparently informing the major that Chivington led the regiment, asked: "Where are the Indians?"

"I am damned glad you have come," Anthony replied as he pointed to the northeast, "I have got them over here about twenty-five miles until I could send to Denver for assistance."[17]

For Chivington, time was of the essence. He halted the command about a mile below the commissary and gave directions to set up camp. Without wasting any time, he drafted General Field Order No. 2, which stated: (1) "[N]o officer will be allowed to leave his command . . . and no soldier without a written pass" unless given proper authority by Chivington for the officers and for the soldiers from their company commanders with approval by the battalion commander; (2) No fires were permitted; and (3) "Any person giving the Indians information of the movements of troops will be deemed a spy and shot to death."[18] Chivington stationed pickets around the entire perimeter of Fort Lyon to prevent anyone from entering or exiting the post. Chivington's intent was to prevent any knowledge that he and his army were in the area, for fear that his presence might become known to the Cheyennes and Arapahos.

Although Chivington did not announce his plans immediately, rumors soon spread that the colonel intended to attack the Indians camped at Sand Creek.

Sometime that afternoon, after Chivington's command was in bivouac, Lieutenant Cramer received orders from Anthony that informed him to have Company K ready to move out between seven and eight that evening "with three days' cooked rations."[19] Cramer approached the major in his office. "I was perfectly willing to obey orders," he later said, "but that I did it under protest, for I believed that he [Anthony] directly, and all officers who accompanied Major Wynkoop to the Smoky Hill indirectly, would perjure themselves both as officers and men." Not finished, Cramer stated that he "believed it to be murder to go out and kill those Indians, as I felt that Major Wynkoop's command owed their lives to this same band of Indians."

According to Cramer, Anthony "stated that he had made no pledges that would compromise his honor." Moreover, "the promise he had given the Indians [at the commissary] he did not consider binding, inasmuch as he had not heard from General Curtis or Washington, and that was as far as his argument extended, to let them know when he did hear." Anthony then presented a better reason for the campaign. According to Cramer, Anthony "was opposed to killing those Indians [Black Kettle, White Antelope, Left Hand] if it went no further, but [Chivington's] intention was to go on to the Sioux camp." He meant the war camp farther to the north with the Dog Men, Northern Cheyennes, Arapahos, and Sioux. "[I]f they [Chivington's command] did that," Anthony stated, he "was in favor of killing everything they came to." When Cramer pressed the major in regard to the chief, Anthony said that "Black Kettle would not be killed," because Chivington had promised to spare the chief's life, as well as his friends. Anthony eased his subordinate's fears. "[O]n those grounds," Cramer told Anthony, "I was perfectly willing to go."

As soon as Cramer informed Captain Soule that his Company K was ordered to join the Fort Lyon First Colorado battalion that Anthony would command, the captain became angry. As Soule soon wrote Wynkoop, "I was indignant as you would have been were you here."[20] At this time Anthony took orders from the District of the Upper Arkansas. This meant that Chivington had no control over anyone stationed at Fort Lyon. Soule immediately went to the quarters of Lieutenant James Cannon, who would function as Anthony's adjutant on the expedition, and here he found a number of officers from both the First and Third Colorado. "[I] told them that any man who would take part in the murders," Soule wrote Wynkoop, "knowing the circumstances as we did, was a low lived cowardly son of a bitch."

Soule had to have known that his outrage would have repercussions.

Two of the officers present were Lieutenant George Hardin, who had gone to the Smoky Hill with Wynkoop, and Captain Jay Johnson (Company E, Third Colorado). They immediately set out for Chivington's camp and informed him of the meeting, and in particular Soule's comments. Apparently Hardin had trouble stomaching what Chivington said, for he later approached Anthony in his office with his discharge papers in hand. The lieutenant had no intention in participating in an attack on the Cheyenne and Arapaho villages on Sand Creek. He resigned his commission effective immediately.[21]

Soule's anger over what he had heard grew and became known. Both Cramer and Anthony approached him and did what they could to stop the captain from storming Chivington's camp, and he wisely decided not to appear in person. Still, he drafted a note to the colonel, placed it in a sealed envelope, and gave it to Captain Presley Talbot (Company M, Third Colorado), and asked him to deliver it to Chivington. Talbot did, but Chivington handed it back to him unopened and unread. Talbot returned the unseen words to Soule.[22]

Cramer still had problems dealing with the pending attack on the Sand Creek village. Early that evening he approached Colonel Chivington, who was then in the commissary with Major Jacob Downing and Lieutenant John S. Maynard overseeing the distribution of supplies. He boldly told Chivington of Wynkoop's pledges to Black Kettle and Left Hand and also of Anthony's pledges, "and that it would be murder, in every sense of the word, if he attacked those Indians."[23] Chivington exploded as he stepped toward Cramer and brought his fist close to the lieutenant's face. "Damn any man who sympathizes with Indians," Chivington stated. Cramer attempted to continue, but Chivington cut him off. According to Cramer, the colonel then said "That he had come to kill Indians, and believed it to be honorable to kill Indians under any and all circumstances."

THAT NOVEMBER 28 WYNKOOP was totally unaware of what was happening at his former post. He, his family, and escort were still a long distance from Fort Riley. During the day's march, No-ta-nee, who had gone to Denver with the major, and two other Indians found Wynkoop's caravan on the plains, and told him that Black Kettle had sent them. According to Wynkoop, No-ta-nee informed him: "[T]wo hundred Sioux had left the headwaters of the Smoky Hill, and had gone down to strike the road between where I was and Fort Larned, for the purpose of making war upon the whites."[24] By this time Wynkoop would not have had more than a handful of Cheyenne words in his vocabulary, and No-ta-nee did not speak English. Black Kettle knew this. To ensure that Wynkoop understood the message, the chief must have again turned to Edmund Guerrier or George Bent, both of whom then camped on Sand Creek, to write another letter. Black Kettle's warning was clear: return to Fort Lyon or risk being attacked. Wynkoop understood the chief's words. This message had to have weighed heavily on him, for he had his family with him and he knew of the risk to which he exposed them. Still Wynkoop refused to turn back. He felt that he had a strong enough escort to repulse an attack, and he had an appointment with his future that he could no longer postpone.

BY THAT EVENING OF NOVEMBER 28, Smith had traded for "[t]hree ponies, one mule, and one hundred and four buffalo robes."[25] It had been a good trip and profitable, but what, if anything, Smith would report to Anthony remained an unknown, for he never recorded what his "spy" mission discovered.

FIRST LIGHT ON NOVEMBER 29, 1864, had arrived. Colonel John Chivington, who carried a Spencer carbine, and Colonel George Shoup, the normally clean-shaven but now bristled second in command, sat their horses

Just before dawn on November 29, 1864, Colonel John Chivington (pictured) and Colonel George Shoup, who commanded the Third Colorado Volunteer Cavalry, peered at the rising Cheyenne and Arapaho encampment on Sand Creek. Chivington, who savored his victory over the Confederates in 1862 and still hoped to resurrect his political aspirations, craved a major victory over the Indians. After discussing the mode of attack, he and Shoup rushed back to their troops three-quarters of a mile to the rear.

John M. Chivington. History Colorado. Accession # 89.451.5534, 84.89.1.

and studied the just-awakening village before them. Chivington had savored the victory over the rebels and was certain that his fame would soar after he defeated warring Indians, and that it might even resurrect his failed political aspirations. The combined Tsistsista council chief village circles and Left Hand's small Hinono'ei village spread out before him on the opposite side of the Big Sandy, as Chivington knew they would. Plumes of smoke spiraled from some of the tipis. Dogs yipped and barked as they skittered about the lodges. Quickly he and Shoup discussed the mode of attack, turned their mounts around, and hustled back to the command three-quarters of a mile to the rear.[26]

When Chivington reached his command, he saw that all were bundled against the cold. Some struggled to remain awake, for after marching a good portion of the previous morning they had force-marched throughout the night to reach their destination some thirty-five to forty miles northeast of Fort Lyon. Chivington's command consisted of some seven hundred men, the bulk of whom belonged to the Third Colorado, whose hundred-day enlistment was nearing its end (the regiment organized between August 20 and September 21). Undoubtedly Chivington was aware of the dates, and perhaps it sparked his urgency to strike a decisive victory over the

Cheyennes. Actually, he was aware of yet another date that was of major importance to him. His term of service in the First Colorado had already expired on September 23. Major Jacob Downing's enlistment had expired on October 27.[27] There was an Indian war raging. Certainly General Curtis would not begin removing key officers in Colorado Territory at this critical time, had he been aware of this fact. Still, Chivington knew that it was crucial to score a major victory before the war ended.

Most of his men craved blood, because the Indian threat, although blown out of proportion by the press, was real, and people had died horribly. When the Hungate family's butchered bodies had been displayed in Denver the previous June, it had caused a panic. Chivington knew his command would not fail him. Horses snorted.

Mixed-blood Tsistsista Edmund Guerrier awoke that fatal morn when Tsistsista women outside his lodge, which was within Tsistsista council chief Little Rock's village circle, yelled that a buffalo herd was about to charge through the village. Immediately women inside his tipi looked outside "and called to me to get up . . . 'there were a lot of soldiers coming.'"[28] Suddenly awake, alive, and dressing with the sole hope of saving his life, he slipped out of the tipi and ran toward John Smith's tent. A few sporadic rounds from *vi'ho' i* guns had begun to zing about. He was not the first to reach Smith's lodge.

Tsistsistas that had seen *vi'ho' i* soldiers three-quarters of a mile to a mile south of the village had already run to Smith's tipi, which was set up near War Bonnet, and yelled for him. Smith had heard the approaching horses and had already pulled on pants, a soldier's overcoat, and his hat.[29]

Black Kettle and White Antelope emerged from their lodges; an American flag flew from a lodgepole near Black Kettle's tipi. He had sent letters to soldiers to discuss ending the war, and he, White Antelope, Left Hand and others had met with Wynkoop on a tributary of the Bunch of Trees River (Smoky Hill). They had given him four children, and he and others had traveled to Denver to meet the governor. Since then, his people had done as instructed; they had camped near the soldier fort on the Flint Arrowpoint (Arkansas). When the red-eyed soldier chief told them to move to Sand Creek, they did, and they had remained at peace.[30] This was a mistake! Anthony and Wynkoop had guaranteed their safety—soldiers would not attack them. But the *vi'ho' i* troops seemed to be everywhere Black Kettle looked. He saw his people—old and young—stumbling about in the frigid first light as they frantically looked for an escape from the soldiers' guns.

He knew this was a mistake. Black Kettle yelled for the Called Out People not to run, that they were at peace, that they had been promised protection. The first Tsistsistas that stepped from their lodges ignored the chief's words as they began to zigzag every which way as they scrambled to get out of the village. Dismounted soldiers fired at the Indians, while mounted soldiers moved toward the clusters of tipis from different directions.

Guerrier pushed past the Tsistsistas outside Smith's lodge and entered unannounced. He met Louderback, who stated that they needed to talk to the attacking troops. Smith agreed and stepped outside, followed by Guerrier and Louderback. Tsistsistas implored Smith to go to the troops and see who they were and what they wanted. He agreed and immediately moved toward the creek bed hoping that his "presence and explanation could reconcile matters."[31]

R. W. Clarke followed Smith and the others out of the tipi. When he realized what was about to happen, he grabbed a white skin, jumped onto Smith's wagon, and waved "a flag of truce."[32] Smith began to frantically wave his hands as he and Guerrier hustled toward the soldiers in an attempt to get their attention. Guerrier saw some dismount; he thought that these were "artillerymen and were about to shell the camp." Guerrier yelled words in support of Smith.[33]

But it was not to be. There would be no chance of preventing bloodshed.

Chivington signaled for the attack to begin. Shoup moved his command to the southwest of the village to cut off the pony herd to the west of the encampment. Lieutenant Luther Wilson, with three companies of the First Colorado (C, E, and F), charged across what has since been called Sand Creek to the northeast of the lodges to capture that pony herd. Anthony had followed Wilson across the creek and took a position south of the village, dismounted his men, and awaited orders. Wilson quickly captured the herd and drove it toward the village. He then dismounted his men, moved toward the village from the northeast, and began firing to cut off escape. When soldiers recognized John Smith, they began shooting at him. Lieutenant Cramer heard someone behind him shout: "[S]hoot the damned old son of a bitch," meaning Smith.[34] As soon as Wilson's command opened fire, so did Anthony's three companies.

"I had hardly spoken [to Smith] when they began firing with their rifles and pistols," Guerrier remembered.[35] Understanding what was happening, he did not wait, did not attempt to continue speaking. Instead he turned and ran. "I left the soldier [Louderback] and Smith."

"While I was waving it [the white skin] three or four bullets went thru it," Clarke recalled.[36] "I got down and lay under the wagon, as I had nothing to fight with."

Smith whirled around and sprinted back to his lodge without being hit.[37] As soon as Jack Smith saw soldiers shoot at his father, he ran for his life, knowing that "being a half-breed he had but little hope of being spared."[38]

"I got so mad I swore I would not burn powder," Cramer claimed after soldiers fired at Smith, "and I did not."[39] He noted that "Soule did the same." Right then Cramer must have realized that he had been lied to at Fort Lyon. "It is no use for me to try to tell you how the fight was managed, only I think the Officer in command should be hung, and I know when the truth is known it will cashier him."

"I refused to fire and swore that none but a coward would, for by this time hundreds of women and children were coming towards us and getting on their knees for mercy," Soule wrote "Ned" on December 14.[40] "Kill the sons of bitches," Soule heard Anthony yell. "My Co. was the only one that kept their formation, and we did not fire a shot."

White Antelope walked toward the soldiers to talk to them, to tell them that the People were not at war. Soldiers shot him, and he fell into the creek bed—dying. Later his scalp, nose, and ears were cut off as well as his penis and testicles. According to Luther Wilson the latter were used to create a tobacco pouch. Soldiers directed their fire at Black Kettle, who stood near his lodge with his wife, Medicine Woman Later. He knew that the time for talking was gone, grabbed her arm, and they ran. They did not get far. A round—maybe more—hit her and she fell. The chief saw no life in his wife, and, thinking that she was dead, fled.[41]

About this time One-Eye and his wife hustled from their camp circle and toward the creek, toward the soldiers. Perhaps his goal was to show the talking leaf that stated he was a good Indian, perhaps he wanted to say he was a spy for the red-eyed chief. It mattered not. Shortly after both of them crossed Sand Creek, soldiers murdered them.[42]

George Bent lived with his stepmother's people, all of whom were with Black Kettle's band, including his sister Julia. The alarming sounds woke them. George dressed and rushed from their lodge. After seeing White Antelope fall, he ducked back into the tipi, grabbed his weapons, and chased older warriors running away from the dry creek bed and toward sand hills to the northwest of the village. Here Bent and the others made a stand as soldiers converged on them. But there was no cover. When more troops began shooting at them from the west, they dropped back down to the creek bed. Almost immediately soldiers began firing at them from another direction. Caught in a crossfire, Bent and some of the warriors scrambled for a sandpit that Tsistsistas frantically dug with their hands. As Bent ran toward it he saw Black Kettle digging in what would become known as the third sandpit. He had almost reached the protective ditch when a *vi'ho' i* round tore into his hip. He fell but was able to claw and push himself to one of the holes where nineteen or twenty men, women, and children huddled in fear and slid into it.[43]

Major Scott Anthony would later state: "The banks upon the side of the creek were two or three feet high, in some places as high as ten feet."[44]

Frightened people still in their tipis heard the pounding of shod hooves, the yells and curses of the *vi'ho' i*, and the pop-pop-popping of their guns. Balls ripped into lodges. Naked women screamed in fear as they grabbed their children and wrapped them in blankets. They had to run—run for their lives—but to where? Soldiers were to the west, to the east, to the south. Tsistsista and Hinono'ei men, women, and children who could flee ran to the northwest and north.

Soldiers moved to cut off escape and to confine the village.

A Tsistsista girl known as Mo-nahs-e-tah (phonetic spelling of her name), the daughter of Little Rock and Skunk Woman, was about fifteen in 1864.[45] Although she had no clue of what her future would entail, she knew on this freezing dawn that she needed to run for her life, that she needed to lead her siblings to safety, for the *vi'ho' i* had come to kill. For a girl who had already reached puberty but not her first marriage, she was way beyond her years. She grabbed the hands of her younger brother Little Plover and sister Playing Crane (about eight). Another brother Hawk (about ten) most likely ran with her. Skunk Woman did not attempt to escape with her. Instead, she remained behind with her youngest child, Short Teeth, whom she held, as Little Rock attempted to help those of the People that followed his lead to survive the attack. Mo-nahs-e-tah and her siblings joined others that scrambled up the mostly dry creek bed as fast as possible. They fled through an area where perhaps 135 of her people died. After covering over a mile, it looked as if they might escape, but *vi'ho' i* soldiers had reached the top of the bluffs to the west of the ever-growing battleground and shot at fleeing Tsistsistas. A soldier's bullet struck Mo-nahs-e-tah in the back of her leg below the knee, breaking a bone. She fell, and could not get up. Her siblings, most likely aided by an adult, dragged her to a large sand pit that her brethren dug. Here she curled up in pain with her brothers and sister, not knowing if she would see another dawn.[46]

In the meantime, Chivington, with the remainder of his command, had reached the riverbed below the village and behind Anthony's battalion. Chivington halted, dismounted the troops with him, and ordered them to remove their overcoats. He then yelled for them to remember the women and children the Indians had raped and murdered on the Platte.[47]

Chivington ordered his command to remount and began firing through and over the heads of Anthony's men. Warriors scrambled to confront the soldiers. Perhaps one hundred warriors confronted the *vi'ho' i*, maybe more. "About 200 adult or fighting age men were present."[48] The assault quickly dissolved into unorganized and scattered firefights wherever warriors made stands. Because the soldiers in the Third had the absolute minimum of training, they regressed into an uncontrolled mob, and as Cramer later testified, with "every one on his own hook, and shots flying between our own ranks."[49]

Jack Smith stopped running after getting a mile from the camp. He turned around and walked back to his father's lodge. Soldiers were all about, but they did not harm him. John Smith was inside, as were Zerepta and their children, when he slipped quietly inside and sat down.[50]

The soldiers had failed to cut off escape to the north. Some Indians found the gap and fled northward toward a large warring Tsistsista–Dog Man–Hinono'ei–Lakota village on the Smoky Hill. There were three escape routes for the Tsistsistas and Hinono'eino'. The first was from the northwestern portion of the extended village; the second was from roughly the center of the village, then turned north close to the first sand pit that the People dug with their hands near the trickle of the creek's water flow; and the third was near Left Hand and Sand Creek's camps on the eastern side of the encampment. These women, children, old ones, and men suddenly turned to the north and away from the bluffs—most likely because *vi'ho' i* gunfire from the west became too intense to continue skirting the creek. Still others ran past the third sand pit as they followed Sand Creek upriver. Troops followed them for perhaps ten miles attempting to kill everyone they came upon.[51]

Guerrier was one of the lucky ones. At the beginning of the assault he raced north and escaped the carnage unhurt. . . . After running five miles, Guerrier "met an Indian woman driving a herd of ponies."[52] She was White Antelope's daughter, and his cousin. She gave him one of her ten to fifteen horses to ride, and he traveled to the Smoky Hill with her. Others would follow as the day progressed.

As First and Third Colorado Volunteers began to seize the village, the mode of fighting changed, and the battle quickly spun hideously out of control. Five Indian women exposed their breasts to troops to show their sex as they begged for mercy. Soldiers shot them down. Other women, hiding in a hole, sent a little girl toward the soldiers with a white flag. She only walked a few steps before soldiers murdered her.[53]

It would get worse.

As Chivington's command secured the village, troops moved about shooting at anything that moved. Pent-up fear and hatred consumed the whites with a blood lust. Small children were used for target practice, and an unborn child was cut from its dead mother's body and scalped.[54]

Charley Bent was perhaps able reach the fighting at the sand pits above the village. But he knew that this was a lost cause without any chance of escape. Wounded, he worked his way back to the camp. Here he luckily encountered Lieutenant Mariano Autobee (Company H, Third Colorado) and his father, Charles, who was the son of a French Canadian trapper. Although fifty-two years old, Charles served as a guide for Chivington, most likely because of the August 12 Arapaho raid that ran off nineteen of his horses. In 1853 Charles Autobee moved to the mouth of the Huerfano River, where he ranched, farmed, and traded. During these years, Mariano Autobee, a mixed-blood white and Hispanic who was born in 1837 to Serafina Avila, got along with all the Indian tribes in the area, and had an especially good relationship with the Tsistsistas. The People called Mariano "Manni." This connection was key to Charley Bent's survival, as George and Charley knew them well.[55]

The question became how to keep Charley Bent away from the Third Colorado, and more important, how to keep him alive. Word that Captain Silas Soule had ordered Company D not to fire on the Indians had spread. Neither Lieutenant Mariano Autobee nor Charley Bent knew him, but he presented a chance for William's youngest son to survive the ongoing bloodbath.

The shooting in the village decreased as soldiers set out in pursuit of the fleeing Indians. The chasing and killing now extended fifteen miles above the village. Most of the Cheyennes and Arapahos were children and elderly, many were women, and some were wounded. Although fright drove them, many could not outrun the soldiers or their rage. As they did elsewhere

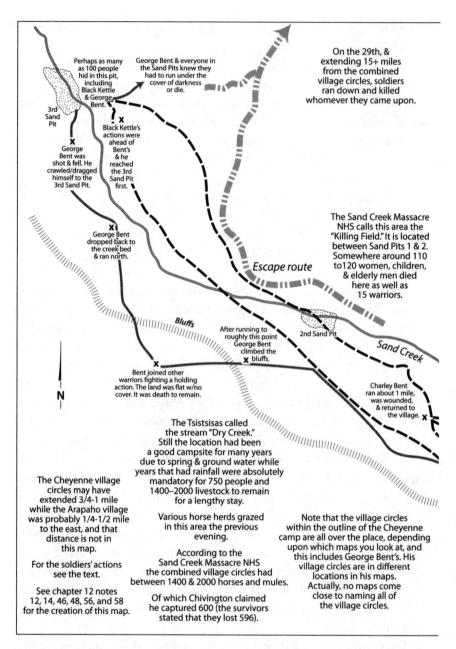

Perhaps as many as 100 people hid in this pit, including Black Kettle & George Bent.

3rd Sand Pit

X
George Bent was shot & fell. He crawled/dragged himself to the 3rd Sand Pit.

George Bent & everyone in the Sand Pits knew they had to run under the cover of darkness or die.

X
Black Kettle's actions were ahead of Bent's & he reached the 3rd Sand Pit first.

On the 29th, & extending 15+ miles from the combined village circles, soldiers ran down and killed whomever they came upon.

X
George Bent dropped back to the creek bed & ran north.

The Sand Creek Massacre NHS calls this area the "Killing Field." It is located between Sand Pits 1 & 2. Somewhere around 110 to120 women, children, & elderly men died here as well as 15 warriors.

Escape route

Bluffs

After running to roughly this point George Bent climbed the **X** bluffs.

2nd Sand Pit

Sand Creek

X
Bent joined other warriors fighting a holding action. The land was flat w/no cover. It was death to remain.

Charley Bent ran about 1 mile, was wounded, & returned to the village. **X**

N

The Tsistsisas called the stream "Dry Creek." Still the location had been a good campsite for many years due to spring & ground water while years that had rainfall were absolutely mandatory for 750 people and 1400–2000 livestock to remain for a lengthy stay.

The Cheyenne village circles may have extended 3/4-1 mile while the Arapaho village was probably 1/4-1/2 mile to the east, and that distance is not in this map.

For the soldiers' actions see the text.

See chapter 12 notes 12, 14, 46, 48, 56, and 58 for the creation of this map.

Various horse herds grazed in this area the previous evening.

According to the Sand Creek Massacre NHS the combined village circles had between 1400 & 2000 horses and mules.

Of which Chivington claimed he captured 600 (the survivors stated that they lost 596).

Note that the village circles within the outline of the Cheyenne camp are all over the place, depending upon which maps you look at, and this includes George Bent's. His village circles are in different locations in his maps. Actually, no maps come close to naming all of the village circles.

Sand Creek village, three sand pits, and the escape routes on November 29, 1864.
Map by Bill Nelson

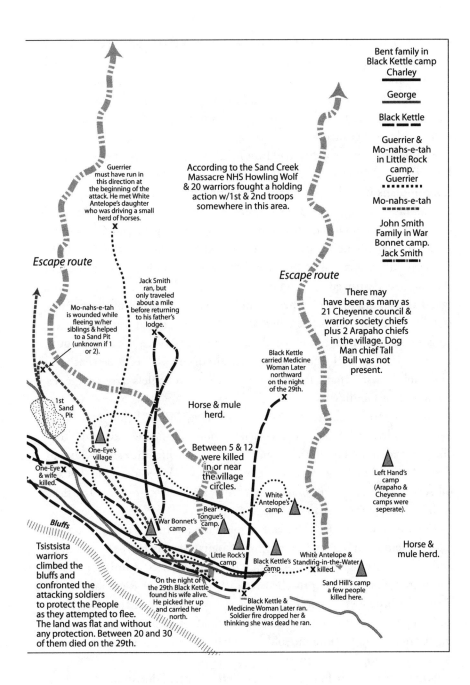

Bent family in
Black Kettle camp
Charley
━━━━━━━━
George
━━━━━━━━
Black Kettle
▄▄▄ ▄▄▄ ▄▄▄

Guerrier &
Mo-nahs-e-tah
in Little Rock
camp.
Guerrier
••••••••••
Mo-nahs-e-tah
▄▄▄ ▄▄▄ ▄▄▄

John Smith
Family in War
Bonnet camp.
Jack Smith
▄▪▄▪▄▪▄▪

Guerrier
must have run in
this direction at
the beginning of the
attack. He met White
Antelope's daughter
who was driving a small
herd of horses.
X

According to the Sand Creek
Massacre NHS Howling Wolf
& 20 warriors fought a holding
action w/1st & 2nd troops
somewhere in this area.

Escape route

Escape route

There may
have been as many as
21 Cheyenne council &
warrior society chiefs
plus 2 Arapaho chiefs
in the village. Dog
Man chief Tall
Bull was not
present.

Jack Smith
ran, but
only traveled
about a mile
before returning
to his father's
lodge.
X

Mo-nahs-e-tah
is wounded while
fleeing w/her
siblings & helped
to a Sand Pit
(unknown if 1
or 2).

X

Black Kettle
carried Medicine
Woman Later
northward
on the night
of the 29th.
X

1st
Sand
Pit

One-Eye's
village

Horse & mule
herd.

Between 5 & 12
were killed
in or near
the village
circles.

White
Antelope's
camp.

Left Hand's
camp
(Arapaho &
Cheyenne
camps were
seperate).

One-Eye
& wife
killed.
X

Bluffs

Bear
Tongue's
camp.

War Bonnet's
camp

Little Rock's
camp

Black Kettle's
camp

White Antelope &
Standing-in-the-Water
X killed.

Horse &
mule herd.

Tsistsista
warriors
climbed the
bluffs and
confronted the
attacking soldiers
to protect the People
as they attempted to flee.
The land was flat and without
any protection. Between 20 and 30
of them died on the 29th.

On the night of
the 29th Black Kettle
found his wife alive.
He picked her up
and carried her
north.

Sand Hill's camp
a few people
killed here.

Black Kettle &
Medicine Woman Later ran.
Soldier fire dropped her &
thinking she was dead he ran.

215

on the bloody field, troopers killed every Indian they came upon and cut their bodies to pieces.[56] The soldiers did not view their actions as heinous. Raiding Indians had butchered friends and neighbors, innocent people, hacking their bodies beyond recognition the previous spring and summer. Motivated by the horrific events, along with a pent-up fear, the soldiers killed with a vengeance.

Just hours after the attack had begun, Chivington had control of the village. The battle now over, except for sporadic firefights where troops came upon Indians who did not escape, the action changed into a mop-up operation, as Chivington and his officers took into account what they had captured. A systematic destruction of the village began, and Chivington began to brag about his victory. He claimed between 500 and 600 Indians were killed, that he had captured 550 ponies, mules, and horses, and that he had destroyed all the lodges and Indian belongings except those taken as trophies of war.[57] There would be many estimates of the number of Cheyennes and Arapahos killed at Sand Creek, and all were well below Chivington's inflated count. Modern calculations place the death count at approximately 230 "men, women, children," of which 75 percent were noncombatants.[58] That left perhaps 67 warriors and chiefs dying while defending their families.

Soldiers moved about the village destroying Indian belongings. Tipis became individual funeral pyres; black smoke funneling skyward. They checked Indian bodies on the ground—if they saw life, they snuffed it out. Then the real butchery came into play. Soldiers stripped the dead, hacked off sexual organs, and decorated themselves with their trophies. The dead were scalped, some as many as five or more times.[59]

But this did not mark the end of the bloodbath. "[D]uring the massacre," Lieutenant James Olney (First Colorado) watched "three squaws and five children, prisoners in charge of some soldiers [who] were being conducted along . . . approached by Lieutenant Harry Richmond." The lieutenant ordered the men to halt. According to Olney, Richmond "killed and scalped the three women and the five children while they were screaming for mercy [and] while the soldiers in whose charge these prisoners were shrank back, apparently aghast."[60]

Still the warriors held out in the sand pits they had dug in the creek bed.

Roughly five hours after the initial attack began, Anthony received orders to move back on the road toward Fort Lyon. At this time he knew that two mixed-blood Cheyennes had surrendered to the soldiers—Charley Bent and Jack Smith. Smith had recently ridden into Fort Lyon and told the major "that a party of Indians were going to make an attack on the settlements down in the vicinity of the mouth of Walnut creek."[61] Before his departure time, Anthony approached Chivington. "[I] told him that Jack Smith was a man he might make very useful to him," Anthony said. "[T]hat he could be made a good guide or scout for us." He then shared his concern, that "unless you give your men to understand that you want the man saved, he is going to be killed."

"I have given my instructions; have told my men not to take any prisoners," Chivington said. "I have no further instructions to give." Knowing that Smith spoke Cheyenne and English, Anthony pushed for his life, but all he did was anger Chivington. "I said at the start that I did not want any prisoners taken," the colonel stated, "and I have no further instructions to give."

Between noon and one on the twenty-ninth Soule approached Anthony and requested additional orders and was directed to take Company D and "put them on guard over some wounded men and property belonging to our men and officers."[62] Anthony also informed him that he would accompany a train back to Fort Lyon. This took Soule and his men out of the fight, which was still ongoing.

Sometime after his meeting with Anthony, Soule received Charley Bent from Lieutenant Autobee. Not knowing of Anthony's earlier interchange with Chivington, around two in the afternoon Soule approached the colonel. "I asked him if I could send Colonel Bent's son Charles, who was taken prisoner with Jack Smith, to his home."[63] Chivington replied "that his (Bent's) brother Robert did not care about having him back." But then he surprised Soule, and "said he had no objections." Colonel George Shoup was present or nearby as he heard Chivington state that "he would allow the half-breed Bent to return to his father."[64]

Soule's request could not have been better timed, as he and Company D moved out with Anthony "between two and three o'clock" that day.

Chivington's reaction to Soule's request was strange, when roughly an hour previous he had told Anthony he did not want any captives taken. Most likely he was so disgusted with Soule for refusing to fire his weapons, he "yessed" the captain simply to get him out of his sight.[65] In his second official report on the Sand Creek attack, he wrote: "I cannot conclude this report without saying that the conduct of Capt. Silas S. Soule, Company D,

George L. Shoup became colonel of the Third Colorado Volunteer Cavalry on September 21, 1864, when he was promoted from First Lieutenant in the First Colorado Volunteer Cavalry. His spectacular jump in rank was due to Colonel John Chivington's view of his capabilities.

George L. Shoup. Photograph by George D. Wakely. History Colorado. Accession # 10031856.

First Cavalry of Colorado, was at least ill-advised, he saying that he thanked God that he had killed no Indians, and like expressions, proving him more in sympathy with those Indians than with the whites."[66]

IN LATE NOVEMBER, WYNKOOP, who had no idea of what had happened after he departed Fort Lyon, approached Fort Dodge, Kansas. When two overland coaches appeared in the distance, he halted his march, as he wanted to alleviate their fears. The passengers included three officers and their wives, Walter Stickney, and Robert L. Lambert and his wife. "I have just completed a treaty with [the Cheyennes], and have a good understanding," Wynkoop supposedly said. "If you see any of them, don't fire on them; allow them to come into your camp, for they are perfectly friendly."[67] Lambert told Wynkoop that they were headed for Fort Union in New Mexico Territory, where he had been ten days earlier. "[As] no trouble had been anticipated," he said, the passengers had not prepared to fight off an attack.

Almost upon Wynkoop's arrival at Fort Riley, Kansas, Major General Curtis wrote Major Henning, who still commanded the post. After complementing him, Curtis got right to his points. "The treaty operations at

Lyon greatly embarrass matters, and I hope you have disposed of Major Wynkoop and directed a change for the better."[68] He then followed with words that hinted at extermination. "Indians must be kept at arm's length. Even if they come in as prisoners of war we are not obliged to receive them, or feed them, or allow them inside the forts. The old and infirm and lazy will come in, while the wicked are allowed to go on with their devilment." Apparently Curtis liked what he had heard about Left Hand, for he again picked on him to highlight the military view of a *good Indian*. Regardless of Black Kettle's efforts he was often referred to as a chief that could not control his warriors. "I suppose Left Hand and some of the Indians who have been in may be sincere, but they must evince their fidelity by strong proofs, such as turning over the culprits, arms, horses, &c., and becoming the foes of hostile bands, ready and willing to fight them." His expectations were beyond the Cheyenne and Arapaho culture, regardless of what Black Kettle, Bull Bear, and Neva supposedly agreed to at the Camp Weld council, and especially now, as the chiefs *had been* speaking for all of the people who had just lost all their belongings and homes.

THIRTEEN

Vengeance and Outrage

SOLDIERS KEPT BLACK KETTLE, George Bent, and those with them in the hand-dug pits, pinned down for hours.[1] When darkness finally arrived, Black Kettle slipped from the breastworks and worked his way back to where he had left Medicine Woman Later. He expected to find her dead—but miraculously she was still alive. Although she had been shot nine times, she had not been scalped. He picked her up onto his back and vanished into the night.[2]

The night of November 29 was extremely cold. The unwounded Tsistsistas who huddled in the sand pits did what they could to keep the children and injured from freezing to death. There was not enough clothing to go around and many were nearly naked. In an attempt to cover those still exposed to the elements, they pulled grass from the riverbed and used it as makeshift blankets. When the soldiers had pulled back, the Tsistsistas created small fires but these were not large enough to warm anyone. All was not in vain, for even though everyone suffered, many continued to live.

Although wounded in the hip, George Bent could walk. He and those with him knew that they could not remain in the sand pits, that they had to brave the frigid weather. For any chance of survival they had to slip by the soldiers and set out for the Tsistsista village in the Big Timbers near the head of the Smoky Hill. Joining others—half of whom were wounded—they stumbled and limped through the black night, fearful of being fallen upon and killed. The refugees moved slowly as they felt their way from the bloody ground. An urgency fueled their efforts, and as George Bent recalled: "[W]e had to dread the pursuit which would probably begin as soon as the coming of day made it possible for the troops to follow our trail, and we knew that if the troops overtook us on the open plain, barely a handful of us could hope to escape."[3] They were lucky, for the soldiers did not follow as they had during the previous day.

A handful of warriors had escaped on horseback at the beginning of the attack. Pushing their mounts, they reached the first of the camps along the Smoky Hill as night fell on the twenty-ninth. Their news spread quickly, and soon many warriors were mounted and riding toward Sand Creek leading horses carrying clothing, food, and buffalo robes. They found the strung-out exodus of Tsistsistas shortly after first light on the thirtieth and clothed, fed, and got everyone mounted and moving to the north-northeast as quickly as possible.

ON THE MORNING OF NOVEMBER 30, Corporal Amos C. Miksch (Company E, First Colorado) wandered about the battlefield. What he saw affected him, and he remembered it in vivid detail. "I saw a little boy covered up among the Indians in a trench, still alive," he stated.[4] He then "saw a major in the 3d regiment take out his pistol and blow off the top of his head." Miksch continued to move about, and as he did, he "saw some men unjointing fingers to get rings off, and cutting off ears to get silver ornaments." He saw the same major from the Third with a group of soldiers, and watched as they dug up "bodies that had been buried in the night to scalp them and take off ornaments." Later he came upon "a squaw with her head smashed in before she was killed."

That morning Jack Smith remained a prisoner in his father's tipi. He was not alone, for his father and stepmother sat with him, as did the mixed-blood African scout Jim Beckwourth, and a number of soldiers. A trooper called for "Uncle John," as the elder Smith was sometimes known. When he stepped from the lodge, the soldier escorted him to see Chivington. "I am sorry to tell you," the soldier said as they walked, "but they are going to kill your son Jack."[5] Smith did not stop as he knew that there was nothing he could do. Jack stepped out of the tipi after his father left and faced a gathering of Thirdsters. One held a cocked carbine, which he pointed at him. While Smith and his escort approached Chivington, the soldiers questioned

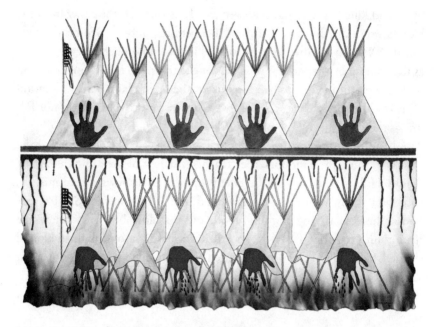

Southern Cheyenne chief Gordon Yellowman is a fifth-generation Sand Creek Massacre descendant. His contemporary painting *Sand Creek* symbolically represents the serenity of the Cheyenne and Arapaho village on the Big Sandy, Colorado Territory, before November 29, 1864, when they thought they had been removed from the current war and were under the protection of the U.S. military, as well as the destruction and butchery that has remained with them throughout time. I met Gordon in 1999 at Fort Larned, Kansas, when both of us spoke at a Fort Larned Old Guard event. It was here that I saw his painting for the first time. I loved it then, and I still love it.

Sand Creek © *Gordon Yellowman, 1996. Reproduced with permission of the artist.*

Jack. Without warning, the soldier with the cocked carbine squeezed the trigger, "the ball passing through Smith's chest, and killing him immediately."[6] Beckwourth disagreed. He later stated under oath that "a pistol [was] fired through [an] opening [previously cut out of the tipi] and the bullet entered below his right breast. He sprung forward and fell dead."[7]

Smith knew he was in a precarious position and kept his mouth shut. But he was not the only one who realized this. "When John Smith's son was shot the regular soldiers belonging to Fort Lyon took Smith, Lauderbeck [*sic*] and myself under their protection," Clarke wrote. "They said Chivington's men would kill us too."[8]

Soon after, Shoup leaped onto a wagon and spoke with his troops, "threatening punishment on any one molesting anything in [Smith's] lodge."[9] The colonel stated that the murder was "accidental."

Sergeant Morse Coffin (Company D, Third Colorado) wrote a detailed memoir. Although he took part in scalping the dead, he shared what he knew. "During the day two of the boys of company D were driving in a small herd of ponies, and following with them was a squaw carrying a child," Coffin wrote. "They encountered Col. Shoup, who told them 'take no prisoners,' or 'we take no prisoner;' or words similar. The squaw seemed to understand the import of the words, and without saying a word turned her back to the boys, who shot them both; as they considered the Colonel's words equal to an order to kill them."[10]

Coffin was honest and open with his view. "I was prepared to remove any Indian's top knot found intact. I know this is not to the credit of myself and others who did it: but it is the truth, and I am disposed to shoulder my share of it."

The battle had ended the previous day, and was long over, but what had happened on that bloody ground would live forever. While Joseph Cramer pointed his finger at officers, accusing at least two of them of atrocities, Soule made it clear what he saw and thought: "White Antelope, War Bonnet and . . . others had Ears and Privates cut off. Squaws['] snatches were cut out for trophies. You would think it impossible for white men to butcher and mutilate human beings as they did there."[11]

CHIVINGTON WAS AWARE that there was an aggressive Indian village on the Republican River, but, contrary to what he had told Major Anthony, he did not move to attack it. As Colonel George Shoup reported, the officers under his command "will obey orders and go to the Smoky Hill and Republican, [if] the colonel commanding . . . so order[s]."[12] He then shared "that an expedition to the above named streams at present must fail" as the command's "horses are worn out, and in an unserviceable condition; most of the animals would fail on the first forced march."

Although Chivington retreated toward the Arkansas on the morning of December 1, he was still in attack mode. Agent Colley had sent him a message that revealed Little Raven's current location.[13]

Major Anthony, with Soule and Charley Bent, reached Fort Lyon with the wounded and dead on December 2. On that day Anthony reported,

"[I] shall immediately rejoin Colonel Chivington's brigade, which is now moving toward the Arapahoe camp, on the Arkansas."[14] Anthony still thought that Chivington's objective was the warring Indians on the Smoky Hill, and was in agreement with what he thought were Chivington's objectives.

When Left Hand moved to Sand Creek, Little Raven initially moved in that direction but changed his mind and returned to the Arkansas. He then moved downriver. Although not yet, many whites would soon disrespect Little Raven as little more than a despot who was more interested in his wives than anything else. They would never attempt to understand him, much less realize that he was not a buffoon—nor was he ever close to being one. Surely his wives were important to him, but he never let concern for them blind him to what he had to do to secure the survival of his people.

EDMUND GUERRIER WAS ALREADY in the village at the Bunch of Timbers/Big Timbers when George Bent and those with him arrived at nightfall on the thirtieth.[15] "As we rode into that camp there was a terrible scene," Bent remembered. "Everyone was crying, even the warriors and the women and children screaming and wailing. Nearly everyone present had lost some relations or friends, and many of them in their grief were gashing themselves with their knives until the blood flowed in streams."[16]

Bent initially saw his people's anger directed at Black Kettle, as they blamed him for the deaths and soldier attack, but then saw it subside when those on the Smoky Hill learned what had happened.

The Tsistsista refugees remained in the Smoky Hill village for a number of days while people healed and mourned. Everyone was angry and wanted revenge, and a war pipe was sent to the Hinono'ei and Brûlé Lakota camps on the Solomon River. Before everyone moved north to the Sioux village, Black Kettle learned that this village planned to join a large war village on the Republican. Even though he, and those who still followed his lead, were bitter over the total loss of their belongings and the murder of their friends and family, they refused to do this. Black Kettle's followers moved south, but before they did, the People in the Smoky Hill village gave them horses and clothing.

At this time George Bent, Guerrier, and the fifteen-year-old Howling Wolf, who had survived the massacre and who had also received horses from friends, set out for William Bent's ranch. The three moved slowly, Bent still suffering from his wound. As they passed Fort Lyon and approached the Bent trading post, they saw a soldier camp nearby. When a nervous Guerrier decided to surrender, Bent tried to talk him out of it but failed. Luckily for Guerrier, he was not mistreated. Later, Guerrier met with Major Anthony at Fort Lyon and spoke about the villages in the north, but according to Bent, he "did not give him any information that was of value."[17] While at Fort Lyon, Guerrier spent time with Colley, and according to the agent he shared the following with him: "Black Kettle . . . laughed at him when he went out," that is, when he ran for his life at Sand Creek. Black Kettle told Guerrier, "You are an old tool; you ought to have stood and been shot down like the rest of us." Harsh words for a young man who was trying to find his identity with half of his lifeblood.

In the meantime Bent and Howling Wolf reached his father's place undetected. He relaxed for almost a week as his wound healed. It was still December when he and Howling Wolf set out for the war camp in the north.

Left Hand (Niwot) had been one of the major players in the peace negotiations with the white man over the years. He could make his views known without an interpreter, although he often used one. All of this had ended on November 29, 1864, when Chivington's volunteers attacked the extended Tsistsista village and his Hinono'ei camp on Sand Creek. Soldier bullets had wounded him, but his people refused to leave him when they fled and carried him to safety. Despite all the Cloud People's efforts to save his life, Left Hand would not survive his wounds. He died at an unknown location—perhaps near the Smoky Hill.[18] Still, their efforts had not been in vain, for they had protected their chieftain's body from horrific sexual mutilation, which meant that he would have an afterlife.

The white men who had attacked the combined Sand Creek villages had no clue that Left Hand had suffered wounds that would end his life. They believed that they had killed Black Kettle, a major goal. They had not, even though Chivington bragged that the most famous Cheyenne was dead. Conversely, Chivington's troops had fired the deadly rounds that would end Left Hand's life, but neither the colonel nor his men claimed a score.

Strange how this played out—a kill was claimed when it never happened, and at the same time a kill that happened was never claimed.

What does this say about the accuracy of military reports?

BY DECEMBER 7, 1864, the victorious John Chivington was back in Denver. He still had no clue that his troops had fatally wounded Left Hand or that Black Kettle had escaped unwounded. Neither did General Curtis in Kansas, for upon the colonel's arrival he wired his initial report, which stated five hundred warring Indians died. He claimed he saw a two- or three-day-old scalp, "and I could mention many more things to show how these Indians, who have been drawing government rations at Fort Lyon, are and have been acting."[19]

Five hundred. In other words, a glorious victory.

On the seventh, Chivington wired John Evans, who then stayed at the National Hotel in Washington, D.C. "Had fight with Cheyennes forty miles north of Lyon. I lost 9 killed and 38 wounded. Killed 500 Indians; destroyed 130 lodges; took 500 mules and ponies. Marched 300 miles in ten days; snow two feet deep for 100 miles."[20] He added a little braggadocio before closing: "Am still after them."

Byers had this to say about Chivington: "This distinguished Colorado soldier . . . is looking fine as usual, though a little fiercer than formerly, and no wonder. Let cowardly snakes and fault-finders carp and slander as they will, the Colonel, as a commander, is a credit to Colorado and the West."[21]

Chivington's bragging was that and no more. His Indian campaigns were over and he was no longer "still after them." He had his victory, *had killed* the leader of the entire Cheyenne nation, and had destroyed his village. All the whites had heard of this chief's name. Still, he was not Bull Bear, he was not Tall Bull, nor was he Stone Forehead (the mystic and perhaps the most powerful Tsistsista on the plains), nor Roman Nose (the Northern Tsistsista war leader who would soon move south to the central plains). Still, Chivington had killed *the most infamous* Cheyenne on the plains, the *evil chief* known as Black Kettle. He never bothered to say that he knew his target was under the protection of the U.S. military, and more important, that this segment of the Upper Arkansas Cheyennes and Arapahos had done everything possible to avoid war.

While Chivington played up his "Indian-fighter" image, Major Henning, who still commanded the District of the Upper Arkansas but now filled in for Colonel James Ford, was in line with this thought. However, much of the information he operated from was totally outdated. In his December 7 report to Curtis (and before he was privy to Chivington's November 29 report) he thought that Little Raven and Left Hand's bands still lived near Fort Lyon and received food per Wynkoop's directive. He wanted them detained by Anthony and sent to Fort Riley or Fort Leavenworth. He then moved to another name that was recognized on the frontier, George Bent. After sharing some of his background—some accurate and some not—he hinted at an unstated but clear view: "George Bent . . . is now foremost in leading those wild tribes in their depredations. He is a noted rebel and ought to have been killed long ago."[22]

That December, Dog Men, Tsistsistas, their Lakota allies, and Hinono'eino' (eighty lodges from the north) came together and created a huge village near the Republican River. The war had been one to protect loved ones and to retain the Tsistsista and Hinono'ei homeland. It still was, but now it was also one of vengeance—similar to tribal warfare against the Pawnees. They had one goal: kill whites. Tall Bull and Bull Bear were in the village, as were Oglala chief Pawnee Killer and Brûlé chief Spotted Tail. George and Charley Bent were also present. Charley had become a full Tsistsista shortly after he quit school and returned to his homeland. George had preferred the Confederacy over the whites who stole his people's land, but he had vacillated. He no longer did. Although he had been living with Black Kettle's band well before the tragedy, he was now 100 percent Tsistsista. He dressed as his people did (alas, his hair braids were short, which made him stand out), and he would fight as they did. It was war to the death—no counting coups. Kill! For that was the only way to survive.[23]

War parties began targeting wagon trains and stations along the Platte; some of the raids were sanctioned, while others led by young hotheads were not. The soldier societies had their hands full preventing unauthorized raids. A plan of deception was beginning to take shape, and secrecy was of major importance.

Captain Silas Soule stewed after he returned to Fort Lyon with Anthony. By mid-December, taking care of Company D's paperwork dominated his time.[24] Twice he had requested to be removed from command of Company

D, once in October and again in November. Indeed, his three years of enlistment had passed, and his thoughts constantly drifted to seeing his mother and family, as soon as he was no longer was an officer in the First Colorado. Even though his term of enlistment had expired on September 17, 1864, he continued to perform his duties and deal with paperwork that mustered out soldiers whose enrollment had also ended (a task any clerk could have performed).[25] Although Cramer was still present at the fort, as were some of the others who had taken part in the peace mission the previous September, Soule found himself a lonely man, especially since Wynkoop was long gone—disgraced for attempting to end a war.

At this time Wynkoop passed his time at Fort Riley with nothing to do. The evidence damning his actions in September had made him a "persona non grata," a forgotten exile that the military shunned. If he had any doubt of what his future held, he no longer did. Wynkoop had no intention of being drummed out of the service without at least presenting his case. He wrote Curtis and requested permission to meet with him. At first the general ignored the request, but then consented to an interview. In late December Wynkoop traveled to Fort Leavenworth to meet with the commanding general. Curtis listened and looked at Wynkoop's documentation. Soule and Cramer's letters, the Arkansas Valley settlers' letter, and the petition that Cramer created. Still Curtis seemed distant, closed off. Wynkoop refused to accept his fate. As in the past, his speaking capability, combined with his demands that Chivington be punished for the murder of innocent people, won out. Surprisingly Curtis agreed. The general felt that Wynkoop's mistake had been in taking the Cheyenne and Arapaho leaders to Evans—that the major should have brought them to him. Suddenly a man who had faced being cashiered out of the military found himself ordered back to Fort Riley to assume command. But he was not totally exonerated, for Curtis informed him that the military would investigate his actions.[26]

Surprisingly, William Byers was mum about Chivington's victory. Most likely this was because the "Laws of the United States" dominated the front page, which made his Indian wars news sporadic. Many days passed after Chivington's arrival in the city before Byers began to publish pieces of the victory. On the seventeenth he finally printed an article on the battle based upon Chivington's two battle reports. Although it still erroneously listed Black Kettle's death, he added Left Hand's demise.[27]

On the twenty-second, Chivington met ten companies of the Third Colorado when it reached Denver. With the First Colorado band leading the way, "Colonels Chivington and Shoup, Lieut. Col. Bowen and Major Sayr, the rank and file of the 'bloody Thirdsters' made a most imposing procession" as they triumphantly marched through the streets of the city.[28] Men and women cheered the returning heroes.

The following day Byers printed in his afternoon daily: "Our streets, hotels, saloons and stores to-day were thronged with strangers, chiefly 'Indian killers.' A high old time there was last night, around!"[29] More important, on that day the *News* reported that an effort was in progress to muster out and pay the Third Colorado, that was "to obtain proper authority that will secure the immediate discharge and prompt payment of this regiment, which has rendered so efficient service."[30] But this was easier said than done, as Captain Loudon Mullin pointed out to Byers on the twentieth. "While I am not anxious to perform duties belonging to another officer, I am ever ready and willing to perform such duties as pertain to my office; and as Mustering and Disbursing officer of this District, I am ready any minute to muster out the Third regiment on presentation of their papers, as I have full authority to do."[31] Although mustering out in the coming days would prove easy, Mullin pointed out that payment of monies owed the troops would not.

On December 24 Lieutenant Harry Richmond, who arrived with his regiment on the twenty-second, trod the boards at the Denver Theatre when he appeared in *Orphan of Geneva*.[32] The Sand Creek hero only had a few rehearsals to practice reenacting his glorious moment at Sand Creek—that is, how to swing his saber and kill three Cheyenne women and four children prisoners without killing any of the seven extras playing the enemy on stage. He also learned how to hold his trophies aloft. Richmond's acting was so popular that he recreated his heroics on the following two nights. Commenting on his third performance, the *News* raved that the lieutenant "played most admirably—better even than we generally have seen him do—and he always acted extra well."[33]

On the twenty-eighth, the Third mustered out, and as Mullin stated, the discharges did not include pay. "This is a great hardship as many of them sorely need what is their due," the *News* published.[34] "All of them cannot immediately procure employment here and they cannot well leave—even if they had the means—until their accounts are settled up. . . . A new paymaster will undoubtedly soon be here to pay them off, and until then our citizens should be generous as possible."

After the massacre at Sand Creek, Second Lieutenant Harry Richmond (Third Colorado Volunteer Cavalry) returned to Denver in December 1864. He had been an actor prior to enlisting in the Third and returned to the stage at the end of the month to reenact his execution and scalping of Cheyenne prisoners (three women and five children) on November 29, 1864. His initial presentation proved so popular that there were additional performances.

Harry Richmond. Photo by W. G. Chamberlain. History Colorado. Accession # 92.297.46.

On that same day the officers of the Third Colorado also began to muster out of service: Captains Jay Johnson, David Nichols, Theodore Cree, and Presley Talbot; as well as Second Lieutenant Harry Richmond. The next day Colonel Shoup; Lieutenant Colonel Leavitt Bowen; Majors William Wilder, Samuel Logan, Hal Sayr; and Captain John McCannon were discharged. The rest of the officers received their discharge before year's end.[35] One exception was Major Jacob Downing, Chivington's friend and close associate.

Byers was on a roll and did not miss the opportunity to announce the presentation of the "Indian drama," *Wept of the Wish-Ton-Wish*, at the Denver Theatre, which would include "Indian costumes, [and] trophies taken in the big battle of Sand Creek."[36] On the same page he printed: "Interwoven with the play will be presented striking trophies taken from the field." Undoubtedly these "trophies" were Indian scalps presented by the heroes of Sand Creek, and perhaps a woman's pubic mound on a stick. The play would prove popular and was extended through the evening of December 30.

These were good times for the heroes of Sand Creek, and the whites in the territory praised and cheered them, especially in Denver. Most of the city's papers did not hold back. Lieutenant Colonel Leavitt Bowen of the now former "Bloody" Third (Companies A, C, H, L, and M) made it known that he had grabbed and held a "papoose" aloft by its hair as he dispatched it with his sword. On the twenty-ninth the *Daily Mining Journal* wanted to know the sex of the colonel's kill.[37]

Everything continued to move at a fast pace. Then, two days later, shocking news announced that Colonel Moonlight would replace Chivington as commander of the District of Colorado, as his "term of service has expired."[38] The announcement preceded Chivington's real exit from the First Colorado by a number of days.

As the year came to an end, Byers gave a large plug for the continuation of theatrical productions moving to Black Hawk and Central City. The key to his pitch was the presentation of "scenes and subject of thrilling interest, in which the Sand Creek battle and the curious trophies of that far famed field will share conspicuously. Look out for it—a new thing, and a 'big thing!'"[39]

The last day of the year turned dark. White traitors to their race had influenced do-gooders in Washington. Suddenly Chivington's triumph was under attack. There was no time to mince words or work for a common ground, for the threat of turning victory into massacre or worse had to be met head-on.

> Those are the men who call for "Congressional investigation" of "the affair at Fort Lyon." They care not what difficulties they may throw around the vital question of securing peace and safety along the Platte and Arkansas roads. They care not for the security of Colorado's frontier settlements, nor for the lives of her defenceless women and children. They would blast the prospects of the Territory for years to come, and for what? Solely and simply to vent their spite upon two or three men against whom they have personal animosities, or whose power and popularity they envy and fear.[40]

By the "Fort Lyon affair," Byers spoke of unnamed officers who dared to speak out against Chivington. He ended his editorial aggressively: "Let the investigation go on."

Colorado Territory was not alone in its view. On the thirty-first the *Nebraska City News* also spoke out on the upcoming investigation of Chivington's actions. "If our National Capitol was located a little nearer the scenes of our Indian depredations, and members of Congress more familiar with the outrages perpetrated on Western settlers, by these dirty, lousy, thieving vagabonds, they would present him [Chivington] with a sword, as a testimonial of their high appreciation, instead of censuring him. No matter what action Congress may take in the affair—the people of Colorado, Idaho, Montana and Nebraska will ever think he did right."[41]

THE MILITARY INVESTIGATION INTO WYNKOOP'S ACTIONS, if any, ended quickly. On December 31, Colonel James Ford, who now commanded the District of the Upper Arkansas, ordered Wynkoop to return to Colorado Territory and again command Fort Lyon. Moreover, Ford directed him to look into Chivington's actions at Sand Creek and report back to him "with as little delay as possible."[42]

On the last day of 1864, Soule's drudgery ended for a few days. With thirty troops he escorted Captain Henry Booth (chief of Cavalry and inspector for the District of the Upper Arkansas) to the Sand Creek massacre site. He, Booth, and some of the troops spent the following day riding through village and exploring the escape routes that the Indians had used to flee the attack. "I spent New year's day on the battle ground counting dead Indians," he later wrote.[43] Undoubtedly Soule's memory again made vivid the horror of what he had watched on November 29. Many of the Cheyenne and Arapaho dead still lay where they had been killed and mutilated. Certainly the passage of thirty-three days—along with the feasting of animals, birds, and insects—had played havoc with the remains. As Soule traversed the dead ground he must have struggled with a vile taste in his mouth, a taste that would remain with him for the rest of his life. The battleground was spread over a large area, and when combined with the Indians' flight to the north and northeast, it made the task of counting the number killed almost impossible.

Soule returned to Fort Lyon early in the new year. Upon his arrival he told Anthony what he saw at the village site. Anthony was at least knowledgeable of what was happening in the military command, so he found Soule's information worth reporting. Actually Anthony had a lot to report, for he had recently spoken with Edmund Guerrier. Although Guerrier's information would have been dated, it held high priority. Anthony wrote that Guerrier told him that "the Indians . . . moved from their camp on the Smoky Hill and . . . have made camp again on Beaver Creek, more to the north and about 170 miles from this post."[44] Guerrier shared his estimate of the size of the combined village. "They are about the same in number as previous reports have stated," Anthony wrote, "viz, 1,080 lodges of Sioux, 400 lodges of Cheyenne, and 40 of Arapaho. This would give them 2,500 fighting men." Anthony waited until almost the end of his report before he shared: "Captain Soule could only find the bodies of sixty-nine Indians, and a large majority of these were women and children." He could not pass up adding an undercut to Chivington's original estimate of Indian dead, adding his view on the death count: "There could not have been 150 killed in all." It mattered not which count was closest to the truth, for both strongly indicated that the colonel had not scored a great victory without actually saying it.

AROUND THE FIRST OF THE NEW YEAR the combined chiefs assembled and determined that they would strike Julesburg, about a mile east of the South Platte and perhaps a mile north of Camp Rankin. The bulk of the combined villages would remain behind on Cherry Creek, a branch of the Republican, while a thousand warriors, a fair number of women, and a herd of extra horses moved stealthily toward their target. Although small raids had been ongoing throughout the month of the Big freezing moon (December), this was now forbidden, as success depended upon surprise. The soldier societies ensured that no young warriors set out in small parties to raid. The huge war party crossed the South Platte about twenty miles south of Julesburg and set up camp (there were no separate village circles here). On January 6 the chiefs and warriors prepared their medicine, painted themselves and their war horses, and rode toward their target under the cover of darkness. Some of the young warriors wore war bonnets. Most carried bow and arrows, lances, tomahawks, and shields. Some had swords. Bent claimed that only older men carried guns—meaning seasoned warriors. This is questionable (certainly he and Charley had guns, as well as others). That night and into the wee hours of the seventh they and the women with extra horses moved toward their prey.[45]

Julesburg Station included the stage stop, eating house, sod corral, granary, blacksmith and repair shop, telegraph office, and a sutler's store. The land was mostly flat with little vegetation or trees. There were hills several miles to the southeast. Before dawn almost all of the Dog Men, Tsistsistas, Hinono'eino' (most from the north), and Lakotas (mainly Pawnee Killer's Oglalas and Spotted Tail's Brûlés) hid behind the hills.[46] They were poised to begin a war of revenge. The well-planned attack would focus on what had become a war for survival—it was no longer a war of bravery and counting coup. From this time onward Black Kettle and others who spoke for living peacefully with the whites were little more than outsiders. How could you live with a race that was bent upon killing you and stealing your land? With the Dog Men leading the way, these tribal bands saw, understood, and agreed with their view. For the first time, Tsistsistas, Hinono'eino', and the two bands of Lakotas came together as one to fight for their freedom.

On that January 7 the massive war party had a definite plan in place. Early that morning Tsistsista Big Crow, with ten warriors, approached Camp Rankin in a dry creek bed that hid their presence in preparation to begin the raid. About this time a westbound stage headed for Julesburg carried a chest with payroll for troops along the road. Earlier it had been chased in a running fight, but the warriors had pulled back, most likely to not ruin the plan to lure the soldiers from the garrison at Camp Rankin.

The station telegraph operator got his lone wire out just before 9:30, when the stage arrived. "The express coach from the east was fired into this morning, about four miles below here. Three of the shots struck the coach, but without doing any injury."[47] He also mentioned a train being attacked in view of Camp Rankin, but this was in total disagreement of the Dog Man–led plans and contrary to anything that the Indians, and in particular George Bent, would claim.

About the time that the stage pulled to a halt at Julesburg, Big Crow's war party left their concealment near the post and fired at sentries. The plan worked. Between thirty-seven and forty troops exited the post. As the soldiers charged, Big Crow and his warriors raced for the hills to the south. The Tsistsistas easily sold that they rode for their lives, while keeping the troops close but out of bullet range. Everything looked perfect as they neared the hills. But then young warriors anxious to fight could not resist temptation and charged out of hiding and toward the oncoming soldiers before the trap was sprung.

Captain Nicholas O'Brien (Company F, Seventh Iowa Cavalry) immediately reversed direction and raced back toward Camp Rankin. Big Crow and his warriors realized what had happened, and they, too, did an about-face and rode after the retreating soldiers. Many of the warriors who waited, hidden by the hills, also joined the charge for the stockade.

Someone at Julesburg saw the moving fight in the distance, and shouted a warning. The pay master without the chest, the station workers, and the sutler and his employees exited the buildings and began to run the mile to Camp Rankin, while stage driver William M. Hudnut cut one of the horses free from the coach, a strange act unless he felt that the team was too jaded to outrun the attacking warriors with the coach. With the animal free he mounted, and using a lead rope and the horse's mane, he kicked it into motion.[48]

Charley and George Bent had hidden behind the hills with everyone else.[49] They, with other warriors, watched the chase, which quickly turned into a stampeding buffalo hunt as warriors closed on fleeing prey. Three hundred yards from the stockade, a number of *vi'ho'i* dismounted to fight on foot, only to be surrounded and quickly killed. O'Brien and the rest of his men had little room for error as they fought to outrun the warriors. By this time the Bents and their companions galloped toward Julesburg, specifically the sutler's store, as Lakotas had said that it was well stocked with supplies.

Once George reached the now-deserted station, he entered the sutler's store. His timing was good, as he and other warriors enjoyed a still-warm breakfast before ransacking the buildings and taking whatever they wanted. Soldiers at the stockade began to launch balls from the two howitzers at the warriors, but the distance was too great, and the explosions fell shy of hitting their targets. The women rode up with the extra horses, and for most of the day they loaded the animals with supplies—everything from canned goods, bacon, sugar, coffee, and flour to guns, ammunition, clothing, linens, and blankets. Bent found a new officer's uniform and claimed it for himself. Later when he stepped outside he saw a warrior chopping up greenbacks from the paymaster's chest or tossing them into the wind and watching them scatter. George ran to the box, "secured [a] good deal of the money," and stuffed it into the pockets of his officer's coat.[50]

Hudnut had lost precious time cutting the horse free, and it almost cost him, for as he neared the front gate there was a free for all outside when the troopers struggled to break free of the surrounding warriors. Big Crow saw him just before he was about to enter the stockade. However, instead of killing him, as had been the plan, he whipped him with his quirt as Hudnut dashed into Camp Rankin and safety.

During the day warriors herded cattle across the frozen South Platte and back to their village on Cherry Creek. Gunners fired howitzers at them but missed. The Dog Men and their allies killed fourteen or fifteen soldiers and three or four civilians.[51] In his letters Bent made it clear that although some warriors were wounded, none were killed. He would later chuckle at some of the whites' reports of dead Indians. After quoting Lieutenant Eugene Ware, who was not present but wrote: "The number of Indians killed and vouched for was fifty-six," Bent added, "while in reality we did not lose a man."[52] He would also mock the reports that he saw or heard, including Ware's, which ignored the sacking of Julesburg, as well as a January 10 report by General Curtis that claimed O'Brien "repulsed" the Indians and "drove them south." One company did this while facing a thousand warriors?

WILLIAM BYERS DID NOT MINCE WORDS in his daily on January 7.

> Since it is settled fact that the friendly—peaceable—surrendered—hightoned—gentle-minded—quiet—inoffensive savages are again "on it" down the Platte, we respectfully suggest that a small and select battalion . . . pacify the devils, receive their arms and negotiate a treaty by which they will bind themselves not to massacre any but the outside settlements this winter. . . . We have no doubt that the gentlemen are ready, willing and waiting to . . . [proceed] under the protection of a white flag, with olive branches in their hands, [contrary] to . . . Messrs. Black Kettle, White Antelope & co., when it will be their pleasure to fix things to suit them.[53]

Byers's sarcasm was extreme, but so was his total ignorance of facts. It was now known that Black Kettle lived while White Antelope did not survive the massacre.

Although Byers was not certain what was about to happen, he had an idea of what was to come. Always one to go on the offensive while making a buck, he announced that the *Rocky Mountain News* had "a hundred copies of the WEEKLY NEWS, containing the complete official reports of the Sand Creek battle, on hand and for sale, wrappers ready for sending east."[54]

On January 8, two days after Anthony reported Captain Silas Soule's description of the battleground, Soule wrote his last letter to his mother. However, here when he spoke of the dead, he used a restrained voice, while making it clear that "most of them were women and children and all of them scalped."[55] Within two days Soule had given two totally disparate body counts. Surprisingly, the body count he gave the major—69—grew to 130 for his mother. Soule later confirmed the scalping. "All [had been scalped]," he stated under oath, "with the exception of Jack Smith (old man Smith's son) and one squaw that was burnt in a lodge. I could not tell whether she was scalped or not."[56] What he had seen disgusted Soule, and he hoped "the authorities in Washington will investigate the killing of those Indians."[57]

The First Colorado's three-year enlistment had expired, and the situation demanded Soule's time. "[A]ll the officers are relieved from duty at this Post," he told his mother, "and I amongst the rest want to get my papers all square so if I go out I can start for the States right off." Officers still stationed at Fort Lyon had told him they thought "that I will be retained in the Veteran organization," which was what the First Colorado would become. "At any rate I can if I wish, and I have been thinking the matter over and believe it is best, for if I go back I don't know of any thing I could go at that would pay for I am too lazy to work [as] you well know." Although not intended, "Sile" devastated his mother. Still he made her smile. "I am reforming in regard to my bad habits Mother for I have left off chewing tobacco and smoking a pipe but I will smoke cigars when I can get them[.] I don't drink so you see I am getting quite respectable."

On the evening of January 8, acting governor Elbert returned to Denver from Golden City. Upon being advised of the actions of the last two days, he immediately wired Evans in Washington. "The Indians are again murdering travelers and burning trains on the plains. Get authority to raise a regiment of cavalry for one year's service. We must have five thousand troops to clean out these savages or the people of this Territory will be compelled to leave it. Everything is already at starvation prices. The General Government must help us or give up the Territory to the Indians."[58]

Extreme words, and ones that Byers liked. "It is only to be hoped that the Governor can obtain promptly the aid that is asked. We believe that he can, but our case is badly complicated by the lying reports of interested parties and sore heads which have been sent to Washington respecting the Fort Lyon battle and other matters."

Major Jacob Downing, Chivington's lawyer friend, mustered out of the Third Colorado on January 9, 1865.[59] Events would soon occur that would affect John Chivington's life, and Downing would become a major player for his former colonel.

Two days later the *Rocky Mountain News* again pitched the display and sale of Cheyenne possessions. "Capt. Foy, of the Diana, has any amount of Sand Creek trophies on exhibition at his place,—arrows, buffalo spoons, calumets of war, scalps and so forth."[60]

UNKNOWN TO SOULE, WYNKOOP, Cramer, and others who had spoken out against Chivington's "massacre," events began to fall into place that would tear Colorado Territory asunder. Major General Henry Wager Halleck, who then served as chief of staff of the U.S. armies in Washington, D.C., wired General Curtis at Fort Leavenworth on January 11, making it clear that he wanted Chivington's "conduct" investigated. That day Curtis wired Colonel Thomas Moonlight (Eleventh Kansas Cavalry) in Denver: "I am directed by General Halleck to investigate the conduct of Colonel Chivington in recent campaign against Indians. Also preserve the plunder taken. If out of service, a commission should be ordered. If still in the service, a court of inquiry could be ordered at his request, or a court-martial could be ordered."[61] Although it has been printed that Chivington was "released" from the military on January 6, 1865, he, in a sworn statement in which he answered questions for the Joint Committee on the Conduct of the War, claimed he mustered out on January 8.[62]

Curtis did not want an investigation, for, as he wrote Halleck the next day, Chivington had been replaced by Moonlight "and is probably out of the service, under provisions of Circular No. 36, War Department."[63] Curtis realized the danger of being associated with Chivington's actions, while not agreeing with the view that the attack had added fire to the war. "Although the colonel may have transgressed my field orders concerning

Indian warfare," he wrote, ". . . and otherwise acted very much against my views of propriety in his assault at Sand Creek, still it is not true, as Indian agents and Indian traders are representing, that such extra severity is increasing Indian war." The military kept a close eye on the movements of the Indians, and promised that "another effort to destroy them" would be made. He quickly added: "I will be glad to save the few honest and kindly disposed, and protest against the slaughter of women and children." In a final attempt to derail the investigation of Chivington, Curtis wrote: "It is almost impossible to try officers in my command if they have a high rank, my troops all being widely scattered and much employed." He did not state that the Third Colorado no longer existed, that most of the First Colorado were out of service, or that many of them had distanced themselves from Colorado Territory. He did say that the order "to investigate Colonel Chivington's conduct toward the Indians is received and will be obeyed."

By January 13 Wynkoop had still not reached Fort Lyon. On that day Curtis contacted Colonel Moonlight in Denver with a startling post assignment change. His order was short and to the point: "Fort Lyon and vicinity is attached to your district command."[64] Curtis found himself privy to what would happen, and with higher orders or not, he realized that the military staff at Fort Lyon prior to the attack would be instrumental to the upcoming investigation into Chivington's actions. He wanted to ensure that key participants would not be lost in a stack of paperwork. Later that day he contacted Moonlight a second time. "If the colonel did attack that camp," Curtis stated, "knowing it to be under the instructions of the commander at Lyon, or the Indian agent, he committed a grave error, and may have very much embarrassed our Indian affairs."[65] Curtis wanted witness views that disagreed to the official transcripts of the battle. He did not want participating members of the First Colorado in the events of the last six months to become lost and forgotten. "I desire that a fair and full exposure of the facts be made."

The following evening when Ned Wynkoop reached Fort Lyon, he found a renewed fear of the Cheyenne war sweeping southward after everything along the Platte was destroyed. On the morning of January 15 he replaced Scott Anthony as commandant of the post. Although he had shared information the previous November, Anthony did not reciprocate. Although Anthony had eagerly joined the attack on the Sand Creek village, he had soured on Chivington when no effort had been made to go after the warring Indians between the Smoky Hill and Republican rivers. He could have helped Wynkoop's investigation that began that morning, especially with two items that he had shared with his brother (that a *supposed* two-day-old scalp found in the village was a false claim and that he felt Chivington attacked a peaceful village), but he refused. Anthony intended to protect himself until he mustered out of service.[66]

Wynkoop faced a daunting task, especially so with the territory being on edge. Questioning Chivington's victory was not popular. Worse, the officers, enlisted men, and civilians that had been involved were few, and Wynkoop now commanded an undermanned post with mostly unfamiliar faces. As such, much of his report focused on his own actions, beginning with the Indian meeting on the Smoky Hill through his exile to Kansas and return to Fort Lyon. He obtained statements with as many soldiers and civilians as possible that day and the following, and it did not help that his two key comrades in arms were gone—Silas Soule and Joseph Cramer had departed for Denver prior to his arrival at Fort Lyon.[67] He did not know when his report would travel east, so he decided to let the affidavits speak for themselves. David Louderback; civilians John Smith and R. Watson Clarke; Agent Samuel Colley; Lieutenants Chauncey Cossitt, James Cannon, and William Minton; and Captain R. A. Hill (First New Mexico Volunteers) provided sworn statements. As the affidavits were taken on January 15, 16, and 27, Wynkoop's report was not en route until the twenty-seventh at the earliest.[68]

Wynkoop's reasoning for doing this was his fear of an Indian attack on a fort that had no walls, making fortifying it his immediate concern. He finalized his report by stating: "It will take many more troops to give security to travellers and settlers in this country, and to make any kind of successful warfare against these Indians. I am at work placing Fort Lyon in a state of defense, having all, both civilians and soldiers, located here employed upon the works."[69] The officer of the day and soldiers on guard duty were the only exceptions. Wynkoop focused on resisting a siege by holding out in the stone and adobe commissary on the hill. He built a stone wall down to the Arkansas to safely evacuate everyone at Fort Lyon to the former Bent's New Fort, raised breastworks on the east and north borders of the building, and placed cannons on the northeast and northwest corners of the structure.[70]

FOURTEEN

The Cost of Glory

AFTER CAPTAIN SILAS SOULE completed his paperwork at Fort Lyon, he and Lieutenant Joseph Cramer took a coach to Denver, arriving on the seventeenth.[1] The former captain's view of his future proved true. He was retained in the military and, on January 26, 1865, appointed assistant provost marshal of Denver as a member of the newly named Veteran Battalion First Colorado Cavalry.[2]

On February 1 Colonel Moonlight destroyed all hope that the investigation into Sand Creek would remain in the East. That day he issued orders that would set in motion a military investigation of the massacre in Denver and Fort Lyon. To John Chivington's shock, the tribunal that would oversee the Colorado inquiry were all officers of the Veteran Battalion First Colorado Cavalry. The two captains, George H. Stilwell, who served as recorder for the upcoming proceedings, and Edward A. Jacobs, were bad enough, but Lieutenant Colonel Samuel Tappan chaired the committee.[3]

DURING THE WEEKS FOLLOWING THE ATTACK on Camp Rankin and Julesburg, the Tsistsistas and their allies raided along the Platte while remaining at Cherry Creek. They feasted and danced and enjoyed what they had captured. As the Hoop-and-stick game moon (January) neared its end, a

Lieutenant Colonel Samuel F. Tappan while he was in Washington, D.C., in 1864. He was at Fort Lyon when Chivington and his army arrived on November 28, 1864, but due to a riding accident on the twenty-sixth that broke his foot, he was not forced to join the expedition. In early 1865 he was selected to head the military tribunal that would hold hearings in Denver and Fort Lyon in an attempt to understand what led up to the Sand Creek Massacre (November 29–30, 1864) and what happened on those two days. Chivington objected to Tappan's appointment but failed to have him removed from the inquiry.

Colonel Samuel F. Tappan. Photo by Brady and Company. History Colorado. Accession # 95.200.1579.

huge war party again converged on Camp Rankin, reaching it on February 2. As these *vi'ho' i* soldiers were not a threat, secrecy was not an issue. All was quiet as George Bent and those with him counted eighteen new graves south of the post. "Soldiers were peeping over the Stockade at us but would not come out," he wrote.[4] Nor did they fire at the massive war party when Bent and a group of warriors drove off more cattle.

The lone purpose of this visit was Julesburg Station. As such, the war party had not destroyed it the previous January, and now they looked forward to seeing if the sutler's store had been restocked. It had been, and after talking all they wanted, they burned every building.

AS THE INDIAN WAR AGAIN HEATED UP, William Byers castigated Ned Wynkoop in the *News*. The editor had turned on the major like a woman scorned. He now regarded Wynkoop as little more than a yes-man to Black Kettle and the Cheyennes. Byers now attacked everything he had done beginning with securing the release of white children through being replaced at Fort Lyon by Anthony. Byers claimed that the Cheyennes had "hoodwinked him just as they pleased week after week and month after month."[5]

While Byers tore into his former friend, the committee moved quicker than its Washington counterpart, meeting first on February 9. At this time Chivington was present, and Moonlight's order creating the commission was read to him.[6] Three days later Moonlight issued additional orders for the committee to follow, mainly "investigating all matters connected with the action between Colonel Chivington and the Indians, known as the Sand Creek fight, to ascertain, as far as possible, who are the aggressors, whether the campaign was conducted by Colonel Chivington according to the recognized rules of civilized warfare, and whether based upon the law of equity from the commencement of Indian hostilities to the present time."[7] Moonlight pointed out other items, such as whether "the Indians [were] under the protection of the government, and by what authority." Also, he questioned whether Chivington was aware that these Indians were protected, and "whether the Indians were in a state of open hostility and prepared to resist any and all of the United States troops." Finally he presented two important items that were key for Chivington. "This commission is not intended for the trial of any person, but to simply investigate and accumulate facts called for by the government, to fix the responsibility, if any, and to insure justice to all parties." Finally Moonlight wrote: "Colonel Chivington under these circumstances, has not the right of challenge." If this held true, it would handcuff the colonel.

Moonlight's dictum was read to Chivington on February 13. He had a good idea of what was coming and was prepared. "I would most respectfully request the commission to delay their organization until I can prepare objections to their organization of the court as a commission," Chivington stated, "and to object to one of the members, on the grounds of prejudice open and avowed, as I have only this minute heard what the instructions of the colonel commanding were, and what the court intended to investigate."[8] Chivington had every right to complain about Tappan's appointment, as they had been at odds since the Glorieta campaign. The lieutenant colonel held grudges and never forgave the preacher-turned-warrior for usurping what he thought should have been his by right of rank. Chivington briefly left the room while his request was discussed. When he returned, he was informed that it "was not complied with."

Chivington probably expected as much. His friend Jacob Downing would serve as his legal counsel.[9] He requested a day to file papers that contained his objections, and this was allowed. Chivington then requested "that the proceedings of this commission be public, and the daily or other papers be allowed, if they desire, to have reporters present," but no decision was made before adjournment.

On the fourteenth Chivington presented papers that were read. The first dealt with Moonlight's February 1 directive, and Chivington's point of view regarding why Tappan was unfit to head the commission. According to Chivington: "Tappan is, and for a long time past has been, my open and avowed enemy," and "has repeatedly expressed himself very much prejudiced against the killing of the Indians near Fort Lyon, . . . and has said that it was a disgrace to every officer connected with it, and that he (Tappan) would make it appear so in the end."[10] As the commission's mandate was not to prosecute, Chivington knew that he was at war to preserve his legacy. "I believe, from a full knowledge of his character, that he cannot divest himself of his prejudices sufficiently to render an impartial verdict, and is, therefore, not such a judge as the law contemplates when it directs that all men shall be tried by an impartial tribunal."

Text written by Joseph S. Maynard claimed to have heard Tappan call the Sand Creek fight "one of the greatest blunders ever committed." Chivington then presented an affidavit he wrote along with a document that stated the commission did not have the authority to investigate his actions, as Moonlight did not have the authority to create the commission.

Like the previous day, the commissioners discussed everything Chivington had presented and then called him back into the room. They dismissed opening the inquiry to the press or public. After a second consultation

Tappan ruled that the commission was legal as long as it held to its mandate, that no one could object to the proceedings as there had been no arraignment, and that the commission had been tasked "to collect evidence, information, and facts only." More, "Colonel Chivington is expected to be present during the sessions of the commission, to introduce evidence and cross-question witnesses, in order that all the facts may be collected, and justice done to all parties."

On February 15 Captain Silas Soule became the first to testify in Denver. On the sixteenth he was recalled and was asked: "[H]ave you been at Sand creek since [the battle]; if so, what did you see there?"[11] Soule answered: "Saw sixty-nine dead Indians and about one hundred live dogs, and two live ponies and a few dead ones. I believe that is about all." Memories age with time, but what Soule had written Wynkoop in December was seared in his soul, as was what he wrote his mother. At this time Assistant Provost Marshal Soule walked the streets of Denver, which seethed with hatred for anyone who spoke against glorious victory. Sixty-nine dead was a huge reduction to Chivington's death count, and yet Soule had dared state this with his former commander and friend staring at him. After that he offered little information.

Before Soule's testimony ended on the sixteenth, the commission asked him the following, but Soule did not elaborate.

"Was any demand made upon the Indians prior to the attack, and any attention paid to their signs that they were friends?"

"Not to my knowledge."

"Were the women and children shot while attempting to escape by Colonel Chivington's command?"

"They were."

"Were the women and children followed while attempting to escape, shot down and scalped, and otherwise mutilated, by any of Colonel Chivington's command?"

"They were."

"Were any efforts made by the commanding officers, Colonel Chivington, Shoup, and Major Anthony, to prevent these mutilations?"

"Not that I know of."

On the morning of the seventeenth Soule was again recalled, and he listened while his testimony was read. The commission then continued where they had left off. "Did you witness any scalping and otherwise mutilating of the dead during and after the engagement on Sand creek?"[12]

"I did."

"Did you see any officer engage in this business of scalping and mutilating the dead?"

"I cannot say that I did."

That afternoon Chivington began his cross-examination of Soule. The former colonel pressed that Wynkoop had acted without orders when he met the Cheyennes and Arapahos on the Smoky Hill, and that his command had been threatened by the Indians. Soule confirmed that this was true. Chivington then questioned him in regard to Wynkoop's actions while negotiating with the Indians. "State, if you know, whether Major Wynkoop and other officers of his expedition acted as men having full control of their reasoning faculties at the time the council with the Indians took place?" He had been forced to ask the question in this manner, as the commission had refused to allow queries regarding drunkenness.

"I think that they all did," Soule replied, "except Lieutenant Hardin, who was excited." Hardin was more than excited; he was drunk.[13]

By a MARCH 3, 1865, joint resolution that represented the Senate and House of Representatives, a Joint Special Committee was created to investigate the condition of the Indian Tribes. Six days later, numerous members of Congress were selected to participate in the massive project. Wisconsin Senator James Rood Doolittle was selected to serve as chairman of the committee.[14] Although the details for what would become a colossal investigation into the treatment of American Indians throughout the western portion of the United States had not been worked out yet, Doolittle and a number of other Congress members did not want to pass up the chance of questioning a number of men who had knowledge about the events that led up to the tragedy at Sand Creek. Four days later they began examining those who were then in the capital city. Indian Agent Samuel Colley was the first to answer Doolittle's questions on March 7. Indian Agent Jesse Leavenworth followed him, but his testimony was not directed at the Cheyenne war.[15] The next day, March 8, John Smith and John Evans testified.[16]

On March 10 the Denver Commission moved to adjourn and to travel to Fort Lyon before the streams became too swollen, which would impede travel to the remote post. Chivington was informed of the decision and of the commission's next scheduled meeting on March 20.[17]

The Joint Committee on the Conduct of the War in Washington finally began its hearings on March 13. Leavenworth was the first to testify. Others followed on March 14: Smith, Captain Samuel M. Robbins (who was still active), Colley, Scott Anthony, and Colley again. Governor Evans testified on March 15, followed by U.S. marshal for the District of Colorado A. C. Hunt.[18]

Most of those of still serving in the Colorado Territory military were not called. Certainly Wynkoop's January 15 report sufficed for the moment.[19] While at Fort Lyon, he received notice that he had been brevetted a lieutenant colonel on March 13.[20] This was the man who should have been cashiered out of the army, but thanks to General Curtis was not. That same day, Captain Soule was brevetted a major while patrolling the streets of Denver.

In Washington, Scott Anthony, who had mustered out of the military while still at Fort Lyon on January 21, 1865, began his testimony on March 14. He would answer questions regarding the Indians and the attack on the village. One question was telling: "Now, what I want to know is, what other Indians were at Sand Creek when you advised Black Kettle and his band to go over there?"[21] This was a loaded question for Anthony and nearly everyone involved with the lead-up to the attack. "Band" was the key word here, and other than John Smith and William Bent, everyone else had a vague awareness of what that word meant.

"I think that there were only a very few Arapahoes under Left Hand," Anthony replied.

"How long were they at Sand creek before Colonel Chivington came along with his force?"

"I should think about twelve days," Anthony replied.

"Did you receive any communication from those Indians on Sand creek during those twelve days? Did they furnish you with information of any kind?"

"I received some information," Anthony replied. "I do not know that it came from that band." (It is unclear whether he meant Black Kettle's or One-Eye's band.) "I had employed at that time, on a salary of $125 a month and a ration, One Eye, who was a chief of the Cheyennes. He was to remain in this camp [Sand Creek] as a spy, and give me information from time to time of the movements of this particular band, and also to go over to the Smoke Hill to the Sioux and Cheyenne camp there, and notify me whenever movement was made by those Indians; but he had gone only as far as Sand [C]reek when Colonel Chivington made his attack . . . and he was killed there."

His statement made it clear that he had employed One-Eye *after* he assumed command at Fort Lyon in early November 1864, and most likely in the middle of the month when he told the Cheyennes and Arapahos to move to Sand Creek.[22] As Wynkoop had been ordered to Kansas in disgrace, there was no reason for Anthony to make him privy to this.

The Joint Committee on the Conduct of the War investigation in Washington concluded with the testimony of Governor Evans and Hunt on March 15.[23] At this time Senator Doolittle, whose hearings had already ended, along with Connecticut senator Lafayette S. Foster and Illinois representative Lewis W. Ross, prepared to travel to Kansas and the territories of Colorado, New Mexico, and Utah, as well as Indian Territory. Other Congress members would travel to California, Minnesota, Oregon, Nevada, and the territories of Dakota, Idaho, Montana, Nebraska, and Washington.[24]

BEFORE THE DENVER COMMISSION resumed testimony at Fort Lyon, Isabelle Eubanks died in Denver. Her passing was buried in a dinky obituary list that the *Rocky Mountain News* printed on March 21. "In this city, on the 18th inst., of inflammation of the brain, Mary Ewbanks, aged 4 years. She was the girl captured from the Indians, on the Arkansas, last fall. Her death was caused indirectly from three arrow wounds, in different parts of her body."[25] Certainly the mention of "three arrow wounds" was in total disagreement with what Mollie Sanford, who had housed the little girl the previous September, wrote. She had bathed the child, saw her body, and wanted to adopt her but did not due to her psychological problems—mainly her nightly wide-awake nightmares with staring eyes as she recited her living horror.[26] If William Byers *had* seen the obituary and realized that someone had changed Isabelle's first name to Mary, and if he had seen the mistaken claim that Isabelle/Mary had *been recaptured* from Indians on the Arkansas, her obituary would never have seen print as worded. He never did, for if he had, he would have seen her age, her corrupted last name, and that "Mary" was the "Isabelle" that Wynkoop had received from Black Kettle in Kansas. This would have stood out in bold red letters, and Byers would have sensationalized Isabelle's captivity and resulting death with an inflammatory heading and a detailed article that would have certainly named Black Kettle as the guilty party. At the same time he would have specifically reminded the citizens of Denver that Chivington's victory prevented more such tragedies from happening.

AS PLANNED, THE COLORADO INQUIRY resumed at Fort Lyon on March 20. Major Wynkoop was the first to testify.[27]

When the results of the testimony were later summarized and published, there would be an outcry that the naysayers far outnumbered those who supported what had happened at Sand Creek. Maybe, maybe not, as members of the Third Colorado were mostly gone and unavailable to answer questions or provide sworn statements. Many of the members of the First Colorado were also out of service, but not all. Others had died, but not from wounds in battle. Lieutenant Colonel Leavitt Bowen, late of the Third Colorado, was one such person. At four in the morning on March 22 he died of pneumonia at his home on Larimer Street in Denver.[28]

On the fourth day of Wynkoop's testimony (March 23) Chivington continued his cross-examination. "[D]id not Colonel Chivington manifest a desire for peace with the Indians, provided Major General Curtis would consent, and provided a peace could be made that would afford permanent security to the people of Colorado Territory? [A]nd did not Colonel Chivington state that he was determined the white people of Colorado should be protected in their lives and property, if he had to kill all the Indians on the plains; and was not all Colonel Chivington's conversation with you manifestly for the whites, regardless of the sympathies that others might have for the Indians?"[29]

"I never heard him express himself in that way, manifesting a desire for peace, &c.," Wynkoop said, "or heard him make use of the expressions used in the latter part of the question. I had no conversation with him of importance, except what I had done and intended to do. He expressed no opinion particularly on the subject that I can remember, at any time that I was in Denver."

"Who was present when this conversation occurred between yourself and Colonel Chivington?"

"No person was present but myself."

If Chivington wanted Wynkoop to admit that he had seen General Curtis's September 28, 1864, telegram wherein the general stated that the

Indians had to be punished before war could end, he did not ask the question, and Wynkoop never offered that he had seen it.[30]

Silas Soule had met Hersa Coberly in early October 1864, when Wynkoop's command stopped briefly at the Coberly's road station on their return trip to Fort Lyon. Soule and the young lady reconnected in Denver in late January or February 1865, and quickly became a couple. Her father, James, had started a ranch on a road near the old "Puebla" ruins after it cut north toward Denver from the Arkansas in the early 1860s. The road was well traveled, and soon he and wife, Sarah, established a stopping station for travelers. Tragedy struck in mid-August 1864, when Indians killed James. This led to Hersa's brother Joe enlisting in the Third Colorado to avenge his father's murder. Before the year had ended, Sarah Coberly hired a man named Mays to run the ranch. When Sarah moved to nearby Huntsville, Hersa relocated in Denver.[31]

Sarah Coberly was not pleased when she learned that Hersa was involved with Soule, as his stance against the Sand Creek attack was in total disagreement with her and Joe's view of the battle and results. As Hersa and Soule were much alike and had become kindred spirits, she ignored their objections. By March they had fallen in love and their relationship quickly moved toward marriage. Hersa brought Soule to her mother's home at the end of the month, but the reception was cold. The couple quickly returned to Denver. On the thirty-first Hersa and Soule attended the theater. Before the evening ended, they announced they would marry the following day. This was not an April fool's joke, and they exchanged wedding vows at eight that morning.[32]

The testimony continued at Fort Lyon, and it included First Colorado troopers David Louderback; George Roan, who talked about the butchery; Sergeant Lucian Palmer; and Amos James. During this time the commission pushed to confirm atrocities while Chivington did what he could to protect himself. Former lieutenant William Minton spoke about Wynkoop and Anthony offering Black Kettle and Left Hand protection while at Sand Creek, words that did not help Chivington.[33] Corporal James Adams and Lieutenant Chauncey Cossitt completed the testimony at Fort Lyon. The commission adjourned on April 8 and returned to Denver to complete the investigation.

Although fun-loving and easygoing, Captain Silas Soule had the courage to speak up for what he considered right. He had placed himself at risk just prior to the attack on the Sand Creek village, during the massacre, and again when he testified in Denver. But now, as assistant provost marshal, he found himself in the midst of a city torn asunder by the investigations into Chivington's actions.

Anne E. Hemphill Collection (Des Moines, Iowa), Byron Strom custodian.

The next day, April 9, Confederate general Robert E. Lee surrendered his army at Appomattox Court House in Virginia, officially ending the Civil War. The cheers did not last. Five days later President Abraham Lincoln attended a presentation of *Our American Cousin* at Ford's Theatre in Washington. During the evening's performance, actor John Wilkes Booth slipped behind the president's seat in a private booth and shot him. Lincoln died the following morning, and became the first president assassinated.[34]

Due to shock and wanting to pay respect to their fallen leader, the military commission did not resume in Denver until April 20. On that day Captain Soule became aware that he had been accused of partnering with John Smith to receive buffalo robes stolen from the Sand Creek village. Not surprisingly, Chivington made the accusation. Knowing how tense the streets of Denver had been since the investigation began, and also aware that his viewpoint was in the minority, Soule was nervous. Unlike his friend Wynkoop, who was located far from the agitated emotions that threatened to erupt on the streets of Denver, he found himself dead center.

Worse, he was accused of a crime. On April 20 he wrote the District of Colorado Headquarters from the Provost Marshal's Office:

Respectfully returned to Dist Hd Qts with the explanation that I never had a robe in my possession taken at Sand Creek[,] neither had I any knowledge of the Buffalo Robes taken there[.] [F]urthermore I believe the statement made in the written explanation by J. M. Chivington in regard to a bundle of Robes being marked Capt S S Soule 1st Cav of Col Fort Lyon to be utterly false, and made for malicious intent by said Chivington[.] [A]s for being in partnership with John Smith, I never was in partnership with him or any one else since I entered the service of the United States. [N]either have I ever Defrauded my Government.[35]

Like Soule, Wynkoop knew that his views were not popular, and he made a conscious decision to "remain quiet." This changed on the twentieth, when he became aware of what Lieutenant James Olney (First Colorado) said at Fort Lyon. He had watched Lieutenant Harry Richmond murder and scalp eight captive Cheyennes at Sand Creek (three women and five children) while they begged for their lives.[36] This enraged Wynkoop, and he broke his promise of silence. Knowing that the Black Hawk *Daily Mining Journal* had dared to speak out against Byers's biased presentation of the Cheyenne war, he wrote them that he hoped "that all honest men [would] hound this cold blooded dastardly murderer through the world."[37]

Three days later, on April 23, Soule walked into Byers's office and told him that he was being threatened. Worse, he expected "to be attacked."[38] Soule knew his life was at risk, but he had no clue how short his time walking this earth had become. That evening, while returning home after a night on the town with his bride, Hersa, he heard gunfire. It was about 10:30. He told her to go home, that he would join her soon. Soule ran to the sound of the shots and came upon two men he did not know. They sat in the doorway of a building. When Soule appeared and halted, both stood. One was a man of mystery named Morrow; the other was a member of the Second Colorado, Charles Squiers (sometimes spelled "Squier" or "Squires"). Morrow kept behind Squiers, who held a revolver. When Soule saw the gun, he drew his Colt and shot him in the hand. Almost simultaneously Morrow stepped around Squires and shot Soule.[39] His aim was deadly. The ball hit Soule in the right cheek and did not stop until it reached the back of his head. The ruling: Soule's murder was "deliberately planned [and] systematically carried out."[40] Editors Hollister and Hall believed that his murder was to silence him from testifying. This changed when they received comments that debunked their April 25 paper. Someone calling himself "Register" stated the murder could not and would not have been to stop Soule from testifying, as he had already done so weeks before. With bullets trashing their theory, they corrected the error in their next edition.[41]

The killers fled. No one knew Morrow's destination, but it was hinted to be the Platte River. Wherever he bolted was a good choice, as he vanished from history. Squiers traveled to Las Vegas, New Mexico Territory. Soule was buried on April 26.[42] His friend Wynkoop did not travel to attend the memorial service. He was busy at Fort Lyon dealing with an Indian war, and probably did not learn of Soule's death until after he was buried.[43]

On the day of Soule's interment, Chivington submitted written answers to questions asked of him by the investigation in Colorado Territory. Over the years many participants in the lead-up to the attack and massacre of men, women, and children on November 29, 1864, would testify and document their views of events. Unlike modern times, they did not have the facts at their fingertips, nor did they keep accurate records for what they remembered seeing or participating in during these times. They would say or record words that differed from what they had already stated or had written. Because of this, many have been challenged by modern-day historians and novelists who have labeled the documented statements lies. Memories and recollections of past events change over time, fading from memory or growing. Reminiscences that do not agree with preconceived premises have been pounded for years. These were not lies, for as the participants aged, so did their memories.

Not so for John Chivington. Less than six months after the attack on the Sand Creek village, he answered questions submitted to him by the Denver commission. It is hard to believe that his memory had faded this much; also, it is hard to believe that he would document so many errors in such a short period of time—unless they were intentionally created. "On my arrival at Fort Lyon," Chivington wrote, "in all my conversations with Major Anthony, commanding the post, and Major Colley, Indian agent, I heard nothing of this recent statement that the Indians were under the protection of the government, &c.; but Major Anthony repeatedly stated to me that he had at different times fired upon these Indians, and that they were hostile, and, during my stay at Fort Lyon, urged the necessity of my immediately attacking the Indians before they could learn of the number of troops at Fort Lyon."[44] Lieutenant Joseph Cramer's confrontation with the colonel had magically vanished, at least from Chivington's version of the story. Soule's anger had been such that he did not dare approach Chivington, and yet the colonel was well aware of his view. Strange that these officers, who had angered him so much on November 28 and during the attack, no longer remained a part of the picture. It is doubtful that Chivington's anger over Cramer's insistence that the Sand Creek village was under the protection of the military would disappear from the former colonel's memory.

The military inquiry waited until after Soule was laid to rest before continuing on the twenty-seventh. On April 28 reports and affidavits relative to Wynkoop's September 1864 meeting with the Cheyennes and Arapahos were introduced as evidence. Chivington immediately objected but was overruled.[45]

On May 11 Chivington introduced Captain Presley Talbot (Company M, Third Colorado) to the commission in Denver. Talbot's testimony reeked of not only collusion but of testifying from a drafted script. On this day he stated a lot of supposed facts that had no connection with reality. For starters, he stated that Agent Colley and John Smith had been sympathetic to the wound that he suffered at Sand Creek, while at the same time saying that "they would do anything to damn Colonel John M. Chivington, or Major Downing" as "they had lost at least six thousand each by the Sand Creek fight."[46] This was a huge increase on the worth of what Smith had traded for prior to the attack, even considering Talbot's fairly accurate "one hundred and five robes and two white ponies bought at the time of the attack," which was close, except that Smith had traded for the horses, mules, and robes. He went on to say that Smith had showed him his bill written against the U.S. government. This brings up a question. Why would John Smith share this information with a man whom he did not know, who was an officer of the Third Colorado, and who was indirectly responsible for the murder of his son and the confiscation of his property?

Talbot, while recovering at Fort Lyon, stated that, "in an adjoining room, in which I lay wounded, in which I recognized the voices of Smith [and] Colley, . . . the purport of which was denouncing Colonel Chivington, . . . and that Colonel Chivington had murdered his boy, and that he would be avenged by using every effort with the department possible." If Smith and Colley had been in the post hospital, which was west of the men's barracks on the west side of the parade ground—and there was no reason for them

Hersa Coberly had met Silas Soule briefly in 1864 at her mother's road station near the "Puebla" ruins north of the Arkansas, and then reconnected with the captain upon his arrival in Denver in 1865. Their personalities had made them the perfect match for each other, a romance blossomed, and it led to marriage on April 1, 1865. Then tragedy struck, for while investigating gunfire on the evening of April 23, Assistant Provost Marshal Soule was murdered on the streets of Denver. Hersa is pictured in the dress she wore at her husband's funeral on April 27.

Anne E. Hemphill Collection (Des Moines, Iowa), Byron Strom custodian.

to be there—why would they discuss private information when they knew that prying ears were near? Why not discuss their plans at Colley's agency in the commissary on the hill to the east of the post and prevent their words from being heard? The farce testimony grew, for next Talbot stated, and again without having seen him but supposedly knowing Smith's voice, "he said, with tears in his eyes, that he [Smith said in regard to son Jack] was a bad boy and deserved punishment, but it was hard for a father to endure it. He furthermore stated that he had tried to influence his boy to quit committing depredations. 'I asked him why he could not prevail on him to do so,'" Talbot testified. "He said that it was inherited, not from him, but from the Indian blood." It was a racial statement typical of the time.

All the commission had to do was look back and consider that the Cheyennes were Smith's people of choice and that Talbot's statement was little more than fiction. "I furthermore asked him why he [Jack] did not deserve death," Talbot said, and "Smith stated 'that he did deserve death,'" and according to Talbot, "burst into a flood of tears." Throughout his life Smith had lived using much of the Cheyenne culture, and this included instantaneous and harsh punishment for those who cried. This statement by Talbot was ludicrous. Finally, Talbot testified: "Colley and Smith stated to me in person that they would go to Washington and represent the Sand creek battle as nothing more than a massacre." When Talbot was recovering at Fort Lyon in December 1864, the Washington investigation did not exist.

As the Denver investigation limped toward conclusion, on May 18, a small Indian camp was seen above the North Platte River ten miles east of Fort Laramie. A Mr. Elston took Indian soldiers and investigated. When he saw a white woman in the encampment, he seized Oglala chief Two Face, who had an almost naked twenty-four-year-old Lucinda Eubanks and her infant son, Willie, in his possession. On the approach of Elston and his Native escort, a number of the Oglalas fled, but he rounded them up the following day and brought the small party into Fort Laramie. Colonel Thomas Moonlight then commanded the post.[47]

Lucinda Eubanks and son Willie had survived their ordeal. It had been rough, as Lucinda was sexually taken and beaten by her Cheyenne captors before she was traded to Two Face. Although Two Face did not sexually abuse her, he beat her mercilessly before Black Foot, an Oglala, purchased her before selling her back to him. She had been whipped, sometimes brutally, when she did not perform menial female chores, and although she claimed that the Oglalas fed her better than the Cheyennes, she was in obvious need of more nutrition. Lucinda had no reason to like Black Foot, as he took her sexually. She stated that "because I resisted him his squaws abused and ill-used me."[48] Black Foot also beat her. With anger burning, she stated he camped on Snake Fork. Indian soldiers rushed to his camp roughly one hundred miles northeast of Fort Laramie, and Black Foot surrendered without a fight. After he and his followers reached the post, Black Foot joined Two Face in chains. Four other males were incarcerated with them.[49]

Reportedly Two Face said he had been en route to a military post to surrender Lucinda and Willie; perhaps for supplies or protection. But if so, the chief did not make this clear to Moonlight, for the colonel never mentioned it.

If indeed Two Face intended to free his female captive and her son, and Lucinda did not damn him, what followed should not have happened. Moonlight claimed that, "Both of the chiefs openly boasted that they had killed white men and that they would do it again if let loose."[50] This, along with Lucinda's story, sealed the two chief's future. Moonlight tied "them up by the neck with a trace chain" and dangled them from a wooden beam with nothing below their feet.

On May 26 Two Face and Blackfoot chanted their death songs as a wagon hauled them across the parade ground at Fort Laramie to a gallows on a rise northwest of the post. When the wagon reached its destination under the gallows, the wagon driver and two noncommissioned officers tossed the chains into position. When ordered, the driver whipped the mules into motion, and the Oglala chiefs hung with chains around their necks.[51]

WHILE NOT GRABBING HEADLINES, Wisconsin senator James Doolittle, with committee members Senator Foster and Representative Ross, set out for the frontier to visit various military posts to interview officers, soldiers, and civilians. Their goal was to gather an informal view of the events that surrounded the Sand Creek attack and how it might affect the future. They reached Fort Riley in mid to late May. Here they interviewed Edmund Guerrier on the twenty-fifth.[52] They also took sutler Henry F. Mayer's statement in regard to Guerrier. He had known him since a boy. When his father died in 1858, Mayer became executor of his estate and Edmund's guardian. "I know him to be an upright, intelligent, correct young man," Mayer said.[53] "I trust every word he says."

Doolittle's committee reached Fort Larned in late May. While at the post, Doolittle's team obtained Colonel James Ford's sworn statement.[54] Before continuing their journey, Doolittle wrote James Harlan, the secretary of the interior, of his views. By this time the senator had formed an opinion of Chivington's attack, which he viewed as "brutal, and cowardly butchery."[55]

Although Doolittle had not completed his investigation, he was not pleased. When Major General Grenville M. Dodge (who then commanded the departments of Nebraska, Kansas, and Utah) ordered Colonel Ford to launch a campaign against the Cheyennes, Arapahos, Kiowas, and Comanches who were south of the Arkansas, Doolittle thought the Indians had between 5,000 and 7,000 warriors, and were "well mounted, the greatest horsemen in the world, and in a country they have held for hundreds of years." These tribes had proved time and again to the military that they were great horsemen, but it was doubtful that they had that many warriors, and they certainly did not call the plains home for hundreds of years. Still his words held power, and would not be ignored. What he stated next would strike fear in the heart of any politician, for he placed the cost of confronting a massive Indian war with 5,000 mounted troops at between $25 and $50 million. Doolittle placed the blame of the situation on the United States, as it had forced the tribes into war. By this time, he realized that Black Kettle and Left Hand had thought that they had secured at least a temporary peace. His next words confirmed a man he had not yet met—Wynkoop: "They [Black Kettle and Left Hand] were invited to place themselves under our protection. The sacred honor of our flag was violated. . . ." His disgust grew as he wrote, "and unsuspecting women and children butchered, and their bodies horribly mutilated, and scenes enacted that a fiend should blush to record."

Doolittle telegraphed President Johnson, as he craved the authority to make peace, especially with the Cheyennes, who he figured might refuse. The senator's letter to Harlan set in motion the impetus to arrange for a peace council, for when it was forwarded to commissioner of Indian affairs W. P. Dole, he enlisted support for Doolittle's proposal. Dole pointed out what he considered a "radical difference in the views of most of the military commanders in the West and this office as to the treatment of the Indians," which "constantly thwarted" efforts to "restore peaceful relations."[56] Dole hoped for "a humane and just policy."

While Doolittle's committee slowly worked their way toward Fort Lyon, Ned Wynkoop traveled to the massacre site and saw it for the first time.[57] He had been as racially inclined as most whites on the frontier, but beginning with meeting Black Kettle and other chiefs, Cramer and Soule's letters, through all he had heard, read, and learned since being exonerated, remained with him. Everything, especially when combined with what he saw on the bloody ground became a perfect storm. It filled Wynkoop with outrage.[58] Chivington's massacre would remain with him for the remainder of his life.[59]

Doolittle, Ross, and Foster reached Fort Lyon in early June. By this time Major General A. McDowell McCook had joined their caravan. Their arrival pleased Wynkoop, and he invited them to reside in his quarters. On June 9 the committee listened to Wynkoop's sworn statement. He concluded by saying that he had recently visited Sand Creek. "I saw no evidences of any entrenchments," Wynkoop said. "I do not think the location is suitable for defense."[60]

ALTHOUGH NED WYNKOOP HAD BECOME an unpopular person in Colorado Territory, his military career was on the upswing. On June 12 Colonel James Ford wired Headquarters, Department of the Missouri, requesting that he be reassigned. On June 17 Major General Grenville Dodge issued an extended list of Special Orders No. 162. Number 14 stated: "Maj. E. W. Wynkoop, First Battalion Colorado Cavalry Volunteers, is hereby assigned as chief of cavalry for the District of the Upper Arkansas, and will report forthwith for duty accordingly to Bvt. Brig. Gen. J. H. Ford, commanding the district."[61]

SHORTLY AFTER REGAINING HER FREEDOM, on June 22, 1865, Lucinda Eubanks sat down with two officers at Julesburg, and talked about her captivity. What she said and what she did not say are probably key to the question of whether she was in the village on the Smoky Hill when Wynkoop received four prisoners including her daughter Isabelle and nephew Ambrose Asher. "They [the Cheyennes] took my young daughter from me just after we were captured and I never saw her again."[62] If she had been in the village between September 10–12, she would have known about the meeting, would have stated that she was in the village at the time, but she did not.

Also, she never spoke about Nancy Morton, never said a word about being threatened with death by the Cheyennes if she cried out.

That June, Samuel Elbert, who had been a friend of John Evans prior to becoming the secretary of Colorado Territory, after a two-year courtship married Josephine, the governor's eighteen-year-old daughter. The governor's longtime friend, Bishop Matthew Simpson, performed the ceremony at the Evans home on the shore of Lake Michigan in Evanston. George Armstrong Custer was Elbert's best man.[63]

FIFTEEN

The Beginning of the End

In mid-July 1865 Brigadier General James Carleton, Department of New Mexico, disparaged what he considered commissioner of Indian affairs William P. Dole's "carte blanche to make treaties with all the Indians of the plains." He questioned the teaming of Dole and Agent Leavenworth, per Doolittle's suggestion, after the senator invited the agent to join his investigative team. Leavenworth lacked the lifetime of knowledge that Kit Carson, whom he knew intimately, and William Bent had. Carleton sarcastically wondered, "if Mr. Dole is charged with such extraordinary powers, and if Colonel Leavenworth is also clothed with treaty-making powers as an itinerary plenipotentiary," whether, when joined by Carson and Bent, the combination of "so many diverse views" would do little more than confuse the Indians.[1] His recommendation: recall Dole and Leavenworth, who did not "understand Indian character," and allow Carson and Bent to meet, smoke, and talk with the Indians.

That July, Northern Cheyennes visited the second Fort Berthold, a trading post on the Missouri River in Dakota Territory that had originally began as Fort Atkinson. War clouds seemed to be everywhere, and they wanted to discuss peace. Their desire was forwarded to Colonel Alfred Sully, and he sent word for the Cheyennes to talk with him at Fort Rice. They did, and told Sully that they wanted him to "grant them peace."[2]

Sully could not do this.

After meeting with the not-named Cheyennes, Sully said, "Things look bright for peace, but I can't say positively what will happen. The red man is a hard animal to deal with, and very uncertain." He then shared what Blackfoot chief Fire Heart, whom he considered "one of the most warlike of the Sioux," recently told him in council, "You are a good chief sent out by our Great Father. . . . [W]hy don't you . . . hang all the agents here on this ground in [the] presence of the Indians? It is they who get us into trouble by telling us lies." Sully wanted the congressional committee to hear the Indians' words. "They would learn some wholesome truths."

As GOVERNOR JOHN EVANS had been unaware of the Sand Creek attack until Chivington wired him on December 7, 1864, he felt confident that he would not be associated with the massacre. B. F. Wade, chairman of the Joint Committee on the Conduct of the War, had assured him "that they would *not* inquire into [his] general management" of the Superintendency of Indian Affairs.[3] Knowing this, he had testified before the Washington hearings, and had provided documentation. Like many in Denver he anxiously awaited the findings of all three investigations.

At the same time, the governor was aware that he had become a man with a target on his back. Although the testimony during the inquiries had not been made public, the senators and congressmen involved with the process shared what they learned with President Andrew Johnson, who had no personal or political connection with Evans. Washington was aware that the military inquiry could not touch Chivington. Still, they needed a scapegoat. Evans fit the bill. On July 18 Secretary of State William H. Seward wrote the governor. "I am directed by the President to inform you that your resignation of the office of Governor of Colorado Territory would be acceptable."[4] Seward added that President Johnson wanted "the resignation . . . without delay."

On the evening of July 19 John Evans arrived in Denver after a trip to Cache Creek, where he had looked into a potential Ute uprising against the Mexican community in the southwest portion of the territory. Before returning, he felt certain that there was nothing to the rumors, as the Ute bands were scattered in Middle Park as well as the San Luis and Wet Mountain valleys. The only chief that had a grievance was Colorado, then in South Park, whose brother-in-law had recently been killed. Evans had ordered the accused to be apprehended and tried with Utes in attendance at Fort Garland. The defendants were acquitted, as the evidence proved that they had shot in self-defense. This satisfied the Utes. On the twentieth Evans told Byers he felt that an upcoming "large distribution of goods and provisions" would quell any Ute thoughts of a war.[5]

When Evans read Seward's request, it did not surprise him. He had approached powerful men—religious men (Bishop Matthew Simpson) and congressmen (Indiana representative Schuyler Colfax and former Indiana senator James Harlan)—to speak on his behalf, but after Lincoln's murder their requests fell on deaf ears. Johnson had not been a popular choice to become vice president and was even less so as president. There would be no reprieve, for the president would not put himself at risk to protect a man that the Joint Committee had already damned.[6]

DOOLITTLE RECRUITED CARSON AND BENT, both of whom stated "that if authorized they [could] make peace with the Indians along and below the Arkansas."[7] Bent went farther, telling Doolittle that he would guarantee peace, but only if the military did not hunt the Indians south of the Arkansas.

While Doolittle remained hopeful that the government could reach out to the Cheyennes and other tribes on the central and southern plains, the military had no intention of turning its back on continuing the war, although Major General Dodge did begrudgingly state that those Indians "sanctioned" by officers could receive goods.[8]

While the military vacillated with what to do with the Indians, Secretary of War Edwin Stanton made a decision. His telegram to Doolittle, who had reached Denver on July 24, strangely led off with a surprise. On June 18 Major General Francis Herron had held an informal meeting and had secured a temporary treaty with the warring tribes south of the Overland Mail route, and this included the Indians south of the Arkansas. Five weeks had passed. Doolittle must have wondered what the hell he was doing. He was a power in the Senate, he should not have been kept in the dark. Stanton, after confirming that Lieutenant General Ulysses Grant approved Herron's negotiation, stated that he wanted Carson and Bent, along with Colonel Eli Parker, to represent the United States when a peace council became reality.[9]

BY JULY, WYNKOOP HAD BEEN REASSIGNED to Fort Riley. The respite placed him and his family far from the controversy that raged in Colorado Territory. Needing a break, Wynkoop, with several officers, took his son Edward and his companions' children out to play. During his absence, Louise realized that an Indian stood at a window and watched her in the commanding officer's quarters. He spoke to her, and although she did not understand him, she pointed toward the door. He entered. The warrior held a pair of beaded moccasins while making it clear that he was hungry. She understood, and it appeared as if he wanted to trade as he handed her the shoes. While the food cooked, she tried one on but then hid the other. The warrior ate what she served, but afterward demanded the return of his moccasins. She refused and he searched the quarters, finding one of his belongings but not both. When he moved toward her, she quickly crossed to a holstered Colt that hung on the wall. He understood her intention and left.[10]

ON AUGUST 1 JOHN EVANS WROTE a brief message to Johnson, "In compliance with your request communicated to me through the Hon. the Secretary of State I tender my resignation."[11]

But the worst was still to come, as Evans had still not seen the Joint Committee on the Conduct of the War's unpublished report. It would ravish him. "His testimony before your committee was characterized by such prevarication and shuffling as has been shown by no witness they have examined; . . . and for the evident purpose of avoiding the admission that he was fully aware that the Indians massacred so brutally at Sand creek, were then, and had been, actuated by the most friendly feelings towards the whites, and had done all in their power to restrain those less friendly disposed."[12]

In early August when Evans finally saw B. F. Wade's short summation of the Joint Committee's Washington investigation into the massacre, he must have felt that he had been duped. It basically confirmed Wynkoop's actions to meet with Indian leaders, to bring them to meet with him, and to feed the Indians near Fort Lyon as prisoners of war, but also confirmed that the Indians were then directed to camp on Sand Creek. According to the report One-Eye was employed by Anthony, Jack Smith was employed by the government, and both were in the village, as was interpreter-trader John Smith on November 29. "Everything seems to have been done to remove from the minds of these Indians any fear of approaching danger," the report stated.[13] "[A]nd when Colonel Chivington commenced his movement he took all the precautions in his power to prevent these Indians learning of his approach. For some days all travel on that route was forcibly stopped by him, not even the mail being allowed to pass." The six-page report was scathing. "In conclusion, your committee are of the opinion that for the purpose of vindicating the cause of justice and upholding the honor of the nation, prompt and energetic measures should be at once taken to remove from office those who have thus disgraced the government by whom they are employed, and to punish, as their crimes deserve, those who have been guilty of these brutal and cowardly acts."[14]

Evans had already resigned, but now he knew that he had been forever linked to the massacre, even though he had left Denver long before Chivington set his plan in action. However bad he thought this connection might have been, it was worse.

> The hatred of the whites to the Indians would seem to have been inflamed and excited to the utmost; the bodies of persons killed at a great distance—whether by Indians or not, is not certain—were brought to the capital of the Territory and exposed to the public gaze for the purpose of inflaming still more the already excited feeling of the people. Their cupidity was appealed to, for the governor in a proclamation calls upon all, "either individually or in such parties as they may organize," "to kill and destroy as enemies of the country, wherever they may be found, all such hostile Indians," authorizing them to "hold to their own private use and benefit all the property of said hostile Indians that they may capture." What Indians he would ever term friendly it is impossible to tell.

The ex-governor had, he thought, worked for the good of Colorado Territory. Even though his political career was in ruin, his vision of turning Denver into a magnificent jewel at the center of the country, the central hub for a transcontinental railroad, continued to exist. Still, what he now read must have devastated him.

Chivington had his own problems. "As to Colonel Chivington, your committee can hardly find fitting terms to describe his conduct," the report stated. "Wearing the uniform of the United States, which should be the emblem of justice and humanity; holding the important position of commander of a military district, and therefore having the honor of the government to that extent in his keeping, he deliberately planned and executed a foul and dastardly massacre which would have disgraced the veriest savage among those who were the victims of his cruelty." It would get worse for the colonel. "There were hostile Indians not far distant, against which Colonel

Chivington could have led his command." Next, the committee basically accused him of cowardice for striking the Sand Creek village when he could have marched four days from Fort Lyon and attacked that much-larger village that was "generally believed to be engaged in acts of hostility towards the whites." The committee's words turned sarcastic. "[T]he truth is that he surprised and murdered, in cold blood, the unsuspecting men, women, and children on Sand creek, who had every reason to believe they were under the protection of the United States authorities, and then returned to Denver and boasted of the brave deeds he and the men under his command had performed."

Wanting to reduce his culpability, Evans did not waste time in responding to the report and the accompanying Washington testimony and did so on August 6. "As it does me great injustice," he began, "and by its partial, unfair, and erroneous statements, will mislead the public, I respectfully ask a suspension of opinion in my case until I shall have time to present the facts to said committee, or some equally high authority, and ask a correction."[15] He pointed out that the committee's mandate was to explore the attack on the village. True, but to do this, the committee, as well as the other two investigations, required background information before they could publish their findings. How else could they know if the attack was justified or not? "They had no power to inquire into my management of Indian affairs, except in so far as it related to this battle," Evans continued. "[T]he Chairman of the Committee assured me that they would *not* inquire into such general management." Wade may have believed this when he guaranteed that Evans's Indian management was outside the scope of the committee's mandate. However, when prosecuting a potential criminal act, most often it is not just the action itself but the cause that initiated it. Unfortunately for ex-governor Evans—no matter what he had accomplished for Colorado Territory, including protecting its white population from a potential Indian uprising such as happened in Minnesota in 1862—his actions connected him to Chivington and the subsequent attack. It had nothing to do with his total lack of knowledge of Chivington's plans for he, like editor William Byers, had promoted an "Indian war."

TIME WAS PASSING, and the United States government moved toward ending this war. But it did so by continuing an agenda that had been in place for some time. As summer moved toward fall, U.S. Indian agents began to spread the word that a great council would be held on the Little Arkansas River north of its confluence with the Arkansas in Kansas. The stated goal was to pay for the destruction of the Sand Creek village as well as to create a treaty of peace with the tribes.

With the upcoming peace council quickly approaching, on September 29 Agent Jesse Leavenworth saw an opening to advance his current position. He offered to also serve as agent for the Arapahos and Cheyennes if one was not chosen for them soon.[16] Colley was gone by this time, having returned to Beloit, Wisconsin, where he continued his life.[17]

By early fall the Tsistsistas and Hinono'eino' remained wary of the white man's word. Most wanted nothing more to do with the hated *vi'ho' i* and their efforts to steal their land. Undoubtedly Black Kettle and Little Raven felt this way also, but still they held firm to pursuing peace. Not so for Dog Man leaders Tall Bull and Bull Bear. George and Charley Bent also wanted nothing more to do with the race that murdered their people.

Yet another person had no desire attend this peace council. But his reason was different—he thought it would mean his death. Brevet Lieutenant Colonel Wynkoop's attempt without orders to save hostages and end a war resulted in the savage butchery of people who, upon his and Major Anthony's word, thought that they were safe from the 1864 war if they camped on Sand Creek. They were not, and Wynkoop held himself responsible.

Then he received orders to command the military escort for the peace commissioners. Wynkoop did what he could to stop the assignment, but failed. As he accompanied the commissioners to the Little Arkansas, he envisioned a Cheyenne arrow ending his life. The day after he delivered the peace commissioners to the council grounds, he rode to the Cheyenne camp. Instead of being attacked, women "greeted [him] with the utmost kindness" while at the same time they "raised a most dismal wail," as his appearance reminded them of that fatal day almost eleven months before.[18] Black Kettle, upon seeing the tall soldier, led him to his tipi, where, in front of other Tsistsista chiefs, he said, "that not for one moment had any of them doubts of my good faith."[19]

EVENTS MOVED QUICKLY, and William Byers cringed when he read the Joint Committee on the Conduct of the War report that pointed the finger of guilt at Governor Evans and held him accountable for the massacre. He rejected the government view that Black Kettle's band was friendly toward whites and had not committed depredations. The editor's goal was twofold: prove that Evans had nothing to do with the attack and assert that Black Kettle's band was not peaceful. He completely bought into Evans's replies to the Joint Committee report, such as: "The public documents to which I refer show conclusively that they [Black Kettle's warriors] had been hostile, and had committed many acts of hostility and depredations."[20] Moreover, he wanted to protect a friend who had the same vision for the territory as he had. But he, like the governor, did not confirm facts.

Often whites that survived an Indian raid named chiefs who attacked them—they had been terrorized or seen friends or loved ones killed. Had they ever seen Black Kettle, Bull Bear, or Tall Bull? Most often they repeated names that they had heard. Black Kettle and Bull Bear posed for two images at Camp Weld in September 1864. It is doubtful if many prints were sold.[21] Mixed-blood Cheyennes Charley and George Bent faced a similar situation when someone in a war party spoke English. The name "Bent" rang a bell. Suddenly George or Charley—present or not—was guilty of leading the raid. Forget that they had never seen either Bent. How did they identify them, or any other mixed-blood?

THE COUNCIL WITH THE CHEYENNES AND ARAPAHOS, which officially began on October 12, 1865, on the Little Arkansas River in Kansas, was not well attended by these tribes. Although Black Kettle and Little Raven had agreed to bring their bands to the council grounds, most of the Called Out People and Cloud People refused to listen to the white men. An additional five Tsistsista and six Hinono'ei chiefs attended the council.

Before it officially began, Black Kettle asked John Smith to translate his words when he introduced Medicine Woman Later to General John Sanborn, who served as president of the commission, and former general and commissioner William S. Harney. What she would share was important, and there could be no misunderstanding. Medicine Woman Later disrobed and allowed Sanborn and Harney to see and touch nine scars on her body that she received from soldier bullets at Sand Creek. Of the nine, a number of them were on her back and obviously shot into her prone body while she laid on the sand bed.[22]

The commissioners included Judge James Steele, Superintendent Thomas Murphy, Jesse Leavenworth, Kit Carson, and William Bent. Sanborn began the council by stating "Chiefs and headmen of the Cheyenne and Arapaho nations," while Mrs. Margaret Wilmarth translated his words for the Hinono'eino', and Smith translated for the Tsistsistas.[23] "I desire, as president of this commission, to express our gratification in meeting you in a friendly manner." He then talked about what the Great White Father had heard. "From rumors that have reached his ears, he has become satisfied that great wrongs have been committed without his knowledge at the time. He has heard that you have been attacked by his soldiers, while you have been at peace with his government; that by this you have met great losses in lives and property, and by this you have been forced to make war."

Rumors? Sanborn used the word twice at the beginning of his speech. By this time the massacre at Sand Creek was long beyond rumors. Moreover, Black Kettle did not go to war, and Little Raven did what he could to avoid the conflict.

Sanborn stated the Cheyennes and Arapahos needed to move north of the North Platte or south of the Arkansas Rivers, and preferably the latter, and this was currently Kiowa and Comanche land. The general did not allow discussion. "We are disposed to acknowledge Black Kettle as chief of the Cheyenne nation," he proclaimed. The statement was absurd. Carson, Bent, Leavenworth, Mrs. Wilmarth, and Smith knew it, but none spoke up. "We have understood that some of his people were dissatisfied with his actions before the [massacre]." He quickly added that the government "would protect" Black Kettle, and the implication was from his own people.

Sanborn stated that the government wanted to complete the treaty as quickly as possible, but Little Raven did not want this, as most of the Hinono'eino' and Tsistsistas were in the north. "We will give them five months to come in and join together," Sanborn said.[24] He also promised that the reservation would be so large "that you can subsist by hunting for many years." Again Little Raven was not pleased; the Cloud People did not want to leave the Arkansas River, as too many were buried on that ground. Sanborn would have none of this; the Indians must make way for "emigration and civilization," to which Little Raven said, "It will be better to wait until next spring and have all the tribes meet." Still, he admitted game was less abundant than before.

The Hinono'ei' chief then surprisingly moved in the direction that Sanborn pushed for—giving up the hunt and growing crops. He also pointed out that Left Hand's band and the Tsistsistas should not have been attacked by Chivington, and that their people grieved over so many deaths. He did not want the people in the south blamed for actions done by people in the north. "You can tell the President that we prefer to have this treaty about lands put off till spring, but for peace, &c., we are willing to treat now."[25] Not finished, he again said, "We would prefer to wait until next spring, until all our people come back and talk it over, and then treat about the land."

Little Raven accused the Comanches and Kiowas for starting the troubles, while maintaining Cloud People innocence until after Sand Creek. He blamed Kaws of stealing two mules and sixteen horses at the council grounds. Next he accused their agents of swindling them. Superintendent Murphy immediately wanted to know which agents. "[We] only had one fair agent," Little Raven replied; "that was Major Fitzpatrick." He wanted the government to pay Mrs. Wilmarth to live with the Cloud People and be their interpreter. Sanborn said that his words would be presented to the Great White Father. This gave Little Raven another opportunity to show his anger over the theft of Hinono'ei and Tsistsista land. Even though it was wrong and the government knew it, they allowed men to invade their land and dig for gold. He had previously made this agreement—and Agent Boone had presented the paper—on which he had made his mark without understanding what he had agreed to. Moreover, he was never paid for the land he supposedly sold. He insisted upon having an interpreter in the future so he would understand the words on the pieces of paper.

Little Raven went back to getting a good agent. He wanted William Bent, and if not him, Major Wynkoop, as "he always treated [us] well."[26] Sanborn ignored the request. Instead he spoke about not being able to stop the flow of white men to the gold fields. William Bent attempted to bring the Arapahos and Cheyennes together to obtain a treaty and annuities. Sanborn ignored Bent, and spoke about how difficult it was for commissioners to travel to meet the Indians. Moreover, President Johnson wanted the treaty signed now, as he did not want to again send commissioners. He then said, "We do not expect this treaty to be binding upon those that are not present, but the treaty will be so made that all those that join the band hereafter will come under it." Surprisingly, Little Raven said his people would be ready tomorrow. Leavenworth pointed out that the treaty paper would include both Little Raven's and Black Kettle's bands. Steele jumped in and said that as more of their people came in and agreed to the treaty that the annuities would increase.

Black Kettle crossed to the commissioners and shook their hands. "The Great Father above hears us, and the Great Father at Washington will hear what we say." But like Little Raven he was wary. "Is it true that you came

Jeroen Vogschmidt of the Netherlands has painted many portraits of American Indians. He created this oil painting of Black Kettle per a request from the author. Contrary to belief, Black Kettle was not a useless old man during the last years of his life. Actually he did everything possible to negotiate a safe lifeway for the Tsistsistas with the *vi' ho' i*. He was alert and aware of what was happening at all times. Although he never traveled to Washington, D.C., Black Kettle knew that the People could not defeat the invaders of their land, and he did everything possible to prevent or end war.

Black Kettle © *Jeroen Vogschmidt, 2017, with permission of the artist.*

here from Washington, and is it true what you say here today?" He wanted to believe what he had just heard translated by Smith, but had trouble doing it. "Your young soldiers I don't think they listen to you. You bring presents, and when I come to get them I am afraid they will strike me before I get away. . . . Now we are again together to make peace. My shame (mortification) is as big as the earth, although I will do what my friends advise me to do. I once thought that I was the only man that persevered to be the friend of the white man, but since they have come and cleaned out (robbed) our lodges, horses, and everything else, it is hard for me to believe white men any more. . . . All my friends—the Indians that are holding back—they are afraid to come in; are afraid they will be betrayed as I have been." He did not know the land where Sanborn pushed for the Cheyennes to move to, and he did not want to put his mark on this treaty until the rest of the Southern Tsistsistas agreed to it.

The chief wanted to know if the Tsistsistas gave their word to keep peace—and he spoke only for those who followed his lead—why could they not travel north of the Arkansas? "We want the privilege of crossing the Arkansas to kill buffalo. I have but few men here, but what I say to them they listen, and they will abide by their promise whatever it may be." He told the commission that he had sent runners to the north to invite his people to travel south, but he wanted them not to be attacked if they listened to his words.

Next Black Kettle addressed the oversight of not seeing the children that had been taken at Sand Creek, and this bothered him, and Leavenworth confirmed that this was true. Suddenly Black Kettle turned his attention to former Agent Fitzpatrick, who had told him that once "he [Fitzpatrick] was gone we would have trouble, and it has proved true." He mentioned that the Tsistsistas had gone through many agents after Fitzpatrick died. "I don't know as we have been wronged, but it looks so," as they had been receiving fewer supplies. He wanted William Bent and Charles Rath as the traders for the Tsistsistas living near the Arkansas. "We have brought our women and children, and now we want to see if you are going to have pity on us."

The treaty council adjourned until the next day, October 13.

William Bent addressed both tribes in their tongue, but his words did not sound like his—certainly not after all his years of interaction with them. But then again, when he was their agent, he had suggested that they abandon the hunt and become farmers. "I would advise you not to hesitate one moment in signing whatever propositions this commission may suggest to you, as I am satisfied that there is no deception practiced on their part."[27] He guaranteed that the Hinono'eino' and Tsistsistas would never receive a better treaty than now. Bent was the most important white man that the Indians knew on the frontier; the influence his words wielded was enormous. He joined them and himself as one, and they had both been deceived by the whites. "For instance, in the summer of 1864 I was sent to you by the governor of Colorado . . . to make a temporary treaty with you, which, I am sorry to say, was a deception on the part of the whites . . ." These white men, Bent professed, were different. "I would again advise you to sign the treaty they offer you without hesitation." Without a doubt William Bent was the cornerstone to the commission's pitch for the Indians to move to an undesired land. Certainly they listened closely to his words.

Quickly Steele spoke, not allowing the Indians to fully digest what they just heard. After praising unnamed leaders in Washington—supposedly true Cheyenne and Arapaho friends—he proclaimed that they had "instructed this commission to make a treaty that will secure your best interests for all time." Glorious words, but quickly followed by trashing Little Raven and Black Kettle for not accepting the U.S. government's pitch of a land grab the previous day. "This commission, in the council we had with you yesterday, regretted very much that you were not ready to treat for a cession of your lands, and this regret was not so much on account of white people, but on account of what we consider your true interests. We all fully realize that it is hard for any people to leave their homes and graves of their ancestors; but, unfortunately for you, gold has been discovered in your country, and a crowd of white people have gone there to live, and a great many of these people are the worst enemies of the Indians—men who do not care for their interests, and who would not stop at any crime to enrich themselves." Steele pointed the finger of blame at those who craved gold and desired the land—but that actually included the U.S. government. His words went beyond translation, for his words were never understood.

Steele continued his presentation. "We want to give you a country that is full of game and good for agricultural purposes, and where the hills and mountains are not full of gold and silver." But these were the wind-blown, dry, and desolate flatlands of south-central Kansas and north-central Indian Territory that even the buffalo avoided. This country would exclude the white man, and although Steele did not provide the reason why, it was a simple one—the white man had no desire to live there.

Murphy attempted to end Steele's negative ramble by asking how many Cheyennes and Arapahos belonged to each tribe. Black Kettle stated that he had "280 lodges, five to a lodge, on the Arkansas river," 80 of which were present, and that the Hinono'eino' had "190 lodges on the Arkansas river."[28]

Little Raven spoke up, saying "the last time we had a meeting there were 390 [Arapaho] lodges; since then many young men have married and got lodges."[29] Here he spoke of the intermarriages between his people and the Tsistsistas. Little Raven then addressed why many of his people rejected the 1861 treaty. When Greenwood came to them, he said, "We did not understand him." He talked about the absurdity of moving the Southern Hinono'eino' and Tsistsistas north of the North Platte or south of the Arkansas. The northern land had been "given to the Sioux" and "south of the Arkansas has been given to the Comanches and Kiowas. To place [us] on the same ground would be to make prisoners of us, or like going out of one fire into another." He was not finished. "There is something very strong for us—that fool band of soldiers that cleared out our lodges, and killed our women and children. This is strong (hard) on us. There, at Sand creek, is one chief, Left Hand; White Antelope and many other chiefs lie there; our women and children lie there. Our lodges were destroyed there, and our horses were taken from us there, and I do not feel disposed to go right off in a new country and leave them. What I have to say, I am glad to see you writing it down to take to the Big Chief in Washington."

Black Kettle again stood and addressed the *vi'ho' i* commissioners, and he was very conciliatory. "Our Great Father sent you here with his words to us, and we take hold of them. Although the troops have struck us, we throw it all behind and are glad to meet you in peace and friendship. What you have come here for, and what the President has sent you for, I don't object to, but say yes to it." Before he finished speaking, Black Kettle added: "I want the privilege of roaming around until it is necessary for me to accept the proposed reservation." He wanted the People to range north of the Arkansas to live and hunt buffalo. "Now the path that you mark out is a good one," he continued. "The roads are open, and we consider that we are living as in the olden time when we were one people together for fear of other troubles. Other nations may commit wrongs that we may be blamed for, and to prevent this we want Colonel Bent and Major Wynkoop to live with us."

The council adjourned until the third day, but not meeting until one in the afternoon. Black Kettle began where he left off. He did not want anything more to do with Governor Evans, and requested that Thomas Murphy become superintendent for the Tsistsistas and Hinono'eino'.

Murphy realized the weight Little Raven and Black Kettle's requests carried, and he had the inside track on what the near future might bring. Sensing that he would be part of this future, he told Little Raven, Black Kettle, and the others that whatever happened, they must avoid the white man and war. When there was a problem, they must tell their agent, and he would report it.

When Murphy finished, Sanborn read the entire treaty, with Smith and Wilmarth translating. This reading, no matter how slow, no matter how accurate the translations, was a mouthful of information to digest and understand. One thing was certain—unless the commission was updating the treaty each day, it was already known what Little Raven and Black Kettle would state, for they and their people had been given the right to roam between the Platte and Arkansas Rivers until they were told that they must move onto their new reservation in Indian Territory. There would be strict limitations of where the Indians could travel when north of the Arkansas. But there was much more in the treaty that was never discussed during the council meetings, unless the official report failed to record everything that was said. Both tribes apparently agreed to bring people that were not present to agree to the terms, but they had made it clear why most of their people had avoided the peace council. They had a huge task staring them in the face, and one that both knew would never become totally successful. The chiefs, and especially Little Raven, wanted to be reimbursed for the horrific loss of property at Sand Creek. This would make it into the treaty even though no specifics were talked about at the council. Still, the payment in the treaty was vague and was left up to the secretary of the interior. This also included anyone who lost a relative on November 29, 1964—they would receive 320 acres. Mixed-bloods in the village, such as Mrs. Wilmarth and her children and William Bent's children, would receive 640 acres each.[30]

After the commissioners signed the treaty, Tsistsistas Black Kettle, Seven Bulls, Little Robe, Black White Man, Eagle's Head, and Bull that Hears; and Hinono'eino' Little Raven, Storm, Big Mouth, Spotted Wolf, Black Man, Chief in Everything, and Haversack made their "X" on the paper. Wynkoop and Smith signed as witnesses.

Black Kettle had impressed Harney during the council, and afterward the general gave him a "fine bay [horse]."[31]

Ned Wynkoop, while not directly participating in the peace negotiations, had also been impressive, not only to Black Kettle and Little Raven but also to the commissioners, in that they saw the chiefs' interest in him becoming their agent. Neither he, Black Kettle, nor Little Raven could have guessed that their initial time together in fall 1864 would lead to this point in time. Or that the cultural divide Wynkoop had dared to straddle on the Smoky Hill, along with his aggressive and reckless determination to mediate with a race he knew only as faceless "savages" in an attempt to end a vicious war, would soon change his life forever. A perfect storm of events—stepping across the racial line that separated Anglo-Americans from Cheyennes and Arapahos—had fallen into place, and would soon propel Wynkoop on an unexpected career path. He was about to become a *cultural broker*, that is "a conduit for goods, services, and information" as he walked between the races.[32]

JOHN CHIVINGTON REFUSED TO VANISH quietly into the night, and for good reason. Regardless of how the investigations painted him and the Colorado Volunteers at Sand Creek, his popularity on the frontier continued to thrive. He was well aware of this and had every intention of using it to his advantage. While in Omaha, Nebraska, on October 16 Chivington wired William Byers: "Announce me as a candidate for Congress in the *News*."[33] Byers gladly placed Chivington's request on the front page of that afternoon's daily.

At that time Editor Byers was not enjoying what he had been hearing about himself and the *News*. In the same issue partner John Dailey saw to it that the front page featured a Democratic rally that had happened the previous Saturday evening at the People's Theatre in Denver. The speaker was never named; simply called a "gesticulating serpent," who spouted "a series of posturing, glidings, hissings, and muttering vaguely about the ga-lor-ri-ous Dim-ocrasy, the cruel war, and denouncing the *Rocky Mountain News*. . . . In his speech the serpent enunciated the original idea that an organization of the Democratic party was absolutely necessary to [shield the] people from 'the man Byers.' He dwelt" on "the people being protected from the terrible Byers and gave to his bugaboo the credit of being the arbitrary despot of Colorado."[34]

There was a lawless element in Denver that on more than one occasion attempted to kill Byers, forcing him to alter his routes home at the end of the workday.[35] The *News* reprinted an article about the editor of the *Gazette*, a Democrat named Stanton, who brutally attacked Byers on the streets of Denver, because he had taken offense at some of the recently published articles that poked sarcastic fun at Democratic political meetings. The article claimed he was also "indebted to [Byers] for many personal and pecuniary favors."[36] As the *News* had not publicized the assault, Byers obviously did not want to share what had happened. Still he okayed reprinting the article, most likely as he liked what the *Oquawka Spectator* wrote about him: "Mr. B. [is] one of the most perfect gentlemen we ever know. As a parti[s]an editor he is able, earnest, and sometimes bitter, but as a man he is kind hearted, generous, and the soul of honor."

The statehood convention on the seventeenth drew its own fireworks as delegates targeted the Cheyenne and Arapaho Indians with resolutions—mainly they wanted to see more Sand Creek battles. This resolution won easily by a 54 to 19 vote. As the *News* reported the day's happenings: "[N]o speaker said a word in favor of defending [the] Sand Creek [battle] without receiving a hearty and unbounded applause. These things show how the people stand on this all-important question."[37] As usual Byers took no prisoners. His victim on this day was Amos Steck, who ran for state senator, as he had voted against the resolution. Seeking to destroy Steck's election bid, he asked his readers to look at Steck's record "and see if we have not the truth." Continuing, the *News* claimed that Steck had "vilified, maligned, and made to suffer by his other slanderous attacks" the people of Colorado Territory. Many Coloradans had visited Washington, D.C., since the Sand Creek battle, and Byers had published their experiences. "The universal testimony of these on their return to us, is that when they attempted to defend the people of Colorado against the charges made concerning that fight, they received for answer that the charges of barbarity and massacre came from our own citizens, and if we are abused on account of them, the remedy must be applied at the root of the disease which is here at home." Byers vented his outrage at the traitor Wynkoop, the turncoat Anthony, and the hated John Smith, who slept with the enemy. As far as he was concerned, they were liars and deserved Soule's fate. Wrapping up his editorial, Byers stated: "We have done nothing that should make us ashamed, and the united voice of this people should and will endorse and approve of the course taken by their defenders at Sand Creek."

William Byers's vision for Denver and Colorado Territory had been in place since he published the first issue of the *Weekly Rocky Mountain News*. He did not tiptoe between the fiery stances of civilizing Denver, slavery, the war of rebellion, or Indian land and rights. The stark turnabout on what happened at Sand Creek had shocked most whites living on the frontier. Byers knew and understood the word on the street, knew the pulse of Denver and the territory, and printed it. The recent treaty with the Arapahos and Cheyennes meant nothing, as these Indians still roamed the land. They hindered progress, they needed to be removed, and he did not care how it happened.

On October 18 Byers made certain that everything of importance made the first page. The *News*'s recommendations to the voters as related to Sand Creek included: (1) The U.S. government will reimburse "all losses sustained by citizens of the Territory of Colorado, from depredations committed by hostile Indians"; and (2) "[A]ll debts contracted by the Territorial authorities" would be paid.[38] The voted-upon platform also included the following (among others): (1) "That we will not support for any political office any person who now sympathizes, or has heretofore sympathized with the Indians who have warred upon our people and our commerce, or who have at any time denounced the officers and men who so gallantly fought at the battle of Sand Creek on the 29th November, 1864, and have thereby not only brought reproach upon us as a people, but upon the American name throughout the Christian world"; (2) "That the infamy attempted to be branded upon the brows of our soldiers, we hereby stamp upon the foreheads of their defamers"; and (3) "That the peace of our State and the progress of civilization, demands a repetition of such battles as those at Sand Creek."[39]

Less than a month after Byers had entered Chivington's name to the list of candidates for Congress, Chivington bowed down to the controversy that swirled around Sand Creek. Even though his popularity held strong in Denver and in the territory, he dropped out of the election on November 8. Byers printed: "This praiseworthy and generous act in the Col. will more than ever endear him to his many friends in Colorado."[40] At this time the Methodist Church held a conference in Colorado. Apparently Chivington had hinted that he might like to return to the pulpit. Even though he would have received votes for a return to the ministry, the church wanted nothing to do with the controversy surrounding the massacre and the former preacher.[41]

With the military in his past, and perhaps religion also in his past, John Chivington needed to recreate himself.

Before the year ended, commissioner of Indian affairs D. N. Cooley broached the subject of obtaining supplies to induce Indians who had avoided the Little Arkansas peace council into meeting with trusted agents and Secretary of the Interior James Harlan. General John Pope was in agreement and recommended that Wynkoop be selected, as the Indians respected him. When William Bent shared his concern that Dog Men were attempting to convince Tsistsista and Hinono'ei warriors to remain in the north, ignore the Little Arkansas Peace Treaty, and continue the war, his thoughts added urgency to the plan. The trader also suggested that a white man the Indians trusted should meet with them to explain the benefits of the treaty.[42]

Cooley contacted Wynkoop, who was then in Washington with his family, and informed him that he might receive the assignment. Wynkoop was not in favor of the proposal. Instead of addressing the current situation, he spoke "of the destitute condition caused by the wholesale robbery at Sand Creek."[43] These victims desperately needed "clothing and food," he continued, and should not be dependent upon Congress acting. The decision came quickly, and on December 5 the War Department ordered Wynkoop to report to Harlan for special duty.[44] He did, but did not accept the assignment until December 12, when he submitted his bond to Harlan in New York.[45] On that day Special Orders No. 109 were issued outlining his duties: to interact with Indians. "I was selected," Wynkoop wrote, "to submit the treaty as changed to the Indians for their signatures."[46] As Wynkoop knew that Arapahos and Cheyennes had been raiding the Butterfield Overland Dispatch on the Smoky Hill, he moved as quickly as possible. However, because Louise was nearing the end of her third pregnancy, he took her and their children to his mother's home in Pennsylvania before setting out for the frontier.[47]

Epilogue
The Tragic End of a Lifeway

BY THE END OF 1865 many of the whites associated with the events that led up to the massacre had moved on with their lives. One was John Chivington, but not William Byers.

By mid-February 1866, Tsistsistas Stone Forehead and Black Kettle camped south of the Arkansas on Bluff Creek in a camp that grew in size daily. Poor Bear's Kiowa-Apaches and some Kiowas had joined the growing village circles. Little Raven and Big Mouth's Hinono'eino' camped thirty to forty miles away. So far no Dog Men were present, but they were expected. At this time the cousins had differing views on how to deal with the white man; Black Kettle stood for peace, while Stone Forehead wanted to retain the old ways.[1]

By this time Special Indian Agent Ned Wynkoop had reached Fort Larned. His goal: get those who signed the 1865 treaty to touch the changed document while presenting it to the war faction. Two companies of the Second U.S. Cavalry (I and K, about sixty troopers) under Captain G. M. Gordon escorted him to Bluff Creek.[2] He was greeted with "signs of friendship" when he reached the village on February 25.[3]

Not so the next morning. Dog Men Bull Bear, Bear Tongue, Big Head, Red Iron, Hairy Wolf, and Porcupine Bear glared at Wynkoop when he stepped from his tent. He ignored their attitude and shook hands with them, all except Porcupine Bear, who covered his face with his blanket. Wynkoop soon learned that Porcupine Bear had lost loved ones at Sand Creek, hated white men, and blamed him for his loss. What Wynkoop had feared on the Little Arkansas had finally become reality.[4]

On the twenty-eighth Wynkoop spoke with Cheyenne leaders. John Smith sat next to him, while George Bent, who wore a breechclout and wrapped himself in a trade blanket, sat with the Tsistsistas to confirm Smith's words. No threats were made, and the meeting ended peacefully. That day Big Mouth arrived with his band of Arapahos. Wynkoop announced that he would meet with everyone the next day.[5]

That night while Wynkoop entertained friends in his tent, Margaret Adams (the former Mrs. Wilmarth had taken a new husband), whom he hired to interpret for the Arapahos, rushed in unannounced. She was crying, close to hysteria, and certain that if Wynkoop forced Porcupine Bear to touch the paper, that the Dog Man would kill him and everyone else. On March 1 Wynkoop distributed much-needed supplies to the Cheyennes and Arapahos. However on this day he believed Adams, and he sat with her and Smith facing his tent, which forced Black Kettle, Stone Forehead, George Bent, Porcupine Bear, the rest of the Dog Men, and Big Mouth to sit with their backs to it. His brother George, who had joined him on the trip, hid in the tent with his Spencer aimed at the Bear.[6]

Wynkoop spoke of the Cheyennes' peaceful overtures as well as their aggressiveness the last two years. He read the updated 1865 treaty to them with plenty of pauses, allowing Smith, Bent, and Adams to translate; then discussed the benefits of peace and war. After saying he had never lied to them, he told them that the Union Pacific Railroad, Eastern Division, intended to lay track between the Smoky Hill and Republican Rivers. If they stayed away from the white man and the roads, they could continue to live and hunt between the Platte and Arkansas Rivers. Someday this would end, but not until their new reservation was ready for them. Talking directly to Stone Forehead, Porcupine Bear, Bull Bear, and Big Mouth, Wynkoop asked them to sign the treaty, as it allowed them to live as they always had for an unknown amount of time.[7]

Dog Man Big Head was not in a good mood, as had been attacked while traveling to Bluff Creek. Showing that he understood the presentation, he countered it. He told Wynkoop that he wanted all the roads that the *vi'ho' i* had created through Indian/buffalo land closed. Big Mouth supported Big Head's words. He stated that the Hinono'eino' did not want to walk away from "their best hunting grounds," that they did not want to move to a foreign land.[8] Wynkoop understood and accepted what he heard, and he replied that he would share their words when he returned to Washington. He then told Big Mouth that he needed to remain at peace.

Black Kettle backed the white man, and surprisingly his words won out. Stone Forehead and Big Head agreed to the treaty. Unexpectedly, the Dog Men were agreeable to a new road through their land. Porcupine Bear appeared to be the lone discontent. Wynkoop asked him to change his mind but was greeted by total negativity. George Bent approached the Bear, but still he declined. Then, without warning, Bull Bear aggressively confronted Porcupine Bear, as did others. Suddenly the Bear stood. Fearing that he was about to be attacked, Wynkoop grabbed his Colt, but instead of charging him, the Dog Man stomped to the treaty paper and made his mark. Luckily Wynkoop's action went unnoticed, and George never squeezed the trigger. The novice had his signatures. Captain Gordon later reported that the chiefs "all showed a desire for peace and friendship," but better, there was not one "unfriendly act . . . between them and the command."[9]

That day Little Raven's band arrived at Bluff Creek. On March 2 the chief met with the special agent and signed the updated treaty. Wynkoop then distributed the supplies marked for his people. On the third the colonel and Gordon's command set out for Fort Larned, reaching it on the fifth.

About the time that Wynkoop completed his negotiation, John Chivington had teamed up with his son Thomas and son-in-law Thomas Pollock and became a freighter. That March he set out with a wagon train of 110 wagons for Atchison, Kansas.[10]

Wynkoop had not completed his assignment. Before returning to Washington, he traveled to Wood Creek, fifteen miles north of Fort Larned, and on April 4 he met with Tsistsistas that continued fighting to retain their hunting grounds between the Smoky Hill and Republican Rivers. The special agent obtained their signatures and declared this meeting a success, but stated that it was based upon "the government fulfil[ling] its promises to them."[11] Wynkoop's statement defined what the United States had to do in regard to its relationship with American Indians.

After returning to Washington, and with Doolittle's recommendation in hand, he met with President Andrew Johnson and made his desire known that he wanted to become the Cheyenne and Arapaho agent. Months later, on July 11, 1866, Brevet Lieutenant Colonel E. W. Wynkoop mustered out of the First Colorado Cavalry. Fourteen days later, commissioner of Indian affairs D. N. Cooley ordered Wynkoop back to the frontier. Again he found the Cheyennes desirable of peace. More, he realized that they judged "good faith by performance," something the U.S. government never delivered.[12] On September 20 President Johnson appointed Wynkoop agent for the Cheyennes and Arapahos.

BY THE END OF 1866 the violence on the prairie had diminished, but that did not end the strained relations, as white encroachment continued into 1867. The Union Pacific, Eastern Division, concentrated on laying track, which caused trouble. To offset this, or perhaps confront it, Major General Winfield Scott Hancock launched a major expedition to the West in March.

A meeting had been set for April 10 at Fort Larned. But a snowstorm on the eighth made travel impossible for Cheyenne leaders from a joint Dog Man–Tsistsista–Lakota village on the Pawnee Fork, thirty-five miles west of the post. When the chiefs had still not appeared by the twelfth, Hancock declared that he would set out for the village the next day. Before nightfall on that day, twelve hungry and tired members of the "Dog band," as Wynkoop called them, arrived on worn-out horses. This included Tall Bull, White Horse, Bull Bear; Southern Tsistsista Slim Face; and Northern Dog Man Gray Head. They asked for food, and Hancock provided it. The general then insisted upon a meeting that night, which made the chiefs suspicious, as peace councils always took place during the day.[13]

Wynkoop, interpreter Edmund Guerrier, and the chiefs sat on one side of a huge bonfire while Hancock and his officers sat across from them. After a pipe was shared, Hancock started matters by complaining about the small showing of chiefs. "The innocent and those who are truly our friends," he said after stating he intended to visit their village, "we shall treat as brother."[14] He then turned aggressive, saying that "we will strike" anyone that lies "to us." Like many whites before him, Hancock refused to accept the ways of the People and repeated the impossible. He wanted the Cheyennes to have a chief that was above all others, for then he could "hold the chief and his tribe responsible . . . [f]or any depredation committed by any one of his tribe." He would not separate people at peace from those at war. "I will await the end of this council," he said, "to see whether you want war or peace."

Tall Bull stood and faced Hancock. He had little to say but held his anger in check as he spoke. He explained that the buffalo and antelope were disappearing at a frightening pace, that the Called Out People wanted to be friends with the *vi'ho' i*; and that Tsistsistas should not be shot when they travel on roads or when they go to forts to receive food. He then dismissed Hancock. "If you go [to our village], I shall have no more to say to you there, than here. I have said all I want to say here."

After the council ended, Tall Bull, Wynkoop, and Guerrier walked into the blackness. The threat was real, and Tall Bull asked Wynkoop to stop the soldiers from coming. It was after midnight when Wynkoop shared the Dog Man's words.[15] Hancock was not interested. He would "talk war or peace to them, as they may elect."[16]

The first day's march was uneventful until Hancock's command had traveled twenty-one miles. Here the general was forced to cross the Pawnee Fork, as warriors had set the prairie on fire. That day a few Tsistsistas rode with the caravan for a short time, mainly to say that chiefs were on their way to talk. They also said the villagers had begun to panic, especially the women and children, as they feared another Sand Creek. On the fourteenth Bull Bear rode into the white bivouac and repeated that chiefs were coming.[17]

By 9:30 that morning Hancock's patience was gone, as was Wynkoop's. The general had told the agent that he would "defer to me certain matters connected with the Indians of my agency."[18] To this point in time he had ignored Wynkoop in regard to what might happen. British reporter Henry Stanley accompanied Hancock, who he thought had been "kind and courteous to the agents," including Jesse Leavenworth, while he received "acrimonious censure" in return.[19]

Winds blew when Hancock moved out shortly after eleven that morning. Captain Albert Barnitz (Seventh U.S. Cavalry) claimed Hancock's army marched in "order of battle—Infantry in line, cavalry in 'close column' on the flanks, and trains in three columns in the center."[20] A little before noon Hancock's army crested a small hill. In the valley below, between three and four hundred warriors and headmen halted. Seeing the massive army above them, they formed a battle line. "The whole command presenting such an appearance as I have seen just prior to the opening of an engagement," Wynkoop reported.[21]

Tsistsista chiefs rode before their line as they yelled for everyone to stop the *vi'ho' i* from butchering their loved ones.[22] Lieutenant Colonel George Armstrong Custer (Seventh U.S. Cavalry) saw his first view of aggressive Plains Indians. "[I] witnessed one of the finest and most imposing military displays, prepared according to the Indian art of war, which it has ever been my lot to behold," he wrote.[23] "It was nothing more nor less than an Indian line of battle drawn directly across our line of march; as if to say, Thus far and no further."

Wynkoop rode to Hancock and asked permission to ride between the lines. Surprisingly, the general agreed. Wynkoop took Guerrier and galloped into the valley. They first met with a group of chiefs, but after seeing Roman Nose screaming for his warriors to kill, they rode to him. Roman Nose wore an officer's uniform and a buffalo skull cap with one horn and following feathers. The war leader carried four revolvers, a Spencer carbine, and his bow and arrows. The agent's words won out, and Roman Nose agreed to talk.[24]

Hancock and several of his officers rode down the hill to meet with Wynkoop and the chiefs, which included Dog Men Gray Head, White Horse, and Medicine Wolf, along with Lakotas Pawnee Killer, Little Bull, Little Bear, and Bad Wound. Bull Bear, who had remained with the soldiers, joined the meeting.

Hancock stated he was ready to fight. This suited Roman Nose. He touched the general's face and counted coup. Knowing the war leader's intent, Bull Bear grabbed his reins and pulled him away from the assembly, as Hancock's murder would have resulted in the massacre of the village. Soon after, Hancock said that it was too windy to talk, ending the discussion.[25]

The march continued. During one of the halts Wynkoop told Hancock that he feared "that the result would be the flight of the women and children."[26] Hancock ignored him, and that afternoon set up camp one mile from the Indian encampment. The panic, which had begun days earlier, peaked. Women grabbed their children and fled.[27]

A disturbed Hancock demanded the presence of Cheyenne leaders. That night when Tall Bull, Bull Bear, Roman Nose, and others appeared, he complained about the flight of the women and children until a disgusted Roman Nose brought up Sand Creek. This Hancock ignored, angering the war leader. The meeting ended when the general demanded that the chiefs bring their women and children back to the village. They said that they would, but had no intention of doing so, as Sand Creek had been branded into the soul of every Tsistsista.[28]

Later that night Guerrier, who had been in the village, returned to the soldier camp and reported that the chiefs and warriors had fled. A livid Hancock ordered Custer and the Seventh to take the encampment. He

At top is a modern-day photo of the Cheyenne–Dog Man–Lakota Pawnee Fork village site in Kansas. Southern Cheyenne chiefs Lawrence Hart and Gordon Yellowman blessed the Pawnee Fork village site on April 24, 1999, and thanks to historian Leo Oliva and others it was added to the National Register of Historic Places on June 17, 2010. At lower right is Theodore R. Davis's woodcut of Indian Agent Ned Wynkoop (left) and Arapaho interpreter Dick Curtis (right) at the time that Major General Winfield S. Hancock and his army threatened to destroy the village (*Harper's Weekly*, May 11, 1867). Wynkoop did all he could to prevent the destruction, but Hancock refused to listen. At lower left is Davis's woodcut of Little Raven at the time he met with Hancock soon after the village had been destroyed on April 19, 1867 (*Harper's Weekly*, June 8, 1867).

Author's collection for the woodcuts; photo by Louis Kraft © 1999. Louis Kraft Collection, ACP010. Chávez History Library, Santa Fe, N.Mex.

did, capturing a handful of people who were incapable of fleeing.[29] Custer's prisoners included White Horse's insane mother, a broken-legged Lakota warrior and his wife, and a white, mixed-blood, or Cheyenne girl who was eight or twelve. She had been raped time and again, and this probably accounted for her dementia and babbling. Wynkoop did not believe that the girl was white and raped by Cheyennes as he had seen her. He confirmed "that she was ravished" and was found after Custer had control of the village.[30] He questioned who had performed the heinous act. "If by her own race, it is the first instance I have any knowledge of."

At two on the morning of April 15 Hancock proclaimed that he would burn the village, as he felt that the Indians "had acted treacherously towards him, and they deserved punishment."[31] Wynkoop warned that this would cause other tribes to flee. When Hancock refused to listen, Wynkoop told him his wards "were terrified," and he believed "that the result would be an Indian outbreak of the most serious nature; while, at the same time, there is no evidence, in my judgment, that this band of Cheyennes are deserving this severe punishment."[32]

Custer's pursuit had no chance of engaging the fleeing Indians, as they broke into small groups and scattered every which way across the prairie. Over time he sent several reports to Hancock. On the sixteenth he wrote "they are influenced by fear alone, and . . . no council can be held with them in the presence of a large military force."[33] The following day he accused the Cheyennes of the murder of the Lookout Station employees. Two days later Custer wrote a follow-up to Lookout Station, and in it he cleared the Cheyennes of the crime.[34] On April 18, Hancock, who refused to speak with Wynkoop, decided to seize Cheyenne and Sioux property in the villages and then destroy the lodges. He made this decision without ever seeing Custer's April 17 report that accused the Cheyennes of murder. On the nineteenth he destroyed both villages, even though Wynkoop again told him that he would start a war.[35]

On the twenty-first Wynkoop wrote commissioner of Indian affairs Nathaniel Taylor, saying the "Indians of my agency have actually been forced into war."[36] Almost two months later Wynkoop wrote: "Hancock has declared war upon the Cheyennes, and ordered all to be shot who make their appearance north of the Arkansas or south of the Platte Rivers. The question is, what have these Indians done to cause such action?"[37]

Defending himself, Hancock claimed: "I can only say that the villages stood upon the same ground, and I was unable, after an inspection which

I made in person, to distinguish with any certainty the lodges of the Chey-ennes from those of the Sioux."[38] But the general's protest was absurd, as his inspector general released an inventory of exactly what was in the Chey-enne and Sioux villages. Worse, Hancock claimed that he kept the lodges belonging to Bull Bear and Roman Nose.[39]

In July Hancock reported that a war party of eight hundred Pawnees, Cheyennes, and Sioux crossed the Smoky Hill Road.[40] It exposed his lack of knowledge, as the Tsistsistas and Lakotas had been tribal enemies of the Pawnees since before recorded time. Hancock's war continued through most of the summer. It accomplished nothing other than roughly three hundred military and civilian deaths, the destruction of a massive quan-tity of private and public property, and "several millions of dollars in expenses."[41]

AT THE END OF SUMMER or early fall 1867, bride Alice Blackwood Baldwin and her husband, Lieutenant Frank Baldwin, traveled with a military es-cort. He had fought to preserve the Union during the Civil War and was now heading to the frontier to begin his military service in the West.[42]

On September 8 the Baldwins and their escort reached Fort Larned. Their arrival coincided with a meeting that Wynkoop had set up with Cheyennes and Arapahos to discuss Hancock's war, which was directly responsible for the upcoming peace council with them. Wynkoop, with Arapaho interpreter Margaret Adams, and superintendent of Indian af-fairs Thomas Murphy, who had arrived that day, sat near Wynkoop's home and agency building that he rented from the post trader. Poor Bear rep-resented the Kiowa-Apaches. Dog Man chief Tall Bull, Cheyenne coun-cil chief Black Kettle, and Arapaho chiefs Little Raven and Yellow Bear joined them, along with several officers. While a pipe was shared, a white woman from a traveling caravan sat down next to Adams. The interpreter told her to leave, but the woman refused. When the pipe reached the intruder, she inhaled the smoke before passing it to the next person. This bothered Black Kettle, as the woman did not belong there. According to Alice, who watched from a short distance, the woman told Adams "to tell [the Indians] to 'come again,' [before] she withdrew from the circle. Black Kettle was insulted, and frowned with a malignant eye at the fun-loving white squaw. Possibly the presence of several hundred soldiers close at hand insured safety and protection."[43] Nothing would have happened, for over the years Black Kettle, Tall Bull, and Little Raven had cemented a good relationship with Wynkoop.

On the evening of October 9 Roman Nose slipped into the Medicine Lodge peace encampment in Kansas with ten warriors. He held Wynkoop responsible for the destruction of the Pawnee Fork village and intended to kill him. That night the agent dined in Black Kettle's lodge with Superintendent Thomas Murphy and George Bent. The Hinono'eino' learned of Roman Nose's intention and warned the agent of the threat. Wynkoop slipped out of the tipi and stole a fleet-looking horse tethered nearby. It was reported that Roman Nose "had a revolver drawn on" Wynkoop as he rode for his life.[44] No bullets were fired as he disappeared into the night.

Ned Wynkoop's safe return to his agency was well timed, for frightened peace commissioners and reporters reached the post on October 12. Tsistsistas had set the prairie on fire to stop them from reaching the council grounds. Wynkoop, Murphy, and General John Sanborn greeted John Smith, Leavenworth, reporter Stanley, and two other reporters in the room that functioned as his agency. Little Raven and Kiowas Satanta and Stumbling Bear joined the celebration. While Wynkoop served alcohol, the talk ranged from getting the Indians to attend the peace council to Wynkoop's escape. Stanley surprisingly said: "The major is a genial soul and a polished gentleman," and "a skillful concoctor of drinkable beverages, and in his company we whiled away a social hour."[45]

Ignoring the threat upon his life, Wynkoop returned to Medicine Lodge Creek with the peace commissioners, reporters, and their escort. The caravan consisted of 175 to 211 wagons and approximately 600 men, including two companies of the Seventh Cavalry, two companies of Third and Fifth infantry, and camp followers. Little Raven, Satanta, Stumbling Bear, and some of their people joined the train.[46] When Satanta saw whites kill buffalo for sport, he called them children. "When the red men kill," he said, "they do so that they may live."[47]

There were over five thousand Indians camped on the council grounds when the commissioners arrived on October 14. Black Kettle said that it would take eight days to complete the Sacred Arrows ceremony while warning of a potential attack by Tsistsistas camped on the Cimarron River. The threat dampened the commissioners' good humor. Reporters S. F. Hall and George Center Brown wondered if the Indians at Medicine Lodge also

I have seen this image of Magpie Woman and George Bent on the day of their marriage being dated as 1866 and also as 1867, but the second date is most likely wrong, for George wrote historian George E. Hyde, April 25, 1906, Yale, and told him that he married his wife in summer 1866. For the record, there is an image supposedly of Southern Cheyenne Mo-nahs-e-tah reclining on her side and supporting her head with her left hand. There is a problem with this identification. If you have access to the reclining portrait, compare the women's faces in both images. Not only are they of the same person, but they are also wearing the same clothing. Without a doubt both photos are of Magpie Woman.

George Bent and Wife Magpie Woman. History Colorado. Accession number 84.100.1.

considered killing whites. The press and commissioners did not sleep well that night, with Harney being an exception, as he did not see any black paint on the chiefs' faces, which he associated with death.[48]

Stone Forehead had proclaimed that the People should not attend the peace talks until he completed the renewal of the arrows, so the Tsistsistas on the Cimarron avoided the council en masse. But this did not stop Tall Bull and Gray Head from visiting the encampment to check on the meeting's progress. At sundown on the fifteenth they appeared with between fifty and eighty painted warriors across from the commissioners' camp. Harney saw Gray Head and Tall Bull, and realized two friends had come to visit. He invited them to return on October 17, when Wynkoop would be questioned about the Pawnee Fork village.[49]

The seventeenth began with an impromptu meeting between the commissioners, about twenty-five chiefs including Black Kettle and Satanta, and five hundred warriors. Commissioner of Indian Affairs Nathaniel Taylor, who served as president of the peace commission, discussed the gifts and stated he wanted to delay until the Cheyennes arrived. The four other tribes did not want to wait. Many spoke—Satanta twice. Poor Bear was right to the point: his people would wait four more days and then leave. Black Kettle patiently waited for his turn. "We were once friends with the whites, but you nudged us out of the way by your intrigues," he said, "and now when we are in council, you keep nudging each other. Why don't you talk and go straight, and let all be well?"[50]

Just before nightfall Tall Bull and Gray Head appeared. They sat and listened to Wynkoop's translated testimony with Harney. The agent discussed Chivington, Sand Creek, and the aftermath before tearing into how government employees stole from the Indians. He then described "three-point blankets" that were "used as wrappers" at a cost of "$13 per pair," calling them "the most worthless things that I ever saw."[51] He described the annuity distributions as "a most shameless affair. [His wards] were not only killed, but the friendliest were cheated." The fraud included half-full barrels of sugar and useless white women's clothing. He claimed his wards often did not receive a third of the goods they had been promised. Finally he moved to the destruction of the Pawnee Fork village—the reason for Tall Bull and Gray Head's presence. Sanborn wanted to know who raped the girl. "I firmly believe that the soldiers ravished the child," he said, "It was the conclusion I arrived at when I heard that she was ravished. It is my belief now." He closed by saying: "The Cheyennes I have seen lately gave me to understand that the war this summer was in retaliation for the destruction of their village by General Hancock." *Missouri Republican* reporter William Fayel watched Tall Bull and Gray Head shake hands with the agent after his testimony, and reported that they shook with warmth and friendship.[52]

Tall Bull and Gray Head then rode across the creek and met with Black Kettle in his camp. Tall Bull told him to travel to the Cimarron village and explain what he hoped to gain by yet another peace with the *vi'ho' i*—if not, a war party might destroy his horse herd.

Stanley did not like Wynkoop's testimony, reporting that the soldiers did not rape the girl, and that "war was already declared when Hancock appeared [at Fort Larned]."[53] His words created an uproar that would rage across the frontier.

By ten on the morning of October 19, trees had been cut to create an amphitheater within a grove of elms. Tables and chairs were arranged in a semicircle for the commissioners, all of whom were present except for Senator John Henderson of Missouri (the leading speaker). An awning of branches protected them from the sun. Logs were set before the commissioners to seat the key chiefs. Lesser chiefs sat behind them, then warriors, and finally other tribal members. Additional tables had been created and placed on both sides of the commissioners for the journalists to work. The council officially began that day, but the only Tsistsistas present were Black Kettle, his band, and Gray Head, who kept an eye on the council chief. John Smith was the official Cheyenne interpreter, but he was not alone, as George and Charley Bent sat behind the chiefs and also translated. George was listed as an interpreter, while Charley was not. This meant little, for George's younger brother's English was as good as his. They were there to ensure that the words were translated correctly. Satanta (wearing a general's coat) sat on a camp chair in front of other Kiowa chiefs. The Comanches were next, with the bespectacled Ten Bears in front with interpreter Philip McCusker. Little Raven sat on a stool with his interpreter, Margaret Adams, who stood out in a red dress.[54]

While everyone waited, Commissioner Taylor invited impromptu statements. Black Kettle remained silent, perhaps cognizant of Tall Bull's threat, while Gray Head said they could not speak for the People. Henderson arrived as Gray Head's words were translated. The slender and bearded senator stepped in front of the seated commissioners, but instead of sticking to the commission's agenda he spoke of wrongs both sides had committed. He then asked Indian leaders to speak. Satanta claimed that he had not done anything wrong since the Little Arkansas Peace Treaty. "[W]hen I go up to the river, I see a camp of soldiers, and they are cutting my wood down or killing my buffalo. I don't like that, and when I see it, my heart feels like bursting with sorrow."[55] Little Raven was angry over the theft of Hinono'ei ponies at the council. Ten Bears could not understand why the Comanches were present, as they had not broken any treaties. He wanted his annuities and wanted to go home.

The next day Black Kettle and Gray Head did not attend the council. Ten Bears said he wanted to die on his land. Satanta said he wanted everything that was his. He then mounted his horse and rode off. The stage was now Henderson's. He ignored the Arapahos and the Kiowa-Apaches (who were still officially Wynkoop's wards). Directing his talk at the Kiowas and Comanches, he reminded them of a great fear—the buffalo would soon be gone. He then addressed what none of these tribes wanted to hear, living in white-man houses and using the plow. Finally he threatened war if they did not move to their new reservation near the Wichita Mountains on the Red River when directed. Without soliciting a reply he told the Comanches and Kiowas that *they would* sign their treaty on the twenty-first.[56]

On October 21 the interpreters did not translate the entire treaty. It did not matter, for the leaders touched the paper. The Kiowa–Comanche 60,000-square-mile reservation was reduced to 48,000 square miles and moved to southwest Indian Territory. After signing the treaty, the Indians demanded their gifts, especially the guns, but the revolvers were inferior and exploded upon firing. Jesse Leavenworth had Colts with him that, per orders, he had not distributed to his wards on August 7. The commissioners gave the Indians the Colts, which calmed tempers.

A howling wind raked the land, the sky turned black, and rain pounded the earth. After being told that they would receive gifts the following day, the Kiowas and Comanches rode through the storm toward their village circles with their annuities.[57]

Braving the storm, Gray Head (who had returned to the Cimarron village), White Horse, Little Robe, and others reached Black Kettle's lodge before dawn the next morning, and yelled for him to join them. When he did, they rode to the commissioners' camp of ambulances and called for Harney. Reporters and other commissioners were also awakened. The Indians were led into a tent, and while they waited, Gray Head and Little Robe spoke with an agitated Black Kettle, who became livid. No one translated the altercation, but the whites present realized something was wrong.

"[B]eing a peacemaker among the Cheyennes in 1867 was a dangerous occupation," reporters claimed.[58]

When Wynkoop and John Smith or one of the Bent brothers arrived, the Cheyennes were short-tempered. Henderson was in a rage over being awakened. Angered, Little Robe told the commissioner that the renewal of the Sacred Arrows was important and that it was difficult to get all the People together in one place. Black Kettle stepped between them and said that four more days were needed to complete the ceremony. He asked them to shake hands. Henderson turned his back, calling the Sacred Arrows "humbug." "It is life and death with them," General Augur contradicted Henderson. "It is their religion."[59]

Wynkoop did not realize how dangerous the Dog Man threats directed at Black Kettle were until he rode south to the Cimarron village with them. Reporters and commissioners viewed Black Kettle's abduction as a potential Cheyenne attack.

That day Taylor agreed to Kiowa-Apache Poor Bear's request to again be associated with the Comanches and Kiowas and ordered a document drawn up for the chiefs to sign. When Little Raven learned of Black Kettle's kidnapping, he sent a note to Taylor stating that the Cloud People wanted to end their relationship with the Called Out People and sign their own treaty. The commissioner ignored the request.[60]

Days passed, tensions built, and Henderson, Murphy, Stanley, Wynkoop, and everyone else waited for the worse. When October 27 arrived, Stanley claimed that "a filmy haze swam in the air," and that "the earth issued a vapor, in which distant objects seemed to float and assume monstrous proportions. It was a day which invited rest."[61]

But there would be no rest.

Breaking the midmorning calm, warriors charged through Black Kettle's village and the Hinono'ei camp circles shouting that Tsistsistas had come. The Indians did not know what Stone Forehead or the Dog Men planned, and there were not enough soldiers present to protect them. Women screamed as they grabbed their children and ran to escape the impending attack. The peace of the morning erupted into confusion as Tsistsistas, Hinono'eino', and whites ran every which way.[62] The reporters were just as frightened as everyone else. "[W]e got ready," Stanley explained, "loaded our rifles, our revolvers, and our derringers."[63]

Time passed—perhaps an hour. Everyone waited—warriors, soldiers, commissioners—everyone. Finally a dust cloud billowed to the south. A bugle sounded, but it was not blown by a trooper. Mounted Tsistsistas and Dog Men exploded from the trees.

Captain Barnitz watched as the painted warriors formed a battle line at the water's edge. "One portion of the tribe—about a squadron formed in line in front of my camp," the captain wrote, "on a little rise of ground about 150 yards distant, and behind them and on their left flank about 200 Arapahos sat on their ponies, with bows strung, and on the other side of camp the Comanches, . . . Kioways, and Apaches [that had not yet departed the council grounds] were out in force."[64] Barnitz ordered his command to prepare for an assault.

The warriors fired their weapons into the air as they yelled. They then urged their mounts into the creek. Stone Forehead was not present, and neither was Roman Nose, but Wynkoop, much to his relief, saw Black Kettle at the front. The Tsistsistas and Dog Men moved forward in columns similar to the U.S. military as they raced across the water and toward the commissioners' camp. Black Kettle, "his horse covered with foam," led the gallop.[65] The chief was "dressed in a dingy shirt and dingier blanket, [with] his long black hair floating behind him like a bashaw's tail."[66]

"It was the Moon [when the water begins to freeze on the edge of the streams], the Sacred Arrows had been renewed, and the Tsistsistas had arrived to hear what the *vi'ho'i* had to say."[67] The haze cleared and the sun blazed, but it would not last. During this time Black Kettle met briefly with the commissioners.

By late afternoon the wind blew in clouds, darkening the sky and threatening rain. Sanborn held an impromptu interview with Gray Head as John Smith interpreted. Gray Head described the unease when the battle line had confronted Hancock's army, the fear when it came within sight of the Pawnee Fork village, and the destruction of their lodges, which created a war. Knowing how much coverage the press gave the raped Cheyenne girl, Sanborn asked about her. "I was the last one that left the village," Gray Head said, "and she was not hurt then."[68] Sanborn did not accept the answer. "Are you sure that she was a Cheyenne?" he demanded. "Did I not know her parents," Gray Head snapped back, "did I not see her as she grew up, day by day?" Stanley consistently supported the military point of view on the raped girl—she was not Cheyenne. Not changing his view, Stanley now blamed the interpreters on the Pawnee Fork for misrepresenting the girl's race; they had supposedly claimed that she was either mixed-blood or white, even though Wynkoop had insisted she was Cheyenne.

At ten the next morning Dog Men leaders Bull Bear, White Horse, Tall Bull, Gray Head, Little Robe, and Buffalo Chief, along with Black Kettle, sat before the commissioners, and all were dressed in their finest clothing. Other chiefs sat behind them, including Whirlwind, Little Rock, Curly Hair, Little Bear, and Spotted Elk. John Smith was present, as were George and Charley Bent. Across from them but also sitting before the commissioners were Arapaho chiefs Little Raven, Spotted Wolf, Yellow Bear, Storm, Little Big Mouth, Tall Bear, Young Colt, and White Rabbit. C. W. Whitaker was listed as interpreter, but Little Raven again brought Margaret Adams. Superintendent Thomas Murphy was also present, and Wynkoop watched with him.[69]

Senator Henderson, who sat in front of the other commissioners, knew he had to calm the anger over the destruction of the Pawnee Fork village:

> Two years ago, at the mouth of the Little Arkansas, we made peace with you and wished it to last forever, but bad men on one side or the other broke the peace. . . . We have among us wicked men who wish to profit by the calamities of both sides. And these bad men continually seek war. Many tell you lies to excite you, and in the same way to us. We now think these bad men told wicked lies to General Hancock and caused him to march with his soldiers last spring into this country. . . . [T]he Great Father . . . asked him for the reasons of his march, and he [said] that you had broken the peace, . . . that you had committed many outrageous acts upon our people before he had commenced his march. Some of our people said that General Hancock was right, some said that he was wrong. Some said that you wanted war and proposed that we should send soldiers among you to cover the plains like grass. Others said that peace commissioners, and not soldiers, should be sent among you to talk with you. . . .
>
> War long continued must result [in] total destruction to the Indian, because his numbers are less. As long as the buffalo ranges on the plains, we are willing that you should hunt him, as long as you keep to the treaties made at the Little Arkansas.[70]

The chiefs smiled and called out words of enthusiasm when Henderson finished speaking. He then invited them to speak.

Little Raven was the lone speaker for the Cloud People. After talking about them being driven from their country near the mountains, he said: "I hear the whites are getting much gold, cutting fine timber. I make no

According to the Smithsonian Institute, this image of Little Raven (by William S. Soule), who is holding Grass Woman (who was either his daughter or grand-daughter), was taken on August 5, 1869. But this date is incorrect, as William Bent, who is sitting next to the chief, died on May 19, 1869. Little Raven's oldest son Shield (right) would take part in the raids on the Saline and Solomon Rivers in August 1868. Little Bear was also the chief's son. This image shows the friendship between Little Raven and Bent; it also shows the bonding between the trader and Arapaho warriors. Halaas and Masich, *Halfbreed* (2004) dated the image to 1867.

Group portrait at Fort Dodge, Kansas. Photo by William S. (Stinson) Soule. History Colorado. Accession # 89.451.3767.

fuss about it. Let me have my reservation near Fort Lyon. Keep the whites away from it." He kept his words short and to the point. "This winter, when the annuities are sent to us, send out ammunition and guns that we may hunt game. You will by that means convince all my people that you do right." His last major point was traders; he wanted an honest one. "I believe it is the traders that do all the mischief. . . . They are very dishonest people, and you should warn them to do right lest evil should come."

The attention turned to the Southern Cheyennes, but Black Kettle remained seated. Instead, Buffalo Chief stood and spoke. His words were even shorter than Little Raven's. "We sprung from the prairie, we live by it, we prefer to do so, and as yet, we do not want the blessings of civilization. We do not claim this country south of the Arkansas, but that country between the Arkansas and the Platte is ours. We are willing, when we desire to live as you do, to take your advice about that, but until then we will take our chances. It were well that those on the Arkansas road were out of that country, that we might roam over the country as formerly; the bones of our forefathers may rest then. You think that you are doing a great deal for us by giving these presents to us, but we prefer to live as formerly. If you gave us all the goods you could give, yet we would prefer our own life. You give us presents and then take our land; that produces war."

That was it. The treaty was not translated to the Indians. None of the commissioners made an attempt to reply. No one else spoke. When it became obvious that the *vi' ho' i* had no intention of addressing what Little Raven and Buffalo Chief had said, instead of lining up to touch the paper, the Tsistsista leaders stood and began to walk away.

John Smith realized what was happening, and he rushed to the chiefs and spoke with them. So did George Bent. The commissioners spoke among themselves. It was close to bedlam. Henderson saw tragedy bloom before his eyes. He needed Cheyenne marks on the treaty paper. Otherwise it would be little more than a scrap of trash. He caught Bent and Smith's attention and signaled for them to speak with him. Before they moved toward the senator, they stopped the chiefs from following their people toward the piles of gifts. The Tsistsista and Dog Man leaders watched, as did others. Henderson, Bent, and Smith left the brush arbor and walked beyond hearing distance. Henderson gambled and did the only thing he could to save the day. He and the interpreters signaled for Buffalo Chief and others to join them. They did; Henderson spoke and his words were translated. Buffalo Chief took hold of the commissioner's hand and held it as he replied. All looked good as Smith and Bent began to speak to the leaders that surrounded them. Finally, everyone returned to the brush arbor.

Henderson shared what had just happened with the commissioners and reporters.[71] It was exactly what Tall Bull, Bull Bear, Buffalo Chief, and Black Kettle desired: "It was further stipulated that the Indians [this included the Arapahos] should be permitted 'to range at pleasure throughout the unsettled portions of that part of the country they claim as originally theirs, which lies between the Arkansas and Platte Rivers.'"[72] As both the Tsistsistas and Hinono'eino' thought that the buffalo would not disappear, and as Buffalo Chief had just said: "*We do not claim this country south of the Arkansas, but that country between the Arkansas and the Platte is ours,*" this was exactly what they wanted to hear.

While Little Raven and the Arapaho leaders held back, and knowing that they would not be forced to move to a strange land, Black Kettle, Little Bear, Spotted Elk, Buffalo Chief, Slim Face, Gray Head, Little Rock, and Curly Hair formed a line to make their marks on the treaty paper. They chatted and smiled. All looked well, but Bull Bear, Tall Bull, White Horse, Little Robe, Whirlwind, and Heap of Birds refused to get in line. Henderson sent Smith to fix the problem. Tall Bull still fumed over the destruction of the Pawnee Fork village. Worse, Little Robe told Smith that they would not make their marks, as too many Tsistsistas and Dog Men had already touched the paper. When Smith explained the reason to Henderson, Taylor, and the others, they accepted it. However, Murphy, who had worked closely with Wynkoop since 1866, knew better. He told the commissioners that without all the Dog Man signatures, the treaty would not mean much, as their words affected the Southern Cheyenne world. Henderson and Taylor urged Bent and Smith to swing the holdouts back into the fold. This resulted in an explosive but short discussion in the Tsistsista tongue. Neither Bent nor Smith shared what was said, but their words were convincing. Bull Bear stormed to the table and made his mark above Black Kettle's. Tall Bull signed after Curly Hair and the others followed in order.[73]

Little Raven, Yellow Bear, Storm, White Rabbit, Spotted Wolf, Little Big Mouth, Young Colt, and Tall Bear touched the paper, and Senator John Henderson had his treaty. What he had said through Bent and Smith to the Cheyenne leaders had been sincere. The treaty's major points, which were never read to the Indians, would become: (1) Cease all resistance to the building of a railroad along the Platte River; (2) Cease all opposition to the building of roads, railroads, or mail stations; (3) Cease all antagonistic acts against whites, including attacking, abducting, killing, or scalping them; (4) Leave their homeland—at an unspecified time, as the government first needed to remove those Indians then occupying the designated land—and live like white men in Indian Territory; and finally (5) The Indians would retain *their* right to hunt on *their* former land *south* of the Arkansas, just as in the 1865 treaty—*the exact opposite of what Henderson told them and what they understood.*[74]

In early November, Lieutenant General William Sherman issued an order to the Division of the Missouri confirming Henderson. As long as

Wynkoop's wards remained ten miles from a fort or public road, they could hunt buffalo north of the Arkansas up to the South Platte in the "unsettled areas."[75] But the press would publish words contrary to what the Cheyennes and Arapahos thought that they had agreed to with the commissioners.

The treaty would be yet another example of peace in word only.

No one then knew that Henderson's winning words would not make it into the ratified treaty, and certainly not Wynkoop. He did not attest to this treaty as he had in 1865, perhaps as Stanley had called for him being fired as Cheyenne and "Sioux" agent. This threat went nowhere, for Taylor stood strongly behind his employee. By this time Wynkoop realized how valuable George Bent was as an intermediary with the Cheyennes and asked if he might consider working for him. Bent was pleased and accepted, knowing that his father would approve, but that the Dog Men would not. George knew exactly how brother Charles would react.[76]

The treaty had been signed, but Stanley, who almost exclusively agreed with the military and government, no longer did. He blasted the commissioners in print. "The chiefs have signed it merely as a matter of form. Not one word of the treaty was read to them. How, therefore, can the treaty have been a success? Bull Bear and Buffalo Chief, even while they signed, said: 'We will hold that country between the Arkansas and the Platte together. We will not give it up yet, as long as the buffalo and elk are roaming through the country.' Do the above words seem anything like giving up all claims to that country?"[77] He felt certain that the mockery of a treaty would result in yet another war.

"[T]hey have no idea that they are giving up," Barnitz wrote, "or that they have ever given up the country which they claim as their own, the country north of the Arkansas."[78]

By that same October 28 William Byers was aware of what had happened at the treaty council, and, most important to him, Wynkoop's testimony before the commissioners, which infuriated him. "We are able to expect almost any thing from Wynkoop," Byers published.[79] "The words and oaths of some men are always worthless." He accused his former friend of being "partially aware of the fact," and of "tell[ing] as large a falsehood as possible. Wynkoop is such a man, and whether he swear[s] to[o] much or little, it is all the same. No one who knows him will believe his word or his oath."

"Thank God!" declared Lydia Maria Child, an advocate for women's rights, Indian rights, and abolition. "[W]e have, at last, an Official Document, which manifests something like a right spirit toward the poor

Indians."[80] Kansas senator Edmund Ross wrote "The Indian Commission," which stated that the Cheyennes and Arapahos agreed to a "voluntary abandonment of the country between the Arkansas and Platte rivers."[81] Calling the treaty a success, *Harper's Weekly* reiterated the false promise that the Indians could "hunt on the old reservation, south of [the] Arkansas."[82] Totally ignored and forgotten were what Little Raven ("This winter, when the annuities are sent to us, send out ammunition and guns that we may hunt game. You will by that means convince all my people that you do right.") and Buffalo Chief ("We do not claim this country south of the Arkansas, but that country between the Arkansas and the Platte is ours.") had said.[83] In reality, the treaty was nothing less than the death knell for Cheyenne and Arapaho freedom.

Charley Bent, who had risked his life to attend the Medicine Lodge peace talks, caught the attention of Theodore R. Davis, an artist and writer whose work often appeared in *Harper's Weekly*. Davis created a woodcut of him that appeared in his story, "A Summer on the Plains," in the February 1868 issue of *Harper's New Monthly Magazine*. He wrote:

A word should be said with reference to the half-breed Indians that are to be found with every band of warriors. Charley Bent will be a good example. He is the son of Colonel Bill Bent by a Cheyenne squaw. Charley was well brought up, and received a good education at the academy in St. Louis. Shortly after the Sand Creek affair he joined the "Dog-Soldier band" of Cheyenne Indians, with which he has ever since continued to roam. He makes occasional visits to traders' camps, but does not care to frequent Government posts, as there are too many crimes laid at his door to make such localities entirely safe for him. The last visit that he paid to his father's ranch on the Purgatory [Purgatoire] River was not of the most peaceful character. The Colonel [William Bent] tells the story:

"My daughter [Julia] saw something that looked like an Indian's head sticking up over the bank of the main irrigating ditch, through which the water ran past the house. She went out to look at the object and discovered Charley. She told him to stay there until she went to the house and got him some clothes. He said 'No,' that he was after the old man, meaning me. I was off in New Mexico at the time, and she told him so, and asked the durn'd scoundrel to come to the house. 'No,' he said; 'I only wanted the old man,' and, uncocking his rifle, he went off. That's the last that we've seen of him."

Charley Bent speaks English perfectly, and is quite intelligent; but there is no doubt that he is one of the worst Indians on the Plains.[84]

Harsh words for a father to say about his son, but they raise a valid question. Why did Charley, like brother George, choose his mother's people over his father's? He grew up walking between two worlds in a time of extreme racial hatred; one accepted him while the other did not. More, he understood what was happening, and saw firsthand Chivington's butchery and mutilation of *his* people—something that must have seared his soul beyond belief. He had heard what his father had said on the Little Arkansas in fall 1865, he saw what had happened at Medicine Lodge Creek, and he knew that his "people's" life and future had a dim outlook. There would be no turning back. Charley's reason to kill his father was heinous. At the same time, it showed who he was, a young man who had made a final decision on which world would be his.

It would never be.

Charley's world also included intertribal warfare, which was a combination of bravery and manhood while providing for the family. It included defending or capturing women, children, and horses, as well as protecting the Tsistsista buffalo range from invasion. During the peace council Kaws had raided the Hinono'ei horse herd—an insult that required action. Although advised not to seek revenge right after the treaty had been signed, Bent joined a war party of young Dog Men who set out after the raiders. By early November they had tracked the Kaws to the mouth of Walnut Creek in Kansas, but before they found the enemy, the war party came face-to-face with a detachment of U.S. scouts from Fort Harker that searched for missing soldiers.

Both sides recognized the other as mortal enemies and halted. As soon as Charley was recognized as the "chief" of the war party, it became a distant standoff until he and Charles Coridoro agreed to ride forward and meet with nine unarmed companions. The foes closed; then Bent and Coridoro continued alone. According to Major N. D. McGinley, "Bent was insolent," saying "that if the troops would lay down their arms and surrender, they would be escorted to Fort Harker without injury."[85] Coridoro did not find the words amusing. Suddenly Bent recognized him. He cursed, yanked his mount around, and galloped away. Coridoro had ignored their agreement, pulled a revolver from his boot, and shot at the retreating man. "The bullet struck Bent just above the hipbone. He clung to his horse and

Theodore R. Davis created this woodcut of Charley Bent at the Medicine Lodge Peace Council in Kansas in October 1867, less than a month before his death on November 10. The portrait was first published in Davis's article, "A Summer on the Plains," in *Harper's New Monthly Magazine*, February 1868.

Louis Kraft Collection, ACP010. Chávez History Library, Santa Fe, N.Mex.

escaped" with the Dog Men as the other scouts yanked out hidden weapons and fired.

The warriors brought Charley to a Tsistsista village, and although the injury was not originally fatal he did not improve. An infection set in, consuming him with fever, and he grew weaker by the day. The nineteen-year-old Charles Bent died on November 10, 1867.[86] He left behind a young family—his wife Little Woman and daughter Susie, who would eventually marry David Penleton.[87]

THE WINTER OF 1867–68 WAS HARSH on the Tsistsistas and Hinono'eino' living between the Platte and Arkansas Rivers. By February 1868 they were cold and hungry. As in the past, they expected what they had agreed to on the treaty ground—but they received nothing. This had not yet caused a problem, but soon would. Superintendent Murphy informed Wynkoop when he distributed annuities that no weapons were to be passed out. This perturbed the agent, and he sarcastically replied that he had none to distribute.[88] Guns were a necessity for his wards' survival, and as they believed the recent treaty included arms and ammunition, they expected to receive them.[89]

John Smith, who then lived with a Tsistsista band sixty miles south of Fort Dodge, wrote Murphy that Wynkoop had not seen his wards since the previous fall. Murphy ignored the accusation, knowing the agent had already moved among his wards twice by February. Murphy, who also knew that Smith had not received long overdue money owed to him by the Interior Department, must have smiled when the interpreter blamed Wynkoop. Smith then shared an escalating problem that he did not report to the agent—the Cheyennes in his village were "getting all of the whiskey that they wanted."[90]

Trader J. L. Butterfield was in a Cheyenne village when a warrior returned from Fort Dodge with five gallons of whiskey. "[N]early the whole camp [became] drunk," he reported.[91] Soon after, Butterfield visited an Arapaho village when Chief Big Mouth arrived with a keg and eighteen bottles of whiskey. Frightened, he spoke about the "effect whiskey has on Indians and what danger white men are in while in their camp."

By the end of the month, Murphy, via orders from above, allowed the distribution of arms in the future.[92] This was just the beginning of an annuity problem that would get out of hand. When there were goods to distribute, there would be no guns; if there were guns, orders prevented distributing them. The first instance happened in March when General Philip Sheridan, who commanded the Division of the Missouri, visited Fort Larned. Wynkoop accompanied him to Fort Dodge, where over weeks the general held impromptu meetings with chiefs as they visited the post. When it was time to distribute annuities, Sheridan blocked the allocation of weapons delivered to Wynkoop. The Cheyennes and Arapahos did not hide their anger.[93]

On April 25 when Wynkoop dispersed annuities to Black Kettle, Stone Forehead, Little Robe, and Big Jake's Cheyenne bands along with Little Raven, Storm, Big Mouth, and Yellow Bear's Arapaho bands, he did not hand out weapons. There was no demonstration of anger.[94] John Smith witnessed the event, and Special Agent Alex Banks certified it. Although Wynkoop thought his wards were "more peaceably disposed then they have been for years," he addressed the shrunken area and the severely reduced number of buffalo available to hunt, saying they are "almost [in] a state of starvation."[95]

Tall Bull's band had missed the April distribution, but when the Dog Man appeared at Fort Larned on May 12 and Wynkoop saw his people's physical condition, he issued supplies.[96] On May 17 Wynkoop wrote a good conduct letter for Tall Bull, as he considered him "peaceably disposed, and will do nothing that is wrong, unless forced to do so by imprudent acts of white men."[97]

The May Cheyenne-Arapaho supplies were sent to Fort Harker and stored in the Chick & Co. warehouse. When Wynkoop learned of the problem, he alerted Murphy while stressing the urgency of getting the goods to Fort Larned. He then sent runners to inform his wards of the situation. As the end of the month neared, the Tsistsista bands of Black Kettle, Stone Forehead, Little Robe, and Big Jake, along with the Hinono'ei bands of Little Raven, Storm, Spotted Wolf, and Yellow Bear, arrived at the Pawnee Fork to receive their annuities. On the twenty-ninth Wynkoop, Smith, and Banks began the thirty-five-mile trip with a train of goods. When they arrived, the Kiowa-Apaches (Iron Shirt, Cut Nose, and Young Chief) were also present, as they were still in limbo from the 1867 treaty. The distribution took five days, and during that time the agent powwowed with Black Kettle and Stone Forehead. The complaints over not receiving weapons that were promised at Medicine Lodge Creek returned and grew.[98]

JUNE BEGAN WITH THUNDERSTORMS in Kansas. The Saline River flooded while the Solomon River saw a huge increase in water flow. Using the rainfall as cover, Little Robe, Tall Bull, and between three and four hundred Dog Men set out on a revenge raid on the Kaw reservation near Council Grove. The three-to-four-hour skirmish amounted to two Kaw buildings destroyed, plus one Kaw and three Dog Men wounded. Afterward Tall Bull, Little Robe, and their warriors split into small groups as they left the area. It was reported that twenty warriors under Little Robe caused massive damage to white farmsteads, including stealing property, damaging crops, killing cattle, and destroying homes, while not harming any whites. Little Robe's statement told a different story. He admitted that to survive, they killed eleven cattle, but they "did not interfere with any person or thing."[99]

The failed raid was just the beginning of what would become a long hot summer.

Aware that Congress had not yet ratified the 1867 treaty, Lieutenant General Sherman made certain that Senator Henderson's promise that the Cheyennes and Arapahos could hunt buffalo north of the Arkansas would not make it into the treaty. He declared that they would not be allowed to hunt buffalo off their reservation. Claiming that bows and arrows were a better weapon to hunt buffalo, on June 24 he told Secretary of the Interior O. H. Browning that the new treaty did not include the distribution of weapons. Sherman knew that this would keep Wynkoop's wards resentful, and might even provoke a war.[100]

Knowing that he would again not be allowed to distribute weapons to starving people, Wynkoop invited his wards to Fort Larned for the July 20 annuity distribution. His agency was outside the perimeter of the southwest corner of the fort below the curve in the Pawnee Fork. Under an intense sun the Kiowa-Apaches and Arapahos accepted their supplies but voiced their displeasure when they did not receive guns. Not so the Cheyennes. As soon as they realized they would not be issued revolvers and carbines, the chiefs abruptly ended the distribution—and they did not hide their anger. Either Black Kettle or Little Robe said: "[Our] white brothers [are] pulling away from [us] the hand they had given to [us] at Medicine Lodge Creek."[101] After refusing the entire shipment, the chief added that they "would wait with patience for the Great Father to" . . . give them "the arms and ammunition [he] promised them." Wynkoop immediately wired Murphy, who was in Washington to get the arms released.

Three days later the superintendent met with Taylor to discuss the weapon situation. The commissioner understood the urgency and directed Murphy to leave for Fort Larned while wiring Wynkoop to proceed with caution. It would be up to the agent to convince Murphy that "no evil will result from such [a] delivery."[102]

While Thomas Murphy was en route to Fort Larned, Congress ratified the Medicine Lodge Treaty on July 25.[103] The superintendent arrived at Fort Larned no later than August 1, for on that day he and Wynkoop held a special meeting with the Arapahos and Kiowa-Apaches (the Southern Cheyennes had not yet arrived). Murphy's lone goal was to see if he agreed with Wynkoop that his wards sincerely wanted peace. If he did, he intended to release the weapons. Murphy spoke about the failed June raid on the Kaws, telling Little Raven and the other chiefs that war parties could no longer travel over land where settlers lived. There could be no war with the white man, and he wanted them to make peace with the Kaws and Osages.

Little Raven grumbled. The Kaws started the trouble at Medicine Lodge Creek when they raided the Hinono'ei pony herd, and he wanted "to know if he and his people were to blame."[104] He then backed off, saying that he would talk with the Tsistsistas, and if they made peace, that he would join them. Little Raven returned to the reason for the meeting. If Murphy released the weapons, he and the other chiefs "promised these arms should never be used against the whites." Murphy believed Little Raven. The

Arapahos received "160 pistols, 80 Lancaster rifles, 12 kegs of powder, 1½ kegs of lead, and 15,000 caps" while the Kiowa-Apaches received "40 pistols, 20 Lancaster rifles, 3 kegs of powder, ½ keg of lead, and 5,000 caps."

Murphy instructed Wynkoop to tell the Cheyennes why they did not receive arms, "to issue them now, and [tell them] to mak[e] peace with the Osages and Kaws." On August 2 the superintendent left for Atchison.

Unknown to Wynkoop or Murphy, Southern Tsistsista warriors quietly set out from several villages above the forks of Walnut Creek on August 2 and 3 with the intention of raiding Pawnees in Nebraska. They were mostly young warriors from Little Rock, Black Kettle, Stone Forehead, and Bull Bear's bands. Red Nose, a Dog Man, and Man Who Breaks the Marrow Bones (or Oh-e-ah-mohe-a), a member of Black Kettle's band and White Antelope's brother, led the war party. Edmund Guerrier and George Bent were two of the warriors. They were in no rush and carefully avoided being seen while gaining warriors as they traveled. After crossing the Smoky Hill near Fort Hays, which was almost due north of Fort Larned, they continued until they reached a Tsistsista village on the Saline River in north-central Kansas. There were ten Lakota and a few Hinono'ei lodges present. Here they passed the war pipe and recruited support. Twenty Lakotas and four Hinono'eino', including Shield (Little Raven's son), and additional Tsistsistas joined the war party.[105]

It was now about the eighth of the month.

While the war party smoked and danced on the Saline, Tsistsista bands under Stone Forehead, Black Kettle, Little Rock, and Bull Bear appeared on the open plain below and west of Wynkoop's agency and set up their camp circles. On August 9 Wynkoop distributed all the supplies that had been previously refused. He then gave them what they most craved—guns. Immediately the Tsistsistas' demeanor changed from dark and edgy to cheerful. "[N]ever before have I known them to be better satisfied and express themselves as being so well contented," Wynkoop reported to Murphy.[106] An optimistic Wynkoop also wrote: "I am perfectly satisfied that there will be no trouble with them this season."

On that same August 9, Lieutenant General Sherman created a military district for the Cheyennes, Arapahos, Comanches, and Kiowas south of the Arkansas that would be commanded by Lieutenant Colonel William Hazen.[107] There would still be Indian agents. However, "When Indians are on reservations with civilian agents actually present with them, no interferences will be made," Sherman's orders stated, "but military commanders may note any neglects or irregularities on the part of said Indians or their agents."[108]

Commissioner Taylor did not like Sherman's dictum, as he saw it as yet another ploy by the military to pull the Indian Bureau away from the Interior Department. He felt the move to force the four tribes to live at Fort Cobb in Indian Territory would open the door for the military to appropriate "control over issues or disbursements to Indians" from the agents.[109]

Regardless of which department was best suited to control the Indians' future, neither were in a position to do so. Sherman admitted that the War Department did not have nearly enough funds to provide for the Indians. Meanwhile Charles Mix, who was functioning as acting commissioner in Taylor's absence, stated that the Indian Bureau had insufficient funds available to provide for the four tribes as put in place by Sherman. While both departments fought to control the Indians' future, neither had bothered to address the cost of providing for them once they had been herded onto their new reservation.

August 10 arrived, and with it came an event that would change the Southern Cheyennes and Arapahos lives forever. On that day most of the warriors in the war party moved down the Saline toward white settlements. About twenty broke off and continued toward the hated Pawnees in Nebraska. As the main war party neared white homesteads, they halted for the day and pitched camp. Red Nose and Man Who Breaks the Marrow Bones continued on to the first building and found a *vi' ho' i* woman, whom they raped. When they brought her to their camp, it was outraged, and she was returned to her home on the eleventh. That day they were fired upon when they approached other homesteads. On August 12 the war party reached the south fork of the Solomon River and were treated kindly and fed by whites. Later that day they reached the north fork of the Solomon and again whites shot at them. The war party moved on, but the Pawnees had become a forgotten target. Now they attacked white communities in their path. They killed and raped. Two small sisters were abducted, but when chased, warriors abandoned them unharmed. When the onslaught began, warriors who wanted nothing to do with it deserted and rode south. Guerrier and Bent were two of these warriors, and according to Edmund returned "to our homes on the Purgatory [Purgatoire]."[110]

But Guerrier did not tell the entire story of their trek south. After seeing Black Kettle and Little Rock's camp circles abandoned, they followed their trail to Wynkoop's agency. Guerrier and Bent were still on and off the agent's payroll, and at this time Bent was on it. Guerrier lived with Little Rock's band when not on the land granted him by the 1865 Little Arkansas Peace Treaty, while Bent and his wife—Black Kettle's "niece"—Magpie Woman (Mo-he-by-vah) lived with the chief and had since before their marriage in 1866. With Julia Bent also at Fort Larned, both men had reason to rejoin their villages.[111]

News of the depredations spread quickly, and this put Wynkoop in a tough spot, as Black Kettle and Little Rock and most of their people were still camped near his agency and were innocent of the crime. A distraught Black Kettle tore his clothes and yanked his hair when he heard of the raid.[112] For anyone suspecting that he had anything to do with the unfortunate attacks, George Bent had this to say: "Black Kettle was not in the Solom[o]n Valley Raid. I know this to be the fact."[113]

On the evening of August 13 Wynkoop spoke with Little Rock and told the council chief that he needed the names of the responsible parties. On the nineteenth Little Rock again met with the agent. John Smith interpreted, and James Morrison, whom Wynkoop employed as a scout to live with the Arapahos, was present, as was Lieutenant Samuel Robbins (Seventh U.S. Cavalry). Little Rock had put himself at risk to gather what turned out to be a massive exposé of the war parties' journey, leaders, outbreak, murders, rapes, and abductions, which named Porcupine Bear (Big Head's son), Bear That Goes Ahead (Sand Hill's son), Tall Wolf (Stone Forehead's oldest son), Red Nose, and Man Who Breaks the Marrow Bones as having committed depredations. "I consider the whole party guilty," Wynkoop concluded, "but it being impossible to punish all of them, I hold the principal men whom you mention responsible for all."[114] He wanted the Tsistsista chiefs to deliver the guilty for punishment, but knew that this was an impossible request. He told Little Rock: "Should my demands not be complied with, you can bring your lodge and family here, and I will protect you."

Soon after, Bent heard Wynkoop tell Black Kettle that "if he would move to Fort Larned he would take care of him."[115] But the chief did not want this. He and Little Rock wanted to get as far as possible from the violence they knew was about to come and moved south. George Bent and Magpie Woman, along with Guerrier, accompanied their chiefs south. Soon after the Tsistsistas set up their campsites near Fort Dodge on the

Arkansas, Black Kettle said he did not intend to return to the land of the Upper Arkansas. Instead, his and Little Rock's bands would journey into Indian Territory with no plan other than that they would winter on the Lodge Pole River (Washita), which they had done in the past. Neither Bent nor Guerrier wanted to do this, and they left for the Purgatoire and Upper Arkansas with Magpie Woman and Julia.

Regardless of how many Southern Cheyennes and Arapahos were unaware of the raid, much less supported it or took part in it, this ill-advised rapine upon white people gave General Sheridan exactly what he needed to launch a winter campaign. There would be no more explanations, no more second chances, no more treaties, for now the wrath of the United States' might had been unleashed. For the most part, the Hinono'eino' had supported their brothers, the Southern Tsistsistas, during the decade, but as Little Raven had failed to make a separation from them at the 1867 peace council, they were now attached to their aggressive brethren for all time.

UNAWARE THAT LIEUTENANT GENERAL SHERMAN had officially declared war on his wards, on September 17 Wynkoop set out for the East to secure support to end the hostilities before they got out of hand.[116]

In the wee hours of that same day Major George Forsyth (Ninth U.S. Cavalry) with a small command of fifty-two (two officers, one surgeon, and the rest hand-picked plainsmen), camped near the Arickaree Fork of the Republican River in Colorado Territory. His command had been tasked with finding and destroying warring Cheyenne villages. But they were too close to a Dog Man–Lakota village and had been discovered. The hunters became the hunted. When Tall Bull and White Horse began the assault on the white camp, the scouts fled to an island.

What should have been an easy victory was not, for the whites had repeating Spencer carbines, and the island provided at least minimal protection from warrior charges over it. Roman Nose was in the village, but he could not take part in the attack, for his medicine that protected him in battle had been compromised when unknowingly he had broken a taboo. He needed to perform a cleansing ceremony before he could participate in the fight.

The first charge over the whites on the island failed to kill them. Warriors rode to the village and pushed for Roman Nose to join the assault.

He could not, for he had not completed the cleansing ritual. At the same time, he knew that the warriors depended upon him to lead them to victory. Later that day the war leader rode to a hill above where the People had surrounded the *vi' ho' i* on the island. Women watched the battle from this vantage point. By this time a second charge over the whites had failed to kill them. Warriors died; the whites also suffered losses. Forsyth had at least two wounds. His second in command, Lieutenant Frederick Beecher, was fatally wounded, as was the expedition's surgeon. Scouts were dead, and more would die from wounds already received.[117]

Tangle Head, with two or three warriors, joined the war leader on the hill. They sat together, and Roman Nose explained his situation. "[S]omething was done [at the Sioux camp] that I was told must not be done," he said.[118] "The bread I ate was taken out of the frying pan with something made of iron. I have been told not to eat anything so treated. This is what keeps me from making a charge. If I go into this fight, I shall certainly be killed."

White Contrary appeared, and his name revealed who he was.[119] He knew the situation, and at the same time it was his position to challenge it. "Well, here is Roman Nose," he said to the group, "the man that we depend on, sitting behind this hill. He is the man that makes it easy for his men in any fight." White Contrary turned to Roman Nose. "You do not see your men falling out there?" he asked. "Two fell just as I came up." White Contrary dared Roman Nose to join the fight. The war leader repeated his situation, but then painted himself and placed his buffalo-horned war bonnet on his head. His great friend Tall Bull told him to complete the purification ceremony, but his words were ignored.

Roman Nose rode to the battlefield. With many warriors behind him, he led the third charge late that afternoon. As he rode over the scouts, a round struck him in the back above the hip and fell from his war horse. Not dead, he clawed himself onto land. Warriors found him and carried him to safety. Roman Nose, who already knew his life was no more, died at sundown.

The list of Tsistsista leaders had shrunk over the previous years, but now, with Roman Nose's death, it was the beginning of the end of the Called Out People's major leaders. Their war leader was gone, but they still had their major peace and Dog Man chiefs.

That night Forsyth requested volunteers Jack Stillwell and Pierre Trudeau to slip through Indian lines and reach Fort Wallace—approximately ninety-five miles—and return with reinforcements. The following night A. J. Pliley and Jack Donovan set out with the same task.[120] All four completed their journey, and the survivors of Forsyth's command were rescued.

BY THE TIME THAT THE FREEZING MOON (December) arrived, there were numerous tribes and bands camped between six and twelve miles below Black Kettle and Little Rock's combined village on the Washita River in Indian Territory. But the mileage was deceiving, as Little Raven's Hinono'ei village was closest downriver. However, as the Lodge Pole looped first north and then south in an oxbow, the huge Tsistsista village that was below Kicking Bird's small Kiowa village was roughly the same distance from Black Kettle as Little Raven's was as the crow flies. This village included the camp circles of Stone Forehead, Sand Hill, Little Robe, Big Jake, Black White Man, and Stone Calf. Old Whirlwind's Tsistsista village was a short distance below the large camp. Comanche and Kiowa-Apache villages were farther downriver.[121]

In mid-November Black Kettle, Little Robe, Big Mouth, and Spotted Wolf left their villages on the Washita with their escorts and assembled at a predetermined location. Together they rode toward Fort Cobb to meet with the *vi'ho' i* peace chief. Their destination was 119 miles east of Black Kettle's Washita village.[122] Upon their arrival Colonel William Hazen, who had recently arrived from New Mexico Territory to oversee the Indians not engaged in war, met with them.

"I do not feel afraid to go among the white men," Black Kettle told Hazen, "because I feel them to be my friends."[123] He said the Tsistsistas south of the Arkansas "do not trouble Texas, but north of the Arkansas they are almost always at war." He then vaguely spoke of the war party that rode north to raid Pawnees, who, when "fired upon," began the current war. "I have always done my best to keep my young men quiet, but some will not listen, and since the fighting began I have not been able to keep them all at home." He told Hazen that he had 180 lodges on the Washita, but here he spoke of all the Tsistsistas camped along the river. "[W]e all want peace, and I would be glad to move all my people down this way. . . . I speak only for my own people; I cannot speak nor control the Cheyennes north of the Arkansas."

Big Mouth told Hazen, "I came to you because I wish to do right; had I wished to do any wrong I never would have come near you." He was fearful of soldiers attacking his village. "I do not want war, and my people do not, but although we have come back south of the Arkansas, the soldiers follow us and continue fighting." He wanted Hazen to stop the "soldiers from coming against us . . . [and] to send a letter to the Great Father at Washington at once, to tell him to have this fighting stopped."

After explaining that he worked with and liked Indians in New Mexico Territory, Hazen said that the Great Father had sent him to Fort Cobb to "take care of all the Cheyennes, Arapahoes, Apaches, Comanches, and Kiowas." He would not only "look after them and their agents and their traders," but he would "get them [onto] the reservations agreed upon . . . at Medicine Lodge, [and] see that they were treated aright." Of course, there was a problem, for the treaty also stated that the Cheyennes and Arapahos would not move onto their new reservation until houses and other required buildings had been built. To date there was nothing, absolutely nothing— no work whatsoever had been done.

The colonel's first words must have pleased Black Kettle and the others, but then he told them that the Cheyennes and Arapahos had started a war and reignited their fears. "I am sent here as a peace chief," Hazen said, "[and] all here is to be peace," which again was what they wanted to hear. But then the colonel changed directons, telling them that Sheridan was a "great war chief, and I do not control him" or his soldiers. "Therefore, you must go back to your country, and if the soldiers come to fight, . . . with him [Sheridan] you must make peace." Lean Bear had tried to stop an attack on his village and was killed, and White Antelope had tried to stop an attack on his village and was killed. It was as if the past had again become the future.

"I am glad to see you," Hazen said, "and glad to hear that you want peace and not war." He then offered hope. "I cannot stop the war, but will send your talk to the Great Father, and if he sends me orders to treat you like the friendly Indians I will send out for you to come in. But you must not come in again unless I send for you." Not finished, he gave them words to carry back to their people. "I am satisfied that you want peace," he said, "that it has not been you, but your bad men . . . that have made war, and I will do all I can for you to bring peace." This must have pleased Black Kettle and Big Mouth. If perchance Hazen received word to deal with them, "I will go with you and your agent [to] your reservation and care for you there."

The colonel sounded sincere. But was he?

Two days later Hazen wrote Lieutenant General Sherman, and included a copy of his talk with Black Kettle and Big Mouth. "To have made peace with them would have brought to my camp most of those now on the war path south of the Arkansas."[124] More, he was concerned that "a second Chivington affair might occur." Hazen then addressed a major concern. "I do not understand that I am to treat for peace, but would like definite instruction in this and like cases. To make peace with these people would probably close the war, but perhaps not permanently."

Hazen also discussed the Kiowa–Comanche view of the Black Kettle–Big Mouth meeting. They "felt that the suit for peace is not sincere beyond the chiefs who spoke, who were without doubt in earnest." Then Hazen shared something that never made it into his recorded meeting with Black Kettle and Big Mouth. "The young men who accompanied these chiefs expressed pleasure that no peace was made, as they would get more mules, and next spring the Sioux and other northern bands were coming down and would clean out this entire country." It is doubtful that the peace mission would have brought warriors yearning to again ride the warpath, for it would have undermined their entire effort. And if they were that foolish, why would Hazen have given them hope, unless it was to lull them into a false sense of safety?

Regardless, Hazen's words sealed Black Kettle's fate, even though the chief never realized it, as he and the others braved heavy snowfall and bitter cold while they struggled to return to their villages.

On the evening of November 26 Black Kettle had been up late while he and others spoke in council; Medicine Woman Later did not retire until her husband did. The night was freezing. Most likely they held each other under their robes as they used their body heat to combat the icy temperature. Suddenly the yapping of dogs, the sound of pounding hooves, the familiar pop-pop-popping of white-man guns, the shrieks of Tsistsistas, and the gruesome shouts of *vi'ho' i* soldiers jerked them awake. The nightmare of four years past had returned. Everything he had done to protect his band and the rest of the Called Out People had once again failed. Instantly awake and dressed, they stepped from their tipi. The chief fired one lone shot from his weapon, but that was it. Luckily, Black Kettle had tethered his horse near their lodge. He mounted and pulled Medicine Woman Later up behind him.[125]

But this attack, by Lieutenant Colonel George Armstrong Custer and the Seventh U.S. Cavalry, was more organized—the four-pronged strike limited the Tsistsistas' chances of escape. As the troopers charged into the encampment from different directions, they came with guns blazing. Every living human that moved became a target. Black Kettle and Medicine

In this detail from Steven Lang's mural at the Washita Battlefield National Historic Site (Cheyenne, Oklahoma), Lieutenant Colonel George Armstrong Custer and the Seventh U.S. Cavalry charge into Black Kettle's village on the Washita River in Indian Territory on November 27, 1868. Custer appears as he did on that frozen day, dressed in buckskins and sporting a full beard (upper right). In the foreground a Cheyenne woman holds her infant as she and her daughter run for their lives. Although Custer attacked the waking camp unaware of who was present until after he controlled the battle site, to this author's knowledge Custer personally killed only one American Indian, it was on that day, and he was a Cheyenne warrior.

Courtesy National Park Service/artist Steven Lang.

Woman Later had seen this at Sand Creek, and on this predawn morn it was no different. Black Kettle instinctively urged his mount toward the Washita, but he was too late. Just as they reached the river bank, soldier bullets cut them down.[126]

This was just the beginning of the onslaught. Against Custer's orders, soldiers would shoot noncombatants, but perhaps they were combatants.

While not knowing that they had but a minute or two left walking Mother Earth, Cheyenne Chief Black Kettle pulls wife Medicine Woman Later onto his horse at the beginning of the dawn attack on their village as they attempt to flee. This is another detail from Steven Lang's magnificent 2004 mural at the Washita Battlefield National Historic Site.

Courtesy National Park Service/artist Steven Lang.

Ben Clarke, Custer's chief of scouts, ran to him on a small mound on the incline south of the village that the colonel had chosen as an observation post. "Gen[eral,] do you want the women and children killed[?]" he asked.[127] "No, why?" Clarke pointed at where women and children attempted to escape. Custer saw his men shooting at them. He did not hesitate, mounted, and rode toward the troops that disobeyed his orders. When he reached them, he demanded they stop shooting at women and children.

But as in all battles, bullets were fired every which way. People died. Custer's attack upon a village without knowledge of who the occupants were was typical for most of the decade. If Indians were present, attack and kill. Custer later claimed that the trail of a war party led him to the village. A war party? They may have been Kiowas, who had stopped at the village on the way to their own village. Could the warriors have simply been hunting game? The truth or lack of truth means nothing. Custer had no clue whom he attacked until he was securing prisoners, when a middle-aged Tsistsista woman named Mahwissa told him that it was Black Kettle's village. She was not Black Kettle's sister, as often claimed.[128]

What followed means a lot, and it was twofold. Custer had suffered casualties, and although not yet, they would include his arrogant second in command—Major Joel Elliott. When Elliot saw Cheyenne women and children attempting to escape, he, without orders, chased them while infamously yelling, "Here goes for a brevet or a coffin."[129] He got the latter when he allowed himself to be surrounded and killed. Every man with him died.

Back in the village it became a defensive operation for the Seventh as Cheyennes, Arapahos, and perhaps Kiowas below Black Kettle's village moved to surround the soldiers. As their numbers grew, and as the counterattack became alarming, Custer remained calm. He concentrated on destroying the village, pony herd, and all the Cheyennes' belongings, while trying to keep his victory and extricating his command from a bad situation. Ben Clarke boldly suggested that the command move toward the other villages as if to attack them. Custer agreed. Just before dark, the Seventh and fifty-three mounted women and children prisoners moved downriver. The subterfuge worked, forcing the harassing warriors to rush to protect their village circles. Sometime after dark, Custer halted his advance, reversed course, and hustled northward as quickly as possible.[130]

NOVEMBER 29, 1868. Ned Wynkoop halted his trek southward toward Fort Cobb, where he had been ordered to congregate his wards. He again felt that he was leading these people to slaughter, but refused to again be a "pied piper." On that day—and he was totally unaware of Black Kettle's fate—he wrote Commissioner Taylor: "[Volunteer troops] have expressed their determination to kill under all circumstances the Indians of my agency. . . . [The Cheyennes and Arapahos] will readily respond to my call [to congregate at Fort Cobb], but I most certainly refuse to again be the instrument of the murder of innocent women and children. . . . All left me under the circumstances, with the present state of feelings I have in this matter, is now to respectfully tender my resignation."[131]

Wynkoop reversed course and retraced his journey as he traveled northward with his ultimate destination being the East. As soon as possible he wired his resignation. Since fall 1864 everything he did or said had become controversial. Having no intention of remaining quiet, while knowing that he would set off another hullabaloo, he provided his resignation letter to the press. This move received large coverage, ranging from the *Leavenworth Commercial* on December 9 to the *New York Times* on the nineteenth. As he hoped, his actions again set off a maelstrom of disagreement.

GENERAL PHILIP SHERIDAN WAS PRESENT when Custer and his prisoners reached Camp Supply and watched the conquering hero's victory parade.

There was a double standard as far as captured women were concerned. The whites constantly pointed at the "heathens" who raped and battered their women, although not all were brutally treated. This was not a one-way street, for on the evening of Custer's safe return, the future of the captive Cheyenne women turned dark.

Throughout time the victors have reaped the rewards and have written the histories. Custer tasked scout Rafael Romero with distributing Cheyenne women to any of his officers desiring female companionship. These women had no choice, for certainly the threat of death, stated or not, dominated their fears. To survive, they allowed Custer's officers to rape them. The lieutenant colonel joined his staff, and according to Captain Frederic Benteen, "Custer took first choice, and lived with her during winter and spring of 1868 and '69."[132] Her name was Mo-nahs-e-tah. She had survived Sand Creek, as had her father, Little Rock, but he died at the Washita. She was seven and a half months pregnant. Her future had to have been frightening. White women did what they had to do to stay alive, and so did this young Tsistsista woman—she did what was necessary to survive.

OUCHESS (MEANING "CREEPING PANTHER"), as the Southern Tsistsistas named Custer after he destroyed Black Kettle's village, returned to the field on December 7, 1868. Sheridan was present, but Custer retained command of the Seventh and the Nineteenth Kansas Volunteer Cavalry.[133] Three prisoners also joined the expedition: Mahwissa, an unnamed Sioux woman, and surprisingly, Mo-nahs-e-tah, who had not yet delivered her first child.[134] This came about when Custer invited the women to his tent and with Romero translating, "acquainted them with the desire of the government to establish peace with their people and with the Arapahoes."

He wanted them to deliver "friendly message[s] to the absent tribes."[135] Mahwissa was the only choice to perform this task. However, after Mo-nahs-e-tah delivered her child at Fort Sill in Indian Territory on January 12, 1869, she chose to leave her newborn behind with the Sioux woman. During the following months Mo-nahs-e-tah functioned as a scout and intermediary for Custer.[136]

The first destination was the battlefield to confirm Elliott's death. All but one corpse were within a twenty-yard circle. The remains were "exactly as they fell," Custer reported, "except [they were] mutilated * * * in the most savage manner."[137] This was not an exaggeration. He included Dr. Henry Lippincott's description of Elliott's body: "[T]wo bullet holes in head; one in left cheek; right hand cut off; left foot almost cut off; * * * deep gash in right groin; deep gashes in calves of both legs; little finger of le[f]t hand cut off, and throat cut." Custer had two armies at his back: one a battle veteran, the other not battle tested. From this point forward both craved blood.

The Custer-Sheridan army passed deserted campsites as they moved down the Washita. He had a victory but was lucky to be alive. Some bands had hastened to Fort Cobb and safety with Hazen, but not all. Stone Forehead and Little Robe knew of Black Kettle's actions to keep peace, and that he was dead. That alone showed how broken the white man's word was, that soon all their people could be dead. They moved south toward the Red River.

WYNKOOP RETURNED THE GOVERNMENT ASSETS to Thomas Murphy in Atchison, Kansas, then hurried to Washington. After settling his account with the Interior Department, on December 17 he testified before the Senate Committee on Indian Affairs. Angered by Black Kettle's death, he criticized the military for creating another war. Wynkoop then hustled to New York City.[138]

On that same December 17 the Custer-Sheridan army suddenly came face-to-face with a huge procession of Kiowas. Custer and a few officers met Satanta and Lone Wolf, who Hazen felt were at peace. Warriors "could be seen posted in the neighboring ravines and upon the surrounding hilltops," Custer reported. "All were painted and plumed for war, and nearly all were armed with one rifle, two revolvers, bow and arrows and lance. Their bows were strung." Custer felt that the Kiowas' "whole appearance and conduct plainly indicated that they had come for war."[139] But he also had in hand Hazen's December 16 report, which stated: "I send this to say that all the camps this side of the point reported to have been reached [Washita battlefield] are friendly, and have not been on the war-path this season."

Over the next two days Custer made both chiefs prisoner, and when the two armies reached Fort Cobb he put them in irons. Sheridan, who had ordered the Kiowas to come into the post, was fed up with them ignoring him. While refusing to speak with Satanta and Lone Wolf, he told Custer to inform them that if their people did not appear by sundown on December 20, that he would hang them. It was a harsh move by Sheridan, but it succeeded.[140]

WHEN WYNKOOP REACHED NEW YORK CITY, he found himself a cause célèbre. He received some praise while also being chastised by high-ranking officers and the press as little more than an outcast who turned traitor to his race.[141]

If Wynkoop had not been privy to Custer's Washita report, he was now. Custer wrote in part: "The Indians were caught napping for once; the warriors rushed from their lodges and posted themselves behind trees and in the deep ravines, from which they began a most determined defense. The lodges and their contents were in our possession within ten minutes after the charge was ordered, but the real fighting, such as has rarely, if ever, been equaled in Indian warfare, began when attempting to clear out or kill the warriors posted in ravines or underbrush . . . After a desperate conflict of several hours, our efforts were crowned with the most complete and gratifying success. The entire village, numbering forty-seven lodges of Black Kettle's band of Cheyennes, two lodges of Arapahoes, two lodges of Sioux; fifty-one lodges in all, under command of their principal chief, Black Kettle, who fell into our hands."[142]

Custer's words that followed would stand out to Wynkoop. "By actual and careful examination after the battle, the following figures give some of the fruits of our victory: The Indians left on the ground and in our possession the bodies of one hundred and three of their warriors, including Black Kettle himself. . . . In the excitement of the fight, as well as in self-defense, it so happened that some of the squaws and a few children were killed and wounded."

Although in the minority with his negative view of Custer's victory, Wynkoop soon received welcome support from former employee James Morrison. Morrison's wife, Emma, was Arapaho chief Big Mouth's daughter, which made him a welcome member of the tribe.[143] Morrison was at Fort Dodge on December 14 when mixed-blood Arapahos John Poisal Jr. and Jack Fitzpatrick arrived at the post with John Smith.[144] Poisal and Fitzpatrick had been at the Washita with Custer while Smith was not. Poisal and Fitzpatrick did not agree with Custer, stating "official reports of the fight were very much exaggerated; that there was not over 20 bucks killed; the rest, about 40, were women and children. The prisoners have got in to-day. They consist of 53 women and children. One boy is an Arapaho, the rest are all Cheyennes. Mrs. Crocker is among them; she is badly wounded. She says that her child is killed."[145] Mrs. Crocker (Ne-sou-hoe, Are-you-there) was a full-blooded Cheyenne, and she and her mixed-blood daughter Jennie Lund Crocker were in the village visiting relatives when Custer attacked. Custer's men killed Jennie.[146] Like Black Kettle and Medicine Woman Later, Jennie had survived the Sand Creek Massacre, and because of her mixed blood, she had been granted 640 acres by the 1865 Little Arkansas Peace Treaty.[147]

Wynkoop would share Morrison's letter.

On December 21 Peter Cooper of the Cooper Institute in New York City, which included the United States Indian Commission, invited Wynkoop to "share the causes that induced you to resign" as Indian agent, your view of the "causes which led to the recent troubles with [the Cheyennes and Arapahos], and the way in which such troubles may have been avoided."[148] They wanted to hear his "views of the remedy," as well as his "knowledge of Black Kettle, his conduct and designs." Wynkoop met them later that day and Cooper invited him to speak at the Institute.

When Wynkoop was introduced two nights later, he spoke before a standing-room-only crowd. The talk had been a long time coming, and Wynkoop was not reticent. He placed the blame on Chivington's massacre, Hancock's destruction of the Pawnee Fork village, and the failure of the government to make good on its treaty promises, including "withholding of arms and ammunition disabling them from procuring game for subsisting their families, which game was becoming more scarce every day, and the neglect to supply them with the absolute necessaries of life, drove them to desperation."[149]

Wynkoop addressed the remedy to the Indian problem. "[T]o me it is a very simple one. Let us, when we make pledges to these untaught savages who, like children, judge of good faith by performance, redeem those pledges, never fail to fulfill our contracts, and the cure will be complete."

He refused to place the blame on the Indian Bureau or the Department of the Interior, but instead raised the possibility of the citizens of the United States being "aroused for the Indian as they have been for the African, and, irrespective of [the] Indian Bureau or Congress, there will be such a radical change in the condition of the Indian." The U.S. Indian Commission "is taking the proper steps to secure this, and, if you continue, success is certain." Next he pointed out that the Cheyennes and Arapahos had never received "any missionary or instructor whatever." He directly addressed the United States' ongoing efforts to destroy their lifeway and culture and replace it with the white man's world. This included the end of their horse and buffalo migrant life, the end of their religion, and the end of their language with a strange new world of living as white people. Although not implied or stated, it did not include them becoming bankers or shopkeepers or anything other than farmers, for that was all the 1867 treaty insisted upon—and the last thing the Cheyennes and Arapahos wanted.

He spoke about Black Kettle and his death, and praised him, saying "The whole force of his nature was concentrated in the one idea of how best to act for the good of his race." Aware of the chief's status prior to the Sand Creek attack and after, he said: "From that time [the massacre] he lost caste, and fell from the position of a sovereign to that of a subject; but he still continued to strive for peace, and gradually regained his former influence, until he succeeded in bringing [some of] his young men off of the warpath, where they had been terribly avenging the murder of their women and children," and to the 1865 and 1867 treaty councils. The friendship they shared as they fought to prevent or end of war joined them as one. Had Black Kettle lived, he and Wynkoop would have become known as "brothers."

Finished, Wynkoop asked if there were any questions. There were, and one got right to the point. What was the best way to solve the Indian problem? Wynkoop did not back away from potentially explosive words. The best way to end the Indian problem would be "to extend American citizenship to the Indians," he said, "and allow their representatives seats in Congress."[150]

These were strong words, words that set the stage for Wynkoop's next career move, and he had a powerful ally, for Peter Cooper would recommend him to President Ulysses Grant. "I consider him eminently fitted for the post of Superintendent of Indian Affairs and have no hesitation in commending him to your favorable notice."[151]

OVER THREE MOONS HAD PASSED since the day when Black Kettle died. Since then, and while carrying the Sacred Arrows, Stone Forehead had moved his band south and onto the Llano Estacado, the Staked Plains of Texas. By the Light snow moon (March 1869) his band camped on Sweetwater Creek, a tributary of the north fork of the Red River. Little Robe's band camped just beyond his. Wolves (scouts) scoured the land and found no sign of white soldiers. The remnants of the Called Out People in the south appeared to be safe. But they had other enemies. The land was dry, harsh, with little vegetation and much less game. Worse, the wind swept across Mother Earth at lightning speed, and it was cold—deathly cold. Everyone went hungry; their mules and prized horses were little more than skeletons, and daily they lived off those that died from starvation.[152]

But they were free.

Then on the fifteenth day two boys who herded horses galloped into the village shouting that soldiers had come. Women ran to the pony herd and grabbed the animals that hauled their belongings. Frantically, they began to pack. Children scrambled about, screaming. Dogs, if they had not been eaten, barked and snapped. Warriors prepared to defend their loved ones. Other warriors rode to the sand hills south of the village to watch the soldiers. They reported back to the encampment. Not knowing what the day would bring, Stone Forehead dressed, painted himself for life or death, and joined the warriors on the sand hills. There were two white men far in advance of the *vi' ho' i* army. When others joined them, Stone Forehead crested the hill.[153]

The leading soldier was George Armstrong Custer, and he signaled that he wanted to talk. By this time Custer, with a small command of forty men, had trailed and met with Little Raven on Mulberry Creek, which was near the middle fork of Red River. He had sat next to the chief in his tipi and they had shared a pipe of peace. Little Raven agreed to move his band onto the reservation. A few days later the chief and his people set out for their new life.[154]

Custer had tasted success without blood. His goal was to convince the Cheyennes to follow the Arapahos onto the reservation. Still he was a warrior; he came alive on the battlefield, but for some reason he wanted to avoid more death. Maybe he did not like what he saw at the Washita, or maybe what he had seen of the Cheyennes and Arapahos gave him a new perspective of his foe. Maybe.

As no interpreter was present, everything said was via sign language. When Aorta chief Sand Hill approached him, the Creeping Panther asked to speak with Stone Forehead. However, when the Keeper of the Arrows rode forward, the rest of the warriors rushed after him and surrounded the white man. The mystic said that the women and children were crying; he invited Ouchess to show his good faith and visit the village. Custer accepted, and Lieutenant W. W. Cooke accompanied him.

Only the Panther entered the Sacred Arrows lodge, and he sat in the place of honor below Maahótse, which hung from a pole above his head. After Little Robe, Sand Hill, Dog Man chief Dull Knife, and twelve other headmen joined them, Stone Forehead prepared a pipe, held it over the white man's heart, and prayed. He presented the pipe to the four directions and then to Maheo before insisting that Ouchess smoke by himself. When he finished, Stone Forehead sprinkled the ashes on the Creeping Panther's boots while he chanted that Maheo would destroy the white chief if he ever walked "contrary to the peace pipe again."[155] Contented that Ouchess "would be destroyed like ashes" if he broke his promise that he would never point a gun at Tsistsistas again, Stone Forehead refilled the pipe, and everyone shared it.

Afterward Custer stated that the tribe had to move to the reservation and live in peace, that resistance would no longer save them. He did not want to use force but was prepared to do so if necessary. The meeting ended. Stone Forehead told Ouchess that he and the chiefs needed to discuss the situation, that they would give him an answer soon.

Outside the Sacred Arrows lodge, the Called Out People watched soldiers (Nineteenth Kansas Volunteer Cavalry) on bluffs that overlooked the valley. The village had almost 200 lodges with a total of 260 spread along the Sweetwater, and between 1,200 and 1,500 people stood between the Sweetwater and the extended soldier line. While these white men continued to close on the upper end of the encampment, other soldiers (Seventh Cavalry) moved toward the lower end of the village. Mounted warriors rode before soldiers nearest the Tsistsistas' lodges. It was obvious that both sides were ready for war, while neither side wanted to start it.[156]

After Ouchess departed, the mystic watched frightened people calm skittish horses as they began to flee. Needing to cover their flight, that afternoon he led a group of warriors into the soldier camp. Custer met him, and Romero translated. Warriors demonstrated their mastery of the horse, while others played flutes. During the performance Custer instructed armed men to join the gathering. When it ended, the musicians left, as did some of the chiefs and warriors. Custer's men outnumbered Stone Forehead's 100 to 40. The colonel stood, unbuckled his revolver belt and dropped it to the ground. "I [do] not desire or propose to shed blood unless forced to do so," he said, and Romero translated. "[L]ook about . . . and count the armed men whom I [have] posted among and around [you], completely cutting off every avenue of escape."[157]

Stone Forehead saw something "ominous in the perfect silence of the motionless soldiers, their clothes faded and ragged, their faces almost black from campfire and storm, their eyes deep-sunken, their teeth protruding, and their fleshless cheeks like lines of skeletons."[158] He and others stood, and some mounted as Ouchess promised them that "all [will] be well" if the Cheyennes submitted to the "inevitable."[159] Stone Forehead leaped onto his horse. "Arrest those men!" the Panther yelled.[160] Soldiers and Indians yanked out their weapons. A warrior nocked an arrow in his bow; Dull Knife cocked his revolver. Neither side fired. A soldier tried to grab Stone Forehead's reins. The mystic pushed him away, jerked his mount into action, and rode to safety.

Custer yelled for his men to hold their fire while warriors and boys swung their weapons at soldiers. Surprisingly not one round was fired while most of the Indians broke free.[161] Custer captured four men: Fat Bear, Dog Man chiefs Big Head and Dull Knife, and Dull Knife's son, who acted as intermediary and delivered the Panther's demand—release two white women held captive and move to the reservation. Stone Forehead ignored the ultimatum. He wanted the release of the three chiefs, and offered the women in trade. Custer refused.[162]

This created an impasse, as neither side was in condition to attack or flee. The livestock on both sides were in worse condition than the people who rode them. The Tsistsistas starved and so did the soldiers. Hoping to continue the pressure on the slowly retreating Cheyennes, Custer followed them on the seventeenth and halted two miles from their camp circles. He saw the pandemonium in the extended Cheyenne village. The standoff continued on the eighteenth, and the Panther moved his camp closer to the Tsistsistas. Hearing the anger of his troops over not attacking, while knowing that he needed to end the stalemate, Custer told Little Robe that day, "I [will] wait one day longer; but if by sunset [tomorrow] the white women [a]re not delivered up, I [will] hang . . . the men held captives by me."[163]

The nineteenth arrived, and nothing happened. Stone Forehead remained silent. Time reached the noon hour, then three, and four, and closed on nightfall.[164] At the same time, his army screamed to attack. Custer ignored them.

No longer able to stall, Stone Forehead sent warriors toward the white-man camp. The two women mounted on one horse accompanied them. They were released and soon were under the protection of the soldiers. Still, Custer did not release his prisoners. Stone Forehead sent another delegation with Little Robe to the soldier camp. After saying that the Called Out People "were in no condition to travel," Little Robe said that they would move "to Camp Supply and abandon the warpath forever," as they were "heartily sick of war, and [will] submit."[165]

It was over, even though Stone Forehead's warriors spoke of attacking the *vi' ho' i*—it was over. His and Little Robe's villages moved off that night. The following morning Custer's command departed. Stone Forehead felt that Ouchess had broken his pledge in the Sacred Arrows lodge, while Custer boasted: "Had my supplies not been exhausted, I would have moved against the Cheyennes after recoving the two women, but prudential reasons forbade it." More likely his decision not to attack—his shining moment on the plains—mimicked Chivington's, in that he held the power to release two armies on a people, two armies that craved blood, but chose not to butcher children, women, and men.

PAINTER VINCENT COLYER, who had previously served with the United States Indian Commission, accepted an unpaid position as a special U.S. Indian commissioner to view and inspect the condition of tribes on the frontier, as it allowed him to mix his interest in humanitarian causes while he painted water and oil paintings of landscapes and military posts. President Ulysses S. Grant provided him transportation and a military escort. He reached the Wichita Agency in Indian Territory on March 29, 1869.

On April 9 he spent time with Little Raven in Major General Benjamin Grierson's (Tenth U.S. Cavalry) tent. What Colyer learned from their conversation placed a black mark on the treaties made between the U.S. government and the Southern Arapahos and Cheyennes during the decade. Colyer reported that Little Raven made "a distinct statement . . . as to the entire ignorance of himself and his people, and also of the Cheyennes, about the precise location of the reservation set off for them by the United States peace commissioners, in 1867."[166] However, Colyer ignored or did not realize that the two tribes were not expected to begin living on their reservation (which constantly moved) until houses and other mandatory buildings existed and that they had the wherewithal, including tools and

On March 9, 1869, Little Raven met with Major General Benjamin Grierson at the Wichita Agency in Indian Territory. The image is a detail of Indian rights activist and artist Vincent Colyer's *Wichita Agency, I.T.* Colyer was present at the meeting and created this watercolor at that time.

Vincent Colyer (1825–1888); Wichita Agency, Indian Territory in 1869 (Detail); Watercolor on paper; Overall: 5 3/4 x 9 1/2 in. (14.6 x 24.1 cm); GM 0226.1376; Gilcrease Museum, Tulsa, Oklahoma.

instruction, to become farmers. To date, nothing had been built or provided. Still, Colyer stated that since Little Raven and Black Kettle "were not on the reservation, that they, with their tribes, were held guilty, and this was . . . why they were attacked." *Little Raven's village was not attacked.*

"By the following statement," Colyer wrote, "you will see now how easily these people are made to sign treaties of the character of which they are not familiar, and are afterwards so severely dealt with for not understanding":

Little Raven, chief of the Arapahos, being questioned as to his knowledge of the location of the reservation allotted to his people and the Cheyennes, by the Medicine Lodge treaty, in 1867, declared in our presence that at the time he signed the treaty he fully supposed that the land upon the Upper Arkansas, between Bent's Fort and the Rocky Mountains, was the reservation, being the same as previously set apart to them in the treaty of 1865; and he believes the Cheyennes were also of that

Robert Lindneux, who is known for his paintings of the Sand Creek Massacre and Fort Lyon in Colorado Territory, and Juan Menchaca share the credit for this portrait of Little Raven. It presents how he might have looked when he met with Major General Benjamin Grierson at the Wichita Agency in Indian Territory in March 1869, as he knew his peoples' entire lifeway was coming to an end.

Chief Little Raven. Oil Painting Robert Lindneux and Juan Menchaca. History Colorado. Accession # H.6131.2.

opinion. Nor had he any doubt about [this] until he met General Sheridan at Medicine Bluff headquarters, 16th February 1869, and until today he did not know precisely where the new reservation was located.

Little Raven says he supposes that his misunderstanding arose from the hasty way in which the treaty was made and read to them and by mistaken interpretation.

Either Little Raven's memory was off or his confusion over what happened during the 1867 treaty negotiations was spot on in regard to what he knew or did not know. *The 1867 Medicine Lodge Treaty was never read to the Hinono'eino' and Tsistsistas.*

IT HAD NOT YET ENDED, but it would soon.

William Bent died on May 19, 1869, at his stockade on the Purgatoire. What had been was gone, for the bands could no longer visit their friend. Until the end he continued to trade for buffalo robes, but was forced to send traders to their villages.[167] He had been a staunch friend of the Cheyennes and Arapahos. At the same time, he had used his influence to persuade them to turn their backs on their lifeway. His son Charles came to hate him for what he considered traitorous actions toward *their* people. Certainly William felt he did what was best for his adopted people to survive in the white man's world. At the same time Charley's dismissing him as little more than a hated *vi'ho' i* must have caused him a lot of internal pain, and especially so after his son's death.

By May 1869 a fair amount of Tsistsistas and Hinono'eino' began moving to their new reservation (read incarceration), but Dog Man chief Tall Bull refused to give up his freedom. His band had been bolstered by Sioux warriors. This was not new, as the chief was half Lakota, as was his half brother Long Chin. Mixed blood was key for why Tall Bull was often in the north. Also, he spoke both languages, as did many of these mixed-bloods.[168] By the twenty-first he moved through the Solomon and Saline River valleys in Kansas. On that day he attacked a hunting party. It was not a lone instance, and as the days passed he attacked whites at will, and this included a railroad crew of the Kansas Pacific Railway (former Union Pacific Railway, Eastern Division, as of March 3, 1869) on the twenty-eighth. Two days later he attacked a German settlement, killing thirteen and abducting Maria Weichell, Susanna Alderdice, and her infant. He then set out for the Republican, but the white child never stopped crying and was murdered.

Unknown to Tall Bull he had become the hunted.

On June 7 Major Eugene A. Carr (Fifth U.S. Cavalry), a West Point graduate who had won the Medal of Honor during the Civil War, and who was currently a brevet major general, received orders "to clear the Republican country of Indians."[169] He began the campaign with eight undermanned companies of the Fifth and a shorthanded battalion of Pawnee scouts commanded by Major Frank North. His expedition was not built for speed, as it included fifty-four wagons.

Over the coming days there would be a few firefights that amounted to little. On July 8, Carr reversed course and returned to his July 4–5 campground, as the Indian sign was mostly old. This movement fooled Tall Bull, and he mistakenly thought that the *vi'ho' i* soldiers had called off the expedition. But two events on that day convinced Carr that he was near his target. Several soldiers had been attacked by a small war party, and at eleven that night Cheyenne warriors attempted to stampede Carr's horse herd. When they failed, the warriors charged into the camp as they fired their weapons at tents and anything that moved. No one was wounded, and the raiders vanished into the night.[170]

Tall Bull reached what the Tsistsistas called Cherry Creek, which was near White Butte. The following day Tall Bull's band moved to what has since been called Summit Springs. His warriors wanted to cross the South Platte, which was west of their camp. Tall Bull believed the river was too high for a safe crossing but sent warriors to test the water level. They considered it safe to cross. He had been a wise man in war who also attempted to keep peace, but on July 10 Tall Bull vacillated, as he wanted to rest their animals and give the People a respite.[171]

At four in the morning on July 11, Carr and his command moved to attack. They reached a split in the Cheyennes' trail, and he divided his command into three as he moved forward. At noon Carr peered down at the serene village from a concealed vantage point two miles distant. Knowing he had the advantage, Carr ordered the charge, and soon after, the other two segments of his command joined the onslaught.

The attack was a total surprise. Tall Bull had kept scouts watching the south, but never anticipated an attack from the north or east. The Pawnees that were split between the three attacking columns came to kill. Two Crows and Good Bear, Dog Men who survived the fight, felt that more people should have died, and that the Pawnees did most of the killing.[172] Over decades the Pawnees had won battles and lost battles with the Tsistsistas and Lakotas, but this was their day. They would kill every man, woman, and child that crossed their path.

Dog Man Plenty or Wolf Hair staked his Dog Rope to Mother Earth. This simply meant that he would fight until his death. The only way he could be released from his pledge to defend his people to the end was for another warrior to yank the stake free. This never happened, and Pawnee bullets ended his life.[173]

Tall Bull rode into a ravine near the village on his favorite war horse. Only one of his wives was in the camp, and she and their six-year-old daughter were mounted before him. He kept moving until he found a location that seemed safe from the firefight, which had intensified as Frank, brother Luther North, and Pawnees had surrounded the ravine. He left them and rode back to the mouth where the fighting was heavy. Sensing that he had reached the spot where he would die he shot his war horse and slashed the back of one of its forelegs. It would never be ridden by the enemy, and more important would die with him.[174]

Hidden in the ravine, Tall Bull listened to the battle erupting above him. This was his fight, his war. With his carbine leading the way he inched his cocked weapon and head above the crest. Seeing a soldier—an officer—in the distance, he squeezed the trigger and immediately dropped down to safety.

The round missed Major North. But like Tall Bull, he was a longtime war veteran. He knew that the man who had attempted to slay him would again expose himself to see if he succeeded or take another shot. He signaled Luther to back off. North dismounted, settled on the ground, and aimed his carbine toward the spot where the Cheyenne's head had been.

Seconds ticked by. . . perhaps a minute.

Tall Bull slipped his cocked carbine above the ravine, then his head. That was the last thing he ever did, for North squeezed the trigger. His round hit the Dog Man in the head and knocked him back into the ravine. Soon after, Tall Bull's widow and young daughter climbed from the ravine and begged for their lives as they walked toward the white soldiers and Pawnee scouts. Unlike at Sand Creek, their prayers were answered.

BY EXECUTIVE ORDER, the Southern Cheyenne and Southern Arapaho reservation was established in Indian Territory on August 10, 1869. Instead of being located on a portion of what was called the Cherokee Strip as established by the 1867 Medicine Lodge Treaty, it was now some forty miles to the south in an area called El Reno. The new Indian agent was Brinton Darlington. The Comanche and Kiowa reservation was at the north fork of the Red River where it bordered on the south; the Caddo and Wichita reservation was to the east; the Cherokee Strip to the north, and the Panhandle of Texas at 100 degrees longitude to the west.[175]

Totally removed from their homeland between the Platte and Arkansas Rivers, the Tsistsistas and Hinono'eino' had finally been forced to relocate to Indian Territory. Underdressed in rags and starving, they froze and died in a foreign land. Better to have perished, for no longer would they have a say in their future.

There were not many major players left from 1864.

Ned Wynkoop was gone, never to walk or work with the Tsistsistas or Hinono'eino' again. After failing to become superintendent of Indian affairs in spring 1869, Wynkoop returned to his native Pennsylvania and his family.[176] Over the coming years he would twice again attempt to work with Indians. The first time was in May 1875, when he applied to become an Indian agent, and the second was a decade later, when he applied to become the superintendent of the Arizona Superintendency of Indian Affairs.[177] Both times the U.S. government denied his applications. He had never been forgiven for speaking out against what he considered heinous crimes against the Cheyennes and Arapahos. The government wanted "yes" men, wanted employees that toed the line and did not question policy or methods. Wynkoop never understood that the United States government and a massive number of whites living on the frontier believed that the end justified the means. As a man of conscience he would forever remain an outsider.

John Evans was gone but not gone. Although his stance on Indians would forever hover in the shadows, he now focused on his dream of Denver and Colorado Territory becoming a great railway hub. By 1867 he became a board member and one of the driving forces behind the Denver Pacific Railroad & Telegraph Company at a time when securing funds was difficult.[178] But still he suffered tragedy, for on October 28, 1868, cherished daughter Josephine Evans Elbert died. He was a strong man with a vision that never flamed out. Five years later he started building the Evans Memorial Chapel in Denver. When it was completed, he dedicated it to Josephine, and deeded it to the Methodist Church of Colorado.[179]

John Chivington eventually drifted in and out of the territory. Like Evans, his family saw tragedy. His son Thomas drowned in 1866; less than a year later Thomas's daughter (his granddaughter), Lulu, fell off a steamer and was never recovered, and a few months later his wife, Martha, who had been sick, died. His life became bizarre, for that year he married his former daughter-in-law, Sarah Chivington, which allowed him to control his son's estate. The Nebraska press had a field day with his marriage. By 1869 the Nebraska Methodist Episcopal Church brought charges against him concerning his character. The church decided not to terminate him, but they made him inactive.[180] As the years passed, he changed directions as he struggled to survive. The darkness of Sand Creek kept him a man of controversy.

John Smith continued to work with the Southern Cheyennes and Arapahos, and continued to interpret for them, For the final time in 1871 he led a delegation of chiefs to Washington, where he and the Indian leaders, including Little Raven, attended a large rally at the Cooper Institute in New York City. The trip was strenuous, taking them to Boston and Philadelphia before returning them to St. Louis, and then journeying them to Chicago. Little Raven, as always, lightened the moment when he stated that since the Philadelphians had given them horses, they could return to their homeland without walking. Smith was introduced, and lauded for his forty years walking between the races. But he was ill, and was perhaps already sick with pneumonia. He returned to his lodge on his people's land at the Darlington Agency in Indian Territory. Only twenty days passed before he died on June 29, 1871.[181]

William Byers continued to thrive as he used the *Rocky Mountain News* as a weapon. Whereas Evans and Chivington had been pushed to the side in the effort to remove all the Indians from Colorado Territory, he remained a staunch defender of their joint vision. As in the past, whenever he sensed opposition, and especially whenever someone spoke up for the Indians or against Chivington's victory at Sand Creek, Byers immediately lashed out with pen and ink.

Only a few Southern Tsistsista and Hinono'ei leaders survived the deliberate destruction of their people's freedom, and were herded onto their reservation in Indian Territory that none of them wanted. Among them were Little Raven, Bull Bear, Stone Forehead (who died a free man in the north in 1876[182]), and Little Robe. In a little more than two decades these once-proud people—the rulers of the central plains—had lost everything and had been reduced to paupers and prisoners in a foreign land.

Many years later George Bent wrote that Wynkoop "was the best friend [the] Cheyennes and Arapahos ever had."[183] Black Kettle, Little Raven, Tall Bull, Stone Forehead, and Left Hand were magnificent representations of their people and culture, and they would have agreed with him.

At times, historians who write about the Indian wars dismiss those whose point of view differs from theirs, or they do not take into account that people's views change over time. Moreover, they might not consider that many of those living during the tumultuous times of the mid-nineteenth century did not have a means to keep documentation that backed up their view of the history they lived through. Luckily military and government documents have survived, as have some photos, paintings, line art, letters, memoirs, and journals. This said, many living on the frontier often were on the move, living here and then there. Their choices of what to take with them when in transit were sparse, and doubly so if they had a family.

Most who testified or left sworn documents did not have legal counsel (unlike John Chivington, who had lawyer Jacob Downing at his side during the Colorado military inquiry into Sand Creek). When asked questions, they answered as well as their memory allowed. Their views were not exact, as time and distance either heightened their memory of the 1864 violence or mellowed it. Some did an almost complete about-face. Their perspective and memories had changed, but were they intentionally wrong? No.

Additionally, newspapers in the mid-1800s were known to slant their editorial content to support their causes. In the case of William Byers, as well as other editors in the Denver area, their main objective was to secure statehood and precious land.

What about the Tsistsistas and the Hinono'eino'? Their story of what happened is little more than bits and pieces. It is almost as if their lives did not count. They were a hindrance to the white man, a fly to swat and smash into dust. Time and again Little Raven and Black Kettle spoke to white leaders, and they almost always were ignored. Their comments, questions, and requests were not addressed. It was almost as if they did not say anything. The shameless disregard of their words was the white man's total refusal to accept that they only spoke for their people that followed them at that moment. The same can be said about what George Bent left us. Unlike Little Raven's and Black Kettle's, his words were not in the moment but based upon his and other Tsistsista memories. If not for Bent, almost all of the Cheyenne point of view on what happened to their people would have been lost to time. Tall Bull and Stone Forehead left us few words, but their actions defined who they were. Finally, Left Hand through his words and actions shined in regard to how he interacted with the invading white man. Unfortunately, his life ended too early.

Lieutenant General William Sherman's mandate accomplished what three Cheyenne-Arapaho treaties during the 1860s failed to do. Sherman's decree was ironclad, with the lone goal to push these tribes onto a flat, wind-blown land with little water, scarce game, and few trees, and there imprison them without bars. This time there were no phony negotiations. Sherman's demand was deadly if not obeyed. The freedom of the Tsistsistas and Hinono'eino' would come to an end, and they had no say in their future. They would become prisoners of war, and they would do as told or face the consequences. Everything was done to make them into white people, and that included destroying everything that they had been throughout time.

Everything.

YEARS PASSED. ON SEPTEMBER 13, 1883, John Chivington spoke at Jewell Park in Denver before a heritage organization called the "Colorado Pioneers." His talk focused on his November 29, 1864, attack on the Sand Creek village, an assault that he still considered a battle. Long past but not forgotten in the minds of Coloradans or in Chivington's, and he refused to shy away from what he believed until the end of time.

Reginald S. Craig, a lawyer who happened to be Chivington's relative and who wrote a defense of the "fighting parson," claimed that the crowd listened intently to the colonel's telling of the events leading up to that fateful day. Before closing, Chivington spoke about the inhabitants of the village he destroyed. "But were not these Indians peaceable?" he asked the crowd. "Oh, yes, peaceable!" He had always had a way with words, and he had lost none of his touch. "Well, a few hundred of them have been peaceable for almost nineteen years, and none of them has been so troublesome as they were before Sand Creek." His words hinted of sarcasm and ridicule. "What are the facts?" he asked while he manipulated them, and created a fictional reality—that is, a lie. "Aye, what of the scalps of white men, women and children, several of which they had not had time to dry and tan since taking. These, all these, and more were taken from the belts of dead warriors on the battlefield of Sand Creek and from their tepees which fell into our hands on the 29th of November, 1864. What of the Indian blanket that was captured fringed with white women's scalps? What says the sleeping dust of the two hundred and eight men, women and children, ranchers, emigrants, herders and soldiers, who lost their lives at the hands of these Indians? Peaceable!" This built to a crescendo, and here he paused before continuing. "Now we are peaceably disposed, but decline giving such testimonials of our peaceful proclivities, and I say here, as I said in my home town in the Quaker County of Clinton, Ohio, in a speech one night last week, 'I stand by Sand Creek.'"[184]

Actress Barbara Hershey plays a Cheyenne anthropologist and professor in *Last of the Dogmen* (Savoy Pictures, 1995), a film that features a band of Cheyenne Dog Men surviving the attack at Sand Creek and vanishing undiscovered into the mountains of modern-day Montana.[185] A bounty hunter, portrayed by Tom Berenger, sees ghostly riders in the mists of night. When he finds only an Indian arrow and little else of three escaped convicts who had apparently been murdered, he tracks down Hershey. After explaining the situation, Berenger shows Hershey the arrow, and she identifies it as a Cheyenne Dog Man arrow. Berenger wants to know if it is possible for Cheyennes from the long-gone past to still be living but hidden from the modern world. Hershey thinks that the question is absurd. "What about the arrow?" he asks. "Twelve-ninety-five in any gift shop," she replies as she dismisses him. Berenger refuses to take no for an answer, and does research in old newspapers. Later one night he appears at her house and asks Hershey more questions. She takes the time to provide background about the 1860s Cheyenne wars, while making it clear that a band of Dog Men from 1864 could not have survived undetected for all this time.

Time passes, but Berenger is persistent, and eventually Hershey agrees to ride into the wilderness with him to discover the truth. But he did not want her ride with him; he wanted one of her male students. As she is a woman, he is hesitant for her to join him. Hershey will have none of this. "We're burnin' daylight," she cracks as she checks her saddle. The future is out there and they ride into it.

One night while sitting around a campfire, they talk about the past of a people whose future was destroyed well over a century before. "What happened was inevitable," Hershey tells him. "The way it happened was unconscionable."[186]

Notes

1. Keefe, *Ma'heo's Children*, 3–5. Keefe writes, "The results of a recent investigation in which human DNA samples were compared across the Globe, has shown that a modern-day full-[blooded] Greek of ancient Celtic ancestry and a full-[blooded] Cree Indian of Algonquian origin, shared common family ancestors from southern Siberia, with an estimated time scale of at least 20,000 years B.P. [i.e., before the present]." See also 324nn5–10. These migrations may have begun between 30,000 and 25,000 B.P. Various studies have also compared tools and blood types, as well as ancient religions and ceremonies.

2. Keefe, *Ma'heo's Children*, 5, 21–22.

3. Cowell, *Dictionary of the Arapaho Language*, 16. Also see "Arapaho," *Encyclopedia of World Cultures Supplement*, Encyclopedia.com, accessed May 10, 2017, http:// www.encyclopedia.com/history/united-states-and-canada/north-american-indigenous -peoples/arapaho; and "Arapaho Language," Native Languages of the Americas, accessed January 21, 2014, http://www.native-languages.org/arapaho.htm, for other spellings of their names.

4. Salzmann, *Arapaho Indians*, 3–4. See Clarke, "Ethnography," 20, Folder 16c, Grinnell Collection, Resources Center of the Autry (hereafter RCOA), for where the Arapahos crossed the Missouri River. Salzmann states, "The difficulty in choosing between these and other reconstructions of Arapaho prehistory stems from the fact that historical sources do not begin to make clear references to the Arapaho until relatively late." According to Salzmann the Arapahos' movement onto the Great Plains happened before that of the Blackfeet and Cheyennes.

5. Keefe, *Ma'heo's Children*, 25.

6. Glenda F. Torres, a Northern Cheyenne living in Southern California, saw a performance of my play *Cheyenne Blood* (May 22, 2009, Oxnard, Calif.). Afterward she took the time to speak with me, and told me that both the Southern and Northern Cheyennes call themselves "Tsistsistas" today and in the past. Note of this conversation is in the Kraft Collection.

7. Kraft, "Wynkoop Confronts Hancock," 41. Also see Hyde to Grinnell, December 13, 1916, Hyde Research, Folder 51e, Grinnell Collection, RCOA; Hyde, *Bent*, 3.

8. Torres-Kraft meeting, May 22, 2009, Kraft Collection.

9. Moore, *Cheyenne Nation*, 82; see also 80 (table 7, which explains the naming of the three separate groupings of people that would become the Cheyenne tribe; it also explains the symbols used in map 4 on 83). Also see the maps in Jablow, *Cheyenne in Plains Indian Trade Relations*, 5, and West, "Called Out People," 5.

10. Moore, *Cheyenne Nation*, 81; also see 85–86, 232–33. Grinnell spells "Omisis" as "Omissis."

11. Moore, *Cheyenne Nation*, 85–86.

12. Grinnell, *Cheyenne Indians*, 1:9 (hereafter Grinnell, *Cheyennes*).

13. Clarke, "Ethnography," 19–20, Folder 16c, Grinnell Collection, RCOA). Also see Moore et al., "Cheyenne," in *Handbook of North American Indians: Plains*, 863–64, map. Their article vaguely places this movement between 1680 and 1760. Exactly when the separated bands of the future Cheyenne tribe reached the Missouri River in the 1700s has not been confirmed, but at the earliest, it was late midcentury. Moore, *Cheyenne Nation*, 55, used the Sioux migration for timing, and he came up with 1766 for their move to the Missouri.

14. Grinnell, *Cheyennes*, 1:9.

15. Grinnell, "Secrets of War Parties," Folder 41c, Grinnell Collection, RCOA. Grinnell created this document based upon a George Bent letter (February 1, 1907); he used Bent's title. This document is so close to Bent's letter that it is plagiarism. Left Hand Bull, whom Bent recommended to Grinnell, verbally shared information.

16. Moore, *Cheyenne Nation*, 83, map 4.

17. Powell, *Sweet Medicine*, II:863–64. Powell consulted the following people: "Henry Little Coyote, the former Keeper of Is´siwun; Jay Black Kettle and James Medicine Elk, the former and present Keeper of Mahuts [which is the same as "Maahótse," as the word is spelled in this book]; and Willis Medicine Bull, John Hill, John Stands in Timber, Fire Wolf, Henry Tall Bull, Rufus Wallowing, Same Buffalo, and others." Continuing, Powell states: "Heammawihio refers to Jesus, the white man's God Above, rather than to Maheo, the Cheyenne All Father. Henry Tall Bull added that Heammawihio came into Northern Cheyenne usage about the time of the Ghost Dance, 'when the Cheyennes were getting ready to meet their loved ones and to meet Christ.'" Concluding, Powell affirms: "The term Maheo in Cheyenne refers to God in a generic way. Its etymology denotes 'All-Origin, All-Father.' The plural of it, Maheono, Maheonasz, refers to a living, supernatural being."

18. Wolf Chief, "Proph[e]sy Story," Folder 16–11, Grinnell Collection, RCOA. Grinnell claimed that Wolf Chief originally called the "story 'The Creation Story' and something like 'White Man's Bible.'" More important, Wolf Chief stated that the Tsistsistas heard this story before they had ever seen a white man.

19. West, "Called Out People," 8.

20. Clarke, "Ethnography," 19–21, Folder 16c, Grinnell Collection, RCOA.

21. Mooney and Powell, *In Sun's Likeness*, 1:35. See Notebook, "November 1901, Southern Cheyenne Diary," no. 334, Grinnell Collection, RCOA, for "Rock Forehead" as translated from his Cheyenne name. He has also been called the "Man Who Walks With His Toes Turned Out." Also see Kraft, *Wynkoop*, 161, 296n18. In 1869 George Armstrong Custer would call this chief and mystic "Medicine Arrow." Note that some historians do not know that Stone Forehead, Rock Forehead, and Medicine Arrow were the same person. Beware of their documentation, for at times they use two or more of his names in the same book, as they thought they were different people. I will call him Stone Forehead to remain consistent with my books, magazine articles, and talks.

22. Charles Mackenzie called the Tsistsistas "Shawyens" when he documented four expeditions to the Missouri between the years 1804 and 1806, and Edwin James called them "Shiennes" when he wrote about an expedition from Pittsburgh to the Rocky Mountains in 1819–20. On that same expedition Alexander Henry called them "Schians." See Hoig, *Peace Chiefs*, 19–21, 164nn4–5, n8.

23. Grinnell, *Cheyennes*, 1:9.

24. Clarke, "Ethnography," Folder 16c, Grinnell Collection, RCOA. Grinnell refused to give Clarke credit for the dialect and word differences in his work even though he obviously pulled it from Clarke's Cheyenne documentation that he had purchased years before. Actually RCOA contains about 500 pages in Ben Clarke's handwriting, and it is very readable. It includes "Ethnography" (44 pages), "Philology" (9 pages), "Local names" (22 pages), "Gramm[a]r" (28 pages), "English-Cheyenne dictionary" (185 pages), "Cheyenne-English dictionary" (180 pages), as well as numerous letters and answers to questions that Grinnell asked. According to a card attached to the first folder (16a), Clarke prepared this documentation per General Philip Sheridan's request, as he intended to have the War Department publish it, but then the general reneged. With a lot of work under his belt but with no money in hand Clarke informed James Mooney of the Bureau of Ethnology of his current status. Mooney introduced him to Grinnell, who, about 1890, bought Clarke's documentation. Apparently, Grinnell figured that Clarke's words were his; much of what Clarke wrote would appear in Grinnell's work without credit.

25. "Lame Dear 1913" is Wind Woman's statement to Grinnell. He mistakenly placed her birth on the Cheyenne River "northeast" of the Black Hills. Folder 69, Grinnell Collection, RCOA.

26. There has been a lot of confusion over Black Kettle's birth, mainly because the 1803 date has been accepted without question. Grinnell interviews of Wind Woman, "Lame Dear 1913," and Wolf Chief, "Life of Black Kettle," Folder 69, Grinnell Collection, RCOA; E. W. Wynkoop to N. G. Taylor, January 11, 1869, National Archives and Records Administration (hereafter NA) RG75, M234, Roll 880; "Indian Affairs," *New York Times*, December 24, 1868; and Edward W. Wynkoop, "Unfinished Colorado History," 1876, 79, Wynkoop Papers, MSS II-20, History Colorado. Note that I am citing Wynkoop's handwritten document, and not a typescript that is also in the Wynkoop Papers. When he spoke at the Cooper Institute in New York City on December 23, 1868, Wynkoop claimed that Black Kettle was fifty-six when he died. . . . There have been other birth dates: Grinnell, "Names of Noted Cheyennes and the Approximate Dates of Birth & Death," Folder 119, 1, Grinnell Collection, RCOA (hereafter "Cheyenne Names," Folder 119), stated 1797, even though both Wind Woman and Wolf Chief (who thought 1803) did not agree. George Bent could not decide upon a date. In Bent to Samuel Tappan, April 16, 1889, Samuel Tappan Collection, MSS 617, FF 9, History Colorado, he placed Black Kettle's birth in 1807. In Hoig, *Peace Chiefs*, 105 and 173n4, he claimed that an unpublished letter from Bent to Tappan, March 16, 1889, in the Colorado Historical Society (now History Colorado), confirmed this. However, I have never found this letter unless it was misdated and he meant April 16, 1889, for here Bent, who married Black Kettle's niece, Magpie Woman, in 1866, and lived with the chieftain until 1868, claimed that he was sixty-one when he died, placing his birth around 1807. In Hyde, *Bent*, 322, George Bent stated that Black Kettle was sixty-seven when he died, which would place his birth date in 1801. There are three key reasons why I have accepted the 1812–15 time frame for Black Kettle's birth: (1) He

was still leading major raids into the mid-1850s and this would have made him in his early forties, a time wherein warriors quit riding the war trail; (2) The two 1864 images of Black Kettle are dark, which, granted, can hide gray or white hair, but he does not look to be in his sixties at that time; and (3) Wind Woman's statement (she did not die until February or March 1915) agrees with Wynkoop's dating. Powell, *People of the Sacred Mountain*, I:188 (hereafter Powell, *People*), without any supporting proof claims that Wind Woman stated "Wolf or Black Dog, later called Black Kettle, was the fourth child," which would make Black Kettle in his thirties at the time of his death. Neither Wind Woman nor Wolf Chief said that.

27. "Lame Dear 1913," Folder 69, Grinnell Collection, RCOA. Although Wind Woman did not say so, most likely her memory during her early years was based upon what had been told to her by elders. Going with Wynkoop's dating of Black Kettle's birth keeps the timetable of the movement of the Cheyennes onto the central and southern plains closer to what has been printed in the past.

28. See Kraft, *Wynkoop*, 111, 289n25; Kappler, *Indian Affairs: Laws and Treaties*, II:810, 891, 989 (hereafter Kappler, *Treaties*); "Cheyenne Names," Folder 119, 1, Grinnell Collection, RCOA; Kraft, "Ned Wynkoop & Black Kettle," 7, for additional background and spellings of his name. I have chosen to use Wynkoop's phonetic spelling of his Cheyenne name (Make-tava-tah), as they began a relationship in 1864 that led to friendship. Wynkoop had a good knowledge of the English language and had by far the best shot at phonetically spelling the chief's name.

29. See the map in Fowler, "Arapaho," 841, as it provides a great view of the Arapaho locations between 1800 and 1891. Perhaps Little Raven was born somewhere between where Fort Fetterman and Fort Laramie would someday stand. Note that Little Raven's winter 1889 death at Cantonment, Oklahoma, is fairly well documented. See Hardorff, *Washita Memories*, 46n5. Although I have seen his birth years printed in many books, not one of them has provided supporting evidence.

30. George Bent to George Hyde, April 17, 1905, George Bent letters to George E. Hyde (1904–18), Coe Collection. Beinecke Rare Book and Manuscript Library, Yale University (hereafter cited as Yale). Bent stated that Left Hand spoke English. Coel, *Left Hand*, 10–11, adds details. Also see Thrapp, *Frontier Biography*, II:839, 1050; and Kraft, *Wynkoop*, 97, 113, for Left Hand's second Arapaho name and Neva's Arapaho name. Two future trading posts were Bent's Fort and Fort St. Vrain (1838). Over the years many whites would converse with Left Hand and Neva in English.

31. Clarke, "Ethnography," 12, Folder 16c, Grinnell Collection, RCOA. See Mooney and Powell, *In Sun's Likeness*, for examples of tipi and shield heraldry.

32. Grinnell, *Cheyennes*, 1:30. Grinnell was partially correct while understating that the horse and buffalo culture was well underway.

33. Hoebel, *Cheyennes*, 37, including the following quote.

34. Hoig, *Peace Chiefs*, 23; "Indian Treaties and Councils Affecting Kansas," 751. Supposedly the expedition consisted of 476 soldiers. If true, many traveled by land, and were needed at times to pull the vessels with 100-to-200-foot ropes when poles were incapable of moving upriver.

35. Powell, *People*, I:30, 625–26nn1–2. Powell cited several people George Bird Grinnell interviewed, including Black Kettle's sister, Wind Woman (August 14, 1913) as sources, as well as Cheyenne John Stands in Timber to himself (1957). According to Grinnell, "Cheyenne Names," Folder 119, 1, RCOA, White Antelope was born about 1799. Also see Powell, *People*, I:vl, for his version of "Wolf Chief's Naming of the

Months." For consistency I use Powell, which I believe is an improvement—word-wise—over Wolf Chief, "The Months," Folder 69, Grinnell Collection, ROCA.

36. Hoig, *Peace Chiefs*, 23; "Indian Treaties and Councils Affecting Kansas," 751.

37. George Bent to Grinnell, May 20, 1905, Folder 10c, Grinnell Collection, RCOA, stated what retired General William Harney told him at the Medicine Lodge Creek peace council in 1867. Bent called the chief High Back Wolf and High Wolf.

38. The journalist and officer as quoted in Hoig, *Peace Chiefs*, 24.

39. Hoig, *Peace Chiefs*, 23.

40. Page on High Wolf, Folder 69, Grinnell Collection, RCOA; Hoig, *Peace Chiefs*, 22, 24. Painter George Catlin met High Back Wolf in 1832 and called him "Wolf on the Hill." Catlin's portrait shows a magnificent human being.

41. Kappler, *Treaties*, II:232–34. "Indian Treaties and Councils Affecting Kansas," 751, lists the date, location of the treaty, name of the tribe, the commissioners, and the Indians. O'Fallon had no rank listed in the treaty. A total of twenty-two officers, two Indian agents, and a surgeon signed the treaty. The "Sious (sic) and Ogallalah tribes" signed their treaty on July 5.

42. Kappler, *Treaties*, II:234. Powell, *People*, named The One Who Walks Against the Others as Leaving Bear (I:30) and perhaps correctly guessed that White Antelope may have made his mark as the warrior White Deer (I:625n2).

43. *St. Louis Daily Missouri Republican*, October 22, 1867, for the information in Hoig, *Peace Chiefs*, 104, 173n2, that connects Black Kettle to Harney. See Thrapp, *Frontier Biography*, II:617–18, for a partial background on Harney. Note that Harney was listed as a lieutenant on the treaty and was not a captain at this time.

44. See the chapter on "Cheyenne Kinship" in Moore, *Cheyenne Nation*. Moore has gone to great lengths to explain kinship, but it is not as complicated as it sounds. Southern Cheyenne Minoma Littlehawk often speaks about her sisters and brothers, aunts and uncles, and when she does, it refers to a special bond between her and major people in her life. To take this thought further, this is not just a part of the Cheyenne lifeway (or other American Indians' lifeways), for it extends to other portions of the world. My wife, Pailin Subanna-Kraft, is Thai. In 2014 I made my first trip to Thailand and spent twenty-one days with her family and friends in both the north and in Bangkok. The first person we stayed with was her *sister* Daranee Konsin. On the third day of our time with her she said to Pailin: "Don't you think that you should tell him I'm not your sister?" Pailin did, but explained that Daranee *is* her sister—that there is a kinship within the Thai people that goes beyond the natural lineage of a family and a person. Carry this thought back to Ned Wynkoop's words before the United States Indian Commission at the Cooper Institute in New York City on December 23, 1868, when he spoke about his friend Black Kettle's death. Surprisingly he, like Harney, thought that Black Kettle was High Back Wolf's son. Wynkoop's entire talk was printed as "Address of Col. Wynkoop," and an original is in the *Wynkoop Scrapbook*, Edward W. Wynkoop Collection, Chávez History Library (hereafter Wynkoop Collection). Moore also mistakenly thought that "Wolf-on-a-Hill" (another name for High Back Wolf) was Black Kettle's father. Moore, *Cheyenne Nation*, 274, 363n29. He cited ethnologist Albert S. Gatschet's unpublished MS 61, which is in the National Anthropological Archives, Smithsonian Institution. Gatschet, who was born in Switzerland in 1832 and arrived in the United States in 1869, mostly dealt with American Indian vocabularies. He also documented Cheyenne ledger art. Bent to Hyde, May 19, 1914, Yale, provided a hint into this misunderstanding when he wrote that Black Kettle was related to High

Back Wolf. This brings us back to Minoma Littlehawk and what I experienced in Thailand, and that is the understanding of kinship and the accuracy of translation.

45. Clarke, "Ethnography," 19 (*ve'heo* and *a'tha*), Folder 16c. Also see Grinnell, "As to the Meaning of the Word Vihio," Folder 69. Both in Grinnell Collection, RCOA.

46. Thrapp, *Frontier Biography*, III:1333.

47. Hoig, *John Simpson Smith*, 30–33. This included a long quote from Ann W. Hafen, "John Simpson Smith," in *Mountain Men and the Fur Trade*, vol. 5, ed. LeRoy Hafen (Glendale, Calif.: Arthur H. Clark, 1968), 327–29.

48. Hoig, *John Simpson Smith*, 41. Some historians have made a point of stating that John Smith did not speak Arapaho, especially Coel, who states "Smith could not speak Arapaho, according to his own testimony." Coel, *Left Hand*, 118n17. She points to "The Chivington Massacre," which is part of the Sand Creek investigation and included in Carroll, *The Sand Creek Massacre: A Documentary History*, 41. On that page Smith answered a question by Senator James Doolittle: "Do you know the language of the Arapahoes and Cheyennes?" Smith replied: "I do that of the Cheyennes." At that point in time, during the investigation of the attack on the Sand Creek village, Smith was in the Cheyenne village, and his answer implied that he knew the language of the people he was then living with. Not stating that he could speak the Arapaho dialect did not necessarily mean he could not speak their language. He did not name them because his comments and answers dealt directly with the Cheyennes, whom he was with at the time of the attack, and had nothing to do with the Arapahos, as he had seen none of what happened to Left Hand's village circle. John Smith did not say that he did not *know* the Arapaho dialect, and it is an odd assumption, considering how close the two languages are. Coel's assertion supports her premise that Left Hand was so literate at English that he interpreted Arapaho to English and back. That is true, but often he used interpreters. Hoig accepted Coel's view that Smith could not speak Arapaho; he did not check her only citation on this fact, and he ignored Lewis Garrard's memories of Smith saving his party when he spoke with unfriendly Arapahos in their language. Ben Clarke to Grinnell, February 15, 1893, Folder 16a, Grinnell Collection, RCOA, had this to say about the Cheyenne-Blackfeet connection: "The Cheyennes are without doubt of the Algonquin family and I am satisfied the Blackfeet are of the same family. Although to hear a Blackfoot speak, the words sound entirely different from the Cheyenne or Arapaho, a study of their vocabulary or grammar convinces me it is of the same root or family." The key words here are: "Cheyenne or Arapaho," meaning that Clarke did not know for certain. The Sioux accepted the Blackfeet as members of their family, which logically leads one to believe that their dialect was closer to the Siouan dialect.

49. Wolf Chief, "Life of Black Kettle" and "Lame Deer 1913," Folder 69, Grinnell Collection, RCOA; "Indian Affairs," *New York Times*, December 24, 1868; Wynkoop to N. G. Taylor, January 11, 1869, NA RG75, M234, Roll 880; Wynkoop, "Unfinished Colorado History," 79; Bent to Tappan, April 16, 1889, Tappan Collection, MSS 617, FF 9, History Colorado.

Chapter 2. Riding into the Future

1. See Jablow, *Cheyenne in Plains Indian Trade Relations*, for entire section.

2. See Hyde, *Bent*, 58, for William's birth and 58n4 for Charles's birth. See 59, and Grinnell, "Bent's Old Fort and its Builders," 29 (hereafter Grinnell, "Bent's Fort"), for

being in Sioux country and the partnership with St. Vrain. See Thrapp, *Frontier Biography*, III:1260, for St. Vrain's birth.

3. Bent to Hyde, February 20, 1914, Yale; Hoig, *Peace Chiefs*, 27; Grinnell, "Bent's Fort," 31. See Powell, *People*, I:XXXIX, for the Cheyenne names of rivers.

4. With Grinnell, "Bent's Fort," 29, dating all over the place I approached John M. Carson (park ranger—interpretation, Bent's Old Fort NHS, La Junta, Colorado). See an extended email exchange between Carson and Kraft, October 7, 2015, Kraft Collection, for it places William and Charles Bent on the Santa Fe Trail or the Upper Arkansas no earlier than 1829. St. Vrain could have been in Santa Fe on a solo trip earlier.

5. Halaas and Masich, *Halfbreed*, 17, are correct with the location, but off with the dating of 1830. Grinnell, "Bent's Fort," 30, incorrectly placed this on the Purgatoire River, as we shall see.

6. Halaas, *Halfbreed*, 10–11.

7. Carson and Kraft, email exchange, October 7, 2015, Kraft Collection.

8. Hyde, *Bent*, 60–61n7, eliminated some of the confusion that George Bent created in two letters to Hyde, April 10, 1905, and April 14, 1908, Yale, when it discussed the Bent-Yellow Wolf meeting. Also see map, 38–39. Bent claimed that the raid was on the Red River. See Carson and Kraft, email exchange, October 7, 2015, Kraft Collection, which is firm that information at Bent's Old Fort NHS proves the Bents did not reach this area until 1829, and I agree with him. Grinnell, "Bent's Fort," 29, claimed: "Testifying before the joint committee of congress which inquired into Indian affairs in the plains 1865, William Bent stated that he first came to the upper Arkansas in 1824 . . . although it has been generally assumed that the journey was made in 1826." But William Bent's undated sworn statement, in *Condition of the Indian Tribes. Report of the Joint Special Committee, Appointed Under Joint Resolution of March 3, 1865*, disagrees. This document begins with Senator Doolittle's summary, 3–10, but also includes "Appendix: The Chivington Massacre," beginning on 26, (hereafter COIT "Chivington Massacre"), 93. Grinnell should have quoted Bent. "Having been living near the mouth of the Purgatoire on the Arkansas river in Colorado Territory for the last thirty-six years," he stated, "and during all that time have resided near or at what is known as Bent's Old Fort." Subtracting thirty-six from the year 1865 makes the date 1829. Perhaps the Bents and St. Vrain were in the north in Sioux country in 1824, and it may have been as late as 1826. This note includes the Cheyenne warriors being saved.

9. William Bent's undated sworn statement, COIT "Chivington Massacre," 93; Carson and Kraft, email exchange, October 7, 2015, Kraft Collection. "[W]e have 'accounts' as early as 1826 that the fort is being built," Carson wrote, "which is not possible as the Bent Brothers did not come to the Southwest/travel the Santa Fe Trail until 1829." This is logical and also in total agreement with Bent's sworn statement. The second meeting with Yellow Wolf happened in 1829. It also makes William Bent twenty. At the same time, it destroys a lot of the earlier and later dating. Bent to Hyde, February 4, 1913, and February 20, May 22, and June 11, 1914, Yale. In his February 20 letter Bent stated that the meeting took place in 1826 or 1827. In his June 11 letter he stated basically that his best guess was 1828 and the stockade was at the mouth of the Purgatoire. If this was true, why would Yellow Wolf insist that the Bents build at the Purgatoire if they were already there? In Bent's February 4 letter he stated that High Back Wolf and Standing on Hill were with Yellow Wolf at this meeting. Other documentation placed the second meeting with Yellow Wolf in 1832. If Yellow Wolf was interested in trading with the Bents why would he wait two-plus years to do so? As

LeRoy R. Hafen, in "When Was Bent's Fort Built," 108, stated: "The foregoing statements regarding the supposed presence of the Bent brothers and Ceran St. Vrain and of their reputed stockade on the upper Arkansas during the years 1824 to 1828 are almost certainly not true; and the continual repetition of an error does not make it a fact."

10. Bent to Hyde, February 20, 1914, and February 11, 1916, Yale. Yellow Wolf eventually named all four brothers. Although authors have at times stated that William and Charles's younger brothers (George, b. April 13, 1814, and Robert, b. February 23, 1816) joined them at this time, the two teenage boys did not join them until later. See Thrapp, *Frontier Biography*, I:97, 99, for their births. Although I have seen that they did not join Charles and William until after 1840, Thrapp placed them on the frontier in 1832.

11. Grinnell, *Fighting Cheyennes*, 5. See Grinnell, *Cheyennes*, 1:11, for the Cheyennes' name for the Arapahos. According to Powell, *People*, I:xxxix, the Arapahos were known as Hetane-vo'eo'o.

12. Salzmann, *Arapaho Indians*, 4.

13. Dorset, *The New Eldorado*, 9, citing Bent from George F. Willison, *Here They Dug the Gold* (New York: Reynal and Hitchcock, 1946), 6; Jablow, *Cheyenne in Plains Indian Trade Relations*, 64. See West, *Contested Plains*, 71, for a discussion on "middlemen."

14. See Powell, *People*, II:1418 for White Thunder's birth; Halaas, *Halfbreed*, 355n37, for James Mooney's 1903 interview of George Bent, wherein he stated that his grandfather was a Sutai. Kessel, *Piavinnia*, 54, for White Thunder's wife; and Hyde, *Bent*, 48, who placed the killing of the warriors in 1832. Actually Bent stated, "I think it was in 1832 that a small party of Cheyennes . . ." The key words here are, "I think," which means Bent was not certain. Halaas, 18, jumped on this date, and then pushed the large raid into 1833. Both Grinnell, *Fighting Cheyennes*, 72, and Powell, *People*, I:3, are firm with 1830. I agree with them. For some of the arrow keeper's other names, Gray (or Grey) Thunder and Painted Thunder, see Grinnell, 45, and Llewellyn and Hoebel, *Cheyenne Way*, 147. See Kraft to Minoma Littlehawk, May 9, 2009, Kraft Collection, and Kraft, *Wynkoop*, 93, for Ohméséhesos spelling and pronunciation.

15. See Grinnell, *Fighting Cheyennes*, 72, for a listing of the six movements by the entire tribe against enemies. Grinnell wrote, "The Cheyennes were always anxious to exterminate the Pawnees, and their attacks against them were continual."

16. See Powell, *Sweet Medicine*, 1:25, for an alternate spelling of Is´siwun.

17. "The Loss of the Cheyenne Medicine Arrows," Folder 506, Grinnell Collection, RCOA. This document is invaluable (see 1–7 for entire section except where noted), for Grinnell presents his research in one location, and in much greater detail than in *Fighting Cheyennes*, 72–73. He also makes it clear exactly where he obtained this information. He had four informants, and three of the four participated in this fight wherein the Pawnees captured the Sacred Arrows. Gentle Horse (Grinnell missed by a quarter century on his birth in this document), a Cheyenne and Black Kettle's brother; Elk River, a Cheyenne boy who had come of age to participate in war; Pipe Chief, a Skidi Pawnee; and the daughter of Big Eagle, who led the Skidi Pawnees during this 1830 fight. I have based this account upon Grinnell's documentation, as opposed to relying on texts by modern historians who have taken information from Grinnell's works. Powell, *People*, 1:7–8, is an exception. As Grinnell states in this document: "These accounts though differing in minor points agree precisely as to the main facts and in many details have been confirmed by other Cheyennes with whom I have discussed the story," 2. Powell, *Sweet Medicine*, 2:862, pointed out that George Bent claimed that the event took place in 1833, but he agreed with Grinnell's dating.

18. Grinnell, "Loss of the Cheyenne Medicine Arrows," 2, RCOA, called Roasting's brother "High Wolf," but confirmed his identity by stating, "the man afterward painted by Catlin." Catlin only painted two portraits of Cheyennes: Wolf with the High Back (High Back Wolf) and She Who Bathes Her Knees.

19. George A. Dorsey, "How the Pawnee Captured the Cheyenne Medicine Arrows," *American Anthropologist*, October–December 1903, 645. Courtesy of JSTOR. Grinnell, "The Loss of the Cheyenne Medicine Arrows," 4–5. This is from the remembrance of Pipe Chief, a Pawnee, of the Skidi sitting on the ground while Cheyenne Elk River claimed that the Skidi on the ground had broken his leg during the fight. I have chosen to use the Pawnee view by Dorsey, as it seems more logical that his contacts knew more about this man. Moreover, Dorsey documented the Pawnee's point of view, and it is in line with what Grinnell learned, but even more so. Actually I believe that Dorsey's telling is more accurate, and it is his story of the old Wolf warrior in this book's text.

20. Dorsey, "How the Pawnee Captured the Cheyenne Medicine Arrows," *American Anthropologist*, October–December 1903, 646.

21. Grinnell, "Loss of the Cheyenne Medicine Arrows," 6, Grinnell Collection, RCOA.

22. Powell, *People*, I:11. Also see 10. Powell thought that this ceremony could have happened between two and four years after the loss of the Sacred Arrows. It could not have been four years, as High Back Wolf died in 1833.

23. Hyde, *Bent*, 68; Halaas, *Halfbreed*, 12–13;

24. See Carson and Kraft, email exchange, October 7, 2015, Kraft Collection, regarding a document in Bent's Old Fort NHS archives. See Hyde, *Bent*, 61n7, which stated that Charles Bent did not receive the first license to trade until December 13, 1834.

25. Berthrong, *Southern Cheyennes*, 78, has a viable reason for the murder, but he is off by two years per a quote he used by Lieutenant Gaines Kingsbury, who was with Colonel Henry Dodge, who visited Bent's Fort in 1835. See Powell, *People*, I:31, for the second version of the murder. Either version could have happened.

26. Hyde, *Bent*, 324. Bent placed High Back Wolf's death in 1832. This seems too early. But this event happened long before Bent's birth, so it is not surprising that it seems off, considering that he had to not only trust what he heard, but also to remember it accurately. Grinnell, *Cheyennes*, 1:30n34, states "Donaldson in his Catalog of the Catlin Indian Gallery says, p. 88, that Catlin painted Wolf on the hill—High Backed Wolf—in 1834, but this appears to be an error. Donaldson's map of Catlin's routes does not agree with this date. The Cheyennes, including High Backed Wolf's two daughters, say that he died in 1833, and fix the date by the star shower of that year. They knew that High Backed Wolf had been painted by Catlin. It used to be said that the stars fell from the sky because of the death of so important a man."

27. "Phenomenon—Celestial," *Pittsburgh Gazette*, November 18, 1833.

Chapter 3. Dominating a New World

1. Galvin, *Through the Country of the Comanche Indians*, 3, for Abert's quote from his 1845 journal. See Halaas, *Halfbreed*, 25, for the marriage. Also see Hyde, *Bent*, 68.

2. Hyde, *Bent*, 72.

3. Powell, *Sweet Medicine*, 1:39.

4. Powell, *Sweet Medicine*, 1:44–45. Also see Hyde, *Bent*, 72–73. Excuses claimed that they had few arrows and bullets on the day of their deaths.

5. Hyde, *Bent*, 74–75. Powell, *Sweet Medicine*, 1:45, claimed that Arapahos and a Sioux recognized some of the Bowstring scalps when they visited Kiowa, Kiowa-Apache, and Comanche camps. Berthrong, *Southern Cheyennes*, 82, stated that Arapaho traders saw two scalps they recognized while watching a Comanche and Kiowa scalp dance.

6. Minoma Littlehawk asked Southern Cheyenne chief Lawrence Hart if "Dog Men" was the correct name of this military society. He confirmed that it was. See Minoma Littlehawk conversation with author, December 31, 2008, and May 17, 2009, Kraft Collection. Also see Kraft, *Wynkoop*, 285n4.

7. Bent to Hyde, June 11, 1914, Yale.

8. Powell, *People*, I:45.

9. Bent to Hyde, June 2, 1814, Yale, which provides great detail, claimed that Porcupine Bear stabbed Little Creek with his butcher knife, whereas Hyde, *Bent*, 74, which is also detailed, stated that the Dog Man chief killed Little Creek with his own knife. Both are in contrast to Powell, *People*, I:45, as he did not believe that Little Creek was the chief's cousin. Although he also had the two Tsistsistas rolling on the floor during the fight, Little Creek did not have a knife. When Porcupine Bear realized that Around needed help, he rushed to Little Creek, who was sitting on Around, and began stabbing him. The chief then called for his cousins to stab the fallen man until he died.

10. Powell, *People*, I:46, 628n9, differs from Hyde, *Bent*, 73–75, 335, 338.

11. Hyde, *Bent*, 335.

12. Hyde, *Bent*, 75, 78–79; Powell, *People*, I:52–56. Hyde called Yellow Wolf a Dog Man, but I have not seen this in any Bent/Hyde letters.

13. Grinnell, *Fighting Cheyennes*, 56, for the quote and additional support (57) to Hyde in the previous note.

14. Powell, *People*, I:56–57. Porcupine Bear's son, Porcupine Bear, was one of the warriors. Porcupine Bear counted twelve coups in this attack, while Hyde, *Bent*, 82, gave him twenty coups for the entire battle. To the Cheyennes he was an outlaw; his claim of the first coup or any following coups did not count.

15. Hyde, *Bent*, 337–38.

16. Hyde, *Bent*, 79.

17. Grinnell, *Fighting Cheyennes*, 57–58.

18. See Powell, *People*, I:57–64, for the best telling of this battle.

19. Powell, *People*, I:61.

20. Sherow, "Workings of the Geodialectic," 65, 69, 73–75.

21. Grinnell, *Fighting Cheyennes*, 63–69; Llewellyn and Hoebel, *Cheyenne Way*, 91–93, for the entire section.

22. High Backed Wolf was not related to High Back Wolf.

23. Grinnell, *Fighting Cheyennes*, 64.

24. Llewellyn and Hoebel, *Cheyenne Way*, 93.

25. Grinnell, *Fighting Cheyennes*, 65–66, for quote and following two.

26. Hyde, *Bent*, 83.

27. Kelsey, *Frontier Capitalist*, 65, 261n2. Their fourth child, John, was born in 1846.

28. See Julia Bent Heirship testimony, April 23, 1914, in regard to Slow Smoking's estate, Washita County, Oklahoma. On this date Julia was sixty-nine years old. Her

name was Julia Guerrier, a last name she took after she married Edmund Guerrier. Her mark was a fingerprint, which seemed to indicate that she did not go to school in Missouri and did not speak English. From what I know from bits of information I have collected, and from long talks with historian Dee Cordry, who is writing a book about the Bents and Guerriers, she did spend time in Missouri, and more important did speak English. After the Sand Creek Massacre she chose to hide this for one simple reason—she hated the white man for butchering her people at Sand Creek in 1864. Also see Julia Guerrier death certificate (Summary of Report of Heirs), Cheyenne & Arapaho Agency, Department of the Interior Office of Indian Affairs, which states she was eighty-seven years old at her death on March 7, 1932. Subtracting from 1932, her birth happened in 1845. Both documents courtesy of Harvey Pratt, great-grandson of Julia Bent.

29. See George Bent heirship testimony, March 25, 1914, in regard to Slow Smoking's estate, Washita County, Oklahoma. Courtesy of Harvey Pratt, great-grandson of Julia Bent.

30. Kessel, *Piavinnia*, 87.

31. Garrard, *Wah-to-yah*, 5.

32. Hyde, *Bent*, 86–87; Grinnell, "Bent's Fort," 76–77.

33. Garrard, *Wah-to-yah*, 42–43. The arrival date might have been the third.

34. Garrard, *Wah-to-yah*, 45. Also see 46.

35. Garrard, *Wah-to-yah*, 45. See Hoig, *John Simpson Smith*, 113, for Wapoola's name.

36. Garrard, *Wah-to-yah*, 46–47.

37. Garrard, *Wah-to-yah*, 48–49. Possibles bags were a carryover from the days of the mountain men. In this case Smith carried what he thought he might need during the day, which included anything from personal items to a skinning knife to black powder. I have found no cross references to Vip-po-nah or Lean Chief, and wonder how close Garrard was with his phonetic spelling of the chief's name, and if "Lean Chief" was just a name he gave him.

38. See Garrard, *Wah-to-yah*, 54–55, 57, for this and the following three quotes (italics in original). Also see 52–53, 56.

39. Garrard, *Wah-to-yah*, 65. Also see 58–59, 61, 64 for the paragraph.

40. Quoted in Grinnell, "Bent's Fort," 77. Also see 76.

41. Grinnell, "Bent's Fort," 77.

42. Garrard, *Wah-to-yah*, 106–7, for quotes and entire encounter with the Arapahos. The timing here is less than two weeks after January 7, 1847.

43. Grinnell, "Bent's Fort," 77–78, 80. Grinnell's research for his article is laudable regardless of a few errors of knowledge after his time. See Carter, *Dear Old Kit*, 84, 86n134, for Josefa and Carson's marriage.

44. Garrard, *Wah-to-yah*, 117, 119 for quotes (also see 116, 118). Also see Hyde, *Bent*, 87.

45. Hafen and Ghent, *Broken Hand*, 196–97.

46. Hafen and Ghent, *Broken Hand*, 197. They opined that the Cheyennes and Arapahos "highly respected" Smith.

47. Fitzpatrick to Superintendent of Indian Affairs Thomas H. Harvey, September 18, 1847, *Annual Report of the Commissioner of Indian Affairs, 1847–48*, Appendix, 241.

48. See Carson and Kraft, email exchange, October 7, 2015, Kraft Collection, in regard to the completion of the building of Bent's Fort and when an American flag first

flew over the post. Carson was certain that a flag flew as early as 1835 when Colonel Henry Dodge passed by with his command, but he has no proof. Carson's research confirms the first flag was seen on July 1, 1844, when John C. Frémont's second expedition arrived. On his arrival Frémont wrote in his journal (in Carson's email): "And atop the belfry the scorching summer wind whipped the oversized American flag back and forth in a dance of color that threatened to snap the ash flagpole."

49. Fitzpatrick to Harvey, September 18, 1847, *Annual Report of the Commissioner of Indian Affairs*, 1847–48, Appendix, 241.

50. Fitzpatrick to Harvey, September 18, 1847, *Annual Report of the Commissioner of Indian Affairs*, 1847–48, Appendix, 241–43, through the end of the section.

51. Bent to Grinnell (no date; but Lincoln Faller estimated the date to be ca. March 1905), Folder 10b. Wolf Chief, "Life of Black Kettle," Folder 69, confirms Bent's 1848 date for this raid (see n56 below for a full explanation of published errors and proof that this raid took place in 1848). Both in Grinnell Collection, RCOA.

52. This Wolf Chief was not the Wolf Chief who would in later years prove invaluable to Grinnell.

53. Indian Claims Commission 338, "The Jicarilla Apache Tribe of the Jicarilla Apache Reservation, New Mexico v. The United States of America, Additional Findings of Fact, Docket No. 22-A, Decided November 9, 1966," 349–50, 352, 356, 361. Children were mostly raised and taught their positions in life by their grandparents.

54. Bent to Grinnell (n.d.; but Faller estimated the date ca. March 1905), Folder 10b, Grinnell Collection, RCOA.

55. "Jicarillas: Additional Findings of Fact," 361. Also see 349–51.

56. Bent to Grinnell (n.d.; Faller estimated date ca. March 1905), Folder 10b. Wolf Chief, "Life of Black Kettle," Folder 69, confirmed Bent's 1848 date for when the Utes and Jicarilla (and not "Mountain" Apaches as Bent called them) captured Little Sage Woman. Wolf Chief's father died at that time. Grinnell Collection, RCOA. Also see Bent to Hyde, April 17, 1906, Yale. Even though it presents less detail, it confirms both Bent's dating and the disappearance of Little Sage Woman from history when she was captured. These documents also confirm the date of an 1854 raid. Powell did not see all of the documentation and merged two separate events that were years apart into one in *People*, I:189 and I:638n8. Specifically, he claimed that Black Kettle's raid to avenge the two Tsistsista warriors in New Mexico Territory traveled deep into Mexico (which Black Kettle did in 1854 when he and others struck the Mexicans deep within their country). Hatch, in *Black Kettle*, 39–42, 269nn32–33, copied Powell's research, portraying it as one 1854 raid, and even made it his conclusion.

57. Bent to Grinnell (n.d.; Faller estimated date ca. March 1905), Folder 10b, Grinnell Collection, RCOA.

CHAPTER 4. A FAILURE TO GRASP THE FUTURE

1. Kelsey, *Frontier Capitalist*, 65.

2. George Bent testimony, March 25, 1914, Heirship Estate of Slow Smoking (Yellow Woman), Washita County, Oklahoma. Courtesy of Harvey Pratt, great-grandson of Julia Bent. When asked if William Bent and Slow Smoking had any children, Bent stated: "One son named Charley Bent." When asked if he was still alive, Bent said, "No sir, he died in 1867 at the age of 19 years." Simple arithmetic places his birth in 1848

and trashes the 1845 birth fantasies. Also see Kessel, *Piavinnia*, 87. Beware of books that cite obscure sources that sound authoritative, but have nothing to do with Charley's birth and are hard to obtain. Clearly the purpose was to move the year to 1845. For Mary and Robert's births see Hyde, *Bent*, 83; and Lubers, "William Bent's Family," 19.

3. Hyde, *Bent*, 88 and nn8–9.

4. Grinnell, "Bent's Fort," 81n93, 82n94. Grinnell thought that the negotiations were in 1849. Editor Lottinville corrected Hyde, *Bent*, 88–89n10. See Thompson, "Life in an Adobe Castle," 25, for St. Vrain offering the fort at $15,000. Bent to Hyde, February 26, 1906, Yale, mistakenly placed the military counteroffer in 1852.

5. Berthrong, *Southern Cheyennes*, 113–14, used good documentation to support what happened. The most detailed telling of the devastation of the 1849 cholera epidemic is Powell, *People*, I:95–96. On I:631n4 he listed three Southern Cheyennes (Sitting in the Lodge Woman, Porcupine Bull, and Cedar Grove) who survived the cholera epidemic and spoke about it as well as numerous Bent letters to Hyde.

6. Julia Guerrier sworn Heirship Estate statement, April 23, 1914, Washita County, Oklahoma. Courtesy of Harvey Pratt, great-grandson of Julia Bent.

7. Powell, *People*, I:96–97.

8. Mooney, *Calendar History of the Kiowa Indians*, 289. See Powell, *People*, I:98, for the Tsistsista deaths.

9. Bent's Old Fort NHS places the move to the Big Timbers in 1849. Berthrong, *Southern Cheyennes*, 114, 114–15n28, and Hyde, *Bent*, 93 and n14. Unfortunately both cite Lavender, *Bent's Fort*, which is not trustworthy. The evidence points to the cholera epidemic, the survival of most of Bent's family, the destruction of Bent's Fort, and the move down the Arkansas after this tragic time.

10. See Grinnell, "The Medicine Arrows," Folder 29, Grinnell Collection, RCOA. in which he wrote: "Up to the time of Stone Forehead . . . the keeper of the Medicine arrows had to submit to a special mutilation. . . . The cutting could only be done by one who had already been cut." In Grinnell, "The Great Mysteries of the Cheyenne," *American Anthropologist* 12, no. 2 (1910): 544, he stated: "The arrow keeper, when he expected to die, was likely to designate his successor in the care of the arrows." Nearing death, seventy-five-year-old White Thunder selected Elk River, who died in 1838 from poisoning during a ceremony gone bad. Before his death, Elk River had time to select Lame Medicine Man as his successor.

11. Grinnell, "Medicine Arrows," Folder 29, Grinnell Collection, RCOA.

12. Kelsey, *Frontier Capitalist*, 65.

13. Hill, "The Great Indian Treaty Council of 1851," 86.

14. Hafen and Ghent, *Broken Hand*, 193, 302n100.

15. Hill, "The Great Indian Treaty Council of 1851," 87–89.

16. Fitzpatrick report, November 24, 1851, *Annual Report of the Commissioner of Indian Affairs, 1851*, 71–72, for all the quotes through the whip-beating of Lean Bear, the threat of war, and the return of Sumner's command unless noted; Bent to Hyde, February 4, 1913, and October 12, 1915, Yale. The whipping may have been as little as three strokes. Hyde, *Bent*, 98, dated the Lean Bear incident in 1853, which is incorrect. Also see Hill, "The Great Indian Treaty Council of 1851," 89–90, which, although misleading on occasion, appears in other books without being cited.

17. Grinnell, *Fighting Cheyennes*, 145n8 for his names. He was born in 1813. For additional spellings of his name see Hafen and Hafen, *Relations with the Indians*, 298, and Grinnell, "Cheyenne Names," Folder 119, 5, RCOA. Grinnell confirmed "Starving

Bear" as his real name. Although it is a better translation of his name, he has mostly been called Lean Bear by historians and his contemporaries (including George Bent).

18. Hoig, *Peace Chiefs*, 6, and *John Simpson Smith*, 78, discussed the Tsistsistas' view of not hitting a boy with a whip, but his supportive citations do not substantiate what he wrote. None of the extensive documentation that I have gathered from the Grinnell Collection deals with this, and I cannot find a reference to it in Grinnell's *Cheyenne Indians* (but this does not mean that it is not there). All said, the striking of a warrior rings true, and even more so when the thirty-eight-year-old Lean Bear was attacked with a whip. Moreover, it gives credence to Tsistsista warriors being upset enough to contemplate attacking the soldiers.

19. See Bent to Hyde, February 4, 1913, Yale, which makes it clear that Lean Bear and Bear were two different warriors. The black clay was called gunpowder in one book.

20. Berthrong, *Southern Cheyennes*, 118, and McGinnis, *Counting Coup*, 86.

21. Hill, "The Great Indian Treaty Council of 1851," 90, 92, 94–95.

22. Chambers quoted in Berthrong, *Southern Cheyennes*, 118.

23. Berthrong, *Southern Cheyennes*, 119–20.

24. Hoig, *Peace Chiefs*, 8. Also see Hoebel, *Cheyennes*, 37.

25. Kappler, *Treaties*, II:594.

26. Kappler, *Treaties*, II:595. The treaty listed Poisal as "Pizelle."

27. Bent to Samuel Tappan, March 15, 1889, Tappan Collection, History Colorado, provided background on Ar-no-ho-woh (his words and punctuation have not been edited): "Black Kettle's wife's name is an old name. good many Cheyenne names cant not be Interpretered. By any body. Names of women very few can be Interpretered. Men's names are easy Interpretered. Most of them are named after animals or some thing else. . . . Ar-no- means after ho here and woh means or used to in the old language is woman, so her name by rights would be Woman here After, or Woman to be here after."

28. See Grinnell, *Fighting Cheyennes*, 84–85, and n3 for the 1851 treaty. This Little Robe (died 1864) would become a council chief, and he should not be confused with Little Robe (born circa 1828, died 1886), who was also a Dog Man chief before becoming a council chief. Most likely Alights-on-the-Cloud died in 1852, as it seems strange that a revenge war would take so long to initiate. Also see "Cheyenne Chronology," Folder 119b, Grinnell Collection, RCOA; Berthrong, *Southern Cheyennes*, 80. Grinnell named the Crows leading the war party, and he also stated that Comanches joined the advance. See Powell, *People*, I:154–55, and II:1419, for the two Little Robe death dates; he did not include Crows. Powell called the Sacred Buffalo Hat "Ésevone," which is the word for buffalo herds, while using "Is'siwun" in *Sweet Medicine*.

29. Bent to Grinnell, June 25, 1907, Folder 41a, Grinnell Collection, RCOA. This twenty-page letter in Bent's hand also includes the Dog Man passing of wives to obtain dog ropes, Little Robe's passing of his wives, the Sacred Arrows, Long Chin, Black Kettle, and Big Head's actions, as well as the battle. Wolf Tongue was George Bent's cousin. In this letter Bent claimed that twelve Tsistsistas died. However, in Bent to Hyde, February 20, 1905, Yale (transcribed by Faller), the death count was eleven Cheyennes and one Arapaho. Here Bent did not list the Comanches or Crows being present; it included the Sacred Arrows ceremony. For Big Head breaking the medicine of the two sacred objects see Grinnell, *Fighting Cheyennes*, 92–93, and Powell, *People*, I:161, II:1418 (Big Head became a council chief in 1856).

30. Grinnell, *Fighting Cheyennes*, 92. This overrides any documentation in the Grinnell Collection, RCOA, or elsewhere that claims Wooden Leg was a Keeper of the

Sacred Arrows. He never was, for Stone Forehead was the Keeper of the Arrows until his death in 1876.

31. See "Wolf Chief 1905," Folder 69, Grinnell Collection, RCOA, regarding Black Kettle and Stone Forehead being cousins.

32. For this attack and the scalp dance, see Bent to Grinnell, August 30, 1910, Folder 41a, Grinnell Collection, RCOA.

33. In Extract of George Bent to Grinnell, February 8, 1914, Folder 119, he made it clear that there were two War Bonnets. "War Bonnet was chief, and chief of Scabby Band also. He was killed at Sand Creek. He was not related to War Bonnet killed in Old Mexico." See "Cheyenne Names," Folder 119, for the second War Bonnet dates (1804–64); Bent to Grinnell (undated, but per Lincoln Faller between April 24, 1905 and May 1, 1905), Folder 10a, for War Bonnet's raid. Mad Wolf was living near Bent at the time of this letter and he was Bent's consultant on what happened. All in Grinnell Collection, RCOA.

34. Bent to Hyde, February 26, 1906, Yale; Hyde, *Bent*, 83, 94. Editor Lottinville, 94n15, placed their arrival in Westport in fall 1853. I have seen Bent to Grinnell, October 12, 1913, Grinnell Collection, RCOA, cited in a book, but although I requested all the Bent/Grinnell letters I did not receive this letter. I have Lincoln Faller's transcription of the letter, but in it George wrote about the Washita fight, Roman Nose's death, and so on; he never mentioned school, Westport, or his siblings.

35. See Bent to Grinnell (n.d., but between April 24, 1905 and May 1, 1905), Folder 10a for Black Kettle's raid into Mexico to avenge War Bonnet's death. See "Cheyenne Names," Folder 119, as it set 1789 for White Antelope's birth, and this date has been accepted. Both in Grinnell Collection, RCOA.

36. See Mrs. Wm. N. Byers, "The Experiences of One Pioneer Woman," (hereafter Byers, "Pioneer Woman"), 1 for quote, and also see 2. William N. Byers Papers, WH55, Western History Collection, Denver Public Library. For Elizabeth's parents' names, see H. D. T., "Pioneer Journalist," 52.

37. Byers, "Pioneer Woman," 2; also see 1; H. D. T., "Pioneer Journalist," 52.

38. Wolf Chief, "Life of Black Kettle," Folder 69, for when he became a chief; and "Noted Cheyennes Names," Folder 119, Grinnell Collection, RCOA. Powell, *People*, I:207, I:632n7, was at first foggy with Bear Feather's death but then precise as he confirmed when Black Kettle became chief.

39. Quoted in Berthrong, *Southern Cheyennes*, 137. See Powell, *People*, I:187, for when Lean Bear became a council chief.

40. See Hafen and Young, *Fort Laramie*, 280 (also see 281) which quoted R. M. Peck, "Recollections of Early Times in Kansas Territory," in *Transactions of the Kansas State Historical Society* 8, 485.

41. Chalfant, *Cheyennes*, 177; also see 178, 180.

42. "Robert M. Peck Account of the Sedgwick Division," in Hafen and Hafen, *Relations with the Indians*, 116; also see 97, 115. Peck served with Sedgwick during the campaign.

43. Sumner report, July 29, 1857, in Hafen and Hafen, *Relations with the Indians*, 26.

44. "Robert M. Peck Account," in Hafen and Hafen, *Relations with the Indians*, 120–21. Also see Ball, *Army Regulars on the Western Frontier*, 39, 42.

45. Grinnell, *Fighting Cheyennes*, 117; Chalfant, *Cheyennes*, 177. Ice would later be known as White Bull.

46. Harney to Thomas, August 22, 1857, in Hafen and Hafen, *Relations with the Indians*, 146.

47. Kraft, *Wynkoop*, 92–93; Kraft, *Custer and the Cheyenne* (hereafter Kraft, *Custer*), 4.

Chapter 5. Bent's Fear Becomes Reality

1. West, *Contested Plains*, 6–7. For a more in-depth explanation see Van Vleck, *Panic of 1857*, 60–79.

2. Kraft, *Wynkoop*, 14.

3. "Latest Intelligence from the Gold Mines of Western Kansas," *Lawrence Republican*, December 30, 1858, in Hafen, *Colorado Gold Rush*, 131–32; Ubbelohde, Benson, and Smith, *Colorado History*, 57, 59.

4. McGaa, "St. Charles and Denver Town Companies," 125–26; Ubbelohde, Benson, and Smith, *Colorado History*, 59; "An Inventory of the Records of the Auraria Town Company," History Colorado, Collection no. 23, 5, provided the offices held by members; Cobb, "Lawrence Party of Pike's Peakers," 195. Cobb, who was a member of the Lawrence Party, claimed that they were on the South Platte above Cherry Creek on September 4, 1858, saw Russell's party pulling gold from the river, and that he and his partners did the same. Then, four days later, he and Adnah French moved to Cherry Creek and selected the land for their city. He did not mention the Montana location and his timeline was earlier than McGaa's. See Hafen, *Colorado Gold Rush*, 209n255, as the Denver City Town Company record book (History Colorado), "gives his name both as Jones and McGaa."

5. McGaa "Statement," 126–27, to the end of the section. Hoig, *John Simpson Smith*, 110, and "Auraria Town Company," 5, claimed that it was 640 acres. The "Auraria Town Company," which provides some background for Russell's claim, got the destination correct (something McGaa did not do), but did not know that Nichols remained on the land. The document claimed that Smith and McGaa did not uphold their part of the agreement (which they attempted to do).

6. H. C. Rogers to Col. N. C. Claiborne, November 2, 1858, in Hafen, *Colorado Gold Rush*, 148. See Kraft, *Wynkoop*, 274n27, for the controversy and confusion that Larimer created with different entries pointing to different dates, which he combined with messed-up arithmetic.

7. Kraft, *Wynkoop*, 3–8; see 271–72nn1–19 for background on Wynkoop's family.

8. McGaa "Statement," 127. Also see Leonard and Noel, *Denver*, 8, and Hoig, *John Simpson Smith*, 112. As time passed, Larimer refused to admit that he threatened anyone. Forty-two members signed the new constitution.

9. G. N. Hill letter, November 28, 1858, 173–74; J. B. Wisenall letter, December 3, 1858, 177 and n232, 178; and Noel Lajeunesse to father, December 2, 1858, 178, all in Hafen, *Colorado Gold Rush*; Larimer to wife Rachel, November 23, 1858, Davis, *Larimer*, 100, 102, also see 105; G. N. Hill letter in Kansas City *Journal of Commerce*, January 15, 1859; Wynkoop, "Unfinished Colorado History," 31, 33, History Colorado; "Latest From the Gold Region," *Missouri Republican*, February 8, 1859; "The New Eldorado," *Agitator*, February 10, 1859, 2; and Isern, "Controversial Career," 2.

10. Bent to Robinson, December 1, 1858, quoted in Lavender, *Bent's Fort*, 340. Also see 423, where Lavender states that Bent wrote: "Nine letters [in regard to the Upper Arkansas Agency] to A. M. Robinson, Jan. 1859–Feb., 1860," and that they are

in "Records of the Bureau of Indian Affairs, National Archives, Washington." One book stated that sixteen-year-old George Bent confronted his father on this issue, but without supporting documentation. Searching George Bent's letters, I could not find anything to confirm this.

11. Hoig, *John Simpson Smith*, 113, 116, 156, documented a newspaper report of this birth of a new Smith son named John. If Jack Smith, and "Jack" has been a nickname for "John" throughout the ages, this article was in error, for Jack Smith was about sixteen in 1858. This led to Hoig stating that this son was William Gilpin Smith. Hoig's proof was the *Lawrence Republican*, October 21, 1858, but there is a problem with this, and it is that William Gilpin was named after the first territorial governor of Colorado Territory.

12. Jones (i.e. McGaa) to unknown, January 7, 1859, in Hafen, *Colorado Gold Rush*, 208. Coel, *Left Hand*, 79, has Smith beating his wife for dancing with the miner, but inexplicably placed the incident in 1857 even though she cited the same page from Hafen.

13. Garrard, *Wah-to-yah*, 74. Italics in original.

14. Jones to unknown, January 7, 1859, in Hafen, *Colorado Gold Rush*, 208.

15. Byers and Kellom, *Hand Book*. Kellom listed himself as "Sup't of Pub. Instruction of Nebraska." See the entire book, as its contents are decent, albeit mostly speculation.

16. Wynkoop, "Unfinished Colorado History," 46.

17. Byers and Kellom, *Hand Book*, 86, including the following quote. Italics in quote.

18. Byers and Kellom, *Hand Book*, 86–92.

19. Byers and Kellom, *Hand Book*, 91.

20. H. D. T., "Pioneer Journalist," 50. Also see *Portrait and Biographical Record of the State of Colorado*, 45.

21. Byers's report, July 10, 1859, 117–21 for all quotes and information, as printed in Hafen and Hafen, *Reports from Colorado*. Byers's report was published "in a special edition of the *Omaha Nebraskian*, and . . . was copied in the *Council Bluffs Press*" (no dates supplied), 116n29.

22. Lavender, *Bent's Fort*, 340–41, 417n1.

23. See Richardson, *Beyond the Mississippi*, 190–93, for the encounter with Little Raven. Richardson mistakenly thought that Utes killed Little Raven in 1860.

24. Richardson, *Beyond the Mississippi*, 189.

25. See Byers, "Pioneer Woman," 2, for this and the following quote and information.

26. Byers, "Pioneer Woman," 3, through the last quote in the section.

27. Bent to Superintendent of Indian Affairs, October 5, 1859, in *Report of the Commissioner of Indian Affairs*, 1859, 137–38, through end of section.

28. Kraft, *Wynkoop*, 37–38, 50; "Observer," November 24 and December 8, 1859, in *Missouri Democrat*, December 10 and 20, 1859, in Hafen and Hafen, *Reports from Colorado*, 223, 226. See Louise Wynkoop Certificate of Death, November 27, 1923, Wynkoop Pension File. Christopher H. Wynkoop to Kraft, July 30, 2007; and Christopher H. Wynkoop, "Brown-Wakely Family Descendants," both in Kraft Collection. Frank Wynkoop, "Data Concerning . . . Wynkoop," Colorado College, 1.

29. Wynkoop, "Unfinished Colorado History," 47–48.

30. "Correspondence, Departure of Governor Steele," *Weekly Rocky Mountain News*, December 14, 1859, 2. (*Rocky Mountain News* is hereafter abbreviated *RMN*.) Also see "Apollo Theatre," *Weekly RMN*, December 1, 1859, 3; Kraft, *Wynkoop*, 34 (Steinberger wrote the play); Schoberlin, *Footlights*, 29–30.

31. Kraft, *Wynkoop*, 33.

32. Bent to Superintendent of Indian Affairs, October 5, 1859, 138–39.

33. Byers, "Pioneer Woman," 3–5.

34. Byers, "Pioneer Woman," 5.

35. Observer, December 8, 1859, published in *Missouri Democrat*, December 20, 1859, and reprinted in Hafen and Hafen, *Reports from Colorado*, 225–26.

36. Observer report, November 24, 1859, as printed in the *Missouri Democrat*, December 10, 1859, in Hafen and Hafen, *Reports from Colorado*, 221–22; including Warren's quote. Italics in original.

37. Observer, December 1, 1859, as printed in the *Missouri Democrat*, December 12, 1859, in Hafen and Hafen, *Reports from Colorado*, 222–23; through the end of the section.

38. "Church Organi[z]ation," *Weekly RMN*, January 25, 1860; also see "Departed"; and Saint John's Cathedral, Denver Colorado, history brochure.

39. Chorley, "The Beginnings of the Church in Colorado," 1. The article has errors: Kehler did not organize St. John's in the Wilderness on January 17, and the first service was not on January 20.

40. "The Ladies' Union Aid Society," *Weekly RMN*, January 25, 1860. Also see Byers, "Pioneer Woman," 5.

41. See "Church Organi[z]ation," January 25, 1860; and "Local and Miscellaneous," February 15, 1860, both in *Weekly RMN*; and Saint John's Cathedral, Denver Colorado, history brochure. Two of Kehler's daughters married in 1860.

Chapter 6. Welcome to the White Man's World

1. "History of the Reverends John M. & Isaac Chivington," John M. Chivington Papers, M1594, Western History Collection, DPL, 2. See Roberts, *Massacre at Sand Creek*, 61–62 (hereafter Roberts, *Massacre*), for Chivington's birth in Warren County, Ohio.

2. Craig, *Fighting Parson*, 26, 30.

3. Quoted in Roberts, *Massacre*, 69.

4. Roberts, *Massacre*, 85–86, 271n38.

5. "History of the Reverends John M. & Isaac Chivington," 2.

6. Roberts, *Massacre*, 70.

7. Email exchange from Kraft, August 11, 2016, to Fort Larned chief historian George Elmore, who forwarded it to Shawn Gillette, chief of interpretation at the Sand Creek Massacre NHS, who then forwarded the request to Gary Roberts, whose reply went back to Elmore, who then sent the results to Kraft, August 18, 2016. Dr. Roberts's reply destroyed previous Nebraska City departure and Denver arrival dates as well as the date of Chivington's first sermon in Denver at the Masonic Hall on May 13. Roberts's proof follows:

In Chivington's account in "The Prospective" written in 1884 (Bancroft Library Collections), Chivington recalled that he left Nebraska City "on the ninth day of April [1860]," and that he arrived in the Denver area on the "fourth of May" and camp[ed] on the east side of Cherry Creek.

In his multipart series, "Footprints of Methodist Itinerants in Colorado," ROCKY MOUNTAIN CHRISTIAN ADVOCATE, September 26, 1889, Chivington wrote, "On May 8, 1860, I arrived in Denver."

I used more contemporary sources in my recent report on Sand Creek. The Nebraska City PEOPLE'S PRESS, reported on April 24, 1860, "REV. JOHN M. CHIVINGTON, recently appointed Presiding Elder of the Rocky Mountain District, of the Methodist Episcopal Church, started yesterday [April 23], with his family for his future field of labor." The Reverend Jacob Adriance wrote in his diary (housed at DPL) on May 8, that he had arrived in Nebraska City expecting to go west with [Rev.] Chivington, but "he had been gone two weeks." Two weeks earlier would have been roughly April 23, which seemed to me to confirm the April 23 departure.

Taking into account Mr. Kraft's question about travel time, I explored a little further, and I think I have found the answer. On May 23, 1860, the ROCKY MOUNTAIN NEWS (Weekly) published this article: "Rev. J. M. Chivington, Presiding Elder of the Methodist Episcopal Church North, for the Rocky Mountain District, Kansas and Nebraska Conference arrived with his family on Saturday last and has taken up his residence in the city. In a very short time he will arrange and systematize his work throughout the district."

"Saturday last" would be May 19, eleven days later than the May 8 date given in most sources including my most recent work [*Massacre at Sand Creek*, 2016, 70, which includes Chivington's first sermon]. This would mean that if we rely on the contemporary sources (which seems the best course to me), Chivington departed Nebraska City on April 23, 1860 and arrived in Denver on May 19, or a few days shy of a month after he left Nebraska City. I believe this is the correct itinerary. The errors in Chivington's accounts are simply matters of faulty memory.

This email exchange is in Kraft Collection. See Craig, *Fighting Parson*, 46, for the wagons. The distance is strangely listed as 478.9 miles for automobiles, bicycles, walking, and airplanes. If they started out on April 23 they would have averaged a little over eighteen miles per day. See the color illustrated map by William Henry Jackson that was distributed by the Union Pacific Railroad and titled "Pony Express Route April 3, 1860—October 24, 1861," on LMB01.

8. Greenwood to J. Thompson, Secretary of the Interior, October 25, 1860, *Report of the Commissioner of Indian Affairs*, 1860, 228–30. Also see Hafen and Hafen, *Relations with the Indians*, 284–86.

9. Kappler, *Treaties*, II:810.

10. Thrapp, *Frontier Biography*, I:299; Kappler, *Treaties*, II:810. Samuel Colley replaced Boone as agent on July 26, 1861.

11. Coel, *Left Hand*, 110–14, has Left Hand and Little Raven at the September 1860 council with Greenwood, and although she cited Greenwood's three-page October 25, 1960, report she did not list the author or date, nor did she mention that Greenwood did not name one Arapaho present at the September meeting, and yet she listed a handful. Her quotations on 111 and 113 are in Greenwood's report. I agree with Coel that Left Hand and Little Raven were present, but there is no proof that they were. In 110n1 Coel cited Kappler, *Treaties*, II:807–11. Why? This deals with the February 1861 treaty and has nothing to do with 1860 or the unnamed Arapahos who met with Greenwood in September 1860.

12. Kappler, *Treaties*, II:807–10.

13. Hoig, *Peace Chiefs*, 106.

14. Wolf Chief, "Life of Black Kettle," Folder 69, Grinnell Collection, RCOA.

15. "Call for Troops," *Weekly RMN*, May 1, 1861. The *RMN* printed its weekly edition on Wednesdays.

16. "The Indians," *Weekly RMN*, May 1, 1861. This article was originally published in the daily edition of *RMN* on April 24.

17. Hardorff, *Washita Memories*, 283n1, provides background on Poisal. His name has often been misspelled as "Poisel" and "Poysell." See Thrapp, *Frontier Biography*, III:1154–55, for additional background on Poisal. Coel, *Left Hand*, 4, confirmed that Mahom and Snake Woman were the same person.

18. "Indian Matters," *Weekly RMN*, May 1, 1861, 1, documents Left Hand's visit to the *RMN* on April 25, 1861. Many of the stories printed in the *Weekly* were reprints (and sometimes shortened stories) that had previously seen print in the *Daily RMN*. When this was the case, the *Weekly* printed the date of the first printing of the story. In this case, "Daily, 25th ult." Some historians have been confused by the dating and of what they read in the paper. This article is a major case in point. In *Left Hand*, 128, Coel stated that Left Hand erred when he said that Little Raven would arrive in Denver in five days for a meeting. He did not err, but Coel did, as she ignored the date of the initial story. Left Hand included the twenty-fifth in his counting when he said "five or six days." Actually, Little Raven would appear on the twenty-ninth. On 127, Coel wrote, "Left Hand said he could not speak for the Cheyennes," but he never said anything close to this to Byers. The *RMN* stated that upon Little Raven's arrival that "they desire to hold a talk with our people." No, the meeting would be with Boone.

19. "Foolish Rumors," *Weekly RMN*, May 1, 1861, 4, "From the Daily of Friday, 26th."

20. "Indian Council," *Weekly RMN*, May 1, 1861, 2, for the entire Boone-Arapaho council.

21. Cowell, *Dictionary of the Arapaho Language*, 219. This is a modern-day spelling of the word. Also see http://www.native-languages.org/arapaho-legends.htm. Nih'oo3oo is pronounced "nih-ah-thaw."

22. "Theatre Last Evening," *Weekly RMN*, May 1, 1861, for Left Hand speaking after a performance at the Apollo Theatre.

23. "The Indians," *Weekly RMN*, May 1, 1861, 1. This article relates to May 1.

24. Bent to Hyde, March 9, 1905, Yale; Halaas, *Halfbreed*, 82; Hyde, *Bent*, 110.

25. "Indian Meeting," *RMN*, May 22, 1861, 3. See Coel, *Left Hand*, 130–31, for the horse races and the Arapaho-Mexican encounter.

26. Kraft, *Wynkoop*, 42, 60–64.

27. Zamonski, *'59ers*, 261.

28. Ashley, "Colorado in the Early 'Sixties," 219.

29. Chivington, "The Pet Lambs," *Denver Republican*, April 20, 1890, 24. Chivington's article appeared in five consecutive Sunday editions of the paper. Also see "History of the Reverends John M. & Isaac Chivington," 2, Chivington Papers, M1594, DPL.

30. Wynkoop, "Unfinished Colorado History," 56.

31. "Indian Differences," *Weekly RMN*, June 12, 1861, 1.

32. "The Late Indian Troubles," *Weekly RMN*, June 19, 1861, 1.

33. Bent to Hyde, February 26, 1906, Yale; Halaas, *Halfbreed*, 82–83; Hyde, *Bent*, 110.

34. Hollister, *Boldly*, 185–90, lists the ranks of the officers of the First Colorado.

35. Wynkoop Military File, Company Muster Roll, July 29–August 31, 1861. All citations indicating that he received his commission on July 21 are incorrect. See Kraft, *Wynkoop*, for his straddling of the law.

36. Louise Wynkoop to son Frank, May 20, 1920, Wynkoop Collection, Chávez History Library.

37. Kelsey, "Background to Sand Creek," 280–81; Berthrong, *Southern Cheyennes*, 156n8.

38. Ashley, "Colorado in the Early 'Sixties," 219. Also see 221. In 1908 Ashley spoke before the Denver Fortnightly Club about her memories of the early days of Denver City. Twenty-eight years later the *Colorado Magazine* printed her recollections.

39. See Ashley, "Colorado in the Early 'Sixties," 222–23 for the rest of the quotes in this section. Hatch, *Black Kettle*, 90, lifted Ashley's paragraph beginning with "One beautiful Sunday . . ." directly from Hoig, *Sand Creek Massacre*, 21–22, with one difference in his note: He misunderstood "Vol. XIII" for an "8."

Chapter 7. White Man War and Dissonance

1. Chivington, "The Pet Lambs," *Denver Republican*, April 20, 1890, 24; Whitlock, *Distant Bugles*, 171–72.

2. Whitlock, *Distant Bugles*, 172, citing Chivington, "The Pet Lambs," Chivington Papers, M1594, DPL, 9. This quote was not in the newspaper articles.

3. Chivington to Brig. Gen. E. R. S. Canby, March 26, 1862; and Walker to Lt. N. M. MacRae, AAAG, Fourth New Mexico Volunteers, May 20, 1862, both in *The War of the Rebellion: A Compilation of the Official Records of the Union and Confederate Armies* (hereafter *OR*), Series I, Vol. IX, 530–31. Edrington, *Glorieta*, 46 (map); Whitlock, *Distant Bugles*, 172–73. In Alberts, *Glorieta*, 48, the soldier count was larger than Chivington's. The engagement may have begun at 2:45. Walker called Kozlowski's Ranch "Gray's Ranch."

4. Walker to MacRae, May 20, 1862, 532, for quote, and Chivington to Canby, March 26, 1862, 530–31, *OR*, Series I, Vol. IX. Also see Edrington, *Glorieta*, 48 (map).

5. Whitlock, *Distant Bugles*, 173.

6. Hollister, *Boldly*, 62. See Slough to Canby, March 29, 1862, *OR*, Series I, Vol. IX, 533, for the retreat.

7. Roberts, *Massacre*, 88–89; Craig, *Fighting Parson*, 68. Although many past-due bills would be paid, others would never be honored, causing countless business failures in Denver.

8. Signed document of Lincoln's appointment of Evans as governor of Colorado Territory, March 26, 1862, Governor John Evans Papers, WH1724, DPL.

9. Slough to Canby, March 29, 1862, 533; Slough to A.G., U.S. Army, March 30, 1862, 534, *OR*, Series I, Vol. IX.

10. Chivington report, March 28, 1862, *OR*, Series I, Vol. IX, 538. Chivington called Kozlowski's Ranch "Camp Lewis." Whitlock, *Distant Bugles*, 188, claimed, without figures, that Chivington's force had almost five hundred men.

11. Slough to Canby, March 29, 1862, 533; Slough to A.G. U.S. Army, March 30, 1862, 534, *OR*, Series I, Vol. IX. For details about Slough's fight, see Sam. F. Tappan to Capt. G. Chapin, AAAG, Dept. Hdqrs., Santa Fe, N.Mex., May 21, 1862, 536–38; John F. Ritter to Capt. G. Chapin, May 16, 1862, 539–40; and W. R. Scurry to Maj. A. M. Jackson, AG, Army of New Mexico, March 30 and March 31, 1862, 541–45, *OR*, Series I, Vol. IX. Scurry claimed the fight began at 11 A.M. and ended at 5:30 P.M., when the Confederate army forced the federal forces to retreat.

12. Slough to Samuel Tappan, February 6, 1863, Tappan Collection, MSS 617, History Colorado, as cited in Arthur A. Wright, "Colonel John P. Slough and the New Mexico Campaign," *Colorado Magazine*, April 1962, 102.

13. Chivington report, March 28, 1862, 538–39. The Slough report, March 30, 1962, 535, dated two days after Chivington's report, claimed that only sixty wagons were destroyed. Both in *OR*, Series I, Vol. IX. Alberts, *Glorieta*, 131–32, 203–4nn7–8. Edrington, *Glorieta*, 93–94, presented a logical reason why Chivington did not join the charge: "[T]he 260-pound major must have realized that while he personally could get down the cliff, getting back up might well be impossible." Also see 155n17, as Edrington and coauthor Taylor climbed and descended the mesa, and confirmed how difficult it was.

14. Scurry to Maj. A. M. Jackson, March 30, 1862, 541–42; Slough report, March 30, 1962, 535; and Chivington report, March 28, 1862, 539, all in *OR*, Series I, Vol. IX.

15. Hollister, *Boldly*, 86; Whitford, *Battle of Glorieta Pass*, 130.

16. *Report of the John Evans Study Committee*, Northwestern University, May 2014, 18 (hereafter Northwestern Evans Study); Utley, *Indian Frontier*, 41–42; Roche, "Territorial Governor as *Ex-Officio* Superintendent," 16.

17. Alberts, *Glorieta*, 163.

18. "Later From New Mexico," *RMN*, May 28, 1862, 2; Hollister, *Boldly*, 89; Alberts, *Glorieta*, 163; Whitlock, *Distant Bugles*, 229.

19. Bent to Hyde, February 26, 1906, Yale; Halaas, *Halfbreed*, 86–91. Also see Hyde, *Bent*, 110–11. The retreat may have begun on May 27.

20. Chivington to Fisher, June 25, 1862, Chivington Papers, M1594, FF1, DPL. I am not certain of the spelling of "Delegote" and could not find anyone with this name in early Colorado Territory history; however, the fifth letter is definitely a "g," as it matches all the other "g's" in Chivington's letter. Emphasis in letter.

21. Chivington, "The Pet Lambs," *Denver Republican*, May 4, 1890, 15, through the First Colorado quote. Roberts, *Massacre*, 77. Roberts (268n94) wrote, "This has an apocryphal ring to it."

22. Roberts, *Sand Creek*, 1:145.

23. Bent to Hyde, February 26, 1906; for joining Black Kettle, see Bent to Hyde, April 17, 1906, Yale; see Halaas, *Halfbreed*, 90, 370nn50–52, which thought Bent's incarceration was longer than one day.

24. Kelsey, "Background to Sand Creek," 282.

25. Chivington to Tappan, October 23, 1862, Tappan Collection, MSS 617, Box 1, FF 3, History Colorado. Emphasis in quote.

26. Evans to Lincoln, October 31, 1862, in Roberts, *Massacre*, 77, for quote; also see 268n65. Surprisingly Lori Cox-Paul, in "Chivington," *Nebraska History* (2007), 132, 146n31, used the same quote as Roberts but dated the letter October 1, 1862. Although the citation is slightly different in both notes it appears to be from the same archive. Did Evans write two letters to Lincoln in October, or did one of the citations have the wrong date?

27. Alberts, *Glorieta*, 165, 209n2; Whitlock, *Distant Bugles*, 247.

28. Roberts, *Massacre*, 78.

29. Tappan to Chivington, January 23, 1863, Tappan Collection, MSS 617, Box 1, FF 3, History Colorado.

30. See Communication from the Secretary of War Edwin M. Stanton, February 1, 1864, 39th Cong., 1st Sess., 4, for date of appointment. Chivington's name does not appear on the document. Also see Roberts, *Massacre*, 78, 268n99.

31. Niderost, "Great Sioux Uprising," 65.

32. Boone to Evans, January 16, 1863, in Roberts, *Sand Creek*, 1:147.

33. Roberts, *Sand Creek*, 1:147–48.

34. Hoig, *White Man's Paper Trail*, 111, citing the *Leavenworth Times*, March 13, 1863.

35. Roberts, *Sand Creek*, 1:148.

36. Mooney and Powell, *In Sun's Likeness*, 1:144–45. Father Peter J. Powell, who edited the book and wrote most of the text, is a Catholic priest and one of the top Cheyenne historians ever. He chose these images taken in March 1863, and in the image with Colley he identifies Starving Bear (a.k.a. Lean Bear) as sitting between the other two chiefs. In the image with Smith he identifies Starving Bear as standing right, and this coincides with the other image. However, then Powell strangely states that the chief standing with Smith might be War Bonnet (he spells the chief's name as Warbonnet), which in turn means that two of the three chiefs with Colley are incorrectly named.

37. "The Indians Heard From," *Weekly RMN*, April 2, 1863, which reported the March 23 meeting with Dole based upon information supplied by Washington.

38. *Washington Evening Star*, March 27, 1863, quoted in Hoig, *White Man's Paper Trail*, 112, changed Hoig's original dating from the twenty-sixth to the twenty-seventh (*Peace Chiefs*, 70), but Prucha, in *Great Father*, I:413, showed the twenty-seventh was wrong when he used the Washington *Daily Morning Chronicle*, March 27, 1963, as his source for the meeting, which meant the meeting happened on the twenty-sixth to make the morning paper.

39. Washington *Daily Morning Chronicle*, March 27, 1963, as quoted in Prucha, *Great Father*, I:413. This paragraph is based on Prucha's view of Lincoln's situation.

40. Roberts, *Sand Creek*, 1:157, documenting Saville to Holloway, April 15, 1863. Unfortunately there is a problem with Saville's letter, for it states that Neva had been present at this meeting, and that Neva had torn into John Smith as not being an acceptable interpreter for the Arapahos. See Hoig, *Peace Chiefs*, 75, for proof that Neva could not have been present at this meeting, as he and the other chiefs that had visited Washington, D.C., that spring were still in New York City on April 18, 1863. On that date they were making their final appearance on P. T. Barnum's stage. Most logical is that in stating Neva's view of John Smith, somehow Saville thought that Neva was present when he was not. This leads one to wonder if there was some translation performed (and not accurately), or if Left Hand's English was not as accomplished as documented.

41. Cox-Paul, "Chivington," 132, for extended quote. She lists "Colonel Slough's" (he was promoted to general over a year before) letter in her notes but no archive. She also states that Evans again wrote a letter (but she was vague for there is no date, what was in the letter, and there is no citation). Roberts, *Massacre*, 78, used a much shorter quote. However, he listed the letter's archive; his prose confirmed the quotation.

42. Roberts, *Massacre*, 78.

43. "Central News," *Weekly Commonwealth and Republican*, October 1, 1863.

Chapter 8. Unjustified Actions

1. See Powell, *People*, I:xl, for the Cheyenne name of the month for March and, in the following paragraph, for April.

2. Colley testimony, March 14, 1865, *Report of the Joint Committee on the Conduct of the War, Massacre of Cheyenne Indians*, 38th Congress, 2nd Session, 1865, 30 (hereafter "Massacre of Cheyenne Indians").

3. Eayre to Chivington, April 23, 1864, *OR*, Series I, Vol. XXXIV/1, 880–81; Hyde, *Bent*, 124–26.

4. Bent to Hyde, March 6, 1905, March 26, 1906, and September 17, 1914, Yale. Bent once wrote that the war party contained twenty warriors but later dropped the number to ten (citing Little Chief). However, on March 26, 1906, he named himself and four others while stating ten others rode with the war party (I used this number). Also see Hyde, *Bent*, 122; Powell, *People*, I:258, II:1419; and Joseph Cramer testimony, February 23, 1865, 32 in *Report of the Secretary of War . . . by a military commission, ordered to inquire into the Sand Creek massacre, November, 1864*, 39th Congress, 2nd Session, Senate Executive Document No. 26, 1867 (hereafter "Sand Creek Massacre"). Cramer heard the story from Black Kettle. Due to the problem with translation, Cramer was not certain if the animals were mules or horses, which gives credence to Ripley's claim that his stock were horses. Bent later had conversations with Bull-Telling-Tales, Little Chief, whom he spoke with often over the years, and Good Bear; the last two were still living in 1914 and they confirmed what he remembered.

5. Sanborn to Chivington, April 12, 1864, *OR*, Series I, Vol. XXXIV/1, 883.

6. Bent to Hyde, March 5, 1913, Yale; Clark Dunn report, April 18, 1864, *OR*, Series I, Vol. XXXIV/1, 884.

7. Cramer testimony, February 23, 1865, "Sand Creek Massacre," 32; Hyde, *Bent*, 122. Bent was correct that the Indians crossed the river in the morning, but wrong about the time when the soldiers came upon them. Gerry is sometimes spelled "Geary." Also see Thrapp, *Frontier Biography*, II:549–50.

8. Dunn report, April 18, 1864, *OR*, Series I, Vol. XXXIV/1, 884; Dunn testimony, April 27, 1865, "Sand Creek Massacre," 180.

9. Cramer testimony, February 23, 1865, "Sand Creek Massacre," 32; Hyde, *Bent*, 122. Cramer's testimony tracks the Dog Men's movements in more detail than Bent's letters to Hyde.

10. Dunn report, April 18, 1864, *OR*, Series I, Vol. XXXIV/1, 884; Dunn testimony, April 27, 1865, "Sand Creek Massacre," 181. Dunn claimed that he watched the main group of warriors cross to the north side of the river, but this seems unlikely. Military reports often reported inflated numbers of Indians.

11. Bent to Hyde, March 26, 1906, March 5, 1913, and September 17, 1914, Yale; Powell, *People*, I:258. The Indians placed the soldier count between fifteen and twenty.

12. Dunn report, April 18, 1864, *OR*, Series II, Vol. XXXIV/1, 884–85; Dunn testimony, April 27, 1865, "Sand Creek Massacre," 181. At the inquiry Dunn stated that the entire line of warriors moved toward him when he approached them. When he retreated to his command, the warriors followed him. Dunn ordered his men to reholster their revolvers, dismount, and disarm the Indians. As soon as his men dismounted, the Indians attacked.

13. Bent to Hyde, March 26, 1906, March 19, 1912, and September 17, 1914, Yale, citing Little Chief in the first letter, and Little Chief and Good Bear in the second letter. In the Smoky Hill Dog Man village after the fight George Bent spoke with some of the warriors. At times it appeared as if Bent was not at the firefight (Bent to Hyde, November 22, 1908), as he seemed to gather information on a fight in which he was not involved. Powell, *People*, I:258, stated that Bull-Telling-Tales beheaded the soldier he shot.

14. Dunn report, April 18, 1864, *OR*, Series I, Vol. XXXIV/1, 885; Sanborn to Chivington, April 15, 1864, *OR*, Series I, Vol. XXXIV/3, 167. Dunn and Sanborn

confuse exactly when Dunn started and ended his second patrol; I have accepted San-born's timeline, as his details seem logical.

15. Chivington to Evans, April 15, 1864, *OR*, Series I, Vol. XXXIV/3, 166–67.

16. Gerry to Sanborn, April 14, 1864, *OR*, Series I, Vol. XXXIV/3, 167–68.

17. Hyde, *Bent*, 125. On 124, Bent stated: "I never believed this story and do not believe it now. The Indians had no use for the oxen; there were plenty of buffalo on that range that winter, and the Indians never would eat 'tame meat' when they could get buffalo. Besides, I have talked to many men who were in these two Cheyenne camps (the other village was Rac[c]oon's); all denied that the oxen were stolen, and I know they told the truth." Also see 126. Eayre to Chivington, April 23, 1864, *OR*, Series I, Vol. XXXIV/1, 880–81; Asbury Bird (Co. D, First Colorado) sworn statement (n.d.), COIT "Chivington Massacre," 72. Bird, who was with Eayre, confirmed the lieuten-ant except for three large points: He claimed the village consisted of five lodges, that Cheyennes, Kiowas, and Arapahos were present, and that two warriors rode out to meet them but then fled when soldiers loped toward them. He agreed that Eayre sent two men to capture the warrior on their left and that he wounded one of them.

18. Eayre to Chivington, April 23, 1864, *OR*, Series I, Vol. XXXIV/1, 880–81; Hyde, *Bent*, 124–26.

19. "Daily News," *RMN*, April 27, 1864, 3.

20. "Daily News," *RMN*, April 29, 1864, 3.

21. Downing sworn statement, July 21, 1865, COIT "Chivington Massacre," 69, through killing the warrior. In "Business Directory," *RMN*, May 22, 1861, 1, Downing was listed as "Attorney at Law, and Commissioner of Deeds for Kansas."

22. Monahan, *Destination: Denver City*, 141–43. In regard to the capture and threat-ened torture of Spotted Horse she did terrific research (262n36), which began with Ashcraft (Denver *Field and Farm*, December 19, 1891), and Downing's (Denver *Post*, December 31, 1903) articles that dealt with burning the warrior's shins. Monahan de-bunked both articles. (Hyde, *Bent*, 129, and Grinnell, *Fighting Cheyennes*, 143, not 137, as listed in Monahan, 262n36). Without mentioning "dime novels" she made it clear that Ashcraft and Downing took great liberties in later life; Downing bragged about torturing the warrior.

23. Special Orders No. 29, May 2, 1864, Wynkoop Military File.

24. Kraft, *Wynkoop*, 84–89, 91, 284n29, 284–85nn37–38.

25. Downing sworn statement, July 21, 1865, COIT "Chivington Massacre," 69. Although some accounts claim that Dunn and some of his troops joined the expedition and that Downing had sixty men, the major never mentioned the lieutenant and was firm that he had forty men.

26. Monahan, *Destination: Denver City*, 142. This description is Monahan's.

27. Downing sworn statement, July 21, 1865, COIT "Chivington Massacre," 69.

28. "Indian Battle," *RMN*, May 4, 1864, 2. Grinnell, *Fighting Cheyennes*, 143, placed the village north of the river. In Downing's sworn statement, July 21, 1865, he claimed that the attack happened in mid-May. Byers's article debunked the major's dating.

29. Downing sworn statement, July 21, 1865, COIT "Chivington Massacre," 69.

30. "Indian Fighting Commenced in Ernest," Black Hawk *Daily Mining Journal*, May 4, 1864, 2 (hereafter BH*DMJ*).

31. "Major Downing Chastises the Indians," *Daily Commonwealth*, May 4, 1864, 2.

32. Joseph Cramer testimony, February 23, 1865, "Sand Creek Massacre," 30; Ha-laas, *Halfbreed*, 117–18.

33. Grinnell, *Fighting Cheyennes*, 145–46. Grinnell erroneously stated that the trip to Washington was in 1862. For additional information see Grinnell, "Southern Cheyennes," 17, 32, Folder 119, Grinnell Collection, RCOA; Bent to Hyde, March 6, 1905, Yale; Cramer testimony, February 23, 1865, "Sand Creek Massacre," 30; Halaas, *Halfbreed*, 117–18; and Hoig, *Peace Chiefs*, 86, 96.

34. Hyde, *Bent*, 131–33, and Wynkoop testimony, June 9, 1865, COIT "Chivington Massacre," 75, wherein he stated that Eayre told him that he was ordered by Chivington "to kill all Indians he came across." Hoig, *Sand Creek Massacre*, 51n28. Grinnell, *Fighting Cheyennes*, 144–46, supports Bent's retelling of the fight, but places the fight twenty miles north of the Pawnee Fork. Bent to Hyde, March 6, 1905, Yale, placed the fight forty miles north of Fort Larned.

35. Eayre to Chivington, May 19, 1864, *OR*, Series I, Vol. XXXIV/1, 935. Eayre claimed the fight took place three miles from the Smoky Hill.

36. Geo. S. Shoup to Chivington, May 30, 1864, *OR*, Series I, Vol. XXXIV/4, 207–8.

37. Grinnell, *Fighting Cheyennes*, 146. Grinnell felt that this incident was one of the reasons why white officials thought that the Cheyennes were plotting war during the previous winter.

38. Powell, *People*, I:260–61.

39. Soule Military Returns, January and February, March and April, May and June, 1864, Soule Papers, MSS 982, History Colorado (hereafter Soule Papers, History Colorado).

40. Soule to Annie, June 17, 1864. Also see Soule to mother, June 2, 1864. Both in Silas S. Soule Papers, WH 1690, Box 1, FF1, Denver Public Library (hereafter Soule Papers, DPL). Soule signed all his letters to his loved ones as "Sile." See "Great Flood in Denver" for the time that Cherry Creek flooded and began the destruction, and O. J. Goldrick, "Sketch of the Great Deluge in Denver." Both articles are in *Weekly Commonwealth*, May 25, 1864, 3. Goldrick, whose prose is overly dramatic, placed the beginning of the tragedy at midnight.

41. "Great Flood in Denver," *Weekly Commonwealth*, May 25, 1864, 3; reprinted June 1, 1864. At the top of the June 1 reprint, a statement claimed that it was originally printed in the *Daily Commonwealth* on May 21. The reason for the reprint was twofold: The *RMN* office had been destroyed and a lot of people had not seen the initial article, and they used the article as a lead in to "The Flood. More Particulars" in both reprints, which provided confirmed details about people who had died. Goldrick's "Sketch of the Great Deluge in Denver" was also reprinted in the June 1 issue.

42. "Great Flood in Denver," *Weekly Commonwealth*, May 25, 1864. In the same issue Goldrick, in "Sketch of the Great Deluge in Denver," wrote: "Among the sufferers of property are Byers & Dailey, publishers and proprietors of the *Rocky Mountain News*, who lost their entire all, with the building and the lot it stood on."

43. Byers, "Pioneer Woman," 8.

44. Byers, "Pioneer Woman," 9, including Byers's note and Chivington's arrival and departure. "Great Flood in Denver," *Weekly Commonwealth*, June 1, 1864, for Chivington's action.

45. Byers, "Pioneer Woman," 9, for quote, rescue, and purchase of new house; and "Great Flood in Denver," *Weekly Commonwealth*, June 1, 1864, for a confirmation of the boat rescue.

46. Kelsey, *Frontier Capitalist*, 88.

47. "Cherry Creek Telegraph," *Weekly Commonwealth*, June 1, 1864, 1, contained a grouping of various comments received by the paper on May 27. Soule submitted numerous notes to the paper on that date.

48. Thrapp, *Frontier Biography*, III:1557.

49. "Cherry Creek Telegraph," *Weekly Commonwealth*, June 1, 1864, 1.

50. Byers, "Pioneer Woman," 9.

51. Byers and Dailey, "Rocky Mountain News," *Weekly Commonwealth*, June 1, 1864, 1.

52. Chivington to Wynkoop, May 31, 1864, 151. Also see Maynard, AAAG, to Wynkoop May 23, 1864, 14. *OR*, Series I, Vol. XXXIV/4.

53. Soule to mother, June 2, 1864, Soule Papers, DPL.

54. Soule Military Returns, May and June, and June 1864, Soule Papers, History Colorado.

55. Berthrong, *Southern Cheyennes*, 190; Grinnell, *Fighting Cheyennes*, 150.

56. Broome, *Cheyenne War*, 54–55, 55nn54–55, pieced together a logical scheme of events.

57. "Executive Order," BH*DMJ*, June 15, 1864, 3.

58. "Indian vs. Indian," *Weekly Commonwealth*, June 15, 1864, 2, including Evans's quotes. At this time the whites did not think that the Arapahos were involved. Italics in quote.

59. "Only Nine Indians Seen," *Weekly Commonwealth*, June 15, 1864, 2.

60. "Indian Depredations—Murder of an Entire Family," *Weekly Commonwealth*, June 15, 1864, 2. Also see Grinnell, *Fighting Cheyennes*, 150–51, 153; Berthrong, *Southern Cheyennes*, 191.

Chapter 9. A Frantic Summer

1. Curtis to Cox, June 6, 1864, *OR*, Series I, XXXIV/4, 250–52.

2. Evans to Indians, June 27, 1864, "Massacre of Cheyenne Indians," 61.

3. Evans to Colley, June 29, 1864, "Massacre of Cheyenne Indians," 60–61.

4. Robinson, *Satanta*, 31–32.

5. Mooney, *Calendar History of the Kiowa Indians*, 314.

6. Joseph Cramer testimony, February 23, 1865, "Sand Creek Massacre," 32–33. Although Cramer could not remember the date of the incident, he repeated what he remembered Left Hand said during a September 10, 1864, meeting on the Smoky Hill.

7. This statement is Coel's in *Left Hand*, 193, and I agree with her.

8. Two pieces of evidence place a timeline on when the events in this section happened. Fort Larned NHS chief historian George Elmore to Kraft, December 19, 2017, stated that Parmetar was discharged on July 7, 1864, Kraft Collection (he also provided a dated list of the other commanding officers in 1864); Col. James Ford's sworn statement, May 31, 1865, COIT "Chivington Massacre," 65, did not provide details other than Indians were not allowed in forts and that Parmetar was the commanding officer.

9. Cramer testimony, February 23, 1865, "Sand Creek Massacre," 33. Coel, *Left Hand*, 192–93, cited Cramer and Ford but added information that neither stated— mainly that women performed traditional dances for the soldiers while Satanta raided the horse herd after the Kiowas began to flee their village.

10. Hyde, *Bent*, 135n24.

11. William Bent sworn statement (n.d.), COIT "Chivington Massacre," 94.

12. "Chapter Four," a draft of Grinnell's *Fighting Cheyennes* based upon George Bent's memories, is raw Bent material. Most of the eleven typed pages did not make it into the printed book. Folder 538a, Grinnell Collection, RCOA. Some books claim that after speaking with Colley, William Bent picked up George at his stockade before setting out for Kansas. George Bent, while not knowing what they would write decades after his death totally disagreed with them. This text includes the bulk of information and quotes for this section except for singularly cited documents. Although George Bent placed his father's efforts to end the war in May, these events happened in July.

13. Walter Camp interview of Guerrier, October 24, 1916, Camp MSS, 1873–1918, Collection No. LMC 1167, Box 4, Envelope 3, Lilly Library, University of Indiana.

14. William Bent sworn statement (n.d.), COIT "Chivington Massacre," 94, which includes him returning to his ranch.

15. Elmore to Kraft, December 19, 2017, in answer to a phone question on December 18 requesting the commanding officers at the post during the summer of 1864. George wrote: "Parmetar assumed command April 1864. July 7th 1864 Parmetar is . . . discharged. Command went to Captain W.H. Backus; in command at least up to Aug. 18. [when he] signs Order as Post CO. Aug 23rd 1864 Anthony signs as Post CO and again on Sept 2nd 1864." George pulled this information from the Fort Larned Post Orders, Roll 1, Record Group 92. George Bent's view on the negativity was accurate but the commanding officer was not Major Scott Anthony.

16. "Denver Correspondence," BH*DMJ*, July 14, 1864, 2, for the soldier's quote and the paper's stance. See Roberts, *Sand Creek*, 1:330, for additional background as well as additional quotes from the BH*DMJ* that spoke out against the so-called Indian war and statehood. The "Ides of September" date back to the Roman Empire and refer to the dividing of the waters; that is material, fed by desire, people, and what would become destiny.

17. "The Soldiers' Vote," *RMN*, July 25, 1864.

18. See "From the Soldiers," BH*DMJ*, July 29, 1864, 2, which reprinted a letter by "Pilsukeminango" (July 19, 1864), which was a pseudonym. Also see "Public Meeting at Fort Lyon," *RMN*, July 26, 1864, 2.

19. As quoted in George C. Caryl, G Company, letter, July 18, 1864, which was printed as "Public Meeting at Fort Lyon," *RMN*, July 26, 1864, 2. "From the Soldiers," BH*DMJ*, July 29, 1864, 2, confirmed this.

20. "From the Soldiers," BH*DMJ*, July 29, 1864, 2. See "Public Meeting at Fort Lyon," *RMN*, July 26, 1864, 2, to the end of the meeting.

21. "The Soldiers' Vote," *RMN*, July 25, 1864.

22. "Slanders Against Colorado," *RMN*, July 26, 1864, 2.

23. Subheading "Dear Friend Jim:—*Give Them Hell*," under "The Soldier Vote," which repeated and mocked Byers's prose of the twenty-fifth, BH*DMJ*, July 28, 1864, 2. Italics in title.

24. As quoted in Roberts, *Sand Creek*, 1:330.

25. Dyer, *Compendium of the War of the Rebellion*, 1:578.

26. Rath, *Rath Trail*, 1, 11–13, 45–54. Supposedly Satank, who was over fifty, led the Kiowa attack. See Thrapp, *Frontier Biography*, III:1192–93, for additional information on Rath.

27. Moore, "Incident on the Upper Arkansas," 417. George Bent had seen an article by Colonel Moore that discussed a raid on a train south of Fort Dodge in August 1864

and wrote him (January 17, 1908), as he wanted to share what he knew. Moore reprinted Bent's letter in this reprint of his article, along with additional details. Although Bent often referred to his brother as "Charley," in this letter he called him "Charles."

28. Laura Roper wrote "Captured by the Indians" in 1918. It was originally published in the Maryville, Nebraska, *Advocate-Democrat*, December 30, 1926, as part of twelve separate articles written by John G. Ellenbecker beginning on December 2, 1926, and concluding on February 24, 1927. It included Roper's manuscript, letters written by Laura Roper Vance (her married name), and others that had knowledge of the events. Lyn Ryder assembled the published newspaper articles, studied them, annotated them, and presented them in *Tragedy at the Little Blue* (hereafter Ryder, *Little Blue*). What follows is Laura's memory as documented in Ryder, viii, 16, 20–29. Unfortunately, at times Roper's memory failed her; when her dating of events was inaccurate the correct dates have been used. But it does not mean that Roper lied. Our memories are what they are, and sometimes the exact details are lost to time.

29. William J. Eubank[s] (Willie) to Ellenbecker, September 2, 1926, Ryder, *Little Blue*, 16, stated that he was nine months old in August 1864; Laura thought he was six months old. Also see Broome, "Massacre Along the Little Blue," 10, for William J. (Willie) changed his family name from Eubanks to Eubank before he died.

30. John Gilbert wrote several letters to Ellenbecker in 1917. At the time of the August 1864 raids he worked at various stations along the Little Blue and joined a volunteer company to confront the attacking Indians. About a week after the murders he was a member of the party that buried the Eubanks dead. He reported that William Eubanks Sr. and Dora had not been scalped. They buried William Sr., who had white hair, his twelve-year-old son, and Dora in one grave. They buried Eubanks Jr., whom he called "Bill," on the sandbar where he died. See Ryder, *Little Blue*, 10, 12.

31. Ryder, *Little Blue*, 22. Also see 40n35.

32. "Nancy Morton's Own Story of the Plum Creek Massacre 1864," with transcript edited by Musetta Gilman and Clyde Wallace, 4–5, in Nancy Jane Fletcher Morton, 1845–1912, RG3467.AM, microfilm no. 16337, History Nebraska (hereafter Morton, "Own Story"). Also see Czaplewski, *Captive of the Cheyenne* (hereafter Czaplewski, *Captive*), section 1:7, 17. She did not name her brother or cousin. However, her 1868 depredation claim in Czaplewski, section 1:68, does.

33. Morton, "Own Story," 5–6, including the attack. For the record, "Own Story" contains different text and quotes than I have seen elsewhere, and all the quotes are from this document. See photo of plaque of Plum Creek Massacre on 748 Road in Northwestern Phelps County, Nebraska, by Rebecca S. Gratz, *Omaha World-Herald*, August 10, 2014. This plaque identifies William Marble as Daniel's father.

34. 1st Lt. Charles Porter (Nebraska Veteran Cavalry) August 8, 9, and 15 letters in Omaha *Weekly Republican*, August 12 and 17, 1864, in Czaplewski, *Captive*, section 1:12–14, 67 (for Bull Bear) put the dead at "thirteen men killed, several scalped and horribly mutilated, nearly all stripped of clothing." Five men, "three women, and several children" supposedly missing, but Nancy and Daniel never mentioned any survivors.

35. Morton, "Own Story," 8–9 for quotes. Also see 7. She did not name the white man while saying he was William Bent's son. It was not George, as he did not participate in the rampage, and it was not Charley, who was sixteen.

36. Often in Nancy Morton's telling of her captivity she quoted words in English that she and the Cheyennes said. She did this to move the telling of her story forward,

but the conversations must have been a combination of pointing, the waving of arms, and sounds, as she did not know sign language.

37. Ryder, *Little Blue*, 22. Strangely Laura did not mention holding Isabelle, although the Cheyennes believed that the little girl was her child.

38. Morton, "Own Story," 10.

39. Morton, "Own Story," 9–10.

40. Mitchell to Curtis, August 8, 1864, *OR*, Series I, Vol. XLI/2, 612.

41. Mitchell to Curtis, second communication on August 8, 1864, *OR*, Series I, Vol. XLI/2, 613.

42. Evans to Curtis, August 8, 1864, *OR*, Series I, Vol. XLI/2, 613.

43. Carleton to Curtis and Chivington, August 8, 1864, *OR*, Series I, Vol. XLI/2, 615.

44. Curtis to Evans, August 11, 1864, *OR*, Series I, Vol. XLI/2, 661.

45. Evans to Curtis, August 11, 1864, *OR*, Series I, Vol. XLI/2, 661.

46. Curtis to Evans, August 11, 1864, *OR*, Series I, Vol. XLI/2, 661.

47. Evans, "Proclamation," August 11, 1864, "Massacre of Cheyenne Indians," 47.

48. Wynkoop to J. C. Maynard, AAAG, District of Colorado, August 13, 1864, *OR*, Series I, Vol. XLI/1, 238.

49. "General Orders—No. 9," *RMN*, August 16, 1864, 2.

50. "Henry Blake Diaries, 1862–1870, 1911," transcribed by Steven J. Rorabaugh and William Light, 37 and v, for the quotes and diary entries for August 17–25. Boulder Historical Society Collections, Carnegie Branch Library for Local History, Boulder Public Library, Colorado.

51. Capt. Joe. C. Davidson, "Circular" (also August 18, 1864), printed in a special "News-Extra" of the *RMN*, August 23, 1864, 1.

52. Special Orders, No. 65, August 18, 1864, printed in a special "News-Extra" of the *RMN*, August 23, 1864. "The Situation," in this "News-Extra," featured the quote with "Denver is at last thoroughly military." The last full edition that the *News* printed that I have seen had an August 16 date, while I have seen "News-Extra" editions for August 18, 20, 22–23.

53. Lucinda Ewbanks [*sic*], June 22, 1965, COIT "Chivington Massacre," 90–91, including Lucinda's comment about Isabelle.

54. I listed these chiefs, as they were present at the September 10, 1864, meeting on the Smoky Hill. Also see Powell, *People*, I:xl, for the month of August, which has no official name, but is often "referred to as 'the time when the cherries are ripe.'"

55. Guerrier's sworn statement, May 25, 1865, COIT "Chivington Massacre," 65–66, for quotes. Hyde, *Bent*, 142; Wynkoop testimony, March 20, 1865, "Sand Creek Massacre," 84.

CHAPTER 10. A DISOBEDIENT PLAY FOR PEACE

1. Wynkoop to J. C. Maynard, AAAG, District of Colorado, August 13, 1864, *OR*, Series I, Vol. XLI/1, 238.

2. Colley testimony, March 14, 1865, "Massacre of Cheyenne Indians," 32, 14. Wynkoop to J. E. Tappan, AAAG, District of Upper Arkansas, January 15, 1865, *OR*, Series I, Vol. XLI/1, 959. There is no evidence that links Wynkoop with One-Eye prior to their September 4 meeting, that Wynkoop was privy to Agent Colley's dealings with the Cheyennes, or that he was present when Chivington wrote a safe conduct pass for

One-Eye. A study of Wynkoop, his letters, reports, and writing confirms this. Historians that link him to One-Eye prior to September 4, 1864, use erroneous secondary publications or mix-and-match primary word bytes. Why would Colley say to Wynkoop that One-Eye supplied information to his father, if the major already knew?

3. Wynkoop, "Unfinished Colorado History," 84–85. Also see Wynkoop to Tappan, January 15, 1865, *OR*, Series I, Vol. XLI/1, 959.

4. Hyde, *Bent*, 142. Also see Wynkoop testimony, March 20, 1865, "Sand Creek Massacre," 84. One was addressed to Agent Colley and the other to the commander of Fort Lyon. Guerrier sworn statement, May 25, 1865, COIT "Chivington Massacre," 66, said that he wrote his "letter to Wynkoop," and Bent, in "Chapter Four," 6, Folder 538a, Grinnell Collection, RCOA, confirmed it.

5. Photograph of Black Kettle's letter to Maj. Colley, August 29, 1864, Special Collections, Tutt Library, Colorado College, Colorado Springs.

6. See Robert Bent sworn statement (n.d.), COIT "Chivington Massacre," 96, for an example of Agent Colley's dealings. There is no evidence that Wynkoop and Smith had any dealings with each other after the 1858 confrontation until this time.

7. John Smith sworn statement, January 15, 1865, "Sand Creek Massacre," 125.

8. Wynkoop, "Unfinished Colorado History," 88.

9. John Smith statement, January 15, 1865, "Massacre of Cheyenne Indians," 84.

10. Wynkoop, "Unfinished Colorado History," 88–89.

11. Wynkoop testimony, March 20, 1965, 84, and Smith statement, January 15, 1865, 125, "Sand Creek Massacre"; Wynkoop to J. E. Tappan, AAAG, District of Upper Arkansas, September 18, 1864, *OR*, Series I, Vol. XLI/3, 242; Wynkoop to Tappan, January 15, 1865, 81, "Massacre of Cheyenne Indians." West, "Called Out People," 6, stated a nomadic life required "a critical mass of about six horses for every man, woman, and child, with considerably more, as many as a dozen per person, for a secure life."

12. Guerrier statement, May 25, 1865, COIT "Chivington Massacre," 66.

13. Wynkoop testimony, March 20, 1865, 84, and Smith statement, January 15, 1865, 125, "Sand Creek Massacre"; Wynkoop, "Unfinished Colorado History," 89; Wynkoop to Tappan, January 15, 1865, 81, "Massacre of Cheyenne Indians." See Grinnell, *Cheyennes*, 2:79–80, for background on contraries.

14. Guerrier statement, May 25, 1865, COIT "Chivington Massacre," 66. Guerrier's memory was off in that he thought the Indians met Wynkoop the night before everyone met in council. None of the white testimony confirms this.

15. "Daily News," September 9, 1864, *RMN*, 3, which includes William Bent fleeing his ranch.

16. Ryder, *Little Blue*, 24–25.

17. Bent to Hyde, March 15, 1905, Yale; Wynkoop testimony March 20, 1865, 84, and B. N. Forbes testimony, May 11, 1865, 205, "Sand Creek Massacre." Also see Kraft, *Wynkoop*, 108–9.

18. Soule testimony, February 17, 1865, "Sand Creek Massacre," 16, through Wynkoop's quote of defending himself. Also see Forbes testimony, May 11, 1865, 205.

19. Bent to Hyde, March 15, 1905, Yale.

20. Joseph Cramer testimony, February 23, 1865, "Sand Creek Massacre," 31, through the question of bringing men and guns. Also see Wynkoop, "Unfinished Colorado History," 91, and Kraft, *Wynkoop*, 109–10.

21. Ryder, *Little Blue*, 23; Lucinda Ewbanks [*sic*] statement at Julesburg, June 22, 1865, COIT "Chivington Massacre," 90–91. Both Laura and Lucinda confirmed the

separation early on, and acknowledged never seeing each other again. Also, Lucinda claimed she did not know what had happened to Isabelle until after her release in May 1865. If she had been in the Smoky Hill village, she would have been aware of what was happening, as Laura had been.

22. Czaplewski, *Captive*, section 2:22–23. This fiction is not in Morton, "Own Story." See Czaplewski, section 1:65–66, for the beginning of Morton's depredation claim (May 11 and June 3, 1865). In the full text of her depredation claim, April 2, 1891, section 1:68–74, she used her then-married name (Nancy Jane Stevens). This claim did not include any of the "dime novel" fiction that her original story propagated, nor did it mention Lucinda, Bull Bear, the Smoky Hill village. Her original story was absurd from the get-go. If Lucinda Eubanks had been present in the village, it seems highly unlikely her Sioux owner would have allowed her to visit Tsistsista prisoners.

23. Forbes testimony, May 11, 1865, "Sand Creek Massacre," 205.

24. Soule testimony, February 17, 1865, 16, and Forbes testimony, May 11, 1865, 205, "Sand Creek Massacre."

25. Cramer testimony, February 23, 1865, "Sand Creek Massacre," 30; Powell, *People*, I:xl, which states that "[t]here are no names for" the months of May and June, "but they are referred to as 'the time when the horses get fat.'"

26. Wynkoop, "Unfinished Colorado History," 93–94.

27. Cramer testimony, March 2, 1865, "Sand Creek Massacre," 56, which includes Wynkoop using Bent as an interpreter. Also see Wynkoop, "Unfinished Colorado History," 93.

28. Wynkoop, "Unfinished Colorado History," 93, which includes his description of Black Kettle's behavior.

29. "Indian Affairs," *New York Times*, December 24, 1868, 1.

30. Wynkoop, "Unfinished Colorado History," 93.

31. Cramer testimony, February 23, 1865, "Sand Creek Massacre," 30, 32–33, including Left Hand, Little Raven, and Bull Bear's comments. Also see Wynkoop, "Unfinished Colorado History," 95.

32. Cramer testimony, February 23, 1865, "Sand Creek Massacre," 30–31; Wynkoop, "Unfinished Colorado History," 95.

33. Wynkoop, "Unfinished Colorado History," 96–97. Also see 95.

34. Wynkoop, "Unfinished Colorado History," 97–98, which includes Wynkoop shaking hands with the chiefs. Also see Wynkoop to Tappan, September 18, 1864, *OR*, Series I, Vol. XLI/3, 243. Neither Black Kettle nor Wynkoop knew that the troops had moved in that direction.

35. John Smith statement, January 15, 1865, COIT "Chivington Massacre," 50–51, for Black Kettle's quote and Wynkoop's repeated statement regarding his authority. Smith stated that Wynkoop would wait two days.

36. Wynkoop, "Unfinished Colorado History," 98.

37. Forbes testimony, May 11, 1865, "Sand Creek Massacre," 206, which includes the next quote. See 205 for his rank on that day.

38. Wynkoop, "Unfinished Colorado History," 98–99.

39. Forbes testimony, May 11, 1865, "Sand Creek Massacre," 206.

40. Wynkoop, "Unfinished Colorado History," 99.

41. Wynkoop, "Unfinished Colorado History," 99–100; Forbes testimony, May 11, 1865, "Sand Creek Massacre," 206; Wynkoop to Tappan, September 18, 1864, *OR*, Series I, Vol. XLI/3, 243. I originally thought that Neva brought Roper to Wynkoop,

but was wrong. Deeper study of Wynkoop's words reveal that the chief who surrendered Roper to him was, according to Wynkoop, "Norwatch." This name is not close to "Neva." However, it is close to "Niwot," Left Hand's Arapaho name. I believe that Left Hand was the key person in this exchange. History is a living science; that is, as additional information is discovered and confirmed, our past as we know it changes. History can never be static, for if so we will never learn the truth. Wynkoop originally thought that Roper was seventeen.

42. See Wynkoop, "Unfinished Colorado History," 100–102, for the prisoner quotes in this section and Wynkoop's return to camp. Also see Kraft, *Wynkoop*, 114.

43. Samuel Colley testimony, March 14, 1865, 31, and Smith sworn statement, January 15, 1865, 86, "Massacre of Cheyenne Indians." See Simeon Whiteley, Camp Weld meeting, September 28, 1864, COIT "Chivington Massacre," 87, for Left Hand's relatives.

44. "Anti-State Arguments," September 9, 1864, 2; "State" and "Election Returns," September 15, 1864, 2, *RMN*.

45. Carey, "Colonel Chivington," 115.

CHAPTER 11. A PEACE IN NAME ONLY

1. Military Return, September 30, 1864, Wynkoop Military File.

2. Samuel Colley testimony, March 14, 1865, 31; John Smith statement, January 15, 1865, 86, "Massacre of Cheyenne Indians."

3. Samuel Colley sworn statement, January 27, 1865, "Massacre of Cheyenne Indians," 91.

4. Wynkoop to Lt. J. E. Tappan, AAAG, District of the Upper Arkansas, September 18, 1864, *OR*, Series I, Vol. XLI/3, 243. Also see Wynkoop testimony, March 21, 1865, "Sand Creek Massacre," 89. Major General James Blunt assumed command of the District of the Upper Arkansas on August 2, 1864. See Blunt, "General Blunt's Account," 251.

5. Wynkoop to Evans, September 18, 1864, COIT "Chivington Massacre," 80.

6. Chivington to Curtis, September 18, 1864, *OR*, Series I, Vol. XLI/3, 261.

7. Lambert, "Plain Tales," Chapter 4, 7, is in total disagreement with Ryder, *Little Blue*, 21–29, for Roper never mentioned Anna Snyder. I have been in many Plains Indian lodges over the years, including the lodge of late friend Southern Cheyenne Ivan Hankler on numerous occasions. Although some writers claim that Snyder used a "cross" lodge pole to end her life, I have never seen one.

8. Wynkoop testimony, March 21, 1865, "Sand Creek Massacre," 89–90; Wynkoop sworn statement, June 9, 1865, COIT "Chivington Massacre," 77; Military Return, September 30, 1864, Wynkoop Military File. Wynkoop may have left for Denver on September 19.

9. Shoup deposition, February 3, 1865, "Sand Creek Massacre," 175.

10. Wynkoop testimony, March 21, 1865, "Sand Creek Massacre," 89–90; Wynkoop statement, June 9, 1865, COIT "Chivington Massacre," 77; Edward Estill Wynkoop, "Wynkoop," 76; Military Return, September 30, 1864, Wynkoop Military File. Booneville was created as a stage station on the Santa Fe Trail in 1860. It was named after Albert Boone.

11. "Editorial Correspondence," BH*DMJ*, September 23, 1864, 2.

12. "Election Frauds," *RMN*, September 26, 1864, 2.

13. Chivington to Maj. C. S. Charlot, September 26, 1864, *OR*, Series I, Vol. XL-VIII/1, 399.

14. Ryder, *Little Blue*, 25, stated "Taken in Denver at the request of Major Wynkoop, this photo has Ambrose Asher, left, Daniel Marble, right, and Laura Roper, center, holding Isabelle Eubank[s]." I totally disagree with Ryder's arrangement of the two boys.

Broome, *Cheyenne War*, 92–94 and 93n9, claimed that Laura Roper cut her copy of the print of her and the three children to send the image of Daniel Marble (d. November 9, 1864) to Ann Marble, his mother. (Broome stated that Marble's death was "less than a month after his rescue," an error as Wynkoop received him on September 12.) Per Broome, this is documented in an undated and unnumbered depredation claim ("Ann Marble Indian Depredation Claim, Record Group 75" while elsewhere depredation claims include identifying claim numbers). Continuing, Broome claimed: "In Coel's research [for *Left Hand*; on page 224, Coel misidentifies Asher as "Archer"] she was given the original photograph that Laura Roper kept, which had Daniel's picture cut out, on the right, confirming Laura's promise to send Daniel's mother the image of him from her own photograph if she was unable to procure another copy." This information is not in Coel's book. Where did it come from? More important, and if true, why did Coel state that the boy on the left—Laura's right—in the printed image of three in her book (227) was Marble? Broome implied that Coel told him all she knew. If so, why was this interview or documentation not dated? Moving forward, Broome stated that OU Press never returned the photos that Coel submitted for *Left Hand*, which means that no evidence exists to date the print that she at one time owned to the 1860s or the 1980s when her book was published. If the photo as printed in *Left Hand* at one time belonged to Laura Roper, she extensively cropped the image and not just the boy on the right (Laura's left) but the bottom, left, and top portions of the print. Looking at other images printed in *Left Hand*, some have been cropped, but not this drastically.

According to John Monnett to Kraft, April 17, 2014, Kraft Collection, quoting Ryder, *Little Blue*, 25, with his bracketed comments (but not the letter "[s]"):

> [T]his photo shows Ambrose Asher, left, Danny Marble, right, and Laura Roper, center, holding Isabelle Eubank[s]. The photo has appeared in the literature omitting Danny Marble and showing only the three on the left, all captives of the Little Blue Raid. The boy on the left has also been identified as Ambrose Asher, but because of the facial resemblance between the boy on the left [I assume Roper's left] and the little girl on the lap of Laura Roper, it is believed that Danny Marble, who was captured at Plum Creek, is shown on the right [of Roper]. . . . Eubank[s] family descendants have also identified the boy on the left [of Roper] as "a Eubank[s] through and through."

I totally agree with John's conclusion. Look at the two boys, and which looks like Isabelle? The final key for my understanding of the identities of the boys is Wynkoop's identification of them. Wynkoop, who did not know the boys' ages, identified Marble as one to two years older than Asher due to his larger size. It is doubtful that Wynkoop would have concluded that Asher was older because he was smaller. Do not forget that Wynkoop's father-in-law took all of the key photos taken on September 28, 1864. Although I have no proof that Wynkoop had prints of these images, it is a safe bet that he did. Also, Wynkoop stated that Marble was talkative while Asher was uncommunicative, a fact that has often been stated. This points to Marble sitting to Roper's right with Asher to her left. See Wynkoop's "Unfinished Colorado History," 100–102, for his description of the two boys. Although Gerboth's additional text for *The Tall Chief* is error-riddled, his transcription of Wynkoop's handwritten document is decent. If you do not have the original, see Gerboth, 95–96.

15. "The Indian Commission on Sand Creek" included the Wynkoop/Evans meeting on the twenty-eighth, *RMN*, January 18, 1865, 2; Wynkoop statement, June 9, 1865, COIT "Chivington Massacre," 77. Also see Kraft, *Wynkoop*, 118.

16. Simeon Whiteley transcription of the Camp Weld meeting, September 28, 1864, COIT "Chivington Massacre," 87–90. Quotes and information not from the government document are separately cited. Kersey, "Background to Sand Creek," 297, wrote, "In spite of Whiteley's repeated assertions that his record was a verbatim transcript of the conference, it very obviously was not."

17. See Hoig, *John Simpson Smith*, 147, for Jack Smith's presence.

18. "Indian Council," *Daily RMN*, September 29, 1864, 2.

19. "Indian Council," *RMN*, September 29, 1864, 2, claimed that "Black Kettle . . . made his proposition for peace in a lengthy and animated speech."

20. Some Cheyenne war books actually have him riding the war trail in 1864, which is ludicrous.

21. This does not agree with what has been documented earlier.

22. Note that this quote was blind edited in Kraft, *Wynkoop*, 122. There should have been brackets as shown in this quote.

23. Wynkoop testimony, March 21, 1865, "Sand Creek Massacre," 91. Wynkoop never stated that Black Kettle hugged him.

24. Wynkoop to Tappan, AAAG, January 15, 1865, "Massacre of Cheyenne Indians," 82.

25. Wynkoop testimony, March 22, 1865, "Sand Creek Massacre," 96, in answer to a direct question if he shared what he intended to do at that time. "I mentioned this fact particularly to Colonel John M. Chivington, as made to Governor John Evans."

26. Curtis to Chivington, September 28, 1864, *OR*, Series I, Vol. XL1/3, 462.

27. "Indian Council," September 29, 1864, *RMN*, 2.

28. Evans to Colley, September 29, 1864, *OR*, Series I, Vol. XL1/3, 495.

29. Wynkoop to Curtis, October 8, 1864, "Sand Creek Massacre," 121. Also see Roberts, "Sand Creek," 1:371, 2:828n63.

30. Wynkoop to Tappan, AAAG, January 15, 1865, "Massacre of Cheyenne Indians," 82; Cramer testimony, February 28, 1865, "Sand Creek Massacre," 45; Anthony to AAG, District of Upper Arkansas, November 7, 1864, Wynkoop Military File; "From the Arkansas," *RMN*, October 20, 1864, 2.

31. Wynkoop to Curtis, October 8, 1864, "Sand Creek Massacre," 121.

32. Danker, introduction, *Mollie Dorsey Sanford*, 189–90 for the quotes, and 91–92, 109–11, 188, 192–93. On December 22, 1865, she gave birth to a daughter that she named Dora Bell.

33. Chivington to Wynkoop, October 16, 1864, *OR*, Series I, Vol. XLI/4, 23–24.

34. Soule to Annie, October 30, 1864, Soule Papers, DPL. His headcount of the Cheyennes and Arapahos was high.

35. Bent to Hyde, April 30, 1906, Yale. Bent credited Robert Bent with Wynkoop bringing his family to the Arapaho village.

36. Special Orders No. 4, October 7, 1864, Anthony Collection, MSS 14, History Colorado. See Anthony to AAAG, District of Upper Arkansas, November 6, 1964, "Massacre of Cheyenne Indians," 70, for his arrival date.

37. Anthony to AAG, District of Upper Arkansas, November 7, 1964, Wynkoop Military File.

38. Special Orders No. 4, October 7, 1864, Anthony Collection, MSS 14, History Colorado.

39. Special Orders No. 13, November 4, 1864, *OR*, Series I, Vol. XL1/4, 433. Also see Wynkoop testimony, March 20, 1865, "Sand Creek Massacre," 87. In Anthony's testimony, March 14, 1865, "Massacre of Cheyenne Indians," 17, he said he assumed command on November 2.

40. Anthony to Maj. B. S. Henning, commanding the District, November 6, 1864, *OR*, Series I, Vol. XL1/1, 912–13, which covers through waiting for word from Curtis. In Anthony's testimony, March 14, 1865, "Massacre of Cheyenne Indians," 17–18, he stated that Left Hand spoke for the Arapahos, that the village was one mile distant, and the stock grew to twenty.

41. Anthony testimony, March 14, 1865, "Massacre of Cheyenne Indians," 18.

42. Minton testimony, April 3, 1865, "Sand Creek Massacre," 146, 148. Minton arrived at Fort Lyon on September 10, 1864. There were other chiefs present but Minton did not know their names. When asked at the inquiry how he knew what the Indians said, he replied that both Smith and Prowers told him. Minton stated that the meeting took place in the middle of November or two weeks before the Sand Creek attack. See Kraft, *Wynkoop*, 127–28, for Anthony's red eyes.

43. Soule testimony, February 21, 1865, "Sand Creek Massacre," 28–29.

44. See Powell, *People*, I:XXXIX , for the Cheyenne name of the creek.

45. Combs testimony, March 29, 1865, "Sand Creek Massacre," 117.

46. Joe Big Medicine, a Southern Cheyenne Sand Creek descendant during a National Park Service oral history interview with Emma Red Hat and William Red Hat Jr., August 18, 1999, *Sand Creek Massacre Project*, 213.

47. Anthony Testimony, March 14, 1865, "Massacre of Cheyenne Indians," 21. He thought the Cheyennes reached Sand Creek twelve days prior to Chivington's attack.

48. Joe Big Medicine, August 18, 1999, *Sand Creek Massacre Project*, 213, thinks that this distance between the camps was correct, as the Cheyennes would not have camped closer to the Arapahos. Historic and modern maps do not make it appear as if Left Hand's camp was that far from the Cheyennes.

49. Citizens of the Arkansas Valley letter, n.d., "Sand Creek Massacre," 95.

50. Cramer letter, November 25, 1864, in "Sand Creek Massacre," 93–94.

51. Anthony recommendation, November 26, 1864, "Sand Creek Massacre," 94.

CHAPTER 12. THE WHITE MAN'S WORD

1. "Proclamation of a Day of Thanksgiving," *RMN*, November 16, 1864, 2.

2. "His Excellency Gov. Evans," *RMN*, November 16, 1864, 2. Also see Report of the John Evans Study Committee, University of Denver, November 2014, 53, for a confirmation of the date.

3. Kelsey, *Frontier Capitalist*, 115, 117.

4. Soule to Anthony, November 25, 1964, Soule Papers, DPL.

5. Anthony's forwarding of Soule's request, November 25, 1864, Soule Papers, DPL.

6. Wynkoop testimony, March 20, 1965, 87; Louderback testimony, March 30, 1865, 134, "Sand Creek Massacre." See Kraft, *Wynkoop*, 68, 81, for the children's ages. Note that Cramer (December 19, 1864) and Soule (December 14, 1864) letters to Wynkoop (*RMN*, September 15, 2000, 7A) stated: "Your family are all well" (Cramer), and "Your family is well" (Soule), which seems to imply that Louise and their two children remained at Fort Lyon. Wynkoop, never anticipating returning to Fort Lyon, took his family with him when he departed on November 26. Cramer and Soule were referring to the close-knit camaraderie between the officers at Fort Lyon beginning with the Smoky Hill council.

7. J. E. Tappan, AAAG, to Commanding Officer, Fort Lyon, November 26, 1864, Wynkoop Papers, MSS 696, History Colorado. See Wynkoop testimony, March 21, 1865, "Sand Creek Massacre," 88, for who commanded Fort Riley.

8. Kappler, *Treaties*, II:889. As both William Gilpin and Armama were mixed-blood Cheyennes who had survived the Sand Creek Massacre, the 1865 Little Arkansas Treaty would award them 640 acres of land.

9. Louderback testimony, March 30, 1865, 134–35; Smith statement, January 15, 1864, 128, "Sand Creek Massacre." Smith did not mention that Anthony wanted him to spy on the Indians while Louderback did. As Gilpin arrived in Denver on May 27, 1861, his son had to have been born around this date, making him no older than three and a half at the time of the massacre. See West, *Contested Plains*, 238; Kraft, *Wynkoop*, 64, 281n4.

10. In two letters to Grinnell (March 8 and April 11, 1929) Clarke signed his last name with an "e." Folder 273, Grinnell Collection, RCOA.

11. Louderback testimony, March 30, 1865, "Sand Creek Massacre," 135.

12. Based on Bent to Hyde, March 15, 1905, Yale; Grinnell, *Fighting Cheyennes*, 171, 173. Hyde, *Bent*, reprinted this map, 150. However, this map is not complete, for both Yellow Wolf and Little Rock were present and were not part of Black Kettle's camp circle. See Greene and Scott, *Finding Sand Creek*, 36–37, for some of Bent's maps. For the record, Bent's maps are also incomplete and do not mimic each other. Moreover, they are not in agreement with Grinnell's printed map, which must have been created from research over the years. Also see Dee Cordry, phone call with Kraft, March 4, 2019, wherein we spoke about Jeff C. Campbell's map that is displayed at the Sand Creek NHS, and which both of us had jotted notes about while studying it. We also spoke about George Bent's maps (some of which I had not seen yet) that are housed at the University of Colorado, Boulder. See Cordry, email to Kraft, on the same date (Dee sent me the links to Bent's maps at CU Boulder). Also see Jeff C. Campbell, "Sand Creek Massacre NHS 150th Commemoration Press Release," revised November 14, 2014, 3–4. Subject matter experts Gary Roberts, Craig Moore (Sand Creek Massacre NHS), Tom Meier (University of Colorado, Boulder), and David Halaas contributed to this document.

13. Hyde, *Bent*, 153.

14. Campbell, "Sand Creek Massacre NHS 150th Commemoration Press Release," revised November 14, 2014, 3–4. In Jeff C. Campbell's talk, "Myths & Misconceptions," at the National Museum of the American Indian, October 9, 2014, p. 4, Sand Creek Massacre NHS, he stated that Dog Man chief Tall Bull was present at the massacre. Tall Bull did not attend the September 10, 1864, Wynkoop–Cheyenne–Arapaho meeting, he did not travel to Denver for the September 28 meeting at Camp Weld, and his village

circle was not camped anywhere near Fort Lyon prior to November 29, 1864. I have never seen anything confirming that he was at Sand Creek, and I emailed two trusted Cheyenne experts. See email exchanges between Kraft and John Monnett, June 23 and 24, 2019; and Kraft and Leo Oliva, June 23, 2019. Both are in the Kraft Collection. John wrote, "I have never seen anything about Tall Bull being at Sand Creek. He was a Dog Man leader and at that time they were at winter Camp on Cherry Creek at modern St. Francis, Kansas." Leo wrote, "I've never seen any evidence that Dog Soldier [c]hief Tall Bull was at Sand Creek. Somewhere I recall reading that he was located at one of the Cheyenne camps in northwest Kansas where many survivors of Sand Creek fled after the massacre. . . . There are two possibilities that I know of for the confusion. Tall Bull was not an uncommon name among the Cheyenne. . . . The other confusion may come from Bill Tall Bull[,] who later claimed his grandfather was killed at Sand Creek. Actually, his great-great-grandfather was White Antelope, not anyone named Tall Bull."

15. Samuel Colley testimony, March 7, 1865, COIT "Chivington Massacre," 27–28; Soule testimony, February 15, 1865, "Sand Creek Massacre," 10. Also see Michno, *Sand Creek*, 194–96, for Soule's two patrols and Chivington's arrival at Fort Lyon.

16. Soule testimony, February 15, 1865, 10; also see Soule testimony, February 18, 20, 1865, 20–21, 24, "Sand Creek Massacre."

17. See Richmond testimony, May 16, 1865, "Sand Creek Massacre," 212, for the quotes and meeting. Also see Samuel Colley testimony, March 7, 1865, COIT "Chivington Massacre," 27. Richmond had stated that the meeting took place when "the command was between Fort Lyon and the commissary building." Per a detailed line drawing of Fort Lyon and two maps given to Kraft by Scott M. Forsythe, National Archives and Records Administration, Great Lakes Region, Chicago, Illinois, in August 2007, and now in the Kraft Collection, Richmond's words were misleading, for there was no reason to squeeze between the hill and the post and dodge the corrals, and moreover, there was nowhere to go for the hill butted up to the river per the detailed drawing created prior to the abandonment of the post in 1870. Both of the maps detail the Santa Fe Stage Route, which had two detours from the road proper that moved south to the northeast and northwest sides of the fort. The maps date to 1863 and 1870. Also, the commissary was not a mile below the fort; actually it was so close that Wynkoop felt that he could abandon the post during an Indian attack and hold off a siege from the commissary (Kraft, *Wynkoop*, 143). Undated Luther Wilson sworn statement documents when Chivington reached Fort Lyon, COIT "Chivington Massacre," 67. For the lack of mail, see Colley's testimony. The Indians were farther away than Anthony thought.

18. Michno, *Sand Creek*, 194. See 195n21 for his discovery that numerous books "erroneously say the penalty for leaving [Fort Lyon] was death," while Chivington's orders are clear on who would be executed. The books and page numbers are listed in Michno's note, and it appears that the error was often repeated without confirming research. Per Luther Wilson's undated sworn statement, COIT "Chivington Massacre," 67, he was not aware that pickets surrounded Fort Lyon.

19. Cramer testimony, February 28–March 1, 1865, "Sand Creek Massacre," 46–47. Cramer claimed that some of this conversation was in Anthony's office and the rest during the night march. Soule testimony, February 16, 1865, "Sand Creek Massacre," 11, confirmed the cooked rations "and twenty uncooked."

20. See Soule to Wynkoop, December 14, 1864, in *RMN*, September 15, 2000, 7A, which continues through officers going to see Chivington.

21. Roberts, "Sand Creek," 1:418, 2:841n20.

22. Soule testimony, February 18, 1864, "Sand Creek Massacre," 21.

23. Cramer sworn statement at Fort Lyon (n.d.), COIT "Chivington Massacre," 74; Cramer testimony, March 1, 1864, "Sand Creek Massacre," 47. Anthony was not present at this meeting, for if he had been, Cramer would not have met with him later that night. Michno, *Sand Creek*, 198n28, points out that "several authors" wrote that Cramer said basically the same words to Chivington twice, and then concludes: "Chivington does not appear to have been in any mood to listen to his subordinates carping over the same issues again and again. A close reading of the sources shows the same men to be present, and almost identical statements made. There was but one meeting." I agree 100 percent with Michno; there was but one Cramer-Chivington meeting, but later Cramer met with Anthony.

24. Wynkoop testimony, March 20, 1865, "Sand Creek Massacre," 87.

25. Louderback Fort Lyon testimony, March 30, 1865, "Sand Creek Massacre," 135.

26. Shoup deposition, February 3, 1865, "Sand Creek Massacre," 176; Hoig, *Sand Creek Massacre*, 130. See Greene and Scott, *Finding Sand Creek*, 130, for Chivington's carbine.

27. *Official Army Register of the Volunteer Force of the United States Army for the Years 1861, '62, '63, '64, '65*, Part VIII:22, 26 (hereafter *Official Army Register*).

28. Guerrier statement, May 25, 1865, COIT "Chivington Massacre," 66. See Harrison and Leonard, *Monahsetah*, 17, for Guerrier's location in the village.

29. Smith testimony, March 14, 1865, "Massacre of Cheyenne Indians," 5.

30. Kraft, *Wynkoop*, 105–7, 109–16, 119, 121–23, 128.

31. Smith testimony, March 14, 1865, "Massacre of Cheyenne Indians," 5. Guerrier statement, May 25, 1865, COIT "Chivington Massacre," 66; Camp interview of Guerrier, October 24, 1916, Camp MSS, Box 4, Envelope 3, Lilly Library. Guerrier claimed that Smith was sick on the twenty-ninth.

32. Clarke, quoted in "Saw Sand Creek Massacre; R. W. Clark[e], a pioneer, does not recall any portion of city which is familiar after long absence." Clarke sent Grinnell this 1916 newspaper clipping on April 11, 1929. In his letter to Grinnell that accompanied the article, Clarke wrote: "I write to say that the papers get things wrong." Here he referred to the spelling of his name, some of the dates in the article, as well as an Indian lodge at the massacre that turned into a cabin. Folder 273, Grinnell Collection, RCOA.

33. Guerrier statement, May 25, 1865, COIT "Chivington Massacre," 66.

34. Cramer sworn statement, n.d., COIT "Chivington Massacre," 73; Shoup deposition, February 3, 1865, "Sand Creek Massacre," 176; Smith testimony, March 14, 1865, "Massacre of Cheyenne Indians," 5; Soule, December 14, 1864, and Cramer December 19, 1864, to Wynkoop, *RMN*, September 15, 2000, 7A. Wilson's men could not have fired at Smith as they were on the eastern side of the village while War Bonnet's camp was near the center of the village circles.

35. Guerrier statement, May 25, 1865, COIT "Chivington Massacre," 66. Beware of books that state that Julia Bent was married to Guerrier in 1864. These writers create history, and are clueless that they only met a few months before or that Cheyenne marriages did not happen quickly. If Guerrier and Julia were married, why did Edmund not sleep with her in Black Kettle's village circle? If they were married he would have tried to find his bride before running for his life, something he never did. Finally, he never said, "My wife—Julia—was in the Sand Creek village." There are two key reasons why historians have erred here. For Julia Bent being in the village, see Kappler, *Treaties*,

II:889, as Article 5 of the 1865 Cheyenne-Arapaho treaty states in part, "At the special request of the Cheyenne and Arrapahoe [*sic*] Indians, . . . the United States agree to grant, by patent in fee-simple, the following-named persons, all of whom are related to the Cheyennes or Arapahoes by blood, to each an amount of land equal to one section of six hundred and forty acres, viz: . . . to Julia Bent." She was granted this land for one reason; she was in the village on November 29. What follows is also from Kappler, II:889: six hundred and forty acres are granted to "Edmund Guerrier, Rosa Guerrier, and Julia Guerrier." For confirmation of Rosa (or Rosanna) and Julia being Edmund's sisters, see Kessel, *Piavinnia*, 321n14. At no time have the two Julias been confirmed as one person, and there is no reason to believe the government would give one person 1,280 acres. It did not help that Hyde, *Bent*, 164, erroneously stated that Guerrier and George were brothers-in-law in 1864. See Kessel, 203, and 325nn4-5, for their wedding at Fort Reno, Indian Territory. According to the 1900 United States Census they had been married for twenty-five years, placing their wedding in 1875.

36. Clarke, "Saw Sand Creek Massacre," Folder 273, Grinnell Collection, RCOA.

37. Smith statement, January 15, 1865, COIT "Chivington Massacre," 51.

38. Smith testimony, March 14, 1865, "Massacre of Cheyenne Indians," 10.

39. Cramer to Wynkoop, December 19, 1864, in *RMN*, September 15, 2000, 7A.

40. Soule to Wynkoop, December 14, 1864, in *RMN*, September 15, 2000, 7A. The number of women and children approaching the troops seems high for this was just the start of the attack. Soule to mother, December 18, 1864, Soule Papers, DPL, states: "The day you wrote I was present at a massacre . . . and I would not let my Company fire."

41. Bent to Hyde, April 24, 1906, Yale; Hyde, *Bent*, 151–55; Wilson sworn statement, n.d., COIT "Chivington Massacre," 67; Hoig, *Sand Creek Massacre*, 153n9.

42. Dee Cordry and Kraft phone call on March 4, 2019, wherein we discussed our notes of the Jeff Campbell Sand Creek map at the Sand Creek Massacre NHS. Notes of Cordry–Kraft, March 4, 2019, phone call in Kraft Collection.

43. Bent to S. F. Tappan, February 23, 1889, Tappan Collection, MSS 617, Box 1, FF 9, History Colorado; Hyde, *Bent*, 152–53. Also see Halaas, *Halfbreed*, 142, 144–45, which is different than Hyde, but that is because *Halfbreed* tapped into additional Bent letters that Hyde did not see. Per a hand-drawn map by Jeff Campbell at the Sand Creek NHS, this was the third sand pit moving north. See Kraft Sand Creek Massacre NHS notes, October 3, 2014, Kraft Collection. The NHS placed the number of people in this pit at one hundred. According to Bent, one of the children in the hand-dug bulwarks, a Cheyenne girl, was taken captive later that day.

44. Anthony testimony, March 14, 1865, "Massacre of Cheyenne Indians," 22. Anthony estimated that the creek bed was between "200 to 500 yards wide," which, if true, meant that a good portion of the village circles were also in the creek bed.

45. Great Southern Cheyenne historian and educator Dr. Henrietta Mann, whom I met and befriended at the Washita Battlefield NHS (December 4–6, 2008) shared the pronunciation and phonetic spelling of Mo-nahs-e-tah's name with me as I needed it before my play, *Cheyenne Blood*, went into rehearsal and premiered in Southern California in spring 2009. We met on the second of the three days of festivities and spent a lot of time together. On April 11, 2012, I visited Henry at the Cheyenne-Arapaho Tribal College in Weatherford, Oklahoma, and she confirmed what she had previously shared of Mo-nahs-e-tah's name.

46. Harrison and Leonard, *Monahsetah*, 19. Also see 27n25. Harrison spent time with Mo-nahs-e-tah's great-great-granddaughter, Mary Pearl Wolfchief, in October

1999. She was born during Mo-nahs-e-tah's lifetime, and, although quite old, remembered the details of the escape attempt, including that she "had made her run hand-in-hand with two younger members of the family, one of whom was a sister." Also see notes of Cordry–Kraft March 4, 2019, phone call, Kraft Collection.

47. Cramer sworn statement, n.d., COIT "Chivington Massacre," 73; Hoig, *Sand Creek Massacre*, 146–47.

48. Campbell, "Sand Creek Massacre NHS 150th Commemoration Press Release," revised 2014, 3, claimed this was "confirmed by persons actually in the village prior to the attack and proportionate to the number of adult men killed."

49. Cramer sworn statement, on or before June 9, 1865, COIT "Chivington Massacre," 73. Also see Jacob Downing sworn statement, July 21, 1865, 70.

50. Smith testimony, March 14, 1865, "Massacre of Cheyenne Indians," 10.

51. Campbell map at Sand Creek NHS; Kraft notes at the NHS, October 3, 2014, Kraft Collection.

52. Guerrier statement, May 25, 1865, COIT "Chivington Massacre," 66.

53. Robert Bent sworn statement, undated, COIT "Chivington Massacre," 96. He had been forced by Chivington to lead the way to the Sand Creek village on the night and morning of November 28–29.

54. Soule to Wynkoop, December 14, 1864, and Cramer to Wynkoop, December 19, 1864, in *RMN*, September 15, 2000, 7A.

55. See Bent to Hyde, February 19, 1913, Yale; and Bent to Grinnell, October 20, 1902, Grinnell Collection, RCOA, for the Huerfano location and great trading relationship with the Indians, including the Utes, as well as Mariano's Cheyenne name. See Janet Lecompte, "Charles Autobees [*sic*], IX," *Colorado Magazine*, October 1958, 303, for the horse raid and Mariano's rank in the Third Colorado; Lecompte, "Charles Autobees [*sic*], I," *Colorado Magazine*, July 1957, 163–64, for a physical description of Charles Autobee, along with him being a mixed-blood based upon a photo of him that perhaps dated to 1864 while stating his mother was English, Irish, mulatto, or an Indian; and Janet Lecompte, "Charles Autobees [*sic*]," in *Trappers of the Far West*, ed. LeRoy R. Hafen, 242, 253, including Serafina not marrying Charles until after their second son (José Tomás or Tom) was born in 1842. Autobee, although smart, was illiterate, and did not know how to spell his last name; thus various spellings of it. A number of books claim that "New Mexican" or "Mexican" scouts rescued Charley. Mariano Autobee was second in command of Company H of the Third Colorado with zero connections with Fort Lyon. Halaas, *Halfbreed*, 146, erred when it stated that Silas Soule was well acquainted with the Bents; actually it was the opposite as neither George nor Charley dared to appear at Fort Lyon in 1864. The lone George/Soule connection was the September 10 meeting on the Big Timbers. See Michno, *Sand Creek*, 298–99, for at least nineteen members of Company H having Hispanic surnames.

56. Campbell map at Sand Creek NHS. Also see Kraft notes at the NHS, October 3, 2014, and Cordry–Kraft phone conversation, March 4, 2019, Kraft Collection.

57. Chivington to Headquarters District of Colorado, December 16, 1864, "Massacre of Cheyenne Indians," 49. Chivington sent two official reports, and this, the second, was much longer and more detailed of the two reports. The first report (November 29, 1864, 48) was brief. Both reports were bloated with braggadocio and error-riddled. (For example, The Indian death count did not come close to five hundred.)

58. Campbell, "Sand Creek Massacre NHS 150th Commemoration Press Release," revised 2014, 4. In 2014 the estimate was 200 killed, and this included the percentages

of noncombatants, warriors, and chiefs. During a conversation with Jeff on June 22, 2018, he told me that this estimate has increased to 230. Jeff later emailed me a talk that he delivered on October 19, 2014, "Myths & Misconceptions." See p. 6, which had the death count at 230 and confirmed the percentages.

59. See Cramer to Wynkoop, December 19, 1864, in *RMN*, September 15, 2000, 7A, for the number of scalps taken from the bodies.

60. Olney sworn statement, April 20, 1865, COIT "Chivington Massacre," 61.

61. Anthony testimony, March 14, 1865, "Massacre of Cheyenne Indians," 21–23, including his conversation with Chivington.

62. Soule testimony, February 19–20, 1865, "Sand Creek Massacre," 21, 23.

63. Soule cross-examination by Chivington, February 20, 1865, "Sand Creek Massacre," 22–23. He was not asked, nor did he state how Charles Bent came into his possession.

64. Shoup deposition, February 3, 1865, "Sand Creek Massacre," 177.

65. Soule to Wynkoop, December 14, 1864, in *RMN*, September 15, 2000, 7A.

66. Chivington to Headquarters District of Colorado, December 16, 1864, *OR*, Series I, Vol. XLVIII/1, 950. This includes Chivington's view of Soule, and adds validity to what the captain wrote Wynkoop on December 14, 1864, as it makes it obvious that the colonel was well aware of his views.

67. *History of the Arkansas Valley, Colorado*, 838–39. Lambert supplied Wynkoop's quote.

68. Curtis to Henning, December 2, 1864, *OR*, Series I, Vol. XLI/4, 751. This communication shoots holes through publications that claim Wynkoop traveled to Kansas to command Fort Riley.

Chapter 13. Vengeance and Outrage

1. Hyde, *Bent*, 152–53.
2. Bent to Hyde, April 24, 1906, Yale; Hyde, *Bent*, 155.
3. Bent to Hyde, December 21, 1905, Yale; Hyde, *Bent*, 158. Also see 157.
4. Miksch sworn statement, COIT "Chivington Massacre," 74–75.
5. Smith testimony, March 14, 1865, "Massacre of Cheyenne Indians," 10.
6. Coffin, *Sand Creek*, 28.
7. Beckw[our]th testimony, March 6, 1865, "Sand Creek Massacre," 71.
8. Clarke to Grinnell, April 11, 1929, Folder 273, Grinnell Collection, RCOA.
9. Coffin, *Sand Creek*, 28.
10. Coffin, *Sand Creek*, 29; 36 for Coffin's quotes.
11. Soule to Wynkoop, December 14, 1864; Cramer to Wynkoop, December 19, 1864, *RMN*, September 15, 2000, 7A. Lieutenant Colonel Leavitt Bowen and Majors Hal Sayre, Samuel Logan, Scott Anthony, William F. Wilder, and Jacob Downing all fought at Sand Creek; Cramer implied that two of them committed atrocities.
12. Shoup to Capt. J. S. Maynard, AAAG, December 6, 1864, "Massacre of Cheyenne Indians," 50.
13. Chivington "sworn and subscribed" written answers to requested questions, April 26, 1865, "Sand Creek Massacre," 108.
14. Anthony to Lt. A. Helliwell, AAAG, December 2, 1864, *OR*, Series I, Vol. XLI/1, 952.

15. Halaas, *Halfbreed*, 155, citing Bent to Hyde, March 15, 1905, Yale, claimed that George Bent was already resting "on a soft bed of buffalo robes" when Guerrier reached the camp the following day. There is no mention of this in Bent's letter, and no mention of Guerrier.

16. Hyde, *Bent*, 158–59. Also see 164. Here Hyde erred twice more. He called the Bunch of Timbers "Bunch Timbers" even though Bent supplied the correct name (164n1). He also misspelled Guerrier's first name.

17. Hyde, *Bent*, 164–65. See Colley testimony, March 7, 1865, COIT "Chivington Massacre," 30, for his comments on Guerrier. Also see Halaas, *Halfbreed*, 158, for Howling Wolf's name.

18. See Coel, *Left Hand*, 300–301, for her version of his death. I do not know exactly where or when he died, but I believe that he was carried from the bloody ground before his life ended.

19. Chivington to Headquarters District of Colorado, November 29, 1864, "Massacre of Cheyenne Indians," 40.

20. Chivington to Evans, December 7, 1864, *OR*, Series I, Vol. XLI/4, 797. This is twenty lodges less than the estimate in Campbell, "Sand Creek Massacre NHS 150th Commemoration Press Release," revised 2014, 3.

21. "Col. Chivington," *RMN*, December 13, 1864, 3.

22. Henning to Maj. C. S. Charlot, AAG, Department of Kansas, December 7, 1864, *OR*, Series I, Vol. XLI/4, 796–97. Ford assumed command before the end of the month.

23. Bent to George Hyde, May 3, 1905, History Colorado; Bent to Hyde, May 7, 1906, Yale. Also see Berthrong, *Southern Cheyennes*, 225–27; Grinnell, *Fighting Cheyennes*, 190–91; Halaas, *Halfbreed*, 161.

24. Soule to his mother, December 18, 1864, Soule Papers, DPL.

25. Hersa A. Soule Pension Claim; two applications for a soldier's pension, September 13, and November 25, 1865, Soule Papers, FF 14, History Colorado.

26. Wynkoop testimony, March 21, 1865, "Sand Creek Massacre," 92; Kraft, *Wynkoop*, 139.

27. "The Battle of Sand Creek," *RMN*, December 17, 1864, 2.

28. "Arrival of the Third Regiment—Grand March Thro-town [*sic*]," *RMN*, December 22, 1864, 2. Companies 11 and 12 were "stationed at the Junction Valley Station, on the Platte."

29. Untitled, *RMN*, December 23, 1864, 3.

30. "Muster Out and Pay of the Third," *RMN*, December 23, 1864, 3.

31. Mullin letter, "Muster Out of the Third Regiment," *RMN*, December 24, 1864, 2. Italics removed from text.

32. "Theatre To-night," *RMN*, December 24, 1864, 3.

33. Blurb on Richmond's performance, *RMN*, December 27, 1864, 3.

34. "The Third," *RMN*, December 29, 1864, 2.

35. *Official Army Register*, VIII:26.

36. "Unusual Attraction," and "striking trophies" note, *RMN*, December 28, 1864, 3. Also see "The Indian Piece," *RMN*, December 30, 1864, 3; Luther Wilson sworn statement, perhaps July 21,1865, COIT "Chivington Massacre," 67.

37. BH*DMJ*, December 29, 1864, 3.

38. "A New Commander," *RMN*, December 30, 1864, 3.

39. "Fun for Mountaineers," *RMN*, December 31, 1864, 3.

40. "Its Effect," *RMN*, December 31, 1864, 2.

41. "Colonel Chivington," reprinted in *RMN*, January 10, 1865, 3.

42. Ford order, December 31, 1864, *OR*, Series I, Vol. XLI/4, 971. Also see Ford's Special Orders No. 43, January 2, 1865, Anthony Papers, FF7, History Colorado.

43. Soule to mother Sophia Soule, January 8, 1865, Soule Papers, DPL. Also see Soule testimony, February 16, 1865, "Sand Creek Massacre," 11.

44. Anthony to AAAG, District of Upper Arkansas, January 6, 1865, *OR*, Series I, Vol. XLVIII/1, 436.

45. This note is for the entire section except where noted. Hyde, *Bent*, 167 (Hyde map w/Bent notations), 168–75. Bent to Hyde, April 24, 1905; May 10, 1906; October 18, 1906; October 27, 1914, Yale. Bent to Hyde, May 3, 1905, History Colorado. At times Bent's letters are in disagreement with one another and also with Hyde's text. Still, considering the length of time between the letters they are fairly consistent.

46. See Price, *Oglala People*, 59, for Spotted Tail's band.

47. "Indian Troubles Down the Platte—Loss of Life and Property," *RMN*, January 7, 1865, 2.

48. See Afton, Halaas, and Masich, *Cheyenne Dog Soldiers*, 164–65, 232–33, 359n1. Plate 113 shows ledger art of Big Crow counting coup on Hudnut, who wore a yellow sack coat and a broad-brimmed hat. Art by Bear Man, 166, states: "Bear Man is a consummate artist, and his drawings prove a reasonable standard for comparison with all other Dog Soldier warrior-artists in the Ledgerbook." See Halaas, *Halfbreed*, 167–68, 386n18, for Hudnut's frantic escape and Big Crow's coup on him. However, between 1997, when the Dog Soldier Ledgerbook was published, and 2004, when *Halfbreed* was published, Halaas had second thoughts about Hudnut being at Camp Rankin prior to the attack and the stage having a fresh team and begging for an escort to Denver, and O'Brien's refusal (359n1), which listed the "Testimony as to the Claim of Ben Holladay" document for damages. If Hudnut had a fresh team that had only traveled from Julesburg to the post and back, everyone would have leaped onto the coach and reached the post before charging warriors caught up with them.

49. Bent to Hyde, May 10, 1906, Yale.

50. Hyde, *Bent*, 173.

51. Halaas, *Halfbreed*, 168.

52. See Hyde, *Bent*, 174, which includes Curtis's comments. See Ware, *The Indian War of 1864*, 326, for his words that Bent quoted. Ware continued, writing: "That may or may not be correct At any rate, the Indians held most of the battle-field; the fighting was not far from the post; within the range of the artillery the Indians did not come. . . . Some of our men were killed in the territory of their control, and were scalped. The Indians carried off their dead, and disappeared." Also see Powell, *People*, I:xl, for the Cheyenne name for the December moon—the "Big freezing moon."

53. "A Suggestion," *RMN*, January 7, 1865, 2.

54. Sales blurb, *RMN*, January 7, 1865, 2.

55. Soule to Sophia Soule, January 8, 1865, Soule Papers, DPL. This is the last-dated Soule letter that I have seen in the DPL. I mention this because Michno, *Sand Creek*, uses Bruce Cutler's poetry and fiction, *The Massacre at Sand Creek: Narrative Voices* (Norman: University of Oklahoma Press, 1995), 114, 117, where he cites two *fictional* letters Soule wrote (to Walt Whitman, February 12, 1865, and his mother on April 15). In these letters Soule "supposedly" stated to Whitman, "The governor sent out our Colonel Chivington and a regiment of Hundred Daysers just to kill the ones that camped under our

protection down at Sand Creek." Evans was in Washington and had no clue of current events. By the time that Soule supposedly wrote this letter, he would have known that Evans was absent from the territory long before the November 29 attack. Also, Cutler pushed the factual limit with such sentences as, "The colonel-preacher went at me like I was 666 itself." In the "supposed" letter to his mother he wrote: "You won't believe that Colonel Chivington alas mustered out. I'd say he's shown his heels. He left the Army flat, he's off to preaching to the frenzied, while I, the one who swore all up and down I'd muster out, I'm still in blue." Chivington mustering out was not new news in April. More important he was the leading player in the U.S. military investigation of the Sand Creek Massacre at Denver and Fort Lyon, a fact that Soule knew only too well.

56. Soule Testimony, February 17, 1864, "Sand Creek Massacre," 15.

57. Soule to Sophia, January 8, 1865, Soule Papers, DPL.

58. "Preparing for War," *RMN*, January 9, 1865, 2; including Byers's quote.

59. Untitled, *RMN*, January 11, 1865, 3.

60. "Capt. Foy," *RMN*, January 11, 1865, 3.

61. Curtis to Moonlight, January 11, 1865, *OR*, Series I, Vol. XLVIII/1, 490. Halleck served as chief of staff from March 12, 1864, until April 18, 1865.

62. Craig, *Fighting Parson*, 231, citing "Record of Service of John M. Chivington, War Dept., Record & Pension Division, National Archives, Record Group No. 15B, WC 416–181." Chivington's written answers to questions, April 26, 1865, sworn and subscribed before Alexander W. Atkins, notary public, on that day, "Massacre of Cheyenne Indians," 101.

63. Curtis to Halleck, January 12, 1865, *OR*, Series I, Vol. XLVIII/1, 502–3.

64. Curtis to Moonlight, January 13, 1865, *OR*, Series I, Vol. XLVIII/1, 510.

65. Curtis to Moonlight, second January 13, 1865, communication, *OR*, Series I, Vol. XLVIII/1, 511.

66. S.O. No. 43 Hd Qts Dist of Up Arkansas, January 5, 1865; Military Return, January 31, 1865; and Wynkoop General Orders No. 3, January 15, 1865, all in Wynkoop Military File. Wynkoop to Lt. Tappan, AAAG, District of Upper Arkansas, January 15, 1865, "Massacre of Cheyenne Indians," 81; Anthony to brother, December 23, 30, 1864, Anthony Papers, Correspondence, MSS 14, History Colorado.

67. Wynkoop to Tappan, AAAG, January 15, 1865, "Massacre of Cheyenne Indians," 82. For Soule and Cramer's absence at Fort Lyon see the first note in chapter 14.

68. For Wynkoop's report and the affidavits, see "Massacre of Cheyenne Indians," 81–93.

69. Wynkoop to Tappan, AAAG, January 15, 1865, "Massacre of Cheyenne Indians," 84.

70. Lambert, "Plain Tales," Chapter 5, 16.

CHAPTER 14. THE COST OF GLORY

1. Soule Military Returns, months of Jan. 1865 and Jan.-Feb. 1865, Soule Papers, History Colorado; Untitled article, *RMN*, January 18, 1865, 3.

2. General Orders, No. 9. Hdqrs. District of Colorado, Denver, Colo. Ter., February 4, 1865, *OR*, Series I, Vol. XLVIII/1, 748.

3. Special Order No. 23, February 1, 1865, Senate Ex. Doc. 26, 39th Congress, 2nd Sess., 2.

4. Bent to Hyde, October 27, 1914, Yale; Hyde, *Bent*, 174.

5. "The Journal," *RMN*, February 8, 1865, 2.

6. Commission first meeting, February 9, 1865, "Sand Creek Massacre," 2.

7. Moonlight orders, February 12, 1865, "Sand Creek Massacre," 3–4.

8. Chivington to Commission, February 13, 1865, "Sand Creek Massacre," 4, which includes through his request to have reporters present.

9. Although Downing had a small presence during the inquiry," his views and silent recommendations were of value to Chivington.

10. Two undated Chivington statements, one on Tappan and the other on Moonlight's authority, presented on February 14, 1865, "Sand Creek Massacre," 5–7. This included Chivington's affidavit and Maynard's sworn statement, both February 9, 1865, as well as the commission's ruling.

11. Soule testimony, January 16, 1865, "Sand Creek Massacre," 11, 14. See 8 for the start of his testimony.

12. Soule testimony, February 17, 1865, "Sand Creek Massacre," 14, 16–17.

13. Hardin was cashiered out of the service on August 9, 1864, for drunkenness and the inability to perform his duties. See *Official Army Register*, VIII:22, and *Army and Navy Journal*, 1864, vol. 2, 10. I have not learned how he was reinstated.

14. Doolittle report, January 26, 1867, COIT, 3.

15. Colley (26–36) and Leavenworth testimonies (36–40), COIT "Chivington Massacre." Colley was also deposed at Fort Lyon on January 27, 1865, "Sand Creek Massacre," 131.

16. Smith (41–43) and Evans (43–49) testimonies, COIT "Chivington Massacre."

17. Twenty-sixth day of the Military inquiry, March 10, 1864, "Sand Creek Massacre," 83.

18. "Massacre of Cheyenne Indians," Washington testimony: Leavenworth, 3–4; Smith, 4–12; Robbins, 12–14; Colley, 14–16, 29–32; Anthony, 16–29; Evans, 32–43; Hunt, 43–46.

19. Wynkoop report, January 15, 1864, "Massacre of Cheyenne Indians," 81–84.

20. See *Official Army Register*, VIII:22, which includes Soule.

21. Anthony testimony, March 14, 1865, "Massacre of Cheyenne Indians," 21. See Scott Anthony "Declaration for an Original Invalid Pension," Anthony Papers, MSS 14, History Colorado, and *Official Army Register*, VIII:22, for his muster-out date.

22. As One-Eye died at Sand Creek on November 29, he was Anthony's employee for less than a month, and was never a longtime spy for the military as some historians claim.

23. See note 18.

24. Doolittle report, January 26, 1867, COIT, 3.

25. "Died," *RMN*, March 21, 1865, 2.

26. Danker, *Mollie Dorsey Sanford*, 189–90.

27. Wynkoop testimony, March 20, 1864, "Sand Creek Massacre," 83.

28. "Died," *RMN*, March 22, 1865, 2.

29. Wynkoop testimony, March 23, 1864, "Sand Creek Massacre," 100, for Chivington's questions and Wynkoop's answers through "present but myself," which related to their meeting shortly after the Camp Weld council.

30. Chivington's cross-examination of Wynkoop began on March 22 and ended on the twenty-third, "Sand Creek Massacre," 96–102.

31. Bensing, *Soule*, 117–18; Cramer testimony, February 28, 1865, "Sand Creek Massacre," 45. The city of Pueblo was founded in 1885. See Kraft, *Wynkoop*, 17, 274n25 for background on Puebla.

32. Milavec, "Alias Emma S. Soule," 3; Bensing, *Soule*, 118. See Field and Staff Muster Roll, April 1865, Wynkoop Military File, which shows the major spent the entire month at Fort Lyon. See *Official Army Register*, VIII:22 for Cramer being able to attend the wedding, as he mustered out of the First Colorado in Denver on April 4.

33. Minton testimony, April 3, 1865, "Sand Creek Massacre," 146. Also see 147–59.

34. "Assassination of President Lincoln," *RMN*, April 15, 1865, 2. Evans, *Legend of John Wilkes Booth*, presents a totally different viewpoint of Lincoln's assassination, 101–2.

35. Soule to Dist Hd Qts, April 20, 1865, Soule Papers, History Colorado.

36. Olney sworn statement, April 20, 1865, COIT, "Chivington Massacre," 61.

37. Wynkoop to Hollister and Hall, April 20, 1865, Wynkoop Papers, FF6, History Colorado. They wisely did not print it.

38. "The Homicide Last Night," *RMN*, April 24, 1865, 2.

39. Squires statement, *RMN*, June 13, 1865, 2.

40. "The Homicide Last Night," *RMN*, April 24, 1865, 2, which includes the following quote. Hersa Soule's two widow pension applications, September 30 and November 25, 1865. On November 28, 1900, Emma S. Bright, who called herself Emma S. Soule, petitioned for a widow's pension, claiming she was Soule's wife until her departure for Iowa on April 3, 1865. She never knew Soule married Hersa Coberly. Hersa A. Coberly Widow's Declarations (Pension Claims) and Emma S. Soule Widow's Declaration (Pension Claim), Soule Papers, History Colorado. Milavec, "Alias Emma Soule," 3–23, conclusively debunked Bright's claim, while also debunking all articles and books that have called Soule a bigamist. "Capt. Soule's Funeral," *RMN*, April 27, 1865, 2, printed details about Soule's funeral. Also see "The Funeral," *RMN*, April 26, 1865, 2, which stated, "Of the late Captain Soule, demanded more of our editorial space than the time of going to press allowed us, upon return from the burial, so the fact must be an apology for these columns this afternoon."

41. "Who Did It?," BH*DMJ*, April 26, 1865, 2. Also see "Murder of Capt. Soule," BH*DMJ*, April 25, 1865, 2.

42. "Capt. Soule's Funeral," *RMN*, April 27, 1865, 2.

43. Field and Staff Muster Roll, April 1865, Wynkoop Military File, shows he spent the entire month of April at Fort Lyon. Easily 75 percent of the published documentation places Wynkoop at Soule's funeral and all are in error. Do not believe it; check the Denver papers for the month of April as none state that Wynkoop was in Denver that month. For the record, Wynkoop fell from his horse during funeral procession in February 1863 (the Denver papers prove this). See Kraft, *Wynkoop*, 81, 283n14, for details of the accident and the newspapers that reported it.

44. Chivington "sworn and subscribed" written answers to questions, April 26, 1865, "Sand Creek Massacre," 108.

45. "Sand Creek Massacre," 161, 163.

46. Talbot testimony, May 11, 1865, "Sand Creek Massacre," 208–9 for quotes. See the map of Fort Lyon supplied to Kraft by Scott M. Forsythe, archivist, National Archives, Chicago, Illinois, on August 7, 2007. This map showed the location and name for each building at the fort. Copy of the map in the Kraft Collection.

47. Col. Thomas Moonlight to Capt. George F. Price, AAG, Julesburg, CT [Colorado Territory], May 27, 1865, *OR*, Series I, Vol. XLVIII/1, 276–77.

48. Lucinda Ewbanks [*sic*] statement, Julesburg, Colorado Territory, June 22, 1865, COIT "Chivington Massacre," 90.

49. Moonlight to Price, May 27, 1865, *OR*, Series I, Vol. XLVIII/1, 276–77. Also see Johnson, "Hanging of the Chiefs," 60–69, for debunking of a massive amount of erroneous statements made in regard to their executions.

50. Moonlight to Price, May 27, 1865, *OR*, Series I, Vol. XLVIII/1, 276–77.

51. McChristian, *Fort Laramie*, 205–6.

52. Guerrier statement, May 25, 1865, COIT "Chivington Massacre," 65–66. Also see Prucha, *Great Father*, 1:485–87, including n3, for differing views on the committee's findings.

53. Mayer statement, May 25, 1865," COIT "Chivington Massacre," 67.

54. Ford statement, May 31, 1865, COIT "Chivington Massacre," 64–65.

55. Doolittle to Harlan, May 31, 1865, *OR*, Series I, Vol. XLVIII/2, 868–69.

56. Dole to Harlan, June 12, 1865, *OR*, Series I, Vol. XLVIII/2, 870 for quotes. Also see 869.

57. Wynkoop testimony, June 9, 1865, COIT "Chivington Massacre," 77.

58. Edward Estill Wynkoop, "Wynkoop," 77. Writing years after his father's death, he merged numerous facts into one sentence. See Kraft, *Wynkoop*, 294n54, for some of his errors.

59. Harman H. Wynkoop to Dorothy Gardiner, April 20, 1949, Wynkoop Papers, MSS 695, History Colorado. Shortly after Wynkoop's death in 1891, his son Herman worked for the *Rocky Mountain Herald*. One day a white-haired Chivington entered the office and was introduced to him. After Chivington said that he never knew "he would have the pleasure of meeting one of Major Ned Wynkoop's boys," he praised Wynkoop as a soldier and man. Harlan thanked him, and then said: "I will always have the same feeling toward you and your men for the Sand Creek Massacre that my father had to his dying day." Also see Kraft, *Wynkoop*, 266.

60. Wynkoop testimony, June 9, 1865, "Chivington Massacre," 77. Also see Kraft, *Wynkoop*, 150.

61. Dodge Special Orders, June 17, 1865, *OR*, Series I, Vol. XLVIII/2 (Correspondence), 913. Also see Ford to J. W. Barnes, AAG, Dept. of the Missouri, June 12, 1865; Special Orders No. 162, June 14, 1865, Wynkoop Military File (which appears to be the same special orders but carries a June 14, 1865, date).

62. Ewbanks [*sic*] statement, June 22, 1865, COIT "Chivington Massacre," 91; also see 90.

63. Kelsey, *Frontier Capitalist*, 209–10; Cannon, "Josephine Evans Elbert," 265, 267.

Chapter 15. The Beginning of the End

1. Carleton to Maj. Gen. Alexander McCook, July 17, 1865, *OR*, Series I, Vol. XLVIII/2, 1090–91.

2. Sully to Maj. Gen. John Pope, July 17, 1865, *OR*, Series I, Vol. XLVIII/2, 1088–89.

3. Evans reply to the Joint Committee on the Conduct of the War, August 6, 1865, COIT "Chivington Massacre," 78. Italics in quote.

4. Seward to Evans, July 18, 1865, Evans Personal Correspondence Collection, Colorado State Archives.

5. "The Ute Difficulty—Return of Gov. Evans," *RMN*, July 20, 1865, 1.

6. Northwestern Evans Study, 83.

7. Doolittle to Seward and E. M. Stanton, Secretary of War, July 19, 1865, *OR*, Series I, Vol. XLVIII/2, 1094.

8. Dodge to Brevet Maj. Gen. John B. Sanborn, July 19, 1865, *OR*, Series I, Vol. XLVIII/2, 1115.

9. Stanton to Doolittle, July 24, 1865, *OR*, Series I, Vol. XLVIII/2, 1117–18. In July 1865 Herron was selected to serve as a commissioner to meet with Plains Indians and negotiate treaties. Apparently he did not want the assignment as he resigned his commission on the sixteenth. Huff, "Major General F. J. Herron," 806–7.

10. Frank Wynkoop, "Commemoration," 3, Wynkoop Collection, Chávez History Library.

11. Photo of Letter Book copy of Evans resignation, Northwestern Evans Study, 84.

12. Joint Committee on the Conduct of the War report, "Massacre of Cheyenne Indians," IV.

13. Joint Committee report, "Massacre of Cheyenne Indians," III. Also see I–II.

14. Joint Committee report, "Massacre of Cheyenne Indians," VI, IV, and V, including all the quotes through the one that ends with "the men under his command had performed."

15. Evans reply, August 6, 1865, COIT "Chivington Massacre," 78.

16. Leavenworth to acting commissioner of Indian affairs R. B. Van Valkenburgh, September 29, 1865, "Report of the Secretary of the Interior," included with the Message of the President of the United States, 39th Cong., 1st Sess., 1865, 581.

17. Kelsey, "Background to Sand Creek," 299 and n84.

18. Wynkoop, "Unfinished Colorado History," 138–39.

19. Frank Wynkoop, "Intimate Notes," 2. Also see Kraft, "Ned Wynkoop & Black Kettle," 8.

20. Evans reply, August 6, 1865, COIT "Chivington Massacre," 86.

21. George Wakely captured the two images at Camp Weld (one with the chiefs and one with the chiefs and whites). These are the only known photos of Black Kettle. Tall Bull never allowed his image to be taken. The first known image of George Bent was created when he married Magpie Woman in summer 1866. Bent to Hyde, April 24, 1906, Yale. Theodore R. Davis created a woodcut of Charley Bent at the Medicine Lodge Peace council in 1867, but he was dead before it was published. Davis, "Summer on the Plains," 305.

22. Bent to Hyde, April 24, 1906, Yale.

23. Sanborn and all commissioners to James Harlan, Secretary of the Interior, October 16, 1865, in "Report of the Secretary of the Interior," 39th Cong., 1st Sess., 1865, 701–2, through protecting Black Kettle. Also see 699–700. Hereafter cited as Sanborn report, October 16, 1865.

24. Sanborn report, October 16, 1865, 702, through Little Raven's quote, "wait until next spring."

25. Sanborn report, October 16, 1865, 703, including the following paragraph.

26. Sanborn report, October 16, 1865, 704–5, for all the quotes to "pity on us." See 706 for the children in Denver not being located.

27. Sanborn report, October 16, 1865, 706–7, through Steele's presentation.

28. Sanborn report, October 16, 1865, 707.

29. Sanborn report, October 16, 1865, 708–11, through reading the treaty.

30. Kappler, *Treaties*, II:887–91. The treaty was ratified on May 22, 1866, and proclaimed on February 2, 1867.

31. Bent to Hyde, April 25, 1906, Yale.

32. Szasz, *Cultural Broker*, 16. Also see 17, 294, 296. The term did not originate until 1988.

33. "Announcement by Telegraph," *RMN*, October 16, 1865, 1.

34. "A Democratic Rally," *RMN*, October 16, 1865, 1.

35. Kraft, *Wynkoop*, 40.

36. "A Brutal Assault in Denver," *RMN*, October 19, 1865; reprint of *Oquawka Spectator*, unknown date.

37. "Sand Creek—The Test Question," *RMN*, October 18, 1865, 1.

38. "Announcements: To the Voters of Colorado," *RMN*, October 18, 1865, 1.

39. "Platform," *RMN*, October 18, 1865, 1.

40. "Withdrawal of Col. Chivington," *RMN*, November 8, 1865, 1.

41. Roberts, *Massacre*, 192.

42. Zwink, "Bluff Creek Council," 222–23, citing Pope to President Johnson and Pope to Harlan, October 27, 1865; Harlan to Cooley, November 2, 1865; Bent to Thomas Murphy, November 21, 1865.

43. Wynkoop to Cooley, November 22, 1865, NA RG75, M234, Roll 879. See Kraft, *Wynkoop*, 156–57, for Wynkoop being in Washington.

44. War Department Special Orders No. 628, December 5, 1865, Wynkoop Military File.

45. Wynkoop bond submission, December 12, 1865, and Wynkoop bond acceptance, December 21, 1865, NA RG75, M234, Roll 879.

46. Wynkoop, "Unfinished Colorado History," 140. Also see Special Orders No 109, December 21, 1865, Wynkoop Collection, Chávez History Library; Wynkoop Military File; and Harlan to Cooley, December 6, 1865, NA RG75, M234, Roll 879.

47. Christopher H. Wynkoop, "Descendants of Edward Wanshaer Wynkoop," 4. Angeline C. Wynkoop was born in January 1866. See Kraft, *Wynkoop*, 157, for the trip to Pennsylvania.

EPILOGUE

1. Hardorff, *Washita Memories*, 362n16, stated "The Cheyennes regarded [Stone Forehead] as a man of wisdom and peace, whose advice was respected in tribal affairs." He placed Stone Forehead closer to Black Kettle's view of the invading whites. Maybe; maybe not.

2. Wynkoop to Murphy, January 12, 1866; paid bill, January 12, 1866; Wynkoop to Cooley, January 15, 1866; Gordon to AAG, Dist. of Kansas, March 5, 1866 (hereafter Gordon, March 5, 1866, report), all in NA RG75, M234, Roll 879. Zwink, "Bluff Creek Council," 228–29.

3. Gordon, March 5, 1866, report; Halaas, *Halfbreed*, 208.

4. Wynkoop, "Unfinished Colorado History," 141. Porcupine Bear's father had been banished from the tribe when he had killed Little Creek during the winter of 1837–38.

5. Gordon, March 5, 1866, report.

6. Wynkoop, "Unfinished Colorado History," 141–42. For background on Adams, see Kraft, *Wynkoop*, 154, 162, 212, and 228. "Adams" was the Arapaho interpreter's name at this time and not "McAdams" as previously stated.

7. Wynkoop, "Unfinished Colorado History," 144; Gordon, March 5, 1866, report. Also see Halaas, *Halfbreed*, 204, 208–9; Berthrong, *Southern Cheyennes*, 258.

8. Gordon, March 5, 1866, report.

9. Gordon, March 5, 1866, report. Wynkoop, "Unfinished Colorado History," 143–46, through Little Raven.

10. Cox-Paul, "Chivington," 134–35.

11. Wynkoop to John Pope, April 5, 1866; and Wynkoop to Cooley, March 12 and April 8, 1866, all three in NA RG75, M234, Roll 879. Chalfant, *Hancock's War*, 42.

12. Wynkoop, "Unfinished Colorado History," 140. Certificate, Andrew Johnson appointment, September 20, 1866; and Cooley to Wynkoop, March 19, 1866, both in Wynkoop Collection, History Colorado. Wynkoop to Cooley, September 27, 1866, NA RG75, M234, Roll 879; Department of the Interior, Bureau of Pensions No. 749091, June 7, 1890, Wynkoop Pension File, NA, Washington, D.C.; Frank Wynkoop, "Data Concerning . . . Wynkoop," Colorado College, 4.

13. Hancock to Nichols, AAG May 22, 1867, in John M. Carroll, ed., *General Custer and the Battle of the Washita: The Federal View* (Bryan, Tex.: Guidon Press, 1978), 156 (hereafter Carroll, *Fed View*); Wynkoop to Murphy, June 11, September 14, 1867, NA RG75, M234, Roll 879; "Wynkoop on the Indian War," *RMN*, October 29, 1867; Powell, *People*, I:464–65; Barnitz to wife Jennie, April 9, 1867, in Utley, *Life in Custer's Cavalry*, 27 (hereafter Utley, *Life*). Chalfant, *Hancock's War*, 131, presented reasoning why Little Robe and Oglala chief Pawnee Killer were not present.

14. Hancock report, April 12, 1867, NA RG94, M619, Roll 563, for all quotes during the council. Hancock to Nichols May 22, 1867, in Carroll, *Fed View*, 156.

15. Wynkoop to Murphy, June 11, 1867, NA RG75, M234, Roll 879.

16. Barnitz (quoting Hancock) to Jennie, April 12, 1867, in Utley, *Life*, 31.

17. Hancock to Nichols, May 22, 1867, in Carroll, *Fed View*, 156–57.

18. Wynkoop to Murphy, September 14, 1967, in Carroll, *Fed View*, 114.

19. Stanley, *Early Travels*, 1:46–47.

20. Barnitz to Jennie, April 14, 1867, in Utley, *Life*, 32.

21. Wynkoop to Murphy, September 14, 1867, in Carroll, *Fed View*, 115. This hill still exists on farmland. It is called "Confrontation Ridge." There has been an ongoing effort to protect it. As of spring 2019 the land owner, who was already protecting this historic location, allowed two major placards to be placed on a pasture near Confrontation Ridge that describe the Indian and military views of that long gone April 14, 1867. See the Kraft Collection for photos that historian Leo Oliva took of the signs while they were being created and after they had been installed.

22. Stanley, *Early Travels*, 1:36.

23. Custer, *My Life on the Plains*, 32 (hereafter Custer, *Life*).

24. Grinnell, *Fighting Cheyennes*, 250.

25. Hancock to Nichols, May 22, 1867, in Carroll, *Fed View*, 157; Powell, *People*, I:469–70, 668n24; Kennedy, *On the Plains*, 63; Hoig, *Peace Chiefs*, 99–100. Grinnell, *Fighting Cheyennes*, 250, placed the Roman Nose/Hancock incident at the first meeting while Hyde, *Bent*, 259–60, placed it at the second and unmounted meeting. Roman Nose's counting coup must have been a light touch as neither Hancock nor Wynkoop reported it.

26. Wynkoop to Murphy, September 14, 1867, in Carroll, *Fed View*, 115.

27. Powell, *People*, I:470.

28. Wynkoop to Murphy, September 14, 1867, in *Report on Indian Affairs by the Acting Commissioner for the Year 1867*, 312. Wynkoop to Murphy, June 11, 1867; and Jesse Leavenworth to Taylor, April 15, 1867, both in NA RG75, M234, Roll 879; Powell, *People*, I:471; Hyde, *Bent*, 260.

29. Guerrier 1908 comments in Grinnell, *Fighting Cheyennes*, 253; also see Wynkoop to Murphy, September 14, 1867, in *Report on Indian Affairs*, 1867, 312.

30. Wynkoop to Murphy, June 11, 1867, in Carroll, *Fed View*, 107. Also see Wynkoop to Murphy, September 14, 1867, in *Report on Indian Affairs*, 1867, 312; "General A. J. Smith on Colonel Wynkoop's Testimony—Letter to Hon. N. G. Taylor, Superintendent of Indian Affairs," *RMN*, November 12, 1867; Hancock to Sherman, April 17, 1867, in Carroll, *Fed View*, 141; Grinnell, *Fighting Cheyennes*, 253; Powell, *People*, I:471–72; Hyde, *Bent*, 261; Stanley, *Early Travels*, 39–40; Custer, *Life*, 38; Barnitz to Jennie, April 17, 1867, in Utley, *Life*, 35; and Leavenworth to Taylor, April 15, 1867, NA RG75, M234, Roll 879.

31. "Wynkoop on the Indian War," *RMN*, October 29, 1867. Also, see Wynkoop to Murphy, September 14, 1867, *Report on Indian Affairs*, 1867, 312–13.

32. Wynkoop to Hancock, April 13, 1867, *Report on Indian Affairs*, 1867, 313. The dating of this letter is an error, for everything discussed happened on April 14; the date was April 15. See Hancock to Sherman, April 17, 1867, 141; and Wynkoop to Taylor, April 15, 1867, 104, both in Carroll, *Fed View*. Hancock's report included Wynkoop's April 15 protest letter.

33. Custer to Lt. T. B. Weir, April 16, 1867, in Carroll, *Fed View*, 145.

34. Custer to Weir, April 17, 19, 1867, 145–46, 150, in Carroll, *Fed View*.

35. Hancock to Sherman, April 17, 18, 19, 1867, 141, 143, 146; W. G. Mitchell, AAAG, report, April 18, 1867, 172, in Carroll, *Fed View*. See Stanley, *Early Travels*, 40, for the arrival of Custer's April 17 report.

36. Wynkoop to Taylor, April 21, 1867, in Carroll, *Fed View*, 102.

37. Wynkoop to Murphy, June 11, 1867, NA RG75, M234, Roll 879.

38. Hancock to Maj. George K. Leet, AAG, August 31, 1867, in Carroll, *Fed View*, 191.

39. See Carroll, *Fed View*, 171, for the inventory of the two separate villages. Also see Wynkoop to Murphy, September 14, 1867, *Report on Indian Affairs*, 1867, 313.

40. Hancock to Leet, July 31, 1867, in Carroll, *Fed View*, 190.

41. Taylor to O. H. Browning, secretary of the interior, November 23, 1868, *Annual Report of the Commissioner of Indian Affairs*, 1868, 9.

42. Carriker and Carriker, *Army Wife*, 48.

43. Carriker and Carriker, *Army Wife*, 49. Alice Baldwin correctly stated that Cheyennes smoked with Wynkoop but erred when she stated that the other chiefs were Kiowas. She called Wynkoop's interpreter "Celestia" Adams. Wynkoop would have had a Cheyenne interpreter also. At this time John Smith was his employee and was probably present.

44. Henry Stanley, "The March from Larned to Medicine Creek," *Missouri Democrat*, October 21, 1867, 2. Although some of the following claim that the murder attempt happened on October 10, this could not be, as Murphy also needed time to return to Fort Larned. Also see "Escape of Major Wyncoop" [*sic*], *Colorado Transcript*,

October 30, 1867, 3; *Chicago Times*, October 22, 1867; Hoig, *Peace Chiefs*, 100; Powell, *People*, I:509; and Halaas, *Halfbreed*, 243.

45. Stanley, "March from Larned," *Missouri Democrat*, October 21, 1867, 2.

46. Jones, *Treaty*, 66–67.

47. Stanley, *Early Travels*, 1:228–29.

48. Jones, *Treaty*, 70–71, 73–75. Powell, *People*, I:510–11. Powell stuck with Stanley's dating, which is in disagreement with the other papers' timeline of events.

49. Hoig, *Washita*, 27; Jones, *Treaty*, cited the *Missouri Republican*, October 24, 1867, 84–85. Stanley was not present at this meeting.

50. "The Peace Commission: Indian Talks," *Missouri Democrat*, October 23, 1867, 2.

51. "The Peace Commission: Indian Talks," *Missouri Democrat*, October 23, 1867, 2; "Indian Council," *Daily Colorado Tribune*, October 29, 1867, 2; Hoig, *Washita*, 28, for *Chicago Times*, October 29, 1867.

52. *Missouri Republican*, October 24, 1867, in Jones, *Treaty*, 98, including the threat against Black Kettle.

53. "The Peace Commission: Indian Talks," *Missouri Democrat*, October 23, 1867, 2.

54. Stanley, "The Medicine Lodge Peace Council," in Cozzens, *Eyewitnesses to the Indian Wars*, October 19, 1867 (These are the dates that Stanley wrote his articles and not the dates when they were published.), 94–95, 98 (hereafter, Stanley, "Medicine Lodge Peace Council"); Powell, *People*, I:515; Jones, *Treaty*, 80; Kappler, *Treaties*, II:982, 989.

55. Stanley, "Medicine Lodge Peace Council," October 19, 1867, 97; also see 94–96, 98. Jones, *Treaty*, 112 and n2, cites all seven 1867 papers covering the council: *New York Herald* (October 30), *Missouri Republican* (October 25), *Chicago Times* (October 29), *Chicago Tribune* (October 26), *Cincinnati Commercial* (October 29), *Cincinnati Gazette* (October 29), and *Missouri Democrat* (October 25).

56. "The Peace Council: Second Session of the Grand Council," *Missouri Democrat*, October 28, 1867, 2.

57. Jones, *Treaty*, 136–37.

58. Jones, *Treaty*, 138; also see 136–37; Hoig, *Washita*, 30–31.

59. "The Peace Council: Second Session of the Grand Council," *Missouri Democrat*, October 28, 1867, 2. Also see Jones, *Treaty*, 138–39.

60. Jones, *Treaty*, 141–42; Hoig, *Washita*, 31; Kappler, *Treaties*, II:282–84; "The Peace Council: Second Session of the Grand Council," *Missouri Democrat*, October 28, 1867, 2.

61. Stanley, "Medicine Lodge Peace Council," October 27, 1867, 114.

62. Taylor, "Medicine Lodge," 108.

63. Stanley, "Medicine Lodge Peace Council," October 27, 1867, 115, through "exploded from the trees."

64. Barnitz journal, October 27, 1867, in Utley, *Life*, 114.

65. Stanley, "Medicine Lodge Peace Council," October 27, 1867, 115.

66. *New York Tribune*, November 8, 1867, in Hoig, *Peace Chiefs*, 90.

67. Kraft, *Wynkoop*, 214. The original quote used "Moon of the Changing Season," which is a shortened and more usable version of the month's name than Powell's "Moon when the water begins to freeze on the edge of the streams" (in *People*, I:xl). Powell's wording is slightly different from Wolf Chief's, which ended with "edges of the stream."

68. Stanley, "Medicine Lodge Peace Council," October 27, 1867, 112–13, for the interview and quotes.

69. Kappler, *Treaties*, II:989.

70. "The Peace Council: Second Session of the Grand Council," *Missouri Democrat*, October 28, 1867, 2, for Henderson, Little Raven, and Buffalo Chief's quotes. Jones, *Treaty*, 173, only quoted a few of Buffalo Chief's words, which differ slightly: "'We never claimed any land south of the Arkansas,' he said. 'But that country between the Arkansas and the South Platte is ours.'" (See 177n5 for eight newspapers he listed and their dates.)

71. Jones, *Treaty*, 174–76, 177n5. See Stanley, "Medicine Lodge Peace Council," November 2, 1867, 122, for Smith's actions; and Hoig, *Washita*, 36.

72. "The Peace Council: Second Session of the Grand Council," *Missouri Democrat*, October 28, 1867, 2. Emphasis added.

73. Jones, *Treaty*, 177–78, lists three holdouts. Powell, *People*, I:530, agreed, but on I:676n42, he pointed to Hoig, *Washita*, 36, who added Tall Bull refusing to sign but did not add him to the flow of his text. See Kappler, *Treaties*, II:989, as Tall Bull did sign the treaty. Hoig's note on 221 (last one from 36) cites Brown, *Cincinnati Commercial*, November 4, 1867, and two articles by Stanley in the *Kansas Weekly Tribune* (November 11) and *New York Tribune* (November 8). Although the documentation points to four holdouts, Halaas, *Halfbreed*, 240, claimed six held out with superb logic.

74. Kappler, *Treaties*, II:984–89.

75. Jones, *Treaty*, 181–82.

76. Bent to Joseph Thoburn, September 29, 1910, Thoburn Papers; Kappler, *Treaties*, II:989; Stanley, "March from Larned," *Missouri Democrat*, October 21, 1867, 2. Also see Jones, *Treaty*, 63; and Halaas, *Halfbreed*, 244, which presented valid but opposing thoughts on Bent's choice to work for Wynkoop.

77. Hoig, *Washita*, 37, citing *Kansas Weekly Tribune*, November 11, 1867.

78. Barnitz journal, October 28, 1867, in Utley, *Life*, 115.

79. "The Council with the Southern Tribes," *RMN*, October 29, 1867, 1.

80. Cited in Prucha, *Great Father*, I:497.

81. Printed in the *New York Times*, November 5, 1867.

82. "The Indian Peace Treaty," November 16, 1867, 725.

83. "The Peace Council: Second Session of the Grand Council," *Missouri Democrat*, October 28, 1867, 2.

84. Davis, "Summer on the Plains," 305–6. The murder attempt had to have happened after the Medicine Lodge council, because Julia, who was present, would have confronted her brother. Grinnell, "Bent's Old Fort," 47n36, claimed, "A picture printed in *Harper's Magazine* for February 1868, is not Charles Bent. The old Indians thought it looked like a young Arapahoe whose picture was made by a travelling artist." Davis was a professional; it is doubtful that he would have misidentified his portrait of Charley, and doubly so, as it was included in his article, which featured his art.

85. McGinley as quoted in the *Sunday Oklahoman*, October 2, 1910, in Halaas, *Halfbreed*, 245, 397–98n3. This is a good extended note, which included the fact that McGinley "knew and respected" George Bent and "lived near" him when the story was published, and also that George's son, George W., wrote that Kaws wounded Charley on Walnut Creek.

86. In George Bent's Heirship testimony, March 23, 1914, he stated that "he died in 1867 at the age of 19 years." Washita County, Oklahoma. Courtesy of Harvey Pratt, great-grandson of Julia Bent. Bent to Thoburn, September 23, 1910, Thoburn Collection, provided the exact date.

87. George Bent interview, 1914, and a "Parents of Decedent" document that names Susie Penleton, Cheyenne heirship files, Indian Archives. Courtesy of Harvey Pratt, great-grandson of Julia Bent.

88. Wynkoop to Murphy, 2nd letter dated February 1, 1868, NA RG75, M234, Roll 880.

89. Kraft, *Wynkoop*, 223.

90. Smith to Murphy, February 5, 1868, NA RG75, M234, Roll 880.

91. Butterfield to Murphy, February 5, 1868, NA RG75, M234, Roll 880.

92. Taylor to Murphy and Wynkoop (two separate documents), February 25, 1868, NA RG75, M21, Roll 85.

93. Barnitz journal, February 29, March 3, and March 6, 1868, in Utley, *Life*, 136–37; Hutton, *Sheridan*, 27–28. Wynkoop to Taylor, March 5, 1868; Thomas Murphy note, May 23, 1868; and Clerk Ind. Office to Charles E. Mix, Act. Commissioner, May 23, 1868, all in NA RG75, M234, Roll 880.

94. Wynkoop distribution, April 25, 1868, NA RG75, M234, Roll 880.

95. Wynkoop to Banks, May 4, 1868, NA RG75, M234, Roll 880.

96. Wynkoop to Murphy, May 15, 1868, NA RG75, M234, Roll 880.

97. Kraft, *Wynkoop*, 229–30, 306n15.

98. Wynkoop to Murphy, May 22, 23, 1868; and Wynkoop distribution May 29, 1868, witnessed by Smith and certified by Banks, both in NA RG75, M234, Roll 880. Fort Ellsworth was renamed Fort Harker in November 1866. According to Powell, *People*, I:xl, there are two moons for The time when the horses get fat. The first is May and the second is June.

99. Kraft, *Wynkoop*, 233, 306n25; Garfield, "Defense of the Kansas Frontier," 454.

100. Sherman to Browning, June 24, 1868, NA RG75, M234, Roll 880.

101. Wynkoop to Murphy, July 20, 1868, NA RG75, M234, Roll 880.

102. Taylor to Murphy, 67, and Taylor to Wynkoop, 66, July 23, 1868, *Annual Report of the Commissioner of Indian Affairs*, 1868.

103. Kappler, *Treaties*, II:984. The treaty was proclaimed on August 19, 1868.

104. Murphy to Taylor, August 1, 1868, including Murphy's instructions to Wynkoop, *Annual Report of the Commissioner of Indian Affairs*, 1868, 69. Also see 68. Little Raven's statement pointed to Arapahos joining Little Robe on the June raid. Barnitz had heard rumors of the upcoming weapons distribution three days before the distribution, and wrote his wife that Wynkoop on this day will "issue 350 or 375 rifles to them, by order of the Secretary of the Interior." Barnitz to Jennie, July 29, 1868, Barnitz Papers, Yale. Larger portions of the quote are in Kraft, *Wynkoop*, 236, and Utley, *Life*, 174–75. Historians often quote Barnitz, not realizing he knew not what he spoke about.

105. Wynkoop report of his interview with Little Rock, August 19, 1868, NA RG75, M234, Roll 880. Robert M. Utley, *Frontier Regulars*, 143, questioned the early departure date while suggesting that the war party set out perhaps two or three days prior to August 10. I tended to agree with him (Kraft, *Wynkoop*, 308n54), however, at this time I am not convinced for the reasons in the text. Either way, these warriors were not present at the August 9 gun distribution. See Edmund Guerrier's affidavit, February 9, 1869, "Difficulties with Indian Tribes," House of Representatives, Ex. Doc. No. 240, 41st Congress, 2nd session, 167, for it not only confirms his firsthand knowledge of the beginning of the raid but also what Little Rock reported to Wynkoop without him being privy to that meeting.

106. Wynkoop to Murphy, August 10, 1868, NA RG75, M234, Roll 880.

107. Sherman to Secretary of War J. M. Schofield, August 9, 1868, NA RG94, M619, Roll 629.

108. General Orders, No. 4, August 10, 1868, NA RG94, M619, Roll 629.

109. Taylor to Browning, August 18, 1868; Sherman to E. D. Townsend, AAG, September 5 and 8, 1868; Mix to Acting Secretary of the Interior W. F. Otto, September 12, 1868, NA RG94, M619, Roll 629.

110. Guerrier statement to Bvt. Lt. Col. J Schuyler Crosby, February 9, 1869, House of Representatives, 41st Cong., 2nd Sess., Ex. Doc. 240, 171. See Wynkoop's Little Rock report, August 19, 1868, NA RG75, M234, Roll 880, for the larger warrior count; and Greene, *Washita*, 49–50, 222nn13, 15, for a warrior count of 115 white deaths, and warriors who "raped and wounded several women." Hoig, *Washita*, 46–50, provided additional details based upon newspapers. Also see Powell, *People*, I:568–69. Hatch, *Black Kettle*, 235, is an error-riddled distortion of facts and events.

111. See Hardorff, *Washita Memories*, 360 and n12, for Bent to Robert Peck, December 1906, regarding the Washita attack. In it he referred to his wife as Black Kettle's "stepdaughter." As mentioned in an earlier note, kinship was a blurring of relationships and a sister could be a real sister or a good friend, and in this kinship example the chief's niece became his stepdaughter. Hardorff pointed to Halaas, *Halfbreed*, 259 (see also 260), which dealt with kinship and Magpie Woman's mother, Nis-tah-nah (Corn Tassel Woman), who was in the Washita village but not killed. However, I have never seen Wind Woman, Black Kettle's sister, called by either of these names, so this leads me to believe that the relationship was totally dependent upon kinship. See Kraft, *Wynkoop*, for Guerrier (181, 182, 219, 225) and Bent (181) being on the agent's payroll. But it went beyond this, as both knew how important they were to bridge the language gap between their chiefs and Wynkoop. Barnitz to Jennie, July 15, 1868, in Utley, *Life*, 171, places Julia Bent in Black Kettle's village. Finally, see Bent to Hyde, April 25, 1906, Yale. George states that in summer 1866, when he married Magpie Woman, Black Kettle gave him a gift—the "fine bay" horse that retired general William Harney had given the chief at the Little Arkansas Treaty in 1865.

112. Powell, *People*, I:570.

113. Bent to Thoburn, January 9, 1912, Thoburn Papers.

114. Wynkoop report, August 19, 1868, NA RG75, M234, Roll 880. According to Powell, *People*, I:570, 667n22, "Later Wynkoop stated that Stone Forehead also promised that the men who had committed the rapes and killings would be turned over to the whites."

115. Bent to Thoburn, December 27, 1911, Thoburn Papers, which includes through Bent and Guerrier leaving Black Kettle.

116. Kraft, *Wynkoop*, 243, 308n62.

117. Monnett, *Beecher Island*, 131–35, 137, 141.

118. See Grinnell, *Fighting Cheyennes*, 286–88, for quotes and action through Roman Nose's death.

119. See an earlier note about Cheyenne contraries and how they functioned within the tribe.

120. Monnett, *Beecher Island*, 152–57, 160.

121. See Greene, *Washita*, 102, for the chiefs and the positioning of the villages on the Washita, plus my viewing of many maps.

122. See Hardorff, *Washita Memories*, 273n3, for the distance.

123. Black Kettle–Big Mouth–Hazen meeting, November 20, 1868, recorded by Capt. Henry E. Alvord (Tenth U.S. Cavalry), Senate Ex. Doc. No. 18, 40th Cong., 3rd Sess., 22–23, for all quotes. Little Robe and Spotted Wolf did not speak. Neither Black Kettle nor Big Mouth offered to trade or ransom captives to Hazen for peace, even though I have seen it printed that they did. For an example, see Michno, "Cheyenne Chief Black Kettle Reassessed," *Wild West*, December 2005, 72, which stated: "On November 20, Black Kettle, Big Mouth and a number of chiefs representing the Cheyennes and Arapahos, came to see Hazen to discuss peace and talk about ransoming the white captives."

124. Hazen to Sherman, November 22, 1868, Senate Ex. Doc. No. 18, 40th Cong., 3rd Sess., 24–25. There was no mention of Black Kettle attempting to ransom white prisoners.

125. Powell, *People*, I:602.

126. Custer to Sheridan, November 28, 1868, House of Representatives, 41st Cong., 2nd Sess., Ex. Doc. 240, 163–64. Also see 162, 165, for what appears to have been an inflated and yet amazingly detailed description of everything he captured and destroyed. He was in a battle zone, which included being under attack, and yet his men counted every bullet, weighed the powder, and so on. Hereafter cited as Custer report, November 28, 1868.

127. Ben Clark[e] interview by Walter Mason Camp, Lilly Library, Indiana University, Bloomington, Indiana. For Custer's actions during the attack see Kraft, *Custer*, 49–62; and Greene, *Washita*, 116–28. A portion of Custer Hill still exists at the Washita Battlefield NHS in Cheyenne, Oklahoma. Clarke claimed that Custer sent him to stop the murder of women and children.

128. See chapter 1 for Black Kettle's only sister, "Wind Woman." Custer, *Life*, 252, erred calling Mahwissa Black Kettle's "sister."

129. Kraft, *Custer*, 53, for quote; Barnard, *Elliott*, 261–74, for details of Elliot's death. Also see Hoig, *Washita*, 141, 210.

130. Custer report, November 28, 1868, 164; Custer, *Life*, 258–59; Greene, *Washita*, 127–28.

131. Wynkoop to Taylor, November 29, 1868, House of Representatives, 41st Cong., 2nd Sess., Ex. Doc. 240, 5. Many publications have erroneously inverted the dates of Wynkoop's resignation and Custer's Washita attack.

132. Benteen to Theodore Goldin, February 17, 1896, in Carroll, *Benteen-Goldin Letters*, 271; Walter Mason Camp interview of Ben Clark[e], Lilly Library; Brill, *Conquest*, 46; Frost, *Custer Legends*, 64–65, 69. Kraft, *Custer*, 68n21, presents details about various views of what or what did not happen. Also see Stiles, *Custer's Trials*, 327, 332–33, 523n11.

133. Custer to J. Schuyler Crosby, AAAG, Department of the Missouri, December 22, 1868, in Carroll, *Fed View*, 67. See Kraft, *Custer*, xi, for Custer's names.

134. Benteen to Goldin, February 17, 1896, in Carroll, *Benteen-Goldin Letters*, 271.

135. Custer, *Life*, 312.

136. Frost, *Custer Legends*, 66; See Custer, *Life*, for some of Mo-nahs-e-tah's actions in the field, 350–51, 365–66. Also see Benteen to Goldin, February 14, 1896, in Carroll, *Benteen-Goldin Letters*, 258. "What does your brother mean by putting on all those thrills?" Benteen claimed he said to Capt. Tom Custer. "Doesn't he know that Dr. Renick has seen him 'not only' sleeping with that Indian girl all winter long, but has seen him many times in the very act of copulating with her!"

137. Custer to Crosby, December 22, 1868, in Carroll, *Fed View*, 68–69. Did "* * *" mean Elliott was missing his sexual organs as many of his companions were, or were the words more gruesome? Carroll's *Fed View* is a collection of military and government reports that detail the 1867–68 lead-up to the battle of the Washita, the destruction of Black Kettle's village, and some of the aftermath. They are pulled from three Senate reports (40th Congress) and one House of Representatives report (41st Congress). It was a massive undertaking by Carroll to place hundreds of documents together in one book. I use *Fed View* whenever I do not have the original document, for it is a goldmine. This said, I do not know if "* * *" was Carroll's censorship, or if the original reports were graphic, originally censored by Custer and Dr. Lippincott, or later censored. Also see Spotts, *Campaigning*, for his journal entry on December 22, 1868, 75. Elliott's death created a chasm within the Seventh that would continue until long after Custer's death.

138. "9,000 Indians on Reservation," *Quincy Daily Whig*, December 16, 1868, 1; "From Washington," *Daily Kansas State Journal*, December 17, 1868, 1; Kraft, *Wynkoop*, 246.

139. Custer, *Life*, 292; Custer report, December 22, 1868, in Carroll, *Fed View*, 69–70. See Kraft, *Custer*, 84–85. Sharp Grover, Tom Custer, Kicking Bird, and Little Heart appear in Charles Schreyvogel's magnificent painting "Custer's Demand," but were not at this meeting.

140. Sheridan to W. A. Nichols, December 19, 1868, in Carroll, *Fed View*, 50.

141. *Weekly RMN*, December 23, 1868, 3; Kraft, *Wynkoop*, 246. Also see Kraft talk, "Wynkoop's Last Stand," April 20, 2013, Order of the Indian Wars Symposium, Centennial, Colorado, also as "Louis Kraft Speaks about Wynkoop Lashing Out Against the Murder of Cheyennes," on Kraft's YouTube channel.

142. Custer report, November 28, 1868, 163–64. Also see 162, 165. Sheridan reports, November 29, 1868, and January 1, 1869, House of Representatives, 41st Cong., 2nd Sess., Ex. Doc. 240, 165–66, supported Custer's actions. For those interested in battle fictions that have been perpetrated for decades, see Greene, *Washita*, chapter 9, "Controversies."

143. Hardorff, *Washita Memories*, 282.

144. Bent to Thoburn, December 27, 1911, Thoburn Papers. Bent stated that Jack Fitzpatrick (b. October 8, 1850) was Thomas Fitzpatrick's son. Also see Hardorff, *Washita Memories*, 283nn1–2; Thrapp, *Frontier Biography*, I:495. Jack's name was Andrew Jackson Fitzpatrick; his mother was Margaret Poisal (b. 1834), mixed-blood daughter of Snake Woman (Left Hand's sister) and John Poisal, who had married Fitzpatrick in November 1849. John Poisal Jr. (b. 1850) was Margaret's brother.

145. Morrison to Wynkoop, December 14, 1868, Senate, 40th Cong., 3rd Sess., Ex. Doc. 36, 2. Morrison's letter to Wynkoop is also in NA RG75, M234, Roll 880. Greene, *Washita*, 212–14, has a larger warrior and smaller women and children death toll than Morrison's letter. Greene did state, "Some individuals listed below might have had two or more names, so a few entries might be duplicative." Still his list is way below Custer's "one hundred and three" warrior death count.

146. Hardorff, *Washita Memories*, 283n3. Her husband, Lieutenant Crocker, had been a member of the Second Colorado Volunteers.

147. Kappler, *Treaties*, II:889. Both of Mrs. Crocker's Cheyenne names were listed in the treaty.

148. Peter Cooper, Vincent Colyer, and four others to Wynkoop, December 21, 1868, *Wynkoop Scrapbook*. It was printed on page 2 of Wynkoop's December 23, 1868, talk (details in following note). The Cooper Union, as it is now called, still exists in New York City.

149. "Address of Col. E. W. Wynkoop, before the Indian Peace Commission of the Cooper Institute, New York, December 23, 1868," 6–8, for all quotes. It includes Wynkoop's entire talk. An original is in the *Wynkoop Scrapbook* (Kraft Collection includes a copy). Wynkoop's words reflect those in vogue during the 1860s, such as "savages," and should not be taken out of context and dragged into the twenty-first century, where their connotation is extreme prejudice. What Wynkoop heard of High Back Wolf and knew of Black Kettle allowed him to state that their "administrative ability and wisdom, rather than by deeds of prowess in the field, [made them] . . . great chieftain[s]."

150. "Indian Affairs," *New York Times*, December 24, 1868, 1.

151. Cooper to Grant, March 19, 1869, Wynkoop Collection, Chávez History Library.

152. Kraft, "Confrontation on the Sweetwater," 42. See Kraft, *Custer*, for the events that led up to the Stone Forehead–Custer confrontation and aftermath. Also see Powell, *People*, I:xl, for the Light snow moon, sometimes called the Dusty moon.

153. Custer report, March 21, 1869, Box R-41, Packet 1, 222–23 [641–42], Carl Coke Rister Collection, Western History Collections, University of Oklahoma Libraries, Norman, Oklahoma (hereafter Rister Collection); Custer, *Life*, 354; Powell, *People*, II:707, 709.

154. Custer, *Life*, 326–28, 330; Chandler, *Of Garryowen in Glory*, 39; Kraft, *Custer*, 106–9; Hutton, *Sheridan*, 103.

155. Brill, *Conquest*, 228 and n2 for the quotes; also see 226–27. Sprinkling the ashes on Custer's boots made the peace pipe stronger. Tsistsista Magpie was Brill's 1930 source for what happened during the powwow. See Powell, *Sweet Medicine*, 1:120, for another version of the quote. Custer, *Life*, 356–57, had an unnamed holy man perform the ceremony and Powell, *People*, II:708–10, accepted this. Brill used Magpie's verbal testimony and claimed that Stone Forehead performed the ceremony. I agree with Brill, as the ceremony was too important. Also see Bent to Hyde, September (n.d.) 1905, History Colorado.

156. Hadley, "Nineteenth Kansas Cavalry," 450; Spotts, *Campaigning*, March 15, 1868, 152; Brill, *Conquest*, 224.

157. Custer, *Life*, 361–62, and 360; Custer report, March 21, 1869, 224 [644], Rister Collection; Berthrong, *Southern Cheyennes*, 337.

158. Hadley, "Nineteenth Kansas Cavalry," 451. Also see Brill, *Conquest*, 238.

159. Custer, *Life*, 362. Also Brill, *Conquest*, 238.

160. Hadley, "Nineteenth Kansas Cavalry," 451. Also see Custer, *Life*, 362–63; Brill, *Conquest*, 238.

161. Custer report, March 21, 1869, 224 [644], Rister Collection.

162. Hadley, "Nineteenth Kansas Cavalry," 452; Custer report, March 21, 1869, 224 [644], Rister Collection; Brill, *Conquest*, 239, 241; Custer, *Following the Guidon*, 98; Dixon, "Sweetwater Hostages," 99; and Spotts, March 16, 1869, *Campaigning*, 154. There is a lot of confusion with the prisoners' identities.

163. Custer report, March 21, 1869, 225–26 [645–46], Rister Collection. Also see Custer, *Life*, 368; Custer to Libbie, March 24, 1869, in Custer, *Following the Guidon*, 56; Powell, *People*, II:716; Kraft, *Custer*, 158–61.

164. Custer, *Life*, 370; Brill, *Conquest*, 245.

165. Custer report, March 21, 1869, 228 [648], also see 226–27 [646–47], Rister Collection; Custer, *Life*, 371; Spotts, *Campaigning*, March 19, 1868, 158; Brill, *Conquest*, 245; Custer, *Following the Guidon*, 58.

166. Extract of Colyer, April 9, 1869, report in Hardorff, *Washita Memories*, 367–68. Grierson, U.S. interpreter H. P. Jones, and Capt. Henry Alvord (Tenth U.S. Cavalry) endorsed Little Raven's mark.

167. Hyde, *Bent*, 291–92.

168. Bent to Grinnell, May 1, 1905, Grinnell Collection, RCOA; and Bent to Hyde, June 11, 1914, Yale.

169. Filipiak, "Battle of Summit Springs," 347, quoted a portion of the orders. Also see 347n11 for the source, and 346 for Tall Bull.

170. King, *War Eagle*, 3, 109–10; Hayes, "Story of an Indian Campaign," 407. Hayes was a second lieutenant in the Fifth Cavalry in 1869 and commanded the supply train on the expedition.

171. Grinnell, *Fighting Cheyennes*, 310–11, including the beginning of the attack.

172. Bent to Hyde, December 11, 1905, Yale.

173. Bent to Hyde, February 23, 1904, and December 11, 1905, Yale.

174. Alfred Sorenson, "A Quarter-Century on the Frontier, or the Adventures of Major Frank North, the 'White Chief of the Pawnees,'" (Nebraska State Historical Society), in King, *War Eagle*, 114; and Grinnell, *Fighting Cheyennes*, 316–17, for Tall Bull's death. Grinnell's version is almost a verbatim retelling of Sorenson without citing him. Sorenson based his manuscript on Frank North's "recollections," while he based his *Two Great Scouts and their Pawnee Battalion* on Luther's memories. King thought that Sorenson's document dated to the late 1870s. Carr to Bvt. Brig. Gen. G. D. Ruggles, July 20, 1869, in King, 113, had Tall Bull's wife on one horse with him eventually handing their daughter to her while telling "her to escape and take the white woman who was prisoner, and she might use her to make terms for herself when peace was made." He also stated that Tall Bull killed his horse. King (114–15) shot holes through William Cody's claim that he captured Tall Bull's horse when he killed the chief.

175. Clarke, "Ethnography," 1, Folder 16c, Grinnell Collection, RCOA.

176. Kraft, *Wynkoop*, 252–54. President Grant refused to respond to his application.

177. Whipple to Wynkoop, May 24, 1875; Martin to Wynkoop, May 8, 1875; and Thomas Vail to Wynkoop, May 20, 1875, all in Wynkoop Collection, Chávez History Library; and ARC identifier 5744453, MLR number A1 15, NA RG48, M750, Roll 17, 45, 47, Records of the Office of the Secretary of the Interior, 1826–2006, College Park, Maryland, for Arizona.

178. Thomas J. Noel, "All Hail the Denver Pacific," 97, 99–100; *History of Colorado Biographical*, IV:15.

179. Cannon, "Josephine Evans Elbert," 269.

180. Cox-Paul, "Chivington," 135–37, 142.

181. Hoig, *John Simpson Smith*, 225–26. Near the end of Cutler's *Massacre at Sand Creek*, 217–34, John Smith has a conversation with the Devil when he returns to the frontier for the last time. Historical figures do not have dialogues with the Devil. Any nonfiction book that cites Cutler's fiction is suspect.

182. Powell, *People*, II:884–85, 895–96, and Kraft, *Custer*, 198, for how he escaped to the north in 1874 by having those with him wear their buffalo robes with the fur

side out as he chanted a holy song, which made soldiers think that they were a herd of bison in the distance.

183. Bent to Thoburn, September 29, 1910, Thoburn Papers, OHS.

184. Craig, *Fighting Parson*, 234–35. In a talk, "A Misplaced Massacre: Struggling Over the Memory of Sand Creek," that Ari Kelman delivered to the Civil War Institute's "The Civil War in 1864" conference, Gettysburg College, Pennsylvania, June 21, 2014, he stated: "Finally in 1883 as he was nearing the end of his life Chivington spoke publicly for the last time about Sand Creek," and closed with "I stand by Sand Creek." Chivington lived another eleven years. Kelman saw Craig's two pages but did not look at 235n6. Craig pulled the 1883 talk information and quotes from the *Denver Republican*, October 5, 1894, an extended obituary on the colonel, who died on October 4, 1894. C-SPAN taped Kelman's talk: https://www.c-span.org/video/?319538–3/sand-creek-massacre&start=729.

185. There were few Dog Men at Sand Creek, but that is American cinema. It was almost as if director Tab Murphy was totally in line with the great film director John Ford and his dictum: "Print the legend."

186. Murphy wrote the screenplay.

Bibliography

Archival Sources

Anne E. Hemphill Collection. Byron Strom, custodian. Des Moines, Iowa.
  Silas and Hersa Coberly Soule letters and photos.
Resources Center of the Autry, Burbank, California, a facility of the Autry Museum of the American West, Los Angeles, California. (I completed my research at the Braun Research Library at the Southwest Museum in June 2014, and received photocopies and digital copies of my research request in September and October 2015. The Braun closed in 2015 and the entire archive now resides at the Resources Center, which is set to open to historians in late 2020 or early 2021.)
  George Bird Grinnell Collection, MS.5.
    "As to the Meaning of the Word Vihio (as spelled)." Folder 69.
    Bent, George. Additional letters to Grinnell. Folders 10a, 10b, 10c. (Note that some are copies, typescripts, but some are duplicates of the letters in Folders 41a through 4d.)
    Bent, George. "George Bent's Correspondence with Grinnell on Cheyennes." Folders 41a, 41b, 41c, 41d.
    "Cheyenne Band Names From the Clark[e] Manuscript." Folder 69.
    "Cheyenne Chronology." Folder 119b.
    "Cheyenne Notes/Biographies." Folder 69.
    Clarke, Ben. "Ethnography." Fort Reno, Indian Territory, February 10, 1887. Folder 16c.
    "Lame Deer 1913." Folder 69.
    "The Loss of the Cheyenne Medicine Arrows." Folder 506.
    "The Medicine Arrows." Folder 29.
    "Names of Noted Cheyennes and the Approximate Dates of Birth & Death." Folder 119. (Note that the Braun History Library at the Southwest Museum used to have Folders 119, 119a, and 119b. These folders have been merged to just 119. This document now has two page 5s.)
    "Noted Cheyennes—Cheyenne Chronology." Folder 119.
    "November 1901, Southern Cheyenne" Notebook. Folder/Diary 334.

Page on High Wolf, Folder 69.

"Secrets of War Parties." Folder 41c.

Wolf Chief. "Life of Black Kettle." Folder 69.

Wolf Chief. "Proph[e]sy Story." Folder 16–11.

Wolf Chief. "The Months." Folder 69.

Beinecke Rare Book & Manuscript Library, Yale University, New Haven, Connecticut.

George Bent Papers, Coe Collection.

George Bent letters to George E. Hyde, 1904–18.

Boulder Historical Society Collections, Carnegie Branch Library for Local History, Boulder Public Library, Colorado.

"Henry Blake Diaries, 1862–1870, 1911." Transcribed by Steven J. Rorabaugh and William Light, edited by Todd Ellison.

Colorado College, Colorado Springs. Tutt Library.

Black Kettle. Letter dictated to Indian agent Samuel Colley requesting a meeting to discuss peace, August 29, 1964.

Colley, Samuel. Letters to and from.

Wynkoop, Frank M. "Data Concerning Col. Edward Wanshear [sic] Wynkoop and Louise Brown Wynkoop." Special Collections and Manuscripts, File Mf 0109. 7 pages.

Colorado State Archives Public Records Register.

John Evans Personal Correspondence Collection, 1833–85. FF9, Folio 94.

Denver Public Library. Western History Collection.

George Bent Papers. WH1704.

Governor John Evans Papers. WH1724.

John M. Chivington Papers. M1594.

"History of the Reverends John M. & Isaac Chivington in Their Relationship to the Early Methodist Church in Kansas and Nebraska," n.d. FF5.

Various letters.

Silas Soule Papers. WH1690.

William N. Byers Papers. WH55.

Byers, Mrs. Wm. N. "The Experiences of One Pioneer Woman." Series 2, Box 3.

Fort Larned National Historical Site, Larned, Kansas.

Fort Larned Post Orders. Roll 1, NA RG 92.

Fray Angélico Chávez History Library, History Museum of New Mexico, Santa Fe.

Edward W. Wynkoop Collection. AC247.

Various documents and correspondence related to Wynkoop's life and career created by him and his contemporaries.

Wynkoop, Edward Estill. "Edward Wanshear [sic] Wynkoop," n.d. Typescript. File nos. 2–3.

Wynkoop, Frank (Francis) Murray. "Commemoration: Mrs. Louise M. Wynkoop; A Biographical Sketch," 1938. Box 112.

Wynkoop Scrapbook.

"Address of Col. E. W. Wynkoop, before the Indian Peace Commission of the Cooper Institute, New York, December 23, 1868." Philadelphia: A. C. Bryson, Printers, 1869, 1–8.

Wynkoop, Frank M. "Intimate Notes Relative to the Career of Colonel Edward Wynkoop Which Are Not at All or Incompletely

Included in This Scrapbook," n.d. (This document accompanied the scrapbook that Edward W. Wynkoop began in 1876 but never completed.)

Louis Kraft Collection. AC402; photos ACP010.

Louis Kraft correspondence and research related to people and events associated with the Sand Creek Massacre.

Louis Kraft correspondence, research, lectures, articles, plays, and books related to Ned Wynkoop and the Cheyennes.

Louis Kraft photos and art related to the Cheyenne Indian wars of the 1860s.

Ned Wynkoop and the Lonely Road from Sand Creek, manuscript drafts, and book reviews.

Sand Creek and the Tragic End of a Lifeway, manuscript drafts, and book reviews.

Wynkoop, Christopher H. "Brown-Wakely Family Descendants."

Wynkoop, Christopher H. "Descendants of Edward Wanshaer Wynkoop."

History Colorado, Denver.

An Inventory of the Records of the Auraria Town Company. Collection no. 23.

George Bent Papers. MSS 54.

John H. Kehler Collection. MSS 721, FF2, 1864.

Samuel F. Tappan Collection. MSS 617.

George Bent to Tappan, March 15, 1889. Box 1, FF 9.

Scott J. Anthony Papers. MSS 14.

Correspondence, 1864. FF2.

Cramer, Jean H. "A Calendar of the Papers of Scott J. Anthony, 1830–1903: A Holding of the Library of the State Historical Society of Colorado," 1967, 3. MSS 14.

Declaration for Original Invalid Pension. FF15.

Special Orders 1863–1864. FF5.

Special Orders 1864–1865. FF6, FF7.

Silas S. Soule Papers. MSS 982.

Emma S. Soule Pension Claim. Box 1, FF 14.

Hersa A. Soule Pension Claim. Box 1, FF 14.

Military Returns. Box 1, FF 14.

Wynkoop Papers. MSS 695.

Correspondence. FF5, FF6.

Wynkoop, Edward W. "Unfinished Colorado History," 1876. MSS 2–20. (In Wynkoop's and others' handwriting.) There is also a typescript, but I did not use it.

Wynkoop, Frank Murray. "Reminiscences," 1953. FF5.

History Nebraska, Lincoln

"Nancy Jane Fletcher Morton, 1845–1912." RG3467.AM, one folder (including photos) and one roll of microfilm (16337).

"Nancy Morton's Own Story of the Plum Creek Massacre 1864." With transcript edited by Musetta Gilman and Clyde Wallace.

Lilly Library, University of Indiana, Bloomington.

Camp MSS, 1873–1918. Collection no. LMC 1167.

Walter Mason Camp interview of Ben Clark[e], Field Notes. Transcribed by Kenneth Hammer, 190–206. Box 3, Folder 11.

Walter Mason Camp interview of Edmund Guerrier, Unclassified. Transcribed by Kenneth Hammer, 217–25. Box 4, Folder 2, Envelope 3.

National Archives and Records Administration, Washington, D.C.

Edward W. Wynkoop Military File.

Edward W. Wynkoop Pension File.

"Letters Received by the Office of Indian Affairs, 1824–1881." RG75, M234, Rolls 879–80.

"Letters Sent by the Ninth Military Department, Department of New Mexico, 1849–1890."

RG48, M750, Roll 17.

RG75, M21, Roll 85.

RG94, M619, Rolls 563, 629.

RG393, M1072, Roll 3.

Oklahoma Historical Society, Oklahoma City.

Joseph B. Thoburn Collection. 86.01, Box 8, Folder 9.

Bent, George. Letters to Thoburn.

Sand Creek Massacre NHS, Eads, Colorado.

Campbell, Jeff C. "Myths & Misconceptions," paper delivered at the "Sand Creek Massacre: 150 Year Remembrance," National Museum of the American Indian, Washington, D.C., October 9, 2014.

———. "Sand Creek Massacre NHS 150th Commemoration Press Release," revised November 14, 2014.

Western History Collections, University of Oklahoma Libraries, Norman, Oklahoma.

George Armstrong Custer report, March 21, 1869, Box R-41, Packet 1, 222–23 [641–42], Carl Coke Rister Collection.

GOVERNMENT DOCUMENTS

Annual Report of the Commissioner of Indian Affairs, 1847–1848. Washington, D.C.: Wendell and Van Benthuysen, 1848. This includes an appendix.

Annual Report of the Commissioner of Indian Affairs, 1851. Washington, D.C.: Gideon, 1851.

Annual Report of the Commissioner of Indian Affairs, 1868. Washington, D.C.: Government Printing Office, 1868.

Annual Report of the Secretary of the Interior for the Year 1860, The Commissioner of Indian Affairs. Washington, D.C.: George W. Bowman, 1860.

Communication from the Secretary of War in Regard to the Number of Appointments of Brigadier and Major Generals. 38th Congress, 1st Session. Executive R. Washington, D.C.: U.S. War Dept., 1864.

Condition of the Indian Tribes. Report of the Joint Special Committee, Appointed Under Joint Resolution of March 3, 1865. With an Appendix. Washington, D.C.: Government Printing Office, 1867. (Note that this appendix, which includes "The Chivington Massacre," is huge and documents investigations into the status of other American Indian tribes in the West that are not related to the massacre.)

"Difficulties with Indian Tribes." In *Message of the President of the United States*. House of Representatives, 41st Congress, 2nd Session. Executive Document No. 240. Washington, D.C.: Government Printing Office, 1870.

Official Army Register of the Volunteer Force of the United States Army for the Years 1861, '62, '63, '64, '65. Part 8. Washington, D.C.: Adjutant General's Office, 1867.

Report on Indian Affairs by the Acting Commissioner for the Year 1867. Washington, D.C.: Government Printing Office, 1868.

Report of the Commissioner of Indian Affairs, 1859. Washington, D.C.: George W. Bowman, 1860.

Report of the Commissioner of Indian Affairs, 1860. Washington, D.C.: George W. Bowman, 1860.

Report of the Commissioner of Indian Affairs for the Year 1865. Washington, D.C.: Government Printing Office, 1865.

Report of the Commissioner of Indian Affairs for the Year 1866. Washington, D.C.: Government Printing Office, 1866.

"Report of the Commissioner of Indian Affairs." In *Message of the President of the United States, and Accompanying Documents, to the Two Houses of Congress at the Commencement of the First Session of the Thirty-ninth Congress.* Washington, D.C.: Government Printing Office, 1865.

"Report of the Secretary of the Interior." Included with the *Message of the President of the United States.* 39th Congress, 1st Session. 2 volumes. Washington, D.C.: Government Printing Office, 1865–66.

Report of the Secretary of War, Communicating, In compliance with a resolution of the Senate of February 4, 1867, a copy of the evidence taken at Denver and Fort Lyon, Colorado Territory, by a military commission, ordered to inquire into the Sand Creek massacre, November, 1864. 39th Congress, 2nd Session. Senate Executive Document No. 26, 1867. Also known as "Sand Creek Massacre."

Sand Creek Massacre Project, Volume 1: Site Location Study. Denver: National Park Service, Intermountain Region, 2000.

U.S. Congress. House. *Message from the President of the United States.* 41st Congress, 2nd Session.

———. *Report of the Joint Committee on the Conduct of the War, Massacre of Cheyenne Indians.* 38th Congress, 2nd Session. Washington, D.C.: Government Printing Office, 1865. This is frequently known as "Massacre of Cheyenne Indians."

U.S. Congress. Senate. 40th Congress, 3rd Session. Executive Document No. 13.

The War of the Rebellion: A Compilation of the Official Records of the Union and Confederate Armies. 4 series, 128 volumes. Washington, D.C.: United States War Department, 1880–1901.

BOOKS

Afton, Jean, David Fridtjof Halaas, and Andrew E. Masich, with Richard N. Ellis. *Cheyenne Dog Soldiers: A Ledgerbook History of Coups and Combat.* Denver: Colorado Historical Society and University Press of Colorado, 1997.

Alberts, Don E. *The Battle of Glorieta: Union Victory in the West.* College Station: Texas A&M University Press, 1998.

Ball, Durwood. *Army Regulars on the Western Frontier, 1848–1861.* Norman: University of Oklahoma Press, 2001.

Barnard, Sandy. *A Hoosier Quaker Goes to War: The Life & Death of Major Joel H. Elliott, 7th Cavalry.* Wake Forest, N.C.: AST Press, 2010.

Bensing, Tom. *Silas Soule: A Short, Eventful Life of Moral Courage*. Indianapolis: Dog Ear, 2012.

Berthrong, Donald J. *The Southern Cheyennes*. Norman: University of Oklahoma Press, 1963.

Brill, Charles J. *Conquest of the Southern Plains: Uncensored Narrative of the Battle of the Washita and Custer's Southern Campaign*. Oklahoma City: Golden Saga Publishers, 1938.

Broome, Jeff. *Cheyenne War: Indian Raids on the Roads to Denver, 1864–1869*. Sheridan, Colo.: Aberdeen Books, 2013.

Byers, William N., and John H. Kellom. *Hand Book of the Gold Fields of Nebraska and Kansas: Being a Complete Guide to the Gold Regions of the North and South Platte, and Cherry Creek*. New York: Derby and Jackson; Chicago: D. B. Cooke, 1859.

Carriker, Robert C., and Eleanor R. Carriker, eds. *An Army Wife on the Frontier: The Memoirs of Alice Blackwood Baldwin 1867–1877*. Salt Lake City: University of Utah, 1975.

Carroll, John M., ed. *The Benteen-Goldin Letters on Custer and His Last Battle*. New York: Liveright, 1974.

———, ed. *General Custer and the Battle of the Washita: The Federal View*. Bryan, Tex.: Guidon Press, 1978.

———. Introduction. *The Sand Creek Massacre: A Documentary History*. New York: Sol Lewis, 1973. Includes "The Chivington Massacre."

Carter, Harvey Lewis. *"Dear Old Kit": The Historical Christopher Carson*. Norman: University of Oklahoma Press, 1968.

Chalfant, William Y. *Cheyennes and Horse Soldiers: The 1857 Expedition and the Battle of Solomon's Fork*. Norman: University of Oklahoma Press, 1989.

———. *Hancock's War: Conflict on the Southern Plains*. Norman, Okla.: Arthur H. Clark, 2010.

Chandler, Lt. Col. Melbourne C. *Of Garryowen in Glory, History of the Seventh United States Cavalry*. 1981. Anndale, Va.: Turnpike Press, 1960.

Coel, Margaret. *Chief Left Hand: Southern Arapaho*. 1981. Reprint, Norman: University of Oklahoma Press, 1987.

Coffin, Morse H. *The Battle of Sand Creek*. Waco, Tex.: W. M. Morrison, 1965.

Cowell, Andrew, with Alonzo Moss Sr., William C'Hair, Wayne C'Hair, Arapahoe Immersion School, and elders of the Northern Arapaho Tribe. *Dictionary of the Arapaho Language*. 1st ed. published 1983. 4th ed., Ethete, Wyo.: Northern Arapaho Tribe, 2012.

Craig, Reginald S. *The Fighting Parson: A Biography of Col. John M. Chivington*. 1959. Reprint, Tucson: Westernlore Press, 1994.

Custer, Elizabeth Bacon. *Following the Guidon*. 1890. Reprint, Norman: University of Oklahoma Press, 1966.

Custer, George Armstrong. *My Life on the Plains or, Personal Experiences with Indians*. 1874. Reprint, Norman: University of Oklahoma Press, 1962.

Czaplewski, Russ. *Captive of the Cheyenne: The Story of Nancy Jane Morton and the Plum Creek Massacre*. Lexington, Neb.: Dawson County Historical Museum, 1993.

Danker, Donald F. Introduction and Notes. *Mollie: The Journal of Mollie Dorsey Sanford in Nebraska and Colorado Territories, 1857–1866*. Lincoln: University of Nebraska Press, 1959.

Davis, Herman S., comp. *Reminiscences of General William Larimer and of His Son William H. H. Larimer: Two of the Founders of Denver City.* Lancaster, Pa.: Press of the New Era, 1918.

Dorset, Phyllis Flanders. *The New Eldorado: The Story of Colorado's Gold and Silver Rushes.* New York: Macmillan, 1970.

Dyer, Frederick H. *A Compendium of the War of the Rebellion.* Vol. 1. Des Moines: Dyer Publishing, 1908.

Edrington, Thomas S., and John Taylor. *The Battle of Glorieta Pass: A Gettysburg in the West, March 26–28, 1862.* Albuquerque: University of New Mexico Press, 1998.

Evans, C. Wyatt. *The Legend of John Wilkes Booth: Myth, Memory, and a Mummy.* Lawrence: University of Kansas, 2004.

Frost, Lawrence A. *Custer Legends.* Bowling Green, Ohio: Bowling Green University Popular Press, 1981.

Galvin, John G., ed. *Through the Country of the Comanche Indians in the Fall of the Year 1845: The Journal of a U.S. Army Expedition by Lieutenant James W. Abert of the Topographical Engineers; Artist extraordinary whose paintings of Indians and Their Wild West illustrate this book.* San Francisco, Calif.: John Howell Books, 1970.

Garrard, Lewis H. *Wah-to-yah and the Taos Trail, or Prairie Travel and Scalp Dances, with a Look at Los Rancheros from Muleback and the Rocky Mountain Campfire.* Norman: University of Oklahoma Press, 1955.

Gerboth, Lewis H., ed. *The Tall Chief: The Autobiography of Edward W. Wynkoop.* Denver: Colorado Historical Society, 1994.

Greene, Jerome A. *Washita: The U.S. Army and the Southern Cheyennes, 1867–1869.* Norman: University of Oklahoma Press, 2004.

Greene, Jerome A., and Douglas D. Scott. *Finding Sand Creek: History, Archeology, and the 1864 Massacre Site.* Norman: University of Oklahoma Press, 2004.

Grinnell, George Bird. *The Cheyenne Indians: Their History and Ways of Life.* 2 vols. 1923. Reprint, New York: Cooper Square, 1962.

———. *The Fighting Cheyennes.* 1915. Reprint, Norman: University of Oklahoma Press, 1983.

Hafen, LeRoy R., and W. J. Ghent. *Broken Hand: The Life Story of Thomas Fitzpatrick, Chief of the Mountain Men.* Denver: Old West, 1931.

Hafen, LeRoy R., and Francis Marion Young. *Fort Laramie and the Pageant of the West, 1834–1890.* Reprint 1984. Lincoln: University of Nebraska Press, 1938.

Hafen, LeRoy R., ed. *Colorado Gold Rush: Contemporary Letters and Reports 1858–1859.* Glendale, Calif.: Arthur H. Clark, 1941.

Hafen, LeRoy R., and Ann W. Hafen, eds. *Relations with the Indians of the Plains, 1857–1861.* Glendale, Calif.: Arthur H. Clark, 1959.

———. *Reports from Colorado: The Wildman Letters 1859–1865, with other related letters and newspaper reports, 1859.* Glendale, Calif.: Arthur H. Clark, 1961.

Halaas, David Fridtjof, and Andrew E. Masich. *Halfbreed: The Remarkable True Story of George Bent Caught between the Worlds of the Indian and the White Man.* Cambridge, Mass.: Da Capo Press, 2004.

Hardorff, Richard G. *Washita Memories: Eyewitness Views of Custer's Attack on Black Kettle's Village.* Norman: University of Oklahoma Press, 2006.

Harrison, Peter. *Monahsetah: The Life of a Custer Captive.* Edited by Gary Leonard. London: English Westerners' Society, 2014.

Hatch, Thom. *Black Kettle: The Cheyenne Chief Who Sought Peace but Found War.* Hoboken, N.J.: John Wiley and Sons, 2004.

History of Colorado Biographical. 5 vols. Vol. 4. Denver: O. Linderman, 1927.

History of the Arkansas Valley, Colorado. Chicago: O. L. Baskin, Historical Publishers, 1881.

Hodge, Frederick Webb, ed. *Handbook of American Indians North of Mexico.* 2 vols. Washington, D.C.: Government Printing Office, fourth impression, September 1912.

Hoebel, E. Adamson. *The Cheyennes: Indians of the Great Plains.* New York: Holt, Rinehart and Winston, 1960.

Hoig, Stan. *The Battle of the Washita: The Sheridan-Custer Campaign of 1867–69.* Garden City, N.Y.: Doubleday, 1976.

———. *The Peace Chiefs of the Cheyennes.* Norman: University of Oklahoma Press, 1980.

———. *The Sand Creek Massacre.* Norman: University of Oklahoma Press, 1961.

———. *The Western Odyssey of John Simpson Smith.* Glendale, Calif.: Arthur H. Clark, 1974.

———. *White Man's Paper Trail: Grand Councils and Treaty-making on the Central Plains.* Boulder: University Press of Colorado, 2006.

Hollister, Ovando J. *Boldly They Rode: A History of the First Colorado Regiment of Volunteers.* Lakewood, Colo.: Golden Press, 1949.

Hutton, Paul Andrew. *Phil Sheridan and His Army.* Lincoln and London: University of Nebraska Press, 1985.

Hyde, George E. *A Life of George Bent: Written from His Letters.* Norman: University of Oklahoma Press, 1967.

Jablow, Joseph. *The Cheyenne in Plains Indian Trade Relations, 1795–1840.* 1950. Reprint, Seattle: University of Washington Press, 1966.

Jones, Douglas C. *The Treaty of Medicine Lodge: The Story of the Great Treaty Council as Told by Eyewitnesses.* Norman: University of Oklahoma Press, 1966.

Kappler, Charles J., comp. and ed. *United States Indian Affairs: Laws and Treaties.* 2 vols. Washington, D.C.: Government Printing Office, 1904.

Keefe, Brian L. *Ma'heo's Children: The Early History of the Cheyenne and Suhtaio Indians from Prehistoric Times to AD 1700.* Gloucester, United Kingdom: Choir Press, 2014.

Kelman, Ari. *A Misplaced Massacre: Struggling over the Memory of Sand Creek.* Cambridge, Mass.: Harvard University Press, 2013.

Kelsey, Harry E. *Frontier Capitalist: The Life of John Evans.* Denver: State Historical Society of Colorado and Pruett Publishing, 1969.

Kennedy, W. J. D. *On the Plains with Custer and Hancock: The Journal of Isaac Coates, Army Surgeon.* Boulder, Colo.: Johnson Books, 1997.

Kessel, Jo Ann. *Piavinnia: The Bent-Guerrier Connection.* Oklahoma City: Oklahoma Horizons Series, 2014.

King, James T. *War Eagle: A Life of General Eugene A. Carr.* Lincoln: University of Nebraska Press, 1963.

Kraft, Louis. *Custer and the Cheyenne: George Armstrong Custer's Winter Campaign on the Southern Plains.* El Segundo, Calif.: Upton and Sons, Publishers, 1995.

———. *Ned Wynkoop and the Lonely Road from Sand Creek.* Norman: University of Oklahoma Press, 2011.

Lavender, David. *Bent's Fort*. Garden City, N.Y.: Doubleday, 1954.

Leonard, Stephen J., and Thomas J. Noel. *Denver: Mining Camp to Metropolis*. Niwot: University Press of Colorado, 1990.

Llewellyn, Karl N., and E. Adamson Hoebel. *The Cheyenne Way*. Norman: University of Oklahoma Press, 1941.

McChristian, Douglas C. *Fort Laramie, Military Bastion of the High Plains*. Norman, Okla.: Arthur H. Clark, 2008.

McGinnis, Anthony. *Counting Coup and Cutting Horses*. Lincoln: University of Nebraska Press, 1990.

Memoirs of the American Anthropological Association. Volume 1, part 6. Reprint (no original date listed), New York: Kraus Reprint Corporation, 1964. Includes an index for volume 1, and James Mooney, "The Cheyenne Indians," 357–442.

Michno, Gregory F. *Battle at Sand Creek: The Military Perspective*. El Segundo, Calif.: Upton and Sons, Publishers, 2004.

Monahan, Doris. *Destination: Denver City, The South Platte Trail*. Athens, Ohio: Swallow Press, 1985.

Monnett, John H. *The Battle of Beecher Island and the Indian War of 1867–1969*. Niwot: University Press of Colorado, 1992.

Mooney, James. *Calendar History of the Kiowa Indians*. Extract from the Seventeenth Annual Report of the Bureau of American Ethnology. Washington, D.C.: Government Printing Office, 1898.

———. *In Sun's Likeness and Power: Accounts of Shield and Tipi Heraldry*. Transcribed and edited by Father Peter J. Powell. 2 vols. Lincoln: University of Nebraska Press, 2013.

Moore, John H. *The Cheyenne Nation: A Social and Demographic History*. Lincoln: University of Nebraska Press, 1987.

Perkin, Robert L. *The First Hundred Years: An Informal History of Denver and the Rocky Mountain News*. Garden City, N.Y.: Doubleday, 1959.

Portrait and Biographical Record of the State of Colorado. Chicago: Chapman, 1899.

Powell, Peter John. *People of the Sacred Mountain: A History of the Northern Cheyenne Chiefs and Warrior Societies, 1830–1879; with an Epilogue, 1969–1974*. 2 vols. San Francisco: Harper and Row, 1981.

Powell, Peter J. *Sweet Medicine*. 2 vols. 1969. Reprint, Norman: University of Oklahoma Press, 1979.

Price, Catherine. *The Oglala People, 1841–1879: A Political History*. Lincoln: University of Nebraska Press, 1996.

Prucha, Francis Paul. *The Great Father: The United States Government and the American Indians*. 2 vols. 1884. Reprint, Lincoln: University of Nebraska Press, 1986.

Rath, Ida Ellen. *The Rath Trail*. Wichita, Kans.: McCormick-Armstrong, 1961.

Richardson, Albert D. *Beyond the Mississippi: From the Great River to the Great Ocean*. Hartford, Conn.: American Publishing, 1867.

Roberts, Gary L. *Massacre at Sand Creek: How Methodists Were Involved in an American Tragedy*. Nashville: Abingdon Press, 2016.

Robinson, James M., III. *Satanta: Life and Death of a War Chief*. Austin: State House Press, 1997.

Ryder, Lyn, ed., and John G. Ellenbecker. *Tragedy at the Little Blue: The Oak Grove Massacre and the Captivity of Lucinda Eubank and Laura Roper*. Introduction, maps, photos, annotations, and references by Lyn Ryder. Rev. 2nd ed. Niwot, Colo.: Prairie Lark Publications, 1993.

Salzmann, Zdeněk, comp. *The Arapaho Indians: A Research Guide and Bibliography.* New York: Greenwood Press, 1988.

Schoberlin, Melvin. *From Candles to Footlights: A Biography of the Pike's Peak Theatre, 1859–1876.* Denver: Old West, 1941.

Schultz, Duane. *Month of the Freezing Moon: The Sand Creek Massacre, November 1864.* New York: St. Martin's Press, 1990.

Spotts, David L. *Campaigning with Custer and the Nineteenth Kansas Volunteer Cavalry on the Washita Campaign, 1868–1869.* Edited by E. A. Brininstool. 1928. Reprint, Lincoln: University of Nebraska Press, 1988.

Stanley, Henry M. *My Early Travels and Adventures in America and Asia.* 2 vols. New York: Charles Scribner's Sons, 1895.

Stiles, T. J. *Custer's Trials: A Life on the Frontier of a New America.* New York: Alfred A. Knopf, 2016.

Szasz, Margaret Connell, ed. *Between Indian and White Worlds: The Cultural Broker.* Norman: University of Oklahoma Press, 1994.

Thrapp, Dan L. *Encyclopedia of Frontier Biography.* 3 vols. Glendale, Calif.: Arthur H. Clark, 1988.

Ubbelohde, Carl, Maxine Benson, and Duane A. Smith. *A Colorado History.* 1965. 9th ed., Boulder: Pruett Publishing, 2006.

Utley, Robert M. *Frontier Regulars: The United States Army and the Indian, 1866–1890.* New York: Macmillan, 1973.

———. *The Indian Frontier of the American West 1846–1890.* 1965. Albuquerque: University of New Mexico Press, 1984.

———, ed. *Life in Custer's Cavalry: Diaries and Letters of Albert and Jennie Barnitz, 1867–1868.* New Haven: Yale University Press, 1977.

Van Vleck, George W. *The Panic of 1857: An Analytical Study.* New York: Columbia University Press, 1943.

Ware, Eugene F. *The Indian War of 1864,* with an introduction and notes by Clyde C. Walton. 1911. Reprint, New York: St. Martin's Press, 1960.

West, Elliott. *The Contested Plains: Indians, Goldseekers, and the Rush to Colorado.* Lawrence: University Press of Kansas, 1998.

Whitford, William C. *The Battle of Glorieta Pass: The Colorado Volunteers in the Civil War, March 26, 27, 28, 1862.* 1906. Reprint, Glorieta, N.Mex.: Rio Grande Press, 1971.

Whitlock, Flint. *Distant Bugles, Distant Drums: The Union Response to the Confederate Invasion of New Mexico.* Boulder: University Press of Colorado, 2006.

Zamonski, Stanley W., and Teddy Keller. *The '59ers: Roaring Denver in the Gold Rush Days.* 1961. Reprint, Denver: Stanza-Harp, 1967.

Articles and Book Chapters

Ashley, Susan Riley. "Reminiscences of Colorado in the Early 'Sixties." *Colorado Magazine* 13, no. 6 (November 1936): 219–30.

Blunt, James G. "General Blunt's Account of His Civil War Experiences." *Kansas Historical Quarterly* 1, no. 3 (May 1932): 211–65.

Broome, Jeff. "Massacre Along the Little Blue, August 7, 1864." Part One. *The Denver Westerner Roundup* 75, no. 3 (May–June 2019): 3–20.

Cannon, Helen. "First Ladies of Colorado: Josephine Evans Elbert (Governor Samuel Hitt Elbert—1873–1874)." *Colorado Magazine* 39, no. 4 (October 1962): 263–69.

Carey, Raymond G. "Another View of the Sand Creek Affair." *Roundup* 16 (February 1960): 4–15.

———. "Colonel Chivington, Brigadier General Conner, and Sand Creek." *The Westerners Denver Posse 1960 Brand Book*, vol. 16, 105–36. Boulder: Johnson Publishing, 1961.

———. "The 'Bloodless Third' Regiment, Colorado Volunteer Cavalry." *Colorado Magazine* 38, no. 4 (October 1961): 275–300.

———. "The Puzzle of Sand Creek." *Colorado Magazine* 41, no. 4 (Fall 1964): 279–98.

Chorley, E. Clowes. "The Beginnings of the Church in Colorado." *Historical Magazine of the Protestant Episcopal Church* 3, no. 2 (June 1934): 65–75.

Cobb, Frank R. "The Lawrence Party of Pike's Peakers (1858) and the Founding of St. Charles (Predecessor of Denver)." *Colorado Magazine* 10, no. 5 (September 1933): 194–97.

Cox-Paul, Lori. "John M. Chivington: The 'Reverend Colonel' 'Marry-Your-Daughter' 'Sand Creek Massacre'." *Nebraska History* 88 (2007): 126–37, 142–47.

Davis, Theodore R. "A Summer on the Plains." *Harper's New Monthly Magazine* XXXVI, no. 212 (February 1868): 292–307.

Dorsey, George A. "How the Pawnee Captured the Cheyenne Medicine Arrows." *American Anthropologist*, new series 5, no. 4 (October–December 1903): 644–58.

Filipiak, Jack D. "The Battle of Summit Springs." *Colorado Magazine* 41, no. 4 (Fall 1964): 343–54.

Flores, Dan. "Bringing Home All the Pretty Horses." *Montana: The Magazine of Western History* 58, no. 2 (Summer 2008): 3–21, 94–96.

Fowler, Loretta. "Arapaho." In *Handbook of North American Indians*, edited by William C. Sturtevant, vol. 13, part 2, *Plains*, edited by Raymond J. DeMallie, 840–62. Washington, D.C.: Smithsonian Institution, 2001.

Garfield, Marvin H. "Defense of the Kansas Frontier, 1868–1869." *Kansas Historical Quarterly* 1, no. 5 (November 1932): 451–73.

Gower, Calvin W. "Gold Fever in Kansas Territory: Migration to the Pikes Peak Gold Fields, 1858–1860." *Kansas Historical Quarterly* 39, no. 1 (Spring 1973): 58–74.

Grinnell, George Bird. "Bent's Old Fort And Its Builders." *Kansas Historical Collections*, vol. XV, 28–91. Topeka: B. P. Walker, 1923.

Hadley, James A. "The Nineteenth Kansas Cavalry and the Conquest of the Plains Indians." *Kansas Historical Collections*, vol. X, 428–56. Topeka: State Printing Office, 1908.

Hafen, LeRoy R. "When Was Bent's Fort Built?" *Colorado Magazine* 31, no. 2 (April 1954): 105–19.

Halaas, David F. "'All the Camp Was Weeping': George Bent and the Sand Creek Massacre." *Cheyenne Dog Soldiers*, 49–64. Denver: Colorado Historical Society, 1997.

Hayes, Edward M. "The Story of an Indian Campaign: Carr's Republican River Expedition of 1869." In *Eyewitnesses to the Indian Wars 1865–1890, Conquering the Southern Plains*, edited by Peter Cozzens, 407–9. Mechanicsburg, Pa.: Stackpole Books, 2003.

H. D. T. "Pioneer Journalist; or the Founder of the *Rocky Mountain News*." *Magazine of Western History Illustrated* 10 (May–October 1889): 52.

Hill, Burton S. "The Great Indian Treaty Council of 1851." *Nebraska History* 47 (1966): 85–101.

Huff, Sanford W. "Major General F. J. Herron." *The Annals of Iowa* 1867, no. 1 (1867): 801–7.

"Indian Treaties and Councils Affecting Kansas." In *Collections of the Kansas State Historical Society*, vol. XVI, 746–72. Topeka: B. P. Walker, State Printer, 1925. Note that this document is compiled from Charles J. Kappler, *Indian Affairs, Laws and Treaties*, vol. 2 (Washington, D.C., Government Printing Office, 1904) and other authentic sources.

Isern, Thomas D. "The Controversial Career of Edward W. Wynkoop." *Colorado Magazine* 56, nos. 1–2 (Winter–Spring 1979): 1–18.

Johnson, Dorothy M. "The Hanging of the Chiefs." *Montana: The Magazine of Western History* 20, no. 3 (Summer 1970): 60–69.

Kelsey, Harry. "Background to Sand Creek." *Colorado Magazine* 45, no. 4 (Fall 1968): 279–300.

Kingman, Samuel A. "The Diary of Samuel A. Kingman at Indian Treaty in 1865." *Kansas Historical Quarterly* 1, no. 5 (November 1932): 442–50.

Kraft, Louis. "Confrontation on the Sweetwater." *Wild West* 11, no. 3 (October 1998): 42–47.

———. "Ned Wynkoop & Black Kettle," *Research Review* 9, no. 2 (June 1995): 7–17.

———. "Ned Wynkoop's Lonely Walk between the Races." In *Custer and His Times*, book 5, edited by John P. Hart, 85–108. Cordova, Tenn.: Little Big Horn Associates, 2008.

———. "Wynkoop Confronts Hancock." In *Custer and His Times*, book 4, edited by John P. Hart, 38–62. LaGrange Park, Ill.: Little Big Horn Associates, 2002.

Lambert, Julia S. "Plain Tales of the Plains." Chapter 2. *The Trail* 8, no. 10 (March 1916): 5–13.

———. "Plain Tales of the Plains." Chapter 4. *The Trail* 8, no. 12 (May 1916): 5–13.

———. "Plain Tales of the Plains." Chapter 5. *The Trail* 9, no. 13 (June 1916): 16–24.

LeCompte, Janet. "Charles Autobees." *Trappers of the Far West: Sixteen Biographical Sketches*, edited by LeRoy R, Hafen, 242–58. 1965. Reprint, Lincoln: University of Nebraska Press, 1983.

———. "Charles Autobees, I." *Colorado Magazine* 34, no. 3 (July 1957): 163–79.

———. "Charles Autobees, IX." *Colorado Magazine* 35, no. 4 (October 1958): 303–8.

———. "Sand Creek." Chapter 2. *Colorado Magazine* 51, no. 4 (Fall 1964): 315–35.

Lubers, H. L. "William Bent's Family and the Indians of the Plains." *Colorado Magazine* 13, no. 1 (January 1936): 19–22.

McGaa, William. "A Statement Regarding the Formation of the St. Charles and Denver Town Companies." *Colorado Magazine* 22, no. 3 (May 1945): 125–29.

Michno, Gregory. "Cheyenne Chief Black Kettle Reassessed: General Phil Sheridan Called Him a 'Worthless Old Cipher.'" *Wild West* 18, no. 4 (December 2005): 16, 71–73.

Milavec, Pam. "Alias Emma S. Soule: Corrected Historical Fictions Surrounding Silas Soule and the Sand Creek Massacre." *The Denver Westerners Roundup* 61, no. 4 (July–August 2005): 3–22.

Moore, Ely. "The Lecompton Party Which Located Denver." In *Transactions of the Kansas State Historical Society, 1907–1908*, vol. 7, 446–52. Topeka: Morgan State Printers, 1902.

Moore, John H., Margot P. Liberty, and A. Terry Straus. "Cheyenne." In *Handbook of North American Indians*, edited by William C. Sturtevant, vol. 13, part 2 of 2, *Plains*, edited by Raymond J. DeMallie, 863–64. Washington, D.C.: Smithsonian Institution, 2001.

Moore, Milton. "An Incident on the Upper Arkansas in 1864." In *Transactions of the Kansas State Historical Society, 1901–1902*, vol. 10, 414–18. Topeka: State Printing Office, 1908.

Niderost, Eric. "The Great Sioux Uprising of 1862." *Military Heritage* 12, no. 1 (December 2010): 58–65.

Noel, Thomas J. "All Hail the Denver Pacific: Denver's First Railroad." *Colorado Magazine* (Spring 1973): 91–116.

Sherow, James E. "Workings of the Geodialectic: High Plains Indians and Their Horses in the Region of the Arkansas River Valley, 1800–1870." *Environmental History Review* 16, no. 2 (Summer 1992): 61–84. doi:10.2307/3984929.

Stanley, Henry Morton. "The Medicine Lodge Peace Council" (series of dispatches printed in the *Missouri Democrat*). *Eyewitnesses to the Indian Wars 1865–1890: Conquering the Southern Plains*, edited by Peter Cozzens, 74–126. Mechanicsburg, Pa.: Stackpole Books, 2003.

Taylor, Alfred A. "Medicine Lodge Peace Council." *Chronicles of Oklahoma* 2, no. 2 (June 1924): 98–118.

Thompson, Enid. "Life in an Adobe Castle." *Colorado Magazine* 54, no. 4 (Fall 1977): 6–27.

West, Elliott. "Called Out People: The Cheyennes and the Central Plains." *Montana: The Magazine of Western History* 48, no. 2 (Summer 1998): 2–15.

REPORTS

Report of the John Evans Study Committee. Evanston, Ill.: Northwestern University, May 2014.

Report of the John Evans Study Committee. Denver, Colo.: University of Denver, November 2014.

THESES

Roberts, Gary Leland. "Sand Creek: Tragedy and Symbol." PhD dissertation, University of Oklahoma, 1984.

Roche, William Howard. "The Territorial Governor as *Ex-Officio* Superintendent of Indian Affairs and the Decline of American-Indian Relations." MA dissertation, University of Montana, 1991.

ONLINE SOURCES

"Arapaho." *Encyclopedia of World Cultures Supplement*, Encyclopedia.com, accessed May 10, 2017. http://www.encyclopedia.com/history/united-states-and-canada/north-american-indigenous-peoples/arapaho.

"Arapaho Legends and Traditional Stories," accessed July 12, 2019. http://www.native
 -languages.org/arapaho-legends.htm.

Kelman, Ari. "A Misplaced Massacre: Struggling Over the Memory of Sand Creek."
 Presented at "The Civil War in 1864" conference, Civil War Institute, Gettysburg
 College, Pennsylvania, June 21, 2014. https://www.c-span.org/video/?319538–3/
 sand-creek-massacre&start=729.

Kraft, Louis, "Wynkoop's Last Stand." Presented at Order of the Indian Wars Symposium, Centennial, Colorado, April 20, 2013. Available on the YouTube channel
 of Louis Kraft as "Louis Kraft Speaks about Ned Wynkoop Lashing Out Against
 Murder of Cheyennes," published March 15, 2014.

Index

Abert, James, describes Owl Woman, 31

Adams, A. B., and Arapaho incident at Ohio House, 103–5

Adams, James, and Fort Lyon Sand Creek testimony, 250

Adams, Margaret: Bluff Creek council, 281; Fort Larned council, 288; Medicine Lodge peace council, translates at, 292, 296. *See also* Wilmarth, Margaret

Adriance, Jacob (Chivington friend), Methodist missionary to gold region, 92

Alderdice, Susanna, 329

Alfarita (Little Raven's daughter; Arapaho), 87

Algonquian people, early migrations, 3–5, 337n1

Anglo-Americans: Arapaho and Cheyenne cultural differences, 61, 138; one chief, 61

Antelope Skin (Cheyenne), and Eayre assault on Crow Chief's village, 130

Anthony, Scott, 131; Arapahos, meetings with, 195, 196; changed view of, 239; Cheyennes' arrival at Sand Creek, 372n47; Chivington, attack "Sioux camp" or Smoky Hill camp, 204, 224; Civil War and Glorieta campaign, 105, 110, 112; Colorado statehood vote, 145–46; Cramer, killing Sand Creek Indians, 204–5; deserves Soule's fate, 277; Fort Larned, commands, 364n15; Fort Lyon, commands, 194–95, 203; guarantees Sand Creek village safety, 196, 205, 208, 250, 267; Guerrier, interview, 233; John Smith, spy for, 201, 206; Joint Committee on the Conduct of the War testimony, 247–48; musters out of military, 247; not privy to One-Eye, 248; protects self, 240; One-Eye, spy, 247–48, 264, 382n22; "red-eyed chief," 196; replaced by Wynkoop

at Fort Lyon, 239; reports to District of the Upper Arkansas, 205; safely delivers Charley Bent to Fort Lyon, 223; Sand Creek, 209–10, 211, 212, 216–17; Soule, 200, 202, 232–33; Wynkoop, 194–96, 198, 239–40

Arapaho Indians, 24, 33, 58, 80; background of, 4–5, 8; Cheyenne name for, 23; and Cheyennes, 23, 34; Comanches, Kiowas, and Kiowa-Apaches peace, 22, 37–38; councils, 47; environment, 36; farming and turning back on lifeway, 48; Fitzpatrick, 47–49; Horse Creek peace council, 58; Hungate murders, 138–39; and Medicine Lodge peace council, 279, 296–99; migration of, 4; names of, 4, 23; raids, 139; U.S.-defined territory of in 1851, 61–62; war with Utes, 82–83, 107–8; white man, peaceful toward, 74

Arickaree Fork, Colo. Terr., battle, 310–11

Around (Cheyenne), 33–34

Ashcraft, Samuel (farmer), scouts for Jacob Downing, 131

Asher, Ambrose, 157; freed, 172; Little Blue raid, 149; Marble-Asher confusion, 172, 370–71n14; Mollie Dorsey, 193

Ashley, Eli M. (surveyor general's office), 103, 106

Ashley, Susan Riley (Eli M. Ashley's wife): description of Denver, 106–7; fear of Arapahos and Cheyennes, 107–8

a'tha (Arapaho word for white man), 14

Atkinson, Henry, and High Back Wolf meeting, 11–13

Augur, Christopher C., contradicts Henderson, 294

Autobee, Charles, 187, 213; background of, 377n55

Autobee, Mariano: background of, 377n55; Sand Creek, 213, 217

Backus, W. H., Evans friendly Indian letter, Fort Larned commander, 144–45, 364n15
Bad Wound (Sioux), at Pawnee Fork/Hancock meeting, 285
Baldwin, Alice Blackwood, and Fort Larned council, 288
Baldwin, Frank, 288
Banks, Alex, annuities, 304
Barnitz, Albert: erroneous 1868 gun distribution, 391n104; Hancock expedition comments, 284; Medicine Lodge peace council attack threat, 295; rips treaty, 300
Barroldo, Joe (mixed-blood Cheyenne), 150
Bear Feather (aka Old Bark; Cheyenne), death, 68
Bear Man (Cheyenne), 148; Sand Creek village, 202
Bear Robe (Cheyenne), Sand Creek village, 202
Bear That Goes Ahead (Sand Hill's son; Cheyenne), Saline and Solomon raid, 309
Bear Tongue (Cheyenne), Sand Creek village, 202, 280
Beckwourth, James, 87, 221
Bend of Timbers (164). See Big Timbers, Kans.
Bent, Charles (William's brother), 19–20, 41; Bent's Fort license, 28, 29; birth of, 18; death of, 46, 53; Taos revolt, 44, 45–46; Yellow Wolf, 22
Bent, Charley (aka Charles; George Bent's half-brother; mixed-blood Cheyenne), 55, 300, 365n35; background, 227, 301–2; birth of, 53, 348–49n2; Charles Rath, 147–48; choice of race, 302; cholera epidemic, 54; Confederacy, 102, 105; Davis portrait of, 390n84; death wound, 302–3, 348–49n2, 390nn85–86; Fort Lyon, 223, 377n55; and George Bent, 148, 364–65n27; Julesburg raid, 233, 235; Little Woman (wife), 303; Medicine Lodge peace council, 292, 294, 296; misidentification of, 268; Sand Creek, 213, 217; St. Louis massacre, 102; Susie Penleton (daughter), 303, 391n87; white men, view of, 267; William Bent, attempt to kill, 301, 329, 390n84
Bent, George (William's brother), death of, 53, 343n10
Bent, George (William Bent's son; mixed-blood Cheyenne), 22, 28, 29, 55, 115, 181, 213, 365n35; background of, 227; birth, 38, 40, 352–53n10; Black Kettle, 117, 158–59, 224, 289, 310; Big Timbers, 164–65, 168, 224;

Bluff Creek council, 281–82; Charley Bent, 148; choice of race, 302; cholera epidemic, 54; Civil War, 117; Confederacy, 102, 105, 115, 117 (fight another day); contribution to Cheyenne history, 334; Crows, joins revenge raid against, 127; Eugene Ware, ridicules Julesburg death count, 236; Fort Lyon, no connection with, 377n55; Guerrier, 144, 224; honors dead, 64; Howling Wolf, 224–25; Julesburg raid, 233–35, 242; Magpie Woman, marries, 392n11; Medicine Lodge peace council, 294; misidentification of, 268; raids, 144, 148; Republican River village, 227; Saline and Solomon raid, 307–8, 309; Sand Creek village, 202, 206, 210–11, 220–21; saves day, 298; St. Louis massacre, 102; sworn statement, 40; translates at, 292, 296; white men, view of, 267; William Bent, 117, 144, 225, 364n12; Wynkoop, 168, 289, 300, 309, 333; Yellow Woman, 40
Bent, Julia (wife of Edmund Guerrier; mixed-blood Cheyenne): birth, 40, 55, 346–47n28, 392n11; Black Kettle, 309, 310; Charley Bent attempt to kill father, 301, 390n84; hatred of whites, 346–47n28; Island, 54; Guerrier, 144; marries in 1875, 375–76n35; Sand Creek, sworn statement, 40; village, 210
Bent, Maria Ignacia Jaramillo (Charles Bent's wife), 45–46
Bent, Mary (George Bent's sister; mixed-blood Cheyenne), 54–55, 348–49n2
Bent, Robert (George Bent's brother; mixed-blood Cheyenne), 54, 55, 80, 117, 196, 217, 348–49n2, 377n53; Fort Wise peace council, 95; George Bent, 177
Bent, Robert (William's brother), death, 53, 344n10
Bent, William, 38, 41, 43, 44, 117, 180, 182, 217, 247, 352–53n10; background of, 18; Bent's Fort, 28, 53, 54, 55, 343–44nn8–9, 347–48n48; Bent's Ranch, flees, 162; Big Timbers on Arkansas, moves to, 55; birth of, 18; birth of children, 38, 40; Charley Bent attempt to kill, 301, 329; cholera epidemic, 54, 349n9; death of, 329; Dog Men, remain in North, 279; Evans friendly Indian letter, 143–45, 157, 160; Fitzpatrick, interprets for, 60; George Bent, 144, 225, 364n12; gold, fear of, 23, 75; Indian agent, 75, 80, 84–85, 86; Indians, become farmers, 75, 85, 329; Indians, starvation, 87; Island, 40; Little Arkansas peace council, 268, 269, 270, 272–73, 275; names of, 22; Owl Woman, 31–32,

38, 40; southern tribes, peace, 261, 263; St. Vrain, buys out, 54; white encroachment on Indian land, 86–87; Yellow Wolf, 20, 22, 55; Yellow Woman, 40, 54

Benteen, Frederic: Custer, comments on, 318; Mo-nahs-e-tah–Custer relationship, 393n136

Bent's Fort, Colo. Terr., 22, 40, 43, 46–47, 53; Bent's Old Fort, 55; cholera epidemic, 349n9; completed, 28, 47; description of, 41, 347–48n48; destruction of, 55; illegal trade, 28; obtains license, 28; offered to military, 54

Bent's New Fort. See Fort Lyon, Colo. Terr.

Bent's Old Fort. See Bent's Fort, Colo. Terr.

Bent's Ranch, Colo. Terr., 117

Berenger, Tom (Last of the Dogmen), 336

Big Crow (Cheyenne), Camp Rankin/Julesburg raid, 234–35

Big Eagle (Pawnee), 24, 27, 344n17

Big Head (Cheyenne): Bluff Creek council, 280–82; Sweetwater village, 325

Big Head (d. 1853; Cheyenne), 63–65

Big Jake (Cheyenne), 66; annuities, 304, 305; Washita village, 312

Big Mouth (Arapaho), 164, 191; annuities, 304; Bluff Creek council, 280–82; daughter, 320; Fort Wise peace council, 95; Hazen meeting, 312–14, 393n123; whiskey, 304

Big Sandy (soon known as Sand Creek), Colo. Terr., 196, 207

Big Timbers, Colo. Terr., 117, 143; Bent flees, 162; Bent relocates to, 55; Bent wants troops in, 86; trading stockade at, 66

Big Timbers, Kans., 181; Wynkoop–Cheyenne–Arapaho council at, 163–64

Big Wolf (Cheyenne), 164

Black Foot (Oglala Sioux), 256–57

Black Hawk (Black Kettle's father; Cheyenne), 9

Black Hawk (aka Stone Chief; Black Kettle's brother; Cheyenne), 9

Black Hawk Daily Mining Journal, and Cheyenne war, 132

Black Kettle (Cheyenne), 117, 121, 153, 163, 173, 175, 194, 200, 219, 248, 258, 267, 268, 322, 323, 333; 1854 raid, 66–67, 348n56; annuities, 304, 305, 306; arrival at Sand Creek, 372n47; attempts to stop fighting, 132–33; background of, 14, 16; Big Timbers council, 164–70, 171; birth, 9, 339–40n26, 395n149; Bluff Creek council, 280–82; and Byers, 236, 267–68; Camp Weld council, 180–84, 186, 190, 192, 371n19; council of forty-four, head chief of six, 97; death of, 314–15; 1848 raid, 50–52, 348n56; Evans

friendly Indian letter, 144, 157; false death of, 225, 228; Fitzpatrick, 272; Fort Larned council, 288; Fort Lyon meeting, 196; Fort Wise peace council, 95–97; George Bent, 289, 309, 359n40; Gray Head, 292; Greenwood 1860 treaty agenda to remove from buffalo land, 93–94, 95; Guerrier 309; Harney, 14, 276; Hazen meeting, 312–14, 393nn123–24; honors dead, 64; John Smith, 268; Julesburg, not present/outsider to tribe, 234; letters to end war, 158, 173; Little Arkansas peace council, 268–70, 272–75; Little Rock, move south, 309–10; Little Sage Woman, 16, 50–52, 62; Mahwissa (not sister), 317, 393n128; Medicine Lodge peace council, 292, 293–94, 295–96, 297–98, 299; Medicine Woman Later, passes, 63; names of, 9; peace, 194; Sacred Arrows, 63, 289; Sand Creek village, 196–97, 202, 204, 208–11, 220, 224, 247; Saline raid and move south, 309; Stone Forehead, cousin, 63; Tall Bull threat, 292; tribal outsider, 234; village after Sand Creek, 224; villages attacked, 132; white invasion threat, 138; war proponent, 313–14; Washita village, 312; William Bent, wants as trader or agent, 272, 274; Wind Woman (sister), 64; Wuh'tapiu, chief of, 68; and Wynkoop, 161–62, 274, 276, 289, 309, 258, 267

Blake, Henry, Third Colorado Volunteer Cavalry, 156

Bluff Creek villages, Kans.: Cheyenne–Arapaho–Wynkoop councils, 280–82; cholera, 54

Blunt, James G., 147, 175, 369n4; Henning as temporary replacement, 200

Boone, Albert, 106, 120, 369n10; Bents, longtime friend, 105; Boone–Left Hand and Little Raven meetings, 356n18; Byers, fake Indian war, 98; Fort Wise peace council, 95, 97; Little Raven–Poisal meeting, 99–101; slavery, 105

Booneville, Colo. Terr., 177

Booth, Henry, and Sand Creek massacre site, 232

Booth, John Wilkes, assassinates President Lincoln, 251

Bosse (Arapaho), 173

Bowen, Leavitt, 229; Sand Creek murder, 231; death, 249

Bowstring warrior society (Cheyenne), 32–33, 37–38

Bright, Emma S., fraudulent widow's claim, 383n40

Brown, George Center (reporter), and Medicine Lodge peace council, fearful of being killed, 289

Browning, O. H. (secretary of the interior), and 1867 treaty, no weapons, 305

Brûlé Sioux (Lakota) Indians, 60, 139, 224, 234; Julesburg raid, 234

Buchanan, James, appoints William Bent Indian agent, 80

buffalo, 17, 80, 182, 296, 300; decrease in numbers, 47, 85, 283, 293, 304; name of, 11; whites kill for sport, 289

Buffalo Chief (Cheyenne), and Medicine Lodge peace council, 296, 297–301

Bull (Arapaho chief), 37

Bull (Cheyenne), loss of Sacred Arrows, 26–27

Bull Bear (Cheyenne), 133, 153, 219, 268; Big Timbers council, 164, 166, 167–69, 173; Bluff Creek council, 280–82; Camp Weld council, 180, 181, 183–84, 189–90, 192; Cheyenne–Sioux battle line, 285; Dog Men band raid, 152; 1869 reservation, 333; Evans friendly Indian letter, 157; Fort Larned council, 283; Fort Wise peace council, did not attend, 95–96; Hancock expedition, 284; Medicine Lodge peace council, 296, 298, 299, 300; Republican River village, 227; tipi, Hancock trophy, 288; white men, view of, 267

Bull Hump (Comanche), 38; tracks Yellow Wolf, 20

Bull-Telling-Tales (Dog Man), 126–29

Bunch of Timbers, Kans., 224. See also Big Timbers, Kans.

Butterfield, J. L. (trader), nervous in Cheyenne and Arapaho villages, 304

Butterfield Overland Dispatch, Kans., Cheyennes and Arapahos raiding, 279

Byers, Elizabeth Minerva Sumner (wife), 79; background of, 67; bias of, 87, 88, 89–90; birth, 67; Denver flood, 134–36, 137; dinner party, 87; on Indians, 83, 88; Ladies Union Aid Society, 90; on "Negroes," 89; trip to Denver, 83–84; and William Byers, 67–68, 88

Byers, William Newton, 89–90, 153, 229, 280; attacks whiskey sales, 101, 102–3; Adams's Ohio House Arapaho incident, 104; background of, 67, 84; birth, 67; and Black Kettle, 236, 267–68; Bloodless Third, 174; Boone–Little Raven–Poisal meeting, 99–101; Camp Weld council, end

of war, 191–92; Cheyenne war, 132, 162; Chivington, relationship with, 136, 141, 228, 278; Colorado statehood, 145, 173–74; debunks Downing battle date, 132, 361n28; demands repetition of Sand Creek fight, 278; Denver/Colorado vision, 278; Denver flood, 134–36, 137; despot of Colorado, 276; Elbert, prints plea for more troops, 238; Elizabeth Byers, 67–68, 90; and Evans, 136, 141, 162, 178, 199, 267–68; fake Indian war, unbiased reporting of, 98; "Fort Lyon affair," 230; gold region and book, 76–80; Hollister, 145, 146–47, 178; Isabelle Eubanks death, 248–49; life at risk, 88–89, 107, 277; *Rocky Mountain News* as weapon, 83, 88, 97, 277, 333; Sand Creek, 230–31, 278; Soule, deserves fate, 277; Steck, 277; Third Colorado Volunteer enlistment, 156, 174; views and goals for Denver, 88–89; weekly *Rocky Mountain News*, all Sand Creek details for sale, 237; White Antelope, ridicules, 236; Winchester, *Rocky Mountain News*, failure to pay for, 88–89; and Wynkoop, 77, 78, 130–31, 192, 300

Camp Rankin, Colo. Terr.: included in Julesburg raids, 234–36, 241–42; revenge target, 233

Canby, Edward, 114, 115

Cannon, James, 197, 205; Fort Lyon, Sand Creek affidavits, 240

Captain Foy, Sand Creek trophies for sale, 238

Carleton, James, 154; questions Leavenworth's Indian knowledge, 261

Carr, Eugene A., hunts Tall Bull, 329–30

Carson, Christopher H. (Kit), 45, 87, 147, 268, 269; southern tribes, peace, 261, 263

Carson, Josefa Jaramillo (wife), 45

Case, Francis M. (surveyor), arrives in Denver with Governor Gilpin, 103

Cheyenne council of forty-four, 10–11, 34, 50, 61; six head chiefs, 97

Cheyenne Indians, 29, 30, 58, 80, 139; Arapahos, relationship with, 23; background of, 5–8, 10; chief's control, 166; cholera epidemic, 54–55; council chiefs, 61; councils, 47; customs and dress, 42–44; description of, 61; 1851 U.S.-defined territory of, 61–62; environment, 36; farming and turning back on lifeway, 48–49; Fitzpatrick, 47–49; migrations, 17–18; names of, 5, 7; Pawnees, 23–27, 62–64; peace with Comanches, Kiowas, and Kiowa-Apaches, 37–38; Platte

River Road raids, 153–54; relationship with Arapahos, 23; raids, 68, 148; Sand Creek, 204; trade, 18; war with Utes, 107–8. *See also* Algonquian people, early migrations

Child, Lydia Maria, on Medicine Lodge Peace Treaty, 300–301

Chivington, John Milton, 129, 136, 153, 154, 247, 250, 254–55, 279, 280, 321 326, 334; Anthony, 239, 253; attacks "Sioux camp" or Smoky Hill camp, 204, 224; background and description, 91–92; Bloodless Third, 174; brigadier generalship, 115–17, 119, 124–25; Byers, 136, 141, 228, 276; Camp Weld council, 180, 184, 186, 190, 192; Cheyennes, view of, 137–38; children and grandchildren of, 91, 332; Civil War and Glorieta campaigns, 105, 109–15, 358n13; Colorado Sand Creek inquiry, 238, 241, 243–45, 246; Cramer, protest of, 205–6; Curtis, Cheyenne war, 175, 178, 191; Denver, trip to, 92; Denver flood, 135; Downing, 230, 238; Evans, relationship with, 92, 118, 124–25, 136, 141; First Colorado enlistment expired, 208; Fort Lyon, arrival, 203, 204, 205, 204; General Field Order No. 2, 204; Governor Gilpin, praises, 103; "Indian fighter" image, 226; "I stand by Sand Creek," 335–36, 397n184; Joint Committee on the Conduct of the War, unpublished report, condemnation of, 264–66; marries daughter-in-law, 332; Methodist Episcopal Church, 332–33; military, musters out, 238; One-Eye safe conduct pass, 159; politics, 145, 146, 173, 175, 276, 278; popularity of, 276; praise of, 232; re-creates self, 279; Sand Creek, 202, 206–9, 212–13, 216, 217, 231; Samuel Colley, 253; Shoup, 177; Soule, 202, 253–54; Stanton, 116; Tappan conflict, 114–15, 118–19, 244; teamster, 282; Third Colorado Volunteer Cavalry enlistment, 156–57, 175; views of slavery, 91, 103, 109; written testimony, Cramer missing, 253; and Wynkoop, changing relationship, 137–38, 145, 147, 184, 192, 193, 228, 240, 246, 249–50, 259, 291, 384n59

Chivington, Martha Rollason (wife), 91; death of, 332

Chivington, Thomas (son), 282; death of, 332

Civil War, 97

Clarke, Ben: background of, 339n24; correct spelling of last name, 373n10; Washita village attack, 316–17, 393n127

Clarke, R. Watson (R. W.): Fort Lyon, Sand Creek affidavits, 240; name misspelled, 375n32; Sand Creek village, 201, 209–10

Coal Creek, Colo. Terr., Cheyennes attack (10 miles from Denver), 139

Coberly, Sarah (Hersa Coberly Soule's mother), 250

Coffin, Morse, Sand Creek village, 223

Colfax, Schuyler, Evans approaches, 263

Colley, Dexter (son), 106, 177, 178, 180; John Smith partnership, 201; joins father at Fort Lyon, 117–18; One-Eye, 159

Colley, Samuel, 196, 197, 253; background of, 106; Black Kettle letter to end war, 158; congressional Joint Special Committee, 246; Evans, 126, 192; Fort Lyon, Sand Creek affidavits, 240; friendly Indian letter, 142, 143; Indian scam, 117–18; Joint Committee on the Conduct of the War, 247; Little Raven, reveals location of, 223; One-Eye, 159; Sand Creek letter, exposes Little Raven's location, 223; Southern Cheyennes, fearful of Sioux war, 126; Talbot false testimony, 254–56; Washington, D.C., trip, 120–21

Colorado (Ute), Evans places killers of his brother on trial, 262–63

Colorado Territory, created, 95

Colyer, Vincent, 395n148; background of, 326; Little Raven–Grierson meeting, 326–29

Comanche Indians, 22, 33–36, 58, 65, 87, 144; Evans friendly Indian letter, 142; Medicine Lodge peace council, 292–93; new reservation, 293; peace with Cheyennes and Arapahos, 37–38; raids of, 148; Washita village, 312

Combs, James M., Left Hand's health, 196–97

Commonwealth, June 1864 raids, 140

congressional Joint Special Committee on condition of Indian tribes, 246; Washington, D.C., testimony, 246

Cook, Samuel H., 110

Cooke, W. W., 324

Cooley, Dennis N. (commissioner of Indian affairs), 279, 282

Cooper, Peter, 321; Wynkoop, recommends, 322

Cooper Institute, New York City, 333, 395nn148–49; Wynkoop speech, 321–22

Coridoro, Charles, and Charley Bent confrontation, 302–3

Cossitt, Chauncey (C. M.), 195; Fort Lyon, Sand Creek affidavits, 240; Sand Creek testimony, 250

Council Grove, Kans. Terr., Dog Man raid on Kaws, 305

Cramer, Joseph, 177, 180, 192, 196; Anthony, killing Sand Creek Indians, 204–5; Big Timbers council, 163, 165, 170; Chivington, missing from written statement, 253; Denver, 241; Fort Lyon, 240, 373n6; Henning, 200; musters out of service, 383n32; protest to, 205–6; Sand Creek, 209–10, 212, 228; Sand Creek, meeting, 205; Soule, 228; Wynkoop, endorses, 197–99

Cree, Theodore, musters out of Third Colorado, 230

Cree Indians, 5

Crocker, Jennie Lund (mixed-blood Cheyenne), 321, 394n146

Crocker, Mrs. (full-blood Cheyenne), 321; Cheyenne names of listed in 1865 peace treaty ("Ne-sou-hoe or Are-you-there"), 394n147; husband, Lieutenant Crocker, 394n146

Crow Chief (Cheyenne), village destroyed by Eayre, 130

Crow Indians, Northern Cheyennes, revenge raid, 126; horse thieves, 58

Curly Hair (Cheyenne), Medicine Lodge peace council, 296, 299

Curtis, Dick, Arapaho interpreter, 286

Curtis, Samuel Evans, 142, 154–55, 203; Chivington, 175, 178, 179, 192; Colorado investigation of, 238–39; and first Julesburg raid, 236; investigation of Sand Creek actions, 238–39; Left Hand, 219; Wynkoop, 192, 219

Custer, George Armstrong, 260; Chivington, 326; commands of, crave blood, 319; Hazen report/Kiowas, 319–20; Little Raven, 323; Little Robe, 324–26; Mo-nahs-e-tah, 317–19, 393n136; names of, 318; Pawnee Fork battle line and village, 284–85, 287; peaceful intentions, 318–19; pursues Cheyennes, reports of, 287; rape of Cheyenne women, 318; Schreyvogel's painting Custer's Demand, 394n139; Sheridan, 318–19; Stone Forehead–Sweetwater confrontation, 323–26, 395n155; Washita village, 314–17, 320–21, 393n126, 393n131

Cut Nose (Kiowa-Apache), annuities, 305

Dark (Cheyenne), sacred prayers fail to stop saber charge, 69, 71

Darlington, Brinton, Southern Cheyenne–Arapaho agent, 331

Darlington Agency, Southern Cheyenne–Arapaho Reservation, Ind. Terr., 333

Davis, Theodore (artist and writer), 301, 390n84

Denver, Colo. Terr.: Cheyenne–Arapaho arrival to speak with Evans, 180; Civil War, anger and armed men, 97, 103, 106; fear of Indian uprising, 141; First Colorado Volunteers, 105; flood, 134–36; Hungate bodies create panic, 140–41, 153; parade with Ute scalps, 107; Sand Creek hearings, 241, 243–46, 251, 254, 256; Third Colorado victory parade, 229

Denver City. See Denver, Colo. Terr.

Denver City Town Company, Larimer-Smith-Wynkoop group threatens St. Charles Town Company, 74

District of Colorado, Colo. Terr., 137, 156; Fort Lyon moved to District of the Upper Arkansas, 147

District of the Upper Arkansas, created, and Fort Lyon moved to, 147

Division of the Missouri, Sheridan commands, 304

Dodge, Grenville M., 258, 259, 263

Dog Man Plenty (Cheyenne-Sioux), 330–31

Dog Men (Cheyenne warrior society), 37–38, 130, 139, 143; Arickaree Fork, 310–11; Black Kettle, abducted, 293–94; Bluff Creek council, 280–82; central division within tribe, 35, 71; Dog Soldiers term, 33, 346n6; Dunn fight, 127–29; Fort Larned councils, 283–84, 288; Frémont's Orchard incident, 126–29; Hancock expedition, 285; Julesburg raid, 234–36; Medicine Lodge Creek peace council, 291–99; mixed-blood background, 33; passing of wives for dog ropes, 62–63, 250n29; raids, 139, 307–8; remain in North, 279; Summit Springs, 330–31; war parties and raids, 139, 302–3, 305

Dole, William P., 106, 119, 258, 261

Doolittle, James Rood: Chivington, view of, 558; Harlan, 258; Indian campaign cost estimate, 258; Joint Special Committee/Sand Creek, chairs, 246; southern tribes, peace council, 258, 261, 263; travels to West, 248, 257; Wynkoop, 282, 259

Downing, Jacob, 110, 244, 254, 334, 361n22; background of, 361n21; Chivington, 230, 238; Chivington–Cramer meeting, 205; destroys Southern Cheyenne village, 131–32, 361n28; First Colorado enlistment expired, 208; Third Colorado, musters out, 230, 238

Dull Knife (Cheyenne), 324–25

Dunn, Clark, 127–29

Eagle Feather (Kiowa), 38

Eagle Head (Cheyenne), 159, 163, 170; Sand Creek village, 202

Eayre, George S., 126; attacks Black Kettle and Lean Bear's village, 132–33; destroys two Southern Cheyenne villages, 130

Elbert, Samuel H., 200; marries Josephine Evans, 260; plea for troops, 237–38

Elliott, Joel: creates chasm within Seventh, 394n137; death of, 317, 319

Eubanks, Dora: and Little Blue raid, 149–50; not scalped, 365n30

Eubanks, Isabelle: death of, 248; freed, 173; Little Blue raid, 149–50; Mollie Sanford and condition of, 193; separated from Lucinda, 259

Eubanks, Lucinda: Big Timbers council, not present at, 166, 258; freed from captivity, 256–57; Isabelle, separated from, 157, 259; Laura Roper, separated from, 157, 367–68n21; Little Blue raid, 148–50, 153; Nancy Morton, 166, 260, 368n22; sworn statement, 259

Eubanks, William, Jr., Little Blue raid, 148–49

Eubanks, William, Sr.: Little Blue raid, 149; not scalped, 365n30

Eubanks, William J. (Willie), 157; Big Timbers council, not present, 166; changes last name, 365n29; freed from captivity, 256–57; Little Blue raid, 149–50

Eubanks family: members killed, 149; spelling of last name, 365n29

Evans, Hannah (wife), 40, 56, 135

Evans, John, 135, 153, 346n27; attacks Indians proclamation, 155; background of, 40; Bloodless Third, 174; Byers, 136, 141 178, 199; Camp Weld council, 173, 180, 182–90, 192; Chivington, relationship with, 92, 118, 124–25, 136, 141; Colorado politics, 146, 147, 173; congressional Joint Special Committee, 246; Curtis, 142, 154–55; death of children, 40, 53, 332; executive order to organize, 139–40; few June 1864 Indian raids, 139; friendly Indian letter, 142, 143; future after Denver, 332; Indian delegation to Washington, D.C., 119–20, 237–38; Joint Committee on the Conduct of the War, 247, 248, 264–65, 266; Josephine, 56–57, 162; plea for military help, 154, 155; proclamation of thanks, 199; railroads, 117, 265; resignation, 262, 263, 264; Sand Creek, not associated with, 262; second territorial governor of Colorado, 111, 114; Sioux war, 126; Utes, 140, 178, 262–63;

Washington, D.C., 199; Wynkoop, 175, 178, 180

Evans, Josephine (daughter): birth of, 40; death of, 332; father's muse, 56–57; horse incident, 162; marries Elbert, 260; memorial chapel in Denver, 332

Evans, Margaret Gray (wife), 135–36

extermination cry, 141

Fat Bear (Cheyenne), Sweetwater village, 325

Fayel, William (*Missouri Republican* reporter), Gray Head–Tall Bull–Wynkoop, 292

Feathered Shin (Cheyenne), and 1848 Black Kettle raid, 50, 52

Fire Heart (Blackfoot Sioux), hang Indian agents, 262

First Colorado Volunteer Cavalry, 203, 229; Sand Creek village, 207–13, 216–18, 221–23

Fisher, George W., performs first Methodist services in gold region, 92

Fitzpatrick, Andrew Jackson (Jack) (son; mixed-blood Arapaho): background of, 394n144; Washita death count, 321

Fitzpatrick, Thomas, 46, 272; Arapahos, opinion of, 49; councils, 47–48, 60; death, 75; Horse Creek peace council, 61; John Smith interprets for, 47–48; Platte River forts undermanned, 57; proposes "great" council, 58

Fletcher, John (Nancy Morton's cousin), and Plum Creek raid, 151–52

Fletcher, William (Nancy Morton's brother), and Plum Creek raid, 151–52

Fontaine Qui Bouille, 22, 110

"Fool, The" (Cheyenne contrary), 170; definition of contraries, 161

Forbes, B. N., 166–67

Ford, James H., 112, 147–48, 227, 259; sworn statement and launch of Indian campaign, 258; Wynkoop to investigate Chivington, 232

Foster, Lafayette S.: and Joint Special Committee/Sand Creek committee, 246; travels to West, 248, 257, 259

Forsyth, George, Arickaree Fork, 310–12

Fort Laramie, Nebr. Terr.: and Evans's friendly letter to Indians, 142; Lucinda Eubanks brought to after rescue, 256–57; moves to Horse Creek, 61; site for 1851 peace council, 60; U.S. buys trading post, 58

Fort Laramie peace council, Nebr. Terr., 58, 60; moves to Horse Creek, 61. *See also* Horse Creek peace council, Nebr. Terr.

Fort Larned, Kans.: Cheyenne–Arapaho council, 288; Hancock–Dog Men–Tall Bull council, 283–84; Left Hand shot at, 143; Satanta raids horse herd, 143; summer 1864 commanders, 364n15; William Bent translates Evans's friendly Indians letter, 143–44

Fort Lyon, Colo. Terr., 117; access to from north, 374n17; Chivington seals off, 204; fortified in case of attack, 240; "Fort Lyon affair," 232; name change from Fort Wise, 117–18; Sand Creek affidavits obtained (January 1865), 240; Sand Creek inquiry, 246, 249–50

Fort Wise peace council, 95–97

Fountain Creek. See Fontaine Qui Bouille

Frémont, John C., 40

Frémont's Orchard, Colo. Terr., 127, 128, 187

French, Adnah, 73

Frog (Cheyenne), and 1848 Black Kettle raid, 50, 52

Garrard, Lewis Hector, 76; background of, 40–41; Cheyennes, description of, 43; and John Smith, 41–46; William Bent, 41, 44, 46

Georgia Company, Byers-Kellom book reveals gold region dollar earnings, 78

Gentle Horse (Cheyenne; Black Kettle's brother), 9, 344n17

Gerry (sometimes spelled "Geary"), Elbridge, 127–30, 131, 188

Gilpin, William (first territorial governor of Colorado), 97, 103, 105, 111, 114

gold region, Colo. Terr., 73–74, 76–80, 92

Goldrick, O. J., overly dramatic prose details flood demise of Rocky Mountain News, 362nn40–42

Good, William H., Methodist missionary in gold region, 92

Gordon, G. M., Bluff Creek council, 280, 282

Grant, Ulysses S., 263, 322, 326

Grass Woman (Little Raven's daughter or granddaughter; Arapaho), 297

Gray Head (Cheyenne): and Black Kettle, 292, 293–94; Cheyenne–Sioux battle line, 285; Fort Larned council, 283; Medicine Lodge peace council, 291–92, 293, 296, 299293; testimony and raped girl, 295

Gregory, John H., gold discovery, 79

Greenwood, Alfred Burton, Southern Cheyennes–Arapahos, 1860 treaty agenda to remove from buffalo land, 93–95

Grierson, Benjamin, Little Raven final surrender, 326–29

Guerrier, Edmund, 181; Anthony interview, 233; background of, 144, 257–58; Big Timbers village after Sand Creek, 224; and Black Kettle, 158–59, 309, 310; Cheyenne–Sioux battle line, 285; George Bent, 144; Julia Bent, 144, 309, 375–76n35; Little Rock, 144, 309; Saline and Solomon raid, 307–8, 391n105; Sand Creek village, 206, 208–9, 212–13, 224; and Wynkoop, 162, 283–84, 309

Guerrier, Julia (Edmund Guerrier's sister), 375–76n35

Hall, S. F. (reporter), Medicine Lodge peace council, fearful of being killed, 289

Halleck, Henry Wager, investigates Chivington's Sand Creek actions, 238, 381n61

Hancock, Winfield Scott, 321; Cheyenne–Sioux battle line, 285, 295; 1867 expedition, 283, 296; Fort Larned council and threats of, 283–84; Indians, ignorance of, 288; and Pawnee Fork village, 287–88; tipi trophies, 288; and Wynkoop, 284, 285, 287

Hancock's war, cost of, 288

Hankler, Ivan (Cheyenne), 176

Hardin, George, 167, 246; cashiered out of service, 381n13; drunk at September 10 Cheyenne–Arapaho council, 246; resigns commission, 205

Harlan, James (senator, secretary of the interior), 111, 279; and Doolittle, 258; Evans, 263; Wynkoop, 279

Harney, William S., 12; Black Kettle (Make-tava-tah), 14, 276; Little Arkansas peace council, 268; Medicine Lodge peace council, 291; William Sumner, negative comments on, 71

Harrison, Charlie, Criterion Saloon Confederate "unofficial headquarters," 103

Hawk (Little Rock's son; Cheyenne), Sand Creek village, 211

Hazen, William: and Black Kettle–Big Mouth meeting, 312–14; friendly Indian report, 319–20; Indian military district, 307

Head Fox (Cheyenne), and 1853 Mexico raid, 65

Heap of Birds (Cheyenne), and Medicine Lodge peace council, 299

Heap of Buffalo (Arapaho), 173

Heeaweea (Little Raven's daughter, Arapaho), 87

Henderson, John B.: buffalo and promise to hunt, 296, 298, 299, 300, 305; Little Robe confrontation, 294; and Medicine Lodge peace council, 292–93, 299; Sherman confirms, 299

Henning, Benjamin. S., 200; Curtis, dispose of Wynkoop, 218–19; operates with outdated information, 226–27

Herron, Francis, 385n9, 263

Hershey, Barbara (*Last of the Dogmen*), 336

High Backed Wolf (Cheyenne), 37–38; not related to High Back Wolf, 346n22

High Back Wolf (Cheyenne), 10–11, 21, 27, 345n18, 395n149; Atkinson meeting, 12–14; death of, 28–30, 345nn25–26; names of, 12, 14

Hill, R. A., and Fort Lyon, Sand Creek affidavits, 240

Hinono'ei Indians. *See* Arapaho Indians

Hollister, Ovando J., 177; anti–Colorado statehood, 145; election fraud, 178; fake Indian war, 147; Soule murder, 252–53

Horse Creek peace council, Nebr. Terr., 61

horses, 7, 17, 36

Howland, George W. (Third U.S. Cavalry), and Glorieta campaign, 109, 110

Howling Wolf (Cheyenne), travels with George Bent, 224–25

Hudnut, William M., and first Julesburg raid, 235–36

Hungate family, 153, 208; background and death of, 138–39, 140, 187; Denver panic, 141, 153

Hunt, A. C., and Joint Committee on the Conduct of the War, 247, 248

Ice (Cheyenne), sacred prayers fail to stop saber charge, 69–70

Indian agents, accusations against, 261

Interior Department/War Department: Indian control infighting, 308

Iron Shirt (Kiowa-Apache), annuities, 305

Island (William Bent's wife; White Thunder's daughter; Cheyenne), 53, 55; Julia Bent, 54; marries William Bent, 40

Is'siwun. *See* Sacred Buffalo Hat

Jackman and Irwin (government freighters), 126

Jacobs, Edward A., and Colorado Sand Creek inquiry committee, 241

James, Amos, and Fort Lyon Sand Creek testimony, 250

Jefferson House, Auraria, Kans. Terr., outraged Elizabeth Byers exited ball, 89

Jicarilla Apache Indians, background of, 50–51; Black Kettle raid, 51–52, 348n56

Johnson, Andrew, 258, 264, 270; Evans, resignation as governor, 262, 263, 264; and Wynkoop, 282, 283

Johnson, Jay, Soule, informs on, 205

Johnson's Ranch, N.Mex. Terr., 110, 111; Chivington's Glorieta victory, 112–13

Joint Committee on the Conduct of the War (Washington, D.C.), and Sand Creek investigation, 238, 247–48, 262, 263, 264, 267–68

Jones, Jack. *See* McGaa, William

Julesburg, Colo. Terr.: description of, 234; raided, 234–36, 241, 243; revenge target, 233

Kansa Indians. *See* Kaw Indians

Kansas, statehood, 95

Kansas Pacific Railway (formerly Union Pacific Railway, Eastern Division), 329

Kaw Indians: Arapaho horse herd, 302; Dog Man–Charley Bent reprisal, 302; Dog Man raid, 305

Kearny, Stephen Watts, 41

Kehler, John H. (Episcopal minister), 90

Kellom, John, K., gold region and book, 76–79

Kicking Bird (Kiowa): in Schreyvogel's *Custer's Demand* painting but not at Custer-Kiowa meeting, 394n139; Washita village, 312

kinship, 14, 60, 341–42n44, 392n111

Kiowa-Apache Indians, 33, 35, 37, 50, 58, 144; annuities, 306–7; Washita village, 312; Wynkoop's wards, 293

Kiowa Indians, 22, 33–36, 50, 58, 64–65, 87, 144, 202, 316, 318–19; cholera epidemic, 54–55; Evans friendly Indian letter, 142; Medicine Lodge peace council, 292–93; peace with Cheyennes and Arapahos, 37–38; raids, 68–69, 148

Lakota Indians. *See* Sioux Indians

Lambert, Julia, misquotes Laura Roper, 177, 369n7

Lame Medicine Man (Keeper of the Sacred Arrows; Cheyenne), 55–56

Larimer, William, 73–74

Last of the Dogmen, 336

Leading Bear (Kiowa-Apache), 38

Lean Bear (Bull Bear's brother; Cheyenne), 16; and council of forty-four chiefs, 68, 97; death of, 132, 133, 189–90, 313; Fort Wise peace council, 95, 97; names of, 59; officer's wife incident, 58–59; Washington, D.C., trip, 120–22

Leavenworth, Jesse, 261, 267, 269, 289; congressional Joint Special Committee, 246

Lee, Robert E., surrenders at Appomattox Court House, 251

Left Hand (Arapaho), 74, 99, 153, 181, 190, 191, 194, 200, 219, 258, 333, 334; Adams's Ohio House Arapaho incident, 103–5; Big Timbers council, 168–69; Boone–Left Hand and Little Raven meetings, 356n18; Byers-Poisal meeting, 98; Camp Weld council, refuses to attend, 173; Cheyenne aggressiveness, 98; death of, 225, 228; Denver racetrack, 102; English language, 10, 81, 98, 123; Evans friendly Indian letter, 157; Fort Larned incident, 143; Fort Lyon, "peace," 195, 227; Fort Wise peace council, refuses to attend, 95, 124; growing concern over whites, 74; John Smith, 100; names of, 10; power of "talking leaves," 101; Samuel Colley, anger at, 124; Sand Creek village, 196–97, 202, 204, 207, 208, 212, 247, 258; Saville meeting, 123; speaks at play in his "vernacular," 101; Washington, D.C., delegation, misses, 120; white invasion threat, 138; Wynkoop-Anthony pledge of safety, 205, 208

Left Hand (or Namos; Cheyenne), 95

Left Hand II (Arapaho), and Sand Creek village, 202

Lewis, William, and Glorieta campaign, 111, 113

Light (Cheyenne), death of, 25

Lincoln, Abraham, 106, 111, 116, 118; death of, 251, 263; Santee Sioux outbreak, 119, 122

Lippincott, Henry, Elliot's men's bodies, 319

Little Arkansas peace council, Kans., 266–67, 268–70, 272–75

Little Bear (Bear Tongue's son; George Bent's friend; Cheyenne), and Sand Creek, 202

Little Bear (Little Raven's son; Arapaho), 296, 299

Little Big Mouth (Arapaho), and Medicine Lodge peace council, 296, 299

Little Brown Backed Hawked Woman (Cheyenne, Black Kettle's mother), 9

Little Chief (Cheyenne), 126, 128

Little Creek (Cheyenne), death of, 33–34

Little Mountain (Kiowa), 38

Little Old Man (Cheyenne), 37–38

Little Plover (Little Rock's son; Cheyenne), Sand Creek village 211

Little Raven (Arapaho), 37, 74, 153, 181, 187, 190, 267, 333, 391n104; annuities, 304, 305, 306; Arkansas River location, revealed

to Chivington, 223; Big Timbers council, 169; birth, 10; Bluff Creek council, 280; Boone–Left Hand and Little Raven meetings, 356n18; Boone–Little Raven–Poisal meeting, 99–101; Colley letter, exposes location, 223; Custer, 323; Denver racetrack, 102; description of, 80; 1869 reservation, 333; Evans friendly Indian letter, 157; final surrender, 326–29; Fort Larned council, 288; Fort Lyon, 195, 227; Fort Wise peace council, 95–97; growing concern over whites, 74; ignored, 334; Kaws, 306; Little Arkansas peace council, 268–70, 273–75; Margaret Wilmarth, 270; Medicine Lodge peace council, 292–93, 294, 299, 310; names of, 10; power of "talking leaves," 101; Richardson, 80–82; Sand Creek village, avoids, 196, 224; Sheridan Medicine Bluff meeting, 328; speaks out, 296, 298, 301; Washington, D.C., trip, refuses, 120, 124, 333; Washita village, 312; white invasion threat, 138; whites, disrespect for, 224; William Bent, wants as agent, 270; wives and children, 81, 87; and Wynkoop, 270, 276, 289

Little Robe (d. 1864; Cheyenne): background of, 350n28; and Pawnees, 62–63; Sand Creek village, 202

Little Robe (d. 1886; Cheyenne), 66, 312; and annuities, 304, 305, 306; background of, 350n28; and Black Kettle, 293–94, 319; confronts Henderson, 394; Custer, 324–26; 1869 reservation, 333; Hazen meeting, 393n123; Little Arkansas peace council, 275; Medicine Lodge peace council, 296, 298, 299; raids of, 148, 305, 391n104; Washita village, 312

Little Rock (Cheyenne), 144; Black Kettle, move south, 309–10; death of, 318; Medicine Lodge peace council, 296, 299; Sand Creek village, 202, 208, 211; Washita village, 312; Wynkoop, meetings and safety offer, 309

Little Sage Woman (Black Kettle's wife; Cheyenne), 16, 50–52, 62, 348n56

Little Wolf (Cheyenne), 20, 22, 34, 95; becomes head chief of council of forty-four, 97

Little Woman (Charley Bent's wife; Cheyenne), 303

Logan, Samuel, Third Colorado, musters out, 230

Lone Wolf (Kiowa), 120; Sheridan, threatens to hang, 320

Long Chin (Tall Bull's half brother; Cheyenne-Sioux), 63, 329

Lookout Station, Kans., Custer clears Cheyennes of murders, 287

Lord, Richard (First U.S. Cavalry), Glorieta campaign, 110

Louderback, David Henry, 250; Fort Lyon, Sand Creek affidavits, 240; Sand Creek testimony, 250; Sand Creek village, 201, 209

Maahótse. See Sacred Arrows

Mad Wolf (Cheyenne), and 1853 Mexico raid, 65

Magon (One-Eye's daughter; John Prowers's wife; Cheyenne), 196

Magpie Woman (George Bent's wife, Cheyenne), 309, 392n111; Black Kettle, leaves last time, 310; marries George Bent, 392n11; Mo-nahs-e-tah photo misidentification error, 290

Maheo, 7, 27, 56, 324

Mahom. See Snake Woman (Left Hand's sister; John Poisal's wife; Arapaho)

Mahwissa (Cheyenne), 317, 318–19; not Black Kettle's sister, 393n128

Making-Out-Roads (aka Roadmaker; Kit Carson's and Charles Rath's wife; Cheyenne), 147

Man Who Breaks the Marrow Bones (Cheyenne), and Saline and Solomon raid, 307–9

Marble, Daniel: Asher-Marble confusion, 172, 370–71n14; freed, 172; Plum Creek raid, 151–53

Marble, William D. (Daniel Marble's father), 151

Mayer, Henry F. (Edmund Guerrier's guardian), and Guerrier, view of, 257–58

Maynard, John S., Chivington-Cramer meeting 205

Maynard, Joseph S., Colorado Sand Creek inquiry, Tappan quote on Chivington, 244

McCannon, John, Third Colorado, musters out, 230

McCusker, Philip, Medicine Lodge peace council, translates at, 292

McCook, A. McDowell, 259

McGaa, William, 76; St. Charles Town Company, 73–74

McGinley, N. D., Charley Bent confrontation, 302–3

Medicine Arrow (or Medicine Arrows). See Stone Forehead (Cheyenne)

Medicine Lodge peace council, Kans., 291–98; Roman Nose raids, 289; whites fear attack, 294–95

Medicine Wolf (Cheyenne), and Hancock meeting, 285

Medicine Woman Later (Black Kettle's wife; Cheyenne), 62; Black Kettle, passes, 63; death of, 314–15; and Little Arkansas peace council, 268; name meaning, 350n27; Sand Creek village, 210, 224

memories and recollections, 253

Mexican war, 41

Middle Park, Colo. Terr., Ute agent Whitely refuses to operate in area, 136

Miksch, Amos C., Sand Creek atrocities, 221

Mim-im-mie. See Eagle Head (Cheyenne)

Minton, William, 197, 202; Fort Lyon, Sand Creek affidavits, 240; Wynkoop and Anthony Sand Creek protection, 250

misidentification of Indian chiefs and mixed-blood Indians, 268

Mitchell, David D., 58

Mitchell, Robert B., reports August 1864 raids, 154

Mix, Charles, Indian Bureau money problems, 308

Mo-nahs-e-tah (Little Rock's daughter; Cheyenne): background of, 317; Custer, sexual relationship with, 393n136; Magpie Woman photo misidentification error, 290; phonetic spelling of name, 376n45; Sand Creek village, 211–12; Washita, rape of, 318

Moonlight, Thomas: Colorado Sand Creek inquiry, 238, 241, 243–44; hangs Two Face and Black Foot, 256–57

Morrison, James, 309; Washita death count letter, 320–21, 394n145

Morrison, Emma (Big Mouth's daughter), 320–21

Morrow, kills Silas Soule, 252–53

Morton, Nancy Jane (Fletcher): background of, 150; Big Timbers village, 166; Lucinda Eubanks, 166, 260, 368n22; Plum Creek raid, 150–53

Morton, Thomas F. (Nancy Morton's husband), Plum Creek raid, 150–53

Mullin, Loudon, musters out of the Third Colorado, 229

Murphy, Tab (dir., Last of the Dogmen), 397nn185–86

Murphy, Thomas (superintendent of Indian affairs), 289, 319, 388n44; arms distribution, 304, 306–7; Fort Larned council, 288; John Smith, 303–4; Little Arkansas peace council, 268, 270, 274–75; Medicine Lodge peace council, 294, 296, 299; Nathanial Taylor, 306; Wynkoop, 303–4

Neva (Arapaho), 153, 173, 219; background of, 10; Big Timbers council, 164–65; Camp Weld council, 180, 184, 187–90, 192; English, speaks, 10; Evans friendly Indian letter, 157; Fort Lyon, 195; Laura Roper, 162–63; names of, 10; Washington, D.C., trip, 120, 359n40

Nichols, Charles, and St. Charles Town Company, 73–74

Nichols, David, musters out of Third Colorado, 230

Night when the stars fell, 9, 30

Nis-tah-nah (aka Corn Tassel Woman; Magpie Woman's mother; Cheyenne), at Washita battle, 292n111

"noble savage," 80

North, Frank, 330; Tall Bull, kills, 331

North, Luther, 331

Northern Arapaho Indians: and Evans friendly Indian letter, 142; Julesburg raid, 234; Sand Creek, 204

Northern Cheyenne Indians, 262–63; chief's control, 166; discuss, peace, 261; Evans friendly Indian letter, 142; Fort Wise peace council, 95–97; Julesburg raid, 234; Sand Creek, 204; war with Crows, 126

No-ta-nee (Arapaho), 173, 195, 206

O'Brien, Nicholas, first Camp Rankin raid, 235–36

Oglala Sioux Indians, 60; Big Timbers council, 166; Julesburg raid, 234; Pawnee Fork, 285; Sand Creek, 204

Ohméséhesos. See Northern Cheyenne Indians

Olney, James, and Sand Creek butchery description, 216, 252

One-Eye (Cheyenne), 153, 163, 170, 173, 196; and Big Timbers council, 169; Chivington pass, 159; Colleys, 159; death of, 210; Evans friendly Indian letter, 157; one of six council of forty-four head chiefs, 97; Sand Creek, 202; spy for Anthony, 247–48, 264, 382n22; and Wynkoop, 159–61, 366–67n2

Owl Woman (William Bent's wife; White Thunder's daughter; Cheyenne), 38, 53, 54, 102; children births, 39–40; death of, 40; description of, 31; William Bent, 31–32, 38

Palmer, Lucian, Fort Lyon Sand Creek testimony, 250

Parker, Eli, U. S. Grant choice for peace council, 263

Parmetar, James W., Fort Lyon commander, 143, 144, 363n8, 364n15

Pawnee Fork village, Kans.: Cheyenne girl raped, 287, 291, 295; destruction of by Hancock, 284–85, 287–88, 295, 296, 299, 321; later Cheyenne–Arapaho camps on, 305; location of Wynkoop agency on Pawnee Fork, 306

Pawnee Indians, tribal conflict with Cheyennes, 23–27, 62–64

Pawnee Killer (Oglala Sioux), 234; Hancock expedition, 285; Julesburg raid, 234; Republican River village, 227

Pawnee scouts, 330–31

peace treaties: land grab with no recorded Indian words (1861), 96–97; of 1851, 61–62; of 1861, 95

Peacock, George, Charles Rath takes over trading post after killed by Kiowas, 147

Peck, Robert M., and Sumner's 1857 Cheyenne saber charge, 70

Penleton, David (Susie Bent's husband), 303

Phillips, Charles, 126, 130, 196

Playing Crane (Little Rock's daughter; Cheyenne), Sand Creek village 211

Plum Creek, Nebr. Terr., Morton–Marble train destroyed near, 154

Plum Creek station, Nebr. Terr., Morton–Marble train destroyed near, 150–52

Poisal, John: background of, 98, 394n144; Boone–Little Raven meeting, 99–101; Byers–Left Hand meeting, 98; Horse Creek peace council, 62; interprets for Left Hand, 104; misspellings of name, 356n17

Poisal, John, Jr. (John Poisal's son; mixed-blood Arapaho): background of, 394n144; Washita death count, 321

Poisal, Margaret (mixed-blood Arapaho), background of, 394n144

Pollock, Thomas (John Chivington's son-in-law), 282

Poor Bear (Kiowa-Apache): and Bluff Creek council, 280; Fort Larned council, 288; Medicine Lodge peace council, 291, 294; Washington, D.C., trip, 120

Pope, John, Indians want Wynkoop, 279

Porcupine Bear (Big Head's son; Cheyenne), and Saline and Solomon raid, 309

Porcupine Bear (father of Porcupine Bear; Cheyenne): becomes a tribal outcast, 34, 346n9; breaks sacred taboos, 35, 346n14; leader of Dog Men, 33

Porcupine Bear (son of Porcupine Bear; Cheyenne), 346n14; Bluff Creek council, 280–82

Powder Face (Arapaho), 187

Prowers, John, 196

"Puebla" ruins, Colo. Terr., near Coberly road station, 192

Pueblo, Colo. Terr., detachment of Third Colorado briefly camped at, 177

Pyron, Charles L., Glorieta campaign, 110

Rath, Charles: background of, 147–48; Black Kettle wants as trader, 272

Red Eye Woman (Frog's wife; Cheyenne), 52

Red Iron (Cheyenne), Bluff Creek, 280

Red Moon (Cheyenne), 1848 Black Kettle raid, 51–52

Red Nose (Cheyenne), Saline and Solomon raid, 307–9

Republican River village, war parties, 227

Richardson, Albert Deane: Byers, 83; Little Raven, 80–82; view of Indians, 80

Richmond, Harry, 203, 230; murder reenactments, 229; Sand Creek, murders women and children, 216, 252

Roan, George, and Fort Lyon Sand Creek testimony, butchery, 250

Roasting (High Back Wolf's brother; Cheyenne), death of, 25

Robinson, A. M., 75, 80

Rocky Mountain District, Kans. Terr., Methodist Church creates, 92

Rocky Mountain News, 79, 83, 87, 97, 107, 132, 137; Denver flood, 134; "Hundred Day service," 157; Sand Creek, demands more such battles, 278

Ripley, W. D., 127–28

Robbins, Samuel M., and Joint Committee on the Conduct of the War, 247

Roman Nose (Cheyenne): Arickaree Fork and death, 310–11; Cheyenne–Sioux battle line, 285; counting coup, 285, 387n25; description of, 285; Hancock, 285; Medicine Lodge peace council, does not attend, 295; tipi trophy, 288; Wynkoop, attempts to kill, 289

Romero, Rafael (Custer's scout), 318–19

Roper, Laura: freed, 171, 178; Julia Lambert, 177, 369n7; Left Hand, 171; Little Blue raid, 148–50, 153; Lucinda Eubanks, separation from, 166, 367–68n21; memories fail her, 365n28; Mollie Dorsey, 193; Neva, 162–63; not sexual object, 163

Ross, Edmund, and Cheyenne and Arapaho abandonment of their land, 301

Ross, Lewis W., and Joint Special Committee/ Sand Creek committee, 246; travels to West, 248, 257, 259

Sacred Arrows, 25–28, 32; blinding ceremony, 35; ceremony on new keeper, 56; loss of, 26–27, 344n17, 345n19; not renewed, 49–50; power broken, 36; renewal of, 34, 289; sixth and final movement of, 62–64

Sacred Buffalo Hat, 24, 28, 63

Sanborn, George L., 127

Sanborn, John B., 289; interviews Gray Head, 295; Little Arkansas peace council, 268, 269–70, 272, 275; Medicine Lodge peace council, 291

Sand Creek village, 201, 206–13, 216–18, 220–23, 225; Black Kettle and Left Hand move to, 196–97; chiefs present, 202; size of, 202

Sand Hill (Cheyenne): and Sand Creek, 202, 212; Sweetwater village, 323–24; Washita village, 312

Sanford, Byron, 192–93

Sanford, Mollie Dorsey, 192–93; takes in Little Blue captives, 193

Satank (Kiowa), 38, 143, 364n26

Satanta (Kiowa): buffalo, killing of for sport, 289; Fort Larned horse herd, 143; Medicine Lodge peace council, 291, 292–93; raids of, 143; Sheridan, threatens to hang, 320; and Wynkoop, 289

Saville, John J., 122–24

Sayr (sometimes spelled "Sayre"), Hal: musters out, 230; and Third Colorado, 229

Scott, Levi (Methodist bishop), 92

Scurry, William R., drives Union forces from field at Glorieta, 113–14

Second Texas Mounted Rifles, confronted Chivington during Glorieta campaign, 110

Seven Bulls (Cheyenne), 37

Seventh U.S. Cavalry: 1869 Southern Plains campaign, 318, 324; Pawnee Fork, 284; Washita attack, 314, 317

Seward, William H. (U.S. secretary of state), and Evans resignation, 262, 263

Shaffer, James, Glorieta campaign, 112

Shavehead (Comanche), 38

Sheridan, Philip H.: blocks distribution of weapons, 304; Custer, 318–19; Fort Dodge, impromptu meetings with chiefs, 304; Hazen, makes peace with Sheridan, 313; Little Raven Medicine Bluff meeting, 328; Satanta and Lone Wolf, threatens to hang, 320; winter war, reason to launch, 310

Sherman, William T.: declares war, 310; Hazen report, 313–14; Henderson and Medicine

Sherman, William T. (*continued*)
Lodge, 299, 305; Indian military district, 307–8, 334–35; mandate of, ends Southern Cheyenne and Arapaho freedom, 334–35; military money problems, 308

She Who Baths Her Knees (High Back Wolf's wife; Cheyenne), 24

Shield (Little Raven's son; Arapaho), 297; Saline and Solomon raid, 307

Short Teeth (Little Rock's sibling; Cheyenne), and Sand Creek village, 211

Shoshone Indians: Cheyennes attack, 60; Horse Creek council, 61

Shoup, George L., 203, 229; Camp Weld council, 180, 187; Sand Creek, 206–7, 223; Third Colorado, colonel of, 177

Simpson, Matthew (Methodist bishop), 125, 260, 263

Sioux Indians, 314; Arickaree Fork fight, 310–11; councils, 47; Evans friendly Indian letter, 142; horse thieves, 58; Santee Sioux Minnesota uprising, 119, 122; woman with Custer, 318–19

Skidi Indians. *See* Pawnee Indians

Skunk Woman (Little Rock's wife; Cheyenne), and Sand Creek village, 211

Slim Face (Cheyenne), 283, 299

Slough, John: brigadier generalship, 116, 119, 124–25; and Glorieta campaign, 111–14

Slow Smoking. *See* Yellow Woman

Smith, Armama (John Smith's daughter; mixed-blood Cheyenne), 201; awarded 640 acres, 373n8

Smith, H. P. S., 73–74

Smith, Jack (John Smith's son; mixed-blood Cheyenne), 41–42, 44, 76, 180; appearance of, 47; birth mistake, 353n11; death of, 221–23, 237, 256; government employee, 264; Sand Creek village, 201, 210, 212, 217, 237

Smith, John Simpson, 47, 173, 177, 247, 264, 347n37; and annuities, 304; Anthony spy mission, 201, 206; Arapaho war party, 45; background of, 14–15, 41, 75; Big Timbers council, 164, 167–68, 170; Blackfeet, 15; Bluff Creek council, 281; Camp Weld council, 173, 180, 186, 188 192; Cheyennes, view of, 45, 201; children of, 75, 76; Colleys, partnership with, 118; congressional Joint Special Committee, 246; conversation with Devil, 396n181; death of, 333; description of, 44; deserves Soule's fate, 277; Fort Lyon, Sand Creek affidavits, 240; Fort Wise peace council, 95; Horse Creek peace council, 61–62; interpreter, 47–48, 61, 78, 100,

118, 120, 122, 165, 196; languages spoken (including Arapaho), 16, 44, 100, 122, 165; Little Arkansas peace council, 268, 269, 275; Medicine Lodge peace council, 292, 294, 295, 298–99; names of, 42, 78, 121, 221; not paid, 304; Sand Creek, 201, 206, 208–10, 212, 375n31; Soule, false partnership with, 251–52; St. Charles Town Company, 73–74; Talbot false testimony, 254–56; trading, 42–43, 46, 206; translates for, 160–61, 167–69, 281, 388n43; view of, 347n46; violence of, 76; Washington, D.C., 120–22, 333; whiskey problem, 304; wives of, 42, 75; and Wynkoop, 74, 160, 289, 303–4, 367n6, 391n98

Smith, William Gilpin (John Smith's son; mixed-blood Cheyenne): awarded 640 acres, 373n8; birth, 373n9; birth mistake, 353n11; Sand Creek, 201

Snake Indians. *See* Shoshone Indians

Snake Woman (Left Hand's sister; John Poisal's wife; Arapaho), 98, 394n144

Snyder, Anna, 181, 369n7

Soule, Hersa A. Coberly (Silas Soule's wife), 252; background of, 250; and Coberly, 192

Soule, Silas S., 105, 177–78, 180, 192, 196, 197; Anthony, 205, 232–33; Big Timbers council, 163, 170; brevetted captain, 247; Byers, 252; Chivington, 202, 205, 253–54, 205; Cramer, 205, 228; delivers Charley Bent to Fort Lyon, 223; Denver flood, 133–34, 136–37, 241; Denver Sand Creek testimony, 245–46; false letters, 380–81n55; family, 138; fear of more war, 194; First Colorado, considers/remains member of, 237, 241; Fort Lyon, 202–3, 240, 373n6; Henning, 200; Hersa Coberly, marries, 250; John Smith, false partnership with, 251–52; last letter to mother, 237; leave of absence, 200; not bigamist, 383n40; November patrols, 202–3; recruiting duty, 125, 133; returns to massacre site, different Indian death counts, 232, 237; Sand Creek village, 210, 213, 217–18; threats and murder of, 252–54; Wynkoop, 138, 253, 254, 383n32, 383n43

Southern Arapaho Indians, 202; annuities, 304, 305, 306–7, 318; Big Timbers council, village circles, 166; in Denver, 82; Dog Men, join, 143; 1869 reservation and sad end, 331–32; end of lifeway, 334–35; environment, 36; Evans friendly Indian letter, 142; executive order, creates 1869 reservation, 331–32; farming and turning back on lifeway, 48,

85; Fort Lyon meeting, 196; Fort Wise peace council, 95–97; gold land, to be paid for, 85; Greenwood 1860 treaty agenda to remove from buffalo land, 93–95; Horse Creek peace council, 58; John Smith, interprets for, 173; Little Arkansas peace council, 268; Medicine Lodge peace council, not read to them/not what they agreed to, 279, 296–99; meetings with whites, 84–85; no more treaties, 310; raids of, 391n104; Saline and Solomon raid, 307–8; Sand Creek, travel to/arrival at, 196, 372n47; Sherman mandate, ends freedom, 334–35; starvation, 87, 279, 303, 332; Utes, war with, 83; Washington, D.C., visits, 121–22, 333; white invasion threat, 86–87, 138; white man's word, wary of, 267; William Bent, 28, 84–85

Southern Cheyenne and Arapaho Reservation, Indian Territory, 331

Southern Cheyenne Indians, 80, 202; annuities, 304, 305, 306, 307; Big Timbers council, village circles, 166; Bluff Creek council, 280–82; Camp Weld council, 180–90; chief's control, 166; cold and hungry, 303; council of forty-four, 10–11, 34, 50, 61, 97; Crows, Northern Cheyenne revenge raid, 126; 1869 reservation and sad end, 331–32; end of lifeway, 334–35; Evans friendly Indian letter, 142; executive order, creates 1869 reservation, 331–32; farming and turning back on lifeway, 48, 85; Fort Larned council, 288; Fort Lyon meeting, 196; Fort Wise peace council, 95–97; gold land, to be paid for, 85; Greenwood 1860 treaty agenda to remove from buffalo land, 93–95; Hancock expedition, fear, battle line, and flight, 283–85; Horse Creek peace council, 58; intertribal warfare, 302; January–February 1865 raids, 233–36, 241–42; Kaws and Osages, war with, 302, 307; Little Arkansas peace council, 268; Medicine Lodge peace council, 295, 296–99; meetings with whites, 84–85; no more treaties, 310; one-leader misconception, 180; removal from their land, 182; Saline and Solomon raid, 307–8; Sand Creek, 197, 212, 216, 285, 372n47; Sherman mandate, ends freedom, 334–35; Sioux war, fearful of, 126; starvation, 87, 279, 303, 332; villages attacked/destroyed, 130, 131–33; war parties and raids, 32–33, 36, 139, 279; Washington, D.C., visits, 121–22, 333; Washita battle, death counts, 320–21; white invasion threat, 86–87, 138; white man's word, wary of, 267;

William Bent, 28, 84–85; Wood Creek council, 282; Wynkoop, agent for, 283

Southwest, threat of Confederate invasion, 103

Spotted Crow (Cheyenne), and Sand Creek village, 202

Spotted Elk (Cheyenne), 296, 299

Spotted Horse (perhaps Cheyenne-Sioux), scouts for Jacob Downing, 131

Spotted Tail (Brûlé Sioux): Julesburg raid, 234; Republican River village, 227

Spotted Wolf (Arapaho), 312; and annuities, 305; Hazen meeting, 393n123; Medicine Lodge peace council, 296, 299

Squiers, Charles, and Silas Soule murder, 252–53

Standing-in-the-Water (Cheyenne): and Sand Creek village, 202; Washington, D.C., trip, 120–21

Standing on Hill (Cheyenne), 22

Stanley, Henry Morton (reporter): Hancock expedition, 284; loads guns, 294; Medicine Lodge peace council, blasts treaty, 300; and raped girl, 295; Wynkoop, view of, 289, 292, 295, 300

Stanton, Edwin M. (U.S. secretary of war), 263; Chivington, 116, 124

Star (Cheyenne), death of, 132

Sedgwick, John, and 1857 Cheyenne campaign, 69

St. Charles Town Company, 73

Steck, Amos, and Byers attempt to destroy politically, 277

Steele, James, and Little Arkansas peace council, 268, 270, 273–74

Steinberger, Albert, and gold region, 77–78

Stilwell, George H., Colorado Sand Creek inquiry committee recorder, 241

stock market crash of 1857, 72

Stone Forehead (Cheyenne), 16, 121, 333, 334, 349–50n30, 386n1; and annuities, 304, 305; background of, 8; Black Kettle, 63, 319; Bluff Creek council, 280, 282; Custer-Sweetwater confrontation, 323–26, 395n155; death of, 333; 1869 reservation, 333; escape to north in 1874, 396n182; Fort Wise peace council, did not attend, 95–96; Horse Creek peace council, 60–61; Keeper of the Sacred Arrows, 56, 349n10; Medicine Lodge peace council, not present, 294, 295; names of, 8, 338n21; Sacred Arrows renewal, 63, 291; Saline and Solomon raid, 392n114; Washita village, 312; Wynkoop, 305

Storm (Arapaho), 99, 195; and annuities, 304, 305; Fort Wise peace council, 95; Medicine Lodge peace council, 296, 299

Stumbling Bear (Kiowa), 289

St. Vrain, Ceran, 18, 19, 40–41, 87; William Bent buys out, 54

Sully, Alfred, and Northern Cheyenne meeting, 261–62

Sumner, Edwin Vose, 58–59; and 1857 Cheyenne campaign, 69–71

Susie (Charley Bent's daughter), 303, 391n87

Sutaio Indians, 18; background of, 9

Tail Woman (White Thunder's wife; Cheyenne), 24; cholera epidemic, 54–55

Talbot, Presley, 205; Denver Sand Creek testimony, 254–56

Tall Bear (Arapaho), and Medicine Lodge peace council, 296, 299

Tall Bull (Cheyenne-Sioux), 133, 153, 268, 333, 334; and annuities, 304; Arickaree Fork, 310–11; Black Kettle, 292; Carr, hunted by, 329–30; death of, 331, 396n174; final days of freedom, 329–31; Fort Larned councils, 283–84, 288; good conduct letter, 304; Hancock, 285; Medicine Lodge peace council, 291, 296, 298, 299; raids Kaws, 305; Republican River village, 227; Sand Creek, not at massacre, 373–74n14; white men, view of, 267; Wynkoop, 284, 289, 292

Tall Wolf (Stone Forehead's oldest son; Cheyenne), and Saline and Solomon raid, 309

Tangle Head (Cheyenne), and Arickaree Fork, 311

Taos revolt, 41, 44, 45

Tappan, Samuel S.: Chivington conflict, 114–15, 118–19; Colorado Sand Creek inquiry, 241, 245; Joseph Maynard on "greatest blunder" quote, 244; unfit to head commission, 244

Taylor, Nathanial J. (commissioner of Indian affairs), 287; and Indian Bureau money problems, 308; Little Raven, ignores request, 294; Medicine Lodge peace council, 291, 292, 294, 299; Sherman military district, 308; Thomas Murphy, 306; weapons release, 306; Wynkoop, 287, 300, 306; Wynkoop resignation, 317

Ten Bears (Comanche): and Medicine Lodge peace council, 292–93; Washington, D.C., trip, 120

Third Colorado Volunteer Cavalry, 203, 205; as "bloody Thirdsters," 229; companies in various locations, 177; created, 155–56; Evans needs victory, 180; former "Bloody Third," 231; hundred-day enlistment nears end, 207;

labeled "Bloodless Third,' 174; musters out, 229–30; Sand Creek village, 207–13, 216–17, 221–23; Shoup, appointed colonel, 177; Special Orders No. 65 creates draft, 156–57

Treaty of Fort Wise, Colo. Terr., 96–97

Treaty of Horse Creek, Nebr. Terr., 61–62

Treaty of Little Arkansas River, Kans., 275

Treaty of Medicine Lodge Creek, Kans., 299, 327; Cheyennes/Arapahos, not agreed to and not read to them, 296–99, 328; damnation and praise, 300–301; not ratified, 305; ratified, 306; Sherman kills buffalo-hunting promise/distribution of arms, 305–6

Tsistsistas, meaning of, 5, 7, 337n6. See also Cheyenne Indians; Northern Cheyenne Indians; Southern Cheyenne Indians

Two Face (Oglala Sioux), 166, 256–57

Two Thighs (Cheyenne), and Sand Creek village, 202

Union Pacific Railroad, 117

Union Pacific Railroad, Eastern Division, 281

United States Indian Commission, 321, 326

Upper Arkansas Indian Agency, Colo. Terr.: at Fort Lyon, 106, 117; moved to Fort Larned, Kans., after Wynkoop becomes agent, 288

Ute Indians, 81, 83, 131, 136, 178, 262–63; Black Kettle raid, 51–52, 348n56; enlist to fight Cheyennes, 140

Van Wormer, Isaac, 139

vi 'ho ' i, Cheyenne word for white man, 14

Vip-po-nah (Cheyenne), 42, 43, 347n37

Wade, B. F. (chair, Joint Committee on the Conduct of the War), 262, 266; summation of investigation, 264

Wakely, George D. (Ned Wynkoop's father-in-law; daguerreotypist), 178, 180, 190

Wakely, Louise. See Wynkoop, Louise Wakely (Ned Wynkoop's wife)

Wakely, Flora, and Rose M. (Louise Wynkoop's sisters), 85–86, 89

Walker, Charles, Glorieta campaign, 110

Walking Coyote (Cheyenne), 35; kills wife's lover, 49

Wapoola (John Smith's wife; Cheyenne), 42, 45, 47; and white man dance, 75–76

War Bonnet (d. 1853; Cheyenne): background, 351n33; Mexico raid, 64–65

War Bonnet (d. 1864; Cheyenne): background, 351n33; mutilated, 223; Sand Creek, 201–2, 208; Washington, D.C., trip, 121–22

Ware, Eugene, and false Julesburg Indian causalities, 236

Weichell, Maria, 329

Weld, Lewis Ledyard (Colo. Terr. secretary of state), 103

Whirlwind (Cheyenne): and Medicine Lodge peace council, 296, 299; Sand Creek village, 202; Washita village, 312

Whitaker, C. W. (Arapaho translator), and Medicine Lodge peace council, 296

White Antelope (Cheyenne), 12, 16, 37–38, 138, 313; Byers, ridiculed by, 236; Camp Weld council, 173, 180, 185–90; council of forty-four head chiefs, 97; death of, 210; Fort Wise peace council, 95, 97; Greenwood 1860 treaty agenda to remove from buffalo land, 93–94, 95; Sand Creek, 202, 204, 208, 212

White Contrary (Cheyenne), and Arickaree Fork, 311

White Horse (Cheyenne), 283, 285, 287; and Arickaree Fork, 310; Medicine Lodge peace council, 296, 299

white invasion threat, 86–87, 138

Whiteley, Simeon: background of, 136; Camp Weld council, 180, 183–85, 187

white man, Native names for, 14

White Rabbit (Arapaho), and Medicine Lodge peace council, 296, 299

White Thunder (Cheyenne Keeper of the Sacred Arrows), 25; birth of, 24; death, 36, 55; selects Elk River to replace him, 349n10; warns raid will fail, 32

Wilder, William, Third Colorado, musters out, 230

Wilmarth, Margaret, 281; Little Arkansas peace council, 268, 269, 270, 275. See also Adams, Margaret

Wilson, Luther, and Sand Creek, 209, 210

Winchester, L. J., and Rocky Mountain News, failure to pay for, 88–89

Wind Woman (Black Kettle's sister; Cheyenne), 9, 359n40; death of Wolf Tongue (husband), 64

Wolf Chief (Cheyenne), 20, 22, 50; 1848 death of, 52, 348n56; not Bent's informant, 348n52

Wolf Chief (George Bent's informant; Cheyenne), 132

Wolf Hair. See Dog Man Plenty (Cheyenne-Sioux)

Wood Creek council, Kans., 282

Wynkoop, Edward Estill (Ned Wynkoop's son), 172, 200, 263

Wynkoop, Edward Wanshaer (Ned), 89, 103, 131, 133, 142, 177–78, 227, 248, 263; annuity distribution, 304, 305, 306; Anthony, 194–96, 239–40; appearance of, 77; Arapahos, meetings with, 195, 196; August 9, 1868, gun distribution, 391n105; background and birth, 73–74; battle line, Big Timbers, and Cheyenne–Arapaho council, 163–70, 173; Black Kettle, 169–70, 267, 294, 305, 322; Bluff Creek council, 280–82; Byers, 77, 78, 130–31, 192, 300; brevetted lieutenant colonel, 247; Camp Weld council, 180–82, 184–86, 189–90, 192; chief of cavalry, 259; and Chivington, 137–38, 145, 147, 184, 192, 193, 228, 240, 246, 249–50, 259, 291; Civil War and Glorieta campaign, 105, 109–10, 112–13; Cramer endorses, 197–98; cultural broker, 276; Curtis, 192, 219, 228, 247; Custer report, 321; deserves Soule's fate, 277; Denver City Town Company, 74; detached duty, special agent, 280; Doolittle, 259, 282; 1867 Hancock expedition, 283; end of 1868 war, 310; end of working with Indians, 332; Evans, 175, 178, 180; Fort Larned council, 288; Fort Lyon, 145–47, 239, 240; Fort Lyon Sand Creek testimony, 249–50; George Bent, 168, 300; gold region, 73–74, 77–78, 79; Guerrier, 283–84; Hackberry Creek mutiny and white captives, 170–73; Hancock, 284, 285, 287, 287, 291; as Indian agent, 283, |317–18; investigation of Chivington, 232; "kill all Indians," 155; John Smith, 74, 160–61, 303–4, 367n6, 388n43, 391n98; Joint Committee on the Conduct of the War, confirms actions, 264; letter to end war with Black Kettle's people, 158–60, 173, 161–62; Little Arkansas peace council, 267; Little Rock, meetings, 309; Louise Wynkoop, 86, 103; make Indians citizens, 322; Medicine Lodge peace council, testimony of, 291–92, 294–96; memoir, 160–61; military, critical of, 319; musters out, 282; One-Eye, 160–61, 248, 366–67n2; Peter Cooper and Cooper Institute talk, 321–22, 395nn148–49; removed from command, 200, 206, 218, 228; Richmond, comment on, 252; Roman Nose attempts to kill, 289; Sand Creek letter, 205, 228; Sand Creek village, guarantees safety, 196, 205, 208, 250, 258, 267; Sherman, 300; Soule, 138, 253, 383n32, 383n43; special duty, 279; Stanley, 292, 295, 300; superintendent of Indian affairs, 322, 396n176; Tall Bull, 284, 291, 304; theater, 86, 103; visits massacre site, 259;

Wynkoop, Edward Wanshaer (*continued*)
   Washita attack, inverted dates of attack and
   Wynkoop resignation, 393n131; Wood Creek
   council, 282
Wynkoop, Emily Reveille (Ned Wynkoop's
   daughter), 172, 200
Wynkoop, Louise Wakely (Ned Wynkoop's
   wife), 89, 177, 192, 200, 279; as actress,
   looked down upon, 89; children of, 200;
   Fort Riley Indian encounter, 264; theatrical
   background of, 85–86

Yellow Bear (Arapaho): and annuities, 304, 305;
   Fort Larned council, 288; Medicine Lodge
   peace council, 296, 299
Yellow Boy (Yellow Hair's son; Kiowa), 38
Yellow Hair (Kiowa), 38

Yellow Shield (Cheyenne), and Sand Creek
   village, 202
Yellow Wolf (Cheyenne), 22, 32, 34, 35;
   background of, 18; councils, 48; raids, 19,
   20; Sand Creek village, 202; William Bent,
   20, 22, 55
Yellow Woman (William Bent's wife; White
   Thunder's daughter; Cheyenne), 55, 102;
   birth of Charles Bent, 53; cholera epidemic,
   54, 349n9; marries William Bent, 40
Young Chief (Kiowa-Apache), annuities, 305
Young Colt (Arapaho), and Medicine Lodge
   peace council, 296, 299
Young Bear (Cheyenne), and 1853 Mexico raid, 65

Zerepta (John Smith's wife; Cheyenne), and
   Sand Creek village, 201, 212